28.95

# "The Most Wonderful Work . . ."

## Our Constitution Interpreted

### Thomas E. Baker

WEST PUBLISHING CO.
ST. PAUL, MN

## WEST'S COMMITMENT TO THE ENVIRONMENT

in 1906, West Publishing Company began recycling materials left over from the production of books. This began a tradition of efficient and responsible use of resources. Today, 100 % of our legal bound volumes are printed on acid-free, recycled paper consisting of 50% new fibers. West recycles nearly 27,700,000 pounds of scrap paper annually—the equivalent of 229,300 trees. Since the 1960s, West has devised ways to capture and recycle waste inks, solvents, oils, and vapors created in the printing process. We also recycle plastics of all kinds, wood, glass, corrugated cardboard, and batteries, and have eliminated the use of polystyrene book packaging. We at West are proud of the longevity and the scope of our commitment to the environment.

Copyright © 1996
By
West Publishing Co.
610 Opperman Drive
P.O. Box 64526
St. Paul, MN 55164–0526
1–800–328–9352

**ISBN** 0–314–20339–7

**Permission has been received from the copyrightholder to quote from the following works:**

The Federalist Society, The Great Debate: Interpreting Our Written Constitution (1986).

Irving Dillard, ed., The Spirit of Liberty (Knopf, 1974).

Daniel Farber, The Case Against Brilliance, 70 Minn.L.Rev. 917 (1986).

Forrest McDonald, The American Presidency (U. of Kan. 1996).

Scott Turow, One L (Farrar, Straus & Giroux 1977).

Grant Gilmore, The Ages of American Law (Yale, 1977).

Woodrow Wilson, Constitutional Government in the United States (Columbia Univ. Press, 1908, 1961).

Walter F. Murphy, James E. Fleming & Sotirios A. Barber, American Constitutional Interpretation (Foundation Press, 2d.ed. 1995).

Philip B. Kurland, "Presidential Powers" in Encyclopedia of the American Constitution (McMillan, 1986).

# Dedication

Every good teacher is first and always a student of his subject who, in turn, has many teachers. I have been fortunate, indeed, to have had so many great teachers, both inside and outside the classroom. My own constitutional vocation began when one of my teachers, Professor Fletcher N. Baldwin, Jr., called on a nervous though prepared first year law student to recite on *Marbury v. Madison*. I never got over it, as is evidenced by this book, which I dedicate to all my teachers. May they find it worthy of their inspiration.

# Acknowledgments

First, I want to thank Denis J. Hauptly, friend and editor in that order, for his support and encouragement and for the gentle respect he showed my scholarship. To quote his own book on the Constitutional Convention as my verdict of his editing prowess: "The deed was done and done well." Four student research assistants helped on this project: Desmond Acosta, Fernando Bustos, Eric Gifford (who also worked above and beyond the call of duty on the Bibliography), and Sarah Yost. For their ever-present helpfulness, I thank my secretaries, Norma Tanner and Leona Wyatt. My wife Jane Marie and my son Thomas Athanasius read and commented on these materials in ways that improved the finished project. My valued colleagues Daniel H. Benson, Charles P. Bubany, and James E. Viator helped insure that my professorialness did not come between me and my readers. Several constitutionalist colleagues offered suggestions and encouragement for which I am grateful: Paul D. Carrington, Richard H. Fallon, Daniel A. Farber, Philip P. Frickey, Gerald Gunther, Wythe Holt, Lewis Henry LaRue, Sanford Levinson, Wayne McCormack, Walter F. Murphy, David M. O'Brien, Charles E. Rice, Ronald D. Rotunda, Thomas D. Rowe, Rodney A. Smolla, Mark Tushnet, and William Van Alstyne.

# *Preface*

~~~~~~~~~~~~~~~~~

*This is a book about understanding our Constitution and how it has been interpreted. This is a book for everyone who has ever wondered about the Constitution.*

In 1878, as the Constitution of the United States approached its centennial, British statesman and Prime Minister William E. Gladstone delivered the now-famous *dictum* that I take for the main title of my book. He proclaimed that the Constitution of 1787 was "the most wonderful work ever struck off at a given time by the brain and purpose of man." At the time, Americans paid no mind to Gladstone's complete context, in which he subtly and elaborately qualified his commendation. Likewise, it did not seem to matter that the phrase was not original with Gladstone; Supreme Court Justice William Johnson had used nearly the same words in 1823. Over time, Gladstone's phrase has become "the most commonly quoted observation about the U.S. Constitution," according to constitutional historian Michael Kammen, because generally "Americans have taken too much pride and proportionately too little interest in their frame of government." This book seeks to improve that ratio, though I submit that pride and learning are not inversely related. Indeed, I take great pride in being a constitutionalist.

Constitutional Law Professor Charles L. Black, Jr. poses the rhetorical follow-up question to Gladstone's seeming hyperbole, "Alright, if not the American Constitution, then what is the most wonderful work ever struck off at a given time by the human mind and will?" My own answer is that ours certainly is the most wonderful Constitution in all of history. And the work of interpreting it—the work, if you will, of "making it work"—is an awesome responsibility which, in turn, is deserving of all our wonder. But it is, after all, our Constitution and not the government's. Each of us participates in the sovereignty of "We the People." The Constitution was written to be debated and understood by ordinary citizens and was intended to be relied upon in their everyday self-government. You do not have to be a Supreme Court Justice or a constitutional law professor to understand the Constitution. There are no high priests or secret rituals in our democratic republic. Ultimately, it is every citizen's responsibility to understand and to preserve our constitutional form of government.

Our Constitution truly is an object of wonder. In his classic work THE AGES OF AMERICAN LAW (1977), legal historian Grant Gilmore highlights the phenomenon of a great creative period in literature or the arts which vanishes as suddenly and as unexpectedly as it began. Elizabethan theater at the end of the 16th century and the Viennese school of music at the end of the 18th century are two examples. We continue to marvel at the virtuosity of a Shakespeare or a Mozart. We still perform their works. We still interpret them. We still learn from them. They still speak to us, over historical time and cultural space, despite the intervening generations and in spite of what modernity calls "progress." Professor Gilmore speculates:

> It may be that, for reasons which escape our grasp, the best and most creative minds of a generation are drawn to a particular field—which may be the creation of a new kind of theater or of a new style of music, or, as in the North American colonies after 1750, the creation of a new kind of government. After a generation or two of intense activity the job is done; the best and the most creative minds of the next generation follow their genius into new fields. But it will be a long time before anyone realizes that the last great play has already been written, the last great symphony composed.

So it was with the Constitution of the United States. Our founders framed a new form of government. In a world of monarchy and despotism, they committed themselves to establishing a republic, but a republic superior to those of ancient Greece and Rome, which devolved into tyranny. The Framers were children of the Enlightenment. They were self-consciously and self-critically aware of what they were doing, aware of how important it was, aware of the real risk of failure, and aware of what was at stake for themselves and their posterity. But theirs was an age that believed in the inevitability of progress through the application of right reason. They aspired toward the perfectibility of man. Through their government and institutions, they were founding the shining city on the hill which would be a light to nations and freedom loving people everywhere and for all time.

The Framers' legacy and ours depend on rational discourse, on a political dialogue engaged in by "We the People." The true genius of their efforts was that they understood government could be legitimate and could persevere only with the consent and the active participation of the governed. They did not attempt to solve all governmental problems, or even all constitutional problems, once and for all. They trusted in themselves and in their posterity. We can only do the same. Woodrow Wilson wrote in his book on CONSTITUTIONAL GOVERNMENT IN THE UNITED STATES (1908): "Constitutional government can exist only where there is actual community of interest and of purpose, and cannot, if it be also *self*-government, express the life of any body of people that does not constitute a veritable community."

A constitutionalist cannot help but marvel and wonder at the insights and prowess displayed in THE FEDERALIST PAPERS by their celebrated authors, Alexander Hamilton, James Madison and John Jay. Originally written under the pseudonym "Publius," these 85 essays were published in the New York City newspapers between October 1787 and May 1788 to persuade voters to elect delegates to that State's convention who would support the proposed Constitution. Mind you, these were newspaper articles composed under severe time constraints. They were editorials, political and rhetorical but also didactic. The collection of essays has been credited with successfully influencing the eventual ratification in New York, by the close vote of 30–27. They were influential in the ratification debates in other States, as well. THE FEDERALIST PAPERS remain this country's most significant political treatise. Originally, these newspaper articles were written for a general readership of informed citizens; they were written to inform, to educate, and to persuade. They were written to explain the wonders of the Constitution.

Today's popular constitutional rhetoric, however, often is sterile, even mindless, by comparison to that of the Framers. Of course, our generation has in common with theirs a full complement of fierce partisan politicians. But constitutional law in their day was understood to be the duty and privilege of every citizen. Today, "doing" constitutional law has become more of an elitist enterprise performed in the salons of our time. Today, Supreme Court Justices and lawyers and constitutional law professors do constitutional law. They do it in the obscure pages of inaccessible case reports, read only by lawyers and judges, and in even more obscure law journals, read only by other law professors. For the most part, these are inaccessible and unintelligible to the average citizen. Arguably much of what is written about the Constitution today by scholars, in particular, may be labeled "brilliant," but I adhere to the heretical observation of Constitutional Law Professor Daniel A. Farber:

Most theories of constitutional law rest on some notion of the consent of the governed, either through tacit institutional acquiescence or through some kind of social contract theory. A brilliant theory is by definition one that would not occur to most people. It is hard to see how the vast majority of the population can be presumed to have agreed to something that they could not conceive of. Who would know better than the average person what the average person has consented to? How can someone have consented to a position that is so novel and clever that only one person on earth has ever thought of it?

Constitutional scholars, for the most part, have abdicated the field of popular constitutional commentary to journalists. Some, but not enough, of this journalism is thoughtful and balanced. Too little is didactic. Instead of being educated in how to think about these issues, the average citizen is merely told what to think by commentators and columnists. Popular pundits use the media to play to their friends in the mob, by leading cheers on radio and television call-in shows and by spinning 1,000 word op-eds in newspapers. The most complex and important issues are reduced to almost visceral slogans like "Pro-Life" and "Pro-Choice." More often than not, constitutional discourse regrettably has become all sound bites and headlines. Think about it. Whether the issue be budget-balancing or flag-burning, who is influencing citizens' constitutional opinions? How many of the opinionated inform themselves by the kind of careful study and thought that took place before, during, and after the Constitutional Convention of 1787? My hope for this book is to replace Gallup poll feelings and attitudes with a deeper knowledge and more careful reflection about the Constitution.

As a teacher of constitutional law—who incidentally admits to having done some of the high-falutin' scholarship being discounted here—as I prepared for my constitutional law courses each year, I would marvel at how some of the opinions written by some of the Justices truly speak to the ages. I lamented, however, how practically inaccessible these opinions were to most people. There is not widespread access to the official case reports and they can be quite intimidating, by their sheer volume and by their lawyers' legalese that includes procedural matters, citations, legal research annotations, *et cetera*. Trying to read them would be like trying to drink from a fire hose.

So I decided to do something about it. My idea was to compile a single volume of highly-edited Supreme Court opinions. The purpose is not to summarize the "law" of the Constitution, but to illuminate its underlying principles. This is not a casebook. It is not a book of quotations. It is a book of essays, after the fashion of THE FEDERALIST PAPERS, but these "essays" are taken from the pages of the opinions delivered by the Justices of the Supreme Court.

My intended audience includes lawyers and law students, as well as students of history and government. Someone who remembers a prior constitutional law course with fondness will enjoy these essays. I imagine some college professors and high school teachers might assign this book as primary or secondary reading in their courses, as well. But this book is targeted primarily toward the lay person who is a serious reader—the kind of person who enjoys wandering around in a book store on the weekends. This book is intended for the curious citizen who wants to be better educated and more informed about constitutional issues. A reader who studies these opinions carefully will learn about the wonders of our Constitution, about the first principles that make the United States historically and politically unique. My goal is to make these writings more widely accessible to more people than they otherwise would be.

In a sense, this book harkens back to a previous era of our constitutional life. According to Charles E. Wyzanski, Jr., Justice Louis Dembitz Brandeis, who served with great distinction on the Supreme Court between 1916 and 1939, "emphasized the special responsibility which falls upon a judge of our highest court to contribute in its deepest sense to the political growth of the American people. From the time of Chief Justice Marshall, the opinions of the Supreme Court have been a text unto the people. Read in the daily press, studied in the common school, knotted into the rope of enduring history, they may well be the largest single contribution to the philosophy of the American way of life." For the sake of the Constitution, both the Justices and the people need to rededicate themselves to this lost tradition.

Many Supreme Court decisions are important and historic. Some of the opinions—majority, concurring, and dissenting— prove to be stimulating and interesting reading, when they are made accessible in a readable format. That is the *raison d'etre* for this book. I have carefully selected and edited these opinions to be sure. The official government compilation of Supreme Court decisions, UNITED STATES REPORTS, lines up more than

500 volumes. In recent years, single volumes run in excess of one thousand pages each. I have chosen opinions from only 85 cases, decided over the last 200 years, and I have edited them all down to a book with fewer total pages than are found in a single one of those volumes. Finally, I have organized them into a coherent volume that provides sufficient context and encourages further reflection. Justice William O. Douglas once said, "The Court's great power is its ability to educate, to provide moral leadership." My criterion for selection is whether an opinion teaches a lesson about some important and overarching principle of the Constitution.

What first got me to thinking about this idea was an article I wrote in 1993 for CONSTITUTIONAL COMMENTARY, a professors' magazine, reviewing Yale University Professor Joseph Goldstein's book entitled THE INTELLIGIBLE CONSTITUTION (1992). Here is part of what I wrote:

> The author derives his basic premise from Chief Justice Marshall's admonition in *McCulloch*: "We must never forget, that it is a constitution we are expounding." In performing this "expounding" function, Professor Goldstein insists that Supreme Court "communications [opinions] on behalf of and to We the People who 'decided' to establish the Constitution must be something that We can understand if We are to remain sovereign, if Our consent to the government is to be sustained." The "thesis of this book," in the words of the author, "is that the justices, as members of a collective body, have an obligation to maintain the Constitution, in opinions of the Court and also in concurring and dissenting opinions, as something intelligible—something that We the People of the United States can understand."

\* \* \* \*

> Professor Goldstein's premise is that the Supreme Court has a constitutional responsibility to perform the role Ralph Lerner once described as the "republican schoolmaster." The contemporary Court most certainly confronts the citizenry on the important issues of the day. There is a "proper connection between judicial power and public opinion." One essential role for the High Court is to engage in "high political education," always to be distinguished from the logical fallacy *argumentum ad populum* at the opposite extreme.

What I expect from the present book is more than one can usually find in the popular press which, with the proverbial notable exceptions, usually reports Supreme Court decisions as events and describes cases in terms of outcomes with winners and losers, somewhat reminiscent of the sports pages. Furthermore, as I have said, contemporary scholars writing law review articles simply are not performing the needed educational function. Scholars tend to write to other dwellers in the groves of academe, occasionally adding a postscript addressed to the Justices themselves. Professors have lost the sense of a diverse audience that includes intelligent enquirers among the citizenry. Consequently, their ideas, for the most part, do not influence anyone with power or influence, let alone inform public opinion. Some professors occasionally worry that there is something wrong about this, but I do not suppose that things are likely to change. (My reader will forgive me, if I digress to refer academic reviewers to some academic writings: *Symposium on Constitutional Theory and the Practice of Judging*, 63 U. Colo. L. Rev. 291 (1992); *Symposium on Legal Education*, 91 Mich. L. Rev. 1921 (1993).) My primary point is that the Justices consistently have done more of the needed civic education in the pages of the UNITED STATES REPORTS, and have done it far better than either the press or the professoriate.

My goal is to educate the enquiring reader about constitutional values and principles; not to show my reader what to think, but how to think, about the nation's political charter. It is expressly not my goal to teach about constitutional doctrine, about the details of the Supreme Court's interpretations of particular constitutional provisions. There are many other fine books which accomplish that goal. My reader will have to look elsewhere, for example, to learn about the evolution of the "clear and present danger" test for speech advocating the violent overthrow of the government or to read about the strengths and weaknesses of the three-prong test for determining whether a government program violates the nonestablishment clause.

Rather, my goal for this book is to explicate those important and fundamental principles on which our constitutional republic is based, the shared values of our polity. These first principles are what Americans are willing to march off to war to defend. Yet, we have a remarkable tradition of debate and argument amongst ourselves about these principles. Our constitutional values are rooted in history at the same time they continue to evolve in our day-to-day self-government. It is not overly melodramatic to insist that it is critically important for all Americans to be well-grounded in this constitutional catechism. What Alexander Hamilton wrote in 1787 in *Federalist Paper No. 1*, when the Constitution was still in doubt, is no less true today in its 208th year: "It seems to have been reserved to the people of this country, by their conduct and example, to decide the important question, whether societies of men are really capable or not of establishing good government from reflection and choice, or whether they are forever destined to depend for their political constitutions on accident and force."

It is in the nature of our Constitution that we cannot rest on the laurels of our founding generation. James Wilson, delegate to the Constitutional Convention and one of the six original members of the Supreme Court, made the argument for the study of constitutional law in his inaugural lecture as Professor of Law at the College of Philadelphia:

The science of law should, in some measure, and in some degree, be the study of every free citizen, and of every free man. Every free citizen and every free man has duties to perform and rights to claim. Unless, in some measure, and in some degree, he knows those duties and rights, he can never act a just and an independent part.

Contemporary philosopher Mortimer J. Adler explains, "citizenship is the primary political office under a constitutional government. In a republic, citizens are the ruling class." Thus, every citizen needs to know about the Constitution. Those who founded this country understood this. We ignore the lessons they learned, the lessons they sought to teach us, the lessons we are obliged to teach our posterity, at our own peril. With full appreciation for what is at stake for every generation, Abraham Lincoln at Gettysburg described ours as a "government of the people, by the people, for the people."

This book is arranged to follow the organization of the Constitution of the United States, which is reproduced in the front of the volume, where it belongs, instead of being placed in a kind of "p.s." appendix. The edited opinion excerpts themselves are grouped in five Chapters dealing with: First Principles; Congress; Executive; Judiciary; and Individual Rights. I have written an introductory essay for each Chapter to provide some overview and to highlight the selections. I have included a selective Bibliography at the end. There is an appendix giving some basic information on the Justices of the Supreme Court.

Each opinion excerpt bears a "title" in the form of a capsule quotation to identify its theme. For each entry, I have included complete citations for readers who want to find the full set of opinions in these cases—the first number is the volume number and the second number is the beginning page number. Many large public libraries have one of the case reports. Then I have written a short introduction or explanation of the case, placing it within some context and commenting on its significance. The italicized introduction is intended to help prepare my reader for the Justice's handiwork. While some might quarrel with my selections or my editing or my editorials, like Horace I shrug to observe that "sometimes even excellent Homer nods."

Unlike casebooks written for lawyers and law students, in this book I have omitted most all extraneous material; there are no explanations of procedural history, strings of citations, footnote digressions, or lengthy quotations, *et cetera*, that might get in the way of understanding. Furthermore, although I have edited and altered the opinions, I have done my best to preserve the Justices' expressions of their ideas intact, so that they may speak in their own voice to the reader. These edited versions are substantially shorter than the originals; opinions that cover more than a hundred pages sometimes are reduced to an essence of just a few pages. I have done this without the distracting ellipses and brackets found in constitutional law casebooks edited for law students. When it seemed necessary to understanding, I have changed a word or a phrase in order to clarify meaning or to finesse an omission. Somewhat tongue in cheek, I find support for my approach in *Masson v. New Yorker Magazine, Inc.*, 111 S.Ct. 2419 (1991), in which the Supreme Court held blameless a commentator who edited quotations from interviews, so long as the changes did not materially alter what was actually said. More practically, my purpose is to save my reader from the fate Scott Turow described, upon reading his very first law school assignment, long before he became a successful attorney and best-selling novelist:

OK. It was nine o'clock when I started reading. The case is four pages long and at 10:35 I finally finished. It was something like stirring concrete with my eyelashes. I had no idea what half the words meant. I must have opened *Black's Law Dictionary* twenty-five times and I still can't understand many of the definitions. There are notations and numbers throughout the case whose purpose baffles me. And even now I'm not crystal-clear on what the court finally decided to do.

In conclusion—although I am no Joseph Story—I invoke the same hope for "THE MOST WONDERFUL WORK" which that Supreme Court Justice, Harvard University law professor, and great constitutional treatise writer invoked in his Preface to his

A FAMILIAR EXPOSITION OF THE CONSTITUTION (1840), which was published to promote and to encourage the wider study and understanding of the Constitution of the United States:

> The present Work is designed, not only for private reading, but as a text book for the highest classes in our Common Schools and Academies. It is also adapted to the use of those, who are more advanced, and have left school, after having passed through the common branches of education. It may also be studied with advantage by those, who have arrived at maturer years, but whose pursuits have not allowed them leisure to acquire a thorough knowledge of the Republican Constitution of Government, under which they live.

THOMAS E. BAKER
Lubbock, Texas
tbaker@ttu.edu
17 September 1996

# Table of Contents

## CHAPTER ONE—FIRST PRINCIPLES                        1

*We the People of the United States, in Order to form a more perfect Union, establish Justice, insure domestic Tranquillity, provide for the common defence, promote the general Welfare, and secure the Blessings of Liberty to ourselves and our Posterity, do ordain and establish this Constitution for the United States of America.*

[nationhood and sovereignty resides in the people—a national government of limited and enumerated powers—constitutional law orders the relationship between the government and the individual—constitutional remedies for constitutional wrongs—a government of laws and not of men—separation of powers and the amendment process—judicial reapportionment of State legislatures is not a political question—an indestructible Union composed of indestructible States—federalism is an American invention—all Americans enjoy the privileges of national citizenship wherever they travel—teaching by example and disapproving of government wrongdoing—judicial self-restraint through deciding not to decide cases—the right to criticize government and public officials—civil disobedience to protest unjust laws—the right of revolution from the Declaration of Independence]

## CHAPTER TWO—THE LEGISLATIVE POWER                  107

*All legislative Powers herein granted shall be vested in a Congress of the United States, which shall consist of a Senate and House of Representatives.*

[all laws necessary and proper—the power of the federal purse—States taking federal money with strings attached—U.S. treaties and laws are supreme over State sovereignty—the commerce clause contemplates a national common market—powers reserved to the States preserve State sovereignty—adjusting the contemporary balance of federal and State powers—judicial authority under the legislative commerce power—Congress cannot abdicate or transfer the legislative power to make laws—absolute protections of legislators' speech and debate—enforcing the congressional guarantee of a republican form of government in each State—the plenary congres-

# Table of Contents by Case Name

# The Constitution of the United States

We the People of the United States, in Order to form a more perfect Union, establish Justice, insure domestic Tranquility, provide for the common defence, promote the general Welfare, and secure the Blessings of Liberty to ourselves and our Posterity, do ordain and establish this Constitution for the United States of America.

## Article I

Section 1. All legislative Powers herein granted shall be vested in a Congress of the United States, which shall consist of a Senate and House of Representatives.

Section 2. The House of Representatives shall be composed of Members chosen every second Year by the People of the several States, and the Electors in each State shall have the Qualifications requisite for Electors of the most numerous Branch of the State Legislature.

No Person shall be a Representative who shall not have attained to the Age of twenty five Years, and been seven Years a Citizen of the United States, and who shall not, when elected, be an Inhabitant of that State in which he shall be chosen.

Representatives and direct Taxes shall be apportioned among the several States which may be included within this Union, according to their respective Numbers, which shall be determined by adding to the whole Number of free Persons, including those bound to Service for a Term of Years, and excluding Indians not taxed, three fifths of all other Persons. The actual Enumeration shall be made within three Years after the first Meeting of the Congress of the United States, and within every subsequent Term of ten Years, in such Manner as they shall by Law direct. The Number of Representatives shall not exceed one for every thirty Thousand, but each State shall have at Least one Representative; and until such enumerations shall be made, the State of New Hampshire shall be entitled to chuse three, Massachusetts eight, Rhode-Island and Providence Plantations one, Connecticut five, New-York six, New Jersey four, Pennsylvania eight, Delaware one, Maryland six, Virginia ten, North Carolina five, South Carolina five, and Georgia three.

When vacancies happen in the Representation from any State, the Executive Authority thereof shall issue Writs of Election to fill such Vacancies.

The House of Representatives shall chuse their speaker and other Officers; and shall have the sole Power of Impeachment.

Section 3. The Senate of the United States shall be composed of two Senators from each State, chosen by the Legislature thereof, for six Years; and each Senator shall have one Vote.

Immediately after they shall be assembled in Consequence of the first Election, they shall be divided as equally as may be into three Classes. The Seats of the Senators of the first Class shall be vacated at the Expiration of the second Year, of the second Class at the Expiration of the fourth Year, and of the third Class at the Expiration of the sixth Year, so that one third may be chosen every second Year; and if Vacancies happen by Resignation, or otherwise, during the Recess of the Legislature of any State, the Executive thereof may make temporary Appointments until the next Meeting of the Legislature, which shall then fill such Vacancies.

No Person shall be a Senator who shall not have attained to the Age of thirty Years, and been nine Years a Citizen of the United States, and who shall not, when elected, be an Inhabitant of that State for which he shall be chosen.

The Vice President of the United States shall be President of the Senate, but shall have no Vote, unless they be equally divided.

The Senate shall chuse their other Officers, and also a President pro tempore, in the Absence of the Vice President, or when he shall exercise the Office of President of the United States.

The Senate shall have the sole Power to try all Impeachments. When sitting for that Purpose, they shall be on Oath or Affirmation. When the President of the United States is tried, the Chief Justice shall preside: And no Person shall be convicted without the concurrence of two thirds of the Members present.

Judgment in Cases of Impeachment shall not extend further than to removal from Office, and disqualification to hold and enjoy any Office of honor, Trust or Profit under the United

States: but the Party convicted shall nevertheless be liable and subject to Indictment, Trial, Judgment and Punishment, according to law.

Section 4. The Times, Places and Manner of holding Elections for Senators and Representatives, shall be prescribed in each State by the Legislature thereof; but the Congress may at any time by Law make or alter such Regulations, except as to the Places of chusing Senators.

The Congress shall assemble at least once in every Year, and such Meeting shall be on the first Monday in December, unless they shall by Law appoint a different Day.

Section 5. Each House shall be the Judge of the Elections, Returns and Qualifications of its own Members, and a Majority of each shall constitute a Quorum to do business; but a smaller Number may adjourn from day to day, and may be authorized to compel the Attendance of absent Members, in such Manner, and under such Penalties as each House may provide.

Each House may determine the Rules of its Proceedings, punish its Members for disorderly Behaviour, and, with the Concurrence of two thirds, expel a Member.

Each House shall keep a Journal of its Proceedings, and from time to time publish the same, excepting such Parts as may in their Judgment require Secrecy; and the yeas and Nays of the Members of either House on any question shall, at the Desire of one fifth of those Present, be entered on the Journal.

Neither House, during the Session of Congress, shall, without the Consent of the other, adjourn for more than three days, nor to any other place than that in which the two Houses shall be sitting.

Section 6. The Senators and Representatives shall receive a Compensation for their Services, to be ascertained by Law, and paid out of the Treasury of the United States. They shall in all Cases, except Treason, Felony and Breach of the Peace, be privileged from Arrest during their Attendance at the Session of their respective Houses, and in going to and returning from the same; and for any Speech or Debate in either House, they shall not be questioned in any other Place.

No Senator or Representative shall, during the Time for which he was elected, be appointed to any civil Office under the Authority of the United States, which shall have been created, or the Emoluments whereof shall have been encreased during such time; and no Person holding any Office under the United States, shall be a Member of either House during his Continuance in Office.

Section 7. All Bills for raising Revenue shall originate in the House of Representatives; but the Senate may propose or concur with Amendments as on other Bills.

Every Bill which shall have passed the House of Representatives and the Senate, shall, before it become a Law, be presented to the President of the United States; If he approve he shall sign it, but if not he shall return it, with his Objections to that House in which it shall have originated, who shall enter the Objections at large on their Journal, and proceed to reconsider it. If after such Reconsideration two thirds of that House shall agree to pass the Bill, it shall be sent, together with the Objections, to the other House, by which it shall likewise be reconsidered, and if approved by two thirds of that House, it shall become a Law. But in all such Cases the Votes of both Houses shall be determined by yeas and Nays, and the Names of the Persons voting for and against the Bill shall be entered on the Journal of each House respectively. If any Bill shall not be returned by the President within ten Days (Sundays excepted) after it shall have been presented to him, the Same shall be a Law, in like Manner as if he had signed it, unless the Congress by their Adjournment prevent its Return, in which Case it shall not be a Law.

Every Order, Resolution, or Vote to which the Concurrence of the Senate and House of Representatives may be necessary (except on a question of Adjournment) shall be presented to the President of the United States; and before the Same shall take Effect, shall be approved by him, or being disapproved by him, shall be repassed by two thirds of the Senate and House of Representatives, according to the Rules and Limitations prescribed in the Case of a Bill.

Section 8. The Congress shall have Power To lay and collect Taxes, Duties, Imposts and Excises, to pay the Debts and provide for the common Defence and general Welfare of the United States; but all duties, Imposts and Excises shall be uniform throughout the United States;

To borrow Money on the Credit of the United States;

To regulate Commerce with foreign Nations, and among the several States, and with the Indian Tribes;

To establish an uniform Rule of Naturalization, and uniform Laws on the subject of Bankruptcies throughout the United States;

To coin Money, regulate the Value thereof, and of foreign Coin, and fix the Standard of Weights and Measures;

To provide for the Punishment of counterfeiting the Securities and current Coin of the United States;

To establish Post Offices and post Roads;

To promote the Progress of Science and useful Arts, by securing for limited Times to Authors and Inventors exclusive Right to their respective Writings and Discoveries;

To constitute Tribunals inferior to the supreme Court;

To define and punish Piracies and Felonies committed on the high Seas, and Offences against the Law of Nations;

To declare War, grant Letters of Marque and Reprisal, and make rules concerning Captures on Land and Water;

To raise and support Armies, but no Appropriation of Money to that Use shall be for a longer Term than two Years;

To provide and maintain a Navy;

To make rules for the Government and Regulation of the land and naval Forces;

To provide for calling forth the Militia to execute the Laws of the Union, suppress Insurrections and repel Invasions;

To provide for organizing, arming, and disciplining, the Militia, and for governing such Part of them as may be employed in the Service of the United States, reserving to the States respectively, the Appointment of the Officers, and the Authority of training the Militia according to the discipline prescribed by Congress;

To exercise exclusive Legislation in all Cases whatsoever, over such District (not exceeding ten Miles square), as may, by Cession of particular States, and the Acceptance of Congress, become the Seat of the Government of the United States, and to exercise like Authority over all Places purchased by the Consent of the Legislature of the State in which the Same shall be for the Erection of Forts, Magazines, Arsenals, dock-Yards, and other needful Buildings;—And

To make all Laws which shall be necessary and proper for carrying into Execution the foregoing Powers, and all other Powers vested by this Constitution in the Government of the United States, or in any Department or Officer thereof.

Section 9. The Migration or Importation of such Persons as any of the States now existing shall think proper to admit, shall not be prohibited by the Congress prior to the Year one thousand eight hundred and eight, but a Tax or duty may be imposed on such Importation, not exceeding ten dollars for each Person.

The Privilege of the Writ of Habeas Corpus shall not be suspended, unless when in Cases of Rebellion or Invasion the public Safety may require it.

No Bill of Attainder or ex post facto Law shall be passed.

No Capitation, or other direct, Tax shall be laid, unless in Proportion to the Census or Enumeration herein before directed to be taken.

No Tax or Duty shall be laid on Articles exported from any State.

No Preference shall be given by any Regulation of Commerce or Revenue to the Ports of one State over those of another: nor shall Vessels bound to, or from, one State, be obliged to enter, clear, or pay Duties in another.

No money shall be drawn from the Treasury, but in Consequence of Appropriations made by Law; and a regular Statement and Account of the Receipts and Expenditures of all public Money shall be published from time to time.

No Title of Nobility shall be granted by the United States: And no Person holding any Office of Profit or Trust under them, shall, without the Consent of the Congress, accept of any present, Emolument, Office, or Title, of any kind whatever, from any King, Prince, or foreign State.

Section 10. No State shall enter into any Treaty, Alliance, or Confederation; grant Letters of Marque and Reprisal; coin Money; emit Bills of Credit; make any Thing but gold and silver Coin a Tender in Payment of Debts; pass any Bill of Attainder, ex post facto Law, or Law impairing the Obligation of Contracts, or grant any Title of Nobility.

No State shall, without the Consent of the Congress, lay any Imposts or Duties on Imports or Exports, except what may be absolutely necessary for executing it's inspection Laws: and the net Produce of all Duties and Imposts, laid by any State on Imports or Exports, shall be for the Use of the Treasury of the United States; and all such Laws shall be subject to the Revision and Controul of the Congress.

No State shall, without the Consent of Congress, lay any Duty of Tonnage, keep Troops, or Ships of War in time of Peace, enter into any Agreement or Compact with another State, or with a foreign Power, or engage in War, unless actually invaded, or in such imminent Danger as will not admit of delay.

## Article II

Section 1. The executive Power shall be vested in a President of the United States of America. He shall hold his Office during the Term of four Years, and, together with the Vice President, chosen for the same term, be elected, as follows:

Each State shall appoint, in such Manner as the Legislature thereof may direct, a Number of Electors, equal to the whole Number of Senators and Representatives to which the State may be entitled in the Congress: but no Senator or Representative, or Person holding an Office of Trust or Profit under the United States, shall be appointed an Elector.

The Electors shall meet in their respective States, and vote by Ballot for two Persons, of whom one at least shall not be an Inhabitant of the same State with themselves. And they shall make a List of all the Persons voted for, and of the Number of Votes for each; which List they shall sign and certify, and transmit sealed to the Seat of the Government of the United States, directed to the President of the Senate. The President of the Senate shall, in the Presence of the Senate and House of Representatives, open all the Certificates, and the Votes shall then be counted. The Person having the greatest Number of Votes shall be the President, if such Number be a Majority of the whole Number of Electors appointed; and if there be more than one who have such Majority, and have an equal Number of Votes, then the House of Representatives shall immediately chuse by Ballot one of them for President: and if no Person have a Majority, then from the five highest on the List the said House shall in like Manner chuse the President. But in chusing the President, the Votes shall be taken by States, the Representation from each State having one Vote; A quorum for this Purpose shall consist of a Member or Members from two thirds of the States, and a Majority of all the States shall be necessary to a Choice. In every Case, after the Choice of the President, the Person having the greatest Number of Votes of the Electors shall be the Vice President. But if there should remain two or more who have equal Votes, the Senate shall chuse from them by Ballot the Vice President.

The Congress may determine the Time of chusing the Electors, and the Day on which they shall give their Votes; which Day shall be the same throughout the United States.

No Person except a natural born Citizen, or a Citizen of the United States, at the time of the Adoption of this Constitution, shall be eligible to the Office of President; neither shall any Person be eligible to that Office who shall not have attained to the Age of thirty five Years, and been fourteen Years a Resident within the United States.

In Case of the Removal of the President from Office, or of his Death, Resignation, or Inability to discharge the Powers and Duties of the said Office, the Same shall devolve on the Vice President, and the Congress may by Law provide for the Case of Removal, Death, Resignation or Inability, both of the President and Vice President, declaring what Officer shall then act as President, and such Officer shall act accordingly, until the Disability be removed, or a President shall be elected.

The President shall, at stated Times, receive for his Services, a Compensation, which shall neither be increased nor diminished during the Period for which he shall have been elected, and he shall not receive within that Period any other Emolument from the United States, or any of them.

Before he enter on the Execution of his Office, he shall take the following Oath or Affirmation:—"I do solemnly swear (or affirm) that I will faithfully execute the Office of President of the United States, and will to the best of my Ability, preserve, protect and defend the Constitution of the United States."

Section 2. The President shall be Commander in Chief of the Army and Navy of the United States, and of the Militia of the several States, when called into the actual Service of the United States; he may require the Opinion, in writing, of the principal Officer in each of the executive Departments, upon any Subject relating to the Duties of their respective Offices, and he shall have Power to grant Reprieves and Pardons for Offences against the United States, except in Cases of Impeachment.

He shall have Power, by and with the Advice and Consent of the Senate, to make Treaties, provided two thirds of the Senators present concur; and he shall nominate, and by and with the Advice and Consent of the Senate, shall appoint Ambassadors, other public Ministers and Consuls, Judges of the supreme Court, and all other Officers of the United States, whose Appointments are not herein otherwise provided for, and which shall be established by Law: but the Congress may by Law vest the Appointment of such inferior Officers, as they think proper, in the President alone, in the Courts of Law, or in the Heads of Departments.

The President shall have Power to fill up all Vacancies that may happen during the Recess of the Senate, by granting Commissions which shall expire at the End of their next Session.

Section 3. He shall from time to time give to the Congress Information of the State of the Union, and recommend to their Consideration such Measures as he shall judge necessary and expedient; he may, on extraordinary Occasions, convene both Houses, or either of them, and in Case of Disagreement between them, with Respect to the Time of Adjournment, he may adjourn them to such Time as he shall think proper; he shall receive Ambassadors and other public Ministers; he shall take Care that the Laws be faithfully executed, and shall Commission all the Officers of the United States.

Section 4. The President, Vice President and all civil Officers of the United States, shall be removed from Office on Impeachment for, and Conviction of, Treason, Bribery, or other High Crimes and Misdemeanors.

## Article III

Section 1. The judicial Power of the United States, shall be vested in one supreme Court, and in such inferior Courts as the Congress may from time to time ordain and establish. The Judges, both of the supreme and inferior Courts, shall hold their Offices during good Behaviour, and shall, at stated Times, receive for their Services, a Compensation, which shall not be diminished during their Continuance in Office.

Section 2. The judicial Power shall extend to all Cases, in Law and Equity, arising under this Constitution, the Laws of the United States, and Treaties made, or which shall be made, under their Authority;—to all Cases affecting Ambassadors, other public Ministers and Consuls;—to all Cases of admiralty and maritime Jurisdiction;—to Controversies to which the

United States shall be a Party;—to Controversies between two or more States; between a State and Citizens of another State;— between Citizens of different States;-between Citizens of the same State claiming Lands under Grants of different States, and between a State, or the Citizens thereof, and foreign States, Citizens or Subjects.

In all Cases affecting Ambassadors, other public Ministers and Consuls, and those in which a State shall be Party, the supreme Court shall have original Jurisdiction. In all the other Cases before mentioned, the supreme Court shall have appellate Jurisdiction, both as to Law and Fact, with such Exceptions, and under such Regulations as the Congress shall make.

The Trial of all Crimes, except in Cases of Impeachment, shall be by Jury; and such Trial shall be held in the State where the said Crimes shall have been committed; but when not committed within any State, the Trial shall be at such Place or Places as the Congress may by Law have directed.

Section 3. Treason against the United States, shall consist only in levying War against them, or in adhering to their Enemies, giving them Aid and Comfort. No Person shall be convicted of Treason unless on the Testimony of two Witnesses to the same overt Act, or on Confession in open Court.

The Congress shall have Power to declare the Punishment of Treason, but no Attainder of Treason shall work Corruption of Blood, or Forfeiture except during the Life of the Person attainted.

## Article IV

Section 1. Full Faith and Credit shall be given in each State to the public Acts, Records, and judicial Proceedings of every other State. And the Congress may by general Laws prescribe the Manner in which such Acts, Records and Proceedings shall be proved, and the Effect thereof.

Section 2. The Citizens of each State shall be entitled to all Privileges and Immunities of Citizens in the several States.

A Person charged in any State with Treason, Felony, or other Crime, who shall flee from Justice, and be found in another State, shall on Demand of the executive Authority of the State from which he fled, be delivered up, to be removed to the State having Jurisdiction of the Crime.

No person held to Service or Labour in one State, under the Laws thereof, escaping into another, shall, in Consequence of any Law or Regulation therein, be discharged from such Service or Labour, but shall be delivered up on Claim of the Party to whom such Service or Labour may be due.

Section 3. New States may be admitted by the Congress into this Union; but no new State shall be formed or erected within the Jurisdiction of any other State; nor any State be formed by the Junction of two or more States, or Parts of States, without the Consent of the Legislatures of the States concerned as well as of the Congress.

The Congress shall have Power to dispose of and make all needful Rules and Regulations respecting the Territory or other Property belonging to the United States; and nothing in this Constitution shall be so construed as to Prejudice any Claims of the United States, or of any particular State.

Section 4. The United States shall guarantee to every State in this Union a Republican Form of Government, and shall protect each of them against Invasion; and on Application of the Legislature, or of the Executive (when the Legislature cannot be convened) against domestic Violence.

## Article V

The Congress, whenever two thirds of both Houses shall deem it necessary, shall propose Amendments to this Constitution, or, on the Application of the Legislatures of two thirds of the several States, shall call a Convention for proposing Amendments, which, in either Case, shall be valid to all Intents and Purposes, as Part of this Constitution, when ratified by the Legislatures of three fourths of the several States, or by Conventions in three fourths thereof, as the one or the other Mode of Ratification may be proposed by the Congress; Provided that no Amendment which may be made prior to the Year One thousand eight hundred and eight shall in any Manner affect the first and fourth Clauses in the Ninth Section of the first Article; and that no State, without its Consent, shall be deprived of its equal Suffrage in the Senate.

## Article VI

All Debts contracted and Engagements entered into, before the Adoption of this Constitution, shall be as valid against the United States under this Constitution, as under the Confederation.

This Constitution, and the Laws of the United States which shall be made in Pursuance thereof; and all Treaties made, or which shall be made, under the Authority of the United States, shall be the supreme Law of the Land; and the Judges in every State shall be bound thereby, any Thing in the Constitution or Laws of any State to the Contrary notwithstanding.

The Senators and Representatives before mentioned, and the Members of the several State Legislatures, and all executive and judicial Officers, both of the United States and of the several States, shall be bound by Oath or Affirmation, to support this Constitution; but no religious Test shall ever be required as a Qualification to any Office or public Trust under the United States.

## Article VII

The Ratification of the Conventions of nine States, shall be sufficient for the Establishment of this Constitution between the States so ratifying the Same.

Done in Convention by the Unanimous Consent of the States present the Seventeenth Day of September in the Year of our Lord one thousand seven hundred and Eighty seven and of the Independence of the United States of America the Twelfth. In witness whereof We have hereunto subscribed our Names,

## Amendments
(The first 10 Amendments were ratified December 15, 1791, and form what is known as the Bill of Rights)

## Amendment 1

Congress shall make no law respecting an establishment of religion, or prohibiting the free exercise thereof; or abridging the freedom of speech, or of the press; or the right of the people peaceably to assemble, and to petition the Government for a redress of grievances.

## Amendment 2

A well regulated Militia, being necessary to the security of a free State, the right of the people to keep and bear Arms, shall not be infringed.

## Amendment 3

No Soldier shall, in time of peace be quartered in any house, without the consent of the Owner, nor in time of war, but in a manner to be prescribed by law.

## Amendment 4

The right of the people to be secure in their persons, houses, papers, and effects, against unreasonable searches and seizures, shall not be violated, and no Warrants shall issue, but upon probable cause, supported by Oath or affirmation, and particularly describing the place to be searched, and the persons or things to be seized.

## Amendment 5

No person shall be held to answer for a capital, or otherwise infamous crime, unless on a presentment or indictment of a Grand Jury, except in cases arising in the land or naval forces, or in the Militia, when in actual service in time of War or public danger; nor shall any person be subject for the same offence to be twice put in jeopardy of life or limb; nor shall be compelled in any criminal case to be a witness against himself, nor be deprived of life, liberty, or property, without due process of law; nor shall private property be taken for public use, without just compensation.

## Amendment 6

In all criminal prosecutions, the accused shall enjoy the right to a speedy and public trial, by an impartial jury of the State and district wherein the crime shall have been committed, which district shall have been previously ascertained by law, and to be informed of the nature and cause of the accusation; to be confronted with the witnesses against him; to have compulsory process for obtaining witnesses in his favor, and to have the Assistance of Counsel for his defence.

## Amendment 7

In Suits at common law, where the value in controversy shall exceed twenty dollars, the right of trial by jury shall be preserved, and no fact tried by a jury, shall be otherwise re-examined in any Court of the United States, than according to the rules of the common law.

## Amendment 8

Excessive bail shall not be required, nor excessive fines imposed, nor cruel and unusual punishments inflicted.

## Amendment 9

The enumeration in the Constitution, of certain rights, shall not be construed to deny or disparage others retained by the people.

## Amendment 10

The powers not delegated to the United States by the Constitution, nor prohibited by it to the States, are reserved to the States respectively, or to the people.

## Amendment 11
### (Ratified February 7, 1795)

The Judicial power of the United States shall not be construed to extend to any suit in law or equity, commenced or prosecuted against one of the United States by Citizens of another State, or by Citizens or Subjects of any Foreign State.

## Amendment 12
### (Ratified July 27, 1804)

The Electors shall meet in their respective states, and vote by ballot for President and Vice-President, one of whom, at least, shall not be an inhabitant of the same state with themselves; they shall name in their ballots the person voted for as President, and in distinct ballots the person voted for as Vice-President, and they shall make distinct lists of all persons voted for as President, and of all persons voted for as Vice-President, and of the number of votes for each, which lists they shall sign and certify, and transmit sealed to the seat of the government of the United States, directed to the President of the Senate;-The President of the Senate shall, in the presence of the Senate and House of Representatives, open all the certificates and the votes shall then be counted;—The person having the greatest number of votes for President, shall be the President, if such number be a majority of the whole number of Electors appointed; and if no person have such majority, then from the persons having the highest numbers not exceeding three on the list of those voted for as President, the House of Representatives shall choose immediately, by ballot, the President. But in choosing the President, the votes shall be taken by states, the representation from each state having one vote; a quorum for this purpose shall consist of a member or members from two-thirds of the states, and a majority of all the states shall be necessary to a choice. And if the House of Representatives shall not choose a President whenever the right of choice shall devolve upon them, before the fourth day of March next following, then the Vice-President shall act as President, as in the case of the death or other constitutional disability of the President.—The person having the greatest number of votes as Vice-President, shall be the Vice-President, if such number be a majority of the whole number of Electors appointed, and if no person have a majority, then from the two highest numbers on the list, the Senate shall choose the Vice-President; a quorum for the purpose shall consist of two-thirds of the whole number of Senators, and a majority of the whole number shall be necessary to a choice. But no person constitutionally ineligible to the office of President shall be eligible to that of Vice-President of the United States.

## Amendment 13
### (Ratified December 6, 1865)

Section 1. Neither slavery nor involuntary servitude, except as a punishment for crime whereof the party shall have been duly convicted, shall exist within the United States, or any place subject to their jurisdiction.

Section 2. Congress shall have power to enforce this article by appropriate legislation.

## Amendment 14
### (Ratified July 9, 1868)

Section 1. All persons born or naturalized in the United States, and subject to the jurisdiction thereof, are citizens of the United States and of the State wherein they reside. No State shall make or enforce any law which shall abridge the privileges or immunities of citizens of the United States; nor shall any State deprive any person of life, liberty, or property, without due process of law; nor deny to any person within its jurisdiction the equal protection of the laws.

Section 2. Representatives shall be apportioned among the several States according to their respective numbers, counting the whole number of persons in each State, excluding Indians not taxed. But when the right to vote at any election for the choice of electors for President and Vice President of the United States, Representatives in Congress, the Executive and Judicial officers of a State, or the members of the Legislature thereof, is denied to any of the male inhabitants of such State, being twenty-one years of age, and citizens of the United States, or in any way abridged, except for participation in rebellion, or other crime, the basis of representation therein shall be reduced in the proportion which the number of such male citizens shall bear to the whole number of male citizens twenty-one years of age in such State.

Section 3. No person shall be a Senator or Representative in Congress, or elector of President and Vice President, or hold any office, civil or military, under the United States, or under any State, who, having previously taken an oath, as a member of Congress, or as an officer of the United States, or as a member of any State legislature, or as an executive or judicial officer of any State, to support the Constitution of the United States, shall have engaged in insurrection or rebellion against the same, or given aid or comfort to the enemies thereof. But Congress may by a vote of two-thirds of each House, remove such disability.

Section 4. The validity of the public debt of the United States, authorized by law, including debts incurred for payment of pensions and bounties for services in suppressing insurrection or rebellion, shall not be questioned. But neither the United States nor any State shall assume or pay any debt or obligation incurred in aid of insurrection or rebellion against the United States, or any claim for the loss or emancipation of any slave; but all such debts, obligations and claims shall be held illegal and void.

Section 5. The Congress shall have power to enforce, by appropriate legislation, the provisions of this article.

## Amendment 15
(Ratified February 3, 1870)

Section 1. The right of citizens of the United States to vote shall not be denied or abridged by the United States or by any State on account of race, color, or previous condition of servitude.

Section 2. The Congress shall have power to enforce this article by appropriate legislation.

## Amendment 16
### (Ratified February 3, 1913)

The Congress shall have power to lay and collect taxes on incomes, from whatever source derived, without apportionment among the several States, and without regard to any census or enumeration.

## Amendment 17
### (Ratified April 8, 1913)

The Senate of the United States shall be composed of two Senators from each State, elected by the people thereof for six years; and each Senator shall have one vote. The electors in each State shall have the qualifications requisite for electors of the most numerous branch of the State legislatures.

When vacancies happen in the representation of any State in the Senate, the executive authority of such State shall issue writs of election to fill such vacancies: Provided, That the legislature of any State may empower the executive thereof to make temporary appointments until the people fill the vacancies by election as the legislature may direct.

This amendment shall not be so construed as to affect the election or term of any Senator chosen before it becomes valid as part of the Constitution.

## Amendment 18
### (Ratified January 16, 1919.
### Repealed December 5, 1933 by Amendment 21)

Section 1. After one year from the ratification of this article the manufacture, sale, or transportation of intoxicating liquors within, the importation thereof into, or the exportation thereof from the United States and all territory subject to the jurisdiction thereof for beverage purposes is hereby prohibited.

Section 2. The Congress and the several States shall have concurrent power to enforce this article by appropriate legislation.

Section 3. This article shall be inoperative unless it shall have been ratified as an amendment to the Constitution by the legislatures of the several States as provided in the Constitution, within seven years from the date of the submission hereof to the States by the Congress.

## Amendment 19
### (Ratified August 18, 1920)

The right of citizens of the United States to vote shall not be denied or abridged by the United States or by any State on account of sex.

Congress shall have power to enforce this article by appropriate legislation.

## Amendment 20
### (Ratified January 23, 1933)

Section 1. The terms of the President and Vice President shall end at noon on the 20th day of January, and the terms of Senators and Representatives at noon on the 3d day of January, of the years in which such terms would have ended if this article had not been ratified; and the terms of their successors shall then begin.

Section 2. The Congress shall assemble at least once in every year, and such meeting shall begin at noon on the 3d day of January, unless they shall by law appoint a different day.

Section 3. If, at the time fixed for the beginning of the term of the President, the President elect shall have died, the Vice President elect shall become President. If a President shall not have been chosen before the time fixed for the beginning of his term, or if the President elect shall have failed to qualify, then the Vice President elect shall act as President until a President shall have qualified; and the Congress may by law provide for the case wherein neither a President elect nor a Vice President elect shall have qualified, declaring who shall then act as President, or the manner in which one who is to act shall be selected, and such person shall act accordingly until a President or Vice President shall have qualified.

Section 4. The Congress may by law provide for the case of the death of any of the persons from whom the House of Representatives may choose a President whenever the right of choice shall have devolved upon them, and for the case of the death of any of the persons from whom the Senate may choose a Vice President whenever the right of choice shall have devolved upon them.

Section 5. Sections 1 and 2 shall take effect on the 15th day of October following the ratification of this article.

Section 6. This article shall be inoperative unless it shall have been ratified as an amendment to the Constitution by the legislatures of three-fourths of the several States within seven years from the date of its submission.

## Amendment 21
### (Ratified December 5, 1933)

Section 1. The eighteenth article of amendment to the Constitution of the United States is hereby repealed.

Section 2. The transportation or importation into any State, Territory, or possession of the United States for delivery or use therein of intoxicating liquors, in violation of the laws thereof, is hereby prohibited.

Section 3. This article shall be inoperative unless it shall have been ratified as an amendment to the Constitution by conventions in the several States, as provided in the Constitution, within seven years from the date of the submission hereof to the States by the Congress.

## Amendment 22
### (Ratified February 27, 1951)

Section 1. No person shall be elected to the office of the President more than twice, and no person who has held the office of President, or acted as President, for more than two years of a term to which some other person was elected President shall be elected to the office of the President more than once. But this Article shall not apply to any person holding the office of President when this Article was proposed by the Congress, and shall not prevent any person who may be holding the office of President, or acting as President, during the term within which this Article becomes operative from holding the office of President or acting as President during the remainder of such term.

Section 2. This article shall be inoperative unless it shall have been ratified as an amendment to the Constitution by the legislatures of three-fourths of the several States within seven years from the date of its submission to the States by the Congress.

## Amendment 23
### (Ratified March 29, 1961)

Section 1. The District constituting the seat of Government of the United States shall appoint in such manner as the Congress may direct:

A number of electors of President and Vice President equal to the whole number of Senators and Representatives in Congress to which the District would be entitled if it were a State, but in no event more than the least populous State; they shall be in addition to those appointed by the States, but they shall be considered, for the purposes of the election of President and Vice President, to be electors appointed by a State; and they shall meet in the District and perform such duties as provided by the twelfth article of amendment.

Section 2. The Congress shall have power to enforce this article by appropriate legislation.

## Amendment 24
### (Ratified January 23, 1964)

Section 1. The right of citizens of the United States to vote in any primary or other election for President or Vice President, for electors for President or Vice President, or for Senator or Representative in Congress, shall not be denied or abridged by the United States or any State by reason of failure to pay any poll tax or other tax.

Section 2. The Congress shall have power to enforce this article by appropriate legislation.

## Amendment 25
### (Ratified February 10, 1967)

Section 1. In case of the removal of the President from office or of his death or resignation, the Vice President shall become President.

Section 2. Whenever there is a vacancy in the office of the Vice President, the President shall nominate a Vice President who shall take office upon confirmation by a majority vote of both Houses of Congress.

Section 3. Whenever the President transmits to the President pro tempore of the Senate and the Speaker of the House of Representatives his written declaration that he is unable to discharge the powers and duties of his office, and until he transmits to them a written declaration to the contrary, such powers and duties shall be discharged by the Vice President as Acting President.

Section 4. Whenever the Vice President and a majority of either the principal officers of the executive departments or of such other body as Congress may by law provide, transmit to the President pro tempore of the Senate and the Speaker of the House of Representatives their written declaration that the President is unable to discharge the powers and duties of his office, the Vice President shall immediately assume the powers and duties of the office as Acting President.

Thereafter, when the President transmits to the President pro tempore of the Senate and the Speaker of the House of Representatives his written declaration that no inability exists, he shall resume the powers and duties of his office unless the Vice President and a majority of either the principal officers of the executive department or of such other body as Congress may by law provide, transmit within four days to the President pro tempore of the Senate and the Speaker of the House of Representatives their written declaration that the President is unable to discharge the powers and duties of his office. Thereupon Congress shall decide the issue, assembling within forty-eight hours for that purpose if not in session. If the Congress, within twenty-one days after receipt of the latter written declaration, or, if Congress is not in session, within twenty-one days after Congress is required to assemble, determines by two-thirds vote of both Houses that the President is unable to discharge the powers and duties of his office, the Vice President shall continue to discharge the same as Acting President; otherwise, the President shall resume the powers and duties of his office.

## Amendment 26
### (Ratified July 1, 1971)

Section 1. The right of citizens of the United States, who are eighteen years of age or older, to vote shall not be denied or abridged by the United States or by any State on account of age.

Section 2. The Congress shall have the power to enforce this article by appropriate legislation.

## Amendment 27
(Ratified May 7, 1992)

No law, varying the compensation for the services of the Senators and Representatives, shall take effect, until an election of Representatives shall have intervened.

# Chapter One

# First Principles

*We the People of the United States, in Order to form a more perfect Union, establish Justice, insure domestic Tranquillity, provide for the common defence, promote the general Welfare, and secure the Blessings of Liberty to ourselves and our Posterity, do ordain and establish this Constitution for the United States of America.*

James Madison, admiringly known as the "Father of the Constitution," identified the central dilemma of constitutionalism: how to empower the government sufficiently for its tasks and, at the same time, how to limit it from overreaching the individual. He described this most elegantly in *Federalist Paper No. 51*:

It may be a reflection on human nature that such devices should be necessary to control the abuses of government. But what is government itself but the greatest of all reflections on human nature? If men were angels, no government would be necessary. If angels were to govern men, neither external nor internal controls on government would be necessary. In framing a government which is to be administered by men over men, the great difficulty lies in this: you must first enable the government to control the governed; and in the next place oblige it to control itself.

"Prudence, indeed, will dictate that governments long established should not be changed for light and transient causes," according to our Nation's defining document, the *Declaration of Independence* in 1776. In the Articles of Confederation, the original thirteen colonies had allied themselves in what they called a "perpetual union" ratified in 1781. But, before long, prominent American leaders became convinced that the Nation desperately needed a new charter. The sense was that the national government simply was not equal to the tasks of nationhood and there was a fear that the State legislatures were going out of control. Americans were beset with grave worries that their hard-fought revolution would be for naught, that their country would come apart from within or be conquered from without. After a meeting in Annapolis in September 1786, reformers recommended a national convention and the States agreed. The Continental Congress responded in February 1787 by calling on the States to send delegates the following summer to a convention to be "held at Philadelphia for the sole and express purpose of revising the Articles of Confederation."

The delegates to the Constitutional Convention of 1787 quickly resolved to draft an entirely new Constitution. Their "more perfect union" was designed to solve Madison's dilemma of self-government. They relied on structural mechanisms, a wonderful clockwork design of checks and balances, to protect individual liberty while at the same time energizing the national government. At once, they understood and mistrusted both human nature and power. They feared tyranny, especially the tyranny of the majority. They did not need to read George Orwell to appreciate that government power was the antithesis of individual liberty. They had lived under George III.

The constitutional blueprint of these political architects called for a foundation of republican theory. They would build a new national government to political specifications of limited government. They laid out a governmental structure arranged horizontally in separation of powers and vertically in federalism. It was on this elaborate structure that they depended for the protection of the individual against the seemingly inevitable corruption of all forms of government into despotism.

The story is told that at the end of the Convention an onlooker asked 81 year-old patriarch Benjamin Franklin, "What have you given us?" "A republic," he replied with a timeless challenge, "if you can keep it." The foundational philosophy of our Constitution is republicanism. In their *Declaration of Independence*, the Framers already had rejected monarchy with its grandiose claims of the divine right of kings to rule over men. In a republic such as ours, popular sovereignty is the order of the day. Ours is not a pure democracy, however, like the democracies in ancient Athens or in a New England town meeting, where every person has a say and a vote on every decision, even down to such details as whether to build a road. In a republic, our laws are made by popularly-elected officials who serve for specified limited terms and who must stand for regularly-scheduled elections. The history of the franchise in the United States has been to broaden participation, more accurately, to undo historical discriminations based on class, wealth, race, and gender. There is a decided emphasis on majority rule, but the majority rules within proscribed limits that respect political minorities and protect individual rights.

In our form of limited national government, the appropriate governmental goals or objectives are specifically enumerated. For example, Article I, Section 8 lists the powers of the Congress in some detail, adding at the end the elastic clause "To make all laws necessary and proper for carrying into Execution the foregoing Powers." How the government may decide what goals to pursue and how it will pursue them is thus prescribed in advance. Each of the first three Articles of the Constitution outlines procedures for the three branches of government, the legislative, the executive, and the judicial. Finally, the manner in which the government may pursue those objectives is limited by guarantees of individual liberty to be found in various places in the text, especially in the Bill of Rights. It is not a digression, however, to emphasize that individual rights are not "granted" by the Constitution. Read the 1st amendment, for example. Congress is forbidden from abridging "the freedom of speech," a freedom that is assumed to preexist the Constitution and to be inviolate. The constitutional understanding, carried forward from the *Declaration of Independence*, is that freedom and liberty are the inalienable birthrights of all humankind.

The separation of powers depends on the insight from history that a people who depend on governmental self-restraint to protect their liberty will come to regret their political naivete. In *Federalist Paper No. 48*, Madison lauded the way the Constitution would "guard against those encroachments which lead to a tyrannical concentration of all the powers of government in the same hands." He invoked the "oracle" of separated powers, 18th century French political philosopher Baron Montesquieu, to justify and defend the system of having three separate branches of government "connected and blended" to ensure that each has some "constitutional control over the others." Bicameralism, dividing the legislature into two houses, was added to ensure greater deliberation and to protect against the mischiefs of popular government. But your seventh grade civics class description—"the legislative branch makes laws, the executive branch enforces the laws, and the judicial branch interprets the

laws"—is neither complete nor accurate. Our separation of powers is much more complicated and sophisticated. Functions are
shared. Powers are blended. Consider two examples. Congress
may pass a bill and then the President may veto it, but then
Congress may override the veto by a two-thirds vote. A law duly
passed by Congress and signed into law by the President may be
declared unconstitutional by the Supreme Court, but then Congress and the States may override the High Court with an
amendment to the Constitution.

Like separation of powers, the principle of federalism is not
found in so many words in the text but nonetheless is a basic
feature of the constitutional structure. Even though today we
take it for granted, we should be reminded that the concept that
two sovereign governments could somehow occupy the same territory and govern the same people at the same time was an
invention of our 18th-century political philosophers. Back then
it was a novel experiment, a way of organizing government that
many critics at that time believed could not work in theory and
would not work in practice. Although the Framers disagreed
among themselves and many were uncertain about this division
between the national and the state governments, they all fully
expected that there would be conflicts over sovereignty and
power. Indeed, a profound disagreement over federalism principles contributed greatly to the worst cataclysm in our constitutional history, the Civil War.

Federalism rhetoric often is used like red, white and blue
bunting to hide baser political motives. Federalism philosophy,
as understood by the founding generation, contemplated two
distinct spheres of exclusive powers, one national, the other
state. Each respective government would operate without interference from the other and each would respect the other's sovereignty. History trumps philosophy, however, and federalism
today has come to be understood as being the myriad of interre-
lationships and cooperations between the state and national
governments. Since FDR and his Congress and his Supreme
Court reconfigured the constitutional landscape during the late
1930s, governmental power has flowed from the state capitols to
Washington, D.C., as a river flows to the sea.

Though some national politicians, obese with power, today
sing the end of federalism, the political opera is not over so long
as the States continue to play their constitutional role. The science of government is the science of experimentation. In his day,
Justice Louis D. Brandeis was fond of observing, "It is one of the

happy incidents of the federal system that a single courageous State may, if its citizens choose, serve as a laboratory; and try novel social and economic experiments without risk to the rest of the country." In many areas of public policy, this is still true. Debates in Congress in the present day still reverberate with arguments that the States can do some things better than Washington.

\* \* \* \*

The opinions selected for this Chapter contemplate these foundational principles recorded in the *Preamble*. First, there is the question of sovereignty and the need for continuity. Upon our *Declaration of Independence* from the British Crown, sovereignty devolved on "We the people of the United States." In 1793, Justice Wilson penned an opinion in *Chisholm v. Georgia* explaining that it was the constituent people who exercised the sovereignty inherited from the Crown and that it was they who defined the Nation, not the States. Thus was born the modern notion of nationhood. As for the language in the *Preamble* proper, the constitutional question is whether the national government can do anything "necessary and proper" as a means toward those ornate elaborations. If so, the only question left would be whether there was anything the national government could not do. Justice Harlan carefully explains why this cannot be so in *Jacobson v. Massachusetts (1905)*. He writes a primer on the theory of limited government.

The Framers were devotees of the 18th century English philosopher John Locke, whose notion of social compact informed their understanding that constitutional government was a covenant among the people, a contract between the government and its citizens. The contract does not cover everything, not even everything important. The Constitution does not protect you from being murdered, for example. If one individual takes another person's "life, liberty or property," the Constitution simply has not been violated. What the first individual did might be a crime. The person who suffered the harm might be able to bring a civil lawsuit to be made whole. But the Constitution only protects a person from the government, not from other individuals. Whether the wrongdoing will be regarded as being fairly attributable to the government, however, is not always obvious or easily determined. This is called the doctrine of "state action." The difficulties it causes are illustrated by *DeShaney v. Winnegabo County Dept. of Social Services (1989)*. Chief Justice Rehnquist invokes this foundational principle in a poignantly tragic case of child abuse. At the same time, where there is a constitutional wrong there is a constitutional remedy. It might be possible to sue the government itself for the remedy. *Bivens v. Six Unknown Agents of the Federal Bureau of Narcotics (1971)* is one of the leading decisions affording private citizens a claim for money damages for the violations of their constitutional rights.

How is the separation of powers part of the Constitution's "rule of law"? What, if any, is the role of the Supreme Court to supervise the constitutional roles of the other branches of the federal government? How is the respectfulness the Constitution obliges the Court to show coordinate branches different in kind from the respect owed to the States? Justice Scalia's dissent in *Morrison v. Olson (1988)* takes us back to 18th century first principles. In *Coleman v. Miller (1939)*, the Justices debate what role, if any, the courts should play in the Article V procedures to amend the Constitution, which has to be understood as a quintessentially political process. Justice Brennan's opinion in *Baker v. Carr (1962)* explains how some clauses in the Constitution are beyond the ken of judicial review because they commit an unreviewable political power to Congress or to the President. However, he allows how this limitation has nothing to do with the relationship between the Supreme Court and the States, thus opening the constitutional door to federal judicial supervision of the redistricting of state legislatures.

In his Preface to LEAVES OF GRASS, published on the eve of the Civil War, Walt Whitman proclaimed, "The United States themselves are essentially the greatest poem." The Supreme Court has struggled mightily to rhyme the nature of the Union. Was it "perpetual" in a way the Articles of Confederation were not? Is the Civil War a kind of precedent of history that informs us of the proper understanding? President Lincoln's Chief Justice, Salmon P. Chase, explained the lessons of Gettysburg and Appomattox in *Texas v. White (1868)*. On the other side of the constitutional coin, federalism contemplates the political viability of the sovereign States operating in their own proper sphere. How can the Court determine whether a specified power, for example, the power to limit the terms of members of Congress, belongs in the national or the state sphere? In a recent opinion, *U.S. Term Limits, Inc. v. Thornton (1995)*, Justice Anthony M. Kennedy demonstrates the controlling saliency of the principle of federalism. It provides the rule for decision in a case that once again readjusts the balance between the States and the national government. Finally, what does it mean to be a citizen of the

United States? And is that more important than being a citizen of a State, even more important than being a Texan? Justice Robert H. Jackson instructs the State of California, and reminds the rest of us, what it means to be an American in *Edwards v. California (1941)*. No State can deny us our dignity, and, notwithstanding proud proclamations on bumper stickers, it does not matter whether or not we are its native son or daughter.

In various milieus, the Supreme Court has had to decide questions of constitutional etiquette, so to speak. If our republican government is based on the ideal of limited government, the question to be considered is when and how the government must practice self-restraint. The government must follow the constitutional rules, of course. But the aspirational Constitution expects the government to be a good example to its citizens. Justice Louis D. Brandeis, with characteristic aplomb, describes the government as being our constitutional teacher in *Olmstead v. United States (1928)*. In the Third Branch, principles of self-restraint translate to judicial humility. Judges, even Supreme Court Justices, should restrain themselves to stay within their proper role. They do not govern "We the people," even in constitutional matters—especially in constitutional matters. The High Court has developed formal rules of judicial self-restraint, guidelines for when it should decline to decide constitutional cases. These are summarized in *Ashwander v. Tennessee Valley Authority (1936)*.

The Chapter concludes with three cases demonstrating beyond peradventure that sovereignty—in fact and not just in theory—remains lodged with "We the people." First, in *New York Times Co. v. Sullivan (1964)*, the Court explains how the 1st amendment protects the fundamental right of citizens to criticize government officials and their policies. Second, in *Brown v. Louisiana (1966)*, the Court seeks to reconcile the right of civil disobedience with the rule of law and the Constitution. The issue is whether the Constitution protects those who take the law into their own hands. How can lawbreakers invoke the fundamental law in their defense? Along the way, Justice Fortas proves to be a great storyteller and he has a great story to tell. Third, Justice Hugo H. Black's dissent in *In re Anastaplo (1961)* explores the self-evident truth Thomas Jefferson declared in 1776, that at some point a government loses its legitimacy and ceases to claim the loyalty of its people who have an unalienable "right of revolution." This is not merely some lyric from a Beatles' song. It is profoundly more serious and more important. When is it within the constitutional contemplation for an individual to protest, in effect, that the Constitution is no longer legitimate? This underscores the deeply radical nature of government based on the consent of the governed. It was a radical idea in 1787 and it continues to be a radical idea today. Only the brave can be free.

Constitutionalism once was defined, somewhat tongue in cheek, to be "the name given to the trust men repose in the power of words engrossed on parchment to keep a government in order." In all the opinions in this Chapter, the Justices ostensibly set out to interpret the words of the Constitution to keep the government in order. The process of interpretation, in historical context and perspective, creates meaning from the text, translating parchment propositions into cultural and political reality. In Bishop Hoadly's famous sermon preached before the King in 1717, he proclaimed: "Whoever hath an absolute authority to interpret any written or spoken laws, it is he who is truly the lawgiver, to all intents and purposes, and not the person who first spoke or wrote them." But the Constitution is too important to be left to the Justices. "We the People" must take first responsibility for keeping constitutional faith with the Framers. We must accept Ben Franklin's challenge to us to keep our Republic in order.

*Whoever considers, in a combined and comprehensive view, the general texture of the Constitution, will be satisfied, that the people of the United States intended to form themselves into a nation for national purposes.*

—*James Wilson*

## Chisholm v. Georgia
### 2 U.S. (Dallas) 419 (1793)

*This decision was the first reported case decided by the Supreme Court upon the express authority of the Constitution. As was then the custom, the Justices prepared their opinions and then delivered them from the bench "seriatim," each judge in turn giving what amounted to a speech on the law and the case. When they were done, all but one Justice concluded that a State could be sued in federal court by a citizen of another State. Chisholm was from South Carolina and the executor of the estate of a deceased creditor who had provided Georgia with supplies during the Revolution. There was a valid contract and the State owed the money. The fight was over whether a federal court could hear the dispute. After Georgia, claiming state sovereignty, indignantly refused to appear in any federal court, the Supreme Court entered a default judgment for restitution from the state treasury. To say that the decision was controversial would be putting it mildly. State after State denounced the Court. The legislature of Georgia defied the order and considered passing a statute that would have punished any federal officer who attempted to enforce the decision by "death, without benefit of clergy, by being hanged." The immediate consequence for the Constitution was the 11th amendment—proposed by a near unanimous Congress in March 1794, promptly ratified by the requisite three-fourths of the States less than a year later, and officially certified in 1798—which took away federal court jurisdiction in such cases. Thus, the case also marks the first time the amendment process was used explicitly to disapprove of a Supreme Court decision. Indeed, the Court later went so far as to apply the amendment retroactively and ended up dismissing Chisholm's claim along with all other pending law suits. What was more lasting, and radically mod-*

*ern, was Justice Wilson's concept of the relationship between the state and the individual. His vision of nationalism was far ahead of his time. He even uses the concept of political correctness. This opinion is a difficult reading, but the concept exemplified here made it possible for there to be a United States of America. The people of the United States, rather than the government or the States, had exercised their ultimate sovereignty to ordain and establish for themselves and their posterity a form of government the world had never before seen. They described it in the motto they chose for the Great Seal of the new republic that is still to be found on the $1 bill: "Novus Ordo Seclorum" or "A new order for the ages."*

**Justice Wilson:** This is a case of uncommon magnitude. One of the parties to it is a state; certainly respectable, claiming to be sovereign. The question to be determined is, whether this state, so respectable, and whose claim soars so high, is amenable to the jurisdiction of the Supreme Court of the United States? This question, important in itself, will depend on others, more important still; and, may, perhaps, be ultimately resolved into one, no less radical than this "do the people of the United States form a Nation?"

To the Constitution of the United States the term sovereign, is totally unknown. There is but one place where it could have been used with propriety. But, even in that place it would not, perhaps, have comported with the delicacy of those, who ordained and established that Constitution. They might have announced themselves "sovereign" people of the United States: But serenely conscious of the fact, they avoided the ostentatious declaration. In an instrument well drawn, as in a poem well composed, silence is sometimes most expressive.

Man, fearfully and wonderfully made, is the workmanship of his all-perfect Creator: A state, useful and valuable as the contrivance is, is the inferior contrivance of man; and from his native dignity derives all its acquired importance. When I speak of a state as an inferior contrivance, I mean that it is a contrivance inferior only to that, which is divine: Of all human contrivances, it is certainly most transcendently excellent. It is concerning this contrivance that Cicero says so sublimely, "Nothing which is exhibited upon our globe, is more acceptable to that divinity, which governs the whole universe, than those communities and assemblages of men, which, lawfully associated, are denominated states."

Let a state be considered as subordinate to the People: But let everything else be subordinate to the state. By a state I mean, a complete body of free persons united together for their common benefit, to enjoy peaceably what is their own, and to do justice to others. It is an artificial person. It has its affairs and its interests: it has its rules: it has its rights: and it has its obligations. In all our contemplations, however, concerning this feigned and artificial person, we should never forget, that, in truth and nature, those, who think and speak, and act, are men.

The only reason, I believe, why a free man is bound by human laws, is, that he binds himself. Upon the same principles, upon which he becomes bound by the laws, he becomes amenable to the Courts of Justice, which are formed and authorised by those laws. If one free man, an original sovereign, may do all this; why may not an aggregate of free men, a collection of original sovereigns, do this likewise? If the dignity of each singly is undiminished; the dignity of all jointly must be unimpaired. A state, like a merchant, makes a contract. A dishonest state, like a dishonest merchant, wilfully refuses to discharge it: the latter is amenable to a Court of Justice: upon general principles of right, shall the former when summoned to answer the fair demands of its creditor, be permitted, proteus-like, to assume a new appearance, and to insult him and justice, by declaring I am a Sovereign state? Surely not. Before a claim, so contrary, in its first appearance, to the general principles of right and equality, be sustained by a just and impartial tribunal, the person, natural or artificial, entitled to make such claim, should certainly be well known and authenticated. Who, or what, is a sovereignty? What is his or its sovereignty? On this subject, the errors and the mazes are endless and inexplicable. To enumerate all, therefore, will not be expected: to take notice of some will be necessary to the full illustration of the present important cause. In one sense, the term sovereign has for its correlative, subject. In this sense, the term can receive no application; for it has no object in the Constitution of the United States. Under that Constitution there are citizens, but no subjects: "Citizen of the United States." "Citizens of another State." "Citizens of different States." "A State or citizen thereof." The term "subject" occurs, indeed, once in the instrument; but to mark the contrast strongly, the epithet "foreign" is prefixed. In this sense, I presume the state of Georgia has no claim upon her own citizens: in this sense, I am certain, she can have no claim upon the citizens of another state.

As a citizen of the Union, I know the Government of Georgia to be republican; and my short definition of such a Government is, one constructed on this principle, that the Supreme Power resides in the body of the people. As a Judge of this Court, I know, and can decide upon the knowledge, that the citizens of Georgia, when they acted upon the large scale of the Union, as a part of the "People of the United States," did not surrender the Supreme or Sovereign Power to that State; but, as to the purposes of the Union, retained it to themselves. As to the purposes of the Union, therefore, Georgia is not a sovereign state. If the Judicial decision of this case forms one of those purposes; the allegation, that Georgia is a sovereign state, is unsupported by the fact.

I am chiefly to examine the important question now before us, by the Constitution of the United States, and the legitimate result of that valuable instrument. Under this view, the question is naturally subdivided into two others. 1. Could the Constitution of the United States vest a jurisdiction over the State of Georgia? 2. Has that Constitution vested such jurisdiction in this Court? I find nothing, which tends to evince an exemption of the State of Georgia, from the jurisdiction of the Court. I find everything to have a contrary tendency.

In the practice, and even in the science of politics, there has been frequently a strong current against the natural order of things; and an inconsiderate or an interested disposition to sacrifice the end to the means. Even in almost every nation, which has been denominated free, the state has assumed a supercilious preeminence above the people, who have formed it: hence, the haughty notions of state independence, state sovereignty and state supremacy. In despotic Governments, the Government has usurped, in a similar manner, both upon the state and the people: hence, all arbitrary doctrines and pretensions concerning the supreme, absolute, and incontrolable, power of Government. In each, man is degraded from the prime rank, which he ought to hold in human affairs: In the latter, the state as well as the man is degraded. Of both degradations, striking instances occur in history, in politics, and in common life. And, indeed, that Kings should imagine themselves the final causes, for which men were made, and societies were formed, and Governments were instituted, will cease to be a matter of wonder or surprise, when we find that lawyers, and statesmen, and philosophers, have taught or favoured principles, which necessarily lead to the same conclusion.

In the United States, and in the several states, which compose the Union, we go not so far: but still we go one step farther than we ought to go in this unnatural and inverted order of things. The states, rather than the People, for whose sakes the states exist, are frequently the objects which attract and arrest our principal attention. This, I believe, has produced much of the confusion and perplexity, which have appeared in several proceedings and several publications on state-politics, and on the politics, too, of the United States. Sentiments and expressions of this inaccurate kind prevail in our common, even in our convivial, language. Is a toast asked? "The United States," instead of the "People of the United States," is the toast given. This is not politically correct. The toast is meant to present to view the first great object in the Union: it presents only the second: it presents only the artificial person, instead of the natural persons, who spoke it into existence. A state I cheerfully admit, is the noblest work of Man: But, Man himself, free and honest, is, I speak as to this world, the noblest work of God!

Concerning the prerogative of Kings, and concerning the sovereignty of states, much has been said and written; but little has been said and written concerning a subject much more dignified and important, the majesty of the people. The mode of expression, which I would substitute in the place of that generally used, is not only politically, but also (for between true liberty and true taste there is a close alliance) classically more correct. With the strictest propriety, therefore, classical and political, our national scene opens with the most magnificent object, which the nation could present. "The people of the United States" are the first personages introduced. Who were those people? They were the citizens of thirteen states, each of which had a separate Constitution and Government, and all of which were connected together by articles of confederation. To the purposes of public strength and felicity, that confederacy was totally inadequate. A requisition on the several states terminated its Legislative authority: Executive or Judicial authority it had none. In order, therefore, to form a more perfect union, to establish justice, to ensure domestic tranquillity, to provide for common defence, and to secure the blessings of liberty, those people, among whom were the people of Georgia, ordained and established the present Constitution. By that Constitution Legislative power is vested, Executive power is vested, Judicial power is vested.

The question now opens fairly to our view, could the people of those states, among whom were those of Georgia, bind those states, and Georgia among the others, by the Legislative, Executive, and Judicial power so vested? If the principles, on which I have founded myself, are just and true; this question must unavoidably receive an affirmative answer. If those states were the work of those people; those people, and, that I may apply the case closely, the people of Georgia, in particular, could alter, as they pleased, their former work: To any given degree, they could diminish as well as enlarge it. Any or all of the former state-powers, they could extinguish or transfer. The inference, which necessarily results, is, that the Constitution ordained and established by those people; and, still closely to apply the case, in particular by the people of Georgia, could vest jurisdiction or judicial power over those states and over the State of Georgia in particular.

The next question under this head, is—Has the Constitution done so? Did those people mean to exercise this, their undoubted power? These questions may be resolved, either by fair and conclusive deductions, or by direct and explicit declarations.

In order, ultimately, to discover, whether the people of the United States intended to bind those States by the Judicial power vested by the national Constitution, a previous enquiry will naturally be: Did those people intend to bind those states by the Legislative power vested by that Constitution? The Articles of Confederation, it is well known, did not operate upon individual citizens; but operated only upon states. This defect was remedied by the national Constitution, which, as all allow, has an operation on individual citizens. But if an opinion, which some seem to entertain, be just; the defect remedied, on one side, was balanced by a defect introduced on the other: for they seem to think, that the present Constitution operates only on individual citizens, and not on states. This opinion, however, appears to be altogether unfounded. When certain laws of the states are declared to be "subject to the revision and controul of the Congress;" it cannot, surely, be contended that the Legislative power of the national Government was meant to have no operation on the several states. The fact, uncontrovertibly established in one instance, proves the principle in all other instances, to which the facts will be found to apply. We may then infer, that the people of the United States intended to bind the several states, by the Legislative power of the national Government.

In order to make the discovery, at which we ultimately aim, a second previous enquiry will naturally be—Did the people of the United States intend to bind the several states by the Executive power of the national Government? The affirmative answer to the former question directs, unavoidably, an affirmative answer to this. Ever since the time of Bracton, his maxim, I believe, has been deemed a good one "Supervacuum esset leges condere, nisi esset qui leges tueretur." ("It would be superfluous to make laws, unless those laws, when made, were to be enforced.") When the laws are plain, and the application of them is uncontroverted, they are enforced immediately by the Executive authority of Government. When the application of them is doubtful or intricate, the interposition of the judicial authority becomes necessary. The same principle, therefore, which directed us from the first to the second step, will direct us from the second to the third and last step of our deduction. Fair and conclusive deduction, then, evinces that the people of the United States did vest this Court with jurisdiction over the State of Georgia. The same truth may be deduced from the declared objects, and the general texture of the Constitution of the United States. One of its declared objects is, to form an union more perfect, than, before that time, had been formed. Before that time, the Union possessed Legislative, but uninforced Legislative power over the states. Nothing could be more natural than to intend that this Legislative power should be enforced by powers Executive and Judicial. Another declared object is "to establish justice." This points, in a particular manner, to the Judicial authority. And when we view this object in conjunction with the declaration, "that no State shall pass a law impairing the obligation of contracts;" we shall probably think, that this object points, in a particular manner, to the jurisdiction of the Court over the several states. What good purpose could this Constitutional provision secure, if a state might pass a law impairing the obligation of its own contracts; and be amenable, for such a violation of right, to no controlling judiciary power? We have seen, that on the principles of general jurisprudence, a state, for the breach of a contract, may be liable for damages. A third declared object is "to ensure domestic tranquillity." This tranquillity is most likely to be disturbed by controversies between states. These consequences will be most peaceably and effectually decided by the establishment and by the exercise of a superintending judicial authority. By such exercise and establishment, the law of nations; the rule between contending states; will be enforced among the several states, in the same manner as municipal law.

Whoever considers, in a combined and comprehensive view, the general texture of the Constitution, will be satisfied, that the people of the United States intended to form themselves into a nation for national purposes. They instituted, for such purposes, a national Government, complete in all its parts, with powers Legislative, Executive and Judiciary; and, in all those powers, extending over the whole nation. Is it congruous, that, with regard to such purposes, any man or body of men, any person natural or artificial, should be permitted to claim successfully an entire exemption from the jurisdiction of the national Government? Would not such claims, crowned with success, be repugnant to our very existence as a nation? When so many trains of deduction, coming from different quarters, converge and unite, at last, in the same point; we may safely conclude, as the legitimate result of this Constitution, that the State of Georgia is amenable to the jurisdiction of this Court.

But, in my opinion, this doctrine rests not upon the legitimate result of fair and conclusive deduction from the Constitution: it is finally confirmed, beyond all doubt, by the direct and explicit declaration of the Constitution itself. "The judicial power of the United States shall extend, to controversies between two States." Two states are supposed to have a controversy between them: this controversy is supposed to be brought before those vested with the judicial power of the United States: Can the most consummate degree of professional ingenuity devise a mode by which this "controversy between two States" can be brought before a Court of law; and yet neither of those states be a Defendant? "The judicial power of the United States shall extend to controversies, between a state and citizens of another State." Could the strictest legal language; could even that language, which is peculiarly appropriated to an art, deemed, by a great master, to be one of the most honorable, laudable, and profitable things in our law; could this strict and appropriated language, describe, with more precise accuracy, the cause now depending before the tribunal? Causes, and not parties to causes, are weighed by justice, in her equal scales: on the former solely, her attention is fixed: to the latter, she is, as she is painted, blind.

*Although the preamble indicates the general purposes for which the people ordained and established the Constitution, it has never been regarded as the source of any substantive power conferred on the government of the United States, or on any of its departments.*

—*John M. Harlan*

## Jacobson v. Massachusetts
### 25 S.Ct. 358, 197 U.S. 11 (1905)

*The particular holding was that a State could require a smallpox vaccination over the objection of an individual. That imposition did not deny any constitutionally protected liberty. The decision is cited today as precedent for a State's sovereign police power. It also is an early example of the Supreme Court's persistent skepticism toward claims of absolute rights. In a little known but important portion of the opinion, however, the Court definitively interpreted the Preamble. The only part of the Constitution that many Americans know by heart, the Preamble is merely an introductory filigree added at the conclusion of the Constitutional Convention by the Committee on Style. Justice Harlan understood that it could not be a source of federal judicial power to set aside state laws. Furthermore, the Preamble's broad phrases do not create offices or confer powers on the other branches of the national Government, which unlike the States is a government of enumerated and limited powers. Therefore, the paragraph cannot be invoked to justify any mischievous claim of inherent federal power to "promote the general Welfare," et cetera. Instead, the responsibility of assuring the common good is within the primary province of the State's authority and there the individual's liberty often must give way.*

**Justice Harlan:** This case involves the validity, under the Constitution of the United States, of certain provisions in the statutes of Massachusetts relating to vaccination.

Jacobson, was proceeded against by a criminal complaint in one of the inferior courts of Massachusetts. The defendant, having been arraigned, pleaded not guilty. The defendant, standing upon his offers of proof, and introducing no evidence, asked numerous instructions to the jury: including an instruction that the Massachusetts statute was in derogation of the rights secured to the defendant by the preamble to the Constitution of the United States, and tended to subvert and defeat the purposes of the Constitution as declared in its preamble and that said section was opposed to the spirit of the Constitution. But the court refused, to instruct the jury to return a verdict of not guilty. A verdict of guilty was thereupon returned.

We pass without extended discussion the suggestion that the particular section of the statute of Massachusetts now in question is in derogation of rights secured by the preamble of the Constitution of the United States. Although that preamble indicates the general purposes for which the people ordained and established the Constitution, it has never been regarded as the source of any substantive power conferred on the government of the United States, or on any of its departments. Such powers embrace only those expressly granted in the body of the Constitution, and such as may be implied from those so granted. Although, therefore, one of the declared objects of the Constitution was to secure the blessings of liberty to all under the sovereign jurisdiction and authority of the United States, no power can be exerted to that end by the United States, unless, apart from the preamble, it be found in some express delegation of power, or in some power to be properly implied therefrom.

We also pass without discussion the suggestion that the above section of the statute is opposed to the spirit of the Constitution. Undoubtedly, as observed by Chief Justice Marshall, speaking for the court in 1819: "the spirit of an instrument, especially of a constitution, is to be respected not less than its letter; yet the spirit is to be collected chiefly from its words." We have no need in this case to go beyond the plain, obvious meaning of the words in those provisions of the Constitution which, it is contended, must control our decision.

The authority of the state to enact this statute is to be referred to what is commonly called the police power—a power which the state did not surrender when becoming a member of the Union under the Constitution. Although this court has refrained from any attempt to define the limits of that power, yet it has distinctly recognized the authority of a state to enact quarantine laws and "health laws of every description;" indeed, all laws that relate to matters completely within its territory and which do not by their necessary operation affect the people of other states. According to settled principles, the police power of a state must be held to embrace, at least, such reasonable regulations established directly by legislative enactment as will protect the public health and the public safety. The mode or manner in which those results are to be accomplished is within the discretion of the state, subject, of course, so far as Federal power is concerned, only to the condition that no rule prescribed by a state, nor any regulation adopted by a local governmental agency acting under the sanction of state legislation, shall contravene the Constitution of the United States, nor infringe any right granted or secured by that instrument. A local enactment or regulation, even if based on the acknowledged police powers of a state, must always yield in case of conflict with the exercise by the general government of any power it possesses under the Constitution, or with any right which that instrument gives or secures.

We come, then, to inquire whether any right given or secured by the Constitution is invaded by the statute as interpreted by the state court. The defendant insists that his liberty is invaded when the state subjects him to fine or imprisonment for neglecting or refusing to submit to vaccination; that a compulsory vaccination law is unreasonable, arbitrary, and oppressive, and, therefore, hostile to the inherent right of every freeman to care for his own body and health in such way as to him seems best; and that the execution of such a law against one who objects to vaccination, no matter for what reason, is nothing short of an assault upon his person. But the liberty secured by the Constitution of the United States to every person within its jurisdiction does not import an absolute right in each person to be, at all times and in all circumstances, wholly freed from restraint. There are manifold restraints to which every person is necessarily subject for the common good. On any other basis organized society could not exist with safety to its members. Society based on the rule that each one is a law unto himself would soon be confronted with disorder and anarchy. Real liberty for all could not exist under the operation of a principle which recognizes the right of each individual person to use his own, whether in respect of his person or his property, regardless of the injury that may be done to others. This court has more than once recognized it as a fundamental principle that "persons and property are subjected to all kinds of restraints and burdens in order to secure the general comfort, health, and prosperity of the state; of the perfect right of the legislature to do which no question ever was, or upon acknowledged general principles ever can be, made, so far as natural persons are concerned."

In the Constitution of Massachusetts adopted in 1780 it was laid down as a fundamental principle of the social compact that the whole people covenants with each citizen, and each citizen with the whole people, that all shall be governed by certain laws for "the common good," and that government is instituted "for the common good, for the protection, safety, prosperity, and happiness of the people, and not for the profit, honor, or private interests of any one man, family, or class of men." The good and welfare of the Commonwealth, of which the legislature is primarily the judge, is the basis on which the police power rests in Massachusetts.

There is, of course, a sphere within which the individual may assert the supremacy of his own will, and rightfully dispute the authority of any human government—especially of any free government existing under a written constitution, to interfere with the exercise of that will. But it is equally true that in every well-ordered society charged with the duty of conserving the safety of its members the rights of the individual in respect of his liberty may at times, under the pressure of great dangers, be subjected to such restraint, to be enforced by reasonable regulations, as the safety of the general public may demand. The liberty secured by the 14th Amendment, this court has said, consists, in part, in the right of a person "to live and work where he will" and yet he may be compelled, by force if need be, against his will and without regard to his personal wishes or his pecuniary interests, or even his religious or political convictions, to take his place in the ranks of the army of his country, and risk the chance of being shot down in its defense. It is not, therefore, true that the power of the public to guard itself against imminent danger depends in every case involving the control of one's body upon his willingness to submit to reasonable regulations established by the constituted authorities, under the sanction of the state, for the purpose of protecting the public collectively against such danger.

If there is any such power in the judiciary to review legislative action in respect of a matter affecting the general welfare, it can only be when that which the legislature has done comes within the rule that, if a statute purporting to have been enacted to protect the public health, the public morals, or the public safety, has no real or substantial relation to those objects, or is, beyond all question, a plain, palpable invasion of rights secured by the fundamental law, it is the duty of the courts to so adjudge, and thereby give effect to the Constitution.

Whatever may be thought of the expediency of this statute, it cannot be affirmed to be, beyond question, in palpable conflict with the Constitution. In a free country, where the government is by the people, through their chosen representatives, practical legislation admits of no other standard of action, for what the people believe is for the common welfare must be accepted as tending to promote the common welfare, whether it does in fact or not. Any other basis would conflict with the spirit of the Constitution, and would sanction measures opposed to a Republican form of government. We hold that the statute in question is a health law, enacted in a reasonable and proper exercise of the police power.

We are not prepared to hold that a minority, residing or remaining in any city or town where smallpox is prevalent, and enjoying the general protection afforded by an organized local government, may thus defy the will of its constituted authorities, acting in good faith for all, under the legislative sanction of the state. If such be the privilege of a minority, then a like privilege would belong to each individual of the community, and the spectacle would be presented of the welfare and safety of an entire population being subordinated to the notions of a single individual who chooses to remain a part of that population. We are unwilling to hold it to be an element in the liberty secured by the Constitution of the United States that one person, or a minority of persons, residing in any community and enjoying the benefits of its local government, should have the power thus to dominate the majority when supported in their action by the authority of the state. While this court should guard with firmness every right appertaining to life, liberty, or property as secured to the individual by the supreme law of the land, it is of the last importance that it should not invade the domain of local authority except when it is plainly necessary to do so in order to enforce that law. The safety and the health of the people of Massachusetts are, in the first instance, for that Commonwealth to guard and protect. They are matters that do not ordinarily concern the national government. So far as they can be reached by any government, they depend, primarily, upon such action as the state, in its wisdom, may take; and we do not perceive that this legislation has invaded any right secured by the Federal Constitution.

Before closing this opinion we deem it appropriate, in order to prevent misapprehension as to our views, to observe—perhaps to repeat a thought already sufficiently expressed, namely—that the police power of a state may be exerted in such circumstances, or by regulations so arbitrary and oppressive in particular cases, as to justify the interference of the courts to prevent wrong and oppression. Extreme cases can be readily suggested. Ordinarily such cases are not safe guides in the administration of the law. No such case is here presented.

*The Due Process Clause of the Fourteenth Amendment was intended to prevent government "from abusing its power, or employing it as an instrument of oppression." Its purpose was to protect the people from the State, not to ensure that the State protected them from each other.*

—*William H. Rehnquist*

## DeShaney v. Winnebago County Dept. of Social Services
### 109 S.Ct. 998, 489 U.S. 189 (1989)

*Joshua DeShaney was 4 years old when his abusive father, with whom he was living after his parents' divorce, beat him so violently that he fell into a coma and emerged with permanent brain damage so severe that he would spend the rest of his life in an institution for the profoundly retarded. The father was convicted of the state criminal offense of child abuse. Joshua's mother then brought a civil rights lawsuit on behalf of her son and herself against the county, the state department of social services, and individual social workers, who had received complaints and who had reason to believe that the boy was being abused but who failed to remove him from the father's custody. Since the* Civil Rights Cases (1883), *however, the Supreme Court has read the 14th amendment literally to apply only to "state action," i.e., the conduct causing the deprivation of the federal right must be fairly attributable to the State. This is a fundamental principle of the Constitution: the document only orders the relationship between the government—state or federal—and the individual citizen. When a private individual harms another individual, the person harmed may have a remedy in criminal law or in a lawsuit for damages, but the Constitution has not been violated. Only the government can violate the Constitution. Here the plaintiffs were not suing the father and alleging that his abuse violated the Constitution, rather they were suing the state actors directly to argue that they breached a constitutional duty to protect Joshua. Justice Blackmun, along with Justices Brennan and Marshall, was frustrated in dissent and expressed both his dismay for the majority's formalism and his sympathy for "Poor Joshua!"*

**Chief Justice Rehnquist:** The facts of this case are undeniably tragic. Joshua and his mother brought this civil rights action alleging that defendants had deprived Joshua of his liberty without due process of law, in violation of his rights under the Fourteenth Amendment, by failing to intervene to protect him against a risk of violence at his father's hands of which they knew or should have known.

The Due Process Clause of the Fourteenth Amendment provides that "no State shall deprive any person of life, liberty, or property, without due process of law." Plaintiffs contend that the State deprived Joshua of his liberty interest in "freedom from unjustified intrusions on personal security," by failing to provide him with adequate protection against his father's violence. The claim is one invoking the substantive rather than the procedural component of the Due Process Clause; plaintiffs do not claim that the State denied Joshua protection without according him appropriate procedural safeguards, but that it was categorically obligated to protect him in these circumstances.

But nothing in the language of the Due Process Clause itself requires the State to protect the life, liberty, and property of its citizens against invasion by private actors. The Clause is phrased as a limitation on the State's power to act, not as a guarantee of certain minimal levels of safety and security. It forbids the State itself to deprive individuals of life, liberty, or property without "due process of law," but its language cannot fairly be extended to impose an affirmative obligation on the State to ensure that those interests do not come to harm through other means. Nor does history support such an expansive reading of the constitutional text. Like its counterpart in the Fifth Amendment, the Due Process Clause of the Fourteenth Amendment was intended to prevent government "from abusing its power, or employing it as an instrument of oppression." Its purpose was to protect the people from the State, not to ensure that the State protected them from each other. The Framers were content to leave the extent of governmental obligation in the latter area to the democratic political processes.

Consistent with these principles, our cases have recognized that the Due Process Clauses generally confer no affirmative right to governmental aid, even where such aid may be necessary to secure life, liberty, or property interests of which the government itself may not deprive the individual. If the Due Process Clause does not require the State to provide its citizens with particular protective services, it follows that the State cannot be held liable under the Clause for injuries that could have been averted had it chosen to provide them. As a general matter, then, we conclude that a State's failure to protect an individual against private violence simply does not constitute a violation of the Due Process Clause.

Plaintiffs contend, however, that even if the Due Process Clause imposes no affirmative obligation on the State to provide the general public with adequate protective services, such a duty may arise out of certain "special relationships" created or assumed by the State with respect to particular individuals. Plaintiffs argue that such a "special relationship" existed here because the State knew that Joshua faced a special danger of abuse at his father's hands, and specifically proclaimed, by word and by deed, its intention to protect him against that danger. Having actually undertaken to protect Joshua from this danger—which plaintiffs concede the State played no part in creating—the State acquired an affirmative "duty," enforceable through the Due Process Clause, to do so in a reasonably competent fashion. Its failure to discharge that duty, so the argument goes, was an abuse of governmental power that so "shocks the conscience," as to constitute a substantive due process violation.

We reject this argument. It is true that in certain limited circumstances the Constitution imposes upon the State affirmative duties of care and protection with respect to particular individuals. We have recognized that the Eighth Amendment's prohibition against cruel and unusual punishment, made applicable to the States through the Fourteenth Amendment's Due Process Clause, requires the State to provide adequate medical care to incarcerated prisoners. We reasoned that because the prisoner is unable "by reason of the deprivation of his liberty to care for himself," it is only "just" that the State be required to care for him. We have extended this analysis beyond the Eighth Amendment setting, holding that the substantive component of the Fourteenth Amendment's Due Process Clause requires the State to provide involuntarily committed mental patients with such services as are necessary to ensure their "reasonable safety" from themselves and others.

But these cases afford plaintiffs no help. Taken together, they stand only for the proposition that when the State takes a person into its custody and holds him there against his will, the Constitution imposes upon it a corresponding duty to assume some responsibility for his safety and general well-being. The rationale for this principle is simple enough: when the State by the affirmative exercise of its power so restrains an individual's liberty that it renders him unable to care for himself, and at the same time fails to provide for his basic human needs—e.g., food, clothing, shelter, medical care, and reasonable safety—it transgresses the substantive limits on state action set by the Eighth Amendment and the Due Process Clause. The affirmative duty to protect arises not from the State's knowledge of the individual's predicament or from its expressions of intent to help him, but from the limitation which it has imposed on his freedom to act on his own behalf. In the substantive due process analysis, it is the State's affirmative act of restraining the individual's freedom to act on his own behalf—through incarceration, institutionalization, or other similar restraint of personal liberty—which is the "deprivation of liberty" triggering the protections of the Due Process Clause, not its failure to act to protect his liberty interests against harms inflicted by other means.

This line of analysis simply has no applicability in the present case. Plaintiffs concede that the harms Joshua suffered occurred not while he was in the State's custody, but while he was in the custody of his natural father, who was in no sense a state actor. While the State may have been aware of the dangers that Joshua faced in the free world, it played no part in their creation, nor did it do anything to render him any more vulnerable to them. That the State once took temporary custody of Joshua does not alter the analysis, for when it returned him to his father's custody, it placed him in no worse position than that in which he would have been had it not acted at all; the State does not become the permanent guarantor of an individual's safety by having once offered him shelter. Under these circumstances, the State had no constitutional duty to protect Joshua.

It may well be that, by voluntarily undertaking to protect Joshua against a danger it concededly played no part in creating, the State acquired a duty under state tort law to provide him with adequate protection against that danger. But the claim here is based on the Due Process Clause of the Fourteenth Amendment, which, as we have said many times, does not transform every tort committed by a state actor into a constitutional violation. A State may, through its courts and legislatures, impose such affirmative duties of care and protection upon its agents as it wishes. But not "all common-law duties owed by government actors were constitutionalized by the Fourteenth Amendment." Because, as explained above, the State had no constitutional duty to protect Joshua against his father's violence, its failure to do so—though calamitous in hindsight—simply does not constitute a violation of the Due Process Clause.

Judges and lawyers, like other humans, are moved by natural sympathy in a case like this to find a way for Joshua and his mother to receive adequate compensation for the grievous harm inflicted upon them. But before yielding to that impulse, it is well to remember once again that the harm was inflicted not by the State of Wisconsin, but by Joshua's father. The most that can be said of the state functionaries in this case is that they stood by and did nothing when suspicious circumstances dictated a more active role for them. In defense of them it must also be said that had they moved too soon to take custody of the son away from the father, they would likely have been met with charges of improperly intruding into the parent-child relationship, charges based on the same Due Process Clause that forms the basis for the present charge of failure to provide adequate protection.

The people of Wisconsin may well prefer a system of liability which would place upon the State and its officials the responsibility for failure to act in situations such as the present one. They may create such a system, if they do not have it already, by changing the tort law of the State in accordance with the regular lawmaking process. But they should not have it thrust upon them by this Court's expansion of the Due Process Clause of the Fourteenth Amendment.

**Justice Blackmun:** Today, the Court purports to be the dispassionate oracle of the law, unmoved by "natural sympathy." But, in this pretense, the Court itself retreats into a sterile formalism which prevents it from recognizing either the facts of the case before it or the legal norms that should apply to those facts. The facts here involve not mere passivity, but active state intervention in the life of Joshua DeShaney—intervention that triggered a fundamental duty to aid the boy once the State learned of the severe danger to which he was exposed.

The Court fails to recognize this duty because it attempts to draw a sharp and rigid line between action and inaction. But such formalistic reasoning has no place in the interpretation of the broad and stirring Clauses of the Fourteenth Amendment. Indeed, I submit that these Clauses were designed, at least in part, to undo the formalistic legal reasoning that infected antebellum jurisprudence. Like the antebellum judges who denied relief to fugitive slaves, the Court today claims that its decision, however harsh, is compelled by existing legal doctrine. On the contrary, the question presented by this case is an open one, and our Fourteenth Amendment precedents may be read more broadly or narrowly depending upon how one chooses to read them. Faced with the choice, I would adopt a "sympathetic" reading, one which comports with dictates of fundamental justice and recognizes that compassion need not be exiled from the province of judging.

Poor Joshua! Victim of repeated attacks by an irresponsible, bullying, cowardly, and intemperate father, and abandoned by defendants who placed him in a dangerous predicament and who knew or learned what was going on, and yet did essentially nothing except, as the Court revealingly observes, "dutifully recording these incidents in their files." It is a sad commentary upon American life, and constitutional principles—so full of late of patriotic fervor and proud proclamations about "liberty and justice for all"—that this child, Joshua DeShaney, now is assigned to live out the remainder of his life profoundly retarded. Joshua and his mother, as plaintiffs here, deserve—but now are denied by this Court—the opportunity to have the facts of their case considered in the light of their constitutional protections.

*The question here is whether violation by a federal agent acting under color of his authority gives rise to a cause of action for damages consequent upon his unconstitutional conduct. Today we hold that it does.*

—*William J. Brennan*

# Bivens v. Six Unknown Named Agents of the Federal Bureau of Narcotics
## 91 S.Ct. 1999, 403 U.S. 388 (1971)

*This is the leading precedent establishing what lawyers call an implied cause of action under the Constitution. This means that a citizen whose constitutional rights have been violated by federal agents can sue those agents and recover money damages. F.B.N. agents performed an unconstitutional search and seizure of Webster Bivens' apartment. He was manacled in front of his wife and children, who were also threatened with arrest. Then he was taken into custody, booked, interrogated, and strip-searched. Bivens maintained that there was no warrant, that the agents did not have sufficient probable cause, and that they used excessive force. He wanted the opportunity to present his civil lawsuit in federal district court and asked for $15,000 damages from each agent for his humiliation, embarrassment, and mental and physical suffering. Justice Brennan, speaking for the Court, said Bivens could have his day in court, that the Constitution guaranteed him this much. His opinion harkens back to Chief Justice Marshall's constitutional catechism to believe that where there is a right there ought to be a remedy. Justice Harlan carefully concurred separately to emphasize, "it is important in a civilized society, that the judicial branch of the Nation's government stand ready to afford a remedy in these circumstances." Chief Justice Burger dissented, along with Justices Black and Blackmun, to reject Justice Brennan's judicially-created remedy, favoring instead that Congress establish an administrative procedure to process remedial claims of constitutional wrongs. He certainly was accurate to proclaim that "this case has significance far beyond its facts*

*and its holding." Since 1971, implied causes of action
have been recognized directly under various other constitutional provisions.*

**Justice Brennan:** The Fourth Amendment provides that:
"The right of the people to be secure in their persons, houses,
papers, and effects, against unreasonable searches and seizures,
shall not be violated." The question here is whether violation of
that command by a federal agent acting under color of his
authority gives rise to a cause of action for damages consequent
upon his unconstitutional conduct. Today we hold that it does.

The Defendants do not argue that Plaintiff-Bivens should be
entirely without remedy for an unconstitutional invasion of his
rights by federal agents. In the Defendants' view, however, the
rights that he asserts—primarily rights of privacy—are creations of state and not of federal law. Accordingly, they argue,
Plaintiff-Bivens may obtain money damages to redress invasion
of these rights only by an action in tort, under state law, in the
state courts. In this scheme the Fourth Amendment would serve
merely to limit the extent to which the agents could defend the
state law tort suit by asserting that their actions were a valid
exercise of federal power: if the agents were shown to have
violated the Fourth Amendment, such a defense would be lost to
them and they would stand before the state law merely as private individuals.

We think that the Defendants' thesis rests upon an unduly
restrictive view of the Fourth Amendment's protection against
unreasonable searches and seizures by federal agents, a view
that has consistently been rejected by this Court. The Defendants seek to treat the relationship between a citizen and a
federal agent unconstitutionally exercising his authority as no
different from the relationship between two private citizens. In
so doing, they ignore the fact that power, once granted, does not
disappear like a magic gift when it is wrongfully used. An agent
acting—albeit unconstitutionally—in the name of the United
States possesses a far greater capacity for harm than an individual trespasser exercising no authority other than his own. Accordingly, as our cases make clear, the Fourth Amendment
operates as a limitation upon the exercise of federal power regardless of whether the State in whose jurisdiction that power is
exercised would prohibit or penalize the identical act if engaged
in by a private citizen. It guarantees to citizens of the United
States the absolute right to be free from unreasonable searches
and seizures carried out by virtue of federal authority. And

"where federally protected rights have been invaded, it has been the rule from the beginning that courts will be alert to adjust their remedies so as to grant the necessary relief."

Our cases have long since rejected the notion that the Fourth Amendment proscribes only such conduct as would, if engaged in by private persons, be condemned by state law. And our recent decisions regarding electronic surveillance have made it clear beyond peradventure that the Fourth Amendment is not tied to the niceties of local trespass laws. In light of these cases, the Defendants' argument that the Fourth Amendment serves only as a limitation on federal defenses to a state law claim, and not as an independent limitation upon the exercise of federal power, must be rejected.

The interests protected by state laws regulating trespass and the invasion of privacy, and those protected by the Fourth Amendment's guarantee against unreasonable searches and seizures, may be inconsistent or even hostile. Thus, we may bar the door against an unwelcome private intruder, or call the police if he persists in seeking entrance. The availability of such alternative means for the protection of privacy may lead the State to restrict imposition of liability for any consequent trespass. A private citizen, asserting no authority other than his own, will not normally be liable in trespass if he demands, and is granted, admission to another's house. But one who demands admission under a claim of federal authority stands in a far different position. The mere invocation of federal power by a federal law enforcement official will normally render futile any attempt to resist an unlawful entry or arrest by resort to the local police; and a claim of authority to enter is likely to unlock the door as well. In 1882, the Court observed, "In such cases there is no safety for the citizen, except in the protection of the judicial tribunals, for rights which have been invaded by the officers of the government, professing to act in its name. There remains to him but the alternative of resistance, which may amount to crime." Nor is it adequate to answer that state law may take into account the different status of one clothed with the authority of the Federal Government. For just as state law may not authorize federal agents to violate the Fourth Amendment, neither may state law undertake to limit the extent to which federal authority can be exercised. The inevitable consequence of this dual limitation on state power is that the federal question becomes not merely a possible defense to the state law action, but an independent claim both necessary and sufficient to make out a plaintiff's cause of action.

That damages may be obtained for injuries consequent upon a violation of the Fourth Amendment by federal officials should hardly seem a surprising proposition. Historically, damages have been regarded as the ordinary remedy for an invasion of personal interests in liberty. Of course, the Fourth Amendment does not in so many words provide for its enforcement by an award of money damages for the consequences of its violation. But in a 1946 decision reserving the question we decide today, this Court said, "it is well settled that where legal rights have been invaded, and a federal statute provides for a general right to sue for such invasion, federal courts may use any available remedy to make good the wrong done." The present case involves no special factors counseling hesitation in the absence of affirmative action by Congress. We are not dealing with a question of "federal fiscal policy." Nor are we asked in this case to impose liability upon a congressional employee for actions contrary to no constitutional prohibition, but merely said to be in excess of the authority delegated to him by the Congress. Finally, we cannot accept the Defendants' formulation of the question as whether the availability of money damages is necessary to enforce the Fourth Amendment. For we have here no explicit congressional declaration that persons injured by a federal officer's violation of the Fourth Amendment may not recover money damages from the agents, but must instead be remitted to another remedy, equally effective in the view of Congress. The question is merely whether Plaintiff-Bivens, if he can demonstrate an injury consequent upon the violation by federal agents of his Fourth Amendment rights, is entitled to redress his injury through a particular remedial mechanism normally available in the federal courts. As Chief Justice Marshall proclaimed, "The very essence of civil liberty certainly consists in the right of every individual to claim the protection of the laws, whenever he receives an injury." Having concluded that Plaintiff-Biven's complaint states a cause of action under the Fourth Amendment, we hold that he is entitled to recover money damages for any injuries he has suffered as a result of the agents' violation of the Amendment.

*It is the proud boast of our democracy that we have "a government of laws and not of men."*

*— Antonin Scalia*

## Morrison v. Olson
### 108 S.Ct. 2597, 487 U.S. 654 (1988)

*The technical ruling was to uphold the constitutionality of the Ethics in Government Act of 1978. The Act authorized the appointment of an independent counsel, outside the executive branch, to investigate and to prosecute high-ranking government officials for wrongdoing. Only Justice Scalia dissented. His "solo voce" dissent took an heroic view of separation of powers. He appealed to first principles found in* The Federalist Papers. *This is an example of what Chief Justice Hughes must have had in mind when he said, "A dissent in a court of last resort is an appeal to the brooding spirit of the law, to the intelligence of a future day."*

**Justice Scalia:** It is the proud boast of our democracy that we have "a government of laws and not of men." Many Americans are familiar with that phrase; not many know its derivation. It comes from the Massachusetts Constitution of 1780, which reads as follows:

In the government of this Commonwealth, the legislative department shall never exercise the executive and judicial powers, or either of them: The executive shall never exercise the legislative and judicial powers, or either of them: The judicial shall never exercise the legislative and executive powers, or either of them: to the end it may be a government of laws and not of men.

The Framers of the Federal Constitution similarly viewed the principle of separation of powers as the absolutely central guarantee of a just Government. In No. 47 of The Federalist, Madison wrote that "no political truth is certainly of greater intrinsic value, or is stamped with the authority of more enlightened patrons of liberty." Without a secure structure of separated powers, our Bill of Rights would be worthless, as are the bills of rights of many nations of the world that have adopted, or even improved upon, the mere words of ours.

The principle of separation of powers is expressed in our Constitution in the first section of each of the first three Articles. Article I, § 1, provides that "all legislative Powers herein granted shall be vested in a Congress of the United States, which shall consist of a Senate and House of Representatives." Article III, § 1, provides that "the judicial Power of the United States, shall be vested in one supreme Court, and in such inferior Courts as the Congress may from time to time ordain and establish." And the provision at issue here, Art. II, § 1, cl. 1, provides that "the executive Power shall be vested in a President of the United States of America."

But just as the mere words of a Bill of Rights are not self-effectuating, the Framers recognized "the insufficiency of a mere parchment delineation of the boundaries" to achieve the separation of powers. *Federalist No. 73* (A. Hamilton). "The great security," wrote Madison, "against a gradual concentration of the several powers in the same department consists in giving to those who administer each department the necessary constitutional means and personal motives to resist encroachments of the others. The provision for defense must in this, as in all other cases, be made commensurate to the danger of attack." *Federalist No. 51*. Madison continued:

> But it is not possible to give to each department an equal power of self-defense. In republican government, the legislative authority necessarily predominates. The remedy for this inconvenience is to divide the legislature into different branches; and to render them, by different modes of election and different principles of action, as little connected with each other as the nature of their common functions and their common dependence on the society will admit. As the weight of the legislative authority requires that it should be thus divided, the weakness of the executive may require, on the other hand, that it should be fortified.

The major "fortification" provided, of course, was the veto power. But in addition to providing fortification, the Founders conspicuously and very consciously declined to sap the Executive's strength in the same way they had weakened the Legislature: by dividing the executive power. Proposals to have multiple executives, or a council of advisers with separate authority were rejected. Thus, while "all legislative Powers herein granted shall be vested in a Congress of the United

States, which shall consist of a Senate and House of Representatives," U.S. Const., Art. I, § 1, "the executive Power shall be vested in a President of the United States," Art. II, § 1, cl. 1.

That is what this suit is about. Power. The allocation of power among Congress, the President, and the courts in such fashion as to preserve the equilibrium the Constitution sought to establish—so that "a gradual concentration of the several powers in the same department," *Federalist No. 51* (J. Madison), can effectively be resisted. Frequently an issue of this sort will come before the Court clad, so to speak, in sheep's clothing: the potential of the asserted principle to effect important change in the equilibrium of power is not immediately evident, and must be discerned by a careful and perceptive analysis. But this wolf comes as a wolf.

If to describe this case is not to decide it, the concept of a government of separate and coordinate powers no longer has meaning. The Court devotes most of its attention to such relatively technical details as the Appointments Clause and the removal power, addressing briefly and only at the end of its opinion the separation of powers. As my prologue suggests, I think that has it backwards. Our opinions are full of the recognition that it is the principle of separation of powers, and the inseparable corollary that each department's "defense must be made commensurate to the danger of attack," which gives comprehensible content to the Appointments Clause, and determines the appropriate scope of the removal power. Thus, I begin with a consideration of the fountainhead of that jurisprudence, the separation and equilibration of powers.

Where a private citizen challenges action of the Government on grounds unrelated to separation of powers, harmonious functioning of the system demands that we ordinarily give some deference, or a presumption of validity, to the actions of the political branches in what is agreed, between themselves at least, to be within their respective spheres. But where the issue pertains to separation of powers, and the political branches are (as here) in disagreement, neither can be presumed correct. The reason is stated concisely by Madison: "The several departments being perfectly co-ordinate by the terms of their common commission, neither of them, it is evident, can pretend to an exclusive or superior right of settling the boundaries between their respective powers." *Federalist No. 49*. The playing field for the present case, in other words, is a level one. As one of the interested and coordinate parties to the underlying constitutional dispute, Congress, no more than the President, is entitled to the benefit of the doubt.

To repeat, Article II, § 1, cl. 1, of the Constitution provides: "The executive Power shall be vested in a President of the United States." This does not mean some of the executive power, but all of the executive power. It seems to me, therefore, that the lower court's decision invalidating the present statute must be upheld on fundamental separation-of-powers principles if the following two questions are answered affirmatively: (1) Is the conduct of a criminal prosecution (and of an investigation to decide whether to prosecute) the exercise of purely executive power? (2) Does the statute deprive the President of the United States of exclusive control over the exercise of that power? Surprising to say, the majority appears to concede an affirmative answer to both questions, but seeks to avoid the inevitable conclusion that since the statute vests some purely executive power in a person who is not the President of the United States it is void.

The utter incompatibility of the majority's approach with our constitutional traditions can be made more clear, perhaps, by applying it to the powers of the other two branches. Is it conceivable that if Congress passed a statute depriving itself of less than full and entire control over some insignificant area of legislation, we would inquire whether the matter was "so central to the functioning of the Legislative Branch" as really to require complete control, or whether the statute gives Congress "sufficient control over the surrogate legislator to ensure that Congress is able to perform its constitutionally assigned duties?" Of course we would have none of that. Once we determined that a purely legislative power was at issue we would require it to be exercised, wholly and entirely, by Congress. Or to bring the point closer to home, consider a statute giving to non-Article III judges just a tiny bit of purely judicial power in a relatively insignificant field, with substantial control, though not total control, in the courts. Is there any doubt that we would not pause to inquire whether the matter was "so central to the functioning of the Judicial Branch" as really to require complete control, or whether we retained "sufficient control over the matters to be decided that we are able to perform our constitutionally assigned duties?" We would say that our "constitutionally assigned duties" include complete control over all exercises of the judicial power. We should say here that the President's constitutionally assigned duties include complete control over investigation and prosecution of violations of the law, and that the inexorable command of Article II is clear and definite: the executive power must be vested in the President of the United States.

Is it unthinkable that the President should have such exclusive power, even when alleged crimes by him or his close associates are at issue? No more so than that Congress should have the exclusive power of legislation, even when what is at issue is its own exemption from the burdens of certain laws. No more so than that this Court should have the exclusive power to pronounce the final decision on justiciable cases and controversies, even those pertaining to the constitutionality of a statute reducing the salaries of the Justices. A system of separate and coordinate powers necessarily involves an acceptance of exclusive power that can theoretically be abused. While the separation of powers may prevent us from righting every wrong, it does so in order to ensure that we do not lose liberty. The checks against any branch's abuse of its exclusive powers are twofold: First, retaliation by one of the other branch's use of its exclusive powers: Congress, for example, can impeach the executive who willfully fails to enforce the laws; the executive can decline to prosecute under unconstitutional statutes; and the courts can dismiss malicious prosecutions. Second, and ultimately, there is the political check that the people will replace those in the political branches, the branches more "dangerous to the political rights of the Constitution," *Federalist Paper No. 78*, who are guilty of abuse.

The rest of the Court has, nonetheless, replaced the clear constitutional prescription that the executive power belongs to the President with a "balancing test." What are the standards to determine how the balance is to be struck, that is, how much removal of Presidential power is too much? Many countries of the world get along with an executive that is much weaker than ours—in fact, entirely dependent upon the continued support of the legislature. Once we depart from the text of the Constitution, just where short of that do we stop? The most amazing feature of the Court's opinion is that it does not even purport to give an answer. It simply announces, with no analysis, that the ability to control the decision whether to investigate and prosecute the President's closest advisers, and indeed the President himself, is not "so central to the functioning of the Executive Branch" as to be constitutionally required to be within the President's control. Apparently that is so because we say it is so. Having abandoned as the basis for our decision-making the text of Article II that "the executive Power" must be vested in the

President, the Court does not even attempt to craft a substitute criterion—a "justiciable standard," however remote from the Constitution—that today governs, and in the future will govern, the decision of such questions. Evidently, the governing standard is to be what might be called the unfettered wisdom of a majority of this Court, revealed to an obedient people on a case-by-case basis. This is not only not the government of laws that the Constitution established; it is not a government of laws at all.

In my view, moreover, even as an ad hoc, standardless judgment the Court's conclusion must be wrong. The statute deeply wounds the President, by substantially reducing the President's ability to protect himself and his staff. That is the whole object of the law, of course, and I cannot imagine why the Court believes it does not succeed. Besides weakening the Presidency by reducing the zeal of his staff, it must also be obvious that the institution of the independent counsel enfeebles him more directly in his constant confrontations with Congress, by eroding his public support.

In sum, this statute does deprive the President of substantial control over the prosecutory functions performed by the independent counsel, and it does substantially affect the balance of powers. That the Court could possibly conclude otherwise demonstrates both the wisdom of our former constitutional system, in which the degree of reduced control and political impairment were irrelevant, since all purely executive power had to be in the President; and the folly of the new system of standardless judicial allocation of powers we adopt today.

The purpose of the separation and equilibration of powers in general, and of the unitary Executive in particular, was not merely to assure effective government but to preserve individual freedom. Those who hold or have held offices covered by the Ethics in Government Act are entitled to that protection as much as the rest of us, and I conclude my discussion by considering the effect of the Act upon the fairness of the process they receive.

Only someone who has worked in the field of law enforcement can fully appreciate the vast power and the immense discretion that are placed in the hands of a prosecutor with respect to the objects of his investigation. Under our system of government, the primary check against prosecutorial abuse is a political one. The prosecutors who exercise this awesome discretion are selected and can be removed by a President, whom the people have trusted enough to elect. Moreover, when crimes are not investigated and prosecuted fairly, nonselectively, with a reasonable sense of proportion, the President pays the cost in political damage to his administration. If federal prosecutors "pick people that they think they should get, rather than cases that need to be prosecuted," if they amass many more resources against a particular prominent individual, or against a particular class of political protesters, or against members of a particular political party, than the gravity of the alleged offenses or the record of successful prosecutions seems to warrant, the unfairness will come home to roost in the Oval Office. I leave it to the reader to recall the examples of this in recent years. That result, of course, was precisely what the Founders had in mind when they provided that all executive powers would be exercised by a single Chief Executive. As Hamilton put it, "the ingredients which constitute safety in the republican sense are a due dependence on the people, and a due responsibility." The President is directly dependent on the people, and since there is only one President, he is responsible. The people know whom to blame, whereas "one of the weightiest objections to a plurality in the executive is that it tends to conceal faults and destroy responsibility." *Federalist No. 70.*

The notion that every violation of law should be prosecuted, including—indeed, especially—every violation by those in high places, is an attractive one, and it would be risky to argue in an election campaign that that is not an absolutely overriding value. *Fiat justitia, ruat coelum.* "Let justice be done, though the heavens may fall." The reality is, however, that it is not an absolutely overriding value, and it was with the hope that we would be able to acknowledge and apply such realities that the Constitution spared us, by life tenure, the necessity of election campaigns. I cannot imagine that there are not many thoughtful men and women in Congress who realize that the benefits of this legislation are far outweighed by its harmful effect upon our system of government, and even upon the nature of justice received by those men and women who agree to serve in the Executive Branch. But it is difficult to vote not to enact, and even more difficult to vote to repeal, a statute called, appropriately enough, the Ethics in Government Act. If Congress is controlled by the party other than the one to which the President belongs, it has little incentive to repeal it; if it is controlled by the same party, it dare not. By its shortsighted action today, I fear the Court has permanently encumbered the Republic with an institution that will do it great harm.

Worse than what it has done, however, is the manner in which it has done it. A government of laws means a government of rules. Today's decision on the basic issue of fragmentation of executive power is ungoverned by rule, and hence ungoverned by law. It extends into the very heart of our most significant constitutional function the "totality of the circumstances" mode of analysis that this Court has in recent years become fond of. Taking all things into account, we conclude that the power taken away from the President here is not really too much. The next time executive power is assigned to someone other than the President we may conclude, taking all things into account, that it is too much. That opinion, like this one, will not be confined by any rule. We will describe, as we have today (though I hope more accurately) the effects of the provision in question, and will authoritatively announce: "The President's need to control the exercise of the subject officer's discretion is so central to the functioning of the Executive Branch as to require complete control." This is not analysis; it is ad hoc judgment. And it fails to explain why it is not true that—as the text of the Constitution seems to require, as the Founders seemed to expect, and as our past cases have uniformly assumed—all purely executive power must be under the control of the President.

The ad hoc approach to constitutional adjudication has real attraction, even apart from its work-saving potential. It is guaranteed to produce a result, in every case, that will make a majority of the Court happy with the law. The law is, by definition, precisely what the majority thinks, taking all things into account, it ought to be. I prefer to rely upon the judgment of the wise men who constructed our system, and of the people who approved it, and of two centuries of history that have shown it to be sound. Like it or not, that judgment says, quite plainly, that "the executive Power shall be vested in a President of the United States."

*No such division between the political and judicial branches of the government is made by Article V which grants power over the amending of the Constitution to Congress alone. Undivided control of that process has been given by the Article exclusively and completely to Congress.*

*—Hugo L. Black*

## Coleman v. Miller
### 59 S.Ct. 972, 307 U.S. 433 (1939)

*The background for this case was a campaign to amend the Constitution after the Supreme Court had twice invalidated federal laws restricting child labor. This case was an original proceeding brought directly in the Supreme Court by members of the state legislature of Kansas, after the state supreme court had rebuffed them. When the state Lieutenant Governor broke a tie vote in the State's senate to approve the Child Labor Amendment, plaintiffs complained, he was part of the executive and not part of the "legislature" for purposes of Article V and, furthermore, they argued that the proposal was no longer viable, because it had been thirteen years since Congress first proposed the amendment. The Justices themselves divided equally on the first issue and consequently the role of the Lieutenant Governor was neither approved nor disapproved. Chief Justice Hughes went on to reason that the timing issue was political and not justiciable, i.e., for the Congress and not for the courts to decide. Justice Black, joined by Justices Roberts, Frankfurter and Douglas, concurred but would have gone further to announce a total lack of judicial power to consider any and all issues concerning amendments during the entire Article V process, from proposal through adoption. Justices Butler and McReynolds dissented and would have decided that the ratification was too late. The felt need for the particular amendment disappeared during the New Deal, when the Court took an expansive view of existing congressional powers to enact federal legislation against child labor. Many Article V issues have remained unresolved over the past two centuries. Congress extended its deadline for ratification of the Equal Rights Amendment for a second seven year period; the effect of state rescissions of prior ratification votes was mooted when the measure failed to garner the necessary three-fourths majority of the States. The issue of how contemporaneous in time the States' ratification must be with the congressional proposal of an amendment was debated, without being resolved, regarding the 27th amendment, which was declared ratified in 1992 despite having been drafted by James Madison and first proposed by Congress back in 1789.*

**Chief Justice Hughes:** The state court adopted the view expressed by text-writers that a state legislature which has rejected an amendment proposed by the Congress may later ratify. The argument in support of that view is that Article V says nothing of rejection but speaks only of ratification and provides that a proposed amendment shall be valid as part of the Constitution when ratified by three-fourths of the States; that the power to ratify is thus conferred upon the State by the Constitution and, as a ratifying power, persists despite a previous rejection. The opposing view proceeds on an assumption that if ratification by "Conventions" were prescribed by the Congress, a convention could not reject and, having adjourned sine die, be reassembled and ratify. It is also premised, in accordance with views expressed by text-writers, that ratification if once given cannot afterwards be rescinded and the amendment rejected, and it is urged that the same effect in the exhaustion of the State's power to act should be ascribed to rejection; that a State can act "but once, either by convention or through its legislature."

Historic instances are cited. In 1865, the Thirteenth Amendment was rejected by the legislature of New Jersey which subsequently ratified it, but the question did not become important as ratification by the requisite number of States had already been proclaimed. The question did arise in connection with the adoption of the Fourteenth Amendment. The legislatures of Georgia, North Carolina and South Carolina had rejected the amendment in November and December 1866. New governments were erected in those States (and in others) under the direction of Congress. The new legislatures ratified the amendment in July 1868. Ohio and New Jersey first ratified and then passed resolutions withdrawing their consent. As there were then thirty-seven States, twenty-eight were needed to constitute the requisite three-fourths. The Congress adopted a resolution requesting the Secretary of State to communicate "a list of the

States of the Union whose legislatures have ratified the four-teenth article of amendment." Secretary Seward proclaimed the ratification of twenty-eight States, including North Carolina, South Carolina, Ohio and New Jersey, stating that it appeared that Ohio and New Jersey had since passed resolutions with-drawing their consent and that "it is deemed a matter of doubt and uncertainty whether such resolutions are not irregular, in-valid and therefore ineffectual." The Secretary certified that if the ratifying resolutions of Ohio and New Jersey were still in full force and effect, notwithstanding the attempted withdrawal, the amendment had become a part of the Constitution. On the following day the Congress adopted a concurrent resolution which, reciting that three-fourths of the States having ratified (the list including North Carolina, South Carolina, Ohio and New Jersey), declared the Fourteenth Amendment to be a part of the Constitution and that it should be duly promulgated as such by the Secretary of State. Accordingly, Secretary Seward issued his final official proclamation embracing the States men-tioned in the congressional resolution and adding Georgia.

Thus the political departments of the Government dealt with the effect both of previous rejection and of attempted with-drawal and determined that both were ineffectual in the pres-ence of an actual ratification. While there were special circumstances, because of the action of the Congress in relation to the governments of the rejecting States (North Carolina, South Carolina and Georgia), these circumstances were not re-cited in proclaiming ratification and the previous action taken in these States was set forth in the proclamation as actual pre-vious rejections by the respective legislatures. This decision by the political departments of the Government as to the validity of the adoption of the Fourteenth Amendment has been accepted.

We think that in accordance with this historic precedent the question of the efficacy of ratifications by state legislatures, in the light of previous rejection or attempted withdrawal, should be regarded as a political question pertaining to the political departments, with the ultimate authority in the Congress in the exercise of its control over the promulgation of the adoption of the amendment.

The precise question as now raised is whether, when the legislature of the State, as we have found, has actually ratified the proposed amendment, the Court should restrain the state officers from certifying the ratification to the Secretary of State, because of an earlier rejection, and thus prevent the question from coming before the political departments. We find no basis in either Constitution or statute for such judicial action. Article V, speaking solely of ratification, contains no provision as to rejection. Nor has the Congress enacted a statute relating to rejections. The statutory provision with respect to constitutional amendments presupposes official notice to the Secretary of State when a state legislature has adopted a resolution of ratification. We see no warrant for judicial interference with the performance of that duty.

The more serious question is whether the proposal by the Congress of the Amendment had lost its vitality through lapse of time and hence it could not be ratified by the Kansas legislature in 1937. The argument of plaintiffs stresses the fact that nearly thirteen years elapsed between the proposal in 1924 and the ratification in question. It is said that when the amendment was proposed there was a definitely adverse popular sentiment and that at the end of 1925 there had been rejection by both houses of the legislatures of sixteen States and ratification by only four States, and that it was not until about 1933 that an aggressive campaign was started in favor of the amendment. In reply, it is urged that Congress did not fix a limit of time for ratification and that an unreasonably long time had not elapsed since the submission; that the conditions which gave rise to the amendment had not been eliminated; that the prevalence of child labor, the diversity of state laws and the disparity in their administration, with the resulting competitive inequalities, continued to exist. Reference is also made to the fact that a number of the States have treated the amendment as still pending and that in the proceedings of the national government there have been indications of the same view. It is said that there were fourteen ratifications in 1933, four in 1935, one in 1936, and three in 1937.

We have held that the Congress in proposing an amendment may fix a reasonable time for ratification. *Dillon v. Gloss (1921)*. There we sustained the action of the Congress in providing in the proposed Eighteenth Amendment that it should be inoperative unless ratified within seven years. No limitation of time for ratification is provided in the instant case either in the proposed amendment or in the resolution of submission. But plaintiffs contend that, in the absence of a limitation by the Congress, the Court can and should decide what is a reasonable period within which ratification may be had. We are unable to agree with that contention.

It is true that in 1921 the Court said that nothing was found in Article V which suggested that an amendment once proposed was to be open to ratification for all time, or that ratification in some States might be separated from that in others by many years and yet be effective; that there was a strong suggestion to the contrary in that proposal and ratification were but succeeding steps in a single endeavor; that as amendments were deemed to be prompted by necessity, they should be considered and disposed of presently; and that there is a fair implication that ratification must be sufficiently contemporaneous in the required number of States to reflect the will of the people in all sections at relatively the same period; and hence that ratification must be within some reasonable time after the proposal. These considerations were cogent reasons for the decision that the Congress had the power to fix a reasonable time for ratification. But it does not follow that, whenever Congress has not exercised that power, the Court should take upon itself the responsibility of deciding what constitutes a reasonable time and determine accordingly the validity of ratifications. That question was not involved in *Dillon v. Gloss* and, in accordance with familiar principle, what was there said must be read in the light of the point decided.

Where are to be found the criteria for such a judicial determination? None are to be found in Constitution or statute. In their endeavor to answer this question plaintiffs' counsel have suggested that at least two years should be allowed; that six years would not seem to be unreasonably long; that seven years had been used by the Congress as a reasonable period; that one year, six months and thirteen days was the average time used in passing upon amendments which have been ratified since the first ten amendments; that three years, six months and twenty-five days has been the longest time used in ratifying. To this list of variables, counsel add that "the nature and extent of publicity and the activity of the public and of the legislatures of the several States in relation to any particular proposal should be taken into consideration." That statement is pertinent, but there are additional matters to be examined and weighed. When a proposed amendment springs from a conception of economic needs, it would be necessary, in determining whether a reasonable time had elapsed since its submission, to consider the economic conditions prevailing in the country, whether these had so far changed since the submission as to make the proposal no longer responsive to the conception which inspired it or whether conditions were such as to intensify the feeling of need and the appropriateness of the proposed remedial action. In short, the question of a reasonable time in many cases would involve, as in this case it does involve, an appraisal of a great variety of relevant conditions, political, social and economic, which can hardly be said to be within the appropriate range of evidence receivable in a court of justice and as to which it would be an extravagant extension of judicial authority to assert judicial notice as the basis of deciding a controversy with respect to the validity of an amendment actually ratified. On the other hand, these conditions are appropriate for the consideration of the political departments of the Government. The questions they involve are essentially political and not justiciable. They can be decided by the Congress with the full knowledge and appreciation ascribed to the national legislature of the political, social and economic conditions which have prevailed during the period since the submission of the amendment.

Our decision that the Congress has the power under Article V to fix a reasonable limit of time for ratification in proposing an amendment proceeds upon the assumption that the question, what is a reasonable time, lies within the congressional province. If it be deemed that such a question is an open one when the limit has not been fixed in advance, we think that it should also be regarded as an open one for the consideration of the Congress when, in the presence of certified ratifications by three-fourths of the States, the time arrives for the promulgation of the adoption of the amendment. The decision by the Congress, in its control of the action of the Secretary of State, of the question whether the amendment had been adopted within a reasonable time would not be subject to review by the courts.

It would unduly lengthen this opinion to attempt to review our decisions as to the class of questions deemed to be political and not justiciable. In determining whether a question falls within that category, the appropriateness under our system of government of attributing finality to the action of the political departments and also the lack of satisfactory criteria for a judicial determination are dominant considerations. There are many illustrations in the field of our conduct of foreign relations, where there are "considerations of policy, considerations of extreme magnitude, and certainly entirely incompetent to the examination and decision of a court of justice." Questions involving similar considerations are found in the government of our internal affairs. Thus, under Article IV, § 4, of the Constitution, providing that the United States "shall guarantee to every State in this Union a Republican Form of Government," we have held that it rests with the Congress to decide what government is the established one in a State and whether or not it is republican in form. *Luther v. Borden (1849).* In that case Chief Justice Taney observed that "when the senators and representatives of a State are admitted into the councils of the Union, the authority of the government under which they are appointed, as well as its republican character, is recognized by the proper constitutional authority. And its decision is binding on every other department of the government, and could not be questioned in a judicial tribunal." So, it was held in the same case that under the provision of the same Article for the protection of each of the States "against domestic violence" it rested with the Congress "to determine upon the means proper to be adopted to fulfill this guarantee."

For the reasons we have stated, which we think to be as compelling as those which underlay the cited decisions, we think that the Congress in controlling the promulgation of the adoption of a constitutional amendment has the final determination of the question whether by lapse of time its proposal of the amendment had lost its vitality prior to the required ratifications. The state officials should not be restrained from certifying to the Secretary of State the adoption by the legislature of Kansas of the resolution of ratification.

**Justice Black:** The Constitution grants Congress exclusive power to control submission of constitutional amendments. Final determination by Congress that ratification by three-fourths of the States has taken place "is conclusive upon the courts." In the exercise of that power, Congress, of course, is governed by the Constitution. However, whether submission, intervening procedure or Congressional determination of ratification conforms to the commands of the Constitution, call for decisions by a "political department" of questions of a type which this Court has frequently designated "political." And decision of a "political question" by the "political department" to which the Constitution has committed it "conclusively binds the judges, as well as all other officers, citizens, and subjects of government." Proclamation under authority of Congress that an amendment has been ratified will carry with it a solemn insurance by the Congress that ratification has taken place as the Constitution commands. Upon this assurance a proclaimed amendment must be accepted as a part of the Constitution, leaving to the judiciary its traditional authority of interpretation. To the extent that the Court's opinion in the present case even impliedly assumes a power to make judicial interpretation of the exclusive constitutional authority of Congress over submission and ratification of amendments, we are unable to agree.

The State court below assumed jurisdiction to determine whether the proper procedure is being followed between submission and final adoption. However, it is apparent that judicial review of or pronouncements upon a supposed limitation of a "reasonable time" within which Congress may accept ratification; as to whether duly authorized State officials have proceeded properly in ratifying or voting for ratification; or whether a State may reverse its action once taken upon a proposed amendment; and kindred questions, are all consistent only with an ultimate control over the amending process in the courts. And this must inevitably embarrass the course of amendment by subjecting to judicial interference matters that we believe were intrusted by the Constitution solely to the political branch of government.

The Court here treats the amending process of the Constitution in some respects as subject to judicial construction, in others as subject to the final authority of the Congress. There is no disapproval of the conclusion arrived at in *Dillon v. Gloss (1921)*, that the Constitution impliedly requires that a properly submitted amendment must die unless ratified within a "reasonable time." Nor does the Court now disapprove its prior assumption of power to make such a pronouncement. And it is not made clear that only Congress has constitutional power to determine if there is any such implication in Article V of the Constitution. On the other hand, the Court's opinion declares that Congress has the exclusive power to decide the "political questions" of whether a State whose legislature has once acted upon a proposed amendment may subsequently reverse its position, and whether, in the circumstances of such a case as this, an amendment is dead because an "unreasonable" time has elapsed. No such division between the political and judicial branches of the government is made by Article V which grants power over the amending of the Constitution to Congress alone. Undivided control of that process has been given by the Article exclusively and completely to Congress. The process itself is "political" in its entirety, from submission until an amendment becomes part of the Constitution, and is not subject to judicial guidance, control or interference at any point.

Since Congress has sole and complete control over the amending process, subject to no judicial review, the views of any court upon this process cannot be binding upon Congress, and insofar as *Dillon v. Gloss* attempts judicially to impose a limitation upon the right of Congress to determine final adoption of an amendment, it should be disapproved. If Congressional determination that an amendment has been completed and become a part of the Constitution is final and removed from examination by the courts, as the Court's present opinion recognizes, surely the steps leading to that condition must be subject to the scrutiny, control and appraisal of none save the Congress, the body having exclusive power to make that final determination.

Congress, possessing exclusive power over the amending process, cannot be bound by and is under no duty to accept the pronouncements upon that exclusive power by this Court or by the Kansas courts. Neither State nor Federal courts can review that power. Therefore, any judicial expression amounting to more than mere acknowledgment of exclusive Congressional power over the political process of amendment is a mere admonition to the Congress in the nature of an advisory opinion, given wholly without constitutional authority.

*Deciding whether a matter has in any measure been committed by the Constitution to another branch of government, or whether the action of that branch exceeds whatever authority has been committed, is itself a delicate exercise in constitutional interpretation, and is a responsibility of this Court as ultimate interpreter of the Constitution.*

—*William J. Brennan*

## Baker v. Carr
### 82 S.Ct. 691, 369 U.S. 186 (1962)

*For over six decades, the Tennessee state legislature had not redrawn its districts despite wholesale shifts in population from rural to urban areas, which meant that the relatively fewer voters living in rural districts were over-represented. Those in power in Tennessee and in other States could not be expected to be reform-minded to reapportion themselves out of office. This decision allowed voters in more populous districts to be heard in federal court to complain that malapportionment denied them the "equal protection of the laws" in voting. Before this decision, however, the political question or nonjusticiability doctrine had seemed an insurmountable obstacle under Supreme Court precedents. That doctrine provides that some issues are not the proper subject of judicial decision, that the choices of the political branches cannot be reviewed by judges. Justice Brennan's brilliant opinion resynthesized case law and reinterpreted the relationship of the Supreme Court vis-a-vis the political branches, on the one hand, and the States, on the other. In* Reynolds v. Sims (1964) *the Court delivered an edict to redraw districts with equal populations after each federal decennial census to ensure one-person-one vote. Chief Justice Earl Warren called this "the most vital decision" of his tenure and considered this line of cases to be the most important constitutional achievement of the Warren Court.*

**Justice Brennan:** The mere fact that the suit seeks protection of a political right does not mean it presents a political question. Such an objection "is little more than a play upon words." We hold that the claim pleaded here neither rests upon nor implicates the Guaranty Clause and that its justiciability is therefore not foreclosed by our decisions of cases involving that clause. In the Guaranty Clause cases and in the other "political question" cases, it is the relationship between the judiciary and the coordinate branches of the Federal Government, and not the federal judiciary's relationship to the States, which gives rise to the "political question."

We have said that "In determining whether a question falls within (the political question) category, the appropriateness under our system of government of attributing finality to the action of the political departments and also the lack of satisfactory criteria for a judicial determination are dominant considerations." The nonjusticiability of a political question is primarily a function of the separation of powers. Much confusion results from the capacity of the "political question" label to obscure the need for case-by-case inquiry. Deciding whether a matter has in any measure been committed by the Constitution to another branch of government, or whether the action of that branch exceeds whatever authority has been committed, is itself a delicate exercise in constitutional interpretation, and is a responsibility of this Court as ultimate interpreter of the Constitution. To demonstrate this requires no less than to analyze representative cases and to infer from them the analytical threads that make up the political question doctrine. We shall then show that none of those threads catches this case.

It is apparent that several formulations which vary slightly according to the settings in which the questions arise may describe a political question, although each has one or more elements which identify it as essentially a function of the separation of powers. Prominent on the surface of any case held to involve a political question is found a textually demonstrable constitutional commitment of the issue to a coordinate political department; or a lack of judicially discoverable and manageable standards for resolving it; or the impossibility of deciding without an initial policy determination of a kind clearly for nonjudicial discretion; or the impossibility of a court's undertaking independent resolution without expressing lack of the respect due coordinate branches of government; or an unusual need for unquestioning adherence to a political decision already made; or the potentiality of embarrassment from multifarious pronouncements by various departments on one question.

Unless one of these formulations is inextricable from the case at bar, there should be no dismissal for non-justiciability on the ground of a political question's presence. The doctrine of which we treat is one of "political questions," not one of "political cases." The courts cannot reject as "no law suit" a bona fide controversy as to whether some action denominated "political" exceeds constitutional authority. The cases we have reviewed show the necessity for discriminating inquiry into the precise facts and posture of the particular case, and the impossibility of resolution by any semantic cataloguing.

But it is argued that this case shares the characteristics of decisions that constitute a category not yet considered, cases concerning the Constitution's guaranty, in Art. IV, § 4, of a republican form of government. Guaranty Clause claims involve those elements which define a "political question," and for that reason and no other, they are nonjusticiable. The nonjusticiability of such claims has nothing to do with their touching upon matters of state governmental organization.

*Luther v. Borden (1849)* though in form simply an action for damages for trespass was, as Daniel Webster said in opening the argument for the defense, "an unusual case." The defendants, admitting an otherwise tortious breaking and entering, sought to justify their action on the ground that they were agents of the established lawful government of Rhode Island, which State was then under martial law to defend itself from active insurrection; that the plaintiff was engaged in that insurrection; and that they entered under orders to arrest the plaintiff. The case arose "out of the unfortunate political differences which agitated the people of Rhode Island in 1841 and 1842," and which had resulted in a situation wherein two groups laid competing claims to recognition as the lawful government.

Clearly, several factors were thought by the Court in *Luther* to make the question there "political": the commitment to the other branches of the decision as to which is the lawful state government; the unambiguous action by the President, in recognizing the charter government as the lawful authority; the need for finality in the executive's decision; and the lack of criteria by which a court could determine which form of government was republican.

Even though the Court wrote of unrestrained legislative and executive authority under this Guaranty, thus making its enforcement a political question, the Court plainly implied that the political question barrier was no absolute: "Unquestionably a military government, established as the permanent government of the State, would not be a republican government, and it would be the duty of Congress to overthrow it." Of course, it does not necessarily follow that if Congress did not act, the Court would. For while the judiciary might be able to decide the limits of the meaning of "republican form," and thus the factor of lack of criteria might fall away, there would remain other possible barriers to decision because of primary commitment to another branch, which would have to be considered in the particular fact setting presented. The lack of criteria does not obliterate the Guaranty's extreme limits: The guaranty is of a republican form of government. No particular government is designated as republican, neither is the exact form to be guaranteed, in any manner especially designated. Here, as in other parts of the instrument, we are compelled to resort elsewhere to ascertain what was intended.

In 1875, this Court explained: "The guaranty necessarily implies a duty on the part of the States themselves to provide such a government. All the States had governments when the Constitution was adopted. In all the people participated to some extent, through their representatives elected in the manner specially provided. These governments the Constitution did not change. They were accepted precisely as they were, and it is, therefore, to be presumed that they were such as it was the duty of the States to provide. Thus we have unmistakable evidence of what was republican in form, within the meaning of that term as employed in the Constitution." And in 1891, this Court explained further: "By the Constitution, a republican form of government is guaranteed to every state in the Union, and the distinguishing feature of that form is the right of the people to choose their own officers for governmental administration, and pass their own laws in virtue of the legislative power reposed in representative bodies, whose legitimate acts may be said to be those of the people themselves; but, while the people are thus the source of political power, their governments, national and State, have been limited by written constitutions, and they have themselves thereby set bounds to their own power, as against the sudden impulses of mere majorities."

But the only significance that *Luther v. Borden* could have for our immediate purposes is in its holding that the Guaranty Clause is not a repository of judicially manageable standards which a court could utilize independently in order to identify a State's lawful government. The Court has since refused to resort to the Guaranty Clause—which alone had been invoked for the purpose—as the source of a constitutional standard for invalidating state action. Just as the Court has consistently held that a challenge to state action based on the Guaranty Clause presents no justiciable question so has it held, and for the same reasons, that challenges to congressional action on the ground of inconsistency with that clause present no justiciable question.

We come, finally, to the ultimate inquiry whether our precedents as to what constitutes a nonjusticiable "political question" bring the case before us under the umbrella of that doctrine. A natural beginning is to note whether any of the common characteristics which we have been able to identify and label descriptively are present. We find none: The question here is the consistency of state action with the Federal Constitution. We have no question decided, or to be decided, by a political branch of government coequal with this Court. Nor do we risk embarrassment of our government abroad, or grave disturbance at home if we take issue with Tennessee as to the constitutionality of her action here challenged. Nor need the appellants, in order to succeed in this action, ask the Court to enter upon policy determinations for which judicially manageable standards are lacking. Judicial standards under the Equal Protection Clause are well developed and familiar, and it has been open to courts since the enactment of the Fourteenth Amendment to determine, if on the particular facts they must, that a discrimination reflects no policy, but simply arbitrary and capricious action.

This case does, in one sense, involve the allocation of political power within a State, and the plaintiffs might conceivably have added a claim under the Guaranty Clause. Of course, as we have seen, any reliance on that clause would be futile. But because any reliance on the Guaranty Clause could not have succeeded it does not follow that plaintiffs may not be heard on the equal protection claim which in fact they tender. True, it must be clear that the Fourteenth Amendment claim is not so enmeshed with those political question elements which render Guaranty Clause claims nonjusticiable as actually to present a political question itself. But we have found that not to be the case here.

We conclude that the complaint's allegations of a denial of equal protection present a justiciable constitutional cause of action upon which plaintiffs are entitled to a trial and a decision. The right asserted is within the reach of judicial protection under the Fourteenth Amendment.

*The Constitution, in all its provisions, looks to an indestructible Union, composed of indestructible States.*

—*Salmon P. Chase*

## Texas v. White
### 74 U.S. (7 Wallace) 700 (1868)

*In 1867, the Supreme Court accepted original jurisdiction in this case under Article III, § 2, and sat as the trial court, because a State was a party. The reconstruction government of Texas brought suit to recover state-owned securities that had been sold by the State's confederate government to the defendants during the Civil War. The defendants argued that first, Texas could not bring the suit because the State had seceded and had not yet been fully restored to the Union and second, their agreement with the confederate state was valid. Reaching the merits, Chief Justice Chase ruled against the defendants. The confederate state government was unlawful and its acts in support of the rebellion were invalid, including its agreement with the defendants, so the reconstruction state was entitled to recover the securities. Lincoln's Chief Justice delivered the definitive exegesis on the relationship between a State and the Union under the Constitution. The Union is indeed perpetual and the Congress enjoys a certain primacy in defining the roles of the States.*

**Chief Justice Chase:** This is an original suit in this court, in which the State of Texas, claiming certain bonds of the United States as her property, asks an injunction to restrain the defendants from receiving payment from the National government, and to compel the surrender of the bonds to the State. It is not to be questioned that this court has original jurisdiction of suits by States against citizens of other States, or that the States entitled to invoke this jurisdiction must be States of the Union. But, it is equally clear that no such jurisdiction has been conferred upon this court of suits by any other political communities than such States.

If, therefore, it is true that the State of Texas was not at the time of filing this bill, or is not now, one of the United States, we have no jurisdiction of this suit, and it is our duty to dismiss it.

We are very sensible of the magnitude and importance of this question, of the interest it excites, and of the difficulty, not to say impossibility, of so disposing of it as to satisfy the conflicting judgments of men equally enlightened, equally upright, and equally patriotic. But we meet it in the case, and we must determine it in the exercise of our best judgment, under the guidance of the Constitution alone.

Some not unimportant aid, however, in ascertaining the true sense of the Constitution, may, be derived from considering what is the correct idea of a State, apart from any union or confederation with other States. The poverty of language often compels the employment of terms in quite different significations; and of this hardly any example more signal is to be found than in the use of the word we are now considering. It would serve no useful purpose to attempt an enumeration of all the various senses in which it is used. A few only need be noticed.

It describes sometimes a people or community of individuals united more or less closely in political relations, inhabiting temporarily or permanently the same country; often it denotes only the country or territorial region, inhabited by such a community; not infrequently it is applied to the government under which the people live; at other times it represents the combined idea of people, territory, and government.

It is not difficult to see that in all these senses the primary conception is that of a people or community. The people, in whatever territory dwelling, either temporarily or permanently, and whether organized under a regular government, or united by looser and less definite relations, constitute the state. This is undoubtedly the fundamental idea upon which the republican institutions of our own country are established.

In the Constitution the term state most frequently expresses the combined idea just noticed, of people, territory, and government. A state, in the ordinary sense of the Constitution, is a political community of free citizens, occupying a territory of defined boundaries, and organized under a government sanctioned and limited by a written constitution, and established by the consent of the governed. It is the union of such states, under a common constitution, which forms the distinct and greater political unit, which that Constitution designates as the United States, and makes of the people and states which compose it one people and one country.

But it is also used in its geographical sense, as in the clauses which require that a representative in Congress shall be an inhabitant of the State in which he shall be chosen, and that the trial of crimes shall be held within the State where committed. And there are instances in which the principal sense of the word seems to be that primary one to which we have adverted, of a people or political community, as distinguished from a government. In this latter sense the word seems to be used in the clause which provides that the United States shall guarantee to every State in the Union a republican form of government, and shall protect each of them against invasion. In this clause a plain distinction is made between a State and the government of a State.

Having thus ascertained the senses in which the word state is employed in the Constitution, we will proceed to consider the proper application of what has been said.

The Republic of Texas was admitted into the Union, as a State, on the 27th of December, 1845. By this act the new State, and the people of the new State, were invested with all the rights, and became subject to all the responsibilities and duties of the original States under the Constitution.

From the date of admission, until 1861, the State was represented in the Congress of the United States by her senators and representatives, and her relations as a member of the Union remained unimpaired. In that year, acting upon the theory that the rights of a State under the Constitution might be renounced, and her obligations thrown off at pleasure, Texas undertook to sever the bond thus formed, and to break up her constitutional relations with the United States. In all respects, so far as the object could be accomplished by ordinances of the convention, by acts of the legislature, and by votes of the citizens, the relations of Texas to the Union were broken up, and new relations to a new government were established for them.

The position thus assumed could only be maintained by arms, and Texas accordingly took part, with the other Confederate States, in the war of the rebellion, which these events made inevitable. During the whole of that war there was no governor, or judge, or any other State officer in Texas, who recognized the National authority. Nor was any officer of the United States permitted to exercise any authority whatever under the National government within the limits of the State, except under the immediate protection of the National military forces.

Did Texas, in consequence of these acts, cease to be a State? Or, if not, did the State cease to be a member of the Union? It is needless to discuss, at length, the question whether the right of a State to withdraw from the Union for any cause, regarded by herself as sufficient, is consistent with the Constitution of the United States.

The Union of the States never was a purely artificial and arbitrary relation. It began among the Colonies, and grew out of common origin, mutual sympathies, kindred principles, similar interests, and geographical relations. It was confirmed and strengthened by the necessities of war, and received definite form, and character, and sanction from the Articles of Confederation. By these the Union was solemnly declared to be "perpetual." And when these Articles were found to be inadequate to the exigencies of the country, the Constitution was ordained "to form a more perfect Union." It is difficult to convey the idea of indissoluble unity more clearly than by these words. What can be indissoluble if a perpetual Union, made more perfect, is not?

But the perpetuity and indissolubility of the Union, by no means implies the loss of distinct and individual existence, or of the right of self-government by the States. Under the Articles of Confederation each State retained its sovereignty, freedom, and independence, and every power, jurisdiction, and right not expressly delegated to the United States. Under the Constitution, though the powers of the States were much restricted, still, all powers not delegated to the United States, nor prohibited to the States, are reserved to the States respectively, or to the people. And we have already had occasion to remark at this term, that "the people of each State compose a State, having its own government, and endowed with all the functions essential to separate and independent existence," and that "without the States in union, there could be no such political body as the United States." Not only, therefore, can there be no loss of separate and independent autonomy to the States, through their union under the Constitution, but it may be not unreasonably said that the preservation of the States, and the maintenance of their governments, are as much within the design and care of the Constitution as the preservation of the Union and the maintenance of the National government. The Constitution, in all its provisions, looks to an indestructible Union, composed of indestructible States.

When, therefore, Texas became one of the United States, she entered into an indissoluble relation. All the obligations of perpetual union, and all the guaranties of republican government in the Union, attached at once to the State. The act which consummated her admission into the Union was something more than a compact; it was the incorporation of a new member into the political body. And it was final. The union between Texas and the other States was as complete, as perpetual, and as indissoluble as the union between the original States. There was no place for reconsideration, or revocation, except through revolution, or through consent of the States.

Considered therefore as transactions under the Constitution, the ordinance of secession, adopted by the convention and ratified by a majority of the citizens of Texas, and all the acts of her legislature intended to give effect to that ordinance, were absolutely null. They were utterly without operation in law. The obligations of the State, as a member of the Union, and of every citizen of the State, as a citizen of the United States, remained perfect and unimpaired. It certainly follows that the State did not cease to be a State, nor her citizens to be citizens of the Union. If this were otherwise, the State must have become foreign, and her citizens foreigners. The war must have ceased to be a war for the suppression of rebellion, and must have become a war for conquest and subjugation.

Our conclusion therefore is, that Texas continued to be a State, and a State of the Union, notwithstanding the transactions to which we have referred. And this conclusion, in our judgment, is not in conflict with any act or declaration of any department of the National government, but entirely in accordance with the whole series of such acts and declarations since the first outbreak of the rebellion.

But in order to the exercise, by a State, of the right to sue in this court, there needs to be a State government, competent to represent the State in its relations with the National government, so far at least as the institution and prosecution of a suit is concerned. And it is by no means a logical conclusion, from the premises which we have endeavored to establish, that the governmental relations of Texas to the Union remained unaltered. Obligations often remain unimpaired, while relations are greatly changed. The obligations of allegiance to the State, and of obedience to her laws, subject to the Constitution of the United States, are binding upon all citizens, whether faithful or unfaithful to them; but the relations which subsist while these obligations are performed, are essentially different from those which arise when they are disregarded and set at naught. And the same must necessarily be true of the obligations and relations of States and citizens to the Union. No one has been bold enough to contend that, while Texas was controlled by a government hostile to the United States, and in affiliation with a hostile confederation, waging war upon the United States, senators chosen by her legislature, or representatives elected by her citizens, were entitled to seats in Congress; or that any suit, instituted in her name, could be entertained in this court. All admit that, during this condition of civil war, the rights of the State as a member, and of her people as citizens of the Union, were suspended. The government and the citizens of the State, refusing to recognize their constitutional obligations, assumed the character of enemies, and incurred the consequences of rebellion.

These new relations imposed new duties upon the United States. The first was that of suppressing the rebellion. The next was that of re-establishing the broken relations of the State with the Union. The first of these duties having been performed, the next necessarily engaged the attention of the National government. The authority for the performance of the first had been found in the power to suppress insurrection and carry on war; for the performance of the second, authority was derived from the obligation of the United States to guarantee to every State in the Union a republican form of government. The latter, indeed, in the case of a rebellion which involves the government of a State, and for the time excludes the National authority from its limits, seems to be a necessary complement to the former.

Of this, the case of Texas furnishes a striking illustration. When the war closed there was no government in the State except that which had been organized for the purpose of waging war against the United States. That government immediately disappeared. The chief functionaries left the State. Many of the subordinate officials followed their example. Legal responsibilities were annulled or greatly impaired. It was inevitable that great confusion should prevail. If order was maintained, it was where the good sense and virtue of the citizens gave support to local acting magistrates, or supplied more directly the needful restraints.

A great social change increased the difficulty of the situation. Slaves, in the insurgent States, with certain local exceptions, had been declared free by the Proclamation of

Emancipation; and whatever questions might be made as to the effect of that act, under the Constitution, it was clear, from the beginning, that its practical operation, in connection with legislative acts of like tendency, must be complete enfranchisement. Wherever the National forces obtained control, the slaves became freemen. Support to the acts of Congress and the proclamation of the President, concerning slaves, was made a condition of amnesty by President Lincoln, in December, 1863, and by President Johnson in May, 1865. And emancipation was confirmed, rather than ordained, in the insurgent States, by the amendment to the Constitution prohibiting slavery throughout the Union, which was proposed by Congress in February, 1865, and ratified, before the close of the following autumn, by the requisite three-fourths of the States.

The new freemen necessarily became part of the people, and the people still constituted the State; for States, like individuals, retain their identity, though changed to some extent in their constituent elements. And it was the State, thus constituted, which was now entitled to the benefit of the constitutional guaranty.

There being then no government in Texas in constitutional relations with the Union, it became the duty of the United States to provide for the restoration of such a government. But the restoration of the government which existed before the rebellion, without a new election of officers, was obviously impossible; and before any such election could be properly held, it was necessary that the old state constitution should receive such amendments as would conform its provisions to the new conditions created by emancipation, and afford adequate security to the people of the State.

In the exercise of the power conferred by the guaranty clause, as in the exercise of every other constitutional power, a discretion in the choice of means is necessarily allowed. It is essential only that the means must be necessary and proper for carrying into execution the power conferred, through the restoration of the State to its constitutional relations, under a republican form of government, and that no acts be done, and no authority exerted, which is either prohibited or unsanctioned by the Constitution.

It is not important to review, at length, the measures which have been taken, under this power, by the executive and legislative departments of the National government. It is proper, however, to observe that almost immediately after the cessation of organized hostilities, and while the war yet smoldered in Texas, the President of the United States issued his proclamation appointing a provisional governor for the State, and providing for the assembling of a convention, with a view to the re-establishment of a republican government, under an amended constitution, and to the restoration of the State to her proper constitutional relations. A convention was accordingly assembled, the constitution amended, elections held, and a State government, acknowledging its obligations to the Union, established.

Whether the action then taken was, in all respects, warranted by the Constitution, it is not now necessary to determine. The power exercised by the President was supposed, doubtless, to be derived from his constitutional functions, as commander-in-chief; and, so long as the war continued, it cannot be denied that he might institute temporary government within insurgent districts, occupied by the National forces, or take measures, in any State, for the restoration of State government faithful to the Union, employing, however, in such efforts, only such means and agents as were authorized by constitutional laws.

But, the power to carry into effect the clause of guaranty is primarily a legislative power, and resides in Congress. This Court has said: "Under the fourth article of the Constitution, it rests with Congress to decide what government is the established one in a State. For, as the United States guarantee to each State a republican government, Congress must necessarily decide what government is established in the State, before it can determine whether it is republican or not."

The action of the President must, therefore, be considered as provisional, and, in that light, it seems to have been regarded by Congress. It was taken after the term of the 38th Congress had expired. The 39th Congress, which assembled in December, 1865, followed by the 40th Congress, which met in March, 1867, proceeded, after long deliberation, to adopt various measures for reorganization and restoration. These measures were embodied in proposed amendments to the Constitution, and in the statutes known as the Reconstruction Acts, which have been so far carried into effect, that a majority of the States which were engaged in the rebellion have been restored to their constitutional relations, under forms of government, adjudged to be republican by Congress, through the admission of their "Senators and Representatives into the councils of the Union." Nothing in the case before us requires the Court to pronounce judgment upon the constitutionality of any particular provision of these acts.

But, it is important to observe that these acts themselves show that the governments, which had been established and had been in actual operation under executive direction, were recognized by Congress as provisional, as existing, and as capable of continuance. By these acts, these governments were, indeed, pronounced illegal and were subjected to military control, and were declared to be provisional only; and it was further declared that it was the true intent and meaning of the Congress that the governments then existing were not legal State governments, and if continued, were to be continued subject to the military commanders of the respective districts and to the paramount authority of Congress. We do not inquire here into the constitutionality of this legislation so far as it relates to military authority, or to the paramount authority of Congress. It suffices to say, that the terms of the acts necessarily imply recognition of actually existing governments; and that in point of fact, the governments thus recognized, in some important respects, still exist.

What has thus been said generally describes, with sufficient accuracy, the situation of Texas. The legislature of Texas, at the time of the agreement being challenged here, constituted one of the departments of a State government, established in hostility to the Constitution of the United States. It cannot be regarded, therefore, in the courts of the United States, as a lawful legislature, or its acts as lawful acts. And, yet, it is an historical fact that the government of Texas, then in full control of the State, was its only actual government; and certainly if Texas had been a separate State, and not one of the United States, the new government, having displaced the regular authority, and having established itself in the customary seats of power, and in the exercise of the ordinary functions of administration, would have constituted, in the strictest sense of the words, a *de facto* government, and its acts, during the period of its existence as such, would be effectual, and, in almost all respects, valid. And, to some extent, this is true of the actual government of Texas, though unlawful and revolutionary, as to the United States.

It is not necessary to attempt any exact definitions, within which the acts of such a State government must be treated as valid, or invalid. It may be said, perhaps with sufficient accuracy, that acts necessary to peace and good order among citizens, such for example, as acts sanctioning and protecting marriage and the domestic relations, governing the course of descents, regulating the conveyance and transfer of property, real and personal, and providing remedies for injuries to person and estate, and other similar acts, which would be valid if emanating from a lawful government, must be regarded in general as valid when proceeding from an actual, though unlawful government; and that acts in furtherance or support of rebellion against the United States, or intended to defeat the just rights of citizens, and other acts of like nature, must, in general, be regarded as invalid and void.

What, then, by these general tests, was the character of the transactions before this Court? The arranged sale of the bonds was organized, not for the defence of the State against a foreign invasion, or for its protection against domestic violence, within the meaning of these words as used in the National Constitution, but for the purpose, under the name of defence, of levying war against the United States. This purpose was, undoubtedly, unlawful, for the acts which it contemplated are, within the express definition of the Constitution, treasonable.

*Federalism was our Nation's own discovery. The Framers split the atom of sovereignty. It was the genius of their idea that our citizens would have two political capacities, one state and one federal, each protected from incursion by the other.*
*—Anthony M. Kennedy*

## U.S. Term Limits, Inc. v. Thornton
### 115 S.Ct. 1842 (1995)

*In a 5 to 4 decision, the Supreme Court declared unconstitutional an Arkansas state law which imposed term limits—6 years for the House of Representatives and 12 years for the Senate—on the State's representatives in Congress. Similar laws in 22 States were wiped off the books. The qualifications for members of Congress found in Article I were deemed exclusive and beyond the power of the people of an individual State to change. Thus, proponents could no longer rely on the voters to implement federal term limits State-by-State. Instead, they would have to satisfy the arduous extra-majority requirements for amending the U.S. Constitution: a two-thirds vote in both houses of the Congress and ratification by three-fourths of the state legislatures. That this is one of the most important constitutional decisions of the century is suggested by the fact that the four dissenters were riled enough to write a 40 page opinion contradicting the majority's analysis and conclusions. Justice Kennedy, who cast the deciding fifth vote, harkened back to 18th century principles. For him, the case turned on a proper understanding of federalism and dual citizenship.*

**Justice Kennedy:** It is well settled that the whole people of the United States asserted their political identity and unity of purpose when they created the federal system. Federalism was our Nation's own discovery. The Framers split the atom of sovereignty. It was the genius of their idea that our citizens would have two political capacities, one state and one federal, each protected from incursion by the other. The resulting Constitution created a legal system unprecedented in form and design, establishing two orders of government, each with its own direct relationship, its own privity, its own set of mutual rights and obligations to the people who sustain it and are governed by it.

It is appropriate to recall these origins, which instruct us as to the nature of the two different governments created and confirmed by the Constitution.

A distinctive character of the National Government, the mark of its legitimacy, is that it owes its existence to the act of the whole people who created it. It must be remembered that the National Government too is republican in essence and in theory. John Jay insisted on this point early in *The Federalist Papers*, in his comments on the government that preceded the one formed by the Constitution: "To all general purposes we have uniformly been one people; each individual citizen everywhere enjoying the same national rights, privileges, and protection. A strong sense of the value and blessings of union induced the people, at a very early period, to institute a federal government to preserve and perpetuate it. They formed it almost as soon as they had a political existence." *The Federalist No. 2*. Once the National Government was formed under our Constitution, the same republican principles continued to guide its operation and practice. As James Madison explained, the House of Representatives "derives its powers from the people of America," and "the operation of the government on the people in their individual capacities" makes it "a national government," not merely a federal one. *The Federalist No. 39*. The Court confirmed this principle in *McCulloch v. Maryland (1819)*, when it said, "The government of the Union, then is, emphatically, and truly, a government of the people. In form and in substance it emanates from them. Its powers are granted by them, and are to be exercised directly on them, and for their benefit." The same theory led us in a later case to observe: "In a republican government, like ours, political power is reposed in representatives of the entire body of the people."

In one sense it is true that "the people of each State retained their separate political identities," for the Constitution takes care both to preserve the States and to make use of their identities and structures at various points in organizing the federal union. It does not at all follow from this that the sole political identity of an American is with the State of his or her residence. It denies the dual character of the Federal Government which is its very foundation to assert that the people of the United States do not have a political identity as well, one independent of, though consistent with, their identity as citizens of the State of their residence. It must be recognized, as this Court once pointed out, that "for all the great purposes for which the Federal government was formed, we are one people, with one common country."

It might be objected that because the States ratified the Constitution, the people can delegate power only through the States or by acting in their capacities as citizens of particular States. But in *McCulloch v. Maryland*, the Court set forth its authoritative rejection of this idea: "The Convention which framed the constitution was indeed elected by the State legislatures. But the instrument was submitted to the people. It is true, they assembled in their several States—and where else should they have assembled? No political dreamer was ever wild enough to think of breaking down the lines which separate the States, and of compounding the American people into one common mass. Of consequence, when they act, they act in their States. But the measures they adopt do not, on that account, cease to be the measures of the people themselves, or become the measures of the State governments."

The political identity of the entire people of the Union is reinforced by the proposition, which I take to be beyond dispute, that, though limited as to its objects, the National Government is and must be controlled by the people without collateral interference by the States. *McCulloch* affirmed this proposition as well, when the Court rejected the suggestion that States could interfere with federal powers: "This was not intended by the American people. They did not design to make their government dependent on the States." The States have no power, reserved or otherwise, over the exercise of federal authority within its proper sphere. The *McCulloch* opinion explains, where there is an attempt at "usurpation of a power which the people of a single State cannot give," there can be no question whether the power "has been surrendered" by the people of a single State because "the right never existed." That the States may not invade the sphere of federal sovereignty is as incontestable, in my view, as the corollary proposition that the Federal Government must be held within the boundaries of its own power when it intrudes upon matters reserved to the States.

Of course, because the Framers recognized that state power and identity were essential parts of the federal balance, *The Federalist No. 39*, the Constitution is solicitous of the prerogatives of the States, even in an otherwise sovereign federal province. The Constitution uses state boundaries to fix the size of congressional delegations, U.S. Const., Art. I, § 2, cl. 3, ensures that each State shall have at least one representative, ibid., grants States certain powers over the times, places, and manner of federal elections (subject to congressional revision), Art. I, § 4, cl. 1, requires that when the President is elected by the House of Representatives, the delegations from each State have one vote, Art. II, § 1, cl. 3, and Amend. 12, and allows States to appoint electors for the President, Art. II, § 1, cl. 2. Nothing in the Constitution or *The Federalist Papers*, however, supports the idea of state interference with the most basic relation between the National Government and its citizens, the selection of legislative representatives. Indeed, even though the Constitution uses the qualifications for voters of the most numerous branch of the States' own legislatures to set the qualifications of federal electors, Art. I, § 2, cl. 1, when these electors vote, we have recognized that they act in a federal capacity and exercise a federal right. Addressing this principle in 1884, the Court stated as follows: "The right to vote for a member of Congress" is an "office created by that Constitution, and by that alone. It is not true, therefore, that electors for members of Congress owe their right to vote to the State law in any sense which makes the exercise of the right to depend exclusively on the law of the State." We made the same point in a 1941 decision, when we said, "The right of qualified voters within a state to cast their ballots and have them counted at Congressional elections is a right secured by the Constitution" and "is secured against the action of individuals as well as of states."

The federal character of congressional elections flows from the political reality that our National Government is republican in form and that national citizenship has privileges and immunities protected from state abridgement by the force of the Constitution itself. Even before the passage of the Fourteenth Amendment, the latter proposition was given expression when the Court recognized the right of the Federal Government to call "any or all of its citizens to aid in its service, as members of the Congress, of the courts, of the executive departments, and to fill all its other offices," and further recognized that "this right cannot be made to depend upon the pleasure of a State over whose territory they must pass to reach the point where these services must be rendered." And the rights of national citizenship were upheld again in 1876, when the Court said, "The right of the people peaceably to assemble for the purpose of petitioning Congress for a redress of grievances, or for any thing else connected with the powers or the duties of the national government, is an attribute of national citizenship, and, as such, under the protection of, and guaranteed by, the United States. The very idea of a government, republican in form, implies a right on the part of its citizens to meet peaceably for consultation in respect to public affairs and to petition for a redress of grievances."

In 1873, the Court was careful to hold that federal citizenship in and of itself suffices for the assertion of rights under the Constitution, rights that stem from sources other than the States. Referring to these rights of national dimension and origin the Court observed: "But lest it should be said that no such privileges and immunities are to be found if those we have been considering are excluded, we venture to suggest some which owe their existence to the Federal government, its National character, its Constitution, or its laws." Later cases only reinforced the idea that there are such incidents of national citizenship. Federal privileges and immunities may seem limited in their formulation by comparison with the expansive definition given to the privileges and immunities attributed to state citizenship, but that federal rights flow to the people of the United States by virtue of national citizenship is beyond dispute.

Not the least of the incongruities in the position advanced by Arkansas is the proposition, necessary to its case, that it can burden the rights of resident voters in federal elections by reason of the manner in which they earlier had exercised it. If the majority of the voters had been successful in selecting a candidate, they would be penalized from exercising that same right in the future. Quite apart from any First Amendment concerns, neither the law nor federal theory allows a State to burden the exercise of federal rights in this manner. Indeed, as one of the "rights of the citizens of this great country, protected by implied guarantees of its Constitution," the Court identified the right " to come to the seat of government to share its offices, to engage in administering its functions." This observation serves to illustrate the extent of the State's attempted interference with the federal right to vote (and the derivative right to serve if elected by majority vote) in a congressional election, rights that do not derive from the state power in the first instance but that belong to the voter in his or her capacity as a citizen of the United States.

It is maintained by our dissenting colleagues that the State of Arkansas seeks nothing more than to grant its people surer control over the National Government, a control, it is said, that will be enhanced by the law at issue here. The arguments for term limitations (or ballot restrictions having the same effect) are not lacking in force; but the issue, as all of us must acknowledge, is not the efficacy of those measures but whether they have a legitimate source, given their origin in the enactments of a single State. There can be no doubt, if we are to respect the republican origins of the Nation and preserve its federal character, that there exists a federal right of citizenship, a relationship between the people of the Nation and their National Government, with which the States may not interfere. Because the Arkansas enactment intrudes upon this federal domain, it exceeds the boundaries of the Constitution.

*This Court should, however, hold squarely that it is a privilege of citizenship of the United States, protected from state abridgment, to enter any state of the Union, either for temporary sojourn or for the establishment of permanent residence therein and for gaining resultant citizenship thereof. If national citizenship means less than this, it means nothing.*

*—Robert H. Jackson*

## Edwards v. California
### 62 S.Ct. 164, 314 U.S. 160 (1941)

*"The facts of this case are simple and are not disputed," Justice Byrnes' omitted majority opinion begins. This Depression story could have come out of John Steinbeck's 1939 novel* Grapes of Wrath. *Fred Edwards left his home in Marysville, California, and went to Spur, Texas, to bring back his brother-in-law, Frank Duncan, who was out of work. Duncan spent his last $20 on the trip back to California. He lived with Edwards for a couple of weeks but could not find a job and ended up drawing public assistance. Edwards was charged and convicted under California's "Okie law" for the misdemeanor of knowingly assisting an indigent person to move into the State. The Articles of Confederation, our first constitution, expressly provided "the people of each State shall have free ingress and regress to and from any other State." But there is no such provision in either the Constitution of 1787 or the Bill of Rights. Nonetheless, different Justices have on occasion located this right in the commerce clause, the privileges and immunities clause of Article IV, the privileges or immunities clause of the 14th amendment, the equal protection clause, the liberty protected by the 5th and 14th amendments, the inherent nature of the union of States, and the natural rights that preexisted the Constitution. Here, Justice Jackson's powerful exposition invokes a fundamental right inherent in human dignity. Under our Constitution, no one is a stranger.*

**Justice Jackson:** I concur in the result reached by the Court under the commerce clause, and I agree that the grounds of its decision are permissible ones under applicable authorities. But the migrations of a human being, of whom it is charged that he possesses nothing that can be sold and has no wherewithal to buy, do not fit easily into my notions as to what is commerce. To hold that the measure of his rights is the commerce clause is likely to result eventually either in distorting the commercial law or in denaturing human rights. I turn, therefore, away from principles by which commerce is regulated to that clause of the Constitution by virtue of which Duncan is a citizen of the United States and which forbids any state to abridge his privileges or immunities as such.

This clause was adopted to make United States citizenship the dominant and paramount allegiance among us. The return which the law had long associated with allegiance was protection. The power of citizenship as a shield against oppression was widely known from the example of Paul's Roman citizenship, which sent the centurion scurrying to his higher-ups with the message: "Take heed what thou doest: for this man is a Roman." I suppose none of us doubts that the hope of imparting to American citizenship some of this vitality was the purpose of declaring in the Fourteenth Amendment: "All persons born or naturalized in the United States, and subject to the jurisdiction thereof, are citizens of the United States and of the State wherein they reside. No State shall make or enforce any law which shall abridge the privileges or immunities of citizens of the United States."

While instances of valid "privileges or immunities" must be but few, I am convinced that this is one. I do not ignore or belittle the difficulties of what has been characterized by this Court as an "almost forgotten" clause. But the difficulty of the task does not excuse us from giving these general and abstract words whatever of specific content and concreteness they will bear as we mark out their application, case by case. That is the method of the common law, and it has been the method of this Court with other no less general statements in our fundamental law. This Court has not been timorous about giving concrete meaning to such obscure and vagrant phrases as "due process," "general welfare," "equal protection," or even "commerce among the several States." But it has always hesitated to give any real meaning to the privileges and immunities clause lest it improvidently give too much.

This Court should, however, hold squarely that it is a privilege of citizenship of the United States, protected from state abridgment, to enter any state of the Union, either for temporary sojourn or for the establishment of permanent residence therein and for gaining resultant citizenship thereof. If national citizenship means less than this, it means nothing.

The language of the Fourteenth Amendment declaring two kinds of citizenship is discriminating. It is: "All persons born or naturalized in the United States, and subject to the jurisdiction thereof, are citizens of the United States and of the State wherein they reside." While it thus establishes national citizenship from the mere circumstance of birth within the territory and jurisdiction of the United States, birth within a state does not establish citizenship thereof. State citizenship is ephemeral. It results only from residence and is gained or lost therewith. That choice of residence was subject to local approval is contrary to the inescapable implications of the westward movement of our civilization.

Even as to an alien who had "been admitted to the United States under the Federal law," this Court, through Mr. Justice Hughes, declared that "He was thus admitted with the privilege of entering and abiding in the United States, and hence of entering and abiding in any state in the Union." Why we should hesitate to hold that federal citizenship implies rights to enter and abide in any state of the Union at least equal to those possessed by aliens passes my understanding. The world is even more upside down than I had supposed it to be, if California must accept aliens in deference to their federal privileges but is free to turn back citizens of the United States unless we treat them as subjects of commerce.

The right of the citizen to migrate from state to state which is shown by our precedents to be one of national citizenship is not, however, an unlimited one. In addition to being subject to all constitutional limitations imposed by the federal government, such citizen is subject to some control by state governments. He may not, if a fugitive from justice, claim freedom to migrate unmolested, nor may he endanger others by carrying contagion about. These causes, and perhaps others that do not occur to me now, warrant any public authority in stopping a man where it finds him and arresting his progress across a state line quite as much as from place to place within the state.

It is here that we meet the real crux of this case. Does "indigence" as defined by the application of the California statute constitute a basis for restricting the freedom of a citizen, as crime or contagion warrants its restriction. We should say now, and in no uncertain terms, that a man's mere property status, without more, cannot be used by a state to test, qualify, or limit his rights as a citizen of the United States. "Indigence" in itself is neither a source of rights nor a basis for denying them. The mere state of being without funds is a neutral fact—constitutionally an irrelevance, like race, creed, or color.

Any measure which would divide our citizenry on the basis of property into one class free to move from state to state and another class that is poverty-bound to the place where it has suffered misfortune is not only at war with the habit and custom by which our country has expanded, but is also a short-sighted blow at the security of property itself. Property can have no more dangerous, even if unwitting, enemy than one who would make its possession a pretext for unequal or exclusive civil rights. Where those rights are derived from national citizenship no state may impose such a test, and whether the Congress could do so we are not called upon to inquire.

I think California had no right to make the condition of Duncan's purse, with no evidence of violation by him of any law or social policy which caused it, the basis of excluding him or of punishing one who extended him aid.

If I doubted whether his federal citizenship alone were enough to open the gates of California to Duncan, my doubt would disappear on consideration of the obligations of such citizenship. Duncan owes a duty to render military service, and this Court has said that this duty is the result of his citizenship. Mr. Chief Justice White declared in upholding the military draft laws: "It may not be doubted that the very conception of a just government and its duty to the citizen includes the reciprocal obligation of the citizen to render military service in case of need and the right to compel it." A contention that a citizen's duty to render military service is suspended by "indigence" would meet with little favor. Rich or penniless, Duncan's citizenship under the Constitution pledges his strength to the defense of California as a part of the United States, and his right to migrate to any part of the land he must defend is something she must respect under the same instrument. Unless this Court is willing to say that citizenship of the United States means at least this much to the citizen, then our heritage of constitutional privileges and immunities is only a promise to the ear to be broken to the hope, a teasing illusion like a munificent bequest in a pauper's will.

*Our government is the potent, the omnipresent teacher. For good or for ill, it teaches the whole people by its example. Crime is contagious. If the government becomes a lawbreaker, it breeds contempt for law; it invites every man to become a law unto himself; it invites anarchy.*

—*Louis D. Brandeis*

## Olmstead v. United States
### 48 S.Ct. 564, 277 U.S. 438 (1928)

*Olmstead's bootlegging conviction was based on evidence from federal wiretaps, which he argued violated his 4th amendment right to be free of unreasonable searches and seizures and his 5th amendment right against self-incrimination. Chief Justice Taft, for a five member majority, upheld the government's conduct. Justice Holmes wrote a brief dissent that objected to the "ignoble part" the government played and called the investigation "dirty business." In the following dissent, Justice Brandeis took issue with the majority's legal reasoning and sounded a more general alarm against courts approving government wrongdoing. In 1967, the Court overruled Olmstead and declared that the Constitution protects people not places and protects their reasonable expectations of privacy against government surveillance.*

**Justice Brandeis:** The government makes no attempt to defend the methods employed by its officers. But it relies on the language of the fourth amendment, and it claims that the protection given thereby cannot properly be held to include a telephone conversation.

"We must never forget," said Mr. Chief Justice Marshall, "that it is a Constitution we are expounding." Since then this court has repeatedly sustained the exercise of power by Congress, under various clauses of that instrument, over objects of which the fathers could not have dreamed. We have likewise held that general limitations on the powers of government, like those embodied in the due process clauses of the Fifth and Fourteenth Amendments, do not forbid the United States or the states from meeting modern conditions by regulations which "a century ago, or even half a century ago, probably would have been rejected as arbitrary and oppressive." Clauses guaranteeing to the individual protection against specific abuses of power, must have a similar capacity of adaptation to a changing world. It was with reference to such a clause that this court once said:

> Legislation, both statutory and constitutional, is enacted, it is true, from an experience of evils, but its general language should not, therefore, be necessarily confined to the form that evil had theretofore taken. Time works changes, brings into existence new conditions and purposes. Therefore a principal to be vital must be capable of wider application than the mischief which gave it birth. This is peculiarly true of Constitutions. They are not ephemeral enactments, designed to meet passing occasions. They are, to use the words of Chief Justice Marshall, "designed to approach immortality as nearly as human institutions can approach it." The future is their care and provision for events of good and bad tendencies of which no prophecy can be made. In the application of a Constitution, therefore, our contemplation cannot be only of what has been but of what may be. Under any other rule a Constitution would indeed be as easy of application as it would be deficient in efficacy and power. Its general principles would have little value and be converted by precedent into impotent and lifeless formulas. Rights declared in words might be lost in reality.

When the Fourth and Fifth Amendments were adopted, "the form that evil had theretofore taken" had been necessarily simple. Force and violence were then the only means known to man by which a government could directly effect self-incrimination. It could compel the individual to testify—a compulsion effected, if need be, by torture. It could secure possession of his papers and other articles incident to his private life—a seizure effected, if need be, by breaking and entry. Protection against such invasion of "the sanctities of a man's home and the privacies of life" was provided in the Fourth and Fifth Amendments by specific language. But "time works changes, brings into existence new conditions and purposes." Subtler and more far-reaching means of invading privacy have become available to the government. Discovery and invention have made it possible for the government, by means far more effective than stretching upon the rack, to obtain disclosure in court of what is whispered in the closet.

Moreover, "in the application of a Constitution, our contemplation cannot be only of what has been, but of what may be." The progress of science in furnishing the government with means of espionage is not likely to stop with wire tapping. Ways may some day be developed by which the government, without removing papers from secret drawers, can reproduce them in court, and by which it will be enabled to expose to a jury the most intimate occurrences of the home. Advances in the psychic and related sciences may bring means of exploring unexpressed beliefs, thoughts and emotions. "That places the liberty of every man in the hands of every petty officer" was said by James Otis of much lesser intrusions than these. To Lord Camden a far slighter intrusion seemed "subversive of all the comforts of society." Can it be that the Constitution affords no protection against such invasions of individual security?

The evil incident to invasion of the privacy of the telephone is far greater than that involved in tampering with the mails. Whenever a telephone line is tapped, the privacy of the persons at both ends of the line is invaded, and all conversations between them upon any subject, and although proper, confidential, and privileged, may be overheard. Moreover, the tapping of one man's telephone line involves the tapping of the telephone of every other person whom he may call, or who may call him. As a means of espionage, writs of assistance and general warrants are but puny instruments of tyranny and oppression when compared with wire tapping.

Time and again this court, in giving effect to the principle underlying the Fourth Amendment, has refused to place an unduly literal construction upon it. The narrow language of the Amendment has been consistently construed in the light of its object, "to insure that a person should not be compelled, when acting as a witness in any investigation, to give testimony which might tend to show that he himself had committed a crime. The privilege is limited to criminal matters, but it is as broad as the mischief against which it seeks to guard."

The protection guaranteed by the amendments is much broader in scope. The makers of our Constitution undertook to secure conditions favorable to the pursuit of happiness. They recognized the significance of man's spiritual nature, of his feelings and of his intellect. They knew that only a part of the pain, pleasure and satisfactions of life are to be found in material things. They sought to protect Americans in their beliefs, their thoughts, their emotions and their sensations. They conferred, as against the government, the right to be let alone—the most comprehensive of rights and the right most valued by civilized men. To protect, that right, every unjustifiable intrusion by the government upon the privacy of the individual, whatever the means employed, must be deemed a violation of the Fourth Amendment. And the use, as evidence in a criminal proceeding, of facts ascertained by such intrusion must be deemed a violation of the Fifth.

Applying to the Fourth and Fifth Amendments the established rule of construction, the defendants' objections to the evidence obtained by wire tapping must, in my opinion, be sustained. It is immaterial that the intrusion was in aid of law enforcement. Experience should teach us to be most on our guard to protect liberty when the government's purposes are beneficent. Men born to freedom are naturally alert to repel invasion of their liberty by evil-minded rulers. The greatest dangers to liberty lurk in insidious encroachment by men of zeal, well-meaning but without understanding.

Independently of the constitutional question, I am of opinion that the judgment should be reversed. By the laws of Washington, wire tapping is a crime. To prove its case, the government was obliged to lay bare the crimes committed by its officers on its behalf. A federal court should not permit such a prosecution to continue.

Here the evidence obtained by crime was obtained at the government's expense, by its officers, while acting on its behalf; the officers who committed these crimes are the same officers who were charged with the enforcement of the Prohibition Act; the crimes of these officers were committed for the purpose of securing evidence with which to obtain an indictment and to secure a conviction. The evidence so obtained constitutes the warp and woof of the government's case. The aggregate of the government evidence occupies 306 pages of the printed record. More than 210 of them are filled by recitals of the details of the wire tapping and of facts ascertained thereby. There is literally no other evidence of guilt on the part of some of the defendants except that illegally obtained by these officers. As to nearly all the defendants (except those who admitted guilt), the evidence relied upon to secure a conviction consisted mainly of that which these officers had so obtained by violating the state law.

As the trial Judge said below: "Here we are concerned with neither eavesdroppers nor thieves. Nor are we concerned with the acts of private individuals. We are concerned only with the acts of federal agents, whose powers are limited and controlled by the Constitution of the United States."

When these unlawful acts were committed they were crimes only of the officers individually. The government was innocent, in legal contemplation; for no federal official is authorized to commit a crime on its behalf. When the government, having full knowledge, sought, through the Department of Justice, to avail itself of the fruits of these acts in order to accomplish its own ends, it assumed moral responsibility for the officers' crimes. If this court should permit the government, by means of its officers' crimes, to effect its purpose of punishing the defendants, there would seem to be present all the elements of a ratification. If so, the government itself would become a lawbreaker.

Will this court, by sustaining the judgment below, sanction such conduct on the part of the executive? The governing principle has long been settled. It is that a court will not redress a wrong when he who invokes its aid has unclean hands. The maxim of unclean hands comes from courts of equity. But the principle prevails also in courts of law. Its common application is in civil actions between private parties. Where the government is the actor, the reasons for applying it are even more persuasive. Where the remedies invoked are those of the criminal law, the reasons are compelling.

The door of a court is not barred because the plaintiff has committed a crime. The confirmed criminal is as much entitled to redress as his most virtuous fellow citizen; no record of crime, however long, makes one an outlaw. The court's aid is denied only when he who seeks it has violated the law in connection with the very transaction as to which he seeks legal redress. Then aid is denied despite the defendant's wrong. It is denied in order to maintain respect for law; in order to promote confidence in the administration of justice; in order to preserve the judicial process from contamination. The rule is one, not of action, but of inaction. It is sometimes spoken of as a rule of substantive law. But it extends to matters of procedure as well. A defense may be waived. It is waived when not pleaded. But the objection that the plaintiff comes with unclean hands will be taken by the court itself. It will be taken despite the wish to the contrary of all the parties to the litigation. The court protects itself.

Decency, security, and liberty alike demand that government officials shall be subjected to the same rules of conduct that are commands to the citizen. In a government of laws, existence of the government will be imperiled if it fails to observe the law scrupulously. Our government is the potent, the omnipresent teacher. For good or for ill, it teaches the whole people by its example. Crime is contagious. If the government becomes a lawbreaker, it breeds contempt for law; it invites every man to become a law unto himself; it invites anarchy. To declare that in the administration of the criminal law the end justifies the means-to declare that the government may commit crimes in order to secure the conviction of a private criminal-would bring terrible retribution. Against that pernicious doctrine this court should resolutely set its face.

> *The Court has developed, for its own govern-*
> *ance in the cases confessedly within its*
> *jurisdiction, a series of rules under which it has*
> *avoided passing upon a large part of all the consti-*
> *tutional questions pressed upon it for decision.*
>
> *—Louis D. Brandeis*

# Ashwander v. Tennessee Valley Authority
## 56 S.Ct. 466, 297 U.S. 288 (1936)

*Established in 1933 under the New Deal, the Tennes-see Valley Authority was a government corporation de-signed to improve navigation and flood control and to provide inexpensive electric power for homes, farms and industry in the region. The newspaper headlines the day this case was decided proclaimed that the Justices gave constitutional approval to the TVA. Chief Justice Hughes reasoned for a majority that the U.S. Government had the power under the Constitution to build dams and improve navigation for the national defense and the power to sell electricity for the benefit of interstate commerce. The more lasting contribution, however, is to be found in the con-curring opinion by Justice Brandeis that described rules for deciding when to decide constitutional issues. While someone can "take his case all the way to the Supreme Court," the Justices can decline to exercise their power of judicial review. Justice Brandeis' rules of self-restraint continue to be invoked regularly although in a less princi-pled manner than he likely intended. Majorities unwill-ing to decide a particular case often rely on these rules to defend themselves, insisting that they are not abdicating the responsibility of constitutional decision. Just as often, dissenters are heard to complain about the constitutional impatience of a majority reaching beyond these rules to decide an issue the dissenters insist would be better left undecided. "Deciding when to decide" thus is an impor-tant and controverted aspect of the judicial power.*

**Justice Brandeis:** The fact that it would be convenient for the parties and the public to have promptly decided whether the legislation assailed is valid, cannot justify a departure from set-tled rules and established principles. The Court has developed, for its own governance in the cases confessedly within its jurisdiction, a series of rules under which it has avoided passing upon a large part of all the constitutional questions pressed upon it for decision. They are:

1. The Court will not pass upon the constitutionality of legislation in a friendly, nonadversary, proceeding, declining because to decide such questions "is legitimate only in the last resort, and as a necessity in the determination of real, earnest, and vital controversy between individuals. It never was the thought that, by means of a friendly suit, a party beaten in the legislature could transfer to the courts an inquiry as to the constitutionality of the legislative act."

2. The Court will not "anticipate a question of constitutional law in advance of the necessity of deciding it." "It is not the habit of the court to decide questions of a constitutional nature unless absolutely necessary to a decision of the case."

3. The Court will not "formulate a rule of constitutional law broader than is required by the precise facts to which it is to be applied."

4. The Court will not pass upon a constitutional question although properly presented by the record, if there is also present some other ground upon which the case may be disposed of. This rule has found most varied application. Thus, if a case can be decided on either of two grounds, one involving a constitutional question, the other a question of statutory construction or general law, the Court will decide only the latter. Appeals from the highest court of a state challenging its decision of a question under the Federal Constitution are frequently dismissed because the judgment can be sustained on an independent state ground.

5. The Court will not pass upon the validity of a statute upon complaint of one who fails to show that he is injured by its operation. Among the many applications of this rule, none is more striking than the denial of the right of challenge to one who lacks a personal or property right. Thus, the challenge by a public official interested only in the performance of his official duty will not be entertained.

6. The Court will not pass upon the constitutionality of a statute at the instance of one who has availed himself of its benefits.

7. "When the validity of an act of the Congress is drawn in question, and even if a serious doubt of constitutionality is raised, it is a cardinal principle that this Court will first ascertain whether a construction of the statute is fairly possible by which the question may be avoided."

This Court, while recognizing the soundness of the rule of stare decisis where appropriate, has not hesitated to overrule earlier decisions shown, upon fuller consideration, to be erroneous. Our present keener appreciation is for the wisdom of limiting our decisions rigidly to questions essential to the disposition of the case before the court. This would seem to follow as a corollary of the long established presumption in favor of the constitutionality of a statute.

Mr. Justice Iredell said, in 1798: "If any act of congress, or of the legislature of a state, violates those constitutional provisions, it is unquestionably void; though, I admit, that as the authority to declare it void is of a delicate and awful nature, the court will never resort to that authority, but in a clear and urgent case."

Mr. Chief Justice Marshall said, in 1819: "On more than one occasion, this court has expressed the cautious circumspection with which it approaches the consideration of such questions; and has declared, that in no doubtful case, would it pronounce a legislative act to be contrary to the constitution."

Mr. Justice Washington said, in 1827: "But if I could rest my opinion in favour of the constitutionality of the law on which the question arises, on no other ground than this doubt so felt and acknowledged, that alone, would, in my estimation, be a satisfactory vindication of it. It is but a decent respect due to the wisdom, the integrity and the patriotism of the legislative body, by which any law is passed, to presume in favour of its validity, until its violation of the constitution is proved beyond all reasonable doubt. This has always been the language of this court, when that subject has called for its decision; and I know that it expresses the honest sentiments of each and every member of this bench."

The challenge of the power of the Tennessee Valley Authority rests wholly upon the claim that the act of Congress which authorized the contract is unconstitutional. As the opinions of this Court show, that claim was not a matter "beyond peradventure clear." A fortiori this rule should have been applied here where the power challenged is that of Congress under the Constitution.

*We consider this case against the background of a profound national commitment to the principle that debate on public issues should be uninhibited, robust, and wide-open, and that it may well include vehement, caustic, and sometimes unpleasantly sharp attacks on government and public officials.*

*—William J. Brennan*

## New York Times Co. v. Sullivan
### 84 S.Ct. 710, 376 U.S. 254 (1964)

*When Martin Luther King, Jr. was arrested in Alabama, a group of celebrities and civil rights leaders formed a committee to help finance his defense. They took out a full-page ad in the New York Times asking for contributions. The ad contained a few relatively minor inaccuracies about what the police and public officials had done to King. L. B. Sullivan, a city commissioner in Montgomery, filed a defamation suit in state court against the newspaper and the individuals who placed the ad, and a jury awarded him $500,000. This was but one of several such lawsuits brought to discourage the national media from supporting the civil rights movement; Alabama juries had awarded a total of $5.6 million against the Times. The Supreme Court invalidated these awards of presumed or automatic damages. The rights of free speech and free press trumped the state law of defamation. The right to criticize government is fundamental under the Constitution. Civil libertarians hailed the decision as "an occasion for dancing in the streets."*

**Justice Brennan:** The question before us is whether this rule of liability, as applied to an action brought by a public official against critics of his official conduct, abridges the freedom of speech and of the press that is guaranteed by the First and Fourteenth Amendments.

The general proposition that freedom of expression upon public questions is secured by the First Amendment has long been settled by our decisions. The constitutional safeguard, we have said, "was fashioned to assure unfettered interchange of ideas for the bringing about of political and social changes desired by the people." "The maintenance of the opportunity for

— **85** —

free political discussion to the end that government may be responsive to the will of the people and that changes may be obtained by lawful means, an opportunity essential to the security of the Republic, is a fundamental principle of our constitutional system." "It is a prized American privilege to speak one's mind, although not always with perfect good taste, on all public institutions," and this opportunity is to be afforded for "vigorous advocacy" no less than "abstract discussion." The First Amendment, said Judge Learned Hand, "presupposes that right conclusions are more likely to be gathered out of a multitude of tongues, than through any kind of authoritative selection. To many this is, and always will be, folly; but we have staked upon it our all."

Thus we consider this case against the background of a profound national commitment to the principle that debate on public issues should be uninhibited, robust, and wide-open, and that it may well include vehement, caustic, and sometimes unpleasantly sharp attacks on government and public officials. The present advertisement, as an expression of grievance and protest on one of the major public issues of our time, would seem clearly to qualify for the constitutional protection. The question is whether it forfeits that protection by the falsity of some of its factual statements and by its alleged defamation of Commissioner Sullivan.

Authoritative interpretations of the First Amendment guarantees have consistently refused to recognize an exception for any test of truth—whether administered by judges, juries, or administrative officials—and especially one that puts the burden of proving truth on the speaker. The constitutional protection does not turn upon "the truth, popularity, or social utility of the ideas and beliefs which are offered." As James Madison said, "Some degree of abuse is inseparable from the proper use of every thing; and in no instance is this more true than in that of the press." In 1940, the Court declared: "In the realm of religious faith, and in that of political belief, sharp differences arise. In both fields the tenets of one man may seem the rankest error to his neighbor. To persuade others to his own point of view, the pleader, as we know, at times, resorts to exaggeration, to vilification of men who have been, or are, prominent in church or state, and even to false statement. But the people of this nation have ordained in the light of history, that, in spite of the probability of excesses and abuses, these liberties are, in the long view, essential to enlightened opinion and right conduct on the part of the citizens of a democracy."

Erroneous statement is inevitable in free debate, and it must be protected if the freedoms of expression are to have the "breathing space" that they need to survive. Injury to official reputation error affords no more warrant for repressing speech that would otherwise be free than does factual error. Where judicial officers are involved, this Court has held that concern for the dignity and reputation of the courts does not justify the punishment as criminal contempt of criticism of the judge or his decision. This is true even though the utterance contains "half-truths" and "misinformation." Such repression can be justified, if at all, only by a clear and present danger of the obstruction of justice. If judges are to be treated as "men of fortitude, able to thrive in a hardy climate," surely the same must be true of other government officials, such as elected city commissioners. Criticism of their official conduct does not lose its constitutional protection merely because it is effective criticism and hence diminishes their official reputations.

If neither factual error nor defamatory content suffices to remove the constitutional shield from criticism of official conduct, the combination of the two elements is no less inadequate. This is the lesson to be drawn from the great controversy over the Sedition Act of 1798, which first crystallized a national awareness of the central meaning of the First Amendment. That statute made it a crime, punishable by a $5,000 fine and five years in prison, "if any person shall write, print, utter or publish any false, scandalous and malicious writing or writings against the government of the United States, or either house of the Congress or the President with intent to defame or to bring them, or either of them, into contempt or disrepute; or to excite against them, or either or any of them, the hatred of the good people of the United States." The Act allowed the defendant the defense of truth, and provided that the jury were to be judges both of the law and the facts. Despite these qualifications, the Act was vigorously condemned as unconstitutional in an attack joined in by Jefferson and Madison. In the famous Virginia Resolutions of 1798, the General Assembly of Virginia resolved that it "doth particularly protest against the palpable and alarming infractions of the Constitution, in the two late cases of the "Alien and Sedition Acts," passed at the last session of Congress. The Sedition Act exercises a power not delegated by the Constitution, but, on the contrary, expressly and positively forbidden by one of the amendments thereto—a power which, more than any other, ought to produce universal alarm, because it is levelled against the right of freely examining public characters and measures, and of free communication among the people thereon, which has ever been justly deemed the only effectual guardian of every other right." Madison prepared the Report in support of the protest. His premise was that the Constitution created a form of government under which "The people, not the government, possess the absolute sovereignty." The structure of the government dispersed power in reflection of the people's distrust of concentrated power, and of power itself at all levels. This form of government was "altogether different" from the British form, under which the Crown was sovereign and the people were subjects. "Is it not natural and necessary, under such different circumstances," he asked, "that a different degree of freedom in the use of the press should be contemplated?" Earlier, in a debate in the House of Representatives, Madison had said: "If we advert to the nature of Republican Government, we shall find that the censorial power is in the people over the Government, and not in the Government over the people." Of the exercise of that power by the press, his Report concluded: "In every state, probably, in the Union, the press has exerted a freedom in canvassing the merits and measures of public men, of every description, which has not been confined to the strict limits of the common law. On this footing the freedom of the press has stood; on this foundation it yet stands." The right of free public discussion of the stewardship of public officials was thus, in Madison's view, a fundamental principle of the American form of government.

Although the Sedition Act was never tested in this Court, the attack upon its validity has carried the day in the court of history. Fines levied in its prosecution were repaid by Act of Congress on the ground that it was unconstitutional. John C. Calhoun, reporting to the Senate on February 4, 1836, assumed that its invalidity was a matter "which no one now doubts." Jefferson, as President, pardoned those who had been convicted and sentenced under the Act and remitted their fines, stating: "I discharged every person under punishment or prosecution under the sedition law, because I considered, and now consider, that law to be a nullity, as absolute and as palpable as if Congress had ordered us to fall down and worship a golden image." The invalidity of the Act has also been assumed by Justices of this Court. These views reflect a broad consensus that the Act, because of the restraint it imposed upon criticism of government and public officials, was inconsistent with the First Amendment.

What a State may not constitutionally bring about by means of a criminal statute is likewise beyond the reach of its civil law of libel. The fear of damage awards under a rule such as that invoked by the Alabama courts here may be markedly more inhibiting than the fear of prosecution under a criminal statute. The judgment awarded in this case—without the need for any proof of actual pecuniary loss—was one thousand times greater than the maximum fine provided by under the relevant Alabama criminal statute, and one hundred times greater than that provided by the Sedition Act. And since there is no double-jeopardy limitation applicable to civil lawsuits, this is not the only judgment that may be awarded against petitioners for the same publication. Whether or not a newspaper can survive a succession of such judgments, the pall of fear and timidity imposed upon those who would give voice to public criticism is an atmosphere in which the First Amendment freedoms cannot survive. Plainly the Alabama law of civil libel is "a form of regulation that creates hazards to protected freedoms markedly greater than those that attend reliance upon the criminal law."

The state rule of law is not saved by its allowance of the defense of truth. A defense for erroneous statements honestly made is no less essential here. A rule compelling the critic of official conduct to guarantee the truth of all his factual assertions—and to do so on pain of libel judgments virtually unlimited in amount—leads to a comparable "self-censorship." Allowance of the defense of truth, with the burden of proving it on the defendant, does not mean that only false speech will be deterred. Even courts accepting this defense as an adequate safeguard have recognized the difficulties of adducing legal proofs that the alleged libel was true in all its factual particulars. Under such a rule, would-be critics of official conduct may be deterred from voicing their criticism, even though it is believed to be true and even though it is in fact true, because of doubt whether it can be proved in court or fear of the expense of having to do so. They tend to make only statements which "steer far wider of the unlawful zone." The rule thus dampens the vigor and limits the variety of public debate. It is inconsistent with the First and Fourteenth Amendments.

The constitutional guarantees require, we think, a federal rule that prohibits a public official from recovering damages for a defamatory falsehood relating to his official conduct unless he proves that the statement was made with "actual malice"—that is, with knowledge that it was false or with reckless disregard of whether it was false or not.

Such a privilege for criticism of official conduct is appropriately analogous to the protection accorded a public official when he is sued for libel by a private citizen. This Court has held the utterance of a federal official to be absolutely privileged if made "within the outer perimeter" of his duties. The States accord the same immunity to statements of their highest officers, although some differentiate their lesser officials and qualify the privilege they enjoy. But all hold that all officials are protected unless actual malice can be proved. The reason for the official privilege is said to be that the threat of damage suits would otherwise "inhibit the fearless, vigorous, and effective administration of policies of government" and "dampen the ardor of all but the most resolute, or the most irresponsible, in the unflinching discharge of their duties." Analogous considerations support the privilege for the citizen-critic of government. It is as much his duty to criticize as it is the official's duty to administer. As Madison said, "the censorial power is in the people over the Government, and not in the Government over the people."

It would give public servants an unjustified preference over the public they serve, if critics of official conduct did not have a fair equivalent of the immunity granted to the officials themselves. We conclude that such a privilege is required by the First and Fourteenth Amendments.

*We are here dealing with an aspect of a basic constitutional right . . . . the right in a peaceable and orderly manner to protest by silent and re-proachful presence, in a place where the protestant has every right to be, the unconstitu-tional segregation of public facilities.*

*—Abe Fortas*

## Brown v. Louisiana
### 86 S.Ct. 719, 383 U.S. 131 (1966)

*This plurality opinion by Justice Fortas, joined by Chief Justice Warren and Justice Douglas, illustrates a timeless principle of self-government: civil disobedience is defined as a "public, nonviolent, political act contrary to law usually done with the aim of bringing about a change in the law or policies of the government." The Constitution certainly does not provide complete immu-nity for every act of civil disobedience. Indeed, Reverend Martin Luther King, Jr.'s famous Letter from the Bir-mingham Jail declares: "I submit that an individual who breaks a law that his conscience tells him is unjust, and willingly accepts the penalty by staying in jail to arouse the conscience of the community over its injustice, is in reality expressing the very highest respect for law." How-ever, Justice Fortas explains how and why the higher law of our Constitution does protect peaceful protest against the government and its unjust policies. Justices Brennan and White wrote separate concurring opinions. Justice Black wrote an angry dissent, joined by Justices Clark, Harlan and Stewart, which concluded: "It is an unhappy circumstance in my judgment that the group, which more than any other has needed a government of equal laws and equal justice, is now encouraged to believe that the best way for it to advance its cause, which is a worthy one, is by taking the law into its own hands from place to place and time to time. Governments like ours were formed to substitute the rule of law for the rule of force." The civil rights movement of the 1960s, based as it was on this moral theory, obliged the Justices to reconcile civil disobedience with the law of the Constitution.*

**Justice Fortas:** This is the fourth time in little more than four years that this Court has reviewed convictions by the Louisiana courts for alleged violations, in a civil rights context, of that State's breach of the peace statute. In the three preceding cases the convictions were reversed. In each of these cases the demonstration was orderly. In each, the purpose of the participants was to protest the denial to Negroes of rights guaranteed them by state and federal constitutions and to petition their governments for redress of grievances. In none was there evidence that the participants planned or intended disorder. In none were there circumstances which might have led to a breach of the peace chargeable to the protesting participants.

Participants in an orderly demonstration in a public place are not chargeable with the danger, unprovoked except by the fact of the constitutionally protected demonstration itself, that their critics might react with disorder or violence. Because the incident leading to the present convictions occurred in a public library and might be thought to raise materially different questions, we have heard argument and have considered the case in extenso.

The locus of the events was the Audubon Regional Library in the town of Clinton, Louisiana, Parish of East Feliciana. The front room of the building was used as a public library facility where patrons might obtain library services. It was a small room, containing two tables and one chair (apart from the branch assistant's desk and chairs), a stove, a card catalogue, and open book shelves. The room was referred to by the regional librarian, Mrs. Perkins, as "the adult reading-room, the adult service-room." The library permitted "registered borrowers" to "browse" among the books in the room or to borrow books. A "registered borrower" was one who could produce an identification card showing that he was registered by the Audubon Regional Library. Other space in the building included the headquarters of the regional library.

The Audubon Regional Library is operated jointly by the Parishes of East Feliciana, West Feliciana, and St. Helena. It has three branches and two bookmobiles. The bookmobiles served 33 schools, both white and Negro, as well as "individuals." One of the bookmobiles was red, the other blue. The red bookmobile served only white persons. The blue bookmobile served only Negroes. It is a permissible inference that no Negroes used the branch libraries.

The registration cards issued to Negroes were stamped with the word "Negro." A Negro in possession of such a card was entitled to borrow books, but only from the blue bookmobile. A white person could not receive service from the blue bookmobile. He would have to wait until the red bookmobile came around, or would have to go to a branch library.

This tidy plan was challenged on Saturday, March 7, 1964, at about 11:30 a.m. Five young Negro males, all residents of East or West Feliciana Parishes, went into the adult reading or service room of the Audubon Regional Library at Clinton. The branch assistant, Mrs. Katie Reeves, was alone in the room. She met the men "between the tables" and asked if she "could help." Defendant Brown requested a book, "The Story of the Negro" by Arna Bontemps. Mrs. Reeves checked the card catalogue, ascertained that the Branch did not have the book, so advised Mr. Brown, and told him that she would request the book from the State Library, that he would be notified upon its receipt and that "he could either pick it up or it would be mailed to him." She told him that "his point of service was a bookmobile or it could be mailed to him." Mrs. Reeves testified that she expected that the men would then leave; they did not, and she asked them to leave. They did not. Defendant Brown sat down and the others stood near him. They said nothing; there was no noise or boisterous talking. Mrs. Reeves called Mrs. Perkins, the regional librarian, who was in another room. Mrs. Perkins asked the men to leave. They remained.

Neither Mrs. Reeves nor Mrs. Perkins had called the sheriff, but in "10 to 15 minutes" from the time of the arrival of the men at the library, the sheriff and deputies arrived. The sheriff asked the Negroes to leave. They said they would not. The sheriff then arrested them. The sheriff had been notified that morning that members of the Congress of Racial Equality "were going to sit-in" at the library. Ordinarily, the sheriff testified, CORE tells him when they are going to demonstrate or picket. The sheriff was standing at his "place of business" when he saw "these 5 colored males coming down the street." He saw them enter the library. He called the jail to notify his deputies, and he reached the library immediately after the deputies got there. When the sheriff arrived, there was no noise, no disturbance. He testified that he arrested them "for not leaving a public building when asked to do so by an officer."

The library obtained the requested book and mailed it to Mr. Brown on March 28, 1964. An accompanying card said, "You may return the book either by mail or to the Blue Bookmobile." The reference to the color of the vehicle was obviously not designed to facilitate identification of the library vehicle. The blue bookmobile is for Negroes and for Negroes only.

In the course of argument before this Court, counsel for both the State and Defendants stated that the Clinton Branch was closed after the incident of March 7. Counsel for the State also advised the court that the use of cards stamped "Negro" continues to be the practice of the regional library.

On March 25, 1964, Mr. Brown and his four companions were tried and found guilty. Brown was sentenced to pay $150 and costs, and in default thereof to spend 90 days in the parish jail. His companions were sentenced to $35 and costs, or 15 days in jail. The charge was that they had congregated together in the public library of Clinton, Louisiana, "with the intent to provoke a breach of the peace and under circumstances such that a breach of the peace might be occasioned thereby" and had failed and refused "to leave said premises when ordered to do so" by the librarian and by the sheriff.

The Louisiana breach of peace statute under which they were accused reads as follows: "Whoever with intent to provoke a breach of the peace, or under circumstances such that a breach of the peace may be occasioned thereby: (1) crowds or congregates with others in a public place or building and who fails or refuses to disperse and move on, or disperse or move on, when ordered so to do by any law enforcement officer or any other authorized person shall be guilty of disturbing the peace."

Under Louisiana law, these convictions were not appealable. Defendants sought discretionary review by the Louisiana Supreme Court, which denied their application, finding no error. This Court granted certiorari and we reverse.

We may briefly dispose of certain threshold problems. Defendants cannot constitutionally be convicted merely because they did not comply with an order to leave the library. The statute itself reads in the conjunctive; it requires both the defined breach of peace and an order to move on. Without reference to the statute, it must be noted that Defendants' presence in the library was unquestionably lawful. It was a public facility, open to the public. Negroes could not be denied access since white persons were welcome. Defendants' deportment while in

the library was unexceptionable. They were neither loud, boisterous, obstreperous, indecorous nor impolite. There is no claim
that, apart from the continuation—for ten or fifteen minutes—of
their presence itself, their conduct provided a basis for the order
to leave, or for a charge of breach of the peace.

We come, then, to the barebones of the problem. Defendants,
five adult Negro men, remained in the library room for a total of
ten or fifteen minutes. The first few moments were occupied by
a ritualistic request for service and a response. We may assume
that the response constituted service, and we need not consider
whether it was merely a gambit in the ritual. This ceremony
being out of the way, the Negroes proceeded to the business in
hand. They sat and stood in the room, quietly, as monuments of
protest against the segregation of the library. They were arrested and charged and convicted of breach of the peace under a
specific statute.

If we compare this situation with that in our previous cases,
we must inevitably conclude that here, too, there is not the
slightest evidence which would or could sustain the application
of the statute to Defendants. The statute requires a showing
either of "intent to provoke a breach of the peace," or of "circumstances such that a breach of the peace may be occasioned" by
the acts in question. There is not in this case the slightest hint
of either. We need not be beguiled by the ritual of the request
for a copy of "The Story of the Negro." We need not assume that
Defendant Brown and his friends were in search of a book for
night reading. We instead rest upon the manifest fact that they
intended to and did stage a peaceful and orderly protest demonstration, with no "intent to provoke a breach of the peace."

Nor were the circumstances such that a breach of the peace
might be "occasioned" by their actions, as the statute alternatively provides. The library room was empty, except for the li-
brarians. There were no other patrons. There were no onlookers
except for the vigilant and forewarned sheriff and his deputies.
Defendants did nothing and said nothing even remotely provocative when considered against our previous cases. The danger, if any existed, was surely less than in the course of the
sit-in at the "white" lunch counters. And surely there was less
danger that a breach of the peace might occur from Mrs. Katie
Reeves and Mrs. Perkins in the adult reading room of the Clinton Branch Library than that disorder might result from the
"restless" white people in the bus depot waiting room, or from
the 100 to 300 "grumbling" white onlookers outside the court-

house and jail. But in each of these three cases, this Court refused to countenance convictions under Louisiana's breach of the peace statute.

The argument of the State of Louisiana, however, is that the issue presented by this case is much simpler than our statement would indicate. The issue, asserts the State, is simply that Defendants were using the library room "as a place in which to loaf or make a nuisance of themselves." The State argues that the "test"—the permissible civil rights demonstration—was concluded when Defendants entered the library, asked for service and were served. Having satisfied themselves, the argument runs, that they could get service, they should have departed. Instead, they simply sat there, "staring vacantly," and this was "enough to unnerve a woman in the situation Mrs. Reeves was in."

This is a piquant version of the affair, but the matter is hardly to be decided on points. It was not a game. It could not be won so handily by the gesture of service to this particular request. There is no dispute that the library system was segregated, and no possible doubt that these Defendants were there to protest this fact. But even if we were to agree with the State's ingenuous characterization of the events, we would have to reverse. There was no violation of the statute which Defendants are accused of breaching; no disorder, no intent to provoke a breach of the peace and no circumstances indicating that a breach might be occasioned by Defendants" actions. The sole statutory provision invoked by the State contains not a word about occupying the reading room of a public library for more than 15 minutes, any more than it purports to punish the bare refusal to obey an unexplained command to withdraw from a public street or public building. We can find nothing in the language of the statute, in fact, which would elevate the giving of cause for Mrs. Reeves' discomfort, however we may sympathize with her, to a crime against the State of Louisiana.

But there is another and sharper answer which is called for. We are here dealing with an aspect of a basic constitutional right—the right under the First and Fourteenth Amendments guaranteeing freedom of speech and of assembly, and freedom to petition the Government for a redress of grievances. Even the Constitution of the State of Louisiana reiterates these guaranties. As this Court has repeatedly stated, these rights are not confined to verbal expression. They embrace appropriate types of action which certainly include the right in a peaceable and orderly manner to protest by silent and reproachful presence, in a place where the protestant has every right to be, the unconstitutional segregation of public facilities. Accordingly, even if the accused action were within the scope of the statutory instrument, we would be required to assess the constitutional impact of its application, and we would have to hold that the statute cannot constitutionally be applied to punish Defendants' actions in the circumstances of this case. The statute was deliberately and purposefully applied solely to terminate the reasonable, orderly, and limited exercise of the right to protest the unconstitutional segregation of a public facility. Interference with this right, so exercised, by state action is intolerable under our Constitution.

It is an unhappy circumstance that the locus of these events was a public library—a place dedicated to quiet, to knowledge, and to beauty. It is a sad commentary that this hallowed place in the Parish of East Feliciana bore the ugly stamp of racism. It is sad, too, that it was a public library which, reasonably enough in the circumstances, was the stage for a confrontation between those discriminated against and the representatives of the offending parishes. Fortunately, the circumstances here were such that no claim can be made that use of the library by others was disturbed by the demonstration. Perhaps the time and method were carefully chosen with this in mind. Were it otherwise, a factor not present in this case would have to be considered. Here, there was no disturbance of others, no disruption of library activities, and no violation of any library regulations.

A State or its instrumentality may, of course, regulate the use of its libraries or other public facilities. But it must do so in a reasonable and nondiscriminatory manner, equally applicable to all and administered with equality to all. It may not do so as to some and not as to all. It may not provide certain facilities for whites and others for Negroes. And it may not invoke regulations as to use—whether they are ad hoc or general—as a pretext for pursuing those engaged in lawful, constitutionally protected exercise of their fundamental rights.

*Since the beginning of history there have been governments that have engaged in practices against the people so bad, so cruel, so unjust and so destructive of the individual dignity of men and women that the "right of revolution" was all the people had left to free themselves.*

— *Hugo L. Black*

## In re Anastaplo
### 81 S.Ct. 978, 366 U.S. 82 (1961)

*During the McCarthy era, George Anastaplo was denied admission to the Illinois Bar for refusing to answer questions about his views and associations, even though he had an exemplary record as a student and citizen and passed the bar examination. Anastaplo took his case "all the way to the Supreme Court," arguing on his own behalf to the Justices, but lost by the narrowest margin of a 5 to 4 vote. The majority relied on the sophistry that he had been denied admission for failing to cooperate and not for his beliefs. Justice Black, for the four dissenters, chastised his brethren and expressed admiration for Anastaplo. Anastaplo never was admitted to the practice of law. He went on to a long and illustrious academic career as a scholar and professor of constitutional law.*

**Justice Black:** George Anastaplo has been denied the right to practice law in the State of Illinois for refusing to answer questions about his views and associations. This case provides such a striking illustration of the destruction that can be inflicted upon individual liberty when this Court fails to enforce the First Amendment to the full extent of its express and unequivocal terms.

The personal history form required by state law had been filled out and filed with the State Bar Committee on Character and Fitness prior to his appearance and showed Anastaplo was an unusually worthy applicant for admission. His early life had been spent in a small town in southern Illinois where his parents, who had immigrated to this country from Greece before his birth, still resided. After having received his precollege education in the public schools of his home town, he had discontinued his education, at the age of eighteen, and joined the Air Force during the middle of World War II—flying as a navigator in every major theater of the military operations of that war. Upon receiving an honorable discharge in 1947, he had come to Chicago and resumed his education, obtaining his undergraduate degree at the University of Chicago and entering immediately into the study of law at the University of Chicago Law School. His record throughout his life, both as a student and as a citizen, was unblemished.

The personal history form thus did not contain so much as one statement of fact about Anastaplo's past life or conduct that could have, in any way, cast doubt upon his fitness for admission to the Bar. It did, however, contain a statement of opinion which, in the minds of some of the members of the Committee at least, did cast such doubt and in that way served to touch off this controversy: "State what you consider to be the principles underlying (a) the Constitution of the United States." Anastaplo's response to that command was as follows:

> One principle consists of the doctrine of the separation of powers; thus, among the Executive, Legislative, and Judiciary are distributed various functions and powers in a manner designed to provide for a balance of power, thereby intending to prevent totally unrestrained action by any one branch of government. Another basic principle (and the most important) is that such government is constituted so as to secure certain inalienable rights, those rights to Life, Liberty and the Pursuit of Happiness (and elements of these rights are explicitly set forth in such parts of the Constitution as the Bill of Rights). And, of course, whenever the particular government in power becomes destructive of these ends, it is the right of the people to alter or to abolish it and thereupon to establish a new government. This is how I view the Constitution.

When Anastaplo appeared before a two-man Subcommittee of the Committee on Character and Fitness, one of its members almost immediately engaged him in a discussion relating to the meaning of these words which were substantially taken from that part of the Declaration of Independence set out below.[1] This discussion soon developed into an argument as Anastaplo stood by his statement and insisted that if a government gets bad enough, the people have a "right of revolution."

The Subcommittee then refused to certify Anastaplo for admission to the Bar but, instead, set a further hearing on the matter before the full Committee. That next hearing, as well as all of the hearings that followed, have been little more than repetitions of the first. The rift between Anastaplo and the Committee has grown ever wider with each successive hearing. Anastaplo has steadfastly refused to answer any questions put by the Committee which inquired into his political associations or religious beliefs. A majority of the members of the Committee, faced with this refusal, has grown more and more insistent that it has the right to force him to answer any question it sees fit to ask.

It is true, as the majority points out, that the Committee did not expressly rest its refusal to certify Anastaplo for admission to the Bar either upon his views on the "right of revolution," as that "right" is defined in the Declaration of Independence, or upon his refusal to disclose his beliefs with regard to the existence of God, or upon his refusals to disclose any of his political associations other than his "possible" association with the Communist Party. But it certainly cannot be denied that the other questions were asked and, since we should not presume that these members of the Committee did not want answers to their questions, it seems certain that Anastaplo's refusal to answer them must have had some influence upon the final outcome of the hearings.

---

1. "We hold these truths to be self-evident, that all Men are created equal, that they are endowed by their Creator with certain unalienable Rights, that among these are Life, Liberty, and the Pursuit of happiness— That to secure these Rights, Governments are instituted among Men, deriving their just Powers from the consent of the Governed, that whenever any Form of Government becomes destructive of these Ends, it is the Right of the People to alter or to abolish it, and to institute new Government, laying its Foundation on such Principles, and organizing its Powers in such Form, as to them shall seem most likely to effect their Safety and Happiness."

The reasons for Anastaplo's position have been stated by him time and again—first, to the Committee and, later, in the briefs and oral arguments he presented in his own behalf, both before this Court and before the Supreme Court of Illinois. His position was perhaps best stated before the Committee in his closing remarks at the final session:

> It is time now to close. Differences between us remain. I leave to others the sometimes necessary but relatively easy task of praising Athens to Athenians. Besides, you should want no higher praise than what I have said about the contribution the bar can make to republican government. The bar deserves no higher praise until it makes that contribution. You should be grateful that I have not made a complete submission to you, even though I have cooperated as fully as good conscience permits. To the extent I have not submitted, to that extent have I contributed to the solution of one of the most pressing problems that you, as men devoted to character and fitness, must face. This is the problem of selecting the standards and methods the bar must employ if it is to help preserve and nourish that idealism, that vital interest in the problem of justice, that so often lies at the heart of the intelligent and sensitive law student's choice of career. This is an idealism which so many things about the bar, and even about bar admission practices, discourage and make unfashionable to defend or retain. The worthiest men live where the rewards of virtue are greatest. I leave with you men of Illinois the suggestion that you do yourselves and the bar the honor, as well as the service, of anticipating what I trust will be the judgment of our most thoughtful judges. I move therefore that you recommend to the Supreme Court of Illinois that I be admitted to the bar of this State. And I suggest that this recommendation be made retroactive to November 10, 1950 when a young Air Force veteran first was so foolish as to continue to serve his country by daring to defend against a committee on character and fitness the teaching of the *Declaration of Independence* on the right of revolution.

The reasons for the Committee's position are also clear. Its job, throughout these proceedings, has been to determine whether Anastaplo is possessed of the necessary good moral character to justify his admission to the Bar of Illinois. In that regard, the Committee has been given the benefit of voluminous affidavits from men of standing in their professions and in the community that Anastaplo is possessed of an unusually fine character. Even at the present time, he is still there preparing his doctoral dissertation which, understandably enough, is tentatively entitled "The Historical and Philosophical Background of the First Amendment of the Constitution of the United States."

In addition to the information it had obtained from the affidavits and from its independent investigations, the Committee had one more important source of information about Anastaplo's character. It had the opportunity to observe the manner in which he conducted himself during the many hours of hearings before it. That manner, as revealed by the record before us and undenied by any findings of the Committee to the contrary, left absolutely nothing to be desired. Faced with a barrage of sometimes highly provocative and totally irrelevant questions from men openly hostile to his position, Anastaplo invariably responded with all the dignity and restraint attributed to him in the affidavits of his friends. Moreover, it is not amiss to say that he conducted himself in precisely the same manner during the oral argument he presented before this Court.

Thus, it is against the background of a mountain of evidence so favorable to Anastaplo that the word "overwhelming" seems inadequate to describe it that the action of the Committee in refusing to certify Anastaplo as fit for admission to the Bar must be considered. The majority of the Committee rationalized its position on the ground that without answers to some of the questions it had asked, it could not conscientiously perform its duty of determining Anastaplo's character and fitness to be a lawyer. A minority of the Committee described this explanation as "pure sophistry." And it is simply impossible to read this record without agreeing with the minority.

The opinion of the majority already recognizes that there is not one scrap of evidence in the record before us "which could properly be considered as reflecting adversely upon his (Anastaplo's) character or reputation or on the sincerity of the beliefs he espoused before the Committee," and that the Committee had not received any "information from any outside source which would cast any doubt on applicant's loyalty or which would tend to connect him in any manner with any subversive group." The majority opinion even concedes that Anastaplo was correct in urging that the questions asked by the Committee impinged upon the freedoms of speech and association guaranteed by the First and Fourteenth Amendments. But, the opinion then goes on to hold that Anastaplo can nonetheless be excluded from the

Bar pursuant to "the State's interest in having lawyers who are devoted to the law in its broadest sense." I cannot regard that holding, as applied to a man like Anastaplo, as in any way justified. Consider it, for example, in the context of the following remarks of Anastaplo to the Committee—remarks the sincerity of which the majority does not deny:

> I speak of a need to remind the bar of its traditions and to keep alive the spirit of dignified but determined advocacy and opposition. This is not only for the good of the bar, of course, but also because of what the bar means to American republican government. The bar when it exercises self-control is in a peculiar position to mediate between popular passions and informed and principled men, thereby upholding republican government. Unless there is this mediation, intelligent and responsible government is unlikely. The bar, furthermore, is in a peculiar position to apply to our daily lives the constitutional principles which nourish for this country its inner life. Unless there is this nourishment, a just and humane people is impossible. The bar is, in short, in a position to train and lead by precept and example the American people.

These are not the words of a man who lacks devotion to "the law in its broadest sense."

The majority, apparently considering this fact irrelevant because the State might possibly have an interest in learning more about its Bar applicants, decides that Anastaplo can properly be denied admission to the Bar by purporting to "balance" the interest of the State of Illinois in "having lawyers who are devoted to the law in its broadest sense" against the interest of Anastaplo and the public in protecting the freedoms of the First Amendment, concluding, as it usually does when it engages in this process, that "on balance" the interest of Illinois must prevail. If I had ever doubted that the "balancing test" comes close to being a doctrine of governmental absolutism—that to "balance" an interest in individual liberty means almost inevitably to destroy that liberty—those doubts would have been dissipated by this case.

The effect of the Court's "balancing" here is that any State may now reject an applicant for admission to the Bar if he believes in the *Declaration of Independence* as strongly as Anastaplo and if he is willing to sacrifice his career and his means of livelihood in defense of the freedoms of the First Amendment. But the men who founded this country and wrote our Bill of

Rights were strangers neither to a belief in the "right of revolution" nor to the urgency of the need to be free from the control of government with regard to political beliefs and associations. Thomas Jefferson was not disclaiming a belief in the "right of revolution" when he wrote the *Declaration of Independence*. And Patrick Henry was certainly not disclaiming such a belief when he declared in impassioned words that have come on down through the years: "Give me liberty or give me death." This country's freedom was won by men who, whether they believed in it or not, certainly practiced revolution in the Revolutionary War.

Since the beginning of history there have been governments that have engaged in practices against the people so bad, so cruel, so unjust and so destructive of the individual dignity of men and women that the "right of revolution" was all the people had left to free themselves. As simple illustrations, one government almost 2,000 years ago burned Christians upon fiery crosses and another government, during this very century, burned Jews in crematories. I venture the suggestion that there are countless multitudes in this country, and all over the world, who would join Anastaplo's belief in the right of the people to resist by force tyrannical governments like those.

In saying what I have, it is to be borne in mind that Anastaplo has not indicated, even remotely, a belief that this country is an oppressive one in which the "right of revolution" should be exercised. Quite the contrary, the entire course of his life, as disclosed by the record, has been one of devotion and service to his country—first, in his willingness to defend its security at the risk of his own life in time of war and, later, in his willingness to defend its freedoms at the risk of his professional career in time of peace. The one and only time in which he has come into conflict with the Government is when he refused to answer the questions put to him by the Committee about his beliefs and associations. And I think the record clearly shows that conflict resulted, not from any fear on Anastaplo's part to divulge his own political activities, but from a sincere, and in my judgment correct, conviction that the preservation of this country's freedom depends upon adherence to our Bill of Rights. The very most that can fairly be said against Anastaplo's position in this entire matter is that he took too much of the responsibility of preserving that freedom upon himself.

This case illustrates to me the serious consequences to the Bar itself of not affording the full protections of the First Amendment to its applicants for admission. For this record shows that Anastaplo has many of the qualities that are needed in the American Bar. It shows, not only that Anastaplo has followed a high moral, ethical and patriotic course in all of the activities of his life, but also that he combines these more common virtues with the uncommon virtue of courage to stand by his principles at any cost. It is such men as these who have most greatly honored the profession of the law—men who have dared to speak in defense of causes and clients without regard to personal danger to themselves. The legal profession will lose much of its nobility and its glory if it is not constantly replenished with lawyers like these. To force the Bar to become a group of thoroughly orthodox, time-serving, government-fearing individuals is to humiliate and degrade it.

But that is the present trend, not only in the legal profession but in almost every walk of life. Too many men are being driven to become government-fearing and time-serving because the Government is being permitted to strike out at those who are fearless enough to think as they please and say what they think. This trend must be halted if we are to keep faith with the Founders of our Nation and pass on to future generations of Americans the great heritage of freedom which they sacrificed so much to leave to us. The choice is clear to me. If we are to pass on that great heritage of freedom, we must return to the original language of the Bill of Rights. We must not be afraid to be free.

# CHAPTER TWO

# THE LEGISLATIVE POWER

*All legislative Powers herein granted shall be vested in a Congress of the United States, which shall consist of a Senate and House of Representatives.*

On the 150th anniversary of the first Congress, Chief Justice Charles Evans Hughes began his address to the assembly by saying, "Here in this body we find the living exponents of the principle of representative government—not government by direct mass action but by representation which means leadership as well as responsiveness and accountability." Congress is a constitutional creation designed to be responsive to the people, but like the other branches, Congress cannot go beyond the Constitution, even in the name of the people. "We the people" are the ultimate source of Congress' power.

The very idea of "legislative power" is a relatively modern concept in history. The medieval notion was that all authority was attributable to God, nature, or custom and that human institutions merely discovered and enforced the preexisting will. Part of the Enlightenment rethinking of humankind's place in the universe was that laws were made, not found, and their meaning was derived from the will of the lawmakers. During the founding period, however, this very concept of sovereignty was redefined and relocated. Under the familiar British Constitution, sovereignty was defined as the will of the parliament in assembly. This notion was carried over in the early experiences of the States, whose legislatures took it upon themselves to write and ratify state constitutions upon becoming independent of the mother country. The Federalists were obliged to reimagine these assumptions in order to legitimate a truly national government possessed of its own sovereign powers, independent from and supreme over state sovereignty. They came to believe that the ultimate sovereignty in a republic flowed directly from the people. The people surrendered portions of their ultimate sovereignty directly to the United States in bundled powers and to the state governments in an omnibus sovereign police power, respectively. What remained beyond the people's delegations to their governments defined the inalienable freedoms and liberties of the individual.

Thus, the legitimacy of the Constitution and the national government it created did not, in any way, depend on the States or the state legislatures. Once ratified, the Constitution became "the supreme Law of the Land," Article VI, § 2, and the powers of the national government, within their proper spheres, were superior to the powers of the States. This explains the full import and significance of the *Preamble's* beginning invocation of "We the People." It also explains the hue and cry raised about that wording by the Antifederalists, who placed their loyalty to their own State first and foremost.

These foundational principles of popular sovereignty were nowhere more obvious or more important than in Article I. Early in the Constitutional Convention, James Wilson described the basic dichotomy that "there are only two kinds of bad governments—the one which does too much and is therefore oppressive, and the other which does too little and is therefore too weak."

The Articles of Confederation generally were considered to be the weak variety of bad government, and the delegates believed it imperative that the new national government would be equal to the necessary tasks of government, something they were convinced was not possible without a radical restructuring. This was the period historian John Fiske labelled THE CRITICAL PERIOD IN AMERICAN HISTORY (2d ed. 1916), in his classic book of that title. Many of them believed that their generation faced a turning point in history, that in a world of monarchy their political trial was the last great hope for republican self-government.

At the same time, there was a great anxiety abroad in the land, especially among those who served in the national government, that the state legislatures were developing into bad governments of the other kind Wilson mentioned, guilty of democratical excesses. In his powerful revisionist history, entitled THE CREATION OF THE AMERICAN REPUBLIC, 1776–1787 (1969), contemporary scholar Gordon S. Wood insists that the Framers of the Constitution were primarily motivated to empower the national government in order to restrain the States from doing too much. These "small–r" republicans—like James Madison who served in the Virginia legislature—were appalled at what we might call today the interest group politics practiced in the state houses, for example, debt-forgiveness statutes enacted at the behest of debtors against creditors. Legislators were supposed to be statesman, who should resist factional politics and rule with civic virtue for the common good.

These nationalistic Federalists believed that a natural elite would rise to positions of national leadership, especially in the Congress of the United States, so that was where the greatest political power ought to be located. At least, it would be more difficult, if not impossible, for any single faction to capture the national legislature, because there would be so many factions as to cancel each other out in the competition for influence. Madison concluded *Federalist Paper No. 10*, his treatise on the inevitability of political factions and the vagaries of human nature, with a warranty that "the influence of factious leaders may kindle a flame within their particular States but will be unable to spread a general conflagration." The real power to govern would be placed beyond the reach of the less worthy, those of parochial rather than continental vision.

The legislative article establishes the structure and the general manner of proceedings of the Congress. The accepted principle of bicameralism afforded one more check on government power; under the terms of the so-called "Great Compromise" between the large and small States, the two houses would have different characters. Seats in the House of Representatives were apportioned among the States on the basis of population and filled by popular elections every two years by voters qualified under state election rules. Each state legislature would choose two Senators for staggered six year terms; in 1913, the 17th amendment would make them popularly-elected. Other proscribed procedures include: eligibility requirements for members; meeting requirements; quorum requirements; provision of an oath; authority to supervise the behavior of members; requirement of an official journal; presiding officers; and establishment of general lawmaking procedures, including how to override an executive veto.

The great traditional powers of government, consistent with the separation of executive powers, are to be found in Article I, § 8: to lay and collect taxes, to spend for the general welfare, to borrow money, to regulate commerce, to regulate immigration and naturalization, to regulate bankruptcy, to coin money, to fix standards of weights and measures, to regulate the mail, to regulate patents and copyrights, to establish federal courts, to define crimes, to declare war, to raise and support military forces, to regulate the militia, and to perform several other particular powers. To be sure, there are other clauses in the first Article, dealing with subjects like habeas corpus, ex post facto laws, and bills of attainder, that restrain the Congress. But it was intended that the Congress would wield the great powers of government as the United States began to take its place among the nations of the world.

Perhaps the most expansive power the Constitution vests in Congress is the power "To make all Laws which shall be necessary and proper for carrying into Execution the foregoing Powers, and all other Powers vested by this Constitution in the Government of the United States." Article I, § 8, cl. 18. There are similar provisions in the 13th, 14th, 15th, 19th, 24th, and 26th amendments. But a written Constitution, by its very nature, is a limited Constitution. Article VI specifically obliges Senators and Representatives to be "bound by Oath or Affirmation, to support this Constitution." This is why President Franklin D. Roosevelt was misguided, in an infamous 1935 incident, to lobby a member of Congress for support for a bill by insisting, "Manifestly, no one is in a position to give assurance that the proposed act will withstand constitutional tests. But the situation is so urgent and the benefits of the legislation so evident that all doubts should be resolved in favor of the bill, leaving to the courts, in an orderly fashion, the ultimate question of constitutionality." The President was asking the congressman to ignore the oath they both swore. Under our Constitution, the end does not justify unconstitutional means.

On the other hand, constitutionalist James Bradley Thayer, writing in a turn of this century biography of John Marshall, warned that the pendulum of judicial review ought not be allowed to swing too far toward distrust of legislative judgments, because legislatures "are growing accustomed to this distrust, and more and more readily inclined to justify it, and to shed the consideration of constitutional restraints, turning that subject over to the courts; and what is worse, they insensibly fall into a habit of assuming that whatever they can constitutionally do they must do. The tendency of a common and easy resort to this great function is to dwarf the political capacity of the people, and to deaden its sense of moral responsibility." Constitutionalist Paul Brest, writing more recently, emphasized the obvious to remind Congress that "the Constitution speaks directly to legislatures." Congressional constitutionalism cannot be allowed, much less encouraged, to atrophy.

To recognize that Congress is obliged to make judgments about the meaning of the Constitution, however, is not to suggest a congressional supremacy in the interpretative function. Historically, there have been episodic claims of legislative supremacy. Early on the Jeffersonians brooded with the idea. During the Reconstruction Congress, Radical Republicans moved in the direction of asserting hegemony over the other branches by impeaching President Johnson and by restricting the jurisdiction of the Supreme Court. But it is a basic tenet of constitutionalism that legislatures simply cannot have the final word. Alexander Hamilton explained in *Federalist Paper No. 78*, "It is not otherwise to be supposed that the Constitution could intend the representatives of the people to substitute their will to that of their constituents." The Constitution is the ultimate expression of the people's will. Nonetheless, the Congress shares the responsibility to maintain our constitutional order. Political scientist Louis Fisher points out, "Coordinate construction is more than a theory. Given the nature of our political system, it is a necessity." Interbranch disagreements, therefore, are an inevitability. Constitutional law Professor George Anastaplo offered the provocative bicentennial assessment that "in the great crises over the past two hundred years, when Congress and the Supreme Court have differed on major issues, Congress has been correct."

\* \* \* \*

The first opinion in this Chapter is the Great Chief Justice interpreting the "necessary and proper" clause in *McCulloch v. Maryland (1819)*. This case was only obliquely about the power to charter a national bank. It is not an exaggeration to assert that the history of the United States would have been far different, indeed, the history we have had would have been impossible, without John Marshall's *tour de force* opinion. The Constitution may have gone the way of the failed Articles of Confederation otherwise. Marshall reconciles the national legislative sovereignty with state sovereignty, at the great expense of the States, in such a way as to make possible everything that followed for the last two centuries, culminating in the modern, post-New Deal national government of Brobdingnag.

The constitutionality of one of the important programs of the New Deal was before the Supreme Court in *United States v. Butler (1936)*. Justices Roberts and Stone take sides in the debate over nationalism begun by James Madison and Alexander Hamilton back during President Washington's administration. The power to tax and to spend remains as important and as controversial down to the present time. But notice how the Justices feel obliged to assume a posture of self-restraint in fiscal matters. The power to spend includes a power to attach strings to federal money, according to Chief Justice Rehnquist in *South Dakota v. Dole (1987)*, and the federals can bribe the States into obsequious compliance without violating their sovereignty or offending the Constitution. The States are offered a Hobson's choice: "take it or leave it . . . with strings attached."

Writing for a majority of the Justices in *Missouri v. Holland (1920)*, Justice Holmes gives short shrift to claims of state sovereignty in the area of federal treaties. The Yankee Civil War veteran imagines an organic "living" Constitution that would have been seen as Frankenstein's monster by the 18th century Antifederalists. Supreme Courts before and since have taken out of context Chief Justice Marshall's entreaty in *McCulloch*, "we must never forget that it is a constitution we are expounding." Holmes understood this was said about the interpretation of legislative powers, not the power of judicial review. Alexander Hamilton's logic—that the expression of the people's will in the Constitution is superior to the will of their representatives—applies in kind to their judges.

During the first 150 years of the Nation, the commerce clause, Article I, § 8, cl. 3, accounted for more litigation than any other constitutional provision and it eventually became the single most important source of congressional power. In *H. P. Hood & Sons, Inc. v. Du Mond (1949)*, Justice Jackson waxes eloquently about the importance to the Nation of our common market. He echoes Justice Cardozo, "The Constitution was framed under the dominion of a political philosophy less parochial, upon the theory that the peoples of the several states must sink or swim together, and that in the long run prosperity and salvation are in union and not division." But the Justices themselves are divided in a constitutional free-for-all in *Garcia v. San Antonio Metropolitan Transit Authority (1985)*, choosing up sides, some with Congress and some with the States, in the tug-of-war between the commerce clause and the 10th amendment. *United States v. Lopez (1995)* illustrates the contemporary relevance and importance, as well as the ongoing interpretative disagreements, about the respective roles of the national and the state governments. The last commerce clause essay, Justice Scalia's iconoclastic opinion in *Tyler Pipe Industries, Inc. v. Washington Dept. of Revenue (1987)*, maintains that the Supreme Court has acted far beyond its judicial powers when it has stricken state laws that the Justices believe act as a burden on interstate commerce, in the absence of a federal statute. He is bold, to say the least, to argue that the Justices have been wrong all the way back to Chief Justice Marshall's day.

Two otherwise unrelated opinions explore the proper relations between the Executive and the Legislative branches. First, Chief Justice Hughes ouijas a holding out of the separation of powers to rule that Congress cannot delegate its law making power to the Executive. This delegation doctrine, relied on in *Panama Refining Co. v. Ryan (1935)*, really was more of a spell than a rule of law. But it was a spell that had to be broken in order for the modern administrative state to be possible. Today, Hughes' opinion sounds like so much mumbo-jumbo. Second, the Speech and Debate Clause, is a much taken-for-granted provision in Article I, that guarantees virtually absolute free speech for legislators. Justice White canvasses the history and function of this critical protection of the parliamentary process in *Gravel v. United States (1972)*. "Congress is so strange," a visiting dignitary from another country once marvelled, "A man gets up to speak and says nothing. Nobody listens—and then everybody disagrees."

Three opinions explore the proper relations between the Courts and the Congress. First, *Luther v. Borden (1849)* announces early-on that the Guarantee Clause, which obliges the national government to guarantee "a republican form of government" to the States, is committed first and finally to the political branches. It cannot be enforced in a court under Article III. Second, Chief Justice Chase bows to Congress and its authority over the jurisdiction of the federal courts. In *Ex Parte McCardle (1869)*, the Court let Congress get away with manipulating the jurisdictional statutes to remove a case from the Supreme Court's very own docket, by passing a repealer statute because the members of Congress were worried that the Justices might take the side against Reconstruction. But the third case demonstrates that the Justices will stand up to Congress to protect what is constitutionally theirs. Indeed, in *Plaut v. Spendthrift Farm, Inc. (1995)* the Supreme Court asserts its constitutional prerogative to proclaim a violation of the separation of powers, when Congress has exceeded the legislative sphere and has intruded on the judicial sphere by getting into the business of redetermining court cases that already have been decided. Not infrequently over the years, the give-and-take between the Congress and the Supreme Court has been more of an argument than a dialogue, what Professor Alexander Bickel once euphemistically called "a continuing colloquy." Each side has practiced bluff and bluster. Each side has folded, from time to time.

*Ex parte Milligan (1866)* demonstrates the threat posed by Congress against individual rights and how the Supreme Court will act as the champion of the citizen. Congress may not simply declare an emergency, even with good justification, and then do away with basic civil liberties like civilian courts and jury trials. Finally, Justice Brennan's opinion in *Katzenbach v. Morgan (1966)* offers the provocative theory that under Section 5 of the 14th amendment Congress has a power to define individual rights more broadly and to afford them greater protection than do the Justices and the Supreme Court. This "ratchet theory" is still the stuff of congressional debates and scholarly arguments. Whether one agrees with those scholars who find it to be theoretically well-founded or with those scholars who insist that it is merely a sport of a result-oriented jurist, his analysis once again assigns a central and important role for the Congress in the enterprise of interpreting the Constitution.

An oft-told anecdote has Theodore Roosevelt explaining to an old pol in Congress that the President cannot support his bill because it is unconstitutional. The fellow's incredulous comeback is, "What's the Constitution between friends?" To be sure, the Constitution needs loyal friends in the first branch. Nothing less than the rule of law and constitutionalism are at stake. "With all its defects, delays and inconveniences, men have discovered no technique for long preserving free government," Justice Jackson emphasized in his famous steel seizure opinion, "except that the law be made by parliamentary deliberations."

*Let the end be legitimate, let it be within the scope of the constitution, and all means which are appropriate, which are plainly adapted to that end, which are not prohibited, but consist with the letter and spirit of the constitution, are constitutional.*

— *John Marshall*

## McCulloch v. Maryland
### 17 U.S. (4 Wheaton) 316 (1819)

*In 1816, Congress incorporated the Second Bank of the United States. Maryland enacted a tax on any bank not chartered by the State, but the national Bank continued to operate without paying the state tax. So Maryland sued the federal officials in Baltimore for payment and the Maryland state courts upheld the state tax. Six of the greatest lawyers of the day, including Daniel Webster for the Bank, argued the case for nine days. John Marshall delivered his thirty-six page opinion only three days later, for a unanimous Court, declaring the state tax unconstitutional and void. Here is the great Chief Justice at his Federalist best. However orthodox this reading of the Constitution may seem today, at the time it was audacious to interpret the "necessary and proper" clause so broadly and the 10th amendment so narrowly. This holding confirmed that it was only a matter of time before the worst fears of the Antifederalists would come true, that the national government would ineluctably grow in size and power at the expense of the sovereign States.*

**Chief Justice Marshall:** In the case now to be determined, a sovereign state, denies the obligation of a law enacted by the legislature of the Union, and the federal official, on his part, contests the validity of an act which has been passed by the legislature of that state. The constitution of our country, in its most interesting and vital parts, is to be considered; the conflicting powers of the government of the Union and of its members, as marked in that constitution, are to be discussed; and an opinion given, which may essentially influence the great operations of the government. No tribunal can approach such a question without a deep sense of its importance, and of the awful responsibility involved in its decision.

The first question made in the cause is—has congress power to incorporate a bank?

It has been truly said, that this can scarcely be considered as an open question, entirely unprejudiced by the former proceedings of the nation respecting it. The principle now contested was introduced at a very early period of our history, has been recognized by many successive legislatures, and has been acted upon by the judicial department, in cases of peculiar delicacy, as a law of undoubted obligation.

It will not be denied, that a bold and daring usurpation might be resisted, after an acquiescence still longer and more complete than this. But the power now contested was exercised by the first congress elected under the present constitution. Its principle was completely understood, and was opposed with equal zeal and ability. After being resisted, first, in the fair and open field of debate, and afterwards, in the executive cabinet, with as much persevering talent as any measure has ever experienced, and being supported by arguments which convinced minds as pure and as intelligent as this country can boast, it became a law. The original act was permitted to expire; but a short experience of the embarrassments to which the refusal to revive it exposed the government, convinced those who were most prejudiced against the measure of its necessity, and induced the passage of the present law.

In discussing this question, the counsel for the state of Maryland have deemed it of some importance, in the construction of the constitution, to consider that instrument, not as emanating from the people, but as the act of sovereign and independent states. The powers of the general government, it has been said, are delegated by the states, who alone are truly sovereign; and must be exercised in subordination to the states, who alone possess supreme dominion.

It would be difficult to sustain this proposition. The convention which framed the constitution was indeed elected by the state legislatures. But the instrument, when it came from their hands, was a mere proposal, without obligation, or pretensions to it. By the convention, by congress, and by the state legislatures, the instrument was submitted to the people. They acted upon it in the only manner in which they can act safely, effectively and wisely, on such a subject, by assembling in convention.

The government proceeds directly from the people. To the formation of a league, such as was the confederation, the state sovereignties were certainly competent. But when, "in order to form a more perfect union," it was deemed necessary to change this alliance into an effective government, possessing great and sovereign powers, and acting directly on the people, the necessity of referring it to the people, and of deriving its powers directly from them, was felt and acknowledged by all. The government of the Union, then is, emphatically and truly, a government of the people. In form, and in substance, it emanates from them. Its powers are granted by them, and are to be exercised directly on them, and for their benefit.

This government is acknowledged by all, to be one of enumerated powers. The principle, that it can exercise only the powers granted to it, is now universally admitted. But the question respecting the extent of the powers actually granted, is perpetually arising, and will probably continue to arise, so long as our system shall exist.

If any one proposition could command the universal assent of mankind, we might expect it would be this—that the government of the Union, though limited in its powers, is supreme within its sphere of action. This would seem to result, necessarily, from its nature. It is the government of all; its powers are delegated by all; it represents all, and acts for all. This question is not left to mere reason: the people have, in express terms, decided it, by saying, "this constitution, and the laws of the United States, which shall be made in pursuance thereof," "shall be the supreme law of the land." The government of the United States, then, though limited in its powers, is supreme; and its laws, when made in pursuance of the constitution, form the supreme law of the land, "anything in the constitution or laws of any state to the contrary notwithstanding."

Among the enumerated powers, we do not find that of establishing a bank or creating a corporation. But there is no phrase in the instrument which, like the articles of confederation, excludes incidental or implied powers; and which requires that everything granted shall be expressly and minutely described. Even the 10th amendment, which was framed for the purpose of quieting the excessive jealousies which had been excited, omits the word "expressly," and declares only, that the powers "not delegated to the United States, nor prohibited to the states, are reserved to the states or to the people;" thus leaving the question, whether the particular power which may become the subject of contest, has been delegated to the one government, or prohibited to the other, to depend on a fair construction of the whole instrument. The men who drew and adopted this amendment had experienced the embarrassments resulting from the insertion of this word in the articles of confederation, and probably omitted it, to avoid those embarrassments. A constitution, to contain an accurate detail of all the subdivisions of which its great powers will admit, and of all the means by which they may be carried into execution, would partake of the prolixity of a legal code, and could scarcely be embraced by the human mind. It would, probably, never be understood by the public. Its nature, therefore, requires, that only its great outlines should be marked, its important objects designated, and the minor ingredients which compose those objects, be deduced from the nature of the objects themselves. That this idea was entertained by the framers of the American constitution, is not only to be inferred from the nature of the instrument, but from the language. Why else were some of the limitations, found in the 9th section of the 1st article, introduced? It is also, in some degree, warranted, by their having omitted to use any restrictive term which might prevent its receiving a fair and just interpretation. In considering this question, then, we must never forget that it is a constitution we are expounding.

Although, among the enumerated powers of government, we do not find the word "bank" or "incorporation," we find the great powers, to lay and collect taxes; to borrow money; to regulate commerce; to declare and conduct a war; and to raise and support armies and navies. The sword and the purse, all the external relations, and no inconsiderable portion of the industry of the nation, are intrusted to its government. It can never be pretended, that these vast powers draw after them others of inferior importance, merely because they are inferior. Such an idea can never be advanced. But it may with great reason be contended, that a government, intrusted with such ample powers, on the due execution of which the happiness and prosperity of the nation so vitally depends, must also be intrusted with ample means for their execution. The power being given, it is the interest of the nation to facilitate its execution. It can never be their interest, and cannot be presumed to have been their intention, to clog and embarrass its execution, by withholding the most appropriate means. Can we adopt that construction (unless the words imperiously require it), which would impute to the framers of that instrument, when granting these powers for the public good, the intention of impeding their exercise, by withholding a choice of means? If, indeed, such be the mandate of the constitution, we have only to obey; but that instrument does not profess to enumerate the means by which the powers it confers may be executed; nor does it prohibit the creation of a corporation, if the existence of such a being be essential, to the beneficial exercise of those powers. It is, then, the subject of fair inquiry, how far such means may be employed.

It is not denied, that the powers given to the government imply the ordinary means of execution. That, for example, of raising revenue, and applying it to national purposes, is admitted to imply the power of conveying money from place to place, as the exigencies of the nation may require, and of employing the usual means of conveyance. But it is denied, that the government has its choice of means; or, that it may employ the most convenient means, if, to employ them, it be necessary to erect a corporation.

On what foundation does this argument rest? On this alone: the power of creating a corporation, is one appertaining to sovereignty, and is not expressly conferred on congress. This is true. But all legislative powers appertain to sovereignty. The government which has a right to do an act, and has imposed on it, the duty of performing that act, must, according to the dictates of reason, be allowed to select the means; and those who contend that it may not select any appropriate means, that one particular mode of effecting the object is excepted, take upon themselves the burden of establishing that exception.

In America, the powers of sovereignty are divided between the government of the Union, and those of the states. They are each sovereign, with respect to the objects committed to it, and neither sovereign, with respect to the objects committed to the other. We cannot well comprehend the process of reasoning which maintains, that a power appertaining to sovereignty cannot be connected with that vast portion of it which is granted to the general government, so far as it is calculated to subserve the legitimate objects of that government. The power of creating a corporation, though appertaining to sovereignty, is not, like the power of making war, or levying taxes, or of regulating commerce, a great substantive and independent power, which cannot be implied as incidental to other powers, or used as a means of executing them. It is never the end for which other powers are exercised, but a means by which other objects are accomplished. No sufficient reason is, therefore, perceived, why it may not pass as incidental to those powers which are expressly given, if it be a direct mode of executing them.

But the constitution of the United States has not left the right of congress to employ the necessary means, for the execution of the powers conferred on the government, to general reasoning. To its enumeration of powers is added, that of making "all laws which shall be necessary and proper, for carrying into execution the foregoing powers, and all other powers vested by this constitution, in the government of the United States, or in any department thereof." The counsel for the state of Maryland have urged various arguments, to prove that this clause, though, in terms, a grant of power, is not so, in effect; but is really restrictive of the general right, which might otherwise be implied, of selecting means for executing the enumerated powers. In support of this proposition, they have found it necessary to contend, that this clause was inserted for the purpose of conferring on congress the power of making laws. That, without it, doubts might be entertained, whether congress could exercise its powers in the form of legislation.

But could this be the object for which it was inserted? A government is created by the people, having legislative, executive and judicial powers. Its legislative powers are vested in a congress, which is to consist of a senate and house of representatives. Could it be necessary to say, that a legislature should exercise legislative powers, in the shape of legislation? That a legislature, endowed with legislative powers, can legislate, is a proposition too self-evident to have been questioned.

But the argument on which most reliance is placed, is drawn from that peculiar language of this clause. Congress is not empowered by it to make all laws, which may have relation to the powers conferred on the government, but such only as may be "necessary and proper" for carrying them into execution. The word "necessary" is considered as controlling the whole sentence, and as limiting the right to pass laws for the execution of the granted powers, to such as are indispensable, and without which the power would be nugatory. That it excludes the choice of means, and leaves to congress, in each case, that only which is most direct and simple.

Is it true, that this is the sense in which the word "necessary" is always used? Does it always import an absolute physical necessity, so strong, that one thing to which another may be termed necessary, cannot exist without that other? We think it does not. If reference be had to its use, in the common affairs of the world, or in approved authors, we find that it frequently imports no more than that one thing is convenient, or useful, or essential to another. To employ the means necessary to an end, is generally understood as employing any means calculated to produce the end, and not as being confined to those single means, without which the end would be entirely unattainable. Such is the character of human language, that no word conveys to the mind, in all situations, one single definite idea; and nothing is more common than to use words in a figurative sense. Almost all compositions contain words, which, taken in a their rigorous sense, would convey a meaning different from that which is obviously intended. It is essential to just construction, that many words which import something excessive, should be understood in a more mitigated sense—in that sense which common usage justifies. The word "necessary" is of this description. It has not a fixed character, peculiar to itself. It admits of all degrees of comparison; and is often connected with other words, which increase or diminish the impression the mind receives of the urgency it imports. A thing may be necessary, very necessary, absolutely or indispensably necessary. To no mind would the same idea be conveyed by these several phrases. This comment on the word is well illustrated by the passage cited at the bar, from the 10th section of the 1st article of the constitution. It is, we think, impossible to compare the sentence which prohibits a state from laying "imposts, or duties on imports or exports, except what may be absolutely necessary for executing its inspection laws," with that which authorizes congress "to make all laws which shall be necessary and proper for carrying into execution" the powers of the general government, without feeling a conviction, that the convention understood itself to change materially the meaning of the word "necessary," by prefixing the word "absolutely." This word "necessary," then, like others, is used in various senses; and, in its construction, the subject, the context, the intention of the person using them, are all to be taken into view.

It must have been the intention of those who gave these powers, to insure, so far as human prudence could insure, their beneficial execution. This could not be done, by confiding the choice of means to such narrow limits as not to leave it in the power of congress to adopt any which might be appropriate, and which were conducive to the end. This provision is made in a constitution, intended to endure for ages to come, and consequently, to be adapted to the various crises of human affairs. To have prescribed the means by which government should, in all future time, execute its powers, would have been to change, entirely, the character of the instrument, and give it the properties of a legal code. It would have been an unwise attempt to provide, by immutable rules, for exigencies which, if foreseen at all, must have been seen dimly, and which can be best provided for as they occur. To have declared, that the best means shall not be used, but those alone, without which the power given would be nugatory, would have been to deprive the legislature of the capacity to avail itself of experience, to exercise its reason, and to accommodate its legislation to circumstances.

If we apply this principle of construction to any of the powers of the government, we shall find it so pernicious in its operation that we shall be compelled to discard it. The baneful influence of this narrow construction on all the operations of the government, and the absolute impracticability of maintaining it, without rendering the government incompetent to its great objects, might be illustrated by numerous examples drawn from the constitution, and from our laws.

In ascertaining the sense in which the word "necessary" is used in this clause of the constitution, we may derive some aid from that with which it is associated. Congress shall have power "to make all laws which shall be necessary and proper to carry into execution" the powers of the government. If the word "necessary" was used in that strict and rigorous sense for which the counsel for the state of Maryland contend, it would be an extraordinary departure from the usual course of the human mind, as exhibited in composition, to add the word "proper," the only possible effect of which is, to qualify that strict and rigorous meaning; to present to the mind the idea of some choice of means of legislation, not strained and compressed within the narrow limits for which gentlemen contend.

But the argument which most conclusively demonstrates the error of the construction contended for by the counsel for the state of Maryland, is founded on the intention of the convention, as manifested in the whole clause. To waste time and argument in proving that, without it, congress might carry its powers into execution, would be not much less idle, than to hold a lighted taper to the sun.

We think so for the following reasons: The clause is placed among the powers of congress, not among the limitations on those powers. Its terms purport to enlarge, not to diminish the powers vested in the government. It purports to be an additional power, not a restriction on those already granted. No reason has been, or can be assigned, for thus concealing an intention to narrow the discretion of the national legislature, under words which purport to enlarge it. The framers of the constitution wished its adoption, and well knew that it would be endangered by its strength, not by its weakness.

The result of the most careful and attentive consideration bestowed upon this clause is, that if it does not enlarge, it cannot be construed to restrain the powers of congress, or to impair the right of the legislature to exercise its best judgment in the selection of measures to carry into execution the constitutional powers of the government. If no other motive for its insertion can be suggested, a sufficient one is found in the desire to remove all doubts respecting the right to legislate on that vast mass of incidental powers which must be involved in the constitution, if that instrument be not a splendid bauble.

We admit, as all must admit, that the powers of the government are limited, and that its limits are not to be transcended. But we think the sound construction of the constitution must allow to the national legislature that discretion, with respect to the means by which the powers it confers are to be carried into execution, which will enable that body to perform the high duties assigned to it, in the manner most beneficial to the people. Let the end be legitimate, let it be within the scope of the constitution, and all means which are appropriate, which are plainly adapted to that end, which are not prohibited, but consist with the letter and spirit of the constitution, are constitutional.

That a corporation must be considered as a means not less usual, not of higher dignity, not more requiring a particular specification than other means, has been sufficiently proved. Had it been intended to grant this power, as one which should be distinct and independent, to be exercised in any case whatever, it would have found a place among the enumerated powers of the government. But being considered merely as a means, to be employed only for the purpose of carrying into execution the given powers, there could be no motive for particularly mentioning it.

If a corporation may be employed, indiscriminately with other means, to carry into execution the powers of the government, no particular reason can be assigned for excluding the use of a bank, if required for its fiscal operations. To use one, must be within the discretion of congress, if it be an appropriate mode of executing the powers of government. That it is a convenient, a useful, and essential instrument in the prosecution of its fiscal operations, is not now a subject of controversy.

But were its necessity less apparent, none can deny its being an appropriate measure; and if it is, the decree of its necessity, as has been very justly observed, is to be discussed in another place. Should congress, in the execution of its powers, adopt measures which are prohibited by the constitution; or should congress, under the pretext of executing its powers, pass laws for the accomplishment of objects not intrusted to the government; it would become the painful duty of this tribunal, should a case requiring such a decision come before it, to say, that such an act was not the law of the land. But where the law is not prohibited, and is really calculated to effect any of the objects intrusted to the government, to undertake here to inquire into the decree of its necessity, would be to pass the line which circumscribes the judicial department, and to tread on legislative ground. This court disclaims all pretensions to such a power. The choice of means implies a right to choose a national bank in preference to state banks, and congress alone can make the election.

It being the opinion of the court, that the act incorporating the bank is constitutional; and that the power of establishing a branch in the state of Maryland might be properly exercised by the bank itself, we proceed to inquire—Whether the state of Maryland may, without violating the constitution, tax that branch? That the power of taxation is one of vital importance; that it is retained by the states; that it is not abridged by the grant of a similar power to the government of the Union; that it is to be concurrently exercised by the two governments—are truths which have never been denied.

This great principle is, that the constitution and the laws made in pursuance thereof are supreme; that they control the constitution and laws of the respective states, and cannot be controlled by them. From this, which may be almost termed an axiom, other propositions are deduced as corollaries, on the truth or error of which, and on their application to this case, the cause has been supposed to depend. These are, 1st. That a power to create implies a power to preserve: 2d. That a power to destroy, if wielded by a different hand, is hostile to, and incompatible with these powers to create and to preserve: 3d. That where this repugnancy exists, that authority which is supreme must control, not yield to that over which it is supreme.

These propositions, as abstract truths, would, perhaps, never be controverted. Their application to this case, however, has been denied; and both in maintaining the affirmative and the negative, a splendor of eloquence, and strength of argument, seldom, if ever, surpassed, have been displayed.

The power of congress to create, and of course, to continue, the bank, was the subject of the preceding part of this opinion; and is no longer to be considered as questionable. That the power of taxing it by the states may be exercised so as to destroy it, is too obvious to be denied. The argument on the part of the state of Maryland, is, not that the states may directly resist a law of congress, but that they may exercise their acknowledged powers upon it, and that the constitution leaves them this right, in the confidence that they will not abuse it.

All subjects over which the sovereign power of a state extends, are objects of taxation; but those over which it does not extend, are, upon the soundest principles, exempt from taxation. The sovereignty of a state extends to everything which exists by its own authority, or is introduced by its permission; but does it extend to those means which are employed by congress to carry into execution powers conferred on that body by the people of the United States? We think it demonstrable, that it does not. Those powers are not given by the people of a single state. They are given by the people of the United States, to a government whose laws, made in pursuance of the constitution, are declared to be supreme. Consequently, the people of a single state cannot confer a sovereignty which will extend over them.

If we measure the power of taxation residing in a state, by the extent of sovereignty which the people of a single state possess, and can confer on its government, we have an intelligible standard, applicable to every case to which the power may be applied. We have a principle which leaves the power of taxing the people and property of a state unimpaired; which leaves to a state the command of all its resources, and which places beyond its reach, all those powers which are conferred by the people of the United States on the government of the Union, and all those means which are given for the purpose of carrying those powers into execution. We have a principle which is safe for the states, and safe for the Union. We are relieved, as we ought to be, from clashing sovereignty; from interfering powers; from a repugnancy between a right in one government to pull down, what there is an acknowledged right in another to build up; from the incompatibility of a right in one government to destroy, what there is a right in another to preserve. We are not driven to the perplexing inquiry, so unfit for the judicial department, what degree of taxation is the legitimate use, and what degree may amount to the abuse of the power. The attempt to use it on the means employed by the government of the Union, in pursuance of the constitution, is itself an abuse, because it is the usurpation of a power which the people of a single state cannot give. We find, then, on just theory, a total failure of this original right to tax the means employed by the government of the Union, for the execution of its powers. The right never existed, and the question whether it has been surrendered, cannot arise.

That the power to tax involves the power to destroy; that the power to destroy may defeat and render useless the power to create; that there is a plain repugnance in conferring on one government a power to control the constitutional measures of another, which other, with respect to those very measures, is declared to be supreme over that which exerts the control, are propositions not to be denied. But all inconsistencies are to be reconciled by the magic of the word confidence. Taxation, it is said, does not necessarily and unavoidably destroy. To carry it to the excess of destruction, would be an abuse, to presume which, would banish that confidence which is essential to all government. But is this a case of confidence? Would the people of any one state trust those of another with a power to control the most insignificant operations of their state government? We know they would not. Why, then, should we suppose, that the people of any one state should be willing to trust those of another with a power to control the operations of a government to which they have confided their most important and most valuable interests? In the legislature of the Union alone, are all represented. The legislature of the Union alone, therefore, can be trusted by the people with the power of controlling measures which concern all, in the confidence that it will not be abused. This, then, is not a case of confidence, and we must consider it is as it really is.

The American people have declared their constitution and the laws made in pursuance thereof, to be supreme; but this principle would transfer the supremacy, in fact, to the states. If the states may tax one instrument, employed by the government in the execution of its powers, they may tax any and every other instrument. They may tax all the means employed by the government, to an excess which would defeat all the ends of government. This was not intended by the American people. They did not design to make their government dependent on the states.

The question is, in truth, a question of supremacy; and if the right of the states to tax the means employed by the general government be conceded, the declaration that the constitution, and the laws made in pursuance thereof, shall be the supreme law of the land, is empty and unmeaning declamation.

In the course of the argument, *The Federalist* has been quoted; and the opinions expressed by the authors of that work have been justly supposed to be entitled to great respect in expounding the constitution. No tribute can be paid to them which exceeds their merit; but in applying their opinions to the cases which may arise in the progress of our government, a right to judge of their correctness must be retained; and to understand the argument, we must examine the proposition it maintains, and the objections against which it is directed. The arguments of *The Federalist* are intended to prove the fallacy of these apprehensions; not to prove that the government was incapable of executing any of its powers, without exposing the means it employed to the embarrassments of state taxation. No man, who has read their instructive pages, will hesitate to admit, that their answer must have been in the negative.

The court has bestowed on this subject its most deliberate consideration. The result is a conviction that the states have no power, by taxation or otherwise, to retard, impede, burden, or in any manner control, the operations of the constitutional laws enacted by congress to carry into execution the powers vested in the general government. This is, we think, the unavoidable consequence of that supremacy which the constitution has declared. We are unanimously of the opinion, that the law passed by the legislature of Maryland, imposing a tax on the Bank of the United States, is unconstitutional and void.

*That the governmental power of the purse is a great one is not now for the first time announced. Every student of the history of government and economics is aware of its magnitude and of its existence in every civilized government.*

— *Harlan F. Stone*

## United States v. Butler
### 56 S.Ct. 312, 297 U.S. 1 (1936)

*The Agricultural Adjustment Act of 1933, a key program of the New Deal, was designed to improve the fortunes of farmers by subsidizing them for curtailing production with the expectation this would raise crop prices. Congress obtained revenue for the subsidy by levying an excise tax on the processors of each crop, in this case a cotton mill, which could be expected to pass on the tax to the consumers by increasing prices. The cotton mill challenged the constitutionality of the federal tax. Article I, § 8 gives Congress the "power to lay and collect Taxes, Duties, Imposts and Excises, to pay the Debts and provide for the common Defence and general Welfare of the United States." This power was wholly lacking under the Articles of Confederation and the clause was greatly controverted by the Antifederalists, who opposed the Constitution. Among Federalists, there was sharp disagreement on the scope of this congressional power to tax and spend. James Madison took a narrow view and Alexander Hamilton took a broad view. Justice Roberts' opinion endorsed the broad Hamiltonian view, but nevertheless held the AAA unconstitutional. Justice Stone penned a powerful dissent which exposed Roberts' interpretative ineptness and helped convince President Roosevelt that the New Deal had to overcome the Supreme Court majority, thus setting the stage for the constitutional crisis of the court-packing plan the next year. Over the years, the dissent has been invoked many times by minorities, liberal and conservative, to urge judicial self-restraint. Summing up the case law, a scholar has observed, "No taxing and spending clause statute has ever been invalidated because it did not serve the general welfare, and none is likely to be."*

**Justice Roberts:** The government asserts that article 1, § 8 of the Constitution, authorizes the contemplated expenditure of the funds raised by the tax. This contention presents the great and the controlling question in the case. We approach its decision with a sense of our grave responsibility to render judgment in accordance with the principles established for the governance of all three branches of the government.

There should be no misunderstanding as to the function of this court in such a case. It is sometimes said that the court assumes a power to overrule or control the action of the people's representatives. This is a misconception. The Constitution is the supreme law of the land ordained and established by the people. All legislation must conform to the principles it lays down. When an act of Congress is appropriately challenged in the courts as not conforming to the constitutional mandate, the judicial branch of the government has only one duty; to lay the article of the Constitution which is invoked beside the statute which is challenged and to decide whether the latter squares with the former. All the court does, or can do, is to announce its considered judgment upon the question. The only power it has, if such it may be called, is the power of judgment. This court neither approves nor condemns any legislative policy. Its delicate and difficult office is to ascertain and declare whether the legislation is in accordance with, or in contravention of, the provisions of the Constitution; and, having done that, its duty ends.

The question is not what power the federal government ought to have, but what powers in fact have been given by the people. It hardly seems necessary to reiterate that ours is a dual form of government; that in every state there are two governments; the state and the United States. Each state has all governmental powers save such as the people, by their Constitution, have conferred upon the United States, denied to the states, or reserved to themselves. The federal union is a government of delegated powers. It has only such as are expressly conferred upon it and such as are reasonably to be implied from those granted. In this respect we differ radically from nations where all legislative power, without restriction or limitation, is vested in a parliament or other legislative body subject to no restrictions except the discretion of its members.

Article I, § 8, of the Constitution, vests sundry powers in the Congress. The clause thought to authorize the legislation, the first, confers upon the Congress power "to lay and collect Taxes, Duties, Imposts and Excises, to pay the Debts and provide for the common Defence and general Welfare of the United States." Since the foundation of the nation, sharp differences of opinion have persisted as to the true interpretation of the phrase. Madison asserted it amounted to no more than a reference to the other powers enumerated in the subsequent clauses of the same section; that, as the United States is a government of limited and enumerated powers, the grant of power to tax and spend for the general national welfare must be confined to the enumerated legislative fields committed to the Congress. In this view the phrase is mere tautology, for taxation and appropriation are or may be necessary incidents of the exercise of any of the enumerated legislative powers. Hamilton, on the other hand, maintained the clause confers a power separate and distinct from those later enumerated is not restricted in meaning by the grant of them, and Congress consequently has a substantive power to tax and to appropriate, limited only by the requirement that it shall be exercised to provide for the general welfare of the United States. Each contention has had the support of those whose views are entitled to weight. This court has noticed the question, but has never found it necessary to decide which is the true construction. Mr. Justice Story, in his COMMENTARIES ON THE CONSTITUTION, espouses the Hamiltonian position. We shall not review the writings of public men and commentators or discuss the legislative practice. Study of all these leads us to conclude that the reading advocated by Mr. Justice Story is the correct one. While, therefore, the power to tax is not unlimited, its confines are set in the clause which confers it, and not in those of section 8 which bestow and define the legislative powers of the Congress. It results that the power of Congress to authorize expenditure of public moneys for public purposes is not limited by the direct grants of legislative power found in the Constitution.

But the adoption of the broader construction leaves the power to spend subject to limitations. As Story says: "The Constitution was, from its very origin, contemplated to be the frame of a national government, of special and enumerated powers, and not of general and unlimited powers." Hamilton states that the purpose must be "general, and not local." James Monroe, also an advocate of Hamilton's doctrine, wrote: "Have Congress a right to raise and appropriate the money to any and to every purpose according to their will and pleasure? They certainly have not." Story says that if the tax be not proposed for the common defense or general welfare, but for other objects wholly extraneous, it would be wholly indefensible upon constitutional principles. And he makes it clear that the powers of taxation and appropriation extend only to matters of national, as distinguished from local, welfare.

We are not now required to ascertain the scope of the phrase "general welfare of the United States" or to determine whether an appropriation in aid of agriculture falls within it. Wholly apart from that question, another principle embedded in our Constitution prohibits the enforcement of the Agricultural Adjustment Act. The act invades the reserved rights of the states. It is a statutory plan to regulate and control agricultural production, a matter beyond the powers delegated to the federal government. The tax, the appropriation of the funds raised, and the direction for their disbursement, are but parts of the plan. They are but means to an unconstitutional end.

From the accepted doctrine that the United States is a government of delegated powers, it follows that those not expressly granted, or reasonably to be implied from such as are conferred, are reserved to the states or to the people. To forestall any suggestion to the contrary, the Tenth Amendment was adopted. The same proposition, otherwise stated, is that powers not granted are prohibited. None to regulate agricultural production is given, and therefore legislation by Congress for that purpose is forbidden.

If the taxing power may not be used as the instrument to enforce a regulation of matters of state concern with respect to which the Congress has no authority to interfere, may it, as in the present case, be employed to raise the money necessary to purchase a compliance which the Congress is powerless to command? The government asserts that whatever might be said against the validity of the plan, if compulsory, it is constitutionally sound because the end is accomplished by voluntary co-operation. There are two sufficient answers to the contention. The regulation is not in fact voluntary. The farmer, of course, may refuse to comply, but the price of such refusal is the loss of benefits. The power to confer or withhold unlimited benefits is the power to coerce or destroy. If the cotton grower elects not to accept the benefits, he will receive less for his crops; those who receive payments will be able to undersell him. The result may well be financial ruin. This is coercion by economic pressure. The asserted power of choice is illusory.

But if the plan were one for purely voluntary cooperation it would stand no better so far as federal power is concerned. At best, it is a scheme for purchasing with federal funds submission to federal regulation of a subject reserved to the states. Is a statute less objectionable which authorizes expenditure of federal moneys to induce action in a field in which the United States has no power to intermeddle? The Congress cannot invade state jurisdiction to compel individual action; no more can it purchase such action.

Congress has no power to enforce its commands on the farmer to the ends sought by the Agricultural Adjustment Act. It must follow that it may not indirectly accomplish those ends by taxing and spending to purchase compliance. The Constitution and the entire plan of our government negative any such use of the power to tax and to spend as the act undertakes to authorize.

If the act before us is a proper exercise of the federal taxing power, evidently the regulation of all industry throughout the United States may be accomplished by similar exercises of the same power. It would be possible to exact money from one branch of an industry and pay it to another branch in every field of activity which lies within the province of the states. The mere threat of such a procedure might well induce the surrender of rights and the compliance with federal regulation as the price of continuance in business.

Until recently no suggestion of the existence of any such power in the federal government has been advanced. Hamilton himself, the leading advocate of broad interpretation of the power to tax and to appropriate for the general welfare, never suggested that any power granted by the Constitution could be used for the destruction of local self-government in the states. Story countenances no such doctrine. It seems never to have occurred to them, or to those who have agreed with them, that the general welfare of the United States (which has aptly been termed "an indestructible Union, composed of indestructible States,") might be served by obliterating the constituent members of the Union. But to this fatal conclusion the doctrine contended for would inevitably lead. And its sole premise is that, though the makers of the Constitution, in erecting the federal government, intended sedulously to limit and define its powers, so as to reserve to the states and the people sovereign power, to be wielded by the states and their citizens and not to be invaded by the United States, they nevertheless by a single clause gave power to the Congress to tear down the barriers, to invade the states' jurisdiction, and to become a parliament of the whole people, subject to no restrictions save such as are self-imposed. The argument, when seen in its true character and in the light of its inevitable results, must be rejected.

**Justice Stone:** The power of courts to declare a statute unconstitutional is subject to two guiding principles of decision which ought never to be absent from judicial consciousness. One is that courts are concerned only with the power to enact statutes, not with their wisdom. The other is that while unconstitutional exercise of power by the executive and legislative branches of the government is subject to judicial restraint, the only check upon our own exercise of power is our own sense of self-restraint. For the removal of unwise laws from the statute books appeal lies, not to the courts, but to the ballot and to the processes of democratic government.

The constitutional power of Congress to levy an excise tax upon the processing of agricultural products is not questioned. The present levy is held invalid, not for any want of power in Congress to lay such a tax to defray public expenditures, including those for the general welfare, but because the use to which its proceeds are put is disapproved.

As the present depressed state of agriculture is nation wide in its extent and effects, there is no basis for saying that the expenditure of public money in aid of farmers is not within the specifically granted power of Congress to levy taxes to "provide for the general welfare." The opinion of the Court does not declare otherwise.

The pivot on which the decision of the Court is made to turn is that a levy unquestionably within the taxing power of Congress may be treated as invalid because it is a step in a plan to regulate agricultural production and is thus a forbidden infringement of state power. The levy is not any the less an exercise of taxing power because it is intended to defray an expenditure for the general welfare rather than for some other support of government. Nor is the levy and collection of the tax pointed to as effecting the regulation.

In saying that this method of spending public moneys is an invasion of the reserved powers of the states, the Court does not assert that the expenditure of public funds to promote the general welfare is not a substantive power specifically delegated to the national government, as Hamilton and Story pronounced it to be. It does not deny that the expenditure of funds for the benefit of farmers and in aid of a program of curtailment of production of agricultural products, and thus of a supposedly better ordered national economy, is within the specifically granted power. The presumption of constitutionality of a statute is not to be overturned by an assertion of its coercive effect which rests on nothing more substantial than groundless speculation.

It is insisted that, while the Constitution gives to Congress, in specific and unambiguous terms, the power to tax and spend, the power is subject to limitations which do not find their origin in any express provision of the Constitution and to which other expressly delegated powers are not subject.

The Constitution requires that public funds shall be spent for a defined purpose, the promotion of the general welfare. Their expenditure usually involves payment on terms which will insure use by the selected recipients within the limits of the constitutional purpose. Expenditures would fail of their purpose and thus lose their constitutional sanction if the terms of payment were not such that by their influence on the action of the recipients the permitted end would be attained. The power of Congress to spend is inseparable from persuasion to action over which Congress has no legislative control.

The time-honored principle of constitutional interpretation that the granted power includes all those which are incident to it is reversed. "Let the end be legitimate," said the great Chief Justice Marshall, "let it be within the scope of the constitution, and all means which are appropriate, which are plainly adapted to that end, which are not prohibited, but consist with the letter and spirit of the constitution, are constitutional." This cardinal guide to constitutional exposition must now be rephrased so far as the spending power of the federal government is concerned. Let the expenditure be to promote the general welfare, still if it is needful in order to insure its use for the intended purpose to influence any action which Congress cannot command because within the sphere of state government, the expenditure is unconstitutional. And taxes otherwise lawfully levied are likewise unconstitutional if they are appropriated to the expenditure whose incident is condemned.

Such a limitation is contradictory and destructive of the power to appropriate for the public welfare, and is incapable of practical application. The spending power of Congress is in addition to the legislative power and not subordinate to it. This independent grant of the power of the purse, and its very nature, involving in its exercise the duty to insure expenditure within the granted power, presuppose freedom of selection among diverse ends and aims, and the capacity to impose such conditions as will render the choice effective. It is a contradiction in terms to say that there is power to spend for the national welfare, while rejecting any power to impose conditions reasonably adapted to the attainment of the end which alone would justify the expenditure.

The limitation now sanctioned must lead to absurd consequences. The government may give seeds to farmers, but may not condition the gift upon their being planted in places where they are most needed or even planted at all. The government may give money to the unemployed, but may not ask that those who get it shall give labor in return, or even use it to support their families. It may give money to sufferers from earthquake, fire, tornado, pestilence, or flood, but may not impose conditions, health precautions, designed to prevent the spread of disease, or induce the movement of population to safer or more sanitary areas. All that, because it is purchased regulation infringing state powers, must be left for the states, who are unable or unwilling to supply the necessary relief.

Do all its activities collapse because, in order to effect the permissible purpose in myriad ways the money is paid out upon terms and conditions which influence action of the recipients within the states, which Congress cannot command? The answer would seem plain. If the expenditure is for a national public purpose, that purpose will not be thwarted because payment is on condition which will advance that purpose. The action which Congress induces by payments of money to promote the general welfare, but which it does not command or coerce, is but an incident to a specifically granted power, but a permissible means to a legitimate end. If appropriation in aid of a program of curtailment of agricultural production is constitutional, and it is not denied that it is, payment to farmers on condition that they reduce their crop acreage is constitutional. It is not any the less so because the farmer at his own option promises to fulfill the condition.

That the governmental power of the purse is a great one is not now for the first time announced. Every student of the history of government and economics is aware of its magnitude and of its existence in every civilized government. Both were well understood by the framers of the Constitution when they sanctioned the grant of the spending power to the federal government, and both were recognized by Hamilton and Story, whose views of the spending power as standing on a parity with the other powers specifically granted, have hitherto been generally accepted.

The suggestion that it must now be curtailed by judicial fiat because it may be abused by unwise use hardly rises to the dignity of argument. So may judicial power be abused. "The power to tax is the power to destroy," but we do not, for that reason, doubt its existence, or hold that its efficacy is to be restricted by its incidental or collateral effects upon the states. The power to tax and spend is not without constitutional restraints. One restriction is that the purpose must be truly national. Another is that it may not be used to coerce action left to state control. Another is the conscience and patriotism of Congress and the Executive. Justice Holmes said, "It must be remembered that legislatures are ultimate guardians of the liberties and welfare of the people in quite as great a degree as the courts."

A tortured construction of the Constitution is not to be justified by recourse to extreme examples of reckless congressional spending which might occur if courts could not prevent—expenditures which, even if they could be thought to effect any national purpose, would be possible only by action of a legislature lost to all sense of public responsibility. Such suppositions are addressed to the mind accustomed to believe that it is the business of courts to sit in judgment on the wisdom of legislative action. Courts are not the only agency of government that must be assumed to have capacity to govern. Congress and the courts both unhappily may falter or be mistaken in the performance of their constitutional duty. But interpretation of our great charter of government which proceeds on any assumption that the responsibility for the preservation of our institutions is the exclusive concern of any one of the three branches of government, or that it alone can save them from destruction is far more likely, in the long run, "to obliterate the constituent members" of "an indestructible union of indestructible states" than the frank recognition that language, even of a constitution, may mean what it says: that the power to tax and spend includes the power to relieve a nationwide economic maladjustment by conditional gifts of money.

*The Constitution empowers Congress to "lay
and collect Taxes, Duties, Imposts, and Excises,
to pay the Debts and provide for the common
Defence and general Welfare of the United States."
Incident to this power, Congress may attach
conditions on the receipt of federal funds, and
has repeatedly employed the power "to further
broad policy objectives by conditioning receipt of
federal moneys upon compliance by the recipient
with federal statutory and administrative
directives."*

— *William H. Rehnquist*

## South Dakota v. Dole
### 107 S.Ct. 2793, 483 U.S. 203 (1987)

*The drinking age in South Dakota was 19 years of
age. In 1984, Congress passed a statute directing the Secretary of Transportation, then Elizabeth H. Dole, to withhold a percentage of federal highway funds otherwise
allocable from States with a drinking age below 21. Most
of the States responded by raising their drinking ages
accordingly. But South Dakota sued and argued that
Congress had exceeded its taxing and spending powers
because the federal policy violated the 21st amendment's
grant of control over "intoxicating liquors" to the States.
Although "only 5%" of the federal funds were held back,
millions of dollars were at stake. South Dakota believed
constitutional principles of state sovereignty also were at
stake, as did several other States which joined the case as
amici curiae. With only two Justices dissenting, the majority thought otherwise. Contemporary Justices seem to
perceive merely gossamer limits on the taxing and spending powers. Therefore, Congress can constitutionally attach all sorts of strings to federal moneys. What Congress
cannot do directly, it can accomplish indirectly simply by
bribing the States. This case is somewhat unusual in that
usually the States are all too willing to sell their sovereignty to the federal government, reminiscent of Esau
trading his birthright to Jacob for a mess of pottage.*

**Chief Justice Rehnquist:** In this Court, the parties direct most of their efforts to defining the proper scope of the Twenty-first Amendment. Despite the extended treatment of the question by the parties, however, we need not decide in this case whether that Amendment would prohibit an attempt by Congress to legislate directly a national minimum drinking age. Here, Congress has acted indirectly under its spending power to encourage uniformity in the States' drinking ages. We find this legislative effort within constitutional bounds even if Congress may not regulate drinking ages directly.

The Constitution empowers Congress to "lay and collect Taxes, Duties, Imposts, and Excises, to pay the Debts and provide for the common Defence and general Welfare of the United States." Art. I, § 8, cl. 1. Incident to this power, Congress may attach conditions on the receipt of federal funds, and has repeatedly employed the power "to further broad policy objectives by conditioning receipt of federal moneys upon compliance by the recipient with federal statutory and administrative directives." The breadth of this power was made clear in 1936, when the Court, resolving a longstanding debate over the scope of the Spending Clause, determined that "the power of Congress to authorize expenditure of public moneys for public purposes is not limited by the direct grants of legislative power found in the Constitution." Thus, objectives not thought to be within Article I's "enumerated legislative fields," may nevertheless be attained through the use of the spending power and the conditional grant of federal funds.

The spending power is of course not unlimited, but is instead subject to several general restrictions articulated in our cases. The first of these limitations is derived from the language of the Constitution itself: the exercise of the spending power must be in pursuit of "the general welfare." In considering whether a particular expenditure is intended to serve general public purposes, courts should defer substantially to the judgment of Congress. Indeed, the level of deference to the congressional decision is such that the Court has more recently questioned whether "general welfare" is a judicially enforceable restriction at all. Second, we have required that if Congress desires to condition the States' receipt of federal funds, it "must do so unambiguously, enabling the States to exercise their choice knowingly, cognizant of the consequences of their participation." Third, our cases have suggested (without significant elaboration) that conditions on federal grants might be illegitimate if they are unrelated "to the federal interest in particular national projects or programs." Finally, we have noted that other constitutional provisions may provide an independent bar to the conditional grant of federal funds.

South Dakota does not seriously claim that this federal law is inconsistent with any of the first three restrictions mentioned above. We can readily conclude that the provision is designed to serve the general welfare, especially in light of the fact that "the concept of welfare or the opposite is shaped by Congress." Congress found that the differing drinking ages in the States created particular incentives for young persons to combine their desire to drink with their ability to drive, and that this interstate problem required a national solution. The means it chose to address this dangerous situation were reasonably calculated to advance the general welfare. The conditions upon which States receive the funds, moreover, could not be more clearly stated by Congress. And in its Brief before the Court, South Dakota itself, rather than challenging the germaneness of the condition to federal purposes, admits that it "has never contended that the congressional action was unrelated to a national concern in the absence of the Twenty-first Amendment." Indeed, the condition imposed by Congress is directly related to one of the main purposes for which highway funds are expended—safe interstate travel. This goal of the interstate highway system had been frustrated by varying drinking ages among the States. A Presidential commission appointed to study alcohol-related accidents and fatalities on the Nation's highways concluded that the lack of uniformity in the States' drinking ages created "an incentive to drink and drive" because "young persons commute to border States where the drinking age is lower." By enacting this statute, Congress conditioned the receipt of federal funds in a way reasonably calculated to address this particular impediment to a purpose for which the funds are expended.

The remaining question about the validity of this statute—and the basic point of disagreement between the parties—is whether the Twenty-first Amendment constitutes an "independent constitutional bar" to the conditional grant of federal funds. South Dakota, relying on its view that the Twenty-first Amendment prohibits direct regulation of drinking ages by Congress, asserts that "Congress may not use the spending power to regulate that which it is prohibited from regulating directly under the Twenty-first Amendment." But our cases show that this "independent constitutional bar" limitation on the spending power is not of the kind South Dakota suggests. Our precedents have established that the constitutional limitations on Congress when exercising its spending power are less exacting than those on its authority to regulate directly.

We have also held that a perceived Tenth Amendment limitation on congressional regulation of state affairs did not concomitantly limit the range of conditions legitimately placed on federal grants. Our prior cases establish that the "independent constitutional bar" limitation on the spending power is not, as South Dakota suggests, a prohibition on the indirect achievement of objectives which Congress is not empowered to achieve directly. Instead, we think that the language in our earlier opinions stands for the unexceptionable proposition that the power may not be used to induce the States to engage in activities that would themselves be unconstitutional. Thus, for example, a grant of federal funds conditioned on invidiously discriminatory state action or the infliction of cruel and unusual punishment would be an illegitimate exercise of the Congress' broad spending power. But no such claim can be or is made here. Were South Dakota to succumb to the blandishments offered by Congress and raise its drinking age to 21, the State's action in so doing would not violate the constitutional rights of anyone.

Our decisions have recognized that in some circumstances the financial inducement offered by Congress might be so coercive as to pass the point at which "pressure turns into compulsion." Here, however, Congress has directed only that a State desiring to establish a minimum drinking age lower than 21 lose a relatively small percentage of certain federal highway funds. South Dakota contends that the coercive nature of this program is evident from the degree of success it has achieved. We cannot conclude, however, that a conditional grant of federal money of this sort is unconstitutional simply by reason of its success in achieving the congressional objective.

When we consider, for a moment, that all South Dakota would lose if she adheres to her chosen course as to a suitable minimum drinking age is 5% of the funds otherwise obtainable under specified highway grant programs, the argument as to coercion is shown to be more rhetoric than fact. As we said a half century ago: "Every rebate from a tax when conditioned upon conduct is in some measure a temptation. But to hold that motive or temptation is equivalent to coercion is to plunge the law in endless difficulties. The outcome of such a doctrine is the acceptance of a philosophical determinism by which choice becomes impossible. Till now the law has been guided by a robust common sense which assumes the freedom of the will as a working hypothesis in the solution of its problems."

Here Congress has offered relatively mild encouragement to the States to enact higher minimum drinking ages than they would otherwise choose. But the enactment of such laws remains the prerogative of the States not merely in theory but in fact. Even if Congress might lack the power to impose a national minimum drinking age directly, we conclude that encouragement to state action found in the statute before us is a valid use of the spending power.

*The case before us must be considered in the
light of our whole experience and not merely in
that of what was said a hundred years ago. The
treaty in question does not contravene any
prohibitory words to be found in the Constitution.
The only question is whether it is forbidden by
some invisible radiation from the general terms
of the Tenth Amendment. We must consider what
this country has become in deciding what that
amendment has reserved.*

*— Oliver W. Holmes, Jr.*

## Missouri v. Holland
### 40 S.Ct. 382, 252 U.S. 416 (1920)

*The Migratory Bird Treaty Act was passed to fulfill
United States obligations under a treaty with Great Britain to prevent the indiscriminate hunting of migratory
birds across the border with Canada. Lower federal
courts had invalidated an earlier statute, which Congress
had enacted after the States proved unable or unwilling
to deal with the problem but before the treaty was formally approved, maintaining that it violated the 10th
amendment's reserved powers of the States. Justice Holmes answered this same constitutional challenge against
the new statute, which Congress passed after the treaty
was duly ratified, with what has become a famous federal
supremacy argument. The Constitution delegated the
treaty power to the national government and made the
treaty as well as its implementing federal legislation the
"supreme Law of the Land." State sovereignty must give
way to the federal power to implement treaties. Along the
way, he imagined an organic "living Constitution" which
must be understood in the light of history, tradition and
experience.*

**Justice Holmes:** This is a bill in equity brought by the
State of Missouri to prevent a game warden of the United States
from attempting to enforce the Migratory Bird Treaty Act of
July 3, 1918, and the regulations made by the Secretary of Agriculture in pursuance of the same. The ground of the bill is that
the statute is an unconstitutional interference with the rights
reserved to the States by the Tenth Amendment, and that the
acts of the defendant done and threatened under that authority
invade the sovereign right of the State and contravene its will

manifested in statutes. The State also alleges a pecuniary interest, as owner of the wild birds within its borders and otherwise, admitted by the Government to be sufficient, but it is enough that the bill is a reasonable and proper means to assert the alleged quasi sovereign rights of a State.

On December 8, 1916, a treaty between the United States and Great Britain was proclaimed by the President. It recited that many species of birds in their annual migrations traversed many parts of the United States and of Canada, that they were of great value as a source of food and in destroying insects injurious to vegetation, but were in danger of extermination through lack of adequate protection. It therefore provided for specified closed seasons and protection in other forms, and agreed that the two powers would take or propose to their lawmaking bodies the necessary measures for carrying the treaty out. The above mentioned act of July 3, 1918, entitled an act to give effect to the convention, prohibited killing, capturing or selling any of the migratory birds included in the terms of the treaty except as permitted by regulations compatible with those terms, to be made by the Secretary of Agriculture. Regulations were also proclaimed. It is unnecessary to go into any details, because, as we have said, the question raised is the general one whether the treaty and statute are void as an interference with the rights reserved to the States.

To answer this question it is not enough to refer to the Tenth Amendment, reserving the powers not delegated to the United States, because by Article II, Section 2, the power to make treaties is delegated expressly, and by Article VI treaties made under the authority of the United States, along with the Constitution and laws of the United States made in pursuance thereof, are declared the supreme law of the land. If the treaty is valid there can be no dispute about the validity of the statute under Article I, Section 8, as a necessary and proper means to execute the powers of the Government. The language of the Constitution as to the supremacy of treaties being general, the question before us is narrowed to an inquiry into the ground upon which the present supposed exception is placed.

It is said that a treaty cannot be valid if it infringes the Constitution, that there are limits, therefore, to the treaty-making power, and that one such limit is that what an act of Congress could not do unaided, in derogation of the powers reserved to the States, a treaty cannot do. An earlier act of Congress that attempted by itself and not in pursuance of a treaty to regulate the killing of migratory birds within the States had been held bad in the District Courts. Those decisions were supported by arguments that migratory birds were owned by the States in their sovereign capacity for the benefit of their people, and that this control was one that Congress had no power to displace. The same argument is supposed to apply now with equal force.

Whether those earlier District Court cases declaring the former statute to be bad were decided rightly or not, they cannot be accepted as a test of the treaty power. Acts of Congress are the supreme law of the land only when made in pursuance of the Constitution, while treaties are declared to be so when made under the authority of the United States. It is open to question whether the authority of the United States means more than the formal acts prescribed to make the convention. We do not mean to imply that there are no qualifications to the treaty-making power; but they must be ascertained in a different way. It is obvious that there may be matters of the sharpest exigency for the national well being that an act of Congress could not deal with but that a treaty followed by such an act could, and it is not lightly to be assumed that, in matters requiring national action, "a power which must belong to and somewhere reside in every civilized government" is not to be found. What was said in a previous case with regard to the powers of the States applies with equal force to the powers of the nation in cases where the States individually are incompetent to act. We are not yet discussing the particular case before us but only are considering the validity of the test proposed. With regard to that we may add that when we are dealing with words that also are a constituent act, like the Constitution of the United States, we must realize that they have called into life a being the development of which could not have been foreseen completely by the most gifted of its begetters. It was enough for them to realize or to hope that they had created an organism; it has taken a century and has cost their successors much sweat and blood to prove that they created a nation. The case before us must be considered in the light of our whole experience and not merely in that of what was said a hundred years ago. The treaty in question does not contravene any prohibitory words to be found in the Constitution. The only question is whether it is forbidden by some invisible radiation from the general terms of the Tenth Amendment. We must consider what this country has become in deciding what that amendment has reserved.

The State as we have intimated founds its claim of exclusive authority upon an assertion of title to migratory birds, an assertion that is embodied in statute. No doubt it is true that as between a State and its inhabitants the State may regulate the killing and sale of such birds, but it does not follow that its authority is exclusive of paramount powers. To put the claim of the State upon title is to lean upon a slender reed. Wild birds are not in the possession of anyone; and possession is the beginning of ownership. The whole foundation of the State's rights is the presence within their jurisdiction of birds that yesterday had not arrived, tomorrow may be in another State and in a week a thousand miles away. If we are to be accurate we cannot put the case of the State upon higher ground than that the treaty deals with creatures that for the moment are within the state borders, that it must be carried out by officers of the United States within the same territory, and that but for the treaty the State would be free to regulate this subject itself.

As most of the laws of the United States are carried out within the States and as many of them deal with matters which in the silence of such laws the State might regulate, such general grounds are not enough to support Missouri's claim. Valid treaties of course "are as binding within the territorial limits of the States as they are elsewhere throughout the dominion of the United States." No doubt the great body of private relations usually fall within the control of the State, but a treaty may override its power. We do not have to invoke the later developments of constitutional law for this proposition; it was recognized early with regard to statutes of limitation, and even earlier, as to confiscation. It was assumed by Chief Justice Marshall with regard to the escheat of land to the State. So as to a limited jurisdiction of foreign consuls within a State. Further illustration seems unnecessary, and it only remains to consider the application of established rules to the present case.

Here a national interest of very nearly the first magnitude is involved. It can be protected only by national action in concert with that of another power. The subject matter is only transitorily within the State and has no permanent habitat therein. But for the treaty and the statute there soon might be no birds for any powers to deal with. We see nothing in the Constitution that compels the Government to sit by while a food supply is cut off and the protectors of our forests and our crops are destroyed. It is not sufficient to rely upon the States. The reliance is vain, and were it otherwise, the question is whether the United States is forbidden to act. We are of opinion that the treaty and statute must be upheld.

*Our system, fostered by the Commerce Clause, is that every farmer and every craftsman shall be encouraged to produce by the certainty that he will have free access to every market in the Nation, that no home embargoes will withhold his export, and no foreign state will by customs duties or regulations exclude them. Likewise, every consumer may look to the free competition from every producing area in the Nation to protect him from exploitation by any. Such was the vision of the Founders; such has been the doctrine of this Court which has given it reality.*

— *Robert H. Jackson*

## H. P. Hood & Sons, Inc. v. Du Mond
### 69 S.Ct. 657, 336 U.S. 525 (1949)

*The commerce clause, Article I, § 8, cl. 3, more often than not is triggered by some state regulation that imposes a burden on commerce coming into the State, like a tariff between two countries. This case deals with a state regulation that burdened commerce going out of the State, more like an embargo. In both situations, the Supreme Court balances the burden on commerce against the legitimacy and importance of the State's goal. H. P. Hood & Sons, Inc. was a Massachusetts company that bought milk from producers in New York and sold it in Boston. The company applied and was refused a license to operate an additional milk collection station in New York on the ground that it would reduce the supply of milk in the New York market, and eventually lead to higher prices for New Yorkers. The burden of the measure fell on non-residents, the people of Massachusetts who wanted to buy the milk, who were unrepresented and unprotected in New York politics; at the same time, the people of New York were being benefited by being protected from competition in the marketplace. Hence, the state law was the kind of trade barrier the Court would strike down, though two Justices were not so sure and two others would have upheld the New York law. Speaking for the majority here, Justice Jackson describes the underlying assumptions of the commerce clause: the Constitution commits the country to a common market and the Su-*

*preme Court serves as the constitutional cop on the corner. Along the way, he imagines vivid examples of how things would be like otherwise.*

**Justice Jackson:** This case concerns the power of the State of New York to deny additional facilities to acquire and ship milk in interstate commerce where the grounds of denial are that such limitation upon interstate business will protect and advance local economic interests.

Our decision in a milk litigation most relevant to the present controversy deals with the converse of the present situation. In that case, New York placed conditions and limitations on the local sale of milk imported from Vermont designed in practical effect to exclude it, while here its order proposes to limit the local facilities for purchase of additional milk so as to withhold milk from export. The State agreed then, as now, that the Commerce Clause prohibits it from directly curtailing movement of milk into or out of the State. But in the earlier case, it contended that the same result could be accomplished by controlling delivery, bottling and sale after arrival, while here it says it can do so by curtailing facilities for its purchase and receipt before it is shipped out. In neither case is the measure supported by health or safety considerations but solely by protection of local economic interests, such as supply for local consumption and limitation of competition. This Court unanimously rejected the State's contention and held that the Commerce Clause, even in the absence of congressional action, prohibits such regulations for such ends.

The opinion was by Mr. Justice Cardozo, experienced in the milk problems of New York and favorably disposed toward the efforts of the State to control the industry. It recognized, as do we, broad power in the State to protect its inhabitants against perils to health or safety, fraudulent traders and highway hazards even by use of measures which bear adversely upon interstate commerce. But it laid repeated emphasis upon the principle that the State may not promote its own economic advantages by curtailment or burdening of interstate commerce.

The Constitution, said Mr. Justice Cardozo for the unanimous Court, "was framed upon the theory that the peoples of the several states must sink or swim together, and that in the long run prosperity and salvation are in union and not division."

He reiterated that the economic objective, as distinguished from any health, safety and fair-dealing purpose of the regulation, was the root of its invalidity.

This distinction between the power of the State to shelter its people from menaces to their health or safety and from fraud, even when those dangers emanate from interstate commerce, and its lack of power to retard, burden or constrict the flow of such commerce for their economic advantage, is one deeply rooted in both our history and our law.

When victory relieved the Colonies from the pressure for solidarity that war had exerted, a drift toward anarchy and commercial warfare between states began. In his treatise, Justice Story reported, "Each state would legislate according to its estimate of its own interests, the importance of its own products, and the local advantages or disadvantages of its position in a political or commercial view. This came to threaten at once the peace and safety of the Union." The sole purpose for which Virginia initiated the movement which ultimately produced the Constitution was "to take into consideration the trade of the United States; to examine the relative situations and trade of the said states; to consider how far a uniform system in their commercial regulation may be necessary to their common interest and their permanent harmony" and for that purpose the General Assembly of Virginia in January of 1786 named commissioners and proposed their meeting with those from other states.

The desire of the Forefathers to federalize regulation of foreign and interstate commerce stands in sharp contrast to their jealous preservation of power over their internal affairs. No other federal power was so universally assumed to be necessary, no other state power was so readily relinquished. There was no desire to authorize federal interference with social conditions or legal institutions of the states. Even the Bill of Rights amendments were framed only as a limitation upon the powers of Congress. The states were quite content with their several and diverse controls over most matters but, as James Madison indicated at the Convention, "want of a general power over Commerce led to an exercise of this power separately, by the States, which not only proved abortive, but engendered rival, conflicting and angry regulations."

The necessity of centralized regulation of commerce among the states was so obvious and so fully recognized that the few words of the Commerce Clause were little illuminated by debate. But the significance of the clause was not lost and its effect was immediate and salutary. We are told by so responsible an authority as Mr. Jefferson's first appointee to this Court, Mr. Justice Johnson, that "there was not a State in the Union in which there did not, at that time exist a variety of commercial regulations; concerning which it is too much to suppose, that the whole ground covered by these regulations was immediately assumed by actual legislation, under the authority of the Union. But where was the existing statute on this subject, that a State attempted to execute? Or by what State was it ever thought necessary to repeal those statutes? By common consent, these laws dropped lifeless from their statute books, for want of the sustaining power, that had been relinquished to Congress."

The Commerce Clause is one of the most prolific sources of national power and an equally prolific source of conflict with legislation of the state. While the Constitution vests in Congress the power to regulate commerce among the states, it does not say what the states may or may not do in the absence of congressional action, nor how to draw the line between what is and what is not commerce among the states. Perhaps even more than by interpretation of its written word, this Court has advanced the solidarity and prosperity of this Nation by the meaning it has given to these great silences of the Constitution.

This Court consistently has rebuffed attempts of states to advance their own commercial interests by curtailing the movement of articles of commerce, either into or out of the state, while generally supporting their right to impose even burdensome regulations in the interest of local health and safety. As most states serve their own interests best by sending their produce to market, the cases in which this Court has been obliged to deal with prohibitions or limitations by states upon exports of articles of commerce are not numerous.

The principle that our economic unit is the Nation, which alone has the gamut of powers necessary to control of the economy, including the vital power of erecting customs barriers against foreign competition, has as its corollary that the states are not separable economic units. As this Court has said, "What is ultimate is the principle that one state in its dealings with another may not place itself in a position of economic isolation." In so stating this Court but followed the principle that the state may not use its admitted powers to protect the health and safety of its people as a basis for suppressing competition. In the language of Mr. Justice Brandeis, "Its primary purpose is not regu-

—— 149 ——

lation with a view to safety or to conservation of the highways, but the prohibition of competition." The same argument here advanced, that limitation of competition would itself contribute to safety and conservation, and therefore indirectly serve an end permissible to the state, was there declared "not sound" in his opinion for the Court there. It is no better here. This Court has not only recognized this disability of the state to isolate its own economy as a basis for striking down parochial legislative policies designed to do so, but it has recognized the incapacity of the state to protect its own inhabitants from competition as a reason for sustaining particular exercises of the commerce power of Congress to reach matters in which states were so disabled.

The material success that has come to inhabitants of the states which make up this federal free trade unit has been the most impressive in the history of commerce, but the established interdependence of the states only emphasizes the necessity of protecting interstate movement of goods against local burdens and repressions. We need only consider the consequences if each of the few states that produce copper, lead, high-grade iron ore, timber, cotton, oil or gas should decree that industries located in that state shall have priority. What fantastic rivalries and dislocations and reprisals would ensue if such practices were begun! Or suppose that the field of discrimination and retaliation be industry. May Michigan provide that automobiles cannot be taken out of that State until local dealers' demands are fully met? Would she not have every argument in the favor of such a statute that can be offered in support of New York's limiting sales of milk for out-of-state shipment to protect the economic interests of her competing dealers and local consumers? Could Ohio then pounce upon the rubber-tire industry, on which she has a substantial grip, to retaliate for Michigan's auto monopoly?

Our system, fostered by the Commerce Clause, is that every farmer and every craftsman shall be encouraged to produce by the certainty that he will have free access to every market in the Nation, that no home embargoes will withhold his export, and no foreign state will by customs duties or regulations exclude them. Likewise, every consumer may look to the free competition from every producing area in the Nation to protect him from exploitation by any. Such was the vision of the Founders; such has been the doctrine of this Court which has given it reality.

*In our federal system, the States have a major role that cannot be pre-empted by the National Government.*

*— Lewis F. Powell*

## Garcia v. San Antonio Metropolitan Transit Authority
### 105 S.Ct. 1005, 469 U.S. 528 (1985)

*In 1968, the Supreme Court ruled that the federal Fair Labor Standards Act minimum wage provisions applied to state and local government employees. In* National League of Cities v. Usery (1976), *the Court overruled the 1968 case, voting 5 to 4 to hold that the federal statute could not be constitutionally applied to state and local government employees in areas of "traditional governmental functions." In 1985 in* Garcia, *again by a 5 to 4 vote, the Court again overruled itself, rejecting the 1976 decision to return to the 1968 approach. Justice Blackmun, who had cast the fifth and deciding vote the other way back in 1976, wrote the majority opinion applying the Fair Labor Standards Act to employees of a municipal transit system. Justices Powell and O'Connor wrote reasoned dissents complaining about the Court's federalism flip-flops. Justice Rehnquist bluffed, "I do not think it incumbent on those of us in dissent to spell out further the fine points of a principle that will, I am confident, in time again command the support of a majority of this Court." The* Garcia *dissenters almost made good on this bluff in a later case,* New York v. United States (1992), *ruling for the State and against the federal government, thus evidencing that this area of constitutional law is anything but settled.* Garcia *frames the debate in terms of the commerce clause, Article I, § 8, cl. 3, versus the 10th amendment, but the constitutional debate over sovereignty in a federal system is between the national government versus the states.*

**Justice Blackmun:** Our examination of this and other cases decided over the last eight years now persuades us that our approach is not only unworkable but is also inconsistent with established principles of federalism and, indeed, with those very federalism principles on which *National League of Cites v. Usery* (1976) purported to rest. That case, accordingly, is overruled.

This Court itself has made little headway in defining the scope of the state governmental functions deemed protected under *Usery*. We held that the inquiry into a particular function's "traditional" nature was merely a means of determining whether the federal statute at issue unduly handicaps "basic state prerogatives," but we have not offered an explanation of what makes one state function a "basic prerogative" and another function not basic.

We believe, however, that there is a more fundamental problem at work here. The problem is that neither the governmental/proprietary distinction nor any other that purports to separate out important governmental functions can be faithful to the role of federalism in a democratic society. The essence of our federal system is that within the realm of authority left open to them under the Constitution, the States must be equally free to engage in any activity that their citizens choose for the common weal, no matter how unorthodox or unnecessary anyone else—including the judiciary—deems state involvement to be. Any rule of state immunity that looks to the "traditional," "integral," or "necessary" nature of governmental functions inevitably invites an unelected federal judiciary to make decisions about which state policies it favors and which ones it dislikes.

We therefore now reject, as unsound in principle and unworkable in practice, a rule of state immunity from federal regulation that turns on a judicial appraisal of whether a particular governmental function is "integral" or "traditional." Any such rule leads to inconsistent results at the same time that it disserves principles of democratic self-governance, and it breeds inconsistency precisely because it is divorced from those principles. If there are to be limits on the Federal Government's power to interfere with state functions—as undoubtedly there are—we must look elsewhere to find them.

The central theme of *Usery* was that the States occupy a special position in our constitutional system and that the scope of Congress' authority under the Commerce Clause must reflect that position. Of course, the Commerce Clause by its specific language does not provide any special limitation on Congress' actions with respect to the States. It is equally true, however, that the text of the Constitution provides the beginning rather than the final answer to every inquiry into questions of federalism, for "behind the words of the constitutional provisions are postulates which limit and control." *Usery* reflected the general conviction that the Constitution precludes "the National Government from devouring the essentials of state sovereignty." In order to be faithful to the underlying federal premises of the Constitution, courts must look for the "postulates which limit and control."

What has proved problematic is not the perception that the Constitution's federal structure imposes limitations on the Commerce Clause, but rather the nature and content of those limitations. One approach to defining the limits on Congress' authority to regulate the States under the Commerce Clause is to identify certain underlying elements of political sovereignty that are deemed essential to the States' "separate and independent existence." This approach obviously underlay the Court's use of the "traditional governmental function" concept. The point of the inquiry, however, has remained to single out particular features of a State's internal governance that are deemed to be intrinsic parts of state sovereignty.

We doubt that courts ultimately can identify principled constitutional limitations on the scope of Congress' Commerce Clause powers over the States merely by relying on *a priori* definitions of state sovereignty. In part, this is because of the elusiveness of objective criteria for "fundamental" elements of state sovereignty, a problem we have witnessed in the search for "traditional governmental functions." There is, however, a more fundamental reason: the sovereignty of the States is limited by the Constitution itself. A variety of sovereign powers, for example, are withdrawn from the States.

The States unquestionably do "retain a significant measure of sovereign authority." They do so, however, only to the extent that the Constitution has not divested them of their original powers and transferred those powers to the Federal Government. In the words of James Madison to the Members of the First Congress: "Interference with the power of the States was no constitutional criterion of the power of Congress. If the power was not given, Congress could not exercise it; if given, they might exercise it, although it should interfere with the laws, or even the Constitution of the States."

As a result, to say that the Constitution assumes the continued role of the States is to say little about the nature of that role. With rare exceptions, like the guarantee, in Article IV, § 3, of state territorial integrity, the Constitution does not carve out express elements of state sovereignty that Congress may not employ its delegated powers to displace. The power of the Federal Government is a "power to be respected" as well, and the fact that the States remain sovereign as to all powers not vested in Congress or denied them by the Constitution offers no guidance about where the frontier between state and federal power lies. In short, we have no license to employ freestanding conceptions of state sovereignty when measuring congressional authority under the Commerce Clause.

When we look for the States' "residuary and inviolable sovereignty," *The Federalist No. 39*, in the shape of the constitutional scheme rather than in predetermined notions of sovereign power, a different measure of state sovereignty emerges. Apart from the limitation on federal authority inherent in the delegated nature of Congress' Article I powers, the principal means chosen by the Framers to ensure the role of the States in the federal system lies in the structure of the Federal Government itself. It is no novelty to observe that the composition of the Federal Government was designed in large part to protect the States from overreaching by Congress. The Framers thus gave the States a role in the selection both of the Executive and the Legislative Branches of the Federal Government. The States were vested with indirect influence over the House of Representatives and the Presidency by their control of electoral qualifications and their role in Presidential elections. They were given more direct influence in the Senate, where each State received equal representation and each Senator was to be selected by the legislature of his State. The significance attached to the States' equal representation in the Senate is underscored by the prohibition of any constitutional amendment divesting a State of equal representation without the State's consent.

The effectiveness of the federal political process in preserving the States' interests is apparent even today in the course of federal legislation. On the one hand, the States have been able to direct a substantial proportion of federal revenues into their own treasuries in the form of general and program-specific grants in aid. The federal role in assisting state and local governments is a longstanding one. At the same time that the States have exercised their influence to obtain federal support, they have been able to exempt themselves from a wide variety of obligations imposed by Congress under the Commerce Clause.

We realize that changes in the structure of the Federal Government have taken place since 1789, not the least of which has been the substitution of popular election of Senators by the adoption of the Seventeenth Amendment in 1913, and that these changes may work to alter the influence of the States in the federal political process. Nonetheless, against this background, we are convinced that the fundamental limitation that the constitutional scheme imposes on the Commerce Clause to protect the "States as States" is one of process rather than one of result. Any substantive restraint on the exercise of Commerce Clause powers must find its justification in the procedural nature of this basic limitation, and it must be tailored to compensate for possible failings in the national political process rather than to dictate a "sacred province of state autonomy."

Of course, we continue to recognize that the States occupy a special and specific position in our constitutional system and that the scope of Congress' authority under the Commerce Clause must reflect that position. But the principal and basic limit on the federal commerce power is that inherent in all congressional action—the built-in restraints that our system provides through state participation in federal governmental action. The political process ensures that laws that unduly burden the States will not be promulgated.

These cases do not require us to identify or define what affirmative limits the constitutional structure might impose on federal action affecting the States under the Commerce Clause. We note and accept Justice Frankfurter's observation: "The process of Constitutional adjudication does not thrive on conjuring up horrible possibilities that never happen in the real world and devising doctrines sufficiently comprehensive in detail to cover the remotest contingency. Nor need we go beyond what is required for a reasoned disposition of the kind of controversy now before the Court."

**Justice Powell:** Despite some genuflecting in the Court's opinion to the concept of federalism, today's decision effectively reduces the Tenth Amendment to meaningless rhetoric when Congress acts pursuant to the Commerce Clause.

Today's decision means that the extent to which the States may exercise their authority, when Congress purports to act under the Commerce Clause, henceforth is to be determined from time to time by political decisions made by members of the Federal Government, decisions the Court says will not be subject to judicial review. I note that it does not seem to have occurred to the Court that it—an unelected majority of five Justices—today rejects almost 200 years of the understanding of the constitutional status of federalism. In doing so, there is only a single passing reference to the Tenth Amendment. Nor is so much as a *dictum* of any court cited in support of the view that the role of the States in the federal system may depend upon the grace of elected federal officials, rather than on the Constitution as interpreted by this Court. In concluding that judicial efforts to define state immunity are unsound in principle, the Court radically departs from long-settled constitutional values and ignores the role of judicial review in our system of government.

Today's opinion does not explain how the States' role in the electoral process guarantees that particular exercises of the Commerce Clause power will not infringe on residual state sovereignty. Members of Congress are elected from the various States, but once in office they are Members of the Federal Government. Although the States participate in the Electoral College, this is hardly a reason to view the President as a representative of the States' interest against federal encroachment. We noted recently "the hydraulic pressure inherent within each of the separate Branches to exceed the outer limits of its power." The majority offers no reason to think that this pressure will not operate when Congress seeks to invoke its powers under the Commerce Clause, notwithstanding the electoral role of the States.

One can hardly imagine this Court saying that because Congress is composed of individuals, individual rights guaranteed by the Bill of Rights are amply protected by the political process. Yet, the position adopted today is indistinguishable in principle. The Tenth Amendment also is an essential part of the Bill of Rights.

The fact that Congress generally does not transgress constitutional limits on its power to reach state activities does not make judicial review any less necessary to rectify the cases in which it does do so. The States' role in our system of government is a matter of constitutional law, not of legislative grace. "The powers not delegated to the United States by the Constitution, nor prohibited by it to the States, are reserved to the States, respectively, or to the people." U.S. Const., amend. 10.

More troubling than the logical infirmities in the Court's reasoning is the result of its holding, i.e., that federal political officials, invoking the Commerce Clause, are the sole judges of the limits of their own power. This result is inconsistent with the fundamental principles of our constitutional system. *The Federalist No. 78*. At least since 1803, it has been the settled province of the federal judiciary "to say what the law is" with respect to the constitutionality of Acts of Congress. In rejecting the role of the judiciary in protecting the States from federal overreaching, the Court's opinion offers no explanation for ignoring the teaching of the most famous case in our history.

In our federal system, the States have a major role that cannot be pre-empted by the National Government. As contemporaneous writings and the debates at the ratifying conventions make clear, the States' ratification of the Constitution was predicated on this understanding of federalism. Indeed, the Tenth Amendment was adopted specifically to ensure that the important role promised the States by the proponents of the Constitution was realized.

Much of the initial opposition to the Constitution was rooted in the fear that the National Government would be too powerful and eventually would eliminate the States as viable political entities. As a result, eight States voted for the Constitution only after proposing amendments to be adopted after ratification. All eight of these included among their recommendations some version of what later became the Tenth Amendment. So strong was the concern that the proposed Constitution was seriously defective without a specific bill of rights, including a provision reserving powers to the States, that in order to secure the votes for ratification, the Federalists eventually conceded that such provisions were necessary. It was thus generally agreed that consideration of a bill of rights would be among the first business of the new Congress. Accordingly, the 10 Amendments that we know as the Bill of Rights were proposed and adopted early in the first session of the First Congress.

This history, which the Court simply ignores, documents the integral role of the Tenth Amendment in our constitutional theory. It exposes as well, I believe, the fundamental character of the Court's error today. Far from being "unsound in principle," judicial enforcement of the Tenth Amendment is essential to maintaining the federal system so carefully designed by the Framers and adopted in the Constitution.

The Framers had definite ideas about the nature of the Constitution's division of authority between the Federal and State Governments. In *The Federalist No. 39*, for example, James Madison explained this division by drawing a series of contrasts between the attributes of a "national" government and those of the government to be established by the Constitution. While a national form of government would possess an "indefinite supremacy over all persons and things," the form of government contemplated by the Constitution instead consisted of "local or municipal authorities which form distinct and independent portions of the supremacy, no more subject within their respective spheres to the general authority, than the general authority is subject to them, within its own sphere." Under the Constitution, the sphere of the proposed government extended to jurisdiction of "certain enumerated objects only, leaving to the several States a residuary and inviolable sovereignty over all other objects."

Madison elaborated on the content of these separate spheres of sovereignty in *The Federalist No. 45*: "The powers delegated by the proposed Constitution to the Federal Government, are few and defined. Those which are to remain in the State Governments are numerous and indefinite. The former will be exercised principally on external objects, as war, peace, negotiation, and foreign commerce. The powers reserved to the several States will extend to all the objects, which, in the ordinary course of affairs, concern the lives, liberties and properties of the people; and the internal order, improvement, and prosperity of the State."

Madison considered that the operations of the Federal Government would be "most extensive and important in times of war and danger; those of the State Governments in times of peace and security." As a result of this division of powers, the state governments generally would be more important than the Federal Government.

The Framers believed that the separate sphere of sovereignty reserved to the States would ensure that the States would serve as an effective "counterpoise" to the power of the Federal Government. The States would serve this essential role because they would attract and retain the loyalty of their citizens. The roots of such loyalty, the Founders thought, were found in the objects peculiar to state government. For example, Alexander Hamilton argued that the States "regulate all those personal interests and familiar concerns to which the sensibility of individuals is more immediately awake." *The Federalist No. 17*. Thus, he maintained that the people would perceive the States as "the immediate and visible guardian of life and property," a fact which "contributes more than any other circumstance to impressing upon the minds of the people affection, esteem and reverence towards the government." Madison took the same position, explaining that "the people will be more familiarly and minutely conversant" with the business of state governments, and "with the members of these, will a greater proportion of the people have the ties of personal acquaintance and friendship, and of family and party attachments." *The Federalist No. 46.* Like Hamilton, Madison saw the States' involvement in the everyday concerns of the people as the source of their citizens' loyalty.

Thus, the harm to the States that results from federal overreaching under the Commerce Clause is not simply a matter of dollars and cents. Nor is it a matter of the wisdom or folly of certain policy choices. Rather, by usurping functions traditionally performed by the States, federal overreaching under the Commerce Clause undermines the constitutionally mandated balance of power between the States and the Federal Government, a balance designed to protect our fundamental liberties.

The emasculation of the powers of the States that can result from the Court's decision is predicated on the Commerce Clause as a power "delegated to the United States" by the Constitution. The relevant language states: "Congress shall have power to regulate Commerce with foreign Nations, and among the several States, and with the Indian Tribes." Art. I, § 8, cl. 3. Section eight identifies a score of powers, listing the authority to lay taxes, borrow money on the credit of the United States, pay its debts, and provide for the common defense and the general welfare before its brief reference to "Commerce." It is clear from the debates leading up to the adoption of the Constitution that the commerce to be regulated was that which the States themselves lacked the practical capability to regulate. Indeed, the language of the Clause itself focuses on activities that only a National Government could regulate: commerce with foreign nations and Indian tribes and "among" the several States.

To be sure, this Court has construed the Commerce Clause to accommodate unanticipated changes over the past two centuries. As these changes have occurred, the Court has had to decide whether the Federal Government has exceeded its authority by regulating activities beyond the capability of a single State to regulate or beyond legitimate federal interests that outweighed the authority and interests of the States. In so doing, however, the Court properly has been mindful of the essential role of the States in our federal system.

*Usery* was faithful to history in its understanding of federalism. In contrast, the Court today propounds a view of federalism that pays only lip service to the role of the States. It fails to recognize the broad, yet specific areas of sovereignty that the Framers intended the States to retain. Indeed, the Court barely acknowledges that the Tenth Amendment exists. That Amendment states explicitly that "the powers not delegated to the United States are reserved to the States." The Court recasts this language to say that the States retain their sovereign powers "only to the extent that the Constitution has not divested them of their original powers and transferred those powers to the Federal Government." This rephrasing is not a distinction without a difference; rather, it reflects the Court's unprecedented view that Congress is free under the Commerce Clause to assume a State's traditional sovereign power, and to do so without judicial review of its action. Indeed, the Court's view of federalism appears to relegate the States to precisely the trivial role that opponents of the Constitution feared they would occupy.

Although the Court's opinion purports to recognize that the States retain some sovereign power, it does not identify even a single aspect of state authority that would remain when the Commerce Clause is invoked to justify federal regulation. Justice Douglas, once wrote presciently that the Court's reading of the Commerce Clause would enable "the National Government to devour the essentials of state sovereignty, though that sovereignty is attested by the Tenth Amendment." Today's decision makes Justice Douglas' fear once again a realistic one.

**Justice O'Connor:** In my view, federalism cannot be reduced to the weak "essence" distilled by the majority today. There is more to federalism than the nature of the constraints that can be imposed on the States in "the realm of authority left open to them by the Constitution." The central issue of federalism, of course, is whether any realm is left open to the States by the Constitution—whether any area remains in which a State may act free of federal interference. "The issue is whether the federal system has any legal substance, any core of constitutional right that courts will enforce." The true "essence" of federalism is that the States as States have legitimate interests which the National Government is bound to respect even though its laws are supreme. If federalism so conceived and so carefully cultivated by the Framers of our Constitution is to remain meaningful, this Court cannot abdicate its constitutional responsibility to oversee the Federal Government's compliance with its duty to respect the legitimate interests of the States.

Due to the emergence of an integrated and industrialized national economy, this Court has been required to examine and review a breathtaking expansion of the powers of Congress. In doing so, the Court correctly perceived that the Framers of our Constitution intended Congress to have sufficient power to address national problems. But the Framers were not single-minded. The Constitution is animated by an array of intentions. Just as surely as the Framers envisioned a National Government capable of solving national problems, they also envisioned a republic whose vitality was assured by the diffusion of power not only among the branches of the Federal Government, but also between the Federal Government and the States. In the 18th century these intentions did not conflict because technology had not yet converted every local problem into a national one. A conflict has now emerged, and the Court today retreats rather than reconcile the Constitution's dual concerns for federalism and an effective commerce power.

We would do well to recall the constitutional basis for federalism and the development of the commerce power which has come to displace it. The text of the Constitution does not define the precise scope of state authority other than to specify, in the Tenth Amendment, that the powers not delegated to the United States by the Constitution are reserved to the States. In the view of the Framers, however, this did not leave state authority weak or defenseless; the powers delegated to the United States, after all, were "few and defined." *The Federalist No. 45.* The Framers' comments indicate that the sphere of state activity was to be a significant one. The States were to retain authority over those local concerns of greatest relevance and importance to the people. *The Federalist No. 17.* This division of authority, according to Madison, would produce efficient government and protect the rights of the people: "In a single republic, all the power surrendered by the people, is submitted to the administration of a single government; and usurpations are guarded against by a division of the government into distinct and separate departments. In the compound republic of America, the power surrendered by the people, is first divided between two distinct governments, and then the portion allotted to each, subdivided among distinct and separate departments. Hence a double security arises to the rights of the people. The different governments will controul each other; at the same time that each will be controuled by itself." *The Federalist No. 51.*

Of course, one of the "few and defined" powers delegated to the National Congress was the power "To regulate Commerce with foreign Nations, and among the several States, and with the Indian Tribes." Art. I, § 8, cl. 3. The Framers perceived the interstate commerce power to be important but limited, and expected that it would be used primarily if not exclusively to remove interstate tariffs and to regulate maritime affairs and large-scale mercantile enterprise. This perception of a narrow commerce power is important not because it suggests that the commerce power should be as narrowly construed today. Rather, it explains why the Framers could believe the Constitution assured significant state authority even as it bestowed a range of powers, including the commerce power, on the Congress. In an era when interstate commerce represented a tiny fraction of economic activity and most goods and services were produced and consumed close to home, the interstate commerce power left a broad range of activities beyond the reach of Congress.

In the decades since ratification of the Constitution, interstate economic activity has steadily expanded. Industrialization, coupled with advances in transportation and communications, has created a national economy in which virtually every activity occurring within the borders of a State plays a part. The expansion and integration of the national economy brought with it a coordinate expansion in the scope of national problems. This Court has been increasingly generous in its interpretation of the commerce power of Congress, primarily to assure that the National Government would be able to deal with national economic problems. The Court embraced the notion that Congress can regulate intrastate activities that affect interstate commerce as surely as it can regulate interstate commerce directly. Even if a particular individual's activity has no perceptible interstate effect, it can be reached by Congress through regulation of that class of activity in general as long as that class, considered as a whole, affects interstate commerce.

Incidental to this expansion of the commerce power, Congress has been given an ability it lacked prior to the emergence of an integrated national economy. Because virtually every state activity, like virtually every activity of a private individual, arguably "affects" interstate commerce, Congress can now supplant the States from the significant sphere of activities envisioned for them by the Framers. It is in this context that recent changes in the workings of Congress, such as the direct election of Senators and the expanded influence of national interest groups, become relevant. These changes may well have lessened the weight Congress gives to the legitimate interests of States as States. As a result, there is now a real risk that Congress will gradually erase the diffusion of power between State and Nation on which the Framers based their faith in the efficiency and vitality of our Republic.

It would be erroneous, however, to conclude that the Supreme Court was blind to the threat to federalism when it expanded the commerce power. The Court based the expansion on the authority of Congress, through the Necessary and Proper Clause, "to resort to all means for the exercise of a granted power which are appropriate and plainly adapted to the permitted end." It is through this reasoning that an intrastate activity "affecting" interstate commerce can be reached through the commerce power.

It is worth recalling the cited passage that lies at the source of the recent expansion of the commerce power. "Let the end be legitimate, let it be within the scope of the constitution," Chief Justice Marshall said in 1819, "and all means which are appropriate, which are plainly adapted to that end, which are not prohibited, but consist with the letter and spirit of the constitution, are constitutional." The spirit of the Tenth Amendment, of course, is that the States will retain their integrity in a system in which the laws of the United States are nevertheless supreme.

It is not enough that the "end be legitimate"; the means to that end chosen by Congress must not contravene the spirit of the Constitution. Thus many of this Court's decisions acknowledge that the means by which national power is exercised must take into account concerns for state autonomy. For example, Congress might rationally conclude that the location a State chooses for its capital may affect interstate commerce, but the Court has suggested that Congress would nevertheless be barred from dictating that location because such an exercise of a delegated power would undermine the state sovereignty inherent in the Tenth Amendment. The underlying principle is consistent: state autonomy is a relevant factor in assessing the means by which Congress exercises its powers.

This principle requires the Court to enforce affirmative limits on federal regulation of the States to complement the judicially crafted expansion of the interstate commerce power. *Usery* represented an attempt to define such limits. The Court today rejects *Usery* and washes its hands of all efforts to protect the

States. In the process, the Court opines that unwarranted federal encroachments on state authority are and will remain "'horrible possibilities that never happen in the real world.'"

The last two decades have seen an unprecedented growth of federal regulatory activity, as the majority itself acknowledges. Today, as federal legislation and coercive grant programs have expanded to embrace innumerable activities that were once viewed as local, the burden of persuasion has surely shifted, and the extraordinary has become ordinary. The political process has not protected against these encroachments on state activities, even though they directly impinge on a State's ability to make and enforce its laws. With the abandonment of *Usery*, all that stands between the remaining essentials of state sovereignty and Congress is the latter's underdeveloped capacity for self-restraint.

The problems of federalism in an integrated national economy are capable of more responsible resolution than holding that the States as States retain no status apart from that which Congress chooses to let them retain. The proper resolution, I suggest, lies in weighing state autonomy as a factor in the balance when interpreting the means by which Congress can exercise its authority on the States as States. It is insufficient, in assessing the validity of congressional regulation of a State pursuant to the commerce power, to ask only whether the same regulation would be valid if enforced against a private party. That reasoning, embodied in the majority opinion, is inconsistent with the spirit of our Constitution. It remains relevant that a State is being regulated, as *Usery* and every recent case have recognized. As far as the Constitution is concerned, a State should not be equated with any private litigant. Instead, the autonomy of a State is an essential component of federalism.

It has been difficult for this Court to craft bright lines defining the scope of the state autonomy protected by *Usery*. Such difficulty is to be expected whenever constitutional concerns as important as federalism and the effectiveness of the commerce power come into conflict. Regardless of the difficulty, it is and will remain the duty of this Court to reconcile these concerns in the final instance. That the Court shuns the task today by appealing to the "essence of federalism" can provide scant comfort to those who believe our federal system requires something more than a unitary, centralized government. I would not shirk the duty acknowledged by *Usery* and its progeny, and I share the belief that this Court will in time again assume its constitutional responsibility.

*The history of the judicial struggle to interpret the Commerce Clause during the transition from the economic system the Founders knew to the single, national market still emergent in our own era counsels great restraint before the Court determines that the Clause is insufficient to support an exercise of the national power.*

*— Anthony M. Kennedy*

## United States v. Lopez
### 115 S.Ct. 1624 (1995)

*This 5 to 4 ruling is the latest major reinterpretation of the commerce clause, Article I, § 8, cl. 3. Chief Justice Rehnquist wrote the opinion for the Court, carefully moving through two centuries of contradictory holdings and opinions that mark the judicial tacking back and forth between extreme views of national versus state powers. He concluded that the Gun-Free School Zones Act of 1990, which made it a federal felony to possess a firearm within 1,000 feet of a school zone, exceeded the Congress' authority to regulate interstate commerce. Justice Breyer filed the principal dissent, which amounts to a strident brief with an appendix, longer than the opinion, that goes on for page-after-page of social science and government studies linking violence in schools with commercial concerns. The four Justices in dissent worried that the majority's decision called into question fifty years of judicial decisions as well as countless federal statutes in virtually every area of national life going all the way back to the New Deal. Justice Kennedy wrote a concurring opinion, which is excerpted here. It reads like a lecture by a constitutional law professor, which he once was. He seems to be attempting to make more sense out of the Supreme Court's interpretations than may be possible.*

**Justice Kennedy:** The history of the judicial struggle to interpret the Commerce Clause during the transition from the economic system the Founders knew to the single, national market still emergent in our own era counsels great restraint before the Court determines that the Clause is insufficient to support an exercise of the national power. That history gives me some pause about today's decision, but I join the Court's opinion with these observations on what I conceive to be its necessary though limited holding.

In 1824, Chief Justice Marshall announced that the national authority reaches "that commerce which concerns more States than one" and that the commerce power "is complete in itself, may be exercised to its utmost extent, and acknowledges no limitations, other than are prescribed in the constitution." His statements can be understood now as an early and authoritative recognition that the Commerce Clause grants Congress extensive power and ample discretion to determine its appropriate exercise. The progression of our Commerce Clause cases from 1824 to the present was not marked, however, by a coherent or consistent course of interpretation; for neither the course of technological advance nor the foundational principles for the jurisprudence itself were self-evident to the courts that sought to resolve contemporary disputes by enduring principles.

The history of our Commerce Clause decisions contains at least two lessons of relevance to this case. The first, as stated at the outset, is the imprecision of content-based boundaries used without more to define the limits of the Commerce Clause. The second, related to the first but of even greater consequence, is that the Court as an institution and the legal system as a whole have an immense stake in the stability of our Commerce Clause jurisprudence as it has evolved to this point. *Stare decisis* operates with great force in counseling us not to call in question the essential principles now in place respecting the congressional power to regulate transactions of a commercial nature. That fundamental restraint on our power forecloses us from reverting to an understanding of commerce that would serve only an 18th-century economy, dependent then upon production and trading practices that had changed but little over the preceding centuries; it also mandates against returning to the time when congressional authority to regulate undoubted commercial activities was limited by a judicial determination that those matters had an insufficient connection to an interstate system. Congress can regulate in the commercial sphere on the assumption that we have a single market and a unified purpose to build a stable national economy.

In referring to the whole subject of the federal and state balance, we said this just three Terms ago: "This framework has been sufficiently flexible over the past two centuries to allow for enormous changes in the nature of government. The Federal

Government undertakes activities today that would have been unimaginable to the Framers in two senses: first, because the Framers would not have conceived that any government would conduct such activities; and second, because the Framers would not have believed that the Federal Government, rather than the States, would assume such responsibilities. Yet the powers conferred upon the Federal Government by the Constitution were phrased in language broad enough to allow for the expansion of the Federal Government's role."

It does not follow, however, that in every instance the Court lacks the authority and responsibility to review congressional attempts to alter the federal balance. This case requires us to consider our place in the design of the Government and to appreciate the significance of federalism in the whole structure of the Constitution.

Of the various structural elements in the Constitution, separation of powers, checks and balances, judicial review, and federalism, only concerning the last does there seem to be much uncertainty respecting the existence, and the content, of standards that allow the judiciary to play a significant role in maintaining the design contemplated by the Framers. Although the resolution of specific cases has proved difficult, we have derived from the Constitution workable standards to assist in preserving separation of powers and checks and balances. These standards are by now well accepted. Judicial review is also established beyond question, and though we may differ when applying its principles, its legitimacy is undoubted. Our role in preserving the federal balance seems more tenuous.

There is irony in this, because of the four structural elements in the Constitution just mentioned, federalism was the unique contribution of the Framers to political science and political theory. Though on the surface the idea may seem counterintuitive, it was the insight of the Framers that freedom was enhanced by the creation of two governments, not one. "In the compound republic of America, the power surrendered by the people is first divided between two distinct governments, and then the portion allotted to each subdivided among distinct and separate departments. Hence a double security arises to the rights of the people. The different governments will control each other, at the same time that each will be controlled by itself." *The Federalist No. 51.*

The theory that two governments accord more liberty than one requires for its realization two distinct and discernable lines of political accountability: one between the citizens and the Federal Government; the second between the citizens and the States. If, as Madison expected, the federal and state governments are to control each other, *The Federalist No. 51*, and hold each other in check by competing for the affections of the people, *The Federalist No. 46*, those citizens must have some means of knowing which of the two governments to hold accountable for the failure to perform a given function. This Court has noted, "Federalism serves to assign political responsibility, not to obscure it." Were the Federal Government to take over the regulation of entire areas of traditional state concern, areas having nothing to do with the regulation of commercial activities, the boundaries between the spheres of federal and state authority would blur and political responsibility would become illusory. The resultant inability to hold either branch of the government answerable to the citizens is more dangerous even than devolving too much authority to the remote central power.

To be sure, one conclusion that could be drawn from *The Federalist Papers* is that the balance between national and state power is entrusted in its entirety to the political process. Madison's observation that "the people ought not surely to be precluded from giving most of their confidence where they may discover it to be most due," *The Federalist No. 46*, can be interpreted to say that the essence of responsibility for a shift in power from the State to the Federal Government rests upon a political judgment, though he added assurance that "the State governments could have little to apprehend, because it is only within a certain sphere that the federal power can, in the nature of things, be advantageously administered." Whatever the judicial role, it is axiomatic that Congress does have substantial discretion and control over the federal balance.

For these reasons, it would be mistaken and mischievous for the political branches to forget that the sworn obligation to preserve and protect the Constitution in maintaining the federal balance is their own in the first and primary instance. In the Webster-Hayne Debates of last century, and in the debates of the 1960's over the Civil Rights Acts, some Congresses have accepted responsibility to confront the great questions of the proper federal balance in terms of lasting consequences for the constitutional design. The political branches of the Government must fulfill this grave constitutional obligation if democratic liberty and the federalism that secures it are to endure.

At the same time, the absence of structural mechanisms to require those officials to undertake this principled task, and the momentary political convenience often attendant upon their failure to do so, argue against a complete renunciation of the judicial role. Although it is the obligation of all officers of the Government to respect the constitutional design, the federal balance is too essential a part of our constitutional structure and plays too vital a role in securing freedom for us to admit inability to intervene when one or the other level of Government has tipped the scales too far.

Our ability to preserve this principle under the Commerce Clause has presented a much greater challenge. As Felix Frankfurter once explained, "This clause has throughout the Court's history been the chief source of its adjudications regarding federalism," and "no other body of opinions affords a fairer or more revealing test of judicial qualities." But as the branch whose distinctive duty it is to declare "what the law is," we are often called upon to resolve questions of constitutional law not susceptible to the mechanical application of bright and clear lines. The substantial element of political judgment in Commerce Clause matters leaves our institutional capacity to intervene more in doubt than when we decide cases, for instance, under the Bill of Rights even though clear and bright lines are often absent in the latter class of disputes. But our cases do not teach that we have no role at all in determining the meaning of the Commerce Clause.

The statute before us upsets the federal balance to a degree that renders it an unconstitutional assertion of the commerce power, and our intervention is required. As the Chief Justice explains in the opinion for the Court, unlike the earlier cases to come before the Court here neither the actors nor their conduct have a commercial character, and neither the purposes nor the design of the statute have an evident commercial nexus. The statute makes the simple possession of a gun within 1,000 feet of the grounds of the school a federal criminal offense. In a sense any conduct in this interdependent world of ours has an ultimate commercial origin or consequence, but we have not yet said the commerce power may reach so far. If Congress attempts that extension, then at the least we must inquire whether the exercise of national power seeks to intrude upon an area of traditional state concern.

An interference of these dimensions occurs here, for it is well established that education is a traditional concern of the States. The proximity to schools, including of course schools owned and operated by the States or their subdivisions, is the very premise for making the conduct criminal. In these circumstances, we have a particular duty to insure that the federal-state balance is not destroyed.

While it is doubtful that any State, or indeed any reasonable person, would argue that it is wise policy to allow students to carry guns on school premises, considerable disagreement exists about how best to accomplish that goal. In this circumstance, the theory and utility of our federalism are revealed, for the States may perform their role as laboratories for experimentation to devise various solutions where the best solution is far from clear.

If a State or municipality determines that harsh criminal sanctions are necessary and wise to deter students from carrying guns on school premises, the reserved powers of the States are sufficient to enact those measures. Indeed, over 40 States already have criminal laws outlawing the possession of firearms on or near school grounds.

Other, more practicable means to rid the schools of guns may be thought by the citizens of some States to be preferable for the safety and welfare of the schools those States are charged with maintaining. These might include inducements to inform on violators where the information leads to arrests or confiscation of the guns, programs to encourage the voluntary surrender of guns with some provision for amnesty, penalties imposed on parents or guardians for failure to supervise the child, laws providing for suspension or expulsion of gun-toting students, or programs for expulsion with assignment to special facilities.

The statute now before us forecloses the States from experimenting and exercising their own judgment in an area to which States lay claim by right of history and expertise, and it does so by regulating an activity beyond the realm of commerce in the ordinary and usual sense of that term. The tendency of this statute to displace state regulation in areas of traditional state concern is evident from its territorial operation. There are over 100,000 elementary and secondary schools in the United States. Each of these now has an invisible federal zone extending 1,000 feet beyond the (often irregular) boundaries of the school property. In some communities no doubt it would be difficult to navigate without infringing on those zones. Yet throughout these areas, school officials would find their own programs for the prohibition of guns in danger of displacement by the federal authority unless the State chooses to enact a parallel rule.

This is not a case where the etiquette of federalism has been violated by a formal command from the National Government directing the State to enact a certain policy, or to organize its governmental functions in a certain way. While the intrusion on state sovereignty may not be as severe in this instance as in some of our recent Tenth Amendment cases, the intrusion is nonetheless significant. Absent a stronger connection or identification with commercial concerns that are central to the Commerce Clause, that interference contradicts the federal balance the Framers designed and that this Court is obliged to enforce.

*The fact is that in the 114 years since the doctrine of the negative Commerce Clause was formally adopted as holding of this Court, and in the 50 years prior to that in which it was alluded to in various dicta of the Court, our applications of the doctrine have, not to put too fine a point on the matter, made no sense.*

*— Antonin Scalia*

## Tyler Pipe Industries, Inc. v. Washington Dept. of Revenue
### 107 S.Ct. 2810, 483 U.S. 232 (1987)

*Scholars have engaged in a lively debate over the pros and cons of the High Court's "dormant or negative" commerce clause jurisprudence. But two things are clear: a majority of the Justices continues to invoke this theory regularly and Justice Scalia does not like it. Here he dissents to explain why he thinks the Court has been wrong for the last 170 years, going back to John Marshall's time. This judicially-created doctrine, over time, has reduced the scope of state authority to regulate the economy. The idea is that the commerce clause is not merely an explicit enumeration of an affirmative power to Congress to regulate commerce among the several States by enacting regulatory legislation. When Congress is silent, and has not legislated, the negative power of the clause, as interpreted by the Court, imposes some implied limits on the States in the regulation of interstate commerce. A state regulation cannot impermissibly discriminate against interstate business in favor of local interests; the state regulation may not impose indirect or incidental burdens on interstate commerce that are unduly excessive when compared to the local benefit. The Justices themselves perform this balancing. When the Court declares a violation of the negative commerce clause, it is interpreting the sounds of silence. Congress can contradict the Court's understanding, however, and enact legislation to ratify a state regulation that otherwise would be deemed to be prohibited by the negative commerce clause. This is not really a statutory reversal of the Court's constitutional pronouncement, so the theory posits, but rather the Congress, in effect, is adopting a new, valid federal regu-*

*lation. Congress having spoken, the Court must listen. This aspect of the doctrine highlights what Justice Scalia finds anathema: "I believe that this jurisprudence takes us, self-consciously and avowedly, beyond the judicial role itself."*

**Justice Scalia:** It takes no more than our opinions this Term, and the number of prior decisions they explicitly or implicitly overrule, to demonstrate that the practical results we have educed from the so-called "negative" Commerce Clause form not a rock but a "quagmire." Nor is this a recent liquefaction. The fact is that in the 114 years since the doctrine of the negative Commerce Clause was formally adopted as holding of this Court, and in the 50 years prior to that in which it was alluded to in various dicta of the Court, our applications of the doctrine have, not to put too fine a point on the matter, made no sense.

In his history of the first hundred years of this Court, Professor David Currie's discussion of the Commerce Clause decisions of the Marshall and Taney Courts is summed up by his assessment of one of the leading decisions: "Taken by itself, the decision may appear arbitrary, conclusory, and irreconcilable with the constitutional text. Nevertheless, anyone who has slogged through the Augean agglomeration preceding Justice Curtis's labors must find them scarcely less impressive than those of the old stable-cleaner himself." He concludes his discussion of the Chase Court's Commerce Clause jurisprudence by noting: "In doctrinal terms the Court's efforts in this field can be described only as a disaster." And the Waite Court receives the following testimonial: "It is a relief that with that decision we have reached the end of the commerce clause decisions of the Waite period, for they do not make elevating reading." Future commentators are not likely to treat recent eras much more tenderly.

That uncertainty in application has been attributable in no small part to the lack of any clear theoretical underpinning for judicial "enforcement" of the Commerce Clause. The text of the Clause states that "Congress shall have Power to regulate Commerce with foreign Nations, and among the several States, and with the Indian Tribes." Art. I, § 8, cl. 3. On its face, this is a charter for Congress, not the courts, to ensure "an area of trade free from interference by the States." The pre-emption of state legislation would automatically follow, of course, if the grant of power to Congress to regulate interstate commerce were exclusive, as Charles Pinckney's draft constitution would have provided, and as John Marshall at one point seemed to believe it was. However, unlike the District Clause, which empowers Congress "To exercise exclusive Legislation," Art. I, § 8, cl. 17, the language of the Commerce Clause gives no indication of exclusivity. Nor can one assume generally that Congress' Article I powers are exclusive; many of them plainly coexist with concurrent authority in the States. Furthermore, there is no correlative denial of power over commerce to the States in Art. I, § 10, as there is, for example, with the power to coin money or make treaties. And both the States and Congress assumed from the date of ratification that at least some state laws regulating commerce were valid. The exclusivity rationale is infinitely less attractive today than it was in 1847. Now that we know from our precedents that interstate commerce embraces such activities as growing wheat for home consumption, and local loan sharking, it is more difficult to imagine what state activity would survive an exclusive Commerce Clause than to imagine what would be precluded.

Another approach to theoretical justification for judicial enforcement of the Commerce Clause is to assert, as did Justice Curtis in dicta in 1852 that "whatever subjects of this power are in their nature national, or admit only of one uniform system, or plan of regulation, may justly be said to be of such a nature as to require exclusive legislation by Congress." That would perhaps be a wise rule to adopt (though it is hard to see why judges rather than legislators are fit to determine what areas of commerce "in their nature" require national regulation), but it has the misfortune of finding no conceivable basis in the text of the Commerce Clause, which treats "Commerce among the several States" as a unitary subject. And attempting to limit the Clause's pre-emptive effect to state laws intended to regulate commerce (as opposed to those intended, for example, to promote health), while perhaps a textually possible construction of the phrase "regulate Commerce," is a most unlikely one. Distinguishing between laws with the purpose of regulating commerce and "police power" statutes with that effect is more interesting as a metaphysical exercise than useful as a practical technique for marking out the powers of separate sovereigns.

The least plausible theoretical justification of all is the idea that in enforcing the negative Commerce Clause the Court is not applying a constitutional command at all, but is merely interpreting the will of Congress, whose silence in certain fields of interstate commerce (but not in others) is to be taken as a prohibition of regulation. There is no conceivable reason why congressional inaction under the Commerce Clause should be deemed to have the same pre-emptive effect elsewhere accorded only to congressional action. There, as elsewhere, "Congress' silence is just that—silence." Professor Currie has noted "the recurring fallacy that in some undefined cases congressional inaction was to be treated as if it were permissive or prohibitory legislation—though the Constitution makes clear that Congress can act only by affirmative vote of both Houses." Unfortunately, this "legislation by inaction" theory of the negative Commerce Clause seems to be the only basis for the doctrine, relied upon by this Court, that Congress can authorize States to enact legislation that would otherwise violate the negative Commerce Clause. Nothing else could explain the principle that what was invalid state action can be rendered valid state action through "congressional consent." There is surely no area in which Congress can permit the States to violate the Constitution. Justice Curtis, to whom there had not occurred the theory of congressional legislation by inaction, wrote of the relationship between States and the negative Commerce Clause as follows: "If the States were divested of the power to legislate on this subject by the grant of the commercial power to Congress, it is plain this Act could not confer upon them power thus to legislate. If the Constitution excluded the States from making any law regulating commerce, certainly Congress cannot regrant, or in any manner reconvey to the States that power."

The historical record provides no grounds for reading the Commerce Clause to be other than what it says—an authorization for Congress to regulate commerce. The strongest evidence in favor of a negative Commerce Clause—that version of it which renders federal authority over interstate commerce exclusive—is James Madison's comment during the Convention: "Whether the States are now restrained from laying tonnage duties depends on the extent of the power 'to regulate commerce.' These terms are vague but seem to exclude this power of the States." This comment, however, came during discussion of what became Art. I, § 10, cl. 3: "No State shall, without the Consent of Congress, lay any Duty of Tonnage." The fact that it is difficult to conceive how the power to regulate commerce would not include the power to impose duties; and the fact that, despite this apparent coverage, the Convention went on to adopt a provision prohibiting States from levying duties on tonnage without congressional approval; suggest that Madison's assumption of exclusivity of the federal commerce power was ill considered and not generally shared.

Against this mere shadow of historical support there is the overwhelming reality that the Commerce Clause, in its broad outlines, was not a major subject of controversy, neither during the constitutional debates nor in the ratifying conventions. Instead, there was "nearly universal agreement that the federal government should be given the power of regulating commerce," in much the form provided. In his study of the early commerce clause decisions, then-Professor Felix Frankfurter noted, "The records disclose no constructive criticisms by the states of the commerce clause as proposed to them." In *The Federalist Papers*, Madison and Hamilton wrote numerous discourses on the virtues of free trade and the need for uniformity and national control of commercial regulation, see *The Federalist Papers, Nos. 7, 11, 22, 42 & 53*, but said little of substance specifically about the Commerce Clause—and that little was addressed primarily to foreign and Indian trade. Madison does not seem to have exaggerated when he described the Commerce Clause as an addition to the powers of the National Government "which few oppose and from which no apprehensions are entertained." *The Federalist Papers, No. 45*. I think it beyond question that many "apprehensions" would have been "entertained" if supporters of the Constitution had hinted that the Commerce Clause, despite its language, gave this Court the power it has since assumed. As Justice Frankfurter pungently put it: "the doctrine that state authority must be subject to such limitations as the Court finds it necessary to apply for the protection of the national community is an audacious doctrine, which, one may be sure, would hardly have been publicly avowed in support of the adoption of the Constitution."

In sum, to the extent that we have gone beyond guarding against rank discrimination against citizens of other States—which is regulated not by the Commerce Clause but by the Privileges and Immunities Clause, U.S. Const., Art. IV, § 2, cl. 1 ("The Citizens of each State shall be entitled to all Privileges and Immunities of Citizens in the several States")—the Court for over a century has engaged in an enterprise that it has been unable to justify by textual support or even coherent nontextual theory, that it was almost certainly not intended to undertake, and that it has not undertaken very well. It is astonishing that we should be expanding our beachhead in this impoverished territory, rather than being satisfied with what we have already acquired by a sort of intellectual adverse possession.

*The Congress manifestly is not permitted to abdicate or to transfer to others the essential legislative functions with which it is thus vested.*

*— Charles Evans Hughes*

## Panama Refining Co. v. Ryan
### 55 S.Ct. 241, 293 U.S. 388 (1935)

*Sometimes called the "hot oil case," this was a rather inauspicious debut before the Court for Franklin D. Roosevelt's New Deal program. The National Industrial Recovery Act of 1933 was declared unconstitutional by a vote of 8 to 1 and the opinion was authored by the Chief Justice. During the Great Depression, oil prices plummeted. The oil-producing States pressured Congress for a national solution to raise and stabilize prices. The NIRA authorized the President to prohibit interstate shipment of petroleum produced in excess of established quotas, i.e., "hot oil." This was the first time in history that the Court invalidated federal legislation because it delegated legislative authority to the Executive branch without adequate standards for the exercise of discretion. A second similar holding was contemporaneously delivered in the "sick-chicken case,"* Schechter Poultry Corp. v. United States *(1935). These are the only two invocations of the delegation doctrine by the Supreme Court to invalidate legislation. A few years later the delegation doctrine was transformed, by a Supreme Court which had been transformed by Roosevelt appointments, into nothing more than a rationalizing principle for upholding wholesale transfers of legislative power to executive branch agencies. Thus the modern administrative state was rendered constitutional. In his lone dissent favoring the federal "hot oil" regulations, Justice Cardozo anticipated the tolerant attitude of those future courts: "The separation of powers between the Executive and Congress is not a doctrinaire concept to be made use of with pedantic rigor. There must be sensible approximation, there must be elasticity of adjustment, in response to the practical necessities of government, which cannot foresee today the developments of tomorrow in their nearly infinite variety."*

**Chief Justice Hughes:** Section 9 of the statute is assailed upon the ground that it is an unconstitutional delegation of legislative power. The section purports to authorize the President to pass a prohibitory law. The subject to which this authority relates is defined. It is the transportation in interstate and foreign commerce of petroleum and petroleum products which are produced or withdrawn from storage in excess of the amount permitted by state authority. Assuming for the present purpose, without deciding, that the Congress has power to interdict the transportation of that excess in interstate and foreign commerce, the question whether that transportation shall be prohibited by law is obviously one of legislative policy. Accordingly, we look to the statute to see whether the Congress has declared a policy with respect to that subject; whether the Congress has set up a standard for the President's action; whether the Congress has required any finding by the President in the exercise of the authority to enact the prohibition.

Section 9 is brief and unambiguous. It does not attempt to control the production of petroleum and petroleum products within a state. It does not seek to lay down rules for the guidance of state Legislatures or state officers. It leaves to the states and to their constituted authorities the determination of what production shall be permitted. It does not qualify the President's authority by reference to the basis or extent of the state's limitation of production. Section 9 does not state whether or in what circumstances or under what conditions the President is to prohibit the transportation of the amount of petroleum or petroleum products produced in excess of the state's permission. It establishes no criterion to govern the President's course. It does not require any finding by the President as a condition of his action. The Congress in section 9 thus declares no policy as to the transportation of the excess production. So far as this section is concerned, it gives to the President an unlimited authority to determine the policy and to lay down the prohibition, or not to lay it down, as he may see fit. And disobedience to his order is made a crime punishable by fine and imprisonment.

We turn to the other provisions of the act. The first section is a "declaration of policy." This general outline of policy contains nothing as to the circumstances or conditions in which transportation of petroleum or petroleum products should be prohibited—nothing as to the policy of prohibiting or not prohibiting the transportation of production exceeding what the states allow. The general policy declared is "to remove obstructions to the free flow of interstate and foreign commerce." As to production, the section lays down no policy of limitation. It favors the fullest possible utilization of the present productive capacity of industries. It speaks, parenthetically, of a possible temporary restriction of production, but of what, or in what circumstances, it gives no suggestion. The section also speaks in general terms of the conservation of natural resources, but it prescribes no policy for the achievement of that end. It is manifest that this broad outline is simply an introduction of the act, leaving the legislative policy as to particular subjects to be declared and defined, if at all, by the subsequent sections. We find nothing in the first section which limits or controls the authority conferred by section 9. We pass then to the other sections of the act. None of these provisions can be deemed to prescribe any limitation of the grant of authority in section 9.

The question whether such a delegation of legislative power is permitted by the Constitution is not answered by the argument that it should be assumed that the President has acted, and will act, for what he believes to be the public good. The point is not one of motives, but of constitutional authority, for which the best of motives is not a substitute. While the present controversy relates to a delegation to the President, the basic question has a much wider application. If the Congress can make a grant of legislative authority of the sort attempted by section 9, we find nothing in the Constitution which restricts the Congress to the selection of the President as grantee. The Congress may vest the power in the officer of its choice or in a board or commission such as it may select or create for the purpose. Nor, with respect to such a delegation, is the question concerned merely with the transportation of oil, or of oil produced in excess of what the state may allow. If legislative power may thus be vested in the President or other grantee as to that excess of production, we see no reason to doubt that it may similarly be vested with respect to the transportation of oil without reference to the state's requirements. That reference simply defines the subject of the prohibition which the President is authorized to enact or not to enact as he pleases. And, if that legislative power may be given to the President or other grantee, it would seem to follow that such power may similarly be conferred with respect to the transportation of other commodities in interstate commerce with or without reference to state action, thus giving to the grantee of the power the determination of what is a wise policy as to that transportation, and authority to permit or prohibit it, as the person or board or commission so chosen may think desirable. In that view, there would appear to be no ground for denying a similar prerogative of delegation with respect to other subjects of legislation.

The Constitution provides that "All legislative Powers herein granted shall be vested in a Congress of the United States, which shall consist of a Senate and House of Representatives." Article I, § 1. And the Congress is empowered "To make all Laws which shall be necessary and proper for carrying into Execution" its general powers. Article I, § 8, cl. 18. The Congress manifestly is not permitted to abdicate or to transfer to others the essential legislative functions with which it is thus vested. Undoubtedly legislation must often be adapted to complex conditions involving a host of details with which the national Legislature cannot deal directly. The Constitution has never been regarded as denying to the Congress the necessary resources of flexibility and practicality, which will enable it to perform its function in laying down policies and establishing standards, while leaving to selected instrumentalities the making of subordinate rules within prescribed limits and the determination of facts to which the policy as declared by the Legislature is to apply. Without capacity to give authorizations of that sort we should have the anomaly of a legislative power which in many circumstances calling for its exertion would be but a futility. But the constant recognition of the necessity and validity of such provisions and the wide range of administrative authority which has been developed by means of them cannot be allowed to obscure the limitations of the authority to delegate, if our constitutional system is to be maintained.

The Court has had frequent occasion to refer to these limitations and to review the course of congressional action. The Court has referred with approval to the distinction between "the delegation to make the law, which necessarily involves a discretion as to what it shall be, and conferring authority or discretion as to its execution, to be exercised under and in pursuance of the law." Applying this principle, authorizations given by Congress to selected instrumentalities for the purpose of ascertaining the existence of facts to which legislation is directed have constantly been sustained. Moreover the Congress may not only give such authorizations to determine specific facts, but may establish primary standards, devolving upon others the duty to carry out the declared legislative policy; that is, as Chief Justice Marshall expressed it, "to fill up the details" under the general provisions made by the Legislature. Upon this principle, for example, rests the authority of the Interstate Commerce Commission, in the execution of the declared policy of the Congress in enforcing reasonable rates, in preventing undue preferences and unjust discriminations, in requiring suitable facilities for transportation in interstate commerce, and in exercising other powers held to have been validly conferred by the decisions of this Court.

So also, from the beginning of the government, the Congress has conferred upon executive officers the power to make regulations—"not for the government of their departments, but for administering the laws which did govern." Such regulations become, indeed, binding rules of conduct, but they are valid only as subordinate rules and when found to be within the framework of the policy which the Legislature has sufficiently defined. This Court has observed that "it was impracticable for Congress to provide general regulations for these various and varying details of management," and that, in authorizing a Cabinet Secretary to meet local conditions, Congress "was merely conferring administrative functions upon an agent, and not delegating to him legislative power."

In every case in which the question has been raised, the Court has recognized that there are limits of delegation which there is no constitutional authority to transcend. We think that section 9 goes beyond those limits. As to the transportation of oil production in excess of state permission, the Congress has declared no policy, has established no standard, has laid down no rule. There is no requirement, no definition of circumstances and conditions in which the transportation is to be allowed or prohibited.

If section 9 were held valid, it would be idle to pretend that anything would be left of limitations upon the power of the Congress to delegate its lawmaking function. The reasoning of the many decisions we have reviewed would be made vacuous and their distinctions nugatory. Instead of performing its lawmaking function, the Congress could at will and as to such subjects as it chooses transfer that function to the President or other officer or to an administrative body. The question is not of the intrinsic importance of the particular statute before us, but of the constitutional processes of legislation which are an essential part of our system of government.

There is another objection to the validity of the prohibition laid down by the executive order under section 9. The executive order contains no finding, no statement of the grounds of the President's action in enacting the prohibition. Both section 9 and the executive order are in notable contrast with historic practice, as shown by many statutes and proclamations, by which declarations of policy are made by the Congress and delegations are within the framework of that policy and have relation to facts and conditions to be found and stated by the President in the appropriate exercise of the delegated authority. The point is pertinent in relation to the first section of the National Industrial Recovery Act. We have said that the first section is but a general introduction, that it declares no policy and defines no standard with respect to the transportation which is the subject of section 9. But if from the extremely broad description contained in that section and the widely different matters to which the section refers, it were possible to derive a statement of prerequisites to the President's action under section 9, it would still be necessary for the President to comply with those conditions and to show that compliance as the ground of his prohibition. To hold that he is free to select as he chooses from the many and various objects generally described in the first section, and then to act without making any finding with respect to any object that he does select, and the circumstances properly related to that object, would be in effect to make the conditions inoperative and to invest him with an uncontrolled legislative power.

We are not dealing with action which, appropriately belonging to the executive province, is not the subject of judicial review or with the presumptions attaching to executive action. To repeat, we are concerned with the question of the delegation of legislative power. If the citizen is to be punished for the crime of violating a legislative order of an executive officer, or of a board or commission, due process of law requires that it shall appear that the order is within the authority of the officer, board, or commission, and, if that authority depends on determinations of fact, those determinations must be shown. As this Court once said: "In creating such an administrative agency, the Legislature, to prevent its being a pure delegation of legislative power, must enjoin upon it a certain course of procedure and certain rules of decision in the performance of its function. It is a wholesome and necessary principle that such an agency must pursue the procedure and rules enjoined, and show a substantial compliance therewith to give validity to its action. When, therefore, such an administrative agency is required as a condition precedent to an order, to make a finding of facts, the validity of the order must rest upon the needed finding. If it is lacking, the order is ineffective."

We cannot regard the President as immune from the application of these constitutional principles. When the President is invested with legislative authority as the delegate of Congress in carrying out a declared policy, he necessarily acts under the constitutional restriction applicable to such a delegation.

*The Speech or Debate Clause was designed to assure a co-equal branch of the government wide freedom of speech, debate, and deliberation without intimidation or threats from the Executive Branch. It thus protects Members against prosecutions that directly impinge upon or threaten the legislative process.*

— *Byron R. White*

## Gravel v. United States
### 92 S.Ct. 2614, 408 U.S. 606 (1972)

*This case arose out of the criminal investigation by a federal grand jury into the release and publication of a classified Department of Defense study, popularly known as the Pentagon Papers; the same study also figured in the case by that name:* The Pentagon Papers Case (1971). *At a "meeting" of his subcommittee, Senator Mike Gravel, a Democrat from Alaska, read large portions of the study and then introduced the entire 47 volumes into the official public record. A federal grand jury wanted to question Gravel's aide, Leonard S. Rodberg, about the Senator's conduct and to inquire into the arrangements for the publication of the papers by the Beacon Press, a private commercial publisher. Federal criminal laws forbid the release and publication of materials with the security classification "Top Secret-Sensitive," the classification of the study. Although the majority did interpret the speech and debate clause, Article I, § 6, cl. 1, to protect legislative aides, the Court ruled to allow the grand jury inquiry because the dissemination of the study to the publisher was not deemed a legislative act. The Court has come to recognize that this clause does not create an absolute immunity. For example, a criminal prosecution for corrupt behavior, such as accepting bribes, is allowed. And communications beyond the Congress, even communications with a member's constituents, are not protected and therefore are subject to private defamation actions.*

**Justice White:** Because the claim is that a Member's aide shares the Member's constitutional privilege, we consider first whether and to what extent Senator Gravel himself is exempt from process or inquiry by a grand jury investigating the commission of a crime. Our frame of reference is Art. I, § 6, cl. 1, of the Constitution: "The Senators and Representatives shall in all

Cases, except Treason, Felony and Breach of the Peace, be privileged from Arrest during their Attendance at the Session of their respective Houses, and in going to and returning from the same; and for any Speech or Debate in either House, they shall not be questioned in any other Place."

The last sentence of the Clause provides Members of Congress with two distinct privileges. Except in cases of "Treason, Felony and Breach of the Peace," the Clause shields Members from arrest while attending or traveling to and from a session of their House. History reveals, and prior cases so hold, that this part of the Clause exempts Members from arrest in civil cases only. "When the Constitution was adopted, arrests in civil suits were still common in America. It is only to such arrests that the provision applies." "Since the term treason, felony, and breach of the peace, as used in the constitutional provision relied upon, excepts from the operation of the privilege all criminal offenses, the conclusion results that the claim of privilege of exemption from arrest and sentence was without merit." Nor does freedom from arrest confer immunity on a Member from service of process as a defendant in civil matters, or as a witness in a criminal case. "The constitution gives to every man, charged with an offence, the benefit of compulsory process, to secure the attendance of his witnesses. I do not know of any privilege to exempt members of congress from the service, or the obligations, of a subpoena, in such cases." It is, therefore, sufficiently plain that the constitutional freedom from arrest does not exempt Members of Congress from the operation of the ordinary criminal laws, even though imprisonment may prevent or interfere with the performance of their duties as Members. Indeed, implicit in the narrow scope of the privilege of freedom from arrest is, as Thomas Jefferson noted, the judgment that legislators ought not to stand above the law they create but ought generally to be bound by it as are ordinary persons.

In recognition, no doubt, of the force of this part of § 6, Senator Gravel disavows any assertion of general immunity from the criminal law. But he points out that the last portion of § 6 affords Members of Congress another vital privilege—they may not be questioned in any other place for any speech or debate in either House. The claim is not that while one part of § 6 generally permits prosecutions for treason, felony, and breach of the peace, another part nevertheless broadly forbids them. Rather, his insistence is that the Speech or Debate Clause at the very least protects him from criminal or civil liability and from questioning elsewhere than in the Senate, with respect to the events occurring at the subcommittee hearing at which the Pentagon Papers were introduced into the public record. To us this claim is incontrovertible. The Speech or Debate Clause was designed to assure a co-equal branch of the government wide freedom of speech, debate, and deliberation without intimidation or threats from the Executive Branch. It thus protects Members against prosecutions that directly impinge upon or threaten the legislative process. We have no doubt that Senator Gravel may not be made to answer—either in terms of questions or in terms of defending himself from prosecution—for the events that occurred at the subcommittee meeting. Our decision is made easier by the fact that the United States appears to have abandoned whatever position it took to the contrary in the lower courts.

Even so, the United States strongly urges that because the Speech or Debate Clause confers a privilege only upon "Senators and Representatives," Rodberg himself has no valid claim to constitutional immunity from grand jury inquiry. In our view, both courts below correctly rejected this position. We agree with the Court of Appeals that for the purpose of construing the privilege a Member and his aide are to be "treated as one," or, as the District Court put it: the "Speech or Debate Clause prohibits inquiry into things done by Rodberg as the Senator's agent or assistant which would have been legislative acts, and therefore privileged, if performed by the Senator personally." Both courts recognized what the Senate of the United States urgently presses here: that it is literally impossible, in view of the complexities of the modern legislative process, with Congress almost constantly in session and matters of legislative concern constantly proliferating, for Members of Congress to perform their legislative tasks without the help of aides and assistants; that the day-to-day work of such aides is so critical to the Members' performance that they must be treated as the latter's alter egos; and that if they are not so recognized, the central role of the Speech or Debate Clause—to prevent intimidation of legislators by the Executive and accountability before a possibly hostile judiciary—will inevitably be diminished and frustrated.

The Court has already embraced similar views in a 1959 decision immunizing the Acting Director of the Office of Rent Stabilization from liability for an alleged libel contained in a press release, the Court held that the executive privilege recognized in prior cases could not be restricted to those of cabinet rank. As stated by Mr. Justice Harlan, the "privilege is not a badge or emolument of exalted office, but an expression of a policy designed to aid in the effective functioning of government. The complexities and magnitude of governmental activity have become so great that there must of necessity be a delegation and redelegation of authority as to many functions, and we cannot say that these functions become less important simply because they are exercised by officers of lower rank in the executive hierarchy."

It is true that the Clause itself mentions only "Senators and Representatives," but prior cases have plainly not taken a literalistic approach in applying the privilege. The Clause also speaks only of "Speech or Debate," but the Court's consistent approach has been that to confine the protection of the Speech or Debate Clause to words spoken in debate would be an unacceptably narrow view. Committee reports, resolutions, and the act of voting are equally covered; "in short, things generally done in a session of the House by one of its members in relation to the business before it." Rather than giving the clause a cramped construction, the Court has sought to implement its fundamental purpose of freeing the legislator from executive and judicial oversight that realistically threatens to control his conduct as a legislator. We have little doubt that we are neither exceeding our judicial powers nor mistakenly construing the Constitution by holding that the Speech or Debate Clause applies not only to a Member but also to his aides insofar as the conduct of the latter would be a protected legislative act if performed by the Member himself.

Nor can we agree with the United States that our conclusion is foreclosed by our prior decisions going back to the last century. None of these cases adopted the simple proposition that immunity was unavailable to congressional or committee employees because they were not Representatives or Senators; rather, immunity was unavailable because they engaged in illegal conduct that was not entitled to Speech or Debate Clause protection. These prior cases reflect a decidedly jaundiced view towards extending the Clause so as to privilege illegal or unconstitutional conduct beyond that essential to foreclose executive control of legislative speech or debate and associated matters such as voting and committee reports and proceedings. In each case, protecting the rights of others may have to some extent frustrated a planned or completed legislative act; but relief could be afforded without proof of a legislative act or the motives or purposes underlying such an act. No threat to legislative independence was posed, and Speech or Debate Clause protection did not attach.

None of this, as we see it, involves distinguishing between a Senator and his personal aides with respect to legislative immunity. On the other hand, no prior case has held that Members of Congress would be immune for conduct beyond their legislative duties. Senator Gravel is willing to assume that if he personally had "stolen" the Pentagon Papers, and that act were a crime, he could be prosecuted, as could aides or other assistants who participated in the theft.

The United States fears the abuses that history reveals have occurred when legislators are invested with the power to relieve others from the operation of otherwise valid civil and criminal laws. But these abuses, it seems to us, are for the most part obviated if the privilege applicable to the aide is viewed, as it must be, as the privilege of the Senator, and invocable only by the Senator or by the aide on the Senator's behalf, and if in all events the privilege available to the aide is confined to those services that would be immune legislative conduct if performed by the Senator himself. This view places beyond the Speech or Debate Clause a variety of services characteristically performed by aides for Members of Congress, even though within the scope of their employment. It likewise provides no protection for criminal conduct threatening the security of the person or property of others, whether performed at the direction of the Senator in preparation for or in execution of a legislative act or done without his knowledge or direction. Neither does it immunize Senator or aide from testifying at trials or grand jury proceedings involving third-party crimes where the questions do not require testimony about or impugn a legislative act. It follows that an aide's claim of privilege can be repudiated and thus waived by the Senator. Thus our refusal to distinguish between Senator and aide in applying the Speech or Debate Clause does not mean that Rodberg is for all purposes exempt from grand jury questioning.

We are convinced also that the Court of Appeals correctly determined that Senator Gravel's alleged arrangement with Beacon Press to publish the Pentagon Papers was not protected speech or debate within the meaning of Art. I, § 6, cl. 1, of the Constitution.

Historically, the English legislative privilege was not viewed as protecting republication of an otherwise immune libel on the floor of the House. An English judicial decision in 1839 recognized that "for speeches made in Parliament by a member to the prejudice of any other person, or hazardous to the public peace, that member enjoys complete impunity." But it was clearly stated that "if the calumnious or inflammatory speeches should be reported and published, the law will attach responsibility on the publisher." This was accepted in 1881 by a decision of this Court as a "sound statement of the legal effect of the Bill of Rights and of the parliamentary law of England" and as a reasonable basis for inferring "that the framers of the Constitution meant the same thing by the use of language borrowed from that source."

Our prior cases have read the Speech or Debate Clause "broadly to effectuate its purposes," and have included within its reach anything "generally done in a session of the House by one of its members in relation to the business before it." Thus, voting by Members and committee reports are protected; and we recognize today—as the Court has recognized before—that a Member's conduct at legislative committee hearings, although subject to judicial review in various circumstances, as is legislation itself, may not be made the basis for a civil or criminal judgment against a Member because that conduct is within the "sphere of legitimate legislative activity."

This Court has made it equally clear that the limits of "legislative activity" are not established by the Legislative Branch: "Legislatures may not of course acquire power by an unwarranted extension of privilege. The House of Commons' claim of power to establish the limits of its privilege has been little more than a pretense. This Court has not hesitated to sustain the rights of private individuals when it found Congress was acting outside its legislative role."

But the Clause has not been extended beyond the legislative sphere. That Senators generally perform certain acts in their official capacity as Senators does not necessarily make all such acts legislative in nature. Members of Congress are constantly in touch with the Executive Branch of the Government and with administrative agencies—they may cajole, and exhort with respect to the administration of a federal statute—but such conduct, though generally done, is not protected legislative activity. In 1966 we decided at least this much: "No argument is made, nor do we think that it could be successfully contended, that the Speech or Debate Clause reaches conduct, such as was involved in the attempt to influence the Department of Justice, that is in no wise related to the due functioning of the legislative process."

Legislative acts are not all-encompassing. The heart of the Clause is speech or debate in either House. Insofar as the Clause is construed to reach other matters, they must be an integral part of the deliberative and communicative processes by which Members participate in committee and House proceedings with respect to the consideration and passage or rejection of proposed legislation or with respect to other matters which the Constitution places within the jurisdiction of either House. As the Court of Appeals below put it, the courts have extended the privilege to matters beyond pure speech or debate in either House, but "only when necessary to prevent indirect impairment of such deliberations."

Here, private publication by Senator Gravel through the co-operation of Beacon Press was in no way essential to the deliberations of the Senate; nor does questioning as to private publication threaten the integrity or independence of the Senate by impermissibly exposing its deliberations to executive influence. The Senator had conducted his hearings; the record and any report that was forthcoming were available both to his committee and the Senate. Insofar as we are advised, neither Congress nor the full committee ordered or authorized the publication. We cannot but conclude that the Senator's arrangements with Beacon Press were not part and parcel of the legislative process.

There are additional considerations. Article I, § 6, cl. 1, as we have emphasized, does not purport to confer a general exemption upon Members of Congress from liability or process in criminal cases. Quite the contrary is true. While the Speech or Debate Clause recognizes speech, voting, and other legislative acts as exempt from liability that might otherwise attach, it does not privilege either Senator or aide to violate an otherwise valid criminal law in preparing for or implementing legislative acts. If republication of these classified papers would be a crime under an Act of Congress, it would not be entitled to immunity under the Speech or Debate Clause. It also appears that the grand jury was pursuing this very subject in the normal course of a valid investigation. The Speech or Debate Clause does not in our view extend immunity to Rodberg, as a Senator's aide, from testifying before the grand jury about the arrangement between Senator Gravel and Beacon Press or about his own participation, if any, in the alleged transaction, so long as legislative acts of the Senator are not impugned.

*For as the United States guarantee to each State a republican government, Congress must necessarily decide what government is established in the State before it can determine whether it is republican or not.*

*— Roger B. Taney*

## Luther v. Borden
### 48 U.S. (7 Howard) 1 (1849)

*Ostensibly a suit for common law trespass, the facts behind the pleadings were quite remarkable. Rhode Island had never adopted a new state constitution after independence, but rather retained its colonial charter, which, needless to say, contained a rather archaic and very limited franchise for voting. As Chief Justice Taney's opinion describes, opponents took steps to ordain a modern constitution with expanded suffrage rights. The political situation worsened into an armed insurrection often called Dorr's Rebellion after the leader of the opposition. Dorr's side lost in the streets, although the charter government was pressured into adopting a new state constitution that took effect in May 1843. The federal lawsuit essentially was an attempt to have the Supreme Court approve the actions of the insurgents under Article IV, § 4, which obliges the national government to guarantee "a Republican Form of Government" to the States. What this concept means has changed and expanded over time, but at a minimum it means majority rule through regular elections of representatives. Chief Justice Taney took pains to explain that this clause was not a judicially-enforceable guarantee, that its scope and application were committed first to Congress and then to the President, and thus never to the Third Branch. He left to the political or elected branches such basic issues as what are the essential requirements of the clause and whether the Constitution sanctions revolutionary violence. Since then, the guarantee clause has been invoked, without success or effect, in court challenges to various devices of direct democracy, such as state referenda and initiative provisions, and in efforts to reapportion state legislatures.*

**Chief Justice Taney:** This case has arisen out of the unfortunate political differences which agitated the people of Rhode Island in 1841 and 1842. It is an action of trespass brought by Martin Luther, plaintiff, against Luther M. Borden and others, defendants, in the Circuit Court of the United States for the District of Rhode Island, for breaking and entering the plaintiff's house. The defendants justify upon the ground that large numbers of men were assembled in different parts of the State for the purpose of overthrowing the government by military force, and were actually levying war upon the State; that, in order to defend itself from this insurrection, the State was declared by competent authority to be under martial law; that the plaintiff was engaged in the insurrection; and that the defendants, being in the military service of the State, by command of their superior officer, broke and entered the house and searched the rooms for the plaintiff, who was supposed to be there concealed, in order to arrest him, doing as little damage as possible. The plaintiff replied, that the trespass was committed by the defendants of their own proper wrong, and without any such cause; and upon the issue joined on this replication, the parties proceeded to trial.

This is a new question in this court, and certainly a very grave one; and at the time when the trespass is alleged to have been committed it had produced a general and painful excitement in the State, and threatened to end in bloodshed and civil war.

The evidence shows that the defendants, in breaking into the plaintiff's house and endeavouring to arrest him, as stated in the pleadings, acted under the authority of the government which was established in Rhode Island at the time of the Declaration of Independence, and which is usually called the charter government. For when the separation from England took place, Rhode Island did not, like the other States, adopt a new constitution, but continued the form of government established by the charter of Charles the Second in 1663; making only such alterations, by acts of the legislature, as were necessary to adapt it to their condition and rights as an independent State. It was under this form of government that Rhode Island united with the other States in the *Declaration of Independence*, and afterwards ratified the Constitution of the United States and became a member of this Union; and it continued to be the established and unquestioned government of the State until the difficulties took place which have given rise to this action. In this form of government no mode of proceeding was pointed out by which amendments might be made. It authorized the legislature to prescribe the qualification of voters, and in the exercise of this power the right of suffrage was confined to freeholders, until the eventful adoption of the constitution of 1843.

For some years previous to the disturbances of which we are now speaking, many of the citizens became dissatisfied with the charter government, and particularly with the restriction upon the right of suffrage. Memorials were addressed to the legislature upon this subject, urging the justice and necessity of a more liberal and extended rule. But they failed to produce the desired effect. And thereupon meetings were held and associations formed by those who were in favor of a more extended right of suffrage, which finally resulted in the election of a convention to form a new constitution to be submitted to the people for their adoption or rejection. This convention was not authorized by any law of the existing government. It was elected at voluntary meetings, and by those citizens only who favored this plan of reform; those who were opposed to it, or opposed to the manner in which it was proposed to be accomplished, taking no part in the proceedings. The persons chosen as above mentioned came together and framed a constitution, by which the right of suffrage was extended to every male citizen of twenty-one years of age, who had resided in the State for one year, and in the town in which he offered to vote for six months, next preceding the election. The convention also prescribed the manner in which this constitution should be submitted to the decision of the people—permitting every one to vote on that question who was an American citizen, twenty-one years old, and who had a permanent residence or home in the State, and directing the votes to be returned to the convention.

Upon the return of the votes, the convention declared that the constitution was adopted and ratified by a majority of the people of the State, and was the paramount law and constitution of Rhode Island. And it communicated this decision to the governor under the charter government, for the purpose of being laid before the legislature; and directed elections to be held for a governor, members of the legislature, and other officers under the new constitution. These elections accordingly took place, and the governor, lieutenant-governor, secretary of state, and senators and representatives thus appointed assembled at the city of Providence on May 3, 1842, and immediately proceeded to organize the new government, by appointing the officers and passing the laws necessary for that purpose.

The charter government did not, however, admit the validity of these proceedings, nor acquiesce in them. On the contrary, in January of 1842, when this new constitution was communicated to the governor, and by him laid before the legislature, it passed resolutions declaring all acts done for the purpose of imposing that constitution upon the State to be an assumption of the powers of government, in violation of the rights of the existing government and of the people at large; and that it would maintain its authority and defend the legal and constitutional rights of the people.

In adopting this measure, as well as in all others taken by the charter government to assert its authority, it was supported by a large number of the citizens of the State, claiming to be a majority, who regarded the proceedings of the adverse party as unlawful and disorganizing, and maintained that, as the existing government had been established by the people of the State, no convention to frame a new constitution could be called without its sanction; and that the times and places of taking the votes, and the officers to receive them, and the qualification of the voters, must be previously regulated and appointed by law.

But, notwithstanding the determination of the charter government, and of those who adhered to it, to maintain its authority, Thomas W. Dorr, who had been elected governor under the new constitution, prepared to assert the authority of that government by force, and many citizens assembled in arms to support him. The charter government thereupon passed an act declaring the State under martial law, and at the same time proceeded to call out the militia, to repel the threatened attack and to subdue those who were engaged in it. In this state of the contest, the house of the plaintiff, who was engaged in supporting the authority of the new government, was broken and entered in order to arrest him. The defendants were, at the time, in the military service of the old government, and in arms to support its authority.

The difficulties with the government of which Mr. Dorr was the head were soon over. For after an unsuccessful attempt made by Mr. Dorr in 1842, at the head of a military force, to get possession of the State arsenal at Providence, in which he was repulsed, and an assemblage of some hundreds of armed men under his command at Chepatchet in the June following, which dispersed upon the approach of the troops of the old government, no further effort was made to establish it; and the charter government continued to assert its authority and exercise its powers, and to enforce obedience, throughout the State, arresting and imprisoning, and punishing in its judicial tribunals, those who had appeared in arms against it. The charter government eventually convened a convention and ratified a new constitution effective in May 1843.

We do not understand from the argument that the constitution under which the plaintiff acted is supposed to have been in force after the constitution of May 1843, went into operation. The contest is confined to the year preceding. The plaintiff contends that the charter government was displaced, and ceased to have any lawful power, after the organization, in 1842, of the government which he supported, and although that government never was able to exercise any authority in the State, nor to command obedience to its laws or to its officers, yet he insists that it was the lawful and established government, upon the ground that it was ratified by a large majority of the male people of the State of the age of twenty-one and upwards, and also by a majority of those who were entitled to vote for general officers under the then existing laws of the State.

If this court is authorized to enter upon this inquiry as proposed by the plaintiff, and it should be decided that the charter government had no legal existence during the period of time above mentioned—if it had been annulled by the adoption of the opposing government—then the laws passed by its legislature during that time were nullities; its taxes wrongfully collected; its salaries and compensation to its officers illegally paid; its public accounts improperly settled; and the judgments and sentences of its courts in civil and criminal cases null and void, and the officers who carried their decisions into operation answerable as trespassers, if not in some cases as criminals. When the decision of this court might lead to such results, it becomes its duty to examine very carefully its own powers before it undertakes to exercise jurisdiction.

Certainly, the question which the plaintiff proposed to raise by the testimony he offered has not heretofore been recognized as a judicial one in any of the State courts. In forming the constitutions of the different States, after the *Declaration of Independence*, and in the various changes and alterations which have since been made, the political department has always determined whether the proposed constitution or amendment was ratified or not by the people of the State, and the judicial power has followed its decision. In Rhode Island, the question has been directly decided. Prosecutions were there instituted against some of the persons who had been active in the forcible opposition to the old government. And in more than one of the cases evidence was offered on the part of the defence similar to the testimony offered here, and for the same purpose; that is, for the purpose of showing that the proposed constitution had been adopted by the people of Rhode Island, and had, therefore, become the established government, and consequently that the parties accused were doing nothing more than their duty in endeavouring to support it.

But the Rhode Island courts uniformly held that the inquiry proposed to be made belonged to the political power and not to the judicial; that it rested with the political power to decide whether the charter government had been displaced or not; and when that decision was made, the judicial department would be bound to take notice of it as the paramount law of the State, without the aid of oral evidence or the examination of witnesses; that, according to the laws and institutions of Rhode Island, no such change had been recognized by the political power; and that the charter government was the lawful and established government of the State during the period in contest, and that those who were in arms against it were insurgents, and liable to punishment. This doctrine is clearly and forcibly stated in the opinion of the Supreme Court of the State in the trial of Thomas W. Dorr, who was the governor elected under the opposing constitution, and headed the armed force which endeavoured to maintain its authority.

Indeed, we do not see how the question could be tried and judicially decided in a State court. Judicial power presupposes an established government capable of enacting laws and enforcing their execution, and of appointing judges to expound and administer them. The acceptance of the judicial office is a recognition of the authority of the government from which it is derived. And if the authority of that government is annulled and overthrown, the power of its courts and other officers is annulled with it. And if a State court should enter upon the inquiry proposed in this case, and should come to the conclusion that the government under which it acted had been put aside and displaced by an opposing government, it would cease to be a court, and be incapable of pronouncing a judicial decision upon the question it undertook to try. If it decides at all as a court, it necessarily affirms the existence and authority of the government under which it is exercising judicial power.

Upon what ground could the Circuit Court of the United States which tried this case have departed from this rule, and disregarded and overruled the decisions of the courts of Rhode Island? Undoubtedly the courts of the United States have certain powers under the Constitution and laws of the United States which do not belong to the State courts. But the power of determining that a State government has been lawfully established, which the courts of the State disown and repudiate, is not one of them. Upon such a question the courts of the United States are bound to follow the decisions of the State tribunals, and must therefore regard the charter government as the lawful established government during the time of this contest.

Besides, if the Circuit Court had entered upon this inquiry, by what rule could it have determined the qualification of voters upon the adoption or rejection of the proposed constitution, unless there was some previous law of the State to guide it? It is the province of a court to expound the law, not to make it. And certainly it is no part of the judicial functions of any court of the United States to prescribe the qualification of voters in a State, giving the right to those to whom it is denied by the written and established constitution and laws of the State, or taking it away from those to whom it is given; nor has it the right to determine what political privileges the citizens of a State are entitled to, unless there is an established constitution or law to govern its decision.

And if the then existing law of Rhode Island which confined the right of suffrage to freeholders is to govern, and this question is to be tried by that rule, how could the majority have been ascertained by legal evidence, such as a court of justice might lawfully receive? And if this were attempted, where would such an inquiry have terminated? And how long must the people of Rhode Island have waited to learn from this court under what form of government they were living during the year in controversy?

But this is not all. The question as to the majority is a question of fact. It depends upon the testimony of witnesses, and if the testimony offered by the plaintiff had been received, the defendants had the right to offer evidence to rebut it; and there might, and probably would, have been conflicting testimony as to the number of voters in the State, and as to the legal qualifications of many of the individuals who had voted. The decision would, therefore, have depended upon the relative credibility of witnesses, and the weight of testimony; and as the case before the Circuit Court was an action at common law, the question of fact, according to the seventh amendment to the Constitution of the United States, must have been tried by the jury. In one case a jury might find that the constitution which the plaintiff supported was adopted by a lawful majority. Another jury in another case might find otherwise. The authority and security of the State governments do not rest on such unstable foundations.

Moreover, the Constitution of the United States, as far as it has provided for an emergency of this kind, and authorized the general government to interfere in the domestic concerns of a State, has treated the subject as political in its nature, and placed the power in the hands of that department. The fourth section of the fourth article of the Constitution of the United States provides that the United States shall guarantee to every State in the Union a republican form of government, and shall protect each of them against invasion; and on the application of the legislature or of the executive (when the legislature cannot be convened) against domestic violence.

Under this article of the Constitution it rests with Congress to decide what government is the established one in a State. For as the United States guarantee to each State a republican government, Congress must necessarily decide what government is established in the State before it can determine whether it is republican or not. And when the senators and representatives of a State are admitted into the councils of the Union, the authority of the government under which they are appointed, as well as its republican character, is recognized by the proper constitutional authority. And its decision is binding on every other department of the government, and could not be questioned in a judicial tribunal. It is true that the contest in this case did not last long enough to bring the matter to this issue; and as no senators or representatives were elected under the authority of the government of which Mr. Dorr was the head, Congress was not called upon to decide the controversy. Yet the right to decide is placed there, and not in the courts.

So, too, as relates to the clause in the above-mentioned article of the Constitution, providing for cases of domestic violence. It rested with Congress, too, to determine upon the means proper to be adopted to fulfil this guarantee. They might, if they had deemed it most advisable to do so, have placed it in the power of a court to decide when the contingency had happened which required the federal government to interfere. But Congress thought otherwise, and no doubt wisely; and by the act of February 28, 1795, provided, that, "in case of an insurrection in any State against the government thereof, it shall be lawful for the President of the United States, on application of the legislature of such State or of the executive (when the legislature cannot be convened), to call forth such number of the militia of any other State or States, as may be applied for, as he may judge sufficient to suppress such insurrection."

By this act, the power of deciding whether the exigency had arisen upon which the government of the United States is bound to interfere, is given to the President. He is to act upon the application of the legislature or of the executive, and consequently he must determine what body of men constitute the legislature, and who is the governor, before he can act. The fact that both parties claim the right to the government cannot alter the case, for both cannot be entitled to it. If there is an armed conflict, like the one of which we are speaking, it is a case of domestic violence, and one of the parties must be in insurrection against the lawful government. And the President must, of necessity, decide which is the government, and which party is unlawfully arrayed against it, before he can perform the duty imposed upon him by the act of Congress.

After the President has acted and called out the militia, is a Circuit Court of the United States authorized to inquire whether his decision was right? Could the court, while the parties were actually contending in arms for the possession of the government, call witnesses before it and inquire which party represented a majority of the people? If it could, then it would become the duty of the court (provided it came to the conclusion that the President had decided incorrectly) to discharge those who were arrested or detained by the troops in the service of the United States or the government which the President was endeavouring to maintain. If the judicial power extends so far, the guarantee contained in the Constitution of the United States is a guarantee of anarchy, and not of order. Yet if this right does not reside in the courts when the conflict is raging, if the judicial power is at that time bound to follow the decision of the political, it must be equally bound when the contest is over. It cannot, when peace is restored, punish as offences and crimes the acts which it before recognized, and was bound to recognize, as lawful.

It is true that in this case the militia were not called out by the President. But upon the application of the governor under the charter government, the President recognized him as the executive power of the State, and took measures to call out the militia to support his authority if it should be found necessary for the general government to interfere; and it is admitted in the argument, that it was the knowledge of this decision that put an end to the armed opposition to the charter government, and prevented any further efforts to establish by force the proposed constitution. The interference of the President, therefore, by announcing his determination, was as effectual as if the militia had been assembled under his orders. And it should be equally authoritative. For certainly no court of the United States, with a knowledge of this decision, would have been justified in recognizing the opposing party as the lawful government; or in treating as wrongdoers or insurgents the officers of the government which the President had recognized, and was prepared to support by an armed force. In the case of foreign nations, the government acknowledged by the President is always recognized in the courts of justice. And this principle has been applied by the act of Congress to the sovereign States of the Union.

It is said that this power in the President is dangerous to liberty, and may be abused. All power may be abused if placed in unworthy hands. But it would be difficult, we think, to point out any other hands in which this power would be more safe, and at the same time equally effectual. When citizens of the same State are in arms against each other, and the constituted authorities unable to execute the laws, the interposition of the United States must be prompt, or it is of little value. The ordinary course of proceedings in courts of justice would be utterly unfit for the crisis. And the elevated office of the President, chosen as he is by the people of the United States, and the high responsibility he could not fail to feel when acting in a case of so much moment, appear to furnish as strong safeguards against a wilful abuse of power as human prudence and foresight could well provide. At all events, it is conferred upon him by the Constitution and laws of the United States, and must therefore be respected and enforced in its judicial tribunals. Undoubtedly, if the President in exercising this power shall fall into error, or invade the rights of the people of the State, it would be in the power of Congress to apply the proper remedy. But the courts must administer the law as they find it.

Much of the argument on the part of the plaintiff turned upon political rights and political questions, upon which the court has been urged to express an opinion. We decline doing so. The high power has been conferred on this court of passing judgment upon the acts of the State sovereignties, and of the legislative and executive branches of the federal government, and of determining whether they are beyond the limits of power marked out for them respectively by the Constitution of the United States. This tribunal, therefore, should be the last to overstep the boundaries which limit its own jurisdiction. And while it should always be ready to meet any question confided to it by the Constitution, it is equally its duty not to pass beyond its appropriate sphere of action, and to take care not to involve itself in discussions which properly belong to other forums. No one, we believe, has ever doubted the proposition, that, according to the institutions of this country, the sovereignty in every State resides in the people of the State, and that they may alter and change their form of government at their own pleasure. But whether they have changed it or not by abolishing an old government, and establishing a new one in its place, is a question to be settled by the political power. And when that power has decided, the courts are bound to take notice of its decision, and to follow it.

*We are not at liberty to inquire into the motives of the legislature. We can only examine into its power under the Constitution; and the power to make exceptions to the appellate jurisdiction of this court is given by express words.*

— *Salmon P. Chase*

## Ex parte McCardle
### 74 U.S. (7 Wallace) 506 (1869)

*In February 1867, Congress passed a statute giving the Supreme Court jurisdiction to hear appeals in habeas corpus cases. (Habeas corpus is a writ that a court issues to order the release of a prisoner who is being held in custody illegally.) The 1867 statute was intended to protect federal officers in the states of the former Confederacy against state detentions and pretextual prosecutions. It was ironic then, that William McCardle (who was seeking such a writ) was a newspaper editor and Confederate sympathizer in Vicksburg, Mississippi, who had been arrested and charged before a U.S. military court for impeding federal officials by publishing harangues against the military occupation government. In March 1868, the Court completed oral arguments and took the case under advisement for decision. Later that same month, Congress passed a statute repealing the 1867 jurisdiction statute; President Johnson, who was being tried before the Senate as a court of impeachment with the Chief Justice presiding, vetoed the bill; Congress repassed the repealing statute over his veto. The next week, the Court agreed to hear additional oral arguments on the effect of the repealing statute, but postponed them to the next year's term. In March 1869, the Court heard the postponed arguments and issued the ruling below on April 12th. The provision in Article III, § 2 gave Congress the power to make "Exceptions" to the Supreme Court's appellate jurisdiction. Generally, statutes authorizing appellate jurisdiction are understood to impliedly except any and all jurisdiction not explicitly granted. Specifically, the 1868 repealing statute was an explicit exception that affirmatively forbade the Justices from issuing a decision in this case, even though the Court had already taken the case under advisement. So the Court no longer had juris-*

*diction and it was obliged to dismiss McCardle's appeal
without ruling one way or the other. McCardle never went
to trial, however, because the new military commander
dropped the charges. The High Court's meek submission
to Congressional power over its jurisdiction in this case
often is invoked by contemporary members of Congress
when they propose jurisdiction-stripping legislation that
would take away Supreme Court authority to decide controversial issues like school prayer and abortion.*

**Chief Justice Chase:** The first question necessarily is that
of jurisdiction; for, if the act of March, 1868, takes away the
jurisdiction defined by the act of February, 1867, it is useless, if
not improper, to enter into any discussion of other questions.

It is quite true, as was argued by the counsel for the petitioner, that the appellate jurisdiction of this court is not derived
from acts of Congress. It is, strictly speaking, conferred by the
Constitution. But it is conferred "with such exceptions and under such regulations as Congress shall make." Art. III, § 2.

It is unnecessary to consider whether, if Congress had made
no exceptions and no regulations, this court might not have
exercised general appellate jurisdiction under rules prescribed
by itself. For among the earliest acts of the first Congress, at its
first session, was the act of September 24th, 1789, to establish
the judicial courts of the United States. That act provided for
the organization of this court, and prescribed regulations for the
exercise of its jurisdiction.

The source of that jurisdiction, and the limitations of it by
the Constitution and by statute, have been on several occasions
subjects of consideration here. The principle that the affirmation of appellate jurisdiction implies the negation of all such
jurisdiction not affirmed having been thus established, it was an
almost necessary consequence that acts of Congress, providing
for the exercise of jurisdiction, should come to be spoken of as
acts granting jurisdiction, and not as acts making exceptions to
the constitutional grant of it.

The exception to appellate jurisdiction in the case before us,
however, is not an inference from the affirmation of other appellate jurisdiction. It is made in terms. The provision of the act of
1867, affirming the appellate jurisdiction of this court in cases of
habeas corpus is expressly repealed. It is hardly possible to
imagine a plainer instance of positive exception.

We are not at liberty to inquire into the motives of the legislature. We can only examine into its power under the Constitution; and the power to make exceptions to the appellate jurisdiction of this court is given by express words.

What, then, is the effect of the repealing act upon the case before us? We cannot doubt as to this. Without jurisdiction the court cannot proceed at all in any cause. Jurisdiction is power to declare the law, and when it ceases to exist, the only function remaining to the court is that of announcing the fact and dismissing the cause. And this is not less clear upon authority than upon principle.

Several cases were cited by the counsel for the petitioner in support of the position that jurisdiction of this case is not affected by the repealing act. But none of them, in our judgment, afford any support to it. They are all cases of the exercise of judicial power by the legislature, or of legislative interference with courts in the exercising of continuing jurisdiction.

On the other hand, the general rule, supported by the best elementary writers, is, that "when an act of the legislature is repealed, it must be considered, except as to transactions past and closed, as if it never existed." And the effect of repealing acts upon suits under acts repealed, has been determined by the adjudications of this court.

It is quite clear, therefore, that this court cannot proceed to pronounce judgment in this case, for it has no longer jurisdiction of the appeal; and judicial duty is not less fitly performed by declining ungranted jurisdiction than in exercising firmly that which the Constitution and the laws confer.

Counsel seem to have supposed, if effect be given to the repealing act in question, that the whole appellate power of the court, in cases of habeas corpus, is denied. But this is an error. The act of 1868 does not except from that jurisdiction any cases but appeals from Circuit Courts under the act of 1867. It does not affect the jurisdiction which was previously exercised.

The appeal of the petitioner in this case must be dismissed for want of jurisdiction.

*We know of no previous instance in which Congress has enacted retroactive legislation requiring an Article III court to set aside a final judgment, and for good reason. The Constitution's separation of legislative and judicial powers denies it the authority to do so.*

*—Antonin Scalia*

## Plaut v. Spendthrift Farm, Inc.
### 115 S.Ct. 1447 (1995)

*In a 1987 civil action, plaintiffs alleged that in 1983 and 1984 defendants committed fraud and deceit in the sale of stock in violation of the Securities Exchange Act of 1934 and Rule 10b–5 of the Securities and Exchange Commission. The District Court dismissed the lawsuit in 1991 after the Supreme Court held in another case that these kinds of suits had to be commenced within one year after the discovery of the fraud and within three years after the violation. After the dismissal became final, Congress enacted a new statute which reinstated suits such as this which were filed before the 1991 Supreme Court decision. The Justices voted 7 to 2 that the new statute contravened the separation of powers so far as it required federal courts to reopen final judgments entered before the statute was enacted. Justice Scalia's majority opinion provides a neat summary of the origins of the separation of powers between Congress and the federal courts.*

**Justice Scalia:** We conclude that in this statute Congress has exceeded its authority by requiring the federal courts to exercise "the judicial Power of the United States," U.S. Const., Art. III, § 1, in a manner repugnant to the text, structure and traditions of Article III.

Our decisions to date have identified two types of legislation that require federal courts to exercise the judicial power in a manner that Article III forbids. The first was in 1872 when we refused to give effect to a statute that was said "to prescribe rules of decision to the Judicial Department of the government in cases pending before it." Whatever the precise scope of this ruling, however, later decisions have made clear that its prohibition does not take hold when Congress "amends applicable law." This statute indisputably does set out substantive legal standards for the Judiciary to apply, and in that sense changes the law (even if solely retroactively). The second type of unconstitutional restriction upon the exercise of judicial power was identified in a 1792 case which stands for the principle that Congress cannot vest review of the decisions of Article III courts in officials of the Executive Branch. Yet under any application of this statute only courts are involved; no officials of other departments sit in direct review of their decisions. This statute therefore offends neither of these previously established prohibitions.

We think, however, that this statute offends a postulate of Article III just as deeply rooted in our law as those we have mentioned. Article III establishes a "judicial department" with the "province and duty to say what the law is" in particular cases and controversies. The record of history shows that the Framers crafted this charter of the judicial department with an expressed understanding that it gives the Federal Judiciary the power, not merely to rule on cases, but to decide them, subject to review only by superior courts in the Article III hierarchy—with an understanding, in short, that "a judgment conclusively resolves the case" because "a 'judicial Power' is one to render dispositive judgments." By retroactively commanding the federal courts to reopen final judgments, Congress has violated this fundamental principle.

The Framers of our Constitution lived among the ruins of a system of intermingled legislative and judicial powers, which had been prevalent in the colonies long before the Revolution, and which after the Revolution had produced factional strife and partisan oppression. In the 17th and 18th centuries colonial assemblies and legislatures functioned as courts of equity of last resort, hearing original actions or providing appellate review of judicial judgments. Often, however, they chose to correct the judicial process through special bills or other enacted legislation. It was common for such legislation not to prescribe a resolution of the dispute, but rather simply to set aside the judgment and order a new trial or appeal. Thus, such legislation bears not on the problem of interbranch review but on the problem of finality of judicial judgments.

The vigorous, indeed often radical, populism of the revolutionary legislatures and assemblies increased the frequency of legislative correction of judgments. "The period 1780–1787 was a period of 'constitutional reaction'" to these developments, "which leaped suddenly to its climax in the Philadelphia Convention." Voices from many quarters, official as well as private, decried the increasing legislative interference with the private-law judgments of the courts. In 1786 the Vermont Council of Censors issued an "Address of the Council of Censors to the Freemen of the State of Vermont," to fulfill the Council's duty, under the State Constitution of 1784, to report to the people "'whether the legislative and executive branches of government have assumed to themselves, or exercised, other or greater powers than they are entitled to by the Constitution.'" A principal method of usurpation identified by the Censors was "the instances of judgments being vacated by legislative acts."

So too, the famous report of the Pennsylvania Council of Censors in 1784 detailed the abuses of legislative interference with the courts at the behest of private interests and factions. As the General Assembly had (they wrote) made a custom of "extending their deliberations to the cases of individuals," the people had "been taught to consider an application to the legislature, as a shorter and more certain mode of obtaining relief from hardships and losses, than the usual process of law." The Censors noted that because "favour and partiality have, from the nature of public bodies of men, predominated in the distribution of this relief these dangerous procedures have been too often recurred to, since the revolution."

This sense of a sharp necessity to separate the legislative from the judicial power, prompted by the crescendo of legislative interference with private judgments of the courts, triumphed among the Framers of the new Federal Constitution. The Convention made the critical decision to establish a judicial department independent of the Legislative Branch by providing that "the judicial Power of the United States shall be vested in one supreme Court, and in such inferior Courts as the Congress may from time to time ordain and establish." Before and during the debates on ratification, Madison, Jefferson, and Hamilton each wrote of the factional disorders and disarray that the system of legislative equity had produced in the years before the framing; and each thought that the separation of the legislative from the judicial power in the new Constitution would cure them. Madison's Federalist No. 48, the famous description of the process by which "the legislative department is every where extending the sphere of its activity, and drawing all power into its impetuous vortex," referred to the report of the Pennsylvania Council of Censors to show that in that State "cases belonging to the judiciary department had been frequently drawn within legislative cognizance and determination." Madison relied as well on Jefferson's *Notes on the State of Virginia*, which mentioned, as one example of the dangerous concentration of governmental powers into the hands of the legislature, that "the Legislature in many instances decided rights which should have been left to judiciary controversy."

If the need for separation of legislative from judicial power was plain, the principal effect to be accomplished by that separation was even plainer. As Hamilton wrote in his exegesis of Article III, § 1, in *Federalist No. 81*: "It is not true that the parliament of Great Britain, or the legislatures of the particular states, can rectify the exceptionable decisions of their respective courts, in any other sense than might be done by a future legislature of the United States. The theory neither of the British, nor the state constitutions, authorises the revisal of a judicial sentence, by a legislative act. A legislature without exceeding its province cannot reverse a determination once made, in a particular case; though it may prescribe a new rule for future cases." The essential balance created by this allocation of authority was a simple one. The Legislature would be possessed of power to "prescribe the rules by which the duties and rights of every citizen are to be regulated," but the power of "the interpretation of the laws" would be "the proper and peculiar province of the courts." *The Federalist No. 78.* The Judiciary would be, "from the nature of its functions, the department least dangerous to the political rights of the constitution," not because its acts were subject to legislative correction, but because the binding effect of its acts was limited to particular cases and controversies. Thus, "though individual oppression may now and then proceed from the courts of justice, the general liberty of the people can never be endangered from that quarter: so long as the judiciary remains truly distinct from both the legislative and executive." *Id.*

Judicial decisions in the period immediately after ratification of the Constitution confirm the understanding that it forbade interference with the final judgments of courts. In 1798, this Court decided a case in which the Legislature of Connecticut had enacted a statute that set aside the final judgment of a state court in a civil case. Although the issue before this Court was the construction of the Ex Post Facto Clause, Art. I, § 10, Justice Iredell (a leading Federalist who had guided the Constitution to ratification in North Carolina) noted that "the Legislature of Connecticut has been in the uniform, uninterrupted, habit of exercising a general superintending power over its courts of law, by granting new trials. It may, indeed, appear strange to some of us, that in any form, there should exist a power to grant, with respect to suits depending or adjudged, new rights of trial, new privileges of proceeding, not previously recognized and regulated by positive institutions. The power is judicial in its nature; and whenever it is exercised, as in the present instance, it is an exercise of judicial, not of legislative, authority."

The state courts of the era showed a similar understanding of the separation of powers, in decisions that drew little distinction between the federal and state constitutions. To choose one representative example from a multitude: in 1824, the Vermont Supreme Court reviewed a special Act of the Vermont Legislature which authorized a party to appeal from the judgment of a court even though, under the general law, the time for appeal had expired. The court, noting that the unappealed judgment had become final, set itself the question "Have the Legislature power to vacate or annul an existing judgment between party and party?" The answer was emphatic: "The necessity of a distinct and separate existence of the three great departments of government had been proclaimed and enforced by Blackstone, Jefferson and Madison," and had been "sanctioned by the people of the United States, by being adopted in terms more or less explicit, into all their written constitutions." The power to annul a final judgment, the court held was "an assumption of Judicial power," and therefore forbidden.

By the middle of the 19th century, the constitutional equilibrium created by the separation of the legislative power to make general law from the judicial power to apply that law in particular cases was so well understood and accepted that it could survive even *Dred Scott v. Sandford (1857)*. In his First Inaugural Address, President Lincoln explained why the political branches could not, and need not, interfere with even that infamous judgment: "I do not forget the position assumed by some, that constitutional questions are to be decided by the Supreme Court; nor do I deny that such decisions must be binding in any case, upon the parties to a suit, as to the object of that suit. And while it is obviously possible that such decision may be erroneous in any given case, still the evil effect following it, being limited to that particular case, with the chance that it may be over-ruled, and never become a precedent for other cases, can better be borne than could the evils of a different practice." And the great constitutional scholar Thomas Cooley addressed precisely the question before us in his 1868 treatise: "If the legislature cannot thus indirectly control the action of the courts, by requiring of them a construction of the law according to its own views, it is very plain it cannot do so directly, by setting aside their judgments, compelling them to grant new trials, ordering the discharge of offenders, or directing what particular steps shall be taken in the progress of a judicial inquiry."

This statute effects a clear violation of the separation-of-powers principle we have just discussed. It is, of course, retroactive legislation, that is, legislation that prescribes what the law was at an earlier time, when the act whose effect is controlled by the legislation occurred. When retroactive legislation requires its own application in a case already finally adjudicated, it does no more and no less than "reverse a determination once made, in a particular case." *The Federalist No. 81.* Our decisions—although their precise holdings are not strictly applicable here—have uniformly provided fair warning that such an act exceeds the powers of Congress. Today those clear statements must either be honored, or else proved false.

It is true that Congress can always revise the judgments of Article III courts in one sense: When a new law makes clear that it is retroactive, an appellate court must apply that law in reviewing judgments still on appeal that were rendered before the law was enacted, and must alter the outcome accordingly. Since that is so, petitioners argue, federal courts must apply the "new" law created by this statute in finally adjudicated cases as well; for the line that separates lower court judgments that are pending on appeal (or may still be appealed), from lower-court judgments that are final, is determined by statute, and so cannot possibly be a constitutional line. But a distinction between judgments from which all appeals have been forgone or completed, and judgments that remain on appeal (or subject to being appealed), is implicit in what Article III creates: not a batch of unconnected courts, but a judicial department composed of "inferior Courts" and "one supreme Court." Within that hierarchy, the decision of an inferior court is not (unless the time for appeal has expired) the final word of the department as a whole. It is the obligation of the last court in the hierarchy that rules on the case to give effect to Congress's latest enactment, even when that has the effect of overturning the judgment of an inferior court, since each court, at every level, must "decide according to existing laws." Having achieved finality, however, a judicial decision becomes the last word of the judicial department with regard to a particular case or controversy, and Congress may not declare by retroactive legislation that the law applicable to that very case was something other than what the courts said it was. Finality of a legal judgment is determined by statute, just as entitlement to a government benefit is a statutory creation; but that no more deprives the former of its constitutional significance for separation-of-powers analysis than it deprives the latter of its significance for due process purposes.

To be sure, this statute reopens (or directs the reopening of) final judgments in a whole class of cases rather than in a particular suit. We do not see how that makes any difference. The separation-of-powers violation here, if there is any, consists of depriving judicial judgments of the conclusive effect that they had when they were announced, not of acting in a manner—*viz.*, with particular rather than general effect—that is unusual (though, we must note, not impossible) for a legislature. To be sure, a general statute such as this one may reduce the perception that legislative interference with judicial judgments was prompted by individual favoritism; but it is legislative interference with judicial judgments nonetheless. Not favoritism, nor even corruption, but power is the object of the separation-of-powers prohibition. The prohibition is violated when an individual final judgment is legislatively rescinded for even the very best of reasons, such as the legislature's genuine conviction (supported by all the law professors in the land) that the judgment was wrong; and it is violated 40 times over when 40 final judgments are legislatively dissolved.

Apart from the statute we review today, we know of no instance in which Congress has attempted to set aside the final judgment of an Article III court by retroactive legislation. That prolonged reticence would be amazing if such interference were not understood to be constitutionally proscribed. Separation of powers, a distinctively American political doctrine, profits from the advice authored by a distinctively American poet: "Good fences make good neighbors."

We know of no previous instance in which Congress has enacted retroactive legislation requiring an Article III court to set aside a final judgment, and for good reason. The Constitution's separation of legislative and judicial powers denies it the authority to do so. This statute is unconstitutional to the extent that it requires federal courts to reopen final judgments entered before its enactment.

*Civil liberty and this kind of martial law cannot endure together; the antagonism is irreconcilable; and, in the conflict, one or the other must perish.*

*— David Davis*

## Ex parte Milligan
### 71 U.S. (4 Wallace) 2 (1867)

*In 1864, an Army Court sentenced Lambdin P. Milligan to hang for conspiring with other anti-war, negrophobe civilians to seize federal arsenals in Indiana and to liberate Confederate prisoners in northern prison camps. Indiana was not within the theater of war. The regular civilian courts were available for the treason prosecution, but the military officials feared that civilian jurors would be sympathetic to the conspirators. Milligan sought review in the circuit court in Indiana, with Justice Davis sitting, and that court divided over whether the military tribunal could try a civilian. The case went up to the Supreme Court, where all nine members concluded that the military tribunal lacked jurisdiction and that Milligan must be released. Four Justices based their reasoning on a federal statute, but maintained that Congress had the authority under the war power to replace civilian courts with military tribunals. Five Justices, speaking through Justice Davis, proclaimed that the Constitution forbade a declaration of martial law and military trials of civilians so long as the civilian courts remained open. Controversial in its own day, the decision today is considered a landmark protection of civil liberties against abusive governmental power and assertions of extraordinary emergency authority.*

**Justice Davis:** The importance of the main question presented by this record cannot be overstated; for it involves the very framework of the government and the fundamental principles of American liberty.

During the late wicked Rebellion, the temper of the times did not allow that calmness in deliberation and discussion so necessary to a correct conclusion of a purely judicial question. Then, considerations of safety were mingled with the exercise of power; and feelings and interests prevailed which are happily terminated. Now that the public safety is assured, this question, as well as all others, can be discussed and decided without passion or the admixture of any element not required to form a legal judgment. We approach the investigation of this case, fully sensible of the magnitude of the inquiry and the necessity of full and cautious deliberation.

The controlling question in the case is this: Upon the facts stated in Milligan's petition, and the exhibits filed, had the military commission mentioned in it jurisdiction, legally, to try and sentence him? Milligan, not a resident of one of the rebellious states, or a prisoner of war, but a citizen of Indiana for twenty years past, and never in the military or naval service, is, while at his home, arrested by the military power of the United States, imprisoned, and, on certain criminal charges preferred against him, tried, convicted, and sentenced to be hanged by a military commission, organized under the direction of the military commander of the military district of Indiana. Had this tribunal the legal power and authority to try and punish this man?

No graver question was ever considered by this court, nor one which more nearly concerns the rights of the whole people; for it is the birthright of every American citizen when charged with crime, to be tried and punished according to law. The power of punishment is, alone through the means which the laws have provided for that purpose, and if they are ineffectual, there is an immunity from punishment, no matter how great an offender the individual may be, or how much his crimes may have shocked the sense of justice of the country, or endangered its safety. By the protection of the law human rights are secured; withdraw that protection, and they are at the mercy of wicked rulers, or the clamor of an excited people. If there was law to justify this military trial, it is not our province to interfere; if there was not, it is our duty to declare the nullity of the whole proceedings.

The decision of this question does not depend on argument or judicial precedents, numerous and highly illustrative as they are. These precedents inform us of the extent of the struggle to preserve liberty and to relieve those in civil life from military trials. The founders of our government were familiar with the history of that struggle; and secured in a written constitution every right which the people had wrested from power during a contest of ages. By that Constitution and the laws authorized by it this question must be determined.

The provisions of that instrument on the administration of criminal justice are too plain and direct, to leave room for misconstruction or doubt of their true meaning. Those applicable to this case are found in that clause of the original Constitution which says, "That the trial of all crimes, except in case of impeachment, shall be by jury;" and in the fourth, fifth, and sixth articles of the amendments. The fourth proclaims the right to be secure in person and effects against unreasonable search and seizure; and directs that a judicial warrant shall not issue "without proof of probable cause supported by oath or affirmation." The fifth declares "that no person shall be held to answer for a capital or otherwise infamous crime unless on presentment by a grand jury, except in cases arising in the land or naval forces, or in the militia, when in actual service in time of war or public danger, nor be deprived of life, liberty, or property, without due process of law." And the sixth guarantees the right of trial by jury, in such manner and with such regulations that with upright judges, impartial juries, and an able bar, the innocent will be saved and the guilty punished. It is in these words: "In all criminal prosecutions the accused shall enjoy the right to a speedy and public trial by an impartial jury of the state and district wherein the crime shall have been committed, which district shall have been previously ascertained by law, and to be informed of the nature and cause of the accusation, to be confronted with the witnesses against him, to have compulsory process for obtaining witnesses in his favor, and to have the assistance of counsel for his defence." These securities for personal liberty thus embodied, were such as wisdom and experience had demonstrated to be necessary for the protection of those accused of crime. And so strong was the sense of the country of their importance, and so jealous were the people that these rights, highly prized, might be denied them by implication, that when the original Constitution was proposed for adoption it encountered severe opposition; and, but for the belief that it would be so amended as to embrace them, it would never have been ratified.

Time has proven the discernment of our ancestors; for even these provisions, expressed in such plain English words, that it would seem the ingenuity of man could not evade them, are now, after the lapse of more than seventy years, sought to be avoided. Those great and good men foresaw that troublous times would arise, when rulers and people would become restive under restraint, and seek by sharp and decisive measures to accomplish ends deemed just and proper; and that the principles of constitutional liberty would be in peril, unless established by irrepealable law. The history of the world had taught them that what was done in the past might be attempted in the future. The Constitution of the United States is a law for rulers and people, equally in war and in peace, and covers with the shield of its protection all classes of men, at all times, and under all circumstances. No doctrine, involving more pernicious consequences, was ever invented by the wit of man than that any of its provisions can be suspended during any of the great exigencies of government. Such a doctrine leads directly to anarchy or despotism, but the theory of necessity on which it is based is false; for the government, within the Constitution, has all the powers granted to it, which are necessary to preserve its existence; as has been happily proved by the result of the great effort to throw off its just authority.

Have any of the rights guaranteed by the Constitution been violated in the case of Milligan? and if so, what are they?

Every trial involves the exercise of judicial power; and from what source did the military commission that tried him derive their authority? Certainly no part of judicial power of the country was conferred on them; because the Constitution expressly vests it "in one supreme court and such inferior courts as the Congress may from time to time ordain and establish," and it is not pretended that the commission was a court ordained and established by Congress. They cannot justify on the mandate of the President; because he is controlled by law, and has his appropriate sphere of duty, which is to execute, not to make, the laws; and there is "no unwritten criminal code to which resort can be had as a source of jurisdiction."

But it is said that the jurisdiction is complete under the "laws and usages of war."

It can serve no useful purpose to inquire what those laws and usages are, whence they originated, where found, and on whom they operate; they can never be applied to citizens in states which have upheld the authority of the government, and where the courts are open and their process unobstructed. This court has judicial knowledge that in Indiana the Federal authority was always unopposed, and its courts always open to hear criminal accusations and redress grievances; and no usage of war could sanction a military trial there for any offence whatever of a citizen in civil life, in nowise connected with the military service. Congress could grant no such power; and to the honor of our national legislature be it said, it has never been provoked by the state of the country even to attempt its exercise. One of the plainest constitutional provisions was, therefore, infringed when Milligan was tried by a court not ordained and established by Congress, and not composed of judges appointed during good behavior.

Why was he not delivered to the Circuit Court of Indiana to be proceeded against according to law? No reason of necessity could be urged against it; because Congress had declared penalties against the offenses charged, provided for their punishment, and directed that court to hear and determine them. And soon after this military tribunal was ended, the Circuit Court met, peacefully transacted its business, and adjourned. It needed no bayonets to protect it, and required no military aid to execute its judgments. It was held in a state, eminently distinguished for patriotism, by judges commissioned during the Rebellion, who were provided with juries, upright, intelligent, and selected by a marshal appointed by the President. The government had no right to conclude that Milligan, if guilty, would not receive in that court merited punishment; for its records disclose that it was constantly engaged in the trial of similar offenses, and was never interrupted in its administration of criminal justice. If it was dangerous, in the distracted condition of affairs, to leave Milligan unrestrained of his liberty, because he "conspired against the government, afforded aid and comfort to rebels, and incited the people to insurrection," the law said arrest him, confine him closely, render him powerless to do further mischief; and then present his case to the grand jury of the district, with proofs of his guilt, and, if indicted, try him according to the course of the common law, as a civilian, before the civilian courts. If this had been done, the Constitution would have been vindicated, and the securities for personal liberty preserved and defended.

Another guarantee of freedom was broken when Milligan was denied a trial by jury. The great minds of the country have differed on the correct interpretation to be given to various provisions of the Federal Constitution; and judicial decision has been often invoked to settle their true meaning; but until recently no one ever doubted that the right of trial by jury was fortified in the organic law against the power of attack. It is now assailed; but if ideas can be expressed in words, and language has any meaning, this right—one of the most valuable in a free country—is preserved to every one accused of crime who is not attached to the army, or navy, or militia in actual service. The sixth amendment affirms that "in all criminal prosecutions the accused shall enjoy the right to a speedy and public trial by an impartial jury," language broad enough to embrace all persons and cases; but the fifth, recognizing the necessity of an indictment, or presentment, before any one can be held to answer for high crimes, "excepts cases arising in the land or naval forces, or in the militia, when in actual service, in time of war or public danger;" and the framers of the Constitution, doubtless, meant to limit the right of trial by jury, in the sixth amendment, to those persons who were subject to indictment or presentment in the fifth.

The discipline necessary to the efficiency of the army and navy, required other and swifter modes of trial than are furnished by the common law courts; and, in pursuance of the power conferred by the Constitution, Congress has declared the kinds of trial, and the manner in which they shall be conducted, for offenses committed while the party is in the military or naval service. Every one connected with these branches of the public service is amenable to the jurisdiction which Congress has created for their government, and, while thus serving, surrenders his right to be tried by the civil courts. All other persons, citizens of states where the courts are open, if charged with crime, are guaranteed the inestimable privilege of trial by jury. This privilege is a vital principle, underlying the whole administration of criminal justice; it is not held by sufferance, and cannot be frittered away on any plea of state or political necessity. When peace prevails, and the authority of the government is undisputed, there is no difficulty of preserving the safeguards of liberty; for the ordinary modes of trial are never neglected, and no one wishes it otherwise; but if society is disturbed by civil commotion—if the passions of men are aroused and the restraints of law weakened, if not disregarded—these safeguards need, and should receive, the watchful care of those intrusted with the guardianship of the Constitution and laws. In no other way can we transmit to posterity unimpaired the blessings of liberty, consecrated by the sacrifices of the Revolution.

It is claimed that martial law covers with its broad mantle the proceedings of this military commission. The proposition is this: that in a time of war the commander of an armed force (if in his opinion the exigencies of the country demand it, and of which he is to judge), has the power, within the lines of his military district, to suspend all civil rights and their remedies, and subject citizens as well as soldiers to the rule of his will; and in the exercise of his lawful authority cannot be restrained, except by his superior officer or the President of the United States.

If this position is sound to the extent claimed, then when war exists, foreign or domestic, and the country is subdivided into military departments for mere convenience, the commander of one of them can, if he chooses, within his limits, on the plea of necessity, with the approval of the Executive, substitute military force for and to the exclusion of the laws, and punish all persons, as he thinks right and proper, without fixed or certain rules.

The statement of this proposition shows its importance; for, if true, republican government is a failure, and there is an end of liberty regulated by law. Martial law, established on such a basis, destroys every guarantee of the Constitution, and effectually renders the "military independent of and superior to the civil power"—the attempt to do which by the King of Great Britain was deemed by our fathers such an offence, that they assigned it to the world as one of the causes which impelled them to declare their independence. Civil liberty and this kind of martial law cannot endure together; the antagonism is irreconcilable; and, in the conflict, one or the other must perish.

This nation, as experience has proved, cannot always remain at peace, and has no right to expect that it will always have wise and humane rulers, sincerely attached to the principles of the Constitution. Wicked men, ambitious of power, with hatred of liberty and contempt of law, may fill the place once occupied by Washington and Lincoln; and if this right is conceded, and the calamities of war again befall us, the dangers to human liberty are frightful to contemplate. If our fathers had failed to provide for just such a contingency, they would have been false to the trust reposed in them. They knew—the history of the world told them—the nation they were founding, be its existence short or long, would be involved in war; how often or how long continued, human foresight could not tell; and that unlimited power, wherever lodged at such a time, was especially hazardous to freemen. For this, and other equally weighty reasons, they secured the inheritance they had fought to maintain, by incorporating in a written constitution the safeguards which time had proved were essential to its preservation. Not one of these safeguards can the President, or Congress, or the Judiciary disturb, except the one concerning the writ of habeas corpus.

It is essential to the safety of every government that, in a great crisis, like the one we have just passed through, there should be a power somewhere of suspending the writ of habeas corpus. In every war, there are men of previously good character, wicked enough to counsel their fellow-citizens to resist the measures deemed necessary by a good government to sustain its just authority and overthrow its enemies; and their influence may lead to dangerous combinations. In the emergency of the times, an immediate public investigation according to law may not be possible; and yet, the period to the country may be too imminent to suffer such persons to go at large. Unquestionably, there is then an exigency which demands that the government, if it should see fit in the exercise of a proper discretion to make arrests, should not be required to produce the persons arrested in answer to a writ of habeas corpus. The Constitution goes no further. It does not say after a writ of habeas corpus is denied a citizen, that he shall be tried otherwise than by the course of the common law; if it had intended this result, it was easy by the use of direct words to have accomplished it. The illustrious men who framed that instrument were guarding the foundations of civil liberty against the abuses of unlimited power; they were full of wisdom, and the lessons of history informed them that a trial by an established court, assisted by an impartial jury, was the only sure way of protecting the citizen against oppression and wrong. Knowing this, they limited the suspension to one great right, and left the rest to remain forever inviolable. But, it is insisted that the safety of the country in time of war demands that this broad claim for martial law shall be sustained. If this were true, it could be well said that a country, preserved at the sacrifice of all the cardinal principles of liberty, is not worth the cost of preservation. Happily, it is not so.

It will be borne in mind that this is not a question of the power to proclaim martial law, when war exists in a community and the courts and civil authorities are overthrown. Nor is it a question what rule a military commander, at the head of his army, can impose on states in rebellion to cripple their resources and quell the insurrection. The jurisdiction claimed is much more extensive. The necessities of the service, during the late Rebellion, required that the loyal states should be placed within the limits of certain military districts and commanders appointed in them; and, it is urged, that this, in a military sense, constituted them the theater of military operations; and, as in this case, Indiana had been and was again threatened with invasion by the enemy, the occasion was furnished to establish martial law. The conclusion does not follow from the premises. If armies were collected in Indiana, they were to be employed in another locality, where the laws were obstructed and the national authority disputed. On her soil there was no hostile foot; if once invaded, that invasion was at an end, and with it all pretext for martial law. Martial law cannot arise from a threatened invasion. The necessity must be actual and present; the invasion real, such as effectually closes the courts and deposes the civil administration.

It is difficult to see how the safety for the country required martial law in Indiana. If any of her citizens were plotting treason, the power of arrest could secure them, until the government was prepared for their trial, when the courts were open and ready to try them. It was as easy to protect witnesses before a civil as a military tribunal; and as there could be no wish to convict, except on sufficient legal evidence, surely an ordained and establish court was better able to judge of this than a military tribunal composed of gentlemen not trained to the profession of the law.

It follows, from what has been said on this subject, that there are occasions when martial rule can be properly applied. If, in foreign invasion or civil war, the courts are actually closed, and it is impossible to administer criminal justice according to law, then, on the theatre of active military operations, where war really prevails, there is a necessity to furnish a substitute for the civil authority, thus overthrown, to preserve the safety of the army and society; and as no power is left but the military, it is allowed to govern by martial rule until the laws can have their free course. As necessity creates the rule, so it limits its duration; for, if this government is continued after the courts are reinstated, it is a gross usurpation of power. Martial rule can never exist where the courts are open, and in the proper and unobstructed exercise of their jurisdiction. It is also confined to the locality of actual war. Because, during the late Rebellion it could have been enforced in Virginia, where the national authority was overturned and the courts driven out, it does not follow that it should obtain in Indiana, where that authority was never disputed, and justice was always administered. And so in the case of a foreign invasion, martial rule may become a necessity in one state, when, in another, it would be "mere lawless violence."

We are not without precedents in English and American history illustrating our views of this question; but it is hardly necessary to make particular reference to them. We do not deem it important to examine further the adjudged cases; and shall, therefore, conclude without any additional reference to authorities.

It is proper to say, although Milligan's trial and conviction by a military commission was illegal, yet, if guilty of the crimes imputed to him, and his guilt had been ascertained by an established court and impartial jury, he deserved severe punishment. Open resistance to the measures deemed necessary to subdue a great rebellion, by those who enjoy the protection of government, and have not the excuse even of prejudice of section to plead in their favor, is wicked; but that resistance becomes an enormous crime when it assumes the form of a secret political organization, armed to oppose the laws, and seeks by stealthy means to introduce the enemies of the country into peaceful communities, there to light the torch of civil war, and thus overthrow the power of the United States. Conspiracies like these, at such a juncture, are extremely perilous; and those concerned in them are dangerous enemies to their country, and should receive the heaviest penalties of the law, as an example to deter others from similar criminal conduct. It is said the severity of the laws caused them; but Congress was obliged to enact severe laws to meet the crisis; and as our highest civil duty is to serve our country when in danger, the late war has proved that rigorous laws, when necessary, will be cheerfully obeyed by a patriotic people, struggling to preserve the rich blessings of a free government.

*We emphasize that Congress' power under § 5 is limited to adopting measures to enforce the guarantees of the Fourteenth Amendment; § 5 grants Congress no power to restrict, abrogate, or dilute these guarantees.*

*— William J. Brennan*

## Katzenbach v. Morgan
### 86 S.Ct. 1717, 384 U.S. 641 (1966)

*New York state laws imposed an English literacy requirement to vote. In § 4 of the Voting Rights Act of 1965, Congress prohibited the literacy requirement for voters from Puerto Rico with a sixth grade education. Plaintiffs sued to enforce the state laws and challenged the constitutionality of the federal law. They relied on* Lassiter v. Northampton County Bd. of Election *(1959), a unanimous Supreme Court ruling which had upheld a state literacy test against a 14th amendment challenge, to argue that the New York law was valid and that Congress could not set it aside with a statute. But Justice Brennan cut through the gordian knot. His alternative justification was the theory that Congress could overtly disagree with the Supreme Court and independently conclude that the New York literacy requirement violated the equal protection clause notwithstanding the previous, contrary judicial ruling. To his mind, Section 5 of the 14th amendment is a grant of legislative power that might be likened to a ratchet, i.e., Congress could enforce the amendment by appropriate legislation in the direction of affording greater rights than had the Court, but could not legislate in the other direction to reduce or narrow rights already judicially recognized. Furthermore, he insisted that the Supreme Court was obliged to defer to the Congressional decisionmaking to extend the scope of 14th amendment rights. Justice Brennan's provocative maneuver has been challenged then and since by Justices and scholars, and it remains a controverted interpretation.*

**Justice Brennan:** These cases concern the constitutionality of § 4 of the Voting Rights Act of 1965. That federal statute, in the respects pertinent in these cases, provides that no person who has successfully completed the sixth primary grade in the

Commonwealth of Puerto Rico in which the language of instruction was other than English shall be denied the right to vote in any election because of his inability to read or write English. Plaintiffs, registered voters in New York City, brought this suit to challenge the constitutionality of the statute insofar as it pro tanto prohibits the enforcement of the election laws of New York requiring an ability to read and write English as a condition of voting. Under these laws many of the several hundred thousand New York City residents who have migrated there from the Commonwealth of Puerto Rico had previously been denied the right to vote, and Plaintiffs attack the statute insofar as it would enable many of these citizens to vote.

We hold that, in the application challenged in these cases, the statute is a proper exercise of the powers granted to Congress by § 5 of the Fourteenth Amendment and that by force of the Supremacy Clause, Article VI, the New York English literacy requirement cannot be enforced to the extent that it is inconsistent with the statute.

Under the distribution of powers effected by the Constitution, the States establish qualifications for voting for state officers, and the qualifications established by the States for voting for members of the most numerous branch of the state legislature also determine who may vote for United States Representatives and Senators, Art. I, § 2; Seventeenth Amendment. But, of course, the States have no power to grant or withhold the franchise on conditions that are forbidden by the Fourteenth Amendment, or any other provision of the Constitution. Such exercises of state power are no more immune to the limitations of the Fourteenth Amendment than any other state action. The Equal Protection Clause itself has been held to forbid some state laws that restrict the right to vote.

The Attorney General of the State of New York argues that an exercise of congressional power under § 5 of the Fourteenth Amendment that prohibits the enforcement of a state law can only be sustained if the judicial branch determines that the state law is prohibited by the provisions of the Amendment that Congress sought to enforce. More specifically, he urges that the statute cannot be sustained as appropriate legislation to enforce the Equal Protection Clause unless the judiciary decides—even with the guidance of a congressional judgment—that the application of the English literacy requirement prohibited by the statute is forbidden by the Equal Protection Clause itself. We disagree. Neither the language nor history of § 5 supports such a construction. As was said with regard to § 5 in an opinion from 1884: "It is the power of Congress which has been enlarged. Congress is authorized to enforce the prohibitions by appropriate legislation. Some legislation is contemplated to make the amendments fully effective." A construction of § 5 that would require a judicial determination that the enforcement of the state law precluded by Congress violated the Amendment, as a condition of sustaining the congressional enactment, would depreciate both congressional resourcefulness and congressional responsibility for implementing the Amendment. It would confine the legislative power in this context to the insignificant role of abrogating only those state laws that the judicial branch was prepared to adjudge unconstitutional, or of merely informing the judgment of the judiciary by particularizing the "majestic generalities" of § 1 of the Amendment. The historical evidence suggests that the sponsors and supporters of the Amendment were primarily interested in augmenting the power of Congress, rather than the judiciary.

Thus our task in this case is not to determine whether the New York English literacy requirement as applied to deny the right to vote to a person who successfully completed the sixth grade in a Puerto Rican school violates the Equal Protection Clause. Accordingly, our decision in *Lassiter v. Northampton County Bd. of Election (1959)*, sustaining the North Carolina English literacy requirement as not in all circumstances prohibited by the first sections of the Fourteenth and Fifteenth Amendments, is inapposite. *Lassiter* did not present the question before us here: Without regard to whether the judiciary would find that the Equal Protection Clause itself nullifies New York's English literacy requirement as so applied, could Congress prohibit the enforcement of the state law by legislating under § 5 of the Fourteenth Amendment? In answering this question, our task is limited to determining whether such legislation is, as required by § 5, appropriate legislation to enforce the Equal Protection Clause.

By including § 5 the draftsmen sought to grant to Congress, by a specific provision applicable to the Fourteenth Amendment, the same broad powers expressed in the Necessary and Proper Clause, Art. I, § 8, cl. 18. In fact, earlier drafts of the proposed Amendment employed the "necessary and proper" terminology to describe the scope of congressional power under the Amendment. The substitution of the "appropriate legislation" formula was never thought to have the effect of diminishing the scope of this congressional power. The classic formulation of the reach of those powers was established in 1819 by Chief Justice Marshall: "Let the end be legitimate, let it be within the scope of the constitution, and all means which are appropriate, which are plainly adapted to that end, which are not prohibited, but consist with the letter and spirit of the constitution, are constitutional." A case decided 12 years after the adoption of the Fourteenth Amendment held that congressional power under § 5 had this same broad scope: "Whatever legislation is appropriate, that is, adapted to carry out the objects the amendments have in view, whatever tends to enforce submission to the prohibitions they contain, and to secure to all persons the enjoyment of perfect equality of civil rights and the equal protection of the laws against State denial or invasion, if not prohibited, is brought within the domain of congressional power." Thus Chief Justice Marshall's 1819 standard is the measure of what constitutes "appropriate legislation" under § 5 of the Fourteenth Amendment. Correctly viewed, § 5 is a positive grant of legislative power authorizing Congress to exercise its discretion in determining whether and what legislation is needed to secure the guarantees of the Fourteenth Amendment.

Contrary to the suggestion of the dissent, § 5 does not grant Congress power to exercise discretion in the other direction and to enact "statutes so as in effect to dilute equal protection and due process decisions of this Court." We emphasize that Congress' power under § 5 is limited to adopting measures to enforce the guarantees of the Fourteenth Amendment; § 5 grants Congress no power to restrict, abrogate, or dilute these guarantees. Thus, for example, an enactment authorizing the States to establish racially segregated systems of education would not be—as required by § 5—a measure "to enforce" the Equal Protection Clause since that clause of its own force prohibits such state laws.

We therefore proceed to the consideration whether the statute is "appropriate legislation" to enforce the Equal Protection Clause, that is, whether the statute may be regarded as an enactment to enforce the Equal Protection Clause, whether it is "plainly adapted to that end" and whether it is not prohibited by but is consistent with "the letter and spirit of the constitution."

There can be no doubt that the statute may be regarded as an enactment to enforce the Equal Protection Clause. Congress explicitly declared that it enacted the statute "to secure the rights under the fourteenth amendment of persons educated in American-flag schools in which the predominant classroom lan-

guage was other than English." More specifically, the statute
may be viewed as a measure to secure for the Puerto Rican
community residing in New York nondiscriminatory treatment
by government—both in the imposition of voting qualifications
and the provision or administration of governmental services,
such as public schools, public housing and law enforcement.

The statute may be readily seen as "plainly adapted" to furthering these aims of the Equal Protection Clause. The practical
effect of the statute is to prohibit New York from denying the
right to vote to large segments of its Puerto Rican community.
Congress has thus prohibited the State from denying to that
community the right that is "preservative of all rights." This
enhanced political power will be helpful in gaining nondiscriminatory treatment in public services for the entire Puerto Rican
community. It was for Congress, as the branch that made this
judgment, to assess and weigh the various conflicting considerations—the risk or pervasiveness of the discrimination in governmental services, the effectiveness of eliminating the state
restriction on the right to vote as a means of dealing with the
evil, the adequacy or availability of alternative remedies, and
the nature and significance of the state interests that would be
affected by the nullification of the English literacy requirement
as applied to residents who have successfully completed the
sixth grade in a Puerto Rican school. It is not for us to review
the congressional resolution of these factors. It is enough that
we be able to perceive a basis upon which the Congress might
resolve the conflict as it did. There plainly was such a basis to
support the statute in the application in question in this case.
Any contrary conclusion would require us to be blind to the
realities familiar to the legislators.

The result is no different if we confine our inquiry to the
question whether the statute was merely legislation aimed at
the elimination of an invidious discrimination in establishing
voter qualifications. We are told that New York's English literacy requirement originated in the desire to provide an incentive
for non-English speaking immigrants to learn the English language and in order to assure the intelligent exercise of the franchise. Yet Congress might well have questioned, in light of the
many exemptions provided, and some evidence suggesting that
prejudice played a prominent role in the enactment of the requirement, whether these were actually the interests being
served. Congress might have also questioned whether denial of
a right deemed so precious and fundamental in our society was
a necessary or appropriate means of encouraging persons to

learn English, or of furthering the goal of an intelligent exercise of the franchise. Finally, Congress might well have concluded that as a means of furthering the intelligent exercise of the franchise, an ability to read or understand Spanish is as effective as ability to read English for those to whom Spanish-language newspapers and Spanish-language radio and television programs are available to inform them of election issues and governmental affairs. Since Congress undertook to legislate so as to preclude the enforcement of the state law, and did so in the context of a general appraisal of literacy requirements for voting, to which it brought a specially informed legislative competence, it was Congress' prerogative to weigh these competing considerations. Here again, it is enough that we perceive a basis upon which Congress might predicate a judgment that the application of New York's English literacy requirement to deny the right to vote to a person with a sixth grade education in Puerto Rican schools in which the language of instruction was other than English constituted an invidious discrimination in violation of the Equal Protection Clause.

We therefore conclude that the federal statute, in the application challenged in this case, is appropriate legislation to enforce the Equal Protection Clause.

# CHAPTER THREE

# THE EXECUTIVE POWER

*The Executive Power shall be vested in a*
*President of the United States of America.*

The colorful Alexander Hamilton—born illegitimate in the British West Indies, aide-de-camp to George Washington, author of more than half *The Federalist Papers*, leader of the New York ratification convention, first Secretary of the Treasury, and victim of a duel with Aaron Burr—went to the Constitutional Convention already a devout nationalist and a pragmatic believer in a powerful executive. Unlike his ally James Madison, Hamilton trusted himself and his cohorts and therefore trusted power if it was to be placed in their hands. He and everyone else knew that his mentor George Washington would be selected the first President. Early in the Convention, Hamilton delivered a day-long speech holding up the British constitution as a model to be adapted to the American republic, in particular calling for the election of a Chief Executive to serve a life time term.

While not terribly impressed with Hamilton's anglophile sentiments, the delegates were deeply persuaded of the importance of crafting a strong executive in Article II. Drawing on lessons from the classical education they all shared, Hamilton later articulated this value in *Federalist Paper No. 70*:

Energy in the executive is a leading character in the definition of good government. It is essential to the protection of the community from foreign attacks; it is not less essential to the steady administration of the laws; to the protection of property against those irregular and high-handed combinations which sometimes interrupt the ordinary course of justice; to the security of liberty against the enterprises and assaults of ambition, of faction, and of anarchy. Every man the least conversant in Roman history knows how often that republic was obliged to take refuge in the absolute power of a single man, under the formidable title of dictator, as well against the intrigues of ambitious individuals who aspired to the tyranny, and the seditions of whole classes of the community whose conduct threatened the existence of all government, as against the invasion of external enemies who menaced the conquest and destruction of Rome.

George Washington, like Cincinnatus in ancient Rome, was expected to come to the rescue of the Republic and then could be trusted to surrender power and return to his plow. Indeed, Washington's character and performance in office did more than the Constitution to establish the office of President as the republican opposite of a Caesar. For all subsequent generations the inevitable constitutional worry has been how to restrain broad presidential powers in less worthy hands, to prevent the evils two eminent contemporary scholars of the presidency, Clinton Rossiter and Arthur Schlesinger, describe in their two book-length critiques of presidential behavior, respectively entitled CONSTITUTIONAL DICTATORSHIP (1948) and THE IMPERIAL PRESIDENCY (1973).

The delegates debated the executive article more than any other topic, and that debate has yet to be concluded. They rejected a plural arrangement of ministers in favor of a unitary chief executive. They compromised on the manner of selection by creating the electoral college, which may get the prize for their most byzantine invention. They settled on four year terms and an open ended tenure, though George Washington's tradition of two terms stood until Franklin D. Roosevelt broke it, only to be restored with the 22d Amendment (1951). They situated the presidency within the system of checks and balances with interactive provisions such as the power of the veto, the treaty making power, the power of appointments, and the power of commander-in-chief.

The Framers sought to ensure energy in the national government through its chief executor of the laws. The office was a central feature of their nationalism project. They sought to empower the President against the Congress, which they feared was the most dangerous branch given its patent of powers. At the same time, they sought to make the chief executive accountable to the people. In the process, they rejected, once and for all, the form of executive that was predominant in their time, hereditary monarchs. The office they created in place of a king completely captured the imagination of succeeding generations here and abroad. Constitutional law professor Steven G. Calabresi illustrates this point by observing how countries as disparate as France, Russia, Brazil, and Nigeria, among many others, have all been inspired to adopt presidential forms of government at least in part because of the constitutional experience of the United States. He further observes how recently it has become fashionable among the world's most notorious dictators—Juan Peron, Idi Amin, Mikhail Gorbachev, and Fidel Castro, to name a few—to misappropriate the title President in an attempt to legitimate themselves, much like the German and Russian monarchs called themselves "Kaiser" and "Czar" to appropriate the image of "Caesar."

Fast forward 200 years and consider what the modern American presidency has become. Some contemporary constitutionalists, Philip B. Kurland for example, have concluded that the Constitution has been checkmated, that politics and power have overtaken the 18th century republican design:

> The powers of the American presidency are amorphous and enormous. Perhaps they can be defined only by saying that they are made adequate to the problems to which the power is addressed. Although these powers purportedly derive from the specifications of the Constitution itself, in fact their definition is to be found in the behavior of the American Presidents since 1789. During this time the executive branch, largely with the acquiescence of Congress and the encouragement of the Supreme Court, has come to resemble the monolithic authority to be found in governments that have succeeded to the authority of czars and emperors.

Even if you do not agree with this verdict of history, there is no arguing with Professor Kurland's twin premises that the President wields great, yet still largely undefined, powers and that the other two branches, especially the Supreme Court, have contributed to the aggrandizement of powers in the modern Executive. Justice Jackson once quoted Napoleon's maxim as if to shrug this off, "The tools belong to the man who can use them."

Historically and philosophically, there have been two polar approaches to understanding the import of Article II. The fundamental point of disagreement between the two competing views of the Presidency is how to understand the first sentence of Article II, quoted in the title of this Chapter. Is this first sentence simply a designation of the office as the locus which is assigned the powers listed there, but only those powers specifically enumerated and no others? Or is everything that follows in the Executive article surplusage because the first sentence itself is a grant of all imaginable plenary powers of an omnipotent executive, the clauses following being merely illustrative examples and not an exhaustive list? What does the Constitution contemplate: a President with powers that are limited and enumerated, like the Congress's, or a President with open-ended powers that are equal to unforeseen threats, foreign and domestic, more akin to the powers acceded to the Roman dictators?

This is one time when a close reading of the text cannot resolve the debate. Indeed, adherents of both views of presidential powers invoke the text. Those who take the broad view point out that the first sentence in Article II does not contain the limiting reference to "the powers herein granted," unlike the first sentence in the legislative article, Article I. Those who take the narrow view point out that Article II does not contain an expansive "necessary and proper" clause, like the one found in the list of legislative powers in Article I, § 8, cl. 18.

Presidents themselves have debated this issue in terms of their own incumbency. Theodore Roosevelt took the view that the Executive power was limited only by specific restrictions and prohibitions appearing in the Constitution or congressionally-enacted statutes. His successor, William Howard Taft, who served as President and Chief Justice, took an opposite view that a President can exercise no power unless it is fairly and reasonably based on a specific grant of power in Article II. Grading their papers, Professor Kurland has concluded: "Taft's was the better reading of the origins of the constitutional provisions. But Roosevelt's was the better reading of the history of the presidency and a better prediction of what the presidency would become."

It can be observed without fear of contradiction that the presidency has evolved along with historical changes in the role of the United States in world affairs and in the role of the national government in domestic matters. Both roles were far simpler and much more modest back in 1787, as was the presidency. Today the President of the United States is the most powerful person on earth, possessed of the power to literally destroy all of civilization. The President's authority and influence over the Nation are magnified by all the media, but Teddy Roosevelt's "bully pulpit" has become the ubiquitous television. Expectations for any President are of such Homeric proportions that the question is regularly asked—in the Sunday *Parade*

*Magazine* alongside those "before" and "after" pictures of the incumbent's accelerated aging—whether the American Presidency has become too great for any one person to hold. At the same time, the newspapers are filled with op-ed columns by political analysts lamenting how those who are seeking the office seem to have gotten smaller, in character, integrity, and talent. Presidential politics can only be understood against the constitutional history of the presidency.

\* \* \* \*

This Chapter is all about the Supreme Court's understandings of Article II. The first offering, *Myers v. United States (1926)*, is a notable event in the constitutional and judicial history of the presidency. Chief Justice Taft explores the separation of powers, presumably with the aid of his Executive experience and the mindset of a former occupant of the Oval Office. The President draws power from the constitutional fact that only the President represents us all. He is the ultimate representative of the sovereign "We the people." This authority shields the Chief Executive's performance of all his duties, great and small, including the appointment of the Postmaster for Portland, Oregon. Political scientist Edward S. Corwin described Taft's opinion as "a positive instigation to strife between the President and Congress." The on-going significance of the Appointments Clause, in the Executive Branch chain-of-command "to take Care that the Laws be faithfully executed," is illustrated by the *per curiam* opinion in *Buckley v. Valeo (1976)*. Relying on separation of powers, the High Court struck down the provision of a campaign reform law permitting congressional appointment of members of a regulatory commission.

Justice Robert H. Jackson's concurring opinion in *Youngstown Sheet & Tube Co. v. Sawyer (1952)* marks one of the finest hours of the Supreme Court and, in turn, the Presidency. The Court ruled that President Harry S Truman acted *ultra vires*, beyond his powers, to seize the steel mills and he had to give them back, which he promptly did without further ado. Justice Jackson's carefully-reasoned essay understands governing to be an art, not a science. He expects to find guidance, not results, in the Constitution. This classic opinion remains a primer on first principles relating to the Executive. This episode stands out as an object lesson that Presidents, even when acting as Commander-in-Chief, are subject to the rule of law that is the Constitution.

Three more opinions explore the constitutional relationship between the two elected branches. *The Pocket Veto Case (1929)*, appropriately enough, fills in a gap in the text to explain the effect of a President's refusal to sign a bill into law at the end of a legislative session. Traditions informed the Court's interpretation in favor of the Executive. In two opinions of a more recent vintage, each authored by Chief Justice Burger, the Supreme Court took a strict, almost heroic, view of separation of powers to declare unconstitutional two measures which many insisted were valid and common-sensical as well as greatly needed. *Immigration and Naturalization Service v. Chadha (1983)*, analyzed the so-called "legislative veto," by which one of the houses of Congress could supervise administrative agency decisions. *Bowsher v. Synar (1986)* struck down an elaborate political compromise between the two branches designed to achieve some control over the budget deficit.

Historically, Presidents have bundled recognizable textual powers into rhetorical claims of metaphysical powers argued to be larger than the sum of their parts. The power over "foreign affairs" and the "war making power" are two best or worst examples, depending on one's view of such claims. The Supreme Court has a long history, with few notable exceptions like the steel seizure case, of acquiescing in presidential braggadocio, especially if the Congress is running from a President who is acting the part of the bad-ass bully in the constitutional school yard. Justice Grier's opinion in *The Prize Cases (1863)* is an early example of this attitude of abject judicial deference. Over the history of the United States, by one count, there have been more than 150 military actions of varying dimensions. Yet, the Article I, § 8, cl. 11, procedure for Congress to declare war has been followed only five times. Presidents have been unilaterally responsible for all the others.

Sometimes these bundles of presidential powers have been relied on to justify domestic policies as well. In *United States v. Curtiss-Wright Corp. (1936)*, Justice Sutherland explained the connection between foreign affairs and domestic executive authority. And in what was one of the Supreme Court's worst moments, in *Korematsu v. United States (1944)*, a majority of the Justices approved the internment of more than 120,000 American citizens of Japanese ancestry based on war time hysteria and racial prejudice. Anyone who respects and admires the Supreme Court should pause carefully over this decision.

In a few famous recent constitutional showdowns, the Justices have swelled up to stare down Presidents, but usually Congress is standing just behind them. Two examples are from the troubled presidency of Richard M. Nixon. In *New York Times Co. v. United States (1971)*, the Justices ruled that the Executive Branch could not prevent a newspaper from publishing a government report about the undeclared war in Viet Nam that was classified top secret. Justice Potter Stewart, however, took the opportunity to deliver a chilling warning that the presidency has mutated beyond all constitutional limits of authority, even beyond the power of judicial review. Warren E. Burger, President Nixon's hand-picked Chief Justice, delivered the opinion in *Nixon v. United States (1974)* that ordered the President to turn over tape recordings of his oval office conversations with aides, a ruling that directly hastened Nixon's historic resignation from office.

Relations between the Third Branch and the Executive further complicate separation of powers with mixed consequences. In *Mississippi v. Johnson (1867)*, Chief Justice Chase would not permit a lawsuit against President Johnson. The Court deferred to the textual power to pardon criminals in *Ex parte Grossman (1925)*. The decision leaves us with the question whether there are any constitutional limits on the political considerations behind a presidential pardon. The Constitution by its express terms requires Senate confirmation to make a treaty, but it is silent about setting aside a treaty once confirmed. Justice Powell's concurring opinion in *Goldwater v. Carter (1979)* postpones deciding whether a member of Congress can sue a President in federal court over an Executive decision to abrogate a treaty unilaterally. Finally, modern Presidents have continued the *realpolitik* practice of entering into executive agreements with foreign powers, without Senate approval. *Dames & Moore v. Regan (1981)* upholds an executive agreement that had the effect of suspending court claims against Iran, thus stripping federal courts of cases otherwise within their recognized jurisdiction. Justice Rehnquist's opinion candidly admits that this is more constitutional politics, played on the world stage, than it is constitutional law. Therefore, the High Court is relegated to a spectator's role.

So much for the judicial checks and balances on executive prerogative. From time to time, the Court has acted upon a recognition that the Executive is not the only source of wisdom under the Constitution, but more often than not the Court's immediate purpose has been to embolden Congress to stand up to the Executive Branch, instead of the Court itself picking a fight with the President. Thus the Justices usually play a "let's-you-and-him-fight" constitutional strategy.

Regarding the Constitution and the Presidency proper, my conclusion is borrowed from historian Forrest McDonald's path-breaking intellectual history of the American Presidency:

> The presidency has been and remains a powerful force for ensuring domestic tranquillity among a diverse and sometimes bellicose people, and it has served well to protect the nation in a dangerous and often hostile world. Though the powers of the office have sometimes been grossly abused, though the presidency has become almost impossible to manage, and though the caliber of the people who have served as chief executive has declined erratically but persistently from the day George Washington left office, the presidency has been responsible for less harm and more good, in the nation and in the world, than perhaps any other secular institution in history.

*The President is a representative of the people, just as the members of the Senate and of the House are, and it may be at some times, on some subjects, that the President, elected by all the people, is rather more representative of them all than are the members of either body of the Legislature, whose constituencies are local and not country wide, and as the President is elected for four years, with the mandate of the people to exercise his executive power under the Constitution, there would seem to be no reason for construing that instrument in such a way as to limit and hamper that power beyond the limitations of it, expressed or fairly implied.*

— *William H. Taft*

## Myers v. United States
### 47 S.Ct. 21, 272 U.S. 52 (1926)

*An 1876 statute authorized presidential appointment and removal of postmasters but only with the advice and consent of the Senate. In 1917, President Wilson appointed and the Senate confirmed Frank S. Myers; in 1920, the President removed him without consulting the Senate. Myers sued for the amount of his salary from his firing to the expiration of his four-year term. William Howard Taft, the only man ever to have served both as President (1908–12) and as Chief Justice (1921–30), said later about this case, "I never wrote an opinion that I felt to be so important in its effect." He understood far more was at stake than the political patronage of a lowly postmaster in Portland, Oregon. Filtering the relevant history through his own incumbent philosophy of the Executive, Taft crafted an epic account of the separation of powers over the appointment and removal of executive branch officers. Much of his philosophy of Article II has survived, though somewhat qualified by subsequent history and later Supreme Court holdings, and this opinion has been regularly featured in cases and controversies between the President and the Congress.*

**Chief Justice Taft:** This case presents the question whether under the Constitution the President has the exclusive power of removing executive officers of the United States whom he has appointed by and with the advice and consent of the Senate.

The question where the power of removal of executive officers appointed by the President by and with the advice and consent of the Senate was vested, was presented early in the first session of the First Congress. There is no express provision respecting removals in the Constitution, except as section 4 of article 2, provides for removal from office by impeachment. The specific issue was not discussed in the Constitutional Convention. Under the Articles of Confederation, Congress was given the power of appointing certain executive officers of the Confederation, and during the Revolution and while the articles were given effect, Congress exercised the power of removal.

Consideration of the executive power was initiated in the Constitutional Convention by the seventh resolution in the Virginia Plan introduced by Edmund Randolph. It gave to the executive "all the executive powers of the Congress under the Confederation," which would seem therefore to have intended to include the power of removal which had been exercised by that body as incident to the power of appointment. As modified by the Committee of the Whole this resolution declared for a national executive of one person to be elected by the Legislature, with power to carry into execution the national laws and to appoint to offices in cases not otherwise provided for. It was referred to the committee on detail which recommended that the executive power should be vested in a single person to be styled the President of the United States, that he should take care that the laws of the United States be duly and faithfully executed, and that he should commission all the officers of the United States and appoint officers in all cases not otherwise provided by the Constitution. The committee further recommended that the Senate be given power to make treaties, and to appoint ambassadors and judges of the Supreme Court.

After the great compromises of the convention—the one giving the states equality of representation in the Senate, and the other placing the election of the President, not in Congress, as once voted, but in an electoral college, in which the influence of larger states in the selection would be more nearly in proportion to their population—the smaller states led by Roger Sherman, fearing that under the second compromise the President would constantly be chosen from one of the larger states, secured a change by which the appointment of all officers, which theretofore had been left to the President without restriction, was made subject to the Senate's advice and consent, and the making of treaties and the appointments of ambassadors, public ministers, consuls, and judges of the Supreme Court were transferred to the President, but made subject to the advice and consent of the Senate. This third compromise was affected in a special committee in which Gouverneur Morris of Pennsylvania represented the larger states, and Roger Sherman the smaller states. Although adopted finally without objection by any state in the last days of the convention, members from the larger states, like Wilson and others, criticized this limitation of the President's power of appointment of executive officers and the resulting increase of the power of the Senate.

In the House of Representatives of the First Congress, on Tuesday, May 18, 1789, Mr. Madison moved in the Committee of the Whole that there should be established three executive departments, one of Foreign Affairs, another of the Treasury, and a third of War, at the head of each of which there should be a Secretary, to be appointed by the President by and with the advice and consent of the Senate, and to be removable by the President. The committee agreed to the establishment of a Department of Foreign Affairs, but a discussion ensued as to making the Secretary removable by the President. The question was then taken and carried, by a considerable majority, in favor of the power of removal to be in the President.

Mr. Madison insisted that article 2 by vesting the executive power in the President was intended to grant to him the power of appointment and removal of executive officers except as thereafter expressly provided in that article. He pointed out that one of the chief purposes of the convention was to separate the legislative from the executive functions. He said: "If there is a principle in our Constitution, indeed in any free Constitution more sacred than another, it is that which separates the legislative, executive and judicial powers. If there is any point in which the separation of the legislative and executive powers ought to be maintained with great caution, it is that which relates to officers and offices."

Their union under the Confederation had not worked well, as the members of the convention knew. Montesquieu's view that the maintenance of independence, as between the legislative, the executive and the judicial branches, was a security for the people had their full approval. Accordingly the Constitution was so framed as to vest in the Congress all legislative powers therein granted, to vest in the President the executive power, and to vest in one Supreme Court and such inferior courts as Congress might establish the judicial power. From this division on principle, the reasonable construction of the Constitution must be that the branches should be kept separate in all cases in which they were not expressly blended, and the Constitution should be expounded to blend them no more than it affirmatively requires. This rule of construction has been confirmed by this court in numerous cases.

The debates in the Constitutional Convention indicated an intention to create a strong executive, and after a controversial discussion the executive power of the government was vested in one person and many of his important functions were specified so as to avoid the humiliating weakness of the Congress during the Revolution and under the Articles of Confederation.

Mr. Madison and his associates in the discussion in the House of Representatives dwelt at length upon the necessity there was for construing article 2 to give the President the sole power of removal in his responsibility for the conduct of the executive branch, and enforced this by emphasizing his duty expressly declared in the third section of the article to "take care that the laws be faithfully executed."

The vesting of the executive power in the President was essentially a grant of the power to execute the laws. But the President alone and unaided could not execute the laws. He must execute them by the assistance of subordinates. This view has since been repeatedly affirmed by this court. As he is charged specifically to take care that they be faithfully executed, the reasonable implication, even in the absence of express words, was that as part of his executive power he should select those who were to act for him under his direction in the execution of the laws. The further implication must be, in the absence of any express limitation respecting removals, that as his selection of administrative officers is essential to the execution of the laws by him, so must be his power of removing those for whom he cannot continue to be responsible. It was urged that the natural meaning of the term "executive power" granted the President included the appointment and removal of executive subordinates. If such appointments and removals were not an exercise of the executive power, what were they? They certainly were not the exercise of legislative or judicial power in government as usually understood.

It is quite true that, in state and colonial governments at the time of the Constitutional Convention, power to make appointments and removals had sometimes been lodged in the Legislatures or in the courts, but such a disposition of it was really vesting part of the executive power in another branch of the government. In the British system, the crown, which was the executive, had the power of appointment and removal of executive officers, and it was natural, therefore, for those who framed our Constitution to regard the words "executive power" as including both. Unlike the power of conquest of the British crown, considered and rejected as a precedent for us, the association of removal with appointment of executive officers is not incompatible with our republican form of government.

The requirement of the second section of article 2 that the Senate should advise and consent to the presidential appointments, was to be strictly construed. The words of section 2, following the general grant of executive power under section 1, were either an enumeration and emphasis of specific functions of the executive, not all inclusive, or were limitations upon the general grant of the executive power, and as such, being limitations, should not be enlarged beyond the words used. The executive power was given in general terms strengthened by specific terms where emphasis was regarded as appropriate, and was limited by direct expressions where limitation was needed, and the fact that no express limit was placed on the power of removal by the executive was convincing indication that none was intended. This is the same construction of article 2 as that of Alexander Hamilton.

The view of Mr. Madison and his associates was that not only did the grant of executive power to the President in the first section of article 2 carry with it the power of removal, but the express recognition of the power of appointment in the second section enforced this view on the well-approved principle of constitutional and statutory construction that the power of removal of executive officers was incident to the power of appointment. This principle as a rule of constitutional and statutory construction, then generally conceded, has been recognized ever since. The reason for the principle is that those in charge of and responsible for administering functions of government, who select their executive subordinates, need in meeting their responsibility to have the power to remove those whom they appoint.

Under section 2 of article 2, however, the power of appointment by the executive is restricted in its exercise by the provision that the Senate, a part of the legislative branch of the government, may check the action of the executive by rejecting the officers he selects. Does this make the Senate part of the removing power? And this, after the whole discussion in the House is read attentively, is the real point which was considered and decided in the negative by the vote in 1789.

The history of the clause by which the Senate was given a check upon the President's power of appointment makes it clear that it was not prompted by any desire to limit removals. As already pointed out, the important purpose of those who brought about the restriction was to lodge in the Senate, where the small states had equal representation with the larger states, power to prevent the President from making too many appointments from the larger states.

It was pointed out in this great debate that the power of removal, though equally essential to the executive power is different in its nature from that of appointment. A veto by the Senate—a part of the legislative branch of the government— upon removals is a much greater limitation upon the executive branch, and a much more serious blending of the legislative with the executive, than a rejection of a proposed appointment. It is not to be implied. The rejection of a nominee of the President for a particular office does not greatly embarrass him in the conscientious discharge of his high duties in the selection of those who are to aid him, because the President usually has an ample field from which to select for office, according to his preference, competent and capable men. The Senate has full power to reject newly proposed appointees whenever the President shall remove the incumbents. Such a check enables the Senate to prevent the filling of offices with bad or incompetent men, or with those against whom there is tenable objection.

The power to prevent the removal of an officer who has served under the President is different from the authority to consent to or reject his appointment. When a nomination is made, it may be presumed that the Senate is, or may become, as well advised as to the fitness of the nominee as the President, but in the nature of things the defects in ability or intelligence or loyalty in the administration of the laws of one who has served as an officer under the President are facts as to which the President, or his trusted subordinates, must be better informed than the Senate, and the power to remove him may therefore be regarded as confined for very sound and practical reasons, to the governmental authority which has administrative control. The power of removal is incident to the power of appointment, not to the power of advising and consenting to appointment, and when the grant of the executive power is enforced by the express mandate to take care that the laws be faithfully executed, it emphasizes the necessity for including within the executive power as conferred the exclusive power of removal.

In the discussion in the First Congress fear was expressed that such a constitutional rule of construction would expose the country to tyranny through the abuse of the exercise of the power of removal by the President. Underlying such fears was the fundamental misconception that the President's attitude in his exercise of power is one of opposition to the people, while the Congress is their only defender in the government, and such a misconception may be noted in the discussions had before this court. This view was properly contested by Mr. Madison in the discussion. The President is a representative of the people, just as the members of the Senate and of the House are, and it may be at some times, on some subjects, that the President, elected by all the people, is rather more representative of them all than are the members of either body of the Legislature, whose constituencies are local and not country wide, and as the President is elected for four years, with the mandate of the people to exercise his executive power under the Constitution, there would seem to be no reason for construing that instrument in such a way as to limit and hamper that power beyond the limitations of it, expressed or fairly implied.

Another argument advanced in the First Congress against implying the power of removal in the President alone from its necessity in the proper administration of the executive power was that all embarrassment in this respect could be avoided by the President's power of suspension of officers, disloyal or incompetent, until the Senate could act. In the case before us, the same suggestion has been made for the same purpose, and we think it is well answered in the debate of the First Congress. The implication of removal by the President alone is no more a strained construction of the Constitution than that of suspension by him alone and the broader power is much more needed and more strongly to be implied.

Another argument urged against the constitutional power of the President alone to remove executive officers appointed by him with the consent of the Senate is that, in the absence of an express power of removal granted to the President, power to make provision for removal of all such officers is vested in the Congress by section 8 of article 1.

A reference of the whole power of removal to general legislation by Congress is quite out of keeping with the plan of government devised by the framers of the Constitution. It could never have been intended to leave to Congress unlimited discretion to vary fundamentally the operation of the great independent executive branch of government and thus most seriously to weaken it. It would be a delegation by the convention to Congress of the function of defining the primary boundaries of another of the three great divisions of government. The inclusion of removals of executive officers in the executive power vested in the President by article 2 according to its usual definition, and the implication of his power of removal of such officers from the provision of section 2 expressly recognizing in him the power of their appointment, are a much more natural and appropriate source of the removing power.

It is reasonable to suppose also that had it been intended to give to Congress power to regulate or control removals in the manner suggested, it would have been included among the specifically enumerated legislative powers in article 1, or in the specified limitations on the executive power in article 2. The difference between the grant of legislative power under article 1 to Congress which is limited to powers therein enumerated, and the more general grant of the executive power to the President under article 2 is significant. The fact that the executive power is given in general terms strengthened by specific terms where emphasis is appropriate, and limited by direct expressions where limitation is needed, and that no express limit is placed on the power of removal by the executive is a convincing indication that none was intended.

It is argued that the denial of the legislative power to regulate removals in some way involves the denial of power to prescribe qualifications for office, or reasonable classification for promotion, and yet that has been often exercised. We see no conflict between the latter power and that of appointment and removal, provided of course that the qualifications do not so limit selection and so trench upon executive choice as to be in effect legislative designation. The legislative power here referred to is the legislative power of Congress under the Constitution, not legislative power independently of it. Article 2 expressly and by implication withholds from Congress power to determine who shall appoint and who shall remove except as to inferior offices. To Congress under its legislative power is given the establishment of offices, the determination of their functions and jurisdiction, the prescribing of reasonable and relevant qualifications and rules of eligibility of appointees, and the fixing of the term for which they are to be appointed and their compensation—all except as otherwise provided by the Constitution.

An argument in favor of full congressional power to make or withhold provision for removals of all appointed by the President is sought to be found in an asserted analogy between such a power in Congress and its power in the establishment of inferior federal courts. By article 3 the judicial power of the United States is vested in one Supreme Court and in such inferior courts as the Congress may from time to time establish. By section 8 of article 1 also Congress is given power to constitute tribunals inferior to the Supreme Court. By the second section of article 3 the judicial power is extended to all cases in law and equity under this Constitution and to a substantial number of other classes of cases. Under the accepted construction the cases mentioned in this section are treated as a description and reservoir of the judicial power of the United States and a boundary of that federal power as between the United States and the states, and the field of jurisdiction within the limits of which Congress may vest particular jurisdiction in any one inferior federal court which it may constitute. It is clear that the mere establishment of a federal inferior court does not vest that court with all the judicial power of the United States as conferred in the second section of article 3, but only that conferred by Congress specifically on the particular court. It must be limited territorially and in the classes of cases to be heard, and the mere creation of the courts does not confer jurisdiction except as it is conferred in the law of its creation or its amendments. It is said that similarly in the case of the executive power, which is "vested in the President," the power of appointment and removal cannot arise until Congress creates the office and its duties and powers, and must accordingly be exercised and limited only as Congress shall in the creation of the office prescribe.

We think there is little or no analogy between the two legislative functions of Congress in the cases suggested. The judicial power described in the second section of article 3 is vested in the courts collectively, but is manifestly to be distributed to different courts and conferred or withheld as Congress shall in its discretion provide their respective jurisdictions, and is not all to be vested in one particular court. Any other construction would be impracticable. The duty of Congress, therefore, to make provision for the vesting of the whole federal judicial power in federal courts, were it held to exist, would be one of imperfect obligation and unenforceable. On the other hand, the moment an office and its powers and duties are created, the power of appointment and removal, as limited by the Constitution, vests in the executive. The functions of distributing jurisdiction to courts and the exercise of it when distributed and vested are not at all parallel to the creation of an office, and the mere right of appointment to, and of removal from, the office which at once attaches to the executive by virtue of the Constitution.

Mr. Madison and his associates in the House of Representatives pointed out with great force the unreasonable character of the view that the convention intended, without express provision, to give to Congress or the Senate, in case of political or other differences, the means of thwarting the executive in the exercise of his great powers and in the bearing of his great responsibility by fastening upon him, as subordinate executive officers, men who by their inefficient service under him, by their lack of loyalty to the service, or by their different views of policy might make his taking care that the laws be faithfully executed most difficult or impossible.

Made responsible under the Constitution for the effective enforcement of the law, the President needs as an indispensable aid to meet it the disciplinary influence upon those who act under him of a reserve power of removal. But it is contended that executive officers appointed by the President with the consent of the Senate are bound by the statutory law, and are not his servants to do his will, and that his obligation to care for the faithful execution of the laws does not authorize him to treat them as such. The degree of guidance in the discharge of their duties that the President may exercise over executive officers varies with the character of their service as prescribed in the law under which they act. The highest and most important duties which his subordinates perform are those in which they act for him. In such cases they are exercising not their own but his discretion. This field is a very large one. It is sometimes described as political. Each head of a department is and must be the President's *alter ego* in the matters of that department where the President is required by law to exercise authority.

The extent of the political responsibility thrust upon the President is brought out by Mr. Justice Miller, speaking for the court in 1890: "The Constitution, section 3, article 2, declares that the President 'shall take care that the laws be faithfully executed,' and he is provided with the means of fulfilling this obligation by his authority to commission all the officers of the United States, and by and with the advice and consent of the Senate to appoint the most important of them and to fill vacancies. He is declared to be commander-in-chief of the Army and Navy of the United States. The duties which are thus imposed upon him he is further enabled to perform by the recognition in the Constitution, and the creation by Acts of Congress, of executive departments, which have varied in number from four or five to seven or eight, the heads of which are familiarly called Cabinet ministers. These aid him in the performance of the great duties of his office, and represent him in a thousand acts to which it can hardly be supposed his personal attention is called, and thus he is enabled to fulfill the duty of his great department, expressed in the phrase that 'he shall take care that the laws be faithfully executed.'"

In all such cases, the discretion to be exercised is that of the President in determining the national public interest and in directing the action to be taken by his executive subordinates to protect it. In this field his cabinet officers must do his will. He must place in each member of his official family, and his chief executive subordinates, implicit faith. The moment that he loses confidence in the intelligence, ability, judgment, or loyalty of any one of them, he must have the power to remove him without delay. To require him to file charges and submit them to the consideration of the Senate might make impossible that unity and co-ordination in executive administration essential to effective action.

The duties of the heads of departments and bureaus in which the discretion of the President is exercised and which we have described are the most important in the whole field of executive action of the government. There is nothing in the Constitution which permits a distinction between the removal of the head of a department or a bureau, when he discharges a political duty of the President or exercises his discretion, and the removal of executive officers engaged in the discharge of their other normal duties. The imperative reasons requiring an unrestricted power to remove the most important of his subordinates in their most important duties must therefore control the interpretation of the Constitution as to all appointed by him.

But this is not to say that there are not strong reasons why the President should have a like power to remove his appointees charged with other duties than those above described. The ordinary duties of officers prescribed by statute come under the general administrative control of the President by virtue of the general grant to him of the executive power, and he may properly supervise and guide their construction of the statutes under which they act in order to secure that unitary and uniform execution of the laws which article 2 of the Constitution evidently contemplated in vesting general executive power in the President alone. Laws are often passed with specific provision for adoption of regulations by a department or bureau head to make the law workable and effective. The ability and judgment manifested by the official thus empowered, as well as his energy and stimulation of his subordinates, are subjects which the President must consider and supervise in his administrative control. Finding such officers to be negligent and inefficient, the President should have the power to remove them. Of course there may be duties so peculiarly and specifically committed to the discretion of a particular officer as to raise a question whether the President may overrule or revise the officer's interpretation of his statutory duty in a particular instance. Then there may be duties of a quasi judicial character imposed on executive officers and members of executive tribunals whose decisions after hearing affect interests of individuals, the discharge of which the President cannot in a particular case properly influence or control. But even in such a case he may consider the decision after its rendition as a reason for removing the officer, on the ground that the discretion regularly entrusted to that officer by statute has not been on the whole intelligently or wisely exercised. Otherwise he does not discharge his own constitutional duty of seeing that the laws be faithfully executed.

We have devoted much space to this discussion and decision of the question of the presidential power of removal in the First Congress, not because a congressional conclusion on a constitutional issue is conclusive, but first because of our agreement with the reasons upon which it was avowedly based, second because this was the decision of the First Congress on a question of primary importance in the organization of the government made within two years after the Constitutional Convention and within a much shorter time after its ratification, and third because that Congress numbered among its leaders those who had been members of the convention. It must necessarily constitute a precedent upon which many future laws supplying the machinery of the new government would be based and, if erroneous, would be likely to evoke dissent and departure in future Congresses. It would come at once before the executive branch of the government for compliance and might well be brought before the judicial branch for a test of its validity. It was soon accepted as a final decision of the question by all branches of the government.

It was, of course, to be expected that the decision would be received by lawyers and jurists with something of the same division of opinion as that manifested in Congress, and doubts were often expressed as to its correctness. But the acquiescence which was promptly accorded it after a few years was universally recognized. The acquiescence in the legislative decision of 1789 for nearly three-quarters of a century by all branches of the government has been affirmed by this court in unmistakable terms.

The power to remove inferior executive officers, like that to remove superior executive officers, in an incident of the power to appoint them, and is in its nature an executive power. The authority of Congress given by the excepting clause to vest the appointment of such inferior officers in the heads of departments carries with it authority incidentally to invest the heads of departments with power to remove. It has been the practice of Congress to do so and this court has recognized that power. The court also has recognized that Congress, in committing the appointment of such inferior officers to the heads of departments, may prescribe incidental regulations controlling and restricting the latter in the exercise of the power of removal. But the court never has held, nor reasonably could hold, although it is argued to the contrary in the present case, that the excepting clause enables Congress to draw to itself, or to either branch of it, the power to remove or the right to participate in the exercise of that power. To do this would be to go beyond the words and implications of that clause, and to infringe the constitutional principle of the separation of governmental powers.

Assuming, then, the power of Congress to regulate removals as incidental to the exercise of its constitutional power to vest appointments of inferior officers in the heads of departments, certainly so long as Congress does not exercise that power, the power of removal must remain where the Constitution places it, with the President, as part of the executive power, in accordance with the legislative decision of 1789 which we have been considering.

Our conclusion on the merits is that article 2 grants to the President the executive power of the government—*i.e.*, the general administrative control of those executing the laws, including the power of appointment and removal of executive officers—a conclusion confirmed by his obligation to take care that the laws be faithfully executed; that article 2 excludes the exercise of legislative power by Congress to provide for appointments and removals, except only as granted therein to Congress in the matter of inferior offices; that Congress is only given power to provide for appointments and removals of inferior officers after it has vested, and on condition that it does vest, their appointment in other authority than the President with the Senate's consent; that the provisions of the second section of article 2, which blend action by the legislative branch, or by part of it, in the work of the executive, are limitations to be strictly construed, and not to be extended by implication; that the President's power of removal is further established as an incident to his specifically enumerated function of appointment by and with the advice of the Senate, but that such incident does not by implication extend to removals the Senate's power of checking appointments; and, finally, that to hold otherwise would make it impossible for the President, in case of political or other difference with the Senate or Congress, to take care that the laws be faithfully executed.

What, then, are the elements that enter into our decision of this case? We have, first, a construction of the Constitution made by a Congress which was to provide by legislation for the organization of the government in accord with the Constitution which had just then been adopted, and in which there were, as Representatives and Senators, a considerable number of those who had been members of the convention that framed the Constitution and presented it for ratification. It was the Congress that launched the government. It was the Congress that rounded out the Constitution itself by the proposing of the first 10 amendments, which had in effect been promised to the people as a consideration for the ratification. It was the Congress in which Mr. Madison, one of the first in the framing of the Constitution, led also in the organization of the government under it. It was a Congress whose constitutional decisions have always been regarded, as they should be regarded, as of the greatest weight in the interpretation of that fundamental instrument. This construction was followed by the legislative department and the executive department continuously for 73 years, and this, although the matter in the heat of political differences between the executive and the Senate in President Jackson's time, was the subject of bitter controversy. This court has repeatedly laid down the principle that a contemporaneous legislative exposition of the Constitution, when the founders of our government and framers of our Constitution were actively participating in public affairs, acquiesced in for a long term of years, fixes the construction to be given its provisions.

We are now asked to set aside this construction thus buttressed and adopt an adverse view, because the Congress of the United States once did so during a heated political difference of opinion between the then President and the majority leaders of Congress over the reconstruction measures adopted as a means of restoring to their proper status the states which attempted to withdraw from the Union at the time of the Civil War. The extremes to which the majority in both Houses carried legislative measures in that matter are now recognized by all who calmly review the history of that episode in our government leading to articles of impeachment against President Johnson and his acquittal. Without animadverting on the character of the measures taken, we are certainly justified in saying that they should not be given the weight affecting proper constitutional construction to be accorded to that reached by the First Congress of the United States during a political calm and acquiesced in by the whole government for three-quarters of a century, especially when the new construction contended for has never been acquiesced in by either the executive or the judicial departments. While this court has studiously avoided deciding the issue until it was presented in such a way that it could not be avoided, in the references it has made to the history of the question, and in the presumptions it has indulged in favor of a statutory construction not inconsistent with the legislative decision of 1789, it has indicated a trend of view that we should not and cannot ignore. When on the merits we find our conclusion strongly favoring the view which prevailed in the First Congress, we have no hesitation in holding that conclusion to be correct; and it therefore follows that the Tenure of Office Act of 1867, in so far as it attempted to prevent the President from removing executive officers who had been appointed by him by and with the advice and consent of the Senate, was invalid, and that subsequent legislation of the same effect was equally so.

For the reasons given, we must therefore hold that the provision of the law of 1876 by which the unrestricted power of removal of first-class postmasters is denied to the President is in violation of the Constitution and invalid.

*We think that the term "Officers of the United States" as used in Art. II, defined to include "all persons who can be said to hold an office under the government" is a term intended to have substantive meaning.*

— *Per Curiam*

## Buckley v. Valeo
### 96 S.Ct. 612, 424 U.S. 1 (1976)

*This unsigned per curiam opinion, with varying complements of Justices joining its propositions, was remarkable for its lengthy (nearly 300 pages) and thorough-going revision of the Federal Campaign Act. Far-reaching reforms were added to the federal law in 1974, in the aftermath of the Watergate scandal, out of a concern for the appearance and the reality that heavily-financed campaigns were corrupting the political process. In portions not reproduced here, the Justices rendered a complicated and detailed 1st amendment analysis of the statute, section by section, to approve or disapprove particular provisions. For the most part, the comprehensive powers of the Federal Election Commission to regulate federal campaign financing were upheld. But the Justices found the particular manner of appointing the Commissioners was invalid under the separation of powers and the Appointments Clause in Article I, in the portion excerpted below. The Court felt obliged to finesse the remedy for this constitutional violation, however, since the Commission had been operating for nearly two years, issuing regulations and rendering decisions. Rather than invalidate all of this, the Court gave Congress 30 days to amend the statute to provide that new Commissioners be appointed by the President with the advice and consent of the Senate; Congress promptly amended the statute to conform to the Constitution.*

**Per curiam:** Plaintiffs urge that since Congress has given the Federal Election Commission wide-ranging rulemaking and enforcement powers with respect to the substantive provisions of the Federal Election Campaign Act, Congress is precluded under the principle of separation of powers from vesting in itself the authority to appoint those who will exercise such authority. Their argument is based on the language of Art. II, § 2, cl. 2, of the Constitution—the Appointments Clause.

Plaintiffs' argument to challenge the legislation is that this constitutional provision is the exclusive method by which those charged with executing the laws of the United States may be chosen. Congress, they assert, cannot have it both ways. If the Legislature wishes the Commission to exercise all of the conferred powers, then its members are in fact "Officers of the United States" and must be appointed under the Appointments Clause. But if Congress insists upon retaining the power to appoint, then the members of the Commission may not discharge those many functions of the Commission which can be performed only by "Officers of the United States," as that term must be construed within the doctrine of separation of powers.

In response, the Defendant Commission urges that the Framers of the Constitution, while mindful of the need for checks and balances among the three branches of the National Government, had no intention of denying to the Legislative Branch authority to appoint its own officers. Congress, either under the Appointments Clause or under its grants of substantive legislative authority and the Necessary and Proper Clause in Art. I, is in their view empowered to provide for the appointment to the Commission in the manner which it did because the Commission is performing "appropriate legislative functions."

Our inquiry of necessity touches upon the fundamental principles of the Government established by the Framers of the Constitution, and all litigants and all of the courts which have addressed themselves to the matter start on common ground in the recognition of the intent of the Framers that the powers of the three great branches of the National Government be largely separate from one another.

James Madison, writing in The Federalist No. 47, defended the work of the Framers against the charge that these three governmental powers were not entirely separate from one another in the proposed Constitution. He asserted that while there was some admixture, the Constitution was nonetheless true to Montesquieu's well-known maxim that the legislative, executive, and judicial departments ought to be separate and distinct: "The reasons on which Montesquieu grounds his maxim are a further demonstration of his meaning. 'When the legislative and executive powers are united in the same person or body,' says he, 'there can be no liberty, because apprehensions may arise lest the same monarch or senate should enact tyrannical laws to execute them in a tyrannical manner.' Again: 'Were the power of judging joined with the legislative, the life and liberty of the subject would be exposed to arbitrary control, for the judge would then be the legislator. Were it joined to the executive power, the judge might behave with all the violence of an oppressor.' Some of these reasons are more fully explained in other passages; but briefly stated as they are here, they sufficiently establish the meaning which we have put on this celebrated maxim of this celebrated author."

Yet it is also clear from the provisions of the Constitution itself, and from *The Federalist Papers*, that the Constitution by no means contemplates total separation of each of these three essential branches of Government. The President is a participant in the law-making process by virtue of his authority to veto bills enacted by Congress. The Senate is a participant in the appointive process by virtue of its authority to refuse to confirm persons nominated to office by the President. The men who met in Philadelphia in the summer of 1787 were practical statesmen, experienced in politics, who viewed the principle of separation of powers as a vital check against tyranny. But they likewise saw that a hermetic sealing off of the three branches of Government from one another would preclude the establishment of a Nation capable of governing itself effectively.

The Framers regarded the checks and balances that they had built into the tripartite Federal Government as a self-executing safeguard against the encroachment or aggrandizement of one branch at the expense of the other. As Madison put it in *Federalist No. 51*: "This policy of supplying, by opposite and rival interests, the defect of better motives, might be traced through the whole system of human affairs, private as well as public. We see it particularly displayed in all the subordinate distributions of power, where the constant aim is to divide and arrange the several offices in such a manner as that each may be a check on the other that the private interest of every individual may be a sentinel over the public rights. These inventions of prudence cannot be less requisite in the distribution of the supreme powers of the State."

The principle of separation of powers was not simply an abstract generalization in the minds of the Framers: it was woven into the document that they drafted in Philadelphia in the summer of 1787. Article I, § 1, declares: "All legislative Powers herein granted shall be vested in a Congress of the United

States." Article II, § 1, vests the executive power "in a President of the United States of America," and Art. III, § 1, declares that "The judicial Power of the United States, shall be vested in one supreme Court, and in such inferior Courts as the Congress may from time to time ordain and establish." The further concern of the Framers of the Constitution with maintenance of the separation of powers is found in the so-called "Ineligibility" and "Incompatibility" Clauses contained in Art. I, § 6: "No Senator or Representative shall, during the Time for which he was elected, be appointed to any civil Office under the Authority of the United States, which shall have been created, or the Emoluments whereof shall have been encreased during such time; and no Person holding any Office under the United States, shall be a Member of either House during his Continuance in Office."

It is in the context of these cognate provisions of the document that we must examine the language of Art. II, § 2, cl. 2, which Plaintiffs contend provides the only authorization for appointment of those to whom substantial executive or administrative authority is given by statute. Because of the importance of its language, we set out the provision: The President "shall nominate, and by and with the Advice and Consent of the Senate, shall appoint Ambassadors, other public Ministers and Consuls, Judges of the supreme Court, and all other Officers of the United States, whose Appointments are not herein otherwise provided for, and which shall be established by Law: but the Congress may by Law vest the Appointment of such inferior Officers, as they think proper, in the President alone, in the Courts of Law, or in the Heads of Departments."

The Appointments Clause could, of course, be read as merely dealing with etiquette or protocol in describing "Officers of the United States," but the drafters had a less frivolous purpose in mind. In 1879, this Court explained: "The Constitution for purposes of appointment very clearly divides all its officers into two classes. The primary class requires a nomination by the President and confirmation by the Senate. But foreseeing that when offices became numerous, and sudden removals necessary, this mode might be inconvenient, it was provided that, in regard to officers inferior to those specially mentioned, Congress might by law vest their appointment in the President alone, in the courts of law, or in the heads of departments. That all persons who can be said to hold an office under the government about to be established under the Constitution were intended to be included within one or the other of these modes of appointment there can be but little doubt."

We think that the term "Officers of the United States" as used in Art. II, defined to include "all persons who can be said to hold an office under the government" is a term intended to have substantive meaning. We think its fair import is that any appointee exercising significant authority pursuant to the laws of the United States is an "Officer of the United States," and must, therefore, be appointed in the manner prescribed by § 2, cl. 2, of that Article.

If "all persons who can be said to hold an office under the government about to be established under the Constitution were intended to be included within one or the other of these modes of appointment," it is difficult to see how the members of the Commission may escape inclusion. If, as our prior decisions have held, a postmaster first class and the clerk of a district court are inferior officers of the United States within the meaning of the Appointments Clause, as they are, surely the Commissioners before us are at the very least such "inferior Officers" within the meaning of that Clause. To be sure, "Officers of the United States" does not include all employees of the United States, but there is no claim made that the Commissioners are employees of the United States rather than officers. Employees are lesser functionaries subordinate to officers of the United States, whereas the Commissioners, appointed for a statutory term, are not subject to the control or direction of any other executive, judicial, or legislative authority.

Although two members of the Commission are initially selected by the President, his nominations are subject to confirmation not merely by the Senate, but by the House of Representatives as well. The remaining four voting members of the Commission are appointed by the President *pro tempore* of the Senate and by the Speaker of the House. While the second part of the Clause authorizes Congress to vest the appointment of the officers described in that part in "the Courts of Law, or in the Heads of Departments," neither the Speaker of the House nor the President *pro tempore* of the Senate comes within this language.

The phrase "Heads of Departments," used as it is in conjunction with the phrase "Courts of Law," suggests that the Departments referred to are themselves in the Executive Branch or at least have some connection with that branch. While the Clause expressly authorizes Congress to vest the appointment of certain officers in the "Courts of Law," the absence of similar language to include Congress must mean that neither Congress nor its officers were included within the language "Heads of Departments" in this part of clause 2.

Thus with respect to four of the six voting members of the Commission, neither the President, the head of any department, nor the Judiciary has any voice in their selection.

The Appointments Clause specifies the method of appointment only for "Officers of the United States" whose appointment is not "otherwise provided for" in the Constitution. But there is no provision of the Constitution remotely providing any alternative means for the selection of the members of the Commission or for anybody like them. The Commission has argued that the Appointments Clause of Art. II should not be read to exclude the "inherent power of Congress" to appoint its own officers to perform functions necessary to that body as an institution. But there is no need to read the Appointments Clause contrary to its plain language. Article I, § 3, cl. 5, expressly authorizes the selection of the President *pro tempore* of the Senate, and § 2, cl. 5, of that Article provides for the selection of the Speaker of the House. Ranking nonmembers, such as the Clerk of the House of Representatives, are elected under the internal rules of each House and are designated by statute as "officers of the Congress." There is no occasion for us to decide whether any of these member officers are "Officers of the United States" whose "appointment" is otherwise provided for within the meaning of the Appointments Clause, since even if they were such officers their appointees would not be. Contrary to the fears expressed by the lower court, nothing in our holding with respect to Art. II, § 2, cl. 2, will deny to Congress "all power to appoint its own inferior officers to carry out appropriate legislative functions."

The Commission contends somewhat obliquely that because the Framers had no intention of relegating Congress to a position below that of the coequal Judicial and Executive Branches of the National Government, the Appointments Clause must somehow be read to include Congress or its officers as among those in whom the appointment power may be vested. But the debates of the Constitutional Convention, and *The Federalist Papers*, are replete with expressions of fear that the Legislative Branch of the National Government will aggrandize itself at the expense of the other two branches. The debates during the Convention, and the evolution of the draft version of the Constitution, seem to us to lend considerable support to our reading of the language of the Appointments Clause itself.

An interim version of the draft Constitution had vested in the Senate the authority to appoint Ambassadors, public Ministers, and Judges of the Supreme Court, and the language of Art. II as finally adopted is a distinct change in this regard. We believe that it was a deliberate change made by the Framers with the intent to deny Congress any authority itself to appoint those who were "Officers of the United States." The debates on the floor of the Convention reflect at least in part the way the change came about. In the final version, the Senate is shorn of its power to appoint Ambassadors and Judges of the Supreme Court. The President is given, not the power to appoint public officers of the United States, but only the right to nominate them, and a provision is inserted by virtue of which Congress may require Senate confirmation of his nominees. It would seem a fair surmise that a compromise had been made. But no change was made in the concept of the term "Officers of the United States," which since it had first appeared had been taken by all concerned to embrace all appointed officials exercising responsibility under the public laws of the Nation.

The Commission urges that because of what they conceive to be the extraordinary authority reposed in Congress to regulate elections, this case stands on a different footing than if Congress had exercised its legislative authority in another field. There is, of course, no doubt that Congress has express authority to regulate congressional elections, by virtue of the power conferred in Art. I, § 4. This Court has also held that it has very broad authority to prevent corruption in national Presidential elections. But Congress has plenary authority in all areas in which it has substantive legislative jurisdiction, so long as the exercise of that authority does not offend some other constitutional restriction. We see no reason to believe that the authority of Congress over federal election practices is of such a wholly different nature from the other grants of authority to Congress that it may be employed in such a manner as to offend well-established constitutional restrictions stemming from the separation of powers.

The position that because Congress has been given explicit and plenary authority to regulate a field of activity, it must therefore have the power to appoint those who are to administer the regulatory statute is both novel and contrary to the language of the Appointments Clause. Unless their selection is elsewhere provided for, all Officers of the United States are to be appointed in accordance with the Clause. Principal officers are selected by the President with the advice and consent of the

Senate. Inferior officers Congress may allow to be appointed by the President alone, by the heads of departments, or by the Judiciary. No class or type of officer is excluded because of its special functions. The President appoints judicial as well as executive officers. Neither has it been disputed and apparently it is not now disputed that the Clause controls the appointment of the members of a typical administrative agency even though its functions, as this Court recognized, may be "predominantly quasi-judicial and quasi-legislative" rather than executive. Our Court has carefully emphasized that although the members of such agencies were to be independent of the Executive in their day-to-day operations, the Executive was not excluded from selecting them.

We are also told that Congress had good reason for not vesting in a Commission composed wholly of Presidential appointees the authority to administer the Act, since the administration of the Act would undoubtedly have a bearing on any incumbent President's campaign for re-election. While one cannot dispute the basis for this sentiment as a practical matter, it would seem that those who sought to challenge incumbent Congressmen might have equally good reason to fear a Commission which was unduly responsive to members of Congress whom they were seeking to unseat. But such fears, however rational, do not by themselves warrant a distortion of the Framers' work.

The Commission finally contends that whatever shortcomings the provisions for the appointment of members of the Commission might have under Art. II, Congress had ample authority under the Necessary and Proper Clause of Art. I to effectuate this result. We do not agree. The proper inquiry when considering the Necessary and Proper Clause is not the authority of Congress to create an office or a commission, which is broad indeed, but rather its authority to provide that its own officers may make appointments to such office or commission.

So framed, the claim that Congress may provide for this manner of appointment under the Necessary and Proper Clause of Art. I stands on no better footing than the claim that it may provide for such manner of appointment because of its substantive authority to regulate federal elections. Congress could not, merely because it concluded that such a measure was "necessary and proper" to the discharge of its substantive legislative authority, pass a bill of attainder or ex post facto law contrary to the prohibitions contained in § 9 of Art. I. No more may it vest in itself, or in its officers, the authority to appoint officers of the United States when the Appointments Clause by clear implication prohibits it from doing so.

Thus, on the assumption that all of the powers granted in the statute may be exercised by an agency whose members have been appointed in accordance with the Appointments Clause, the ultimate question is which, if any, of those powers may be exercised by the present voting Commissioners, none of whom was appointed as provided by that Clause. The statutory provisions disclose that the Commission's powers fall generally into three categories: functions relating to the flow of necessary information receipt, dissemination, and investigation; functions with respect to the Commission's task of fleshing out the statute rulemaking and advisory opinions; and functions necessary to ensure compliance with the statute and rules informal procedures, administrative determinations and hearings, and civil suits.

Insofar as the powers confided in the Commission are essentially of an investigative and informative nature, falling in the same general category as those powers which Congress might delegate to one of its own committees, there can be no question that the Commission as presently constituted may exercise them. But when we go beyond this type of authority to the more substantial powers exercised by the Commission, we reach a different result. The Commission's enforcement power, exemplified by its discretionary power to seek judicial relief, is authority that cannot possibly be regarded as merely in aid of the legislative function of Congress. A lawsuit is the ultimate remedy for a breach of the law, and it is to the President, and not to the Congress, that the Constitution entrusts the responsibility to "take Care that the Laws be faithfully executed." Art. II, § 3.

Congress may undoubtedly under the Necessary and Proper Clause create "offices" in the generic sense and provide such method of appointment to those "offices" as it chooses. But Congress' power under that Clause is inevitably bounded by the express language of Art. II, § 2, cl. 2, and unless the method it provides comports with the latter, the holders of those offices will not be "Officers of the United States." They may, therefore, properly perform duties only in aid of those functions that Congress may carry out by itself, or in an area sufficiently removed from the administration and enforcement of the public law as to permit their being performed by persons not "Officers of the United States."

We hold that these provisions of the Act, vesting in the Commission primary responsibility for conducting civil litigation in the courts of the United States for vindicating public rights, violate Art. II, § 2, cl. 2, of the Constitution. Such functions may be discharged only by persons who are "Officers of the United States" within the language of that section.

All aspects of the Act are brought within the Commission's broad administrative powers: rulemaking, advisory opinions, and determinations of eligibility for funds and even for federal elective office itself. These functions, exercised free from day-to-day supervision of either Congress or the Executive Branch, are more legislative and judicial in nature than are the Commission's enforcement powers, and are of kinds usually performed by independent regulatory agencies or by some department in the Executive Branch under the direction of an Act of Congress. Congress viewed these broad powers as essential to effective and impartial administration of the entire substantive framework of the Act. Yet each of these functions also represents the performance of a significant governmental duty exercised pursuant to a public law. While the President may not insist that such functions be delegated to an appointee of his removable at will, none of them operates merely in aid of congressional authority to legislate or is sufficiently removed from the administration and enforcement of public law to allow it to be performed by the present Commission. These administrative functions may therefore be exercised only by persons who are "Officers of the United States."

In summary, we hold that most of the powers conferred by the Act upon the Federal Election Commission can be exercised only by "Officers of the United States," appointed in conformity with Art. II, § 2, cl. 2, of the Constitution, and therefore cannot be exercised by the Commission as presently constituted.

*With all its defects, delays and inconveniences, men have discovered no technique for long preserving free government except that the Executive be under the law, and that the law be made by parliamentary deliberations.*

— *Robert H. Jackson*

## Youngstown Sheet & Tube Co. v. Sawyer
### 72 S.Ct. 863, 343 U.S. 579 (1952)

*In a landmark decision restricting presidential power, the Supreme Court invalidated President Harry S Truman's 1952 seizure of private steel mills. A labor dispute had threatened a nationwide strike and Truman believed that interruption in production would harm the U.S. military role in the United Nations' "police effort" in Korea. Justice Black wrote an opinion for a six member majority that included Justices Jackson and Clark, who had served as Attorneys General for Presidents Roosevelt and Truman before becoming Justices and who had taken expansive views of Executive powers while serving in that branch. Each of the five concurring justices wrote separate opinions to explain why Truman was wrong. The President obeyed the Court and returned control of the mills to the companies, though he later expressed his frustration in a letter to one of the Justices complaining he could not "see how a Court ... could do what the Court did to him" in this case. In numerous later decisions, the Court has relied primarily on Justice Jackson's concurring opinion to reject excessive claims of executive power. This masterful opinion also serves as a testimonial for appointing Justices who have learned their constitutional law at the highest levels of government and not merely from textbooks and court opinions.*

**Justice Jackson:** That comprehensive and undefined presidential powers hold both practical advantages and grave dangers for the country will impress anyone who has served as legal adviser to a President in time of transition and public anxiety. While an interval of detached reflection may temper teachings of that experience, they probably are a more realistic influence on my views than the conventional materials of judicial decision which seem unduly to accentuate doctrine and legal fiction.

A judge, like an executive adviser, may be surprised at the poverty of really useful and unambiguous authority applicable to concrete problems of executive power as they actually present themselves. Just what our forefathers did envision, or would have envisioned had they foreseen modern conditions, must be divined from materials almost as enigmatic as the dreams Joseph was called upon to interpret for Pharaoh. A century and a half of partisan debate and scholarly speculation yields no net result but only supplies more or less apt quotations from respected sources on each side of any question. They largely cancel each other. And court decisions are indecisive because of the judicial practice of dealing with the largest questions in the most narrow way.

The actual art of governing under our Constitution does not and cannot conform to judicial definitions of the power of any of its branches based on isolated clauses or even single Articles torn from context. While the Constitution diffuses power the better to secure liberty, it also contemplates that practice will integrate the dispersed powers into a workable government. It enjoins upon its branches separateness but interdependence, autonomy but reciprocity. Presidential powers are not fixed but fluctuate, depending upon their disjunction or conjunction with those of Congress. We may well begin by a somewhat over-simplified grouping of practical situations in which a President may doubt, or others may challenge, his powers, and by distinguishing roughly the legal consequences of this factor of relativity.

1. When the President acts pursuant to an express or implied authorization of Congress, his authority is at its maximum, for it includes all that he possesses in his own right plus all that Congress can delegate. In these circumstances, and in these only, may he be said (for what it may be worth), to personify the federal sovereignty. If his act is held unconstitutional under these circumstances, it usually means that the Federal Government as an undivided whole lacks power.

2. When the President acts in absence of either a congressional grant or denial of authority, he can only rely upon his own independent powers, but there is a zone of twilight in which he and Congress may have concurrent authority, or in which its distribution is uncertain. Therefore, congressional inertia, indifference or quiescence may sometimes, at least as a practical matter, enable, if not invite, measures on independent presidential

responsibility. In this area, any actual test of power is likely to depend on the imperatives of events and contemporary imponderables rather than on abstract theories of law.

3. When the President takes measures incompatible with the expressed or implied will of Congress, his power is at its lowest ebb, for then he can rely only upon his own constitutional powers minus any constitutional powers of Congress over the matter. Courts can sustain exclusive Presidential control in such a case only by disabling the Congress from acting upon the subject. Presidential claim to a power at once so conclusive and preclusive must be scrutinized with caution, for what is at stake is the equilibrium established by our constitutional system.

Into which of these classifications does this executive seizure of the steel industry fit? It is eliminated from the first by admission, for it is conceded that no congressional authorization exists for this seizure. That takes away also the support of the many precedents and declarations which were made in relation, and must be confined, to this category.

Can it then be defended under flexible tests available to the second category? It seems clearly eliminated from that class because Congress has not left seizure of private property an open field but has covered it by three statutory policies inconsistent with this seizure. In choosing a different and inconsistent way of his own, the President cannot claim that it is necessitated or invited by failure of Congress to legislate upon the occasions, grounds and methods for seizure of industrial properties.

This leaves the current seizure to be justified only by the severe tests under the third grouping, where it can be supported only by any remainder of executive power after subtraction of such powers as Congress may have over the subject. In short, we can sustain the President only by holding that seizure of such strike-bound industries is within his domain and beyond control by Congress. Thus, this Court's first review of such seizures occurs under circumstances which leave Presidential power most vulnerable to attack and in the least favorable of possible constitutional postures.

I did not suppose, and I am not persuaded, that history leaves it open to question, at least in the courts, that the executive branch, like the Federal Government as a whole, possesses only delegated powers. The purpose of the Constitution was not only to grant power, but to keep it from getting out of hand. However, because the President does not enjoy unmentioned powers does not mean that the mentioned ones should be narrowed by a niggardly construction. Some clauses could be made almost unworkable, as well as immutable, by refusal to indulge some latitude of interpretation for changing times. I have heretofore, and do now, give to the enumerated powers the scope and elasticity afforded by what seem to be reasonable practical implications instead of the rigidity dictated by a doctrinaire textualism.

The Solicitor General seeks the power of seizure in three clauses of the Executive Article, the first reading, "The executive Power shall be vested in a President of the United States of America." Lest I be thought to exaggerate, I quote the interpretation which his brief puts upon it: "In our view, this clause constitutes a grant of all the executive powers of which the Government is capable." If that be true, it is difficult to see why the forefathers bothered to add several specific items, including some trifling ones.

The example of such unlimited executive power that must have most impressed the forefathers was the prerogative exercised by George III, and the description of its evils in the Declaration of Independence leads me to doubt that they were creating their new Executive in his image. Continental European examples were no more appealing. And if we seek instruction from our own times, we can match it only from the executive powers in those governments we disparagingly describe as totalitarian. I cannot accept the view that this clause is a grant in bulk of all conceivable executive power but regard it as an allocation to the presidential office of the generic powers thereafter stated.

The clause on which the Government next relies is that "The President shall be Commander in Chief of the Army and Navy of the United States." These cryptic words have given rise to some of the most persistent controversies in our constitutional history. Of course, they imply something more than an empty title. But just what authority goes with the name has plagued Presidential advisers who would not waive or narrow it by nonassertion yet cannot say where it begins or ends. It undoubtedly puts the Nation's armed forces under Presidential command. Hence, this loose appellation is sometimes advanced as support for any Presidential action, internal or external, involving use of force, the idea being that it vests power to do anything, anywhere, that can be done with an army or navy.

That seems to be the logic of an argument tendered at our bar—that the President having, on his own responsibility, sent American troops abroad derives from that act "affirmative power" to seize the means of producing a supply of steel for them. To quote, "Perhaps the most forceful illustrations of the scope of Presidential power in this connection is the fact that American troops in Korea, whose safety and effectiveness are so directly involved here, were sent to the field by an exercise of the President's constitutional powers." Thus, it is said he has invested himself with "war powers."

I cannot foresee all that it might entail if the Court should indorse this argument. Nothing in our Constitution is plainer than that declaration of a war is entrusted only to Congress. Of course, a state of war may in fact exist without a formal declaration. But no doctrine that the Court could promulgate would seem to me more sinister and alarming than that a President whose conduct of foreign affairs is so largely uncontrolled, and often even is unknown, can vastly enlarge his mastery over the internal affairs of the country by his own commitment of the Nation's armed forces to some foreign venture. I do not, however, find it necessary or appropriate to consider the legal status of the Korean enterprise to discountenance argument based on it.

Assuming that we are in a war *de facto*, whether it is or is not a war *de jure*, does that empower the Commander-in-Chief to seize industries he thinks necessary to supply our army? The Constitution expressly places in Congress power "to raise and support Armies" and "to provide and maintain a Navy." This certainly lays upon Congress primary responsibility for supplying the armed forces. Congress alone controls the raising of revenues and their appropriation and may determine in what manner and by what means they shall be spent for military and naval procurement. I suppose no one would doubt that Congress can take over war supply as a Government enterprise. On the other hand, if Congress sees fit to rely on free private enterprise collectively bargaining with free labor for support and maintenance of our armed forces can the Executive because of lawful disagreements incidental to that process, seize the facility for operation upon Government-imposed terms?

There are indications that the Constitution did not contemplate that the title Commander-in-Chief of the Army and Navy will constitute him also Commander-in-Chief of the country, its industries and its inhabitants. He has no monopoly of "war powers," whatever they are. While Congress cannot deprive the President of the command of the army and navy, only Congress can provide him an army or navy to command. It is also empowered to make rules for the "Government and Regulation of land and naval forces," by which it may to some unknown extent impinge upon even command functions.

That military powers of the Commander-in-Chief were not to supersede representative government of internal affairs seems obvious from the Constitution and from elementary American history. Time out of mind, and even now in many parts of the world, a military commander can seize private housing to shelter his troops. Not so, however, in the United States, for the Third Amendment says, "No Soldier shall, in time of peace be quartered in any house, without the consent of the Owner, nor in time of war, but in a manner to be prescribed by law." Thus, even in war time, his seizure of needed military housing must be authorized by Congress. It also was expressly left to Congress to "provide for calling forth the Militia to execute the Laws of the Union, suppress Insurrections and repel Invasions." Such a limitation on the command power, written at a time when the militia rather than a standing army was contemplated as the military weapon of the Republic, underscores the Constitution's policy that Congress, not the Executive, should control utilization of the war power as an instrument of domestic policy. Congress, fulfilling that function, has authorized the President to use the army to enforce certain civil rights. On the other hand, Congress has forbidden him to use the army for the purpose of executing general laws except when expressly authorized by the Constitution or by Act of Congress.

While broad claims under this rubric often have been made, advice to the President in specific matters usually has carried overtones that powers, even under this head, are measured by the command functions usual to the topmost officer of the army and navy. Even then, heed has been taken of any efforts of Congress to negative his authority.

We should not use this occasion to circumscribe, much less to contract, the lawful role of the President as Commander-in-Chief. I should indulge the widest latitude of interpretation to sustain his exclusive function to command the instruments of national force, at least when turned against the outside world for the security of our society. But, when it is turned inward, not because of rebellion but because of a lawful economic struggle between industry and labor, it should have no such indulgence. His command power is not such an absolute as might be implied from that office in a militaristic system but is subject to limitations consistent with a constitutional Republic whose law and policy-making branch is a representative Congress. The purpose of lodging dual titles in one man was to insure that the civilian would control the military, not to enable the military to subordinate the presidential office. No penance would ever expiate the sin against free government of holding that a President can escape control of executive powers by law through assuming his military role. What the power of command may include I do not try to envision, but I think it is not a military prerogative, without support of law, to seize persons or property because they are important or even essential for the military and naval establishment.

The third clause in which the Solicitor General finds seizure powers is that "he shall take Care that the Laws be faithfully executed." That authority must be matched against words of the Fifth Amendment that "No person shall be deprived of life, liberty, or property, without due process of law." One gives a governmental authority that reaches so far as there is law, the other gives a private right that authority shall go no farther. These signify about all there is of the principle that ours is a government of laws, not of men, and that we submit ourselves to rulers only if under rules.

The Solicitor General lastly grounds support of the seizure upon nebulous, inherent powers never expressly granted but said to have accrued to the office from the customs and claims of preceding administrations. The plea is for a resulting power to deal with a crisis or an emergency according to the necessities of the case, the unarticulated assumption being that necessity knows no law.

Loose and irresponsible use of adjectives colors all non-legal and much legal discussion of presidential powers. "Inherent" powers, "implied" powers, "incidental" powers, "plenary" powers, "war" powers and "emergency" powers are used, often interchangeably and without fixed or ascertainable meanings.

The vagueness and generality of the clauses that set forth presidential powers afford a plausible basis for pressures within and without an administration for presidential action beyond that supported by those whose responsibility it is to defend his actions in court. The claim of inherent and unrestricted presidential powers has long been a persuasive dialectical weapon in political controversy. While it is not surprising that counsel should grasp support from such unadjudicated claims of power, a judge cannot accept self-serving press statements of the attorney for one of the interested parties as authority in answering a constitutional question, even if the advocate was himself. But prudence has counseled that actual reliance on such nebulous claims stop short of provoking a judicial test.

The Solicitor General, acknowledging that Congress has never authorized the seizure here, says practice of prior Presidents has authorized it. The appeal, however, that we declare the existence of inherent powers *ex necessitate* to meet an emergency asks us to do what many think would be wise, although it is something the forefathers omitted. They knew what emergencies were, knew the pressures they engender for authoritative action, knew, too, how they afford a ready pretext for usurpation. We may also suspect that they suspected that emergency powers would tend to kindle emergencies. Aside from suspension of the privilege of the writ of habeas corpus in time of rebellion or invasion, when the public safety may require it, they made no express provision for exercise of extraordinary authority because of a crisis. I do not think we rightfully may so amend their work, and, if we could, I am not convinced it would be wise to do so, although many modern nations have forthrightly recognized that war and economic crises may upset the normal balance between liberty and authority. Their experience with emergency powers may not be irrelevant to the argument here that we should say that the Executive, of his own volition, can invest himself with undefined emergency powers.

Our contemporary foreign experience may be inconclusive as to the wisdom of lodging emergency powers somewhere in a modern government. But it suggests that emergency powers are consistent with free government only when their control is lodged elsewhere than in the Executive who exercises them. That is the safeguard that would be nullified by our adoption of the "inherent powers" formula. Nothing in my experience convinces me that such risks are warranted by any real necessity, although such powers would, of course, be an executive convenience.

In the practical working of our Government we already have evolved a technique within the framework of the Constitution by which normal executive powers may be considerably expanded to meet an emergency. Congress may and has granted extraordinary authorities which lie dormant in normal times but may be called into play by the Executive in war or upon proclamation of a national emergency. Under this procedure we retain Government by law—special, temporary law, perhaps, but law nonetheless. The public may know the extent and limitations of the powers that can be asserted, and persons affected may be informed from the statute of their rights and duties.

In view of the ease, expedition and safety with which Congress can grant and has granted large emergency powers, certainly ample to embrace this crisis, I am quite unimpressed with the argument that we should affirm possession of them without statute. Such power either has no beginning or it has no end. If it exists, it need submit to no legal restraint. I am not alarmed that it would plunge us straightway into dictatorship, but it is at least a step in that wrong direction.

As to whether there is imperative necessity for such powers, it is relevant to note the gap that exists between the President's paper powers and his real powers. The Constitution does not disclose the measure of the actual controls wielded by the modern presidential office. That instrument must be understood as an Eighteenth-Century sketch of a government hoped for, not as a blueprint of the Government that is. Vast accretions of federal power, eroded from that reserved by the States, have magnified the scope of presidential activity. Subtle shifts take place in the centers of real power that do not show on the face of the Constitution.

Executive power has the advantage of concentration in a single head in those choice the whole Nation has a part, making him the focus of public hopes and expectations. In drama, magnitude and finality his decisions so far overshadow any others that almost alone he fills the public eye and ear. No other personality in public life can begin to compete with him in access to the public mind through modern methods of communications.

By his prestige as head of state and his influence upon public opinion he exerts a leverage upon those who are supposed to check and balance his power which often cancels their effectiveness.

Moreover, rise of the party system has made a significant extraconstitutional supplement to real executive power. No appraisal of his necessities is realistic which overlooks that he heads a political system as well as a legal system. Party loyalties and interests, sometimes more binding than law, extend his effective control into branches of government other than his own and he often may win, as a political leader, what he cannot command under the Constitution. Indeed, Woodrow Wilson, commenting on the President as leader both of his party and of the Nation, observed, "If he rightly interpret the national thought and boldly insist upon it, he is irresistible. His office is anything he has the sagacity and force to make it." I cannot be brought to believe that this country will suffer if the Court refuses further to aggrandize the presidential office, already so potent and so relatively immune from judicial review, at the expense of Congress.

But I have no illusion that any decision by this Court can keep power in the hands of Congress if it is not wise and timely in meeting its problems. A crisis that challenges the President equally, or perhaps primarily, challenges Congress. If not good law, there was worldly wisdom in the maxim attributed to Napoleon that "The tools belong to the man who can use them." We may say that power to legislate for emergencies belongs in the hands of Congress, but only Congress itself can prevent power from slipping through its fingers.

The essence of our free Government is "leave to live by no man's leave, underneath the law"—to be governed by those impersonal forces which we call law. Our Government is fashioned to fulfill this concept so far as humanly possible. The Executive, except for recommendation and veto, has no legislative power. The executive action we have here originates in the individual will of the President and represents an exercise of authority without law. No one, perhaps not even the President, knows the limits of the power he may seek to exert in this instance and the parties affected cannot learn the limit of their rights. We do not know today what powers over labor or property would be claimed to flow from Government possession if we should legalize it, what rights to compensation would be claimed or recognized, or on what contingency it would end. With all its defects, delays and inconveniences, men have discovered no technique for long preserving free government except that the Executive be under the law, and that the law be made by parliamentary deliberations.

Such institutions may be destined to pass away. But it is the duty of the Court to be last, not first, to give them up.

*It is just as essential a part of the constitu-*
*tional provisions, guarding against ill-considered*
*and unwise legislation, that the President, on his*
*part, should have the full time allowed him for*
*determining whether he should approve or*
*disapprove a bill, and if disapproved, for*
*adequately formulating the objections that*
*should be considered by Congress, as it is*
*that Congress, on its part, should have an*
*opportunity to re-pass the bill over his objections.*

*— Edward Sanford*

## The Pocket Veto Case
### 49 S.Ct. 463, 279 U.S. 655 (1929)

*Although historical practice has varied and special*
*sessions may be called for extraordinary reasons, the*
*modern practice has been to divide each two-year long*
*Congress into two sessions of one calendar year each. A*
*bill having to do with Indian Tribal rights was passed by*
*the Congress and presented to the President on June 24,*
*1926. On July 3d, the first session of the 69th Congress*
*was adjourned; neither house of Congress was in session*
*on July 6th, the 10th day after the bill had been pre-*
*sented. The second session of that Congress began on the*
*first Monday in December. A unanimous Supreme Court*
*joined the opinion of Justice Edward Sanford to hold*
*that a bill passed by Congress, but not signed by the*
*President, had died when the Congress adjourned be-*
*tween its first and second sessions. The so-called "Pocket*
*Veto," under Article I, § 7, cl. 3, by which the President*
*neither signs nor formally vetoes a bill but simply keeps it*
*in his "pocket," can be used after final adjournment of a*
*Congress and, this case decides, after the adjournment*
*between sessions of a Congress. In this way, the President*
*can kill the legislation without any possibility of being*
*formally overridden and without having to give any rea-*
*son whatsoever. This power is all the more significant*
*because it is not uncommon for a great many, often im-*
*portant, bills to be finally passed near the end of a ses-*
*sion. Since James Madison first used the device, thirty*
*Presidents have pocketed more than one thousand pieces*
*of legislation, and roughly one-fourth have occurred, un-*

*der the ruling of this case, in between sessions. Later federal cases would hold that the pocket veto could not be used after the brief adjournments during a session. Then the regular Article I, § 7 procedure, providing that a two-thirds majority in each house of Congress may override a President's formal decision to veto a law, must be followed.*

**Justice Sanford:** This case presents the question whether, under the second clause in section 7 of Article 1 of the Constitution of the United States, a bill which is passed by both Houses of Congress during the first regular session of a particular Congress and presented to the President less than ten days (Sundays excepted) before the adjournment of that session, but is neither signed by the President nor returned by him to the house in which it originated, becomes a law in like manner as if he had signed it. The President neither signed the bill nor returned it to the Senate. And it was not published as a law.

The clause of the Constitution here in question reads as follows: "Every Bill which shall have passed the House of Representatives and the Senate, shall, before it become a Law, be presented to the President of the United States; if he approve he shall sign it, but if not he shall return it, with his Objections to that House in which it shall have originated, who shall enter the Objections at large on their Journal, and proceed to reconsider it. If after such Reconsideration two thirds of that House shall agree to pass the Bill, it shall be sent, together with the Objections, to the other House, by which it shall likewise be reconsidered, and if approved by two thirds of that House, it shall become a Law. If any Bill shall not be returned by the President within ten Days (Sundays excepted) after it shall have been presented to him, the Same shall be a Law, in like manner as if he had signed it, unless the Congress by their Adjournment prevent its Return, in which Case it shall not be a Law."

The specific question here presented is whether, within the meaning of the last sentence, Congress by the adjournment on July 3 prevented the President from returning the bill within ten days, Sundays excepted, after it had been presented to him. If the adjournment did not prevent him from returning the bill within the prescribed time, it became a law without his signature; but, if the adjournment prevented him from so doing, it did not become a law. This is unquestioned.

No light is thrown on the meaning of the constitutional provision in the proceedings and debates of the Constitutional Convention; and there has been no decision of this Court dealing directly with its meaning and effect in respect to the precise question here involved.

The Constitution in giving the President a qualified negative over legislation—commonly called a veto—entrusts him with an authority and imposes upon him an obligation that are of the highest importance, in the execution of which it is made his duty not only to sign bills that he approves in order that they may become law, but to return bills that he disapproves, with his objections, in order that they may be reconsidered by Congress. The faithful and effective exercise of this momentous duty necessarily requires time in which the President may carefully examine and consider a bill and determine, after due deliberation, whether he should approve or disapprove it, and if he disapproves it, formulate his objections for the consideration of Congress. To that end a specified time is given, after the bill has been presented to him, in which he may examine its provisions and either approve it or return it, not approved, for reconsideration. The power thus conferred upon the President cannot be narrowed or cut down by Congress, nor the time within which it is to be exercised lessened, directly or indirectly. And it is just as essential a part of the constitutional provisions, guarding against ill-considered and unwise legislation, that the President, on his part, should have the full time allowed him for determining whether he should approve or disapprove a bill, and if disapproved, for adequately formulating the objections that should be considered by Congress, as it is that Congress, on its part, should have an opportunity to re-pass the bill over his objections.

It will frequently happen, especially when many bills are presented to the President near the close of a session, some of which are complicated or deal with questions of great moment, that when Congress adjourns before the time allowed for his consideration and action has expired, he will not have been able to determine whether some of them should be approved or disapproved, or, if disapproved, to formulate adequately the objections which should receive the consideration of Congress. And it is plain that when the adjournment of Congress prevents the return of a bill within the allotted time, the failure of the bill to become a law cannot properly be ascribed to the disapproval of the President—who presumably would have returned it before the adjournment if there had been sufficient time in which to complete his consideration and take such action—but is attributable solely to the action of Congress in adjourning before the time allowed the President for returning the bill had expired.

There is plainly no warrant for adopting the suggestion of counsel for the petitioners that the phrase "within ten Days (Sundays excepted)," may be construed as meaning, not calendar days, but "legislative days," that is, days during which Congress is in legislative session—thereby excluding all calendar days which are not also legislative days from the computation of the period allowed the President for returning a bill. The words used in the Constitution are to be taken in their natural and obvious sense, and are to be given the meaning they have in common use unless there are very strong reasons to the contrary. The word "days," when not qualified, means in ordinary and common usage calendar days. This is obviously the meaning in which it is used in the constitutional provision, and is emphasized by the fact that "Sundays" are excepted. There is nothing whatever to justify changing this meaning by inserting the word "legislative" as a qualifying adjective. And no President or Congress has ever suggested that the President has ten "legislative days" in which to consider and return a bill, or proceeded upon that theory.

Nor can we agree with the argument that the word "adjournment" as used in the constitutional provision refers only to the final adjournment of the Congress. The word "adjournment' is not qualified by the word "final;" and there is nothing in the context which warrants the insertion of such a limitation. On the contrary, the fact that the word "adjournment" as used in the Constitution is not limited to a final adjournment, is shown by the first clause in section 5 of Article 1, which provides that a smaller number than a majority of each House may "adjourn" from day to day, and by the fourth clause of the same Article, which provides that neither House, during the session of Congress, shall, without the consent of the other, "adjourn" for more than three days. And the Standing Rules of the Senate refer specifically to motions to "adjourn to a day certain;" and the Rules of the House of Representatives, to an "adjournment" at the end of one session.

We think that under the constitutional provision the determinative question in reference to an "adjournment" is not whether it is a final adjournment of Congress or an interim adjournment, such as an adjournment of the first session, but whether it is one that "prevents" the President from returning the bill to the House in which it originated within the time allowed. It is clear, and, as we understand, is not questioned, that since the President may return a bill at any time within the allotted period, he is prevented from returning it, within the meaning of the constitutional provision, if by reason of the adjournment it is impossible for him to return it to the House in which it originated on the last day of that period. It is also conceded, as we understand, that the President is necessarily prevented from returning a bill by a final adjournment of the Congress, since such adjournment terminates the legislative existence of the Congress and makes it impossible to return the bill to either House. And the crucial question here presented is whether an interim adjournment of Congress at the end of the first session, as the result of which, although the legislative existence of the House in which the bill originated has not been terminated, it is not in session on the last day of the period allowed the President for returning the bill, likewise prevents him from returning it to such House. This brings us to the specific question whether, in order to return the bill to the House in which it originated, within the meaning of the constitutional provision, it is necessary, as the Attorney General insists, that it be returned to the House itself while it is in session, or whether, as urged by counsel for the petitioners and by the amicus curiae, it may be returned to the House, although not in session, by delivering it to an officer or agent of the House, to be held by him and delivered to the House when it resumes its sittings at the next session.

Clause 2 specifically provides that if the President does not approve a bill "he shall return it, with his Objections to that House in which it shall have originated, who shall enter the Objections at large on their Journal, and proceed to reconsider it." That is, it provides in the same phrase and with no change in definition, that the "House" to which the bill is to be returned is that which is to enter the objections on its journal and proceed to reconsider the bill.

From a consideration of the entire clause we think that the "House" to which the bill is to be returned, is the House in session. Since the bill is to be returned to the same "House," and none other, that is to enter the President's objections on its journal and proceed to reconsider the bill—there being only one and the same reference to such House—it follows, in our opinion, that under the constitutional mandate it is to be returned to the "House" when sitting in an organized capacity for the transaction of business, and having authority to receive the return,

— 277 —

enter the President's objections on its journal, and proceed to reconsider the bill; and that no return can be made to the House when it is not in session as a collective body and its members are dispersed. This accords with the long established practice of both Houses of Congress to receive messages from the President while they are in session.

We find no substantial basis for the suggestion that although the House in which the bill originated is not in session the bill may nevertheless be returned, consistently with the constitutional mandate, by delivering it, with the President's objections, to an officer or agent of the House, for subsequent delivery to the House when it resumes its sittings at the next session, with the same force and effect as if the bill had been returned to the House on the day when it was delivered to such officer or agent. Aside from the fact that Congress has never enacted any statute authorizing any officer or agent of either House to receive for it bills returned by the President during its adjournment, and that there is no rule to that effect in either House, the delivery of the bill to such officer or agent, even if authorized by Congress itself, would not comply with the constitutional mandate. The House, not having been in session when the bill was delivered to the officer or agent, could neither have received the bill and objections at that time, nor have entered the objections upon its journal, nor have proceeded to reconsider the bill, as the Constitution requires; and there is nothing in the Constitution which authorizes either House to make a nunc pro tunc record of the return of a bill as of a date on which it had not, in fact, been returned. Manifestly it was not intended that, instead of returning the bill to the House itself, as required by the constitutional provision, the President should be authorized to deliver it, during an adjournment of the House, to some individual officer or agent not authorized to make any legislative record of its delivery, who should hold it in his own hands for days, weeks or perhaps months, not only leaving open possible questions as to the date on which it had been delivered to him, or whether it had in fact been delivered to him at all, but keeping the bill in the meantime in a state of suspended animation until the House resumes its sittings, with no certain knowledge on the part of the public as to whether it had or had not been seasonably delivered, and necessarily causing delay in its reconsideration which the Constitution evidently intended to avoid.

In short, it was plainly the object of the constitutional provision that there should be a timely return of the bill, which should not only be a matter of official record definitely shown by the journal of the House itself, giving public, certain and prompt knowledge as to the status of the bill, but should enable Congress to proceed immediately with its reconsideration; and that the return of the bill should be an actual and public return to the House itself, and not a fictitious return by a delivery of the bill to some individual which could be given a retroactive effect at a later date when the time for the return of the bill to the House had expired.

The views which we have expressed as to the construction and effect of the constitutional provision here in question are confirmed by the practical construction that has been given to it by the Presidents through a long course of years, in which Congress has acquiesced. Long settled and established practice is a consideration of great weight in a proper interpretation of constitutional provisions of this character. Without analyzing these more-than-a-hundred instances in detail, we think they show that for a long series of years, commencing with President Madison's administration and continuing until the action of the House Committee of the Whole in 1927, all the Presidents who have had occasion to deal with this question have adopted and carried into effect the construction of the constitutional provision that they were prevented from returning the bill to the House in which it originated by the adjournment of the session of Congress; and that this construction has been acquiesced in by both Houses of Congress until 1927.

For these reasons we conclude that the adjournment of the first session of the 69th Congress on July 3, 1926, prevented the President, within the meaning of the constitutional provision, from returning this Bill within ten days, Sundays excepted, after it had been presented to him, and that it did not become a law.

*The decision to provide the President with a limited and qualified power to nullify proposed legislation by veto was based on the profound conviction of the Framers that the powers conferred on Congress were the powers to be most carefully circumscribed. It is beyond doubt that lawmaking was a power to be shared by both Houses and the President.*

— *Warren E. Burger*

## Immigration and Naturalization Service v. Chadha
### 103 S.Ct. 2764, 462 U.S. 919 (1983)

*Jagdish Rai Khiali Ram Nathod Ram Chadha was born in Kenya of Indian parents. He came to the U.S. under a British passport to attend college. When his student visa expired, neither Britain nor Kenya would let him return, so he applied for permanent residency in the U.S. After a long and involved administrative procedure, Chadha's application, in effect, was approved. But two years later, consistent with the relevant statute, the House of Representatives voted to set aside the Executive branch's decision, on the basis of an unexplained recommendation of a subcommittee chair, and Chadha suddenly was facing deportation. By a 7 to 2 vote, the Court held the so-called "legislative veto," a procedure by which one of the houses of Congress could vote by itself to set aside an Executive Branch decision, could not be squared with the Constitution. Reading the Constitution literally, Chief Justice Burger delivered a high school civics lesson on lawmaking. Justice White nearly could not contain his dissent, concluding: "I regret that I am in disagreement with my colleagues on the fundamental questions that this case presents. But even more I regret the destructive scope of the Court's holding. It reflects a profoundly different conception of the Constitution than that held by the Courts which sanctioned the modern administrative state. Today's decision strikes down in one fell swoop provisions in more laws enacted by Congress than the Court has cumulatively invalidated in its history." In the years since this decision, practical politics and power continue to be brokered, however, by the congressional enactment of no fewer than two hundred new provisions which are only a subtlety different variety of indirect legislative vetoes. Chadha became a U.S. citizen in 1984. He married, started a family, and became a sales manager in a stereo store. About his ten year ordeal with the law, Chadha was heard to proclaim proudly, "As long as the republic of the United States lives, law students will all study my case."*

**Chief Justice Burger:** We turn now to the question whether action of one House of Congress under this statute violates strictures of the Constitution. We begin, of course, with the presumption that the challenged statute is valid. Its wisdom is not the concern of the courts; if a challenged action does not violate the Constitution, it must be sustained: "Once the meaning of an enactment is discerned and its constitutionality determined, the judicial process comes to an end. We do not sit as a committee of review, nor are we vested with the power of veto."

By the same token, the fact that a given law or procedure is efficient, convenient, and useful in facilitating functions of government, standing alone, will not save it if it is contrary to the Constitution. Convenience and efficiency are not the primary objectives—or the hallmarks—of democratic government and our inquiry is sharpened rather than blunted by the fact that Congressional veto provisions are appearing with increasing frequency in statutes which delegate authority to executive and independent agencies. A recent commentary has noted: "Since 1932, when the first veto provision was enacted into law, 295 congressional veto-type procedures have been inserted in 196 different statutes as follows: from 1932 to 1939, five statutes were affected; from 1940–49, nineteen statutes; between 1950–59, thirty-four statutes; and from 1960–69, forty-nine. From the year 1970 through 1975, at least one hundred sixty-three such provisions were included in eighty-nine laws."

Justice White undertakes in his dissent to make a case for the proposition that the one-House veto is a useful "political invention," and we need not challenge that assertion. We can even concede this utilitarian argument although the long range political wisdom of this "invention" is arguable. It has been vigorously debated and it is instructive to compare the views of the protagonists. But policy arguments supporting even useful "political inventions" are subject to the demands of the Constitution which defines powers and, with respect to this subject, sets out just how those powers are to be exercised.

Explicit and unambiguous provisions of the Constitution prescribe and define the respective functions of the Congress and of the Executive in the legislative process. Since the precise terms of those familiar provisions are critical to the resolution of this case, we set them out verbatim. Article I provides: "All legislative Powers herein granted shall be vested in a Congress of the United States, which shall consist of a Senate and a House of Representatives." Art. I, § 1. "Every Bill which shall have passed the House of Representatives and the Senate, shall, before it becomes a Law, be presented to the President of the United States." Art. I, § 7, cl. 2. "Every Order, Resolution, or Vote to which the Concurrence of the Senate and House of Representatives may be necessary (except on a question of Adjournment) shall be presented to the President of the United States; and before the Same shall take Effect, shall be approved by him, or being disapproved by him, shall be repassed by two thirds of the Senate and House of Representatives, according to the Rules and Limitations prescribed in the Case of a Bill." Art. I, § 7, cl. 3.

These provisions of Art. I are integral parts of the constitutional design for the separation of powers. We have recently noted that "the principle of separation of powers was not simply an abstract generalization in the minds of the Framers: it was woven into the documents that they drafted in Philadelphia in the summer of 1787." Just as we relied on the textual provision of Art. II, § 2, cl. 2, to vindicate the principle of separation of powers, we find that the purposes underlying the Presentment Clauses, Art. I, § 7, cls. 2 & 3, and the bicameral requirement of Art. I, § 1 and § 7, cl. 2, guide our resolution of the important question presented in this case. The very structure of the articles delegating and separating powers under Arts. I, II, and III exemplify the concept of separation of powers and we now turn to Art. I.

The records of the Constitutional Convention reveal that the requirement that all legislation be presented to the President before becoming law was uniformly accepted by the Framers. Presentment to the President and the Presidential veto were considered so imperative that the draftsmen took special pains to assure that these requirements could not be circumvented. During the final debate on Art. I, § 7, cl. 2, James Madison expressed concern that it might easily be evaded by the simple expedient of calling a proposed law a "resolution" or "vote" rather than a "bill." As a consequence, Art. I, § 7, cl. 3, was added.

The decision to provide the President with a limited and qualified power to nullify proposed legislation by veto was based on the profound conviction of the Framers that the powers conferred on Congress were the powers to be most carefully circumscribed. It is beyond doubt that lawmaking was a power to be shared by both Houses and the President. In *The Federalist No. 73*, Alexander Hamilton focused on the President's role in making laws: "If even no propensity had ever discovered itself in the legislative body to invade the rights of the Executive, the rules of just reasoning and theoretic propriety would of themselves teach us that the one ought not to be left to the mercy of the other, but ought to possess a constitutional and effectual power of self-defense."

The President's role in the lawmaking process also reflects the Framers' careful efforts to check whatever propensity a particular Congress might have to enact oppressive, improvident, or ill-considered measures. The President's veto role in the legislative process was described later during public debate on ratification: "It establishes a salutary check upon the legislative body, calculated to guard the community against the effects of faction, precipitancy, or of any impulse unfriendly to the public good which may happen to influence a majority of that body. The primary inducement to conferring the power in question upon the Executive is to enable him to defend himself; the secondary one is to increase the chances in favor of the community against the passing of bad laws through haste, inadvertence, or design." *The Federalist No. 73*. The Court also has observed previously that the Presentment Clauses serve the important purpose of assuring that a "national" perspective is grafted on the legislative process: "The President is a representative of the people just as the members of the Senate and of the House are, and it may be, at some times, on some subjects, that the President elected by all the people is rather more representative of them all than are the members of either body of the Legislature whose constituencies are local and not countrywide."

The bicameral requirement of Art. I, §§ 1 & 7 was of scarcely less concern to the Framers than was the Presidential veto and indeed the two concepts are interdependent. By providing that no law could take effect without the concurrence of the prescribed majority of the Members of both Houses, the Framers reemphasized their belief that legislation should not be enacted unless it has been carefully and fully considered by the Nation's elected officials. In the Constitutional Convention debates on the need for a bicameral legislature, James Wilson, later to become a Justice of this Court, commented: "Despotism comes on mankind in different shapes. Sometimes in an Executive, sometimes in a military, one. Is there danger of a Legislative despotism? Theory & practice both proclaim it. If the Legislative authority be not restrained, there can be neither liberty nor stability; and it can only be restrained by dividing it within itself, into distinct and independent branches. In a single house there is no check, but the inadequate one, of the virtue & good sense of those who compose it."

Hamilton argued that a Congress comprised of a single House was antithetical to the very purposes of the Constitution. Were the Nation to adopt a Constitution providing for only one legislative organ, he warned: "we shall finally accumulate, in a single body, all the most important prerogatives of sovereignty, and thus entail upon our posterity one of the most execrable forms of government that human infatuation ever contrived. Thus we should create in reality that very tyranny which the adversaries of the new Constitution either are, or affect to be, solicitous to avert." *The Federalist No. 22.*

This view was rooted in a general skepticism regarding the fallibility of human nature later commented on by Justice Joseph Story: "Public bodies, like private persons, are occasionally under the dominion of strong passions and excitements; impatient, irritable, and impetuous. If a legislature feels no check but its own will, it rarely has the firmness to insist upon holding a question long enough under its own view, to see and mark it in all its bearings and relations to society." These observations are consistent with what many of the Framers earlier had expressed, none more cogently than Hamilton in pointing up the need to divide and disperse power in order to protect liberty: "In republican government, the legislative authority necessarily predominates. The remedy for this inconveniency is to divide the legislature into different branches; and to render them, by different modes of election and different principles of action, as little connected with each other as the nature of their common functions and their common dependence on the society will admit." *The Federalist No. 51.*

However familiar, it is useful to recall that apart from their fear that special interests could be favored at the expense of public needs, the Framers were also concerned, although not of one mind, over the apprehensions of the smaller states. Those states feared a commonality of interest among the larger states would work to their disadvantage; representatives of the larger states, on the other hand, were skeptical of a legislature that could pass laws favoring a minority of the people. It need hardly be repeated here that the Great Compromise, under which one House was viewed as representing the people and the other the states, allayed the fears of both the large and small states. The Great Compromise was considered so important by the Framers that they inserted a special provision to ensure that it could not be altered, even by constitutional amendment, except with the consent of the states affected. Art. V.

We see therefore that the Framers were acutely conscious that the bicameral requirement and the Presentment Clauses would serve essential constitutional functions. The President's participation in the legislative process was to protect the Executive Branch from Congress and to protect the whole people from improvident laws. The division of the Congress into two distinctive bodies assures that the legislative power would be exercised only after opportunity for full study and debate in separate settings. The President's unilateral veto power, in turn, was limited by the power of two thirds of both Houses of Congress to overrule a veto thereby precluding final arbitrary action of one person. It emerges clearly that the prescription for legislative action in Art. I, §§ 1 & 7 represents the Framers' decision that the legislative power of the Federal government be exercised in accord with a single, finely wrought and exhaustively considered, procedure.

The Constitution sought to divide the delegated powers of the new federal government into three defined categories, legislative, executive and judicial, to assure, as nearly as possible, that each Branch of government would confine itself to its assigned responsibility. The hydraulic pressure inherent within each of the separate Branches to exceed the outer limits of its power, even to accomplish desirable objectives, must be resisted.

Although not "hermetically" sealed from one another, the powers delegated to the three Branches are functionally identifiable. When any Branch acts, it is presumptively exercising the power the Constitution has delegated to it. When the Executive acts, it presumptively acts in an executive or administrative capacity as defined in Art. II. And when, as here, one House of Congress purports to act, it is presumptively acting within its assigned sphere.

Beginning with this presumption, we must nevertheless establish that the challenged action under the statute is of the kind to which the procedural requirements of Art. I, § 7 apply.

Not every action taken by either House is subject to the bicameralism and presentment requirements of Art. I. Whether actions taken by either House are, in law and fact, an exercise of legislative power depends not on their form but upon "whether they contain matter which is properly to be regarded as legislative in its character and effect."

Examination of the action taken here by one House pursuant to this statute reveals that it was essentially legislative in purpose and effect. In purporting to exercise power defined in Art. I, § 8, cl. 4 to "establish an uniform Rule of Naturalization," the House took action that had the purpose and effect of altering the legal rights, duties and relations of persons, including the Attorney General, Executive Branch officials and Chadha, all outside the legislative branch. The statute purports to authorize one House of Congress to require the Attorney General to deport an individual alien whose deportation otherwise would be cancelled. The one-House veto operated in this case to overrule the Attorney General and mandate Chadha's deportation; absent the House action, Chadha would remain in the United States. Congress has acted and its action has altered Chadha's status.

The legislative character of the one-House veto in this case is confirmed by the character of the Congressional action it supplants. Neither the House of Representatives nor the Senate contends that, absent the legislative veto provision, either of them, or both of them acting together, could effectively require the Attorney General to deport an alien once the Attorney General, in the exercise of legislatively delegated authority, had determined the alien should remain in the United States. Without the challenged provision, this could have been achieved, if at all, only by legislation requiring deportation. Similarly, a veto by one House of Congress cannot be justified as an attempt at amending the standards for deportation or as a repeal of them as applied to Chadha. Amendment and repeal of statutes, no less than enactment, must conform with Art. I.

The nature of the decision implemented by the one-House veto in this case further manifests its legislative character. After long experience with the clumsy, time consuming private bill procedure, Congress made a deliberate choice to delegate to the Executive Branch, and specifically to the Attorney General, the authority to allow deportable aliens to remain in this country in certain specified circumstances. It is not disputed that this choice to delegate authority is precisely the kind of decision that can be implemented only in accordance with the procedures set out in Art. I. Disagreement with the Attorney General's decision on Chadha's deportation—that is, Congress' decision to deport Chadha—no less than Congress' original choice to delegate to the Attorney General the authority to make that decision, involves determinations of policy that Congress can implement in only one way; bicameral passage followed by presentment to the President. Congress must abide by its delegation of authority until that delegation is legislatively altered or revoked.

Finally, we see that when the Framers intended to authorize either House of Congress to act alone and outside of its prescribed bicameral legislative role, they narrowly and precisely defined the procedure for such action. There are but four provisions in the Constitution, explicit and unambiguous, by which one House may act alone with the unreviewable force of law, not subject to the President's veto: (a) The House of Representatives alone was given the power to initiate impeachments, Art. I, § 2, cl. 6; (b) The Senate alone was given the power to conduct trials following impeachment on charges initiated by the House and to convict following trial, Art. I, § 3, cl. 5; (c) The Senate alone was given final unreviewable power to approve or to disapprove presidential appointments, Art. II, § 2, cl. 2; (d) The Senate alone was given unreviewable power to ratify treaties negotiated by the President, Art. II, § 2, cl. 2.

Clearly, when the Draftsmen sought to confer special powers on one House, independent of the other House, or of the President, they did so in explicit, unambiguous terms. These carefully defined exceptions from presentment and bicameralism underscore the difference between the legislative functions of Congress and other unilateral but important and binding one-House acts provided for in the Constitution. These exceptions are narrow, explicit, and separately justified; none of them authorize the action challenged here. On the contrary, they provide further support for the conclusion that Congressional authority is not to be implied and for the conclusion that the veto provided for in this statute is not authorized by the constitutional design of the powers of the Legislative Branch.

Since it is clear that the action by the House under this statute was not within any of the express constitutional exceptions authorizing one House to act alone, and equally clear that it was an exercise of legislative power, that action was subject to the standards prescribed in Article I. The bicameral requirement, the Presentment Clauses, the President's veto, and Congress' power to override a veto were intended to erect enduring checks on each Branch and to protect the people from the improvident exercise of power by mandating certain prescribed steps. To preserve those checks, and maintain the separation of powers, the carefully defined limits on the power of each Branch must not be eroded. To accomplish what has been attempted by one House of Congress in this case requires action in conformity with the express procedures of the Constitution's prescription for legislative action: passage by a majority of both Houses and presentment to the President.

The legislative veto doubtless has been in many respects a convenient shortcut; the "sharing" with the Executive by Congress of its authority over aliens in this manner is, on its face, an appealing compromise. In purely practical terms, it is obviously easier for action to be taken by one House without submission to the President; but it is crystal clear from the records of the Convention, contemporaneous writings and debates, that the Framers ranked other values higher than efficiency. The records of the Convention and debates in the States preceding ratification underscore the common desire to define and limit the exercise of the newly created federal powers affecting the states and the people. There is unmistakable expression of a determination that legislation by the national Congress be a step-by-step, deliberate and deliberative process.

The choices we discern as having been made in the Constitutional Convention impose burdens on governmental processes that often seem clumsy, inefficient, even unworkable, but those hard choices were consciously made by men who had lived under a form of government that permitted arbitrary governmental acts to go unchecked. There is no support in the Constitution or decisions of this Court for the proposition that the cumbersomeness and delays often encountered in complying with explicit Constitutional standards may be avoided, either by the Congress or by the President. With all the obvious flaws of delay, untidiness, and potential for abuse, we have not yet found a better way to preserve freedom than by making the exercise of power subject to the carefully crafted restraints spelled out in the Constitution.

*The structure of the Constitution does not permit Congress to execute the laws; it follows that Congress cannot grant to an officer under its control what it does not possess.*

*— Warren E. Burger*

## Bowsher v. Synar
### 106 S.Ct. 3181, 478 U.S. 714 (1986)

*By a 7 to 2 vote, the Court struck down a key provision in the Balanced Budget Act of 1985, killing the elaborate legislative compromise designed to eliminate the federal deficit. The Justices focused on the Comptroller General, who would specify budget reductions in the event Congress did not. The separation of powers problem was that this officer was situated in the legislative branch—he was appointed and could be removed by Congress—but the statute gave him executive functions—to determine and implement budget reductions. Neither the high-minded goal nor the subtle political mechanism could save this 20th century congressional invention from the Court's formal 18th century constitutional analysis. Consequently, Congress was back at square one, faced with a budget process that many believe is completely out of control, if not uncontrollable. After this decision, pressure grew considerably for a "Balanced Budget Amendment" to the Constitution.*

**Chief Justice Burger:** The question presented by these appeals is whether the assignment by Congress to the Comptroller General of the United States of certain functions under the Balanced Budget and Emergency Deficit Control Act of 1985 violates the doctrine of separation of powers.

We noted recently that "the Constitution sought to divide the delegated powers of the new Federal Government into three defined categories, Legislative, Executive, and Judicial." The declared purpose of separating and dividing the powers of government, as Justice Jackson once noted, was to "diffuse power the better to secure liberty." Justice Jackson's words echo the famous warning of Montesquieu, quoted by James Madison in The Federalist No. 47, that "'there can be no liberty where the legislative and executive powers are united in the same person, or body of magistrates.'"

Even a cursory examination of the Constitution reveals the influence of Montesquieu's thesis that checks and balances were the foundation of a structure of government that would protect liberty. The Framers provided a vigorous Legislative Branch and a separate and wholly independent Executive Branch, with each branch responsible ultimately to the people. The Framers also provided for a Judicial Branch equally independent with "the judicial Power extending to all Cases, in Law and Equity, arising under this Constitution, and the Laws of the United States." Art. III, § 2.

Other, more subtle, examples of separated powers are evident as well. Unlike parliamentary systems such as that of Great Britain, no person who is an officer of the United States may serve as a Member of the Congress. Art. I, § 6. Moreover, unlike parliamentary systems, the President, under Article II, is responsible not to the Congress but to the people, subject only to impeachment proceedings which are exercised by the two Houses as representatives of the people. Art. II, § 4. And even in the impeachment of a President the presiding officer of the ultimate tribunal is not a member of the Legislative Branch, but the Chief Justice of the United States. Art. I, § 3.

That this system of division and separation of powers produces conflicts, confusion, and discordance at times is inherent, but it was deliberately so structured to assure full, vigorous, and open debate on the great issues affecting the people and to provide avenues for the operation of checks on the exercise of governmental power.

The Constitution does not contemplate an active role for Congress in the supervision of officers charged with the execution of the laws it enacts. The President appoints "Officers of the United States" with the "Advice and Consent of the Senate." Art. II, § 2. Once the appointment has been made and confirmed, however, the Constitution explicitly provides for removal of Officers of the United States by Congress only upon impeachment by the House of Representatives and conviction by the Senate. An impeachment by the House and trial by the Senate can rest only on "Treason, Bribery or other high Crimes and Misdemeanors." Article II, § 4. A direct congressional role in the removal of officers charged with the execution of the laws beyond this limited one is inconsistent with separation of powers.

This was made clear in debate in the First Congress in 1789. When Congress considered an amendment to a bill establishing the Department of Foreign Affairs, the debate centered around whether the Congress "should recognize and declare the power of the President under the Constitution to remove the Secretary of Foreign Affairs without the advice and consent of the Senate." In the House of Representatives, James Madison urged rejection of a congressional role in the removal of Executive Branch officers, other than by impeachment, saying in debate: "Perhaps there was no argument urged with more success, or more plausibly grounded against the Constitution, under which we are now deliberating, than that founded on the mingling of the Executive and Legislative branches of the Government in one body. It has been objected, that the Senate have too much of the Executive power even, by having a control over the President in the appointment to office. Now, shall we extend this connexion between the Legislative and Executive departments, which will strengthen the objection, and diminish the responsibility we have in the head of the Executive?" Madison's position ultimately prevailed, and a congressional role in the removal process was rejected. This "Decision of 1789" provides "contemporaneous and weighty evidence" of the Constitution's meaning since many of the Members of the First Congress "had taken part in framing that instrument."

In light of our precedents, we conclude that Congress cannot reserve for itself the power of removal of an officer charged with the execution of the laws except by impeachment. To permit the execution of the laws to be vested in an officer answerable only to Congress would, in practical terms, reserve in Congress control over the execution of the laws. As the District Court observed: "Once an officer is appointed, it is only the authority that can remove him, and not the authority that appointed him, that he must fear and, in the performance of his functions, obey." The structure of the Constitution does not permit Congress to execute the laws; it follows that Congress cannot grant to an officer under its control what it does not possess. To permit an officer controlled by Congress to execute the laws would be, in essence, to permit a congressional veto. Congress could simply remove, or threaten to remove, an officer for executing the laws in any fashion found to be unsatisfactory to Congress. This kind of congressional control over the execution of the laws is constitutionally impermissible.

The dangers of congressional usurpation of Executive Branch functions have long been recognized. In 1976, this Court noted, "The debates of the Constitutional Convention, and *The Federalist Papers*, are replete with expressions of fear that the Legislative Branch of the National Government will aggrandize itself at the expense of the other two branches." Indeed, we also have observed more recently that "the hydraulic pressure inherent within each of the separate Branches to exceed the outer limits of its power, even to accomplish desirable objectives, must be resisted." With these principles in mind, we turn to consideration of whether the Comptroller General is controlled by Congress.

Plaintiffs urge that the Comptroller General performs his duties independently and is not subservient to Congress. We agree with the District Court that this contention does not bear close scrutiny. The critical factor lies in the provisions of the statute defining the Comptroller General's office relating to removability. Although the Comptroller General is nominated by the President from a list of three individuals recommended by the Speaker of the House of Representatives and the President *pro tempore* of the Senate, and confirmed by the Senate, he is removable only at the initiative of Congress. He may be removed not only by impeachment but also by joint resolution of Congress "at any time" resting on any one of the following statutory bases: permanent disability; inefficiency; neglect of duty; malfeasance; or a felony or conduct involving moral turpitude.

This provision was included, as one Congressman explained in urging passage of the Act, because Congress "felt that the Comptroller General should be brought under the sole control of Congress, so that Congress at any moment when it found he was inefficient and was not carrying on the duties of his office as he should and as the Congress expected, could remove him without the long, tedious process of a trial by impeachment." The removal provision was an important part of the legislative scheme, as a number of Congressmen recognized.

It is clear that Congress has consistently viewed the Comptroller General as an officer of the Legislative Branch. Over the years, the Comptrollers General have also viewed themselves as part of the Legislative Branch. Against this background, we see no escape from the conclusion that, because Congress has retained removal authority over the Comptroller General, he may not be entrusted with executive powers.

The executive nature of the Comptroller General's functions under the Act is perhaps most clearly revealed in the section that gives the Comptroller General the ultimate authority to determine the budget cuts to be made. Indeed, the Comptroller General commands the President himself to carry out, without the slightest variation, the directive of the Comptroller General as to the budget reductions.

Congress of course initially determined the content of the Balanced Budget and Emergency Deficit Control Act; and undoubtedly the content of the Act determines the nature of the executive duty. However, as our understanding of the Constitution makes clear, once Congress makes its choice in enacting legislation, its participation ends. Congress can thereafter control the execution of its enactment only indirectly—by passing new legislation. By placing the responsibility for execution of the Balanced Budget and Emergency Deficit Control Act in the hands of an officer who is subject to removal only by itself, Congress in effect has retained control over the execution of the Act and has intruded into the executive function. The Constitution does not permit such intrusion.

No one can doubt that Congress and the President are confronted with fiscal and economic problems of unprecedented magnitude, but as we have observed before, "the fact that a given law or procedure is efficient, convenient, and useful in facilitating functions of government, standing alone, will not save it if it is contrary to the Constitution. Convenience and efficiency are not the primary objectives—or the hallmarks—of democratic government." We conclude that the powers vested in the Comptroller General under this statute violate the command of the Constitution that the Congress play no direct role in the execution of the laws.

*If a war be made by invasion of a foreign nation, the President is not only authorized but bound to resist force by force. He does not initiate the war, but is bound to accept the challenge without waiting for any special legislative authority. And whether the hostile party be a foreign invader, or States organized in rebellion, it is none the less a war, although the declaration of it be "unilateral."*

— *Robert C. Grier*

## The Prize Cases
### 67 U.S. (2 Black) 635 (1863)

*After the shots on Fort Sumter but before Congress could convene in special session, President Lincoln declared the Southern States of the Confederacy in rebellion and imposed a blockade of their ports. Congress subsequently ratified Lincoln's emergency actions, but he insisted that he had acted within his inherent authority as Commander-in-Chief. The owners of four ships that had been seized pursuant to the blockade challenged the President's authority and sued for the return of their ships and their cargo. The cases turned on very technical issues, but the question basic to each case concerned the constitutionality of Lincoln's interim executive order. Justice Grier, for a bare majority of five Justices, upheld the President. The four dissenters insisted that only Congress possessed the greater power to declare war as well as the lesser power to impose a blockade. This majority decision went a long way toward legitimating various other emergency actions by Lincoln, including his suspension of habeas corpus and the Emancipation Proclamation of 1863, all done in the name of preserving the Union first and the Constitution second. It is an irony of history and technology that this precedent from the era of sailing ships provides a constitutional rationale for placing the thermonuclear war button under the President's thumb.*

**Justice Grier:** Had the President a right to institute a blockade of ports in possession of persons in armed rebellion against the Government, on the principles of international law, as known and acknowledged among civilized States?

That the President, as the Executive Chief of the Government and Commander-in-Chief of the Army and Navy, was the proper person to make such notification, has not been, and cannot be disputed. The right of prize and capture has its origin in the jus belli, and is governed and adjudged under the law of nations. To legitimate the capture of a neutral vessel or property on the high seas, a war must exist *de facto*, and the neutral must have a knowledge or notice of the intention of one of the parties belligerent to use this mode of coercion against a port, city, or territory, in possession of the other.

Let us enquire whether, at the time this blockade was instituted, a state of war existed which would justify a resort to these means of subduing the hostile force.

War has been well defined to be, "That state in which a nation prosecutes its right by force." The parties belligerent in a public war are independent nations. But it is not necessary to constitute war, that both parties should be acknowledged as independent nations or sovereign States. A war may exist where one of the belligerents, claims sovereign rights as against the other.

Insurrection against a government may or may not culminate in an organized rebellion, but a civil war always begins by insurrection against the lawful authority of the Government. A civil war is never solemnly declared; it becomes such by its accidents—the number, power, and organization of the persons who originate and carry it on. When the party in rebellion occupy and hold in a hostile manner a certain portion of territory; have declared their independence; have cast off their allegiance; have organized armies; have commenced hostilities against their former sovereign, the world acknowledges them as belligerents, and the contest a war. They claim to be in arms to establish their liberty and independence, in order to become a sovereign State, while the sovereign party treats them as insurgents and rebels who owe allegiance, and who should be punished with death for their treason.

The laws of war, as established among nations, have their foundation in reason, and all tend to mitigate the cruelties and misery produced by the scourge of war. Hence the parties to a civil war usually concede to each other belligerent rights. They exchange prisoners, and adopt the other courtesies and rules common to public or national wars.

"A civil war," says commentator Emmerich de Vattel, "breaks the bands of society and government, or at least suspends their force and effect; it produces in the nation two independent parties, who consider each other as enemies, and acknowledge no common judge. Those two parties, therefore, must necessarily be considered as constituting, at least for a time, two separate bodies, two distinct societies. Having no common superior to judge between them, they stand in precisely the same predicament as two nations who engage in a contest and have recourse to arms."

"This being the case," Vattel continues, "it is very evident that the common laws of war—those maxims of humanity, moderation, and honor—ought to be observed by both parties in every civil war. Should the sovereign conceive he has a right to hang up his prisoners as rebels, the opposite party will make reprisals, et cetera, et cetera; the war will become cruel, horrible, and every day more destructive to the nation."

As a civil war is never publicly proclaimed, *eo nomine* ("by that name"), against insurgents, its actual existence is a fact in our domestic history which the Court is bound to notice and to know. The true test of its existence, as found in the writings of the sages of the common law, may be thus summarily stated: "When the regular course of justice is interrupted by revolt, rebellion, or insurrection, so that the Courts of Justice cannot be kept open, civil war exists and hostilities may be prosecuted on the same footing as if those opposing the Government were foreign enemies invading the land."

By the Constitution, Congress alone has the power to declare a national or foreign war. It cannot declare war against a State, or any number of States, by virtue of any clause in the Constitution. The Constitution confers on the President the whole Executive power. He is bound to take care that the laws be faithfully executed. He is Commander-in-Chief of the Army and Navy of the United States, and of the militia of the several States when called into the actual service of the United States. He has no power to initiate or declare a war either against a foreign nation or a domestic State. But, by longstanding Acts of Congress, he is authorized to call out the militia and use the military and naval forces of the United States in case of invasion by foreign nations, and to suppress insurrection against the government of a State or of the United States.

If a war be made by invasion of a foreign nation, the President is not only authorized but bound to resist force by force. He does not initiate the war, but is bound to accept the challenge without waiting for any special legislative authority. And whether the hostile party be a foreign invader, or States organized in rebellion, it is none the less a war, although the declaration of it be "unilateral."

This greatest of civil wars was not gradually developed by popular commotion, tumultuous assemblies, or local unorganized insurrections. However long may have been its previous conception, it nevertheless sprung forth suddenly from the parent brain, a Minerva in the full panoply of war. The President was bound to meet it in the shape it presented itself, without waiting for Congress to baptize it with a name; and no name given to it by him or them could change the fact.

It is not the less a civil war, with belligerent parties in hostile array, because it may be called an "insurrection" by one side, and the insurgents be considered as rebels or traitors. It is not necessary that the independence of the revolted province or State be acknowledged in order to constitute it a party belligerent in a war according to the law of nations. Foreign nations acknowledge it as war by a declaration of neutrality. The condition of neutrality cannot exist unless there be two belligerent parties.

As soon as the news of the attack on Fort Sumter, and the organization of a government by the seceding States, assuming to act as belligerents, could become known in Europe, on the 13th of May, 1861, the Queen of England issued her proclamation of neutrality, "recognizing hostilities as existing between the Government of the United States of American and certain States styling themselves the Confederate States of America." This was immediately followed by similar declarations or silent acquiescence by other nations.

After such an official recognition by the sovereign, a citizen of a foreign State is estopped to deny the existence of a war with all its consequences as regards neutrals. They cannot ask a Court to affect a technical ignorance of the existence of a war, which all the world acknowledges to be the greatest civil war known in the history of the human race, and thus cripple the arm of the Government and paralyze its power by subtle definitions and ingenious sophisms.

The law of nations is also called the law of nature; it is founded on the common consent as well as the common sense of the world. It contains no such anomalous doctrine as that which this Court are now for the first time desired to pronounce, to wit: That insurgents who have risen in rebellion against their sovereign, expelled her Courts, established a revolutionary government, organized armies, and commenced hostilities, are not enemies because they are traitors; and a war levied on the Government by traitors, in order to dismember and destroy it, is not a war because it is an "insurrection."

Whether the President in fulfilling his duties, as Commander-in-Chief, in suppressing an insurrection, has met with such armed hostile resistance, and a civil war of such alarming proportions as will compel him to accord to them the character of belligerents, is a question to be decided by him, and this Court must be governed by the decisions and acts of the political department of the Government to which this power was entrusted. "He must determine what degree of force the crisis demands." The proclamation of blockade is itself official and conclusive evidence to the Court that a state of war existed which demanded and authorized a recourse to such a measure, under the circumstances peculiar to the case.

If it were necessary to the technical existence of a war, that it should have a legislative sanction, we find it in almost every act passed at the extraordinary session of the Legislature of 1861, which was wholly employed in enacting laws to enable the Government to prosecute the war with vigor and efficiency. And finally, in 1861, we find Congress, in anticipation of such astute objections, passing an act "approving, legalizing, and making valid all the acts, proclamations, and orders of the President, et cetera, as if they had been issued and done under the previous express authority and direction of the Congress of the United States."

Without admitting that such an act was necessary under the circumstances, it is plain that if the President had in any manner assumed powers which it was necessary should have the authority or sanction of Congress, that on the well known principle of law, *omnis ratihabitio retrotrahitur et mandato equiparatur* ("every ratification relates back and is equivalent to a prior authority"), this ratification has operated to perfectly cure the defect.

The objection made to this act of ratification, that it is *ex post facto*, and therefore unconstitutional and void, might possibly have some weight on the trial of an indictment in a criminal Court. But precedents from that source cannot be received as authoritative in a tribunal administering public and international law.

Therefore we are of the opinion that the President had a right, *jure belli* ("by the right or law of war"), to institute a blockade of ports in possession of the States in rebellion, which neutrals are bound to regard.

*Not only, as we have shown, is the federal power over external affairs in origin and essential character different from that over internal affairs, but participation in the exercise of the power is significantly limited. In this vast external realm, with its important, complicated, delicate and manifold problems, the President alone has the power to speak or listen as a representative of the nation.*

— *George Sutherland*

## United States v. Curtiss-Wright Export Corp.
### 57 S.Ct. 216, 299 U.S. 304 (1936)

*The plenary powers of the federal government over foreign affairs are not well-elaborated in the text of the Constitution, but nonetheless are part and parcel of national sovereignty. Almost two years after a territorial war broke out over the Gran Chaco, a large area of Paraguay claimed by Bolivia, Congress authorized the President to embargo arms shipments to the two countries. Curtiss-Wright Export Corp. and some of its officers were indicted for violating the embargo resolution and President Roosevelt's proclamation, crimes punishable by a fine up to $10,000 and imprisonment for as long as two years. The particular arms sale involved was worth three-quarters of a million dollars, a lot of money in the Depression, and the company needed export sales to stay in business. The Defendants argued that the joint resolution and the proclamation were both unconstitutional, confident that the hostility the Court had manifested toward the domestic policies of the New Deal would move the Justices against the government in their case. But the Justices sided with the government and drew a sharp distinction between domestic and foreign powers. Justice Sutherland had to invoke a metaphysical theory of history and a deductive theory of governmental structure, however, to maintain that these powers passed almost mystically from England to the Continental Congress under the Declaration of Independence and then the Articles of Confederation and then the Constitution, and remained always and exclusively at the federal seat of government. And the judicial branch would defer to their exercise by the politi-*

*cal or elected branches. In 1941, therefore, Congress could see its way clear to pass the Lend-Lease Act, authorizing President Roosevelt to disburse vast sums of aid and equipment to the Allies without yet joining World War II. Justice Sutherland's opinion took an expansive view of Executive power that forms the basis for the multitude of Executive agreements which render the modern President virtually the exclusive agent of U.S. foreign policy.*

**Justice Sutherland:** Whether, if the Joint Resolution had related solely to internal affairs, it would be open to the challenge that it constituted an unlawful delegation of legislative power to the Executive, we find it unnecessary to determine. The whole aim of the resolution is to affect a situation entirely external to the United States, and falling within the category of foreign affairs. The determination which we are called to make, therefore, is whether the Joint Resolution, as applied to that situation, is vulnerable to attack under the rule that forbids a delegation of the lawmaking power. In other words, assuming (but not deciding) that the challenged delegation, if it were confined to internal affairs, would be invalid, may it nevertheless be sustained on the ground that its exclusive aim is to afford a remedy for a hurtful condition within foreign territory?

It will contribute to the elucidation of the question if we first consider the differences between the powers of the federal government in respect of foreign or external affairs and those in respect of domestic or internal affairs. That there are differences between them, and that these differences are fundamental, may not be doubted.

The two classes of powers are different, both in respect of their origin and their nature. The broad statement that the federal government can exercise no powers except those specifically enumerated in the Constitution, and such implied powers as are necessary and proper to carry into effect the enumerated powers, is categorically true only in respect of our internal affairs. In that field, the primary purpose of the Constitution was to carve from the general mass of legislative powers then possessed by the states such portions as it was thought desirable to vest in the federal government, leaving those not included in the enumeration still in the states. That this doctrine applies only to powers which the states had is self-evident. And since the states severally never possessed international powers, such powers could not have been carved from the mass of state powers but obviously were transmitted to the United States from some other source. During the Colonial period, those powers were possessed exclusively by and were entirely under the control of the Crown. By the Declaration of Independence, "the Representatives of the United States of America" declared the United (not the several) Colonies to be free and independent states, and as such to have "full Power to levy War, conclude Peace, contract Alliances, establish Commerce and to do all other Acts and Things which Independent States may of right do."

As a result of the separation from Great Britain by the colonies, acting as a unit, the powers of external sovereignty passed from the Crown not to the colonies severally, but to the colonies in their collective and corporate capacity as the United States of America. Even before the *Declaration*, the colonies were a unit in foreign affairs, acting through a common agency—namely, the Continental Congress, composed of delegates from the thirteen colonies. That agency exercised the powers of war and peace, raised an army, created a navy, and finally adopted the *Declaration of Independence*. Rulers come and go; governments end and forms of government change; but sovereignty survives. A political society cannot endure without a supreme will somewhere. Sovereignty is never held in suspense. When, therefore, the external sovereignty of Great Britain in respect of the colonies ceased, it immediately passed to the Union. That fact was given practical application almost at once. The treaty of peace, made on September 3, 1783, was concluded between his Brittanic Majesty and the "United States of America."

The Union existed before the Constitution, which was ordained and established among other things to form "a more perfect Union." Prior to that event, it is clear that the Union, declared by the Articles of Confederation to be "perpetual," was the sole possessor of external sovereignty, and in the Union it remained without change save in so far as the Constitution in express terms qualified its exercise. The Framers' Convention was called and exerted its powers upon the irrefutable postulate that though the states were several their people in respect of foreign affairs were one. In that convention, the entire absence of state power to deal with those affairs was thus forcefully stated by Rufus King: "The states were not 'sovereigns' in the sense contended for by some. They did not possess the peculiar features of sovereignty,—they could not make war, nor peace, nor alliances, nor treaties. Considering them as political beings, they were dumb, for they could not speak to any foreign sovereign whatever. They were deaf, for they could not hear any propositions from such sovereign. They had not even the organs or faculties of defence or offence, for they could not of themselves raise troops, or equip vessels, for war."

It results that the investment of the federal government with the powers of external sovereignty did not depend upon the affirmative grants of the Constitution. The powers to declare and wage war, to conclude peace, to make treaties, to maintain diplomatic relations with other sovereignties, if they had never been mentioned in the Constitution, would have vested in the federal government as necessary concomitants of nationality. Neither the Constitution nor the laws passed in pursuance of it have any force in foreign territory unless in respect of our own citizens; and operations of the nation in such territory must be governed by treaties, international understandings and compacts, and the principles of international law. As a member of the family of nations, the right and power of the United States in that field are equal to the right and power of the other members of the international family. Otherwise, the United States is not completely sovereign. The power to acquire territory by discovery and occupation, the power to expel undesirable aliens, the power to make such international agreements as do not constitute treaties in the constitutional sense, none of which is expressly affirmed by the Constitution, nevertheless exist as inherently inseparable from the conception of nationality. This court has recognized this, and in several cases has found the warrant for its conclusions not in the provisions of the Constitution, but in the law of nations.

Not only, as we have shown, is the federal power over external affairs in origin and essential character different from that over internal affairs, but participation in the exercise of the power is significantly limited. In this vast external realm, with its important, complicated, delicate and manifold problems, the President alone has the power to speak or listen as a representative of the nation. He makes treaties with the advice and consent of the Senate; but he alone negotiates. Into the field of negotiation the Senate cannot intrude; and Congress itself is powerless to invade it. As Chief Justice Marshall said in his great argument as a member of the House of Representatives in 1800, "The President is the sole organ of the nation in its external relations, and its sole representative with foreign nations." The Senate Committee on Foreign Relations at a very early day in our history, February 15, 1816, reported to the Senate, among other things, as follows: "The President is the constitutional representative of the United States with regard to foreign nations. He manages our concerns with foreign nations and must necessarily be most competent to determine when, how, and upon what subjects negotiation may be urged with the greatest prospect of success. For his conduct he is responsible to the Constitution."

It is important to bear in mind that we are here dealing not alone with an authority vested in the President by an exertion of legislative power, but with such an authority plus the very delicate, plenary and exclusive power of the President as the sole organ of the federal government in the field of international relations—a power which does not require as a basis for its exercise an act of Congress, but which, of course, like every other governmental power, must be exercised in subordination to the applicable provisions of the Constitution. It is quite apparent that if, in the maintenance of our international relations, embarrassment—perhaps serious embarrassment—is to be avoided and success for our aims achieved, congressional legislation which is to be made effective through negotiation and inquiry within the international field must often accord to the President a degree of discretion and freedom from statutory restriction which would not be admissible were domestic affairs alone involved. Moreover, he, not Congress, has the better opportunity of knowing the conditions which prevail in foreign countries, and especially is this true in time of war. He has his confidential sources of information. He has his agents in the form of diplomatic, consular and other officials. Secrecy in respect of information gathered by them may be highly necessary, and the premature disclosure of it productive of harmful results. Indeed, so clearly is this true that the first President refused to accede to a request to lay before the House of Representatives the instructions, correspondence and documents relating to the negotiation of the Jay Treaty—a refusal the wisdom of which was recognized by the House itself and has never since been doubted. In his reply to the request, President Washington said: "The nature of foreign negotiations requires caution, and their success must often depend on secrecy; and even when brought to a conclusion a full disclosure of all the measures, demands, or eventual concessions which may have been proposed or contemplated would be extremely impolitic; for this might have a pernicious influence on future negotiations, or produce immediate inconveniences, perhaps danger and mischief, in relation to other powers. The necessity of such caution and secrecy was one cogent reason for vesting the power of making treaties in the President, with the advice and consent of the Senate, the principle on which that body was formed confining it to a small number of members. To admit, then, a right in the House of Representatives to demand and to have as a matter of course all the papers respecting a negotiation with a foreign power would be to establish a dangerous precedent."

The marked difference between foreign affairs and domestic affairs in this respect is recognized by both houses of Congress in the very form of their requisitions for information from the executive departments. In the case of every department except the Department of State, the resolution directs the official to furnish the information. In the case of the State Department, dealing with foreign affairs, the President is requested to furnish the information "if not incompatible with the public interest." A statement that to furnish the information is not compatible with the public interest rarely, if ever, is questioned.

When the President is to be authorized by legislation to act in respect of a matter intended to affect a situation in foreign territory, the legislator properly bears in mind the important consideration that the form of the President's action—or, indeed, whether he shall act at all—may well depend, among other things, upon the nature of the confidential information which he has or may thereafter receive, or upon the effect which his action may have upon our foreign relations. This consideration, in connection with what we have already said on the subject discloses the unwisdom of requiring Congress in this field of governmental power to lay down narrowly definite standards by which the President is to be governed. As this court has said, "As a government, the United States is invested with all the attributes of sovereignty. As it has the character of nationality it has the powers of nationality, especially those which concern its relations and intercourse with other countries. We should hesitate long before limiting or embarrassing such powers."

In the light of the foregoing observations, it is evident that this court should not be in haste to apply a general rule which will have the effect of condemning legislation like that under review as constituting an unlawful delegation of legislative power. The principles which justify such legislation find overwhelming support in the unbroken legislative practice which has prevailed almost from the inception of the national government to the present day.

Let us examine, in chronological order, the acts of legislation which warrant this conclusion. Practically every volume of the United States Statutes contains one or more acts or joint resolutions of Congress authorizing action by the President in respect of subjects affecting foreign relations, which either leave the exercise of the power to his unrestricted judgment, or provide a standard far more general than that which has always been considered requisite with regard to domestic affairs.

The result of holding that the Joint Resolution here under attack is void and unenforceable as constituting an unlawful delegation of legislative power would be to stamp this multitude of comparable acts and resolutions as likewise invalid. And while this court may not, and should not, hesitate to declare acts of Congress, however many times repeated, to be unconstitutional if beyond all rational doubt it finds them to be so, an impressive array of legislation such as we have just set forth, enacted by nearly every Congress from the beginning of our national existence to the present day, must be given unusual weight in the process of reaching a correct determination of the problem. A legislative practice such as we have here, evidenced not by only occasional instances, but marked by the movement of a steady stream for a century and a half of time, goes a long way in the direction of proving the presence of unassailable ground for the constitutionality of the practice, to be found in the origin and history of the power involved, or in its nature, or in both combined.

The uniform, long-continued and undisputed legislative practice just disclosed rests upon an admissible view of the Constitution which, even if the practice found far less support in principle than we think it does, we should not feel at liberty at this late day to disturb.

We deem it unnecessary to consider, *seriatim*, the several clauses which are said to evidence the unconstitutionality of the Joint Resolution as involving an unlawful delegation of legislative power. It is enough to summarize by saying that, both upon principle and in accordance with precedent, we conclude there is sufficient warrant for the broad discretion vested in the President to determine whether the enforcement of the statute will have a beneficial effect upon the re-establishment of peace in the affected countries; whether he shall make proclamation to bring the resolution into operation; whether and when the resolution shall cease to operate and to make proclamation accordingly; and to prescribe limitations and exceptions to which the enforcement of the resolution shall be subject.

*This exclusion of "all persons of Japanese an-cestry, both alien and non-alien," from the Pacific Coast area on a plea of military necessity in the ab-sence of martial law ought not to be approved. Such exclusion goes over "the very brink of consti-tutional power" and falls into the ugly abyss of racism.*

*— Frank Murphy*

## Korematsu v. United States
### 65 S.Ct. 193, 323 U.S. 214 (1944)

*Anyone who respects and admires the Supreme Court should pause carefully over this decision. By the March following the attack on Pearl Harbor, military and civil-ian leaders had manufactured a "military necessity" to justify an elaborately staged plan to place the approxi-mately 120,000 persons of Japanese descent under a home curfew, to exclude them from "military areas" that included virtually the entire West Coast, and finally to "relocate" them to "internment camps" until their "loy-alty" could be determined by a procedure so torpid that in the last year of the war 70,000 were still awaiting "proc-essing." These were mostly American citizens; many had sons off fighting in Europe. The military effort was led by General John L. DeWitt, whose official report recom-mended evacuation based on racist stereotypes and a pro-found ignorance. On the civilian side, private greed encouraged the Administration to implement the pro-gram, because the Japanese-Americans' jobs, businesses and properties were left up for grabs. Newspapers and labor organizations as well as congressional leaders and state officials, including then California Attorney Gen-eral Earl Warren, supported the plan. The year before, in* Hirabayashi v. United States (1943), *a unanimous Court already had upheld the racial curfew as a minor in-fringement during the exigency of war. Justice Black's majority opinion here established the principle that gov-ernmental racial classifications are presumed to be un-constitutional and must satisfy the highest level of judicial review, a proposition for which this case is cited today. But a majority of the Justices still sided with the Administration. At the time, Justices Roberts, Murphy,*

*and Jackson saw through the government's lies and dis-*
*sented. Decades later, a professor and civil liberties law-*
*yer named Peter Irons discovered irrefutable evidence*
*that the government had deliberately misled the Supreme*
*Court; his proof was relied on by federal courts to set*
*aside the convictions of Hirabayashi and Korematsu.*
*Chief Justice Warren later expressed his deep regret over*
*his involvement. Justice Black defended his position to*
*the end of his judicial career, stating in a 1967 interview,*
*"They all look alike to a person not a jap." In 1988, after*
*a federal commission officially concluded that the pro-*
*gram was "motivated by racial prejudice, wartime hys-*
*teria, and a failure of political leadership," the Congress*
*authorized a formal apology from the United States and*
*a reparation payment of $20,000 to each affected person.*

**Justice Black:** It should be noted, to begin with, that all
legal restrictions which curtail the civil rights of a single racial
group are immediately suspect. That is not to say that all such
restrictions are unconstitutional. It is to say that courts must
subject them to the most rigid scrutiny. Pressing public necessity may sometimes justify the existence of such restrictions;
racial antagonism never can.

In the light of the principles we announced last term, unanimously upholding the military curfew, we are unable to conclude that it was beyond the war power of Congress and the
Executive to exclude those of Japanese ancestry from the West
Coast war area at the time they did. True, exclusion from the
area in which one's home is located is a far greater deprivation
than constant confinement to the home from 8 p.m. to 6 a.m.
Nothing short of apprehension by the proper military authorities of the gravest imminent danger to the public safety can
constitutionally justify either. But exclusion from a threatened
area, no less than curfew, has a definite and close relationship
to the prevention of espionage and sabotage. The military
authorities, charged with the primary responsibility of defending our shores, concluded that curfew provided inadequate protection and ordered exclusion. They did so in accordance with
Congressional authority to the military to say who should, and
who should not, remain in the threatened areas.

Here, as in the curfew case, "we cannot reject as unfounded
the judgment of the military authorities and of Congress that
there were disloyal members of that population, whose number
and strength could not be precisely and quickly ascertained. We

cannot say that the war-making branches of the Government did not have ground for believing that in a critical hour such persons could not readily be isolated and separately dealt with, and constituted a menace to the national defense and safety, which demanded that prompt and adequate measures be taken to guard against it."

Like curfew, exclusion of those of Japanese origin was deemed necessary because of the presence of an unascertained number of disloyal members of the group, most of whom we have no doubt were loyal to this country. It was because we could not reject the finding of the military authorities that it was impossible to bring about an immediate segregation of the disloyal from the loyal that we sustained the validity of the curfew order as applying to the whole group. In the instant case, temporary exclusion of the entire group was rested by the military on the same ground. The judgment that exclusion of the whole group was for the same reason a military imperative answers the contention that the exclusion was in the nature of group punishment based on antagonism to those of Japanese origin. That there were members of the group who retained loyalties to Japan has been confirmed by investigations made subsequent to the exclusion. Approximately five thousand American citizens of Japanese ancestry refused to swear unqualified allegiance to the United States and to renounce allegiance to the Japanese Emperor, and several thousand evacuees requested repatriation to Japan.

We uphold the exclusion order as of the time it was made and when the Defendant violated it. In doing so, we are not unmindful of the hardships imposed by it upon a large group of American citizens. But hardships are part of war, and war is an aggregation of hardships. All citizens alike, both in and out of uniform, feel the impact of war in greater or lesser measure. Citizenship has its responsibilities as well as its privileges, and in time of war the burden is always heavier. Compulsory exclusion of large groups of citizens from their homes, except under circumstances of direst emergency and peril, is inconsistent with our basic governmental institutions. But when under conditions of modern warfare our shores are threatened by hostile forces, the power to protect must be commensurate with the threatened danger.

We are being asked to pass at this time upon the whole subsequent detention program in both assembly and relocation centers, although the only issues framed at the trial related to

Defendant's remaining in the prohibited area in violation of the exclusion order. Had Defendant here left the prohibited area and gone to an assembly center we cannot say either as a matter of fact or law, that his presence in that center would have resulted in his detention in a relocation center. Some who did report to the assembly center were not sent to relocation centers, but were released upon condition that they remain outside the prohibited zone until the military orders were modified or lifted. This illustrates that they pose different problems and may be governed by different principles. The lawfulness of one does not necessarily determine the lawfulness of the others. These separate requirements were that those of Japanese ancestry (1) depart from the area; (2) report to and temporarily remain in an assembly center; (3) go under military control to a relocation center there to remain for an indeterminate period until released conditionally or unconditionally by the military authorities. Each of these requirements, it will be noted, imposed distinct duties in connection with the separate steps in a complete evacuation program.

Since the Defendant has not been convicted of failing to report or to remain in an assembly or relocation center, we cannot in this case determine the validity of those separate provisions of the Military Orders. It is sufficient here for us to pass upon the Order which Defendant violated. To do more would be to go beyond the issues raised, and to decide momentous questions not contained within the framework of the pleadings or the evidence in this case. It will be time enough to decide the serious constitutional issues which Defendant seeks to raise when an assembly or relocation order is applied or is certain to be applied to him, and we have its terms before us.

It is said that we are dealing here with the case of imprisonment of a citizen in a concentration camp solely because of his ancestry, without evidence or inquiry concerning his loyalty and good disposition towards the United States. Our task would be simple, our duty clear, were this a case involving the imprisonment of a loyal citizen in a concentration camp because of racial prejudice. Regardless of the true nature of the assembly and relocation centers—and we deem it unjustifiable to call them concentration camps with all the ugly connotations that term implies—we are dealing specifically with nothing but an exclusion order. To cast this case into outlines of racial prejudice, without reference to the real military dangers which were presented, merely confuses the issue. Korematsu was not excluded from the Military Area because of hostility to him or his race.

He was excluded because we are at war with the Japanese Empire, because the properly constituted military authorities feared an invasion of our West Coast and felt constrained to take proper security measures, because they decided that the military urgency of the situation demanded that all citizens of Japanese ancestry be segregated from the West Coast temporarily, and finally, because Congress, reposing its confidence in this time of war in our military leaders—as inevitably it must—determined that they should have the power to do just this. There was evidence of disloyalty on the part of some, the military authorities considered that the need for action was great, and time was short. We cannot—by availing ourselves of the calm perspective of hindsight—now say that at that time these actions were unjustified.

**Justice Frankfurter:** The provisions of the Constitution which confer on the Congress and the President powers to enable this country to wage war are as much part of the Constitution as provisions looking to a nation at peace. And we have had recent occasion to quote approvingly the statement of former Chief Justice Hughes that the war power of the Government is "the power to wage war successfully." Therefore, the validity of action under the war power must be judged wholly in the context of war. That action is not to be stigmatized as lawless because like action in times of peace would be lawless. To talk about a military order that expresses an allowable judgment of war needs by those entrusted with the duty of conducting war as "an unconstitutional order" is to suffuse a part of the Constitution with an atmosphere of unconstitutionality. The respective spheres of action of military authorities and of judges are of course very different. But within their sphere, military authorities are no more outside the bounds of obedience to the Constitution than are judges within theirs. To recognize that military orders are "reasonably expedient military precautions" in time of war and yet to deny them constitutional legitimacy makes of the Constitution an instrument for dialectic subtleties not reasonably to be attributed to the hard-headed Framers, of whom a majority had had actual participation in war. If a military order such as that under review does not transcend the means appropriate for conducting war, such action by the military is as constitutional as would be any authorized action by the Interstate Commerce Commission within the limits of the constitutional power to regulate commerce. And being an exercise of the war power explicitly granted by the Constitution for safeguarding the national life by prosecuting war effectively, I find nothing in the Constitution which denies to Congress the power to enforce such a valid military order by making its violation an offense triable in the civil courts. To find that the Constitution does not forbid the military measures now complained of does not carry with it approval of that which Congress and the Executive did. That is their business, not ours.

**Justice Murphy:** This exclusion of "all persons of Japanese ancestry, both alien and non-alien," from the Pacific Coast area on a plea of military necessity in the absence of martial law ought not to be approved. Such exclusion goes over "the very brink of constitutional power" and falls into the ugly abyss of racism.

In dealing with matters relating to the prosecution and progress of a war, we must accord great respect and consideration to the judgments of the military authorities who are on the scene and who have full knowledge of the military facts. The scope of their discretion must, as a matter of necessity and common sense, be wide. And their judgments ought not to be overruled lightly by those whose training and duties ill-equip them to deal intelligently with matters so vital to the physical security of the nation.

At the same time, however, it is essential that there be definite limits to military discretion, especially where martial law has not been declared. Individuals must not be left impoverished of their constitutional rights on a plea of military necessity that has neither substance nor support. Thus, like other claims conflicting with the asserted constitutional rights of the individual, the military claim must subject itself to the judicial process of having its reasonableness determined and its conflicts with other interests reconciled.

The judicial test of whether the Government, on a plea of military necessity, can validly deprive an individual of any of his constitutional rights is whether the deprivation is reasonably related to a public danger that is so "immediate, imminent, and impending" as not to admit of delay and not to permit the intervention of ordinary constitutional processes to alleviate the danger. Civilian Exclusion Order No. 34, banishing from a prescribed area of the Pacific Coast "all persons of Japanese ancestry, both alien and non-alien," clearly does not meet that test. Being an obvious racial discrimination, the order deprives all those within its scope of the equal protection of the laws as guaranteed by the Fifth Amendment. It further deprives these individuals of their constitutional rights to live and work where they will, to establish a home where they choose and to move about freely. In excommunicating them without benefit of hearings, this order also deprives them of all their constitutional rights to procedural due process. Yet no reasonable relation to an "immediate, imminent, and impending" public danger is evident to support this racial restriction which is one of the most sweeping and complete deprivations of constitutional rights in the history of this nation in the absence of martial law.

It must be conceded that the military and naval situation in the spring of 1942 was such as to generate a very real fear of invasion of the Pacific Coast, accompanied by fears of sabotage and espionage in that area. The military command was therefore justified in adopting all reasonable means necessary to combat these dangers. In adjudging the military action taken in light of the then apparent dangers, we must not erect too high or too meticulous standards; it is necessary only that the action have some reasonable relation to the removal of the dangers of invasion, sabotage and espionage. But the exclusion, either temporarily or permanently, of all persons with Japanese blood in their veins has no such reasonable relation. And that relation is lacking because the exclusion order necessarily must rely for its reasonableness upon the assumption that all persons of Japanese ancestry may have a dangerous tendency to commit sabotage and espionage and to aid our Japanese enemy in other ways. It is difficult to believe that reason, logic or experience could be marshalled in support of such an assumption.

That this forced exclusion was the result in good measure of this erroneous assumption of racial guilt rather than bona fide military necessity is evidenced by the Commanding General's Final Report on the evacuation from the Pacific Coast area. Justification for the exclusion is sought, instead, mainly upon questionable racial and sociological grounds not ordinarily within the realm of expert military judgment, supplemented by certain semi-military conclusions drawn from an unwarranted use of circumstantial evidence. The main reasons relied upon by those responsible for the forced evacuation, therefore, do not prove a reasonable relation between the group characteristics of Japanese Americans and the dangers of invasion, sabotage and espionage. The reasons appear, instead, to be largely an accumulation of much of the misinformation, half-truths and insinuations that for years have been directed against Japanese Americans by people with racial and economic prejudices—the same people who have been among the foremost advocates of the evacuation. A military judgment based upon such racial and sociological considerations is not entitled to the great weight ordinarily given the judgments based upon strictly military considerations. Especially is this so when every charge relative to race, religion, culture, geographical location, and legal and economic status has been substantially discredited by independent studies made by experts in these matters.

The military necessity which is essential to the validity of the evacuation order thus resolves itself into a few intimations that certain individuals actively aided the enemy, from which it is inferred that the entire group of Japanese Americans could not be trusted to be or remain loyal to the United States. No one denies, of course, that there were some disloyal persons of Japanese descent on the Pacific Coast who did all in their power to aid their ancestral land. Similar disloyal activities have been engaged in by many persons of German, Italian and even more pioneer stock in our country. But to infer that examples of individual disloyalty prove group disloyalty and justify discriminatory action against the entire group is to deny that under our system of law individual guilt is the sole basis for deprivation of rights. Moreover, this inference, which is at the very heart of the evacuation orders, has been used in support of the abhorrent and despicable treatment of minority groups by the dictatorial tyrannies which this nation is now pledged to destroy. To give constitutional sanction to that inference in this case, however well-intentioned may have been the military command on the Pacific Coast, is to adopt one of the cruelest of the rationales used by our enemies to destroy the dignity of the individual and to encourage and open the door to discriminatory actions against other minority groups in the passions of tomorrow.

No adequate reason is given for the failure to treat these Japanese Americans on an individual basis by holding investigations and hearings to separate the loyal from the disloyal, as was done in the case of persons of German and Italian ancestry. Moreover, there was no adequate proof that the Federal Bureau of Investigation and the military and naval intelligence services did not have the espionage and sabotage situation well in hand.

I dissent, therefore, from this legalization of racism. Racial discrimination in any form and in any degree has no justifiable part whatever in our democratic way of life. It is unattractive in any setting but it is utterly revolting among a free people who have embraced the principles set forth in the Constitution of the United States. All residents of this nation are kin in some way by blood or culture to a foreign land. Yet they are primarily and necessarily a part of the new and distinct civilization of the

United States. They must accordingly be treated at all times as the heirs of the American experiment and as entitled to all the rights and freedoms guaranteed by the Constitution.

**Justice Jackson:** Korematsu was born on our soil, of parents born in Japan. The Constitution makes him a citizen of the United States by nativity and a citizen of California by residence. No claim is made that he is not loyal to this country. There is no suggestion that apart from the matter involved here he is not law-abiding and well disposed. Korematsu, however, has been convicted of an act not commonly a crime. It consists merely of being present in the state whereof he is a citizen, near the place where he was born, and where all his life he has lived.

Even more unusual is the series of military orders which made this conduct a crime. They forbid such a one to remain, and they also forbid him to leave. They were so drawn that the only way Korematsu could avoid violation was to give himself up to the military authority. This meant submission to custody, examination, and transportation out of the territory, to be followed by indeterminate confinement in detention camps. A citizen's presence in the locality, however, was made a crime only if his parents were of Japanese birth.

Now, if any fundamental assumption underlies our system, it is that guilt is personal and not inheritable. Even if all of one's antecedents had been convicted of treason, the Constitution forbids its penalties to be visited upon him, for it provides that "no Attainder of Treason shall work Corruption of Blood, or Forfeiture except during the Life of the Person attained." Article 3, § 3, cl. 2. But here is an attempt to make an otherwise innocent act a crime merely because this prisoner is the son of parents as to whom he had no choice, and belongs to a race from which there is no way to resign. If Congress in peace-time legislation should enact such a criminal law, I should suppose this Court would refuse to enforce it.

It would be impracticable and dangerous idealism to expect or insist that each specific military command in an area of probable operations will conform to conventional tests of constitutionality. When an area is so beset that it must be put under military control at all, the paramount consideration is that its measures be successful, rather than legal. The armed services must protect a society, not merely its Constitution. The very essence of the military job is to marshal physical force, to remove every obstacle to its effectiveness, to give it every strategic advantage. Defense measures will not, and often should not, be held within the limits that bind civil authority in peace. No court can require such a commander in such circumstances to act as a reasonable man; he may be unreasonably cautious and exacting. Perhaps he should be. But a commander in temporarily focusing the life of a community on defense is carrying out a military program; he is not making law in the sense the courts know the term. He issues orders, and they may have a certain authority as military commands, although they may be very bad as constitutional law.

But if we cannot confine military expedients by the Constitution, neither would I distort the Constitution to approve all that the military may deem expedient. This is what the Court appears to be doing, whether consciously or not. I cannot say, from any evidence before me, that the these military orders were not reasonably expedient military precautions, nor could I say that they were. But even if they were permissible military procedures, I deny that it follows that they are constitutional. If, as the Court holds, it does follow, then we may as well say that any military order will be constitutional and have done with it.

In the very nature of things military decisions are not susceptible of intelligent judicial appraisal. They do not pretend to rest on evidence, but are made on information that often would not be admissible and on assumptions that could not be proved. Information in support of an order could not be disclosed to courts without danger that it would reach the enemy. Neither can courts act on communications made in confidence. Hence courts can never have any real alternative to accepting the mere declaration of the authority that issued the order that it was reasonably necessary from a military viewpoint.

Much is said of the danger to liberty from the Army program for deporting and detaining these citizens of Japanese extraction. But a judicial construction of the due process clause that will sustain this order is a far more subtle blow to liberty than the promulgation of the order itself. A military order, however unconstitutional, is not apt to last longer than the military emergency. Even during that period a succeeding commander may revoke it all. But once a judicial opinion rationalizes such an order to show that it conforms to the Constitution, or rather rationalizes the Constitution to show that the Constitution sanctions such an order, the Court for all time has validated the principle of racial discrimination in criminal procedure and of transplanting American citizens. The principle then lies about like a loaded weapon ready for the hand of any authority that can bring forward a plausible claim of an urgent need. Every repetition imbeds that principle more deeply in our law and thinking and expands it to new purposes. All who observe the work of courts are familiar with what Judge Cardozo described as "the tendency of a principle to expand itself to the limit of its logic." A military commander may overstep the bounds of constitutionality, and it is an incident. But if we review and approve, that passing incident becomes the doctrine of the Constitution. There it has a generative power of its own, and all that it creates will be in its own image. Nothing better illustrates this danger than does the Court's opinion in this case.

Of course the existence of a military power resting on force, so vagrant, so centralized, so necessarily heedless of the individual, is an inherent threat to liberty. But I would not lead people to rely on this Court for a review that seems to me wholly delusive. The military reasonableness of these orders can only be determined by military superiors. If the people ever let command of the war power fall into irresponsible and unscrupulous hands, the courts wield no power equal to its restraint. The chief restraint upon those who command the physical forces of the country, in the future as in the past, must be their responsibility to the political judgments of their contemporaries and to the moral judgments of history.

My duties as a justice as I see them do not require me to make a military judgment as to whether the evacuation and detention program was a reasonable military necessity. I do not suggest that the courts should have attempted to interfere with the Army in carrying out its task. But I do not think they may be asked to execute a military expedient that has no place in law under the Constitution I would reverse the judgment and discharge the prisoner.

*If the Constitution gives the Executive a large degree of unshared power in the conduct of foreign affairs and the maintenance of our national defense, then under the Constitution the Executive must have the largely unshared duty to determine and preserve the degree of internal security necessary to exercise that power successfully.*

— *Potter Stewart*

## New York Times Co. v. United States
### 91 S.Ct. 2140, 403 U.S. 713 (1971)

*Popularly known as the* Pentagon Papers Case, *there was a brief per curiam opinion that covered the common 1st amendment ground among the majority to the effect that prior restraints on newspapers were presumed unconstitutional and that the government had failed to satisfy its burden of proof. The nine Justices wrote nine separate opinions, however, voting 6 to 3 against the executive branch's request for a court injunction against the N.Y.* Times *to halt the publication of the government study of the history of the U.S. military involvement in Viet Nam. Reading between the lines, however, there may actually have been a majority of the Justices who would have sided with the Executive if Congress had authorized the injunction by a simple statute. Here Justice Potter Stewart calls for a constitutional "reality check," to suggest there no longer are any significant checks and balances on the powers of the modern Executive. The constitutional alarm he sounded still echoes today.*

**Justice Stewart:** In the governmental structure created by our Constitution, the Executive is endowed with enormous power in the two related areas of national defense and international relations. The Executive power, largely unchecked by the Legislative and Judicial branches, has been pressed to the very hilt since the advent of the nuclear missile age. For better of for worse, the simple fact is that a President of the United States possesses vastly greater constitutional independence in these two vital areas of power than does, say, a prime minister of a country with a parliamentary form of government.

The President's power to make treaties and to appoint ambassadors is, of course, limited by the requirement of Art. II, § 2, of the Constitution that he obtain the advice and consent of the Senate. Article I, § 8, empowers Congress to "raise and support Armies" and "provide and maintain a Navy." And, of course, Congress alone can declare war. This power was last exercised almost 30 years ago at the inception of World War II. Since the end of that war in 1945, the Armed Forces of the United States have suffered approximately half a million casualties in various parts of the world.

In the absence of the governmental checks and balances present in other areas of our national life, the only effective restraint upon executive policy and power in the areas of national defense and international affairs may lie in an enlightened citizenry—in an informed and critical public opinion which alone can here protect the values of democratic government. For this reason, it is perhaps here that a press that is alert, aware, and free most vitally serves the basic purpose of the First Amendment. For without an informed and free press there cannot be an enlightened people.

Yet it is elementary that the successful conduct of international diplomacy and the maintenance of an effective national defense require both confidentiality and secrecy. Other nations can hardly deal with this Nation in an atmosphere of mutual trust unless they can be assured that their confidences will be kept. And within our own executive departments, the development of considered and intelligent international policies would be impossible if those charged with their formulation could not communicate with each other freely, frankly, and in confidence. In the area of basic national defense the frequent need for absolute secrecy is, of course, self-evident.

I think there can be but one answer to this dilemma, if dilemma it be. The responsibility must be where the power is. If the Constitution gives the Executive a large degree of unshared power in the conduct of foreign affairs and the maintenance of our national defense, then under the Constitution the Executive must have the largely unshared duty to determine and preserve the degree of internal security necessary to exercise that power successfully. It is an awesome responsibility, requiring judgment and wisdom of a high order. I should suppose that moral, political, and practical considerations would dictate that a very first principle of that wisdom would be an insistence upon avoiding secrecy for its own sake. For when everything is classified, then nothing is classified, and the system becomes one to be disregarded by the cynical or the careless, and to be manipulated by those intent on self-protection or self-promotion. I should suppose, in short, that the hallmark of a truly effective internal security system would be the maximum possible disclosure, recognizing that secrecy can best be preserved only when credibility is truly maintained. But be that as it may, it is clear to me that it is the constitutional duty of the Executive—as a matter of sovereign prerogative and not as a matter of law as the courts know law—through the promulgation and enforcement of executive regulations, to protect the confidentiality necessary to carry out its responsibilities in the fields of international relations and national defense.

This is not to say that Congress and the courts have no role to play. Undoubtedly Congress has the power to enact specific and appropriate criminal laws to protect government property and preserve government secrets. Congress has passed such laws, and several of them are of very colorable relevance to the apparent circumstances of these cases. And if a criminal prosecution is instituted, it will be the responsibility of the courts to decide the applicability of the criminal law under which the charge is brought. Moreover, if Congress should pass a specific law authorizing civil proceedings in this field, the courts would likewise have the duty to decide the constitutionality of such a law as well as its applicability to the facts proved.

But in the cases before us, we are asked neither to construe specific regulations nor to apply specific laws. We are asked, instead, to perform a function that the Constitution gave to the Executive, not the Judiciary. We are asked, quite simply, to prevent the publication by two newspapers of material that the Executive Branch insists should not, in the national interest, be published. I am convinced that the Executive is correct with respect to some of the documents involved. But I cannot say that disclosure of any of them will surely result in direct, immediate, and irreparable damage to our Nation or its people. That being so, there can under the First Amendment be but one judicial resolution of the issues before us. I join the judgments of the Court.

*To read the Article II powers of the President as providing an absolute privilege as against a subpoena essential to enforcement of criminal statutes on no more than a generalized claim of the public interest in confidentiality of nonmilitary and nondiplomatic discussions would upset the constitutional balance of "a workable government" and gravely impair the role of the courts under Article III.*

— *Warren E. Burger*

## Nixon v. United States
### 94 S.Ct. 3090, 418 U.S. 683 (1974)

*The story of the Watergate scandal would later be told and retold in books and movies depicting a President acting as if he were above the law. The Supreme Court proceeding was one of the most critical scenes in this constitutional drama. A federal grand jury had indicted former Attorney General Mitchell, former Chief of Staff Haldeman, former Assistant to the President Ehrlichman, and others—and had named the President himself as an unindicted coconspirator. The Special Prosecutor wanted the tape recordings of White House conversations to use as evidence in the prosecutions for obstruction of justice and other charges. The President refused to comply and argued that the Constitution placed him above the district court's subpoena. Both sides appealed to the principle of separation of powers. Nixon's Chief Justice wrote for a unanimous eight member Court that included two Nixon appointees, Justice Powell and Justice Blackmun (Justice Rehnquist did not participate). The "Nixon Court" of "strict constructionists" that the President had made such a big issue in his "law and order" campaign of 1968 came down on the side of the law of the Constitution. It held that the President was not above the law. The judicial branch would have the last constitutional word. The court-ordered release of the tapes, including a "smoking gun" conversation directly linking him to the conspiracy, was bad enough for the embattled President. With the House of Representatives on the verge of recommending articles of impeachment, he became the first President to resign from office, on August 8, 1974, less than a month after the Supreme Court decision. The 18th century system of checks and balances thus resolved a 20th century constitutional crisis.*

**Chief Justice Burger:** This litigation presents for review the denial of a motion, filed in the District Court on behalf of the President of the United States to quash a third-party *subpoena duces tecum* issued by the United States District Court for the District of Columbia. The *subpoena* directed the President to produce certain tape recordings and documents relating to his conversations with aides and advisers.

In the performance of assigned constitutional duties, each branch of the Government must initially interpret the Constitution, and the interpretation of its powers by any branch is due great respect from the others. The President's counsel reads the Constitution as providing an absolute privilege of confidentiality for all Presidential communications. Many decisions of this Court, however, have unequivocally reaffirmed the holding of *Marbury v. Madison (1803)*, that "it is emphatically the province and duty of the judicial department to say what the law is."

No holding of the Court has defined the scope of judicial power specifically relating to the enforcement of a *subpoena* for confidential Presidential communications for use in a criminal prosecution, but other exercises of power by the Executive Branch and the Legislative Branch have been found invalid as in conflict with the Constitution. In a series of cases, the Court interpreted the explicit immunity conferred by express provisions of the Constitution on Members of the House and Senate by the Speech or Debate Clause, U.S. Const. Art. I, § 6. Since this Court has consistently exercised the power to construe and delineate claims arising under express powers, it must follow that the Court has authority to interpret claims with respect to powers alleged to derive implicitly from enumerated powers.

Our system of government "requires that federal courts on occasion interpret the Constitution in a manner at variance with the construction given the document by another branch." In a leading case decided in 1962, the Court stated: "Deciding whether a matter has in any measure been committed by the Constitution to another branch of government, or whether the action of that branch exceeds whatever authority has been committed, is itself a delicate exercise in constitutional interpretation, and is a responsibility of this Court as ultimate interpreter of the Constitution." Notwithstanding the deference each branch must accord the others, the "judicial Power of the United States" vested in the federal courts by Article III, § 1, of the Constitution can no more be shared with the Executive Branch than the Chief Executive, for example, can share with the Judiciary the veto power, or the Congress share with the Judiciary the power to override a Presidential veto. Any other conclusion would be contrary to the basic concept of separation of powers and the checks and balances that flow from the scheme of a tripartite government. *The Federalist, No. 47.* We therefore reaffirm that it is the province and duty of this Court "to say what the law is" with respect to the claim of privilege presented in this case.

In support of his claim of absolute privilege, the President's counsel urges two grounds, one of which is common to all governments and one of which is peculiar to our system of separation of powers. The first ground is the valid need for protection of communications between high Government officials and those who advise and assist them in the performance of their manifold duties; the importance of this confidentiality is too plain to require further discussion. Human experience teaches that those who expect public dissemination of their remarks may well temper candor with a concern for appearances and for their own interests to the detriment of the decisionmaking process. Whatever the nature of the privilege of confidentiality of Presidential communications in the exercise of Article II powers, the privilege can be said to derive from the supremacy of each branch within its own assigned area of constitutional duties. Certain powers and privileges flow from the nature of enumerated powers; the protection of the confidentiality of Presidential communications has similar constitutional underpinnings.

The second ground asserted by the President's counsel in support of the claim of absolute privilege rests on the doctrine of separation of powers. Here it is argued that the independence of the Executive Branch within its own sphere insulates a President from a judicial *subpoena* in an ongoing criminal prosecution, and thereby protects confidential Presidential communications.

However, neither the doctrine of separation of powers, nor the need for confidentiality of high-level communications, without more, can sustain an absolute, unqualified Presidential privilege of immunity from judicial process under all circumstances. The President's need for complete candor and objectivity from advisers calls for great deference from the courts. However, when the privilege depends solely on the broad, undifferentiated claim of public interest in the confidentiality of such conversations, a confrontation with other values arises. Absent a claim of need to protect military, diplomatic, or sensitive national security secrets, we find it difficult to accept the argument that even the very important interest in confidentiality of Presidential communications is significantly diminished by production of such material for *in camera* inspection with all the protection that a district court will be obliged to provide.

The impediment that an absolute, unqualified privilege would place in the way of the primary constitutional duty of the Judicial Branch to do justice in criminal prosecutions would plainly conflict with the function of the courts under Article III. In designing the structure of our Government and dividing and allocating the sovereign power among three co-equal branches, the Framers of the Constitution sought to provide a comprehensive system, but the separate powers were not intended to operate with absolute independence. "While the Constitution diffuses power the better to secure liberty, it also contemplates that practice will integrate the dispersed powers into a workable government. It enjoins upon its branches separateness but interdependence, autonomy but reciprocity." To read the Article II powers of the President as providing an absolute privilege as against a *subpoena* essential to enforcement of criminal statutes on no more than a generalized claim of the public interest in confidentiality of nonmilitary and nondiplomatic discussions would upset the constitutional balance of "a workable government" and gravely impair the role of the courts under Article III.

Since we conclude that the legitimate needs of the judicial process may outweigh Presidential privilege, it is necessary to resolve those competing interests in a manner that preserves the essential functions of each branch. The right and indeed the duty to resolve that question does not free the Judiciary from according high respect to the representations made on behalf of the President.

The expectation of a President to the confidentiality of his conversations and correspondence, like the claim of confidentiality of judicial deliberations, for example, has all the values to which we accord deference for the privacy of all citizens and, added to those values, is the necessity for protection of the public interest in candid, objective, and even blunt or harsh opinions in Presidential decisionmaking. A President and those who assist him must be free to explore alternatives in the process of shaping policies and making decisions and to do so in a way many would be unwilling to express except privately. These are the considerations justifying a presumptive privilege for Presidential communications. The privilege is fundamental to the operation of Government and inextricably rooted in the separation of powers under the Constitution. We agree with Mr. Chief Justice Marshall's observation, made while presiding at the criminal trial of Aaron Burr, therefore, that "in no case of this kind would a court be required to proceed against the president as against an ordinary individual."

But this presumptive privilege must be considered in light of our historic commitment to the rule of law. This is nowhere more profoundly manifest than in our view that "the twofold aim of criminal justice is that guilt shall not escape or innocence suffer." We have elected to employ an adversary system of criminal justice in which the parties contest all issues before a court of law. The need to develop all relevant facts in the adversary system is both fundamental and comprehensive. The ends of criminal justice would be defeated if judgments were to be founded on a partial or speculative presentation of the facts. The very integrity of the judicial system and public confidence in the system depend on full disclosure of all the facts, within the framework of the rules of evidence. To ensure that justice is done, it is imperative to the function of courts that compulsory process be available for the production of evidence needed either by the prosecution or by the defense.

Only recently the Court restated the ancient proposition of law that "the public has a right to every man's evidence," except for those persons protected by a constitutional, common-law, or statutory privilege. The privileges referred to by the Court are designed to protect weighty and legitimate competing interests. Thus, the Fifth Amendment to the Constitution provides that no man "shall be compelled in any criminal case to be a witness against himself." And, generally, an attorney or a priest may not be required to disclose what has been revealed in professional confidence. These and other interests are recognized in law by privileges against forced disclosure, established in the Constitution, by statute, or at common law. Whatever their origins, these exceptions to the demand for every man's evidence are not lightly created nor expansively construed, for they are in derogation of the search for truth.

In this case, the President challenges a *subpoena* served on him as a third party requiring the production of materials for use in a criminal prosecution; he does so on the claim that he has a privilege against disclosure of confidential communications. He does not place his claim of privilege on the ground they are military or diplomatic secrets. As to these areas of Article II duties the courts have traditionally shown the utmost deference to Presidential responsibilities: "The President, both as Commander-in-Chief and as the Nation's organ for foreign affairs, has available intelligence services whose reports are not and ought not to be published to the world. It would be intolerable that courts, without the relevant information, should review and perhaps nullify actions of the Executive taken on information properly held secret." No case of the Court, however, has extended this high degree of deference to a President's generalized interest in confidentiality. Nowhere in the Constitution, as we have noted earlier, is there any explicit reference to a privilege of confidentiality, yet to the extent this interest relates to the effective discharge of a President's powers, it is constitutionally based.

The right to the production of all evidence at a criminal trial similarly has constitutional dimensions. The Sixth Amendment explicitly confers upon every defendant in a criminal trial the right "to be confronted with the witnesses against him" and "to have compulsory process for obtaining witnesses in his favor. Moreover, the Fifth Amendment also guarantees that no person shall be deprived of liberty without due process of law. It is the manifest duty of the courts to vindicate those guarantees and, to accomplish that, it is essential that all relevant and admissible evidence be produced.

In this case, we must weigh the importance of the general privilege of confidentiality of Presidential communications in performance of the President's responsibilities against the inroads of such a privilege on the fair administration of criminal justice. The interest in preserving confidentiality is weighty indeed and entitled to great respect. However, we cannot conclude that advisers will be moved to temper the candor of their remarks by the infrequent occasions of disclosure because of the possibility that such conversations will be called for in the context of a criminal prosecution.

On the other hand, the allowance of the privilege to withhold evidence that is demonstrably relevant in a criminal trial would cut deeply into the guarantee of due process of law and gravely impair the basic function of the courts. A President's acknowledged need for confidentiality in the communications of his office is general in nature, whereas the constitutional need for production of relevant evidence in a criminal proceeding is specific and central to the fair adjudication of a particular criminal case in the administration of justice. Without access to specific facts a criminal prosecution may be totally frustrated. The President's broad interest in confidentiality of communications will not be vitiated by disclosure of a limited number of conversations preliminarily shown to have some bearing on the pending criminal cases.

We conclude that when the ground for asserting privilege as to subpoenaed materials sought for use in a criminal trial is based only on the generalized interest in confidentiality, it cannot prevail over the fundamental demands of due process of law in the fair administration of criminal justice. The generalized assertion of privilege must yield to the demonstrated, specific need for evidence in a pending criminal trial.

*An attempt on the part of the judicial department of the government to enforce the performance of such duties by the President might be justly characterized, in the language of Chief Justice Marshall, as "an absurd and excessive extravagance."*

— *Salmon P. Chase*

## Mississippi v. Johnson
### 71 U.S. (4 Wallace) 475 (1867)

*When one of the States asks permission of the Supreme Court to file a bill or complaint in an action against the President, fundamental constitutional principles are put into play. The Justices unanimously ruled that legislatively-mandated executive duties were not subject to being judicially enjoined. A few days after the Mississippi officials were rebuffed, officials from Georgia attempted to sue the Secretary of War under the Supreme Court's original jurisdiction, again arguing that the Reconstruction Acts were unconstitutional, and again the Court dismissed the suit. Georgia v. Stanton (1868). These exercises of "the better part of valor" within the tripartite system were based on the Justices' recognition of their own inherently limited judicial power when compared with the inherently greater power of the President to take care that the laws be faithfully executed. After all, as the Chief Justice emphasized, "the President is the executive department." Consequently, the Supreme Court never ruled on the underlying dispute over congressional measures placing the unrestored States of the former Confederacy under military authority.*

**Chief Justice Chase:** A motion was made, some days since, in behalf of the State of Mississippi, for leave to file a bill in the name of the State, praying this court perpetually to enjoin and restrain Andrew Johnson, President of the United States, and E. O. C. Ord, General, commanding in the District of Mississippi and Arkansas, from executing, or in any manner carrying out, certain acts of Congress therein named. The acts referred to are those of March 2d and March 23d, 1867, commonly known as the Reconstruction Acts.

The Attorney-General objected to the leave asked for, upon the ground that no bill which makes a President a defendant, and seeks an injunction against him to restrain the performance of his duties as President, should be allowed to be filed in this court. This point has been fully argued, and we will now dispose of it. We shall limit our inquiry to the question presented by the objection, without expressing any opinion on the broader issues discussed in argument, whether, in any case, the President of the United States may be required, by the process of this court, to perform a purely ministerial act under a positive law, or may be held amenable, in any case, otherwise than by impeachment for crime.

The single point which requires consideration is this: Can the President be restrained by injunction from carrying into effect an act of Congress alleged to be unconstitutional?

It is assumed by the counsel for the State of Mississippi, that the President, in the execution of the Reconstruction Acts, is required to perform a mere ministerial duty. In this assumption, there is, we think, a confounding of the terms ministerial and executive, which are by no means equivalent in import. A ministerial duty, the performance of which may, in proper cases, be required of the head of a department, by judicial process, is one in respect to which nothing is left to discretion. It is a simple, definite duty, arising under conditions admitted or proved to exist, and imposed by law.

The case of *Marbury v. Madison (1803)* furnishes an illustration. A citizen had been nominated, confirmed, and appointed a justice of the peace for the District of Columbia, and his commission had been made out, signed, and sealed. Nothing remained to be done except delivery, and the duty of delivery was imposed by law on the Secretary of State. It was held that the performance of this duty might be enforced by *mandamus* issuing from a court having jurisdiction. In every prior case in which the court furnished relief, there was nothing left to discretion. There was no room for the exercise of judgment. The law required the performance of a single specific act; and that performance, it was held, might be required by *mandamus*.

Very different is the duty of the President in the exercise of the power to see that the laws are faithfully executed, and among these laws the acts named in the bill. By the first of these acts he is required to assign generals to command in the several military districts, and to detail sufficient military force to enable such officers to discharge their duties under the law.

By the supplementary act, other duties are imposed on the several commanding generals, and these duties must necessarily be performed under the supervision of the President as commander-in-chief. The duty thus imposed on the President is in no just sense ministerial. It is purely executive and political. An attempt on the part of the judicial department of the government to enforce the performance of such duties by the President might be justly characterized, in the language of Chief Justice Marshal, as "an absurd and excessive extravagance."

It is true that in the instance before us the interposition of the court is not sought to enforce action by the Executive under constitutional legislation, but to restrain such action under legislation alleged to be unconstitutional. But we are unable to perceive that this circumstance takes the case out of the general principles which forbid judicial interference with the exercise of Executive discretion.

It was admitted in the argument that the application now made to us is without a precedent; and this is of much weight against it. Had it been supposed at the bar that this court would, in any case, interpose, by injunction, to prevent the execution of an unconstitutional act of Congress, it can hardly be doubted that applications with that object would have been heretofore addressed to it.

Occasions have not been wanting. The constitutionality of the act for the annexation of Texas was vehemently denied. It made important and permanent changes in the relative importance of States and sections, and was by many supposed to be pregnant with disastrous results to large interests in particular States. But no one seems to have thought of an application for an injunction against the execution of the act by the President. And yet it is difficult to perceive upon what principle the application now before us can be allowed and similar applications in that and other cases have been denied.

The fact that no such application was ever before made in any case indicates the general judgment of the profession that no such application should be entertained. It will hardly be contended that the courts can interpose, in any case, to restrain the enactment of an unconstitutional law; and yet how can the right to judicial interposition to prevent such an enactment, when the purpose is evident and the execution of that purpose certain, be distinguished, in principle, from the right to such interposition against the execution of such a law by the President? The Congress is the legislative department of the government; the President is the executive department. Neither can be restrained in its action by the judicial department; though the acts of both, when performed, are, in proper cases, subject to its cognizance.

The impropriety of such interference will be clearly seen upon consideration of its possible consequences. Suppose the bill filed and the injunction prayed for allowed. If the President refuse obedience, it is needless to observe that the court is without power to enforce its process. If, on the other hand, the President complies with the order of the court and refuses to execute the acts of Congress, is it not clear that a collision may occur between the executive and legislative departments of the government? May not the House of Representatives impeach the President for such refusal? And in that case could this court interfere, in behalf of the President, thus endangered by compliance with its mandate, and restrain by injunction the Senate of the United States from sitting as a court of impeachment? Would the strange spectacle be offered to the public world of an attempt by this court to arrest proceedings in that court?

These questions answer themselves.

It is true that a State may file an original bill in this court. And it may be true, in some cases, that such a bill may be filed against the United States. But we are fully satisfied that this court has no jurisdiction of a bill to enjoin the President in the performance of his official duties; and that no such bill ought to be received by us.

It has been suggested that the bill contains a prayer that, if the relief sought cannot be had against Andrew Johnson, as President, it may be granted against Andrew Johnson as a citizen of Tennessee. But it is plain that relief as against the execution of an act of Congress by Andrew Johnson, is relief against its execution by the President. A bill praying an injunction against the execution of an act of Congress by the incumbent of the presidential office cannot be received, whether it describes him as President or as a citizen of a State.

The motion for leave to file the bill is, therefore, denied.

*If it be said that the President by successive pardons of constantly recurring contempts in particular litigation might deprive a court of power to enforce its orders in a recalcitrant neighborhood, it is enough to observe that such a course is so improbable as to furnish but little basis for argument. Exceptional cases like this if to be imagined at all would suggest a resort to impeachment rather than to a narrow and strained construction of the general powers of the President.*

— *William H. Taft*

## Ex parte Grossman
### 45 S.Ct. 332, 267 U.S. 87 (1925)

*Philip Grossman was a bootlegger whose Chicago speak-easy was closed under the federal Prohibition laws. He was arrested, tried, and sentenced to serve one year in prison and to pay a $1,000 fine. After the President had commuted the sentence to the fine only and it was paid, the federal court ordered Grossman to prison and he brought a writ of habeas corpus in the Supreme Court. Some of the Framers were somewhat reluctant to include the power to pardon in the Constitution, because it resembled the historically abused royal prerogative to award individuals dispensations from obedience to the laws. However, Chief Justice Taft was not hesitant at all to conclude that the power was plenary in the office of the President, subject only to the political constraint of public opinion. Before and after this decision, Presidents regularly have exercised the power to pardon, not infrequently amid public controversy. The court of public opinion remains fiercely divided over President Gerald Ford's 1974 decision to bestow upon former President Nixon a "full, free, and absolute pardon for all offenses against the United States which he had committed or may have committed or taken part in." Substantial controversy also attended President Carter's 1977 blanket amnesty for anyone who had unlawfully evaded the military draft during the Viet Nam conflict and President Bush's 1992 pardon of former Secretary of the Defense Caspar Wein-*

*berger and five other Reagan Administration officials who were facing criminal charges for their alleged roles in the Iran-Contra scandal.*

**Chief Justice Taft:** The only question raised by the pleadings herein is that of the power of the President to grant the pardon. Article 2, § 2, cl. 1, of the Constitution, dealing with the powers and duties of the President, closes with these words: "And he shall have power to grant reprieves and pardons for offenses against the United States, except in cases of impeachment."

The argument for the re-imprisonment is that the President's power extends only to offenses against the United States and a contempt of court is not such an offense, that offenses against the United States are not common-law offenses but can only be created by legislative act, that the President's pardoning power is more limited than that of the king of England at common law, which was a broad prerogative and included contempts against his courts chiefly because the judges thereof were his agents and acted in his name, that the context of the Constitution shows that the word "offenses" is used in that instrument only to include crimes and misdemeanors triable by jury and not contempts of the dignity and authority of the federal courts, and that to construe the pardon clause to include contempts of court would be to violate the fundamental principle of the Constitution in the division of powers between the legislative, executive and judicial branches, and to take from the federal courts their independence and the essential means of protecting their dignity and authority.

The language of the Constitution cannot be interpreted safely except by reference to the common law and to British institutions as they were when the instrument was framed and adopted. The statesmen and lawyers of the Convention who submitted it to the ratification of the Convention of the Thirteen States, were born and brought up in the atmosphere of the common law, and thought and spoke in its vocabulary. They were familiar with other forms of government, recent and ancient, and indicated in their discussions earnest study and consideration of many of them, but when they came to put their conclusions into the form of fundamental law in a compact draft, they expressed them in terms of the common law, confident that they could be shortly and easily understood.

In a case presenting the question whether a pardon should be pleaded in bar to be effective, Chief Justice Marshall once said of the power of pardon: "As this power had been exercised, from time immemorial, by the executive of that nation whose language is our language, and to whose judicial institutions ours bear a close resemblance, we adopt their principles respecting the operation and effect of a pardon, and look into their books for the rules prescribing the manner in which it is to be used by the person who would avail himself of it."

The king of England before our Revolution, in the exercise of his prerogative, had always exercised the power to pardon contempts of court, just as he did ordinary crimes and misdemeanors and as he has done to the present day. In the mind of a common-law lawyer of the eighteenth century the word "pardon" included within its scope the ending by the king's grace of the punishment of such derelictions, whether it was imposed by the court without a jury or upon indictment, for both forms of trial for contempts were had.

With this authoritative background of the common law and English history before the American Revolution to show that criminal contempts were within the understood scope of the pardoning power of the executive, we come now to the history of the clause in the Constitutional Convention of 1787. There seems to have been no discussion over the substance of the clause except that a motion to except cases of treason was referred to the Committee on Style, was not approved by the Committee and after discussion was defeated in the Convention.

The history of the clause further shows that the words "for offenses against the United States" were inserted by the Committee on Style, presumably to make clear that the pardon of the President was to operate upon offenses against the United States as distinguished from offenses against the states. It cannot be supposed that the Committee on Revision by adding these words, or the Convention by accepting them, intended sub silentio to narrow the scope of a pardon from one at common law or to confer any different power in this regard on our executive from that which the members of the Convention had seen exercised before the Revolution.

Nor is there any substance in the contention that there is any substantial difference in this matter between the executive power of pardon in our government and the king's prerogative. The courts of Great Britain were called the king's courts, as indeed they were; but for years before our Constitution they were as independent of the king's interference as they are today. The extent of the king's pardon was clearly circumscribed by law and the British Constitution, as shown by the cases we have reviewed. The framers of our Constitution had in mind no necessity for curtailing this feature of the king's prerogative in transplanting it into the American governmental structures, save by excepting cases of impeachment; and even in that regard, the common law forbade the pleading a pardon in bar to an impeachment. The suggestion that the President's power of pardon should be regarded as necessarily less than that of the king was pressed upon this court in 1856 and was agreed to by Mr. Justice McLean, in dissent, but it did not prevail with the majority.

Nothing in the ordinary meaning of the words "offenses against the United States" excludes criminal contempts. That which violates the dignity and authority of federal courts such as an intentional effort to defeat their decrees justifying punishment violates a law of the United States, and so must be an offense against the United States. We think the arguments drawn from the common law, from the power of the king under the British Constitution, which plainly was the prototype of this clause, from the legislative history of the clause in the Convention, and from the ordinary meaning of its words, are relevant and convincing. Moreover, criminal contempts of a federal court have been pardoned for 85 years. In that time, the power has been exercised 27 times. Such long practice under the pardoning power and acquiescence in it strongly sustains the construction it is based on.

Finally it is urged that criminal contempts should not be held within the pardoning power because it will tend to destroy the independence of the judiciary and violate the primary constitutional principle of a separation of the legislative, executive and judicial powers.

The federal Constitution nowhere expressly declares that the three branches of the government shall be kept separate and independent. All legislative powers are vested in a Congress. The executive power is vested in a President. The judicial power is vested in one Supreme Court and in such inferior courts as Congress may from time to time establish. The judges are given life tenure and a compensation that may not be diminished during their continuance in office, with the evident purpose of securing them and their courts an independence of Congress and the executive. Complete independence and separation between the three branches, however, are not attained, or intended, as other provisions of the Constitution and the normal operation of government under it easily demonstrate. By affirmative action through the veto power, the executive and one more than one-third of either House may defeat all legislation. One-half of the House and two-thirds of the Senate may impeach and remove the members of the judiciary. The executive can reprieve or pardon all offenses after their commission, either before trial, during trial or after trial, by individuals, or by classes, conditionally or absolutely, and this without modification or regulation by Congress. Negatively one House of Congress can withhold all appropriations and stop the operations of government. The Senate can hold up all appointments, confirmation of which either the Constitution or a statute requires, and thus deprive the President of the necessary agents with which he is to take care that the laws be faithfully executed.

These are some instances of positive and negative restraints possibly available under the Constitution to each branch of the government in defeat of the action of the other. They show that the independence of each of the other is qualified and is so subject to exception as not to constitute a broadly positive injunction or a necessarily controlling rule of construction. The fact is that the judiciary, quite as much as Congress and the executive, are dependent on the co-operation of the other two, that government may go on. Indeed while the Constitution has made the judiciary as independent of the other branches as is practicable, it is, as often remarked, the weakest of the three. It must look for a continuity of necessary co-operation, in the possible reluctance of either of the other branches, to the force of public opinion.

Executive clemency exists to afford relief from undue harshness or evident mistake in the operation or enforcement of the criminal law. The administration of justice by the courts is not necessarily always wise or certainly considerate of circumstances which may properly mitigate guilt. To afford a remedy, it has always been thought essential in popular governments, as well as in monarchies, to vest in some other authority than the courts power to ameliorate or avoid particular criminal judgments. It is a check entrusted to the executive for special cases. To exercise it to the extent of destroying the deterrent effect of judicial punishment would be to prevent it; but whoever is to make it useful must have full discretion to exercise it. Our Constitution confers this discretion on the highest officer in the nation in confidence that he will not abuse it. An abuse in pardoning contempts would certainly embarrass courts, but it is questionable how much more it would lessen their effectiveness than a wholesale pardon of other offenses. If we could conjure up in our minds a President willing to paralyze courts by pardoning all criminal contempts, why not a President ordering a general jail delivery?

If it be said that the President, by successive pardons of constantly recurring contempts in particular litigation, might deprive a court of power to enforce its orders in a recalcitrant neighborhood, it is enough to observe that such a course is so improbable as to furnish but little basis for argument. Exceptional cases like this, if to be imagined at all, would suggest a resort to impeachment rather than to a narrow and strained construction of the general powers of the President.

The power of a court to protect itself and its usefulness by punishing contemnors is of course necessary, but it is one exercised without the restraining influence of a jury and without many of the guaranties which the bill of rights offers to protect the individual against unjust conviction. Is it unreasonable to provide for the possibility that the personal element may sometimes enter into a summary judgment pronounced by a judge who thinks his authority is flouted or denied? May it not be fairly said that in order to avoid possible mistake, undue prejudice or needless severity, the chance of pardon should exist at least as much in favor of a person convicted by a judge without a jury as in favor of one convicted in a jury trial? The pardoning by the President of criminal contempts has been practiced more than three-quarters of a century, and no abuses during all that time developed sufficiently to invoke a test in the federal courts of its validity.

It goes without saying that nowhere is there a more earnest will to maintain the independence of federal courts and the preservation of every legitimate safeguard of their effectiveness afforded by the Constitution than in this court. But the qualified independence which they fortunately enjoy is not likely to be permanently strengthened by ignoring precedent and practice and minimizing the importance of the co-ordinating checks and balances of the Constitution.

*The Judicial Branch should not decide issues affecting the allocation of power between the President and Congress until the political branches reach a constitutional impasse.*

— *Lewis F. Powell*

## Goldwater v. Carter
### 100 S.Ct. 533, 444 U.S. 996 (1979)

*Senator Barry Goldwater and other members of Congress sued President Jimmy Carter claiming that his unilateral termination of the mutual defense treaty with the Republic of China (Taiwan) violated the Constitution. The Constitution expressly gives the power to make treaties to the President, provided that two-thirds of the Senate concur. Article II, § 2, cl. 2. It is silent, however, about the power to abrogate treaties. The Supreme Court summarily reversed the lower federal court's decision to reach the merits and to approve what the President had done. The Supreme Court reasoned that the judicial branch should neither grant nor withhold its constitutional imprimatur on what the President had done. Four Justices shared the view, expressed by Justice Rehnquist, that this was a nonjusticiable political question a la the precedent of* Baker v. Carr (1962). *Justice Powell's was the necessary 5th vote to send the case back to the lower court with directions to dismiss, but he did not think the issue was completely off-limits to the judicial branch. Instead, he concluded that the Plaintiffs had come to court too soon, before Congress had called out the President by passing a formal resolution. The full Senate, however, did not have the stomach for a fight and the controversy evaporated without ever getting back to the courtroom. In dissent, only Justice Brennan offered a definitive opinion on the merits and he would have sided with the President. For Justice Brennan, the authority to abrogate the treaty with Taiwan was incidental to the President's contemporaneous exercise of his exclusive power under the Constitution to recognize and establish diplomatic relations with the Peoples' Republic of China. The issue, therefore, remains unresolved. Here Justice Powell explains how and why a court should not decide a dispute between the other two branches before its time.*

**Justice Powell:** This Court has recognized that an issue should not be decided if it is not ripe for judicial review. Prudential considerations persuade me that a dispute between Congress and the President is not ready for judicial review unless and until each branch has taken action unequivocally asserting its constitutional authority. Differences between the President and the Congress are commonplace under our system. The differences should, and almost invariably do, turn on political rather than legal considerations. The Judicial Branch should not decide issues affecting the allocation of power between the President and Congress until the political branches reach a constitutional impasse. Otherwise, we would encourage small groups or even individual Members of Congress to seek judicial resolution of issues before the normal political process has the opportunity to resolve the conflict.

In this case, a few Members of Congress claim that the President's action in terminating the treaty with Taiwan has deprived them of their constitutional role with respect to a change in the supreme law of the land. Congress has taken no official action. In the present posture of this case, we do not know whether there ever will be an actual confrontation between the Legislative and Executive Branches. Although the Senate has considered a resolution declaring that Senate approval is necessary for the termination of any mutual defense treaty, no final vote has been taken on the resolution. Moreover, it is unclear whether the resolution would have retroactive effect. It cannot be said that either the Senate or the House has rejected the President's claim. If the Congress chooses not to confront the President, it is not our task to do so.

Justice Rehnquist and the plurality suggests, however, that the issue presented by this case is a nonjusticiable political question which can never be considered by this Court. I cannot agree. In my view, reliance upon the political-question doctrine is inconsistent with our precedents.

No constitutional provision explicitly confers upon the President the power to terminate treaties. Further, Art. II, § 2, of the Constitution authorizes the President to make treaties with the advice and consent of the Senate. Article VI provides that treaties shall be a part of the supreme law of the land. These provisions add support to the view that the text of the Constitution does not unquestionably commit the power to terminate treaties to the President alone.

We are asked to decide whether the President may terminate a treaty under the Constitution without congressional approval. Resolution of the question may not be easy, but it only requires us to apply normal principles of interpretation to the constitutional provisions at issue. The present case involves neither review of the President's activities as Commander in Chief nor impermissible interference in the field of foreign affairs. Such a case would arise if we were asked to decide, for example, whether a treaty required the President to order troops into a foreign country. But this Court has pointed out that "it is error to suppose that every case or controversy which touches foreign relations lies beyond judicial cognizance." This case "touches" foreign relations, but the question presented to us concerns only the constitutional division of power between Congress and the President.

A simple hypothetical demonstrates the confusion that I find inherent in Justice Rehnquist's invocation of the political question doctrine. Assume that the President signed a mutual defense treaty with a foreign country and announced that it would go into effect despite its rejection by the Senate. Under Justice Rehnquist's analysis that situation would present a political question even though Art. II, § 2, clearly would resolve the dispute. Although the answer to the hypothetical case seems self-evident because it demands textual rather than interstitial analysis, the nature of the legal issue presented is no different from the issue presented in the case before us. In both cases, the Court would interpret the Constitution to decide whether congressional approval is necessary to give a Presidential decision on the validity of a treaty the force of law. Such an inquiry demands no special competence or information beyond the reach of the Judiciary.

The Court has recognized that, in the area of foreign policy, Congress may leave the President with wide discretion that otherwise might run afoul of the nondelegation doctrine. In a leading precedent decided in 1936, this Court said "the President alone has the power to speak or listen as a representative of the Nation. He makes treaties with the advice and consent of the Senate; but he alone negotiates." Resolution of this case would interfere with neither the President's ability to negotiate treaties nor his duty to execute their provisions. We are merely being asked to decide whether a treaty, which cannot be ratified without Senate approval, continues in effect until the Senate or perhaps the Congress take further action.

Finally, the political-question doctrine rests in part on prudential concerns calling for mutual respect among the three branches of Government. Thus, the Judicial Branch should avoid "the potentiality of embarrassment" that would result from "multifarious pronouncements by various departments on one question." Similarly, the doctrine restrains judicial action where there is an "unusual need for unquestioning adherence to a political decision already made." If this case were ripe for judicial review, none of these prudential considerations would be present. Interpretation of the Constitution does not imply lack of respect for a coordinate branch. If the President and the Congress had reached irreconcilable positions, final disposition of the question presented by this case would eliminate, rather than create, multiple constitutional interpretations. The specter of the Federal Government brought to a halt because of the mutual intransigence of the President and the Congress would require this Court to provide a resolution pursuant to our duty "to say what the law is."

In my view, the suggestion that this case presents a political question is incompatible with this Court's willingness on previous occasions to decide whether one branch of our Government has impinged upon the power of another. Under the criteria enunciated in our leading precedents, we have the responsibility to decide whether both the Executive and Legislative Branches have constitutional roles to play in termination of a treaty. If the Congress, by appropriate formal action, had challenged the President's authority to terminate the treaty with Taiwan, the resulting uncertainty could have serious consequences for our country. In that situation, it would be the duty of this Court to resolve the issue.

*We are obviously deciding only one more epi-*
*sode in the never-ending tension between the*
*President exercising the executive authority in a*
*world that presents each day some new challenge*
*with which he must deal and the Constitution un-*
*der which we all live and which no one disputes*
*embodies some sort of system of checks and bal-*
*ances.*

*— William H. Rehnquist*

## Dames & Moore v. Regan
### 101 S.Ct. 2972, 453 U.S. 654 (1981)

*In November 1979, the American Embassy in Tehran*
*was seized and our diplomatic personnel were captured*
*and held hostage. President Carter declared a national*
*emergency and froze all the assets the government of Iran*
*owned in the U.S. By Executive Order, the President also*
*suspended any and all claims against those assets then*
*pending in American courts. President Reagan ratified*
*these executive orders with one of his own. In January*
*1981, the American hostages were released pursuant to*
*an agreement negotiated and declared by the government*
*of Algeria. The Algerian agreement provided that any*
*claims against Iran's assets would be resolved by interna-*
*tional arbitration and not in U.S. courts. Plaintiff Dames*
*& Moore was owed more than $3 million for services*
*rendered before the crisis under a contract with the Ira-*
*nian government to develop nuclear power plants in that*
*country. Dames & Moore challenged what the President*
*had done but the Justices all agreed that he acted within*
*his constitutional and statutory powers. The President*
*had the power, in effect, to remove a category of cases*
*from the federal courts and to renegotiate private prop-*
*erty rights. The decision seemed to go beyond previous*
*holdings to afford treaty-like authority to presidential ex-*
*ecutive agreements, though they are not ratified by the*
*Senate. This then is an important holding in favor of a*
*broad presidential foreign relations power, and for that it*
*has met with sharp criticism.*

**Justice Rehnquist:** The questions presented by this case touch fundamentally upon the matter in which our Republic is to be governed. Throughout the nearly two centuries of our Nation's existence under the Constitution, this subject has generated considerable debate. We have had the benefit of commentators such as John Jay, Alexander Hamilton, and James Madison writing in The Federalist Papers at the Nation's very inception, the benefit of astute foreign observers of our system such as Alexis de Tocqueville and James Bryce writing during the first century of the Nation's existence, and the benefit of many other treatises as well as more than 400 volumes of reports of decisions of this Court. As these writings reveal, it is doubtless both futile and perhaps dangerous to find any epigrammatical explanation of how this country has been governed. Indeed, as Justice Jackson once had occasion to note, "a judge may be surprised at the poverty of really useful and unambiguous authority applicable to concrete problems of executive power as they actually present themselves."

Our decision today will not dramatically alter this situation, because, as Justice Frankfurter observed, the Framers "did not make the judiciary the overseer of our government." We are confined to a resolution of the dispute presented to us. That dispute involves various Executive Orders and regulations by which the President nullified attachments and liens on Iranian assets in the United States, directed that these assets be transferred to Iran, and suspended claims against Iran that may be presented to an International Claims Tribunal. This action was taken in an effort to comply with an Executive Agreement between the United States and Iran.

But before turning to the facts and law which we believe determine the result in this case, we stress that the expeditious treatment of the issues involved by all of the courts which have considered the President's actions makes us acutely aware of the necessity to rest decision on the narrowest possible ground capable of deciding the case. This does not mean that reasoned analysis may give way to judicial fiat. It does mean that Justice Jackson's famous epigram—that we decide difficult cases presented to us by virtue of our commissions, not our competence—is especially true here. We attempt to lay down no general "guidelines" covering other situations not involved here, and attempt to confine the opinion only to the very questions necessary to decision of the case.

Perhaps it is because it is so difficult to reconcile the foregoing definition of Article III judicial power with the broad range of vitally important day-to-day questions regularly decided by Congress or the Executive, without either challenge or interference by the Judiciary, that the decisions of the Court in this area have been rare, episodic, and afford little precedential value for subsequent cases. The tensions present in any exercise of executive power under the tri-partite system of Federal Government established by the Constitution have been reflected in opinions by Members of this Court more than once.

As we now turn to the factual and legal issues in this case, we freely confess that we are obviously deciding only one more episode in the never-ending tension between the President exercising the executive authority in a world that presents each day some new challenge with which he must deal and the Constitution under which we all live and which no one disputes embodies some sort of system of checks and balances.

The parties and the lower courts, confronted with the instant questions, have all agreed that much relevant analysis is contained in this Court's opinion in the steel seizure case decided in 1952. Justice Jackson's concurring opinion elaborated in a general way the consequences of different types of interaction between the two democratic branches in assessing Presidential authority to act in any given case. When the President acts pursuant to an express or implied authorization from Congress, he exercises not only his powers but also those delegated by Congress. In such a case the executive action "would be supported by the strongest of presumptions and the widest latitude of judicial interpretation, and the burden of persuasion would rest heavily upon any who might attack it."

We also should be mindful of Justice Holmes' admonition that "the great ordinances of the Constitution do not establish and divide fields of black and white." Justice Jackson himself recognized that his categorical approach represented "a somewhat over-simplified grouping," and it is doubtless the case that executive action in any particular instance falls, not neatly in one of three pigeonholes, but rather at some point along a spectrum running from explicit congressional authorization to explicit congressional prohibition. This is particularly true as respects cases such as the one before us, involving responses to international crises the nature of which Congress can hardly have been expected to anticipate in any detail.

The Government has principally relied on the International Emergency Economic Powers Act. Although Congress intended to limit the President's emergency power in peacetime, we do not think the changes brought about by the enactment of the Act in any way affected the authority of the President to take the specific actions taken here. This Court has previously recognized that the congressional purpose in authorizing blocking orders is "to put control of foreign assets in the hands of the President." Such orders permit the President to maintain the foreign assets at his disposal for use in negotiating the resolution of a declared national emergency. The frozen assets serve as a "bargaining chip" to be used by the President when dealing with a hostile country.

Because the President's action in nullifying the attachments and ordering the transfer of the assets was taken pursuant to specific congressional authorization, under Justice Jackson's analysis, it is "supported by the strongest of presumptions and the widest latitude of judicial interpretation, and the burden of persuasion would rest heavily upon any who might attack it." Under the circumstances of this case, we cannot say that Dames & Moore has sustained that heavy burden. A contrary ruling would mean that the Federal Government as a whole lacked the power exercised by the President, and that we are not prepared to say.

Although we have concluded that this Act constitutes specific congressional authorization to the President to nullify the attachments and order the transfer of Iranian assets, there remains the separate and distinct question of the President's authority to suspend claims pending in American courts. Such claims have, of course, an existence apart from the attachments which accompanied them. We conclude that although the Act authorized the nullification of the attachments in the first place, it cannot be read to authorize the suspension of the in personam judicial claims. The terms of the Act simply do not authorize the President to suspend claims in American courts.

The President also purported to enter his Executive Order under the Hostage Act of 1868. We also are reluctant to conclude that this older provision constitutes specific authorization to the President to suspend claims in American courts. Concluding that neither of the two statutes constitutes specific authorization of the President's action suspending claims in federal court, however, is not to say that these statutory provisions are entirely irrelevant to the question of the validity of the President's action. We think both statutes highly relevant in the looser sense of indicating congressional acceptance of a broad scope for executive action in circumstances such as those presented in this case. The International Emergency Economic Powers Act delegates broad authority to the President to act in times of national emergency with respect to property of a foreign country. The Hostage Act similarly indicates congressional willingness that the President have broad discretion when responding to the hostile acts of foreign sovereigns.

Although we have declined to conclude that the two statutes directly authorize the President's suspension of claims for the reasons noted, we cannot ignore the general tenor of Congress' legislation in this area in trying to determine whether the President is acting alone or at least with the acceptance of Congress. Congress cannot anticipate and legislate with regard to every possible action the President may find it necessary to take or every possible situation in which he might act. Such failure of Congress specifically to delegate authority does not, "especially in the areas of foreign policy and national security," imply "congressional disapproval" of action taken by the Executive. On the contrary, the enactment of legislation closely related to the question of the President's authority in a particular case which evinces legislative intent to accord the President broad discretion may be considered, in Justice Jackson's words, to "invite" "measures on independent presidential responsibility." At least this is so where there is no contrary indication of legislative intent and when, as here, there is a history of congressional acquiescence in conduct of the sort engaged in by the President.

Not infrequently in affairs between nations, outstanding claims by nationals of one country against the government of another country are "sources of friction" between the two sovereigns. To resolve these difficulties, nations have often entered into agreements settling the claims of their respective nationals. As one treatise writer puts it, international agreements settling claims by nationals of one state against the government of another "are established international practice reflecting traditional international theory." Consistent with that principle, the United States has repeatedly exercised its sovereign authority to settle the claims of its nationals against foreign countries. Though those settlements have sometimes been made by treaty, there has also been a longstanding practice of settling such claims by executive agreement without the advice and consent of the Senate. Under such agreements, the President has agreed to renounce or extinguish claims of United States nationals against foreign governments in return for lump-sum payments or the establishment of arbitration procedures.

At least since the case of the "Wilmington Packet" in 1799, Presidents have exercised the power to settle claims of United States nationals by executive agreement. In fact, during the period of 1817–1917, "no fewer than eighty executive agreements were entered into by the United States looking toward the liquidation of claims of its citizens." It is clear that the practice of settling claims continues today. Since 1952, the President has entered into at least 10 binding settlements with foreign nations, including an $80 million settlement with the People's Republic of China.

Crucial to our decision today is the conclusion that Congress has implicitly approved the practice of claim settlement by executive agreement. Indeed, Congress has consistently failed to object to this longstanding practice of claim settlement by executive agreement, even when it has had an opportunity to do so.

In addition to congressional acquiescence in the President's power to settle claims, prior cases of this Court have also recognized that the President does have some measure of power to enter into executive agreements without obtaining the advice and consent of the Senate. In a case decided in 1942, for example, the Court upheld the validity of the Litvinov Assignment, which was part of an Executive Agreement whereby the Soviet Union assigned to the United States amounts owed to it by American nationals so that outstanding claims of other American nationals could be paid. The Court explained that the resolution of such claims was integrally connected with normalizing United States' relations with a foreign state: "Power to remove such obstacles to full recognition as settlement of claims of our nationals certainly is a modest implied power of the President. No such obstacle can be placed in the way of rehabilitation of relations between this country and another nation, unless the historic conception of the powers and responsibilities is to be drastically revised."

In light of all of the foregoing—the inferences to be drawn from the character of the legislation Congress has enacted in the area and from the history of acquiescence in executive claims settlement—we conclude that the President was authorized to suspend pending claims pursuant to this Executive Order. As Justice Frankfurter once pointed out, "a systematic, unbroken, executive practice, long pursued to the knowledge of the Congress and never before questioned may be treated as a gloss on 'Executive Power' vested in the President by § 1 of Art. II." Past practice does not, by itself, create power, but "long-continued practice, known to and acquiesced in by Congress, would raise a presumption that the action had been taken in pursuance of its consent." Such practice is present here and such a presumption is also appropriate. In light of the fact that Congress may be considered to have consented to the President's action in suspending claims, we cannot say that action exceeded the President's powers.

Just as importantly, Congress has not disapproved of the particular action taken here. Though Congress has held hearings on the Iranian Agreement itself, Congress has not enacted legislation, or even passed a resolution, indicating its displeasure with the Agreement. Quite the contrary, the relevant Senate Committee has stated that the establishment of the Tribunal is "of vital importance to the United States." We are thus clearly not confronted with a situation in which Congress has in some way resisted the exercise of Presidential authority.

Finally, we re-emphasize the narrowness of our decision. We do not decide that the President possesses plenary power to settle claims, even as against foreign governmental entities. As the lower court stressed, "the sheer magnitude of such a power, considered against the background of the diversity and complexity of modern international trade, cautions against any broader construction of authority than is necessary." But where, as here, the settlement of claims has been determined to be a necessary incident to the resolution of a major foreign policy dispute between our country and another, and where, as here, we can conclude that Congress acquiesced in the President's action, we are not prepared to say that the President lacks the power to settle such claims.

# Chapter Four

# The Judicial Power

*The Judicial Power of the United States,*
*shall be vested in one supreme Court, and in*
*such inferior Courts as the Congress may from*
*time to time ordain and establish.*

In the United States, we take federal courts for granted. But other countries with federal systems do not have two complete sets of federal and state courts coexisting alongside one another. Instead, the trial courts are all state courts and the only federal courts are appellate courts. It is a little remembered fact that the United States came close to adopting this model.

The debate at the Constitutional Convention of 1787 about courts was protracted and intense. The arguments went back and forth, without much prospect for compromise. Things got so heated that at one point the delegates voted to strike a provision previously agreed upon and they agreed to eliminate any and all mention of a national judicial branch in the new Constitution. Their premise was that the existing courts in the States were equal to the judicial tasks of the Nation and therefore all that was needed was to provide for appeals from the state courts to a supreme national court. After a great deal more parliamentary wrangling, another version of compromise was reached, however, which yielded the text quoted in the title of this Chapter. There would be one Supreme Court. Congress was authorized—but not required—to "ordain and establish" a separate and independent system of federal courts, separate from the state courts and independent from the other branches of the federal government.

The delegates' hard fought compromise continued to be the subject of high and full controversy in the subsequent ratification debates in the States. Five full issues of *The Federalist*

*Papers, Nos. 78–82,* defended the idea of a separate and independent federal judiciary, with political passion, against the sustained attacks of the Antifederalists. Federalists insisted that the lack of a federal judiciary was a serious deficiency in the Articles of Confederation and they portrayed the proposed federal courts as guardians of civil liberties.

For their part, Antifederalists mistrusted all three heads of the federal leviathan. They felt especially threatened by the congressional power to create a new federal judiciary because they believed it would aggrandize power toward the central government and away from the state sovereigns, all to the eventual detriment of individual rights. At the same time, they argued that the lack of a written bill of rights was reason enough to oppose the proposed Constitution. In the end, the Federalists prevailed, but the Constitution was ratified though barely and by close margins in several key States: Massachusetts 187–168; Virginia 89–79; and New York 30–27. Thus, from the beginning, the Article III judiciary and civil liberties have been linked in controversy.

One of the transcendent achievements of the first Congress assembled under the newly-ratified Constitution was to enact the Judiciary Act of 1789, a statute which has come to be considered a great law because, once and for all, it established the tradition of a separate and independent system of federal courts. But the role those courts would play within the separation of powers and in our federalism was left to be determined by constitutional experience. History and tradition have elaborated on the delphic generality of Article III. The federal courts themselves, especially the Supreme Court, have done a great deal to shape this history and tradition.

The Supreme Court of the United States, of course, has been from the beginning and remains the most important as well as the most controversial federal court. Justice Oliver Wendell Holmes, Jr., once remarked, "We are very quiet there but it is the quiet of a storm centre."

The Supreme Court is the only court created directly by the Constitution. It has supervisory and appellate jurisdiction over the lower federal courts and reviews cases involving federal issues from the highest courts of the States. It is composed of nine Justices—although the number has been changed no fewer than seven times by congressional statutes and has varied between five and ten members—who are appointed by the President, with the advice and consent of the Senate, and who serve "during good behaviour," effectively until they retire or die. The House of Representatives can impeach and the Senate can remove a Justice upon conviction of "high Crimes and Misdemeanors." Early in our history, however, impeachment became what Thomas Jefferson called "a mere scarecrow." It would be unthinkable today for Congress to impeach and remove a Justice based on some ruling or a judicial opinion.

The Framers' expectation was to create a federal judiciary that was independent, but neither too much nor too long at odds with popular sovereignty. Historically, predicting what specific issues will come before the Court has been impossible, except in the short term, and then only in the most general terms. Furthermore, predicting how any individual jurist will interpret the Constitution has been next to impossible. Nevertheless, Presidents and Senates engage in political branch forecasting each time a vacancy occurs and the nomination and confirmation process is the primary external restraint on the Supreme Court.

Judge Learned Hand once remarked, "For myself it would be most irksome to be ruled by a bevy of Platonic Guardians, even if I knew how to choose them, which I assuredly do not." Recent confirmation battles between a President of one party and a Senate majority of the other party have shed more heat than light on what is at stake for the Constitution. But here there are no constitutional rules beyond Madison's mechanism of "ambition checking ambition," *Federalist Paper No. 51*. A President can nominate a person for the Supreme Court for good reason or for bad reason or for no reason at all. The Constitution is completely silent on qualifications. Merit is almost always the announced criterion, of course, although other reasons that have been invoked over the years have included political and personal patronage, geography, race, religion, and gender. For periods in its history, particular chairs have been temporarily identified, such as "the Jewish (or Catholic) seat" or "the African-American (or Woman's) seat," but these appellations are by and large newspaper constructions. For the most part, a President wants a justice who will be faithful to the President's views about the Constitution on the issues the President deems politically important. And, for the most part, presidential sponsors have been pleased by their judicial proteges. The Senators can confirm or reject for any of the same reasons that a President chooses a nominee. In a controversial nomination battle between the President and the upper chamber, the Senators usually end up bowing to the will of their constituencies, more so now that the proceedings are televised. This is high stakes politics, but politics nonetheless. In the constitutional long run, nomination and confirmation shape the Supreme Court as an institution in the image and likeness, not of the 18th century Framers, but of "ourselves and our posterity."

The Supreme Court sits *en banc*, that is, all the Justices participate and decide every case. Its annual Term begins the first Monday in October (the title of the only movie ever made about the Court itself) and continues usually through the end of June. Its annual docket consists of more than 7,000 cases. Most of the Court's jurisdiction is discretionary, and it exercises great care in selecting which cases to decide. Each October Term, the Court hears oral arguments (usually 30 minutes per side) and reads briefs (a misnomer for book-length written arguments filed by lawyers) in fewer than 100 cases. For these cases, the Justices write detailed, scholarly opinions, like the ones excerpted in this book but many times longer and usually not as interesting. More often than not, some of the Justices will write a concurring opinion, explaining why they agree with the outcome but for different reasons, and others will file a dissenting opinion, explaining why they think the majority is wholly mistaken. The Chief Justice, or the most senior Justice in the majority when the Chief Justice is dissenting, assigns the responsibility of preparing a draft opinion for the Court. Individual Justices, however, are free to write separate opinions, and frequently do so, expressing their own views in a case. A full set of opinions in a major decision can run well over a hundred pages. All documents and briefs are matters of public record. Oral arguments are conducted in public. The decisions are announced in open court and then published. The only secret procedures are the Justices' conference—when the nine meet without any others present to discuss and vote on cases—and their confidential individual work in chambers. The Justices are aided by law clerks, the best and the brightest of recent law school graduates who serve a one year apprenticeship, in the arduous task of preparing opinions: researching the law, checking the lower court record, studying briefs and legal authorities, and exchanging memoranda with each other to argue points of law and to suggest changes in drafts. Not infrequently, this secret back-and-forth can result in one or more of the Justices rethinking an earlier vote thus shifting the ultimate outcome 180° in a closely contested decision.

In the 1994 October Term, the Court resolved ninety-five cases fully on the merits. The nine Justices wrote eighty-six majority opinions, fifty concurring opinions, and sixty-four dissenting opinions. There were twenty-eight (32.6%) unanimous decisions. Sixteen (18.6%) cases were decided by a 5 to 4 vote. Volume 115 of SUPREME COURT REPORTER contains 2,641 pages recording and annotating the Term's decisions. Thus, each year another ponderous Talmudic volume is published commenting on the great charter. Iconoclastic law professor and legal realist Fred Rodell once harrumphed that these lengthy, elaborately documented, carefully crafted, published opinions merely amounted to "fancy rationalizations of legal action."

The cliched lawyer's threat, "I will take this case all the way to the Supreme Court," may be literally possible, but the odds are greatly against obtaining a Supreme Court ruling on the merits of a case. In the vast majority of cases brought before them, the only thing the Justices conclude and announce is that they will not hear or decide the issues. "The petition for a writ of *certiorari* to the court below is denied" is the lawyers' parlance. "*Certiorari*" was the name the common law gave a writ from a higher court to a lower court ordering that the record in a case be sent up for review. This is why newspapers can be very misleading when they report that the Supreme Court "approved" of some ruling by some lower court, when all that the Justices have done is to deny review. By tradition, it takes four Justices to agree to hear a case. Thus, a minority sets the agenda. One thing is certain, whether the Court does or does not decide a case: there is no further appeal. Justice Robert H. Jackson once aptly described the High Court's place in the judicial hierarchy: "We are not final because we are infallible, but we are infallible only because we are final."

But the larger constitutional debate goes on. From the beginning down to modern times, Americans have singled out particularly controversial decisions—on such divisive issues as race relations and abortion—but they consistently have maintained their confidence in the Supreme Court as an institution of government. Over the 200–plus year history of the Constitution, "We the People" seem to have been arguing about its meaning the entire time. The Supreme Court, like a republican schoolmaster, has presided over that debate. I know my own pedagogical and forensic skills are about to be tested when my wife looks over the newspaper at me and asks, "Do you know what *your* Supreme Court has done now?"

Chief Justice Charles Evans Hughes once proudly proclaimed that the Supreme Court is "distinctly American in concept and function." The complex role of the High Court in the

American system derives from its authority to invalidate legislation or executive actions which conflict with the Constitution, the power of judicial review. While this power is not explicitly granted in the Constitution, it had been anticipated at the time the document was written and ratified. The power of judicial review, the ultimate political power of the Supreme Court, must be appreciated within the context of the American regime.

\* \* \* \*

No political institution, least of all a committee of nine lawyers appointed for life, could be expected to exercise a near-absolute power over such a wide range of public policy without political legitimacy and widespread respect. The broad historical tradition of liberalism, based as it is on the consent of the governed, helps account for this. Americans have always been and still are "Lockeans," whether they be labelled Federalists or Antifederalists, Democrats or Republicans, liberals or conservatives. The American people from the beginning have been committed to the rule of law, to republican government, and to a written Constitution. If the Constitution is understood to be "the supreme Law of the Land," then the Nation's highest Court logically is the most appropriate institution to perform the function of interpreter of the law. Alexander Hamilton said as much in *Federalist Paper No. 78* and Chief Justice Marshall proclaimed this authority in the famous decision of *Marbury v. Madison (1803)*, the first selection in this Chapter. The fact is that the primary document is silent on the subject and the reality is that these two secondary documents are less than apodictic. Consequently, it should come as no surprise that intense and sustained controversy would attend the assertion of this power and its proffered justifications, right down to the present day.

That great Chief Justice took great rhetorical and logical pains to justify locating the authority of constitutional interpretation in the Supreme Court. But that was only the beginning. In *Cooper v. Aaron (1958)*, the Justices issued a single, joint opinion, signed by them all, insisting that their interpretations be given the same respect and allegiance as the Constitution itself. Is this constitutional *hubris*? Does judicial review ineluctably lead to what the Antifederalists feared most, assertions of judicial supremacy and court oligarchy? Political scientist Edward S. Corwin irreverently called this judicial *hocus-pocus* "a kind of transubstantiation whereby the Court's opinion becomes the very body and blood of the Constitution."

From the earliest days of the Republic, the Court has understood some clauses in the Constitution to be off limits to the judicial branch. The political question doctrine explains that some constitutional powers are committed to the political branches, either Congress or the Executive, and it would be unconstitutional for the Justices to review the coordinate decisionmaking. This idea is to be found in the deep structure of the Constitution and the separation of powers. But it is the Justices who have the final authority to decide whether a power is committed to one of the other branches and it is the Justices who determine the scope of the power. In *Nixon v. United States (1993)*, Chief Justice Rehnquist explains how and why the curiosities of judicial impeachments fall into this category, in a case brought by an impeached judge by that name.

Much has been made of the counter-majoritarian nature of judicial review: an unelected life-tenured Supreme Court professing to know what is better for the country than the people's elected representatives in Congress or the state legislature. How can we square judicial review and democracy? Should the Court defer to the elected branches of government? The Justices believe there often are special reasons—to protect fundamental rights and to defend political minorities—that justify a more aggressive review of legislation which burdens these rights or disadvantages certain groups. This argument for the Supreme Court to act as a champion of political underdogs can be traced back to a footnote—a rather unassuming place to find such an important first principle—planted into the case reports by Justice Stone in *United States v. Carolene Products (1938)*. As in the Biblical parable of the mustard seed, nearly all of our modern understandings of constitutional law have grown from that footnote.

The jurisprudence of original intent takes as its starting point to divine the meaning intended by those who wrote and ratified the Constitution. But there is no toll free number "1–800–MADISON" to call. How does an originalist Justice attempt to recapture this essence? A member of the present Court, Justice Clarence Thomas, demonstrates this channeling back to the founders in *McIntyre v. Ohio (1995)*. Sixty years ago, in *Home Building & Loan Assoc. v. Blaisdell (1934)*, Chief Justice Hughes complained that such originalist efforts were the constitutional equivalent of searching for the Holy Grail.

Justice William J. Brennan, Jr., arguably the most influential member of the Court in the last fifty years, once delivered a speech in which he labelled originalism "arrogance cloaked as humility." He admitted his own approach to be far more subjective:

> We current Justices read the Constitution in the only way we can: as Twentieth Century Americans. We look to the history of the time of framing and to the intervening history of interpretation. But the ultimate question must be, what do the words of the text mean in our time? For the genius of the Constitution rests not in any static meaning it might have had in a world that is dead and gone, but in the adaptability of its great principles to cope with current problems and current needs. What the constitutional fundamentals meant to the wisdom of other times cannot be their measure to the vision of our time.

Is he suggesting that clauses in the Constitution evolve? That the words of the Constitution have no inherent meaning beyond the policy preference of the Justice interpreting them? That the meaning of the clauses somehow changes over time? That it is for the Justices to know and the rest of us to find out when and how this happens? The notion of a "living Constitution" is a frequently invoked metaphor. But the same 4,400 words remain elegantly engrossed on those fading sheets of parchment kept under glass at the Archives of the United States, in Washington, D.C. What actually changes are the interpreters. Perhaps Charles Evans Hughes was more accurate than cynical to observe, before he became Chief Justice, that "We are under a Constitution, but the Constitution is what the judges say it is."

Are there principles beyond the Constitution that an interpreter may rely on to decide cases? Where else beyond the document should the high priests of the Constitution look for inspiration and revelations? Some Justices have looked to natural law theory, deeply textured in the *Declaration of Independence*. Before the ink was dry on the Constitution, Justice Samuel Chase and Justice James Iredell began a debate that has never subsided over the propriety of judges undertaking this method of interpretation, in *Calder v. Bull (1798)*.

Other Justices have found meaning in the historical practices and traditions of the people. But then there are the twin problems, first, to determine what in history qualifies as a worthy tradition and, second, to choose between competing traditions that inform opposite results. That something has been around a long time does not necessarily make it constitutional, of course. Furthermore, it is equally logical to worry whether some wisdoms though recently discovered nonetheless deserve to be afforded constitutional respect. Two sets of opinions bring this debate up to date. First, the Justices engage in a spirited debate over the derivation and meaning of the "right of privacy," nowhere expressed in so many words in the text of the Constitution, in *Griswold v. Connecticut (1965)*. Second, in *Michael H. and Victoria D. v. Gerald D. (1989)*, Justices Scalia and Brennan argue over when and how the Court can rely on traditions, that is, how our kaleidoscopic American culture informs our understanding of the Constitution over time. In both these decisions, the Justices assume that constitutional law is not limited to the four corners of the 1787 parchment.

Constitution writers do not make it easy on Constitution interpreters. Constitutional language is written in majestic generalities. To be sure, there always is the temptation—a temptation Justice Holmes wished his colleagues had resisted in *Hammer v. Dagenhart (1918)*—for the Justices-as-interpreters to "interpret" into constitutional law their own personal political peccadilloes, in the misguided belief that in their heart of hearts they know what is best for the Nation. His dissent was written before its time, but has since come to be regarded as one of the finest declarations of the principle of judicial deference to majority rule.

Still, "due process of law," guaranteed in the 5th and 14th Amendments at very different times and for very different purposes, like so many other constitutional phrases has an iceberg quality to it. If we suppose it means that the government, federal or state, must treat its citizens fairly, then we still have to decide what is fair under the applicable circumstances. During the 1960s, the Justices engaged in a debate that revolutionized and constitutionalized state criminal procedures. The Bill of Rights, which by its express language and intended history only applied to the national government, was "incorporated" and applied to the States. The debate between Justice Black and Justice Frankfurter, in the landmark decision in *Adamson v. California (1947)*, established the parameters of this interpretive question.

Echoes of the hue and cry that rose up against the "judicial activism" of the Warren Court in the 1960s continue to reverberate in the body politic. More lately, critics from the left have complained about conservative activism on the part of Rehnquist Court majorities interpreting these same majestic generalities. Perhaps, charges of activism amount to nothing more than sour grapes. Among the Justices themselves, it certainly is true that this complaint always is levelled at a majority by dissenters who lack the requisite votes to have it their own way.

When a State violates the rights of one of its citizens and a federal court provides a remedy, it is the State—not the court— that is acting outside the Constitution. The federal courts are the guardians of federal rights, the centurions of the Constitution. Justice Holmes, a veteran of the Civil War, learned about federalism as a Union officer who was wounded at Balls Bluff, Antietam, and Fredericksburg. As a Union judge he later had occasion to observe, "I do not think the United States would come to an end if we lost our power to declare an Act of Congress void. I do think the Union would be imperiled if we could not make that declaration as to the laws of the several States." Principles of "Our Federalism," however, sound a caution that federal judges should not become ombudsmen. The complex of relations between the national government and the States is all the more complicated to the extent that federal courts and state courts have to get along.

Two decisions illustrate the difficulty in deciding issues of judicial federalism. In *Ex parte Young (1908)*, Justice Peckham hypothesizes a way to enforce the 14th Amendment's protections of individual liberty against a State, despite the sovereign immunity bar in the 11th Amendment that plainly says a State cannot be sued in federal court. In his solitary dissent, the first Justice Harlan, a former slaveowner and southern aristocrat who had fought on the side of the Union, marches an antifederalist/states'-rightist's parade of horribles past the Supreme Court bench that has come true in the aftermath of that decision. Federal judges today routinely act as constitutional overseers of schools and prisons, for example, which in Justice Harlan's day were deemed within the exclusive domain of the States. Nonetheless, federal courts still owe a great deal of respect to state courts under the Constitution. Justice Black's opinion in *Younger v. Harris (1971)* hearkens us back to first principles to explain why a federal court generally should not interfere with a state court proceeding, even when the Constitution may be being violated.

Professor Walter F. Murphy, a prominent Supreme Court scholar, reminded us that even Supreme Court Justices are human beings and carry with them all the mystery of what it is to be human:

> In a post-Freudian world, there can be no serious doubt that a judge's personal values influence the way in which he or she interprets the Constitution. Society can require that judges be neutral between parties to a case; but no one can ask a mature adult to be neutral between ideas that go to the heart of political philosophy. Not only do we all carry our peculiar DNA Code and bear the effects of early childhood, religious and moral instruction, family relations, and social class, but we are affected by our more formal education and our experiences in life. These factors shape the values we apply to choices; they also influence the way in which we make choices.

Performing the role of a Justice of the Supreme Court of the United States must indeed be a daunting responsibility. A member of the Court constantly is engaged in an internal debate over the great issues of the day. Not everything a Justice believes, no matter how self-evidently, can be attributed to the Constitution, however. There are times when the Justice must obey the law of the Constitution against personal conscience and desire. That is the philosophy of the rule of law we call the Constitution. That is the Gethsemane oath judges swear: "Not my will but the Constitution's." But at the deepest levels of being and judging, do "We the People" ask the impossible?

On the occasion of his retirement in 1969, Chief Justice Earl Warren spoke of "the very awesome responsibility" the Justices bear to "speak the last word in great governmental affairs," for the Nation and its future:

> It is a responsibility that is made more difficult in this Court because we have no constituency. We serve no majority. We serve no minority. We serve only the public interest as we see it, guided only by the Constitution and our own consciences. And conscience sometimes is a very severe taskmaster.

Rarely do Justices provide us with glimpses into the isolating solitude of their judicial conscience. We are left only to imagine their inner turmoil towards their decisionmaking. The last two selections provide us with rare insights into what it must be like to be a member of the Supreme Court with the responsibility to decide these most difficult issues. Justice Blackmum writes why he decided to change his constitutional mind about the death penalty in *Callins v. Collins (1994)*. Before this opinion, he had accepted its constitutionality, but he announces here that he no longer would do so. True to the American judicial tradition, he feels obliged to give his reasons. And Justice Kennedy wrings his hands over his personal decision to join a ruling that burning the U.S. flag is protected under the 1st and 14th Amendments in *Texas v. Johnson (1989)*. He follows his judicial duty as he sees it, although he admits wishing it could be otherwise.

This is the Supreme Court in the constitutional storm center. Petitions are presented. Cases are accepted. Arguments are made. The Justices make choices. Ultimately their choices affect us all. While still a professor at Princeton University, Woodrow Wilson explained what is at stake:

> So far as the individual is concerned, a constitutional government is as good as its courts; no better, no worse. Its laws are only its professions. It keeps its promises, or does not keep them, in its courts.

*It is emphatically the province and duty of the
judicial department to say what the law is.*

— *John Marshall*

## Marbury v. Madison
### 5 U.S. (1 Cranch) 137 (1803)

*On the surface, the case involved whether Jefferson's
Republican administration could get rid of the so-called
"Midnight judges," justices of the peace for the District of
Columbia appointed in the last days of the Federalist
Adams administration. Serving as Secretary of State,
John Marshall had only a day to deliver more than forty
such commissions. Several remained signed and sealed
but undelivered as Adam's term ended on March 3, 1801.
The new President refused to deliver them, and, William
Marbury, along with three others, sued James Madison,
Secretary of State under Jefferson, in the Supreme Court
for an order to obtain their commissions. The Republicans won the case; the decision went against Marbury.
But Chief Justice Marshall wrote in the grand manner to
establish the power of judicial review, the judicial power
to declare that an act of the legislature or the executive
violates the Constitution and, therefore, is void. In the
next case in this Chapter,* Cooper v. Aaron *(1958), the
Justices rebuked the grandiose claim that the Governor
and Legislature of a State somehow were not bound by
the Supreme Court's school desegregation decision. They
invoked the great Chief Justice's most famous opinion in
this case, "This decision declared the basic principle that
the federal judiciary is supreme in the exposition of the
law of the Constitution, and that principle has ever since
been respected by this Court and the Country as a permanent and indispensable feature of our constitutional system."*

**Chief Justice Marshall:** The peculiar delicacy of this case,
the novelty of some of its circumstances, and the real difficulty
attending the points which occur in it, require a complete exposition of the principles on which the opinion to be given by the
court is founded.

The very essence of civil liberty certainly consists in the right of every individual to claim the protection of the laws, whenever he receives an injury. One of the first duties of government is to afford that protection. In Great Britain the king himself is sued in the respectful form of a petition, and he never fails to comply with the judgment of his court.

The government of the United States has been emphatically termed a government of laws, and not of men. It will certainly cease to deserve this high appellation, if the laws furnish no remedy for the violation of a vested legal right.

If this obloquy is to be cast on the jurisprudence of our country, it must arise from the peculiar character of the case. If some acts be examinable, and others not, there must be some rule of law to guide the court in the exercise of its jurisdiction.

If this be the rule, let us inquire how it applies to the case under the consideration of the court.

It is then the opinion of the court,

1.  That by signing the commission of Mr. Marbury, the president of the United States appointed him a justice of peace for the county of Washington in the district of Columbia; and that the seal of the United States, affixed thereto by the secretary of state, is conclusive testimony of the verity of the signature, and of the completion of the appointment; and that the appointment conferred on him a legal right to the office for the space of five years.

2.  That, having this legal title to the office, he has a consequent right to the commission; a refusal to deliver which is a plain violation of that right, for which the laws of his country afford him a remedy.

It remains to be inquired whether, he is entitled to the remedy for which he applies. This depends on the nature of the writ applied for, and the power of this court.

Still, to render the *mandamus* a proper remedy, the officer to whom it is to be directed, must be one to whom, on legal principles, such writ may be directed; and the person applying for it must be without any other specific and legal remedy.

With respect to the officer to whom it would be directed. The intimate political relation, subsisting between the president of the United States and the heads of departments, necessarily renders any legal investigation of the acts of one of those high officers peculiarly irksome, as well as delicate; and excites some hesitation with respect to the propriety of entering into such investigation. Impressions are often received without much reflection or examination; and it is not wonderful that in such a case as this, the assertion, by an individual, of his legal claims in a court of justice, to which claims it is the duty of that court to attend, should at first view be considered by some, as an attempt to intrude into the cabinet, and to intermeddle with the prerogatives of the executive.

It is scarcely necessary for the court to disclaim all pretensions to such a jurisdiction. An extravagance, so absurd and excessive, could not have been entertained for a moment. The province of the court is, solely, to decide on the rights of individuals, not to inquire how the executive, or executive officers, perform duties in which they have a discretion. Questions, in their nature political, or which are, by the constitution and laws, submitted to the executive, can never be made in this court.

But, if this be not such a question; if so far from being an intrusion into the secrets of the cabinet, it respects a paper, which, according to law, is upon record, and to a copy of which the law gives a right, on the payment of ten cents; if it be no intermeddling with a subject, over which the executive can be considered as having exercised any control; what is there in the exalted station of the officer, which shall bar a citizen from asserting, in a court of justice, his legal rights, or shall forbid a court to listen to the claim; or to issue a *mandamus*, directing the performance of a duty, not depending on executive discretion, but on particular acts of congress and the general principles of law?

It is not by the office of the person to whom the writ is directed, but the nature of the thing to be done, that the propriety or impropriety of issuing a *mandamus* is to be determined. Where the head of a department acts in a case in which executive discretion is to be exercised; in which he is the mere organ of executive will; it is again repeated, that any application to a court to control, in any respect, his conduct, would be rejected without hesitation.

It has already been stated that the applicant has, to that commission, a vested right, of which the Executive cannot deprive him. This, then, is a plain case of a *mandamus*, either to deliver the commission, or a copy of it from the record; and it only remains to be inquired, whether it can issue from this court.

The authority given to the supreme court, by Section 13 of the Judiciary Act of 1789 establishing the judicial courts of the United States, to issue writs of *mandamus* to public officers, appears not to be warranted by the constitution; and it becomes necessary to inquire whether a jurisdiction, so conferred, can be exercised.

The question, whether an act, repugnant to the constitution, can become the law of the land, is a question deeply interesting to the United States; but, happily, not of an intricacy proportioned to its interest. It seems only necessary to recognize certain principles, supposed to have been long and well established, to decide it.

That the people have an original right to establish, for their future government, such principles as, in their opinion, shall most conduce to their own happiness, is the basis on which the whole American fabric has been erected. The exercise of this original right is a very great exertion; nor can it nor ought it to be frequently repeated. The principles, therefore, so established are deemed fundamental. And as the authority, from which they proceed, is supreme, and can seldom act, they are designed to be permanent.

This original and supreme will organizes the government, and assigns to different departments their respective powers. It may either stop here; or establish certain limits not to be transcended by those departments.

The government of the United States is of the latter description. The powers of the legislature are defined and limited; and that those limits may not be mistaken or forgotten, the constitution is written. To what purpose are powers limited, and to what purpose is that limitation committed to writing; if these limits may, at any time, be passed by those intended to be restrained? The distinction between a government with limited and unlimited powers is abolished, if those limits do not confine the persons on whom they are imposed, and if acts prohibited and acts allowed are of equal obligation. It is a proposition too plain to be contested, that the constitution controls any legislative act repugnant to it; or, that the legislature may alter the constitution by an ordinary act.

Between these alternatives there is no middle ground. The constitution is either a superior, paramount law, unchangeable by ordinary means, or it is on a level with ordinary legislative acts, and like other acts, is alterable when the legislature shall please to alter it.

If the former part of the alternative be true, then a legislative act contrary to the constitution is not law: if the latter part be true, then written constitutions are absurd attempts, on the part of the people, to limit a power in its own nature illimitable.

Certainly all those who have framed written constitutions contemplate them as forming the fundamental and paramount law of the nation, and consequently the theory of every such government must be, that an act of the legislature repugnant to the constitution is void.

This theory is essentially attached to a written constitution, and is consequently to be considered by this court as one of the fundamental principles of our society. It is not therefore to be lost sight of in the further consideration of this subject.

If an act of the legislature, repugnant to the constitution, is void, does it, notwithstanding its invalidity, bind the courts and oblige them to give it effect? Or, in other words, though it be not law, does it constitute a rule as operative as if it was a law? This would be to overthrow in fact what was established in theory; and would seem, at first view, an absurdity too gross to be insisted on. It shall, however, receive a more attentive consideration.

It is emphatically the province and duty of the judicial department to say what the law is. Those who apply the rule to particular cases, must of necessity expound and interpret that rule. If two laws conflict with each other, the courts must decide on the operation of each.

So if a law be in opposition to the constitution: if both the law and the constitution apply to a particular case, so that the court must either decide that case conformably to the law, disregarding the constitution; or conformably to the constitution, disregarding the law: the court must determine which of these conflicting rules governs the case. This is of the very essence of judicial duty.

If then the courts are to regard the constitution; and the constitution is superior to any ordinary act of the legislature; the constitution, and not such ordinary act, must govern the case to which they both apply.

Those then who controvert the principle that the constitution is to be considered, in court, as a paramount law, are reduced to the necessity of maintaining that courts must close their eyes on the constitution, and see only the law.

This doctrine would subvert the very foundation of all written constitutions. It would declare that an act, which, according to the principles and theory of our government, is entirely void, is yet, in practice, completely obligatory. It would declare, that if the legislature shall do what is expressly forbidden, such act, notwithstanding the express prohibition, is in reality effectual. It would be giving to the legislature a practical and real omnipotence with the same breath which professes to restrict their powers within narrow limits. It is prescribing limits, and declaring that those limits may be passed at pleasure.

That it thus reduces to nothing what we have deemed the greatest improvement on political institutions, a written constitution, would of itself be sufficient, in America where written constitutions have been viewed with so much reverence, for rejecting the construction. But the peculiar expressions of the constitution of the United States furnish additional arguments in favour of its rejection.

The judicial power of the United States is extended to all cases arising under the constitution.

Could it be the intention of those who gave this power, to say that, in using it, the constitution should not be looked into? That a case arising under the constitution should be decided without examining the instrument under which it arises?

This is too extravagant to be maintained.

In some cases then, the constitution must be looked into by the judges. And if they can open it at all, what part of it are they forbidden to read, or to obey?

There are many other parts of the constitution which serve to illustrate this subject.

It is declared that "no tax or duty shall be laid on articles exported from any state." Suppose a duty on the export of cotton, of tobacco, or of flour; and a suit instituted to recover it. Ought judgment to be rendered in such a case? Ought the judges to close their eyes on the constitution, and only see the law.

The constitution declares that "no bill of attainder or *ex post facto* law shall be passed."

If, however, such a bill should be passed and a person should be prosecuted under it, must the court condemn to death those victims whom the constitution endeavours to preserve?

"No person," says the constitution, "shall be convicted of treason unless on the testimony of two witnesses to the same overt act, or on confession in open court."

Here the language of the constitution is addressed especially to the courts. It prescribes, directly for them, a rule of evidence not to be departed from. If the legislature should change that rule, and declare one witness, or a confession out of court, sufficient for conviction, must the constitutional principle yield to the legislative act?

From these and many other selections which might be made, it is apparent, that the framers of the constitution contemplated that instrument as a rule for the government of courts, as well as of the legislature.

Why otherwise does it direct the judges to take an oath to support it? This oath certainly applies, in an especial manner, to their conduct in their official character. How immoral to impose it on them, if they were to be used as the instruments, and the knowing instruments, for violating what they swear to support!

The oath of office, too, imposed by the legislature, is completely demonstrative of the legislative opinion on this subject. It is in these words: "I do solemnly swear that I will administer justice without respect to persons, and do equal right to the poor and to the rich; and that I will faithfully and impartially discharge all the duties incumbent on me as according to the best of my abilities and understanding, agreeably to the constitution and laws of the United States."

Why does a judge swear to discharge his duties agreeably to the constitution of the United States, if that constitution forms no rule for his government? If it is closed upon him and cannot be inspected by him?

If such be the real state of things, this is worse than solemn mockery. To prescribe, or to take this oath, becomes equally a crime.

It is also not entirely unworthy of observation, that in declaring what shall be the supreme law of the land, the constitution itself is first mentioned; and not the laws of the United States generally, but those only which shall be made in pursuance of the constitution, have that rank.

Thus, the particular phraseology of the constitution of the United States confirms and strengthens the principle, supposed to be essential to all written constitutions, that a law repugnant to the constitution is void, and that courts, as well as other departments, are bound by that instrument.

*The interpretation of the Fourteenth Amendment enunciated by this Court in the* Brown *case is the supreme law of the land, and Art. VI of the Constitution makes it of binding effect on the States "any Thing in the Constitution or Laws of any State to the Contrary notwithstanding."*

— *Earl Warren*

## Cooper v. Aaron
### 78 S.Ct. 1401, 358 U.S. 1 (1958)

*The Little Rock, Arkansas school board proposed a plan for desegregating Central High School beginning in September 1957. Governor Orval Faubus ordered the state National Guard to prevent its implementation. The U.S. Attorney General obtained an injunction against the Governor but when a handful of African-American students attempted to go to class a hostile crowd stopped them. President Eisenhower then sent in U.S. Army troops to protect the children. In February 1958, the school board went back to federal court, at the instigation of the Governor and members of the legislature, and successfully argued that the threat of violence and disruption justified a postponement of any further desegregation for two and one-half years. The case presented the Justices with a direct challenge to their decision in* Brown v. Board of Education *(1954). In an unusual procedure, the Court accelerated its review and convened in a special term during its normal recess. Oral argument was heard on September 11 and the very next day an order was entered disapproving of any further delay and promising a full opinion "in due course." A few weeks later, the Court published the following unanimous opinion, signed by all nine Justices in a rare display of solidarity, as if to emphasize their individual and collective support for the holding in* Brown. *Along the way, the Justices seemed to claim that the power of judicial review was based on a principle of judicial supremacy. One cannot take their supremacy claim literally or logically, however, for the Court in* Brown *in fact overruled one of its own prior holdings. Therefore, we know that Supreme Court opinions—whatever else they are—are not the same as the Constitution.*

**Opinion of the Court:** As this case reaches us, it raises questions of the highest importance to the maintenance of our federal system of government. It necessarily involves a claim by the Governor and Legislature of a State that there is no duty on state officials to obey federal court orders resting on this Court's considered interpretation of the United States Constitution. Specifically it involves actions by the Governor and Legislature of Arkansas upon the premise that they are not bound by our holding in *Brown v. Board of Education (1954)*. That holding was that the Fourteenth Amendment forbids States to use their governmental powers to bar children on racial grounds from attending schools where there is state participation through any arrangement, management, funds or property. We are urged to uphold a suspension of the Little Rock School Board's plan to do away with segregated public schools in Little Rock until state laws and efforts to upset and nullify *Brown* have been further challenged and tested in the courts. We reject these contentions.

In order that the School Board might know, without doubt, its duty in this regard before the opening of school, which had been set for the following Monday, September 15, 1958, we immediately issued the judgment, reserving the expression of our supporting views to a later date. This opinion of all of the members of the Court embodies those views.

On May 17, 1954, in *Brown v. Board of Education*, this Court decided that enforced racial segregation in the public schools of a State is a denial of the equal protection of the laws enjoined by the Fourteenth Amendment. The Court postponed, pending further argument, formulation of a decree to effectuate this decision. That decree was rendered May 31, 1955. In the formulation of that decree, the Court recognized that good faith compliance with the principles declared in *Brown* might in some situations "call for elimination of a variety of obstacles in making the transition to school systems operated in accordance with the constitutional principles set forth in our decision." The Court went on to state: "Courts of equity may properly take into account the public interest in the elimination of such obstacles in a systematic and effective manner. But it should go without saying that the vitality of these constitutional principles cannot be allowed to yield simply because of disagreement with them."

One may well sympathize with the position of the Board in the face of the frustrating conditions which have confronted it, but, regardless of the Board's good faith, the actions of the other state agencies responsible for those conditions compel us to reject the Board's legal position. The constitutional rights of these school children are not to be sacrificed or yielded to the violence and disorder which have followed upon the actions of the Governor and Legislature. As this Court said some 41 years ago in a unanimous opinion in a case involving another aspect of racial segregation: "It is urged that this proposed segregation will promote the public peace by preventing race conflicts. Desirable as this is, and important as is the preservation of the public peace, this aim cannot be accomplished by laws or ordinances which deny rights created or protected by the federal Constitution." Thus law and order are not here to be preserved by depriving the Negro children of their constitutional rights.

The controlling legal principles are plain. The command of the Fourteenth Amendment is that no "State" shall deny to any person within its jurisdiction the equal protection of the laws. "A State acts by its legislative, its executive, or its judicial authorities. It can act in no other way. The constitutional provision, therefore, must mean that no agency of the State, or of the officers or agents by whom its powers are exerted, shall deny to any person within its jurisdiction the equal protection of the laws. Whoever, by virtue of public position under a State government, denies or takes away the equal protection of the laws, violates the constitutional inhibition; and as he acts in the name and for the State, and is clothed with the State's power, his act is that of the State. This must be so, or the constitutional prohibition has no meaning." In short, the constitutional rights of children not to be discriminated against in school admission on grounds of race or color declared by this Court in the *Brown* case can neither be nullified openly and directly by state legislators or state executive or judicial officers, nor nullified indirectly by them through evasive schemes for segregation whether attempted "ingeniously or ingenuously."

What has been said, in the light of the facts developed, is enough to dispose of the case. However, we should answer the premise of the actions of the Governor and Legislature that they are not bound by our holding in the *Brown* case. It is necessary only to recall some basic constitutional propositions which are settled doctrine.

Article VI of the Constitution makes the Constitution the "supreme Law of the Land." In 1803, Chief Justice Marshall, speaking for a unanimous Court, referring to the Constitution as "the fundamental and paramount law of the nation," declared in the notable case of *Marbury v. Madison* that "It is emphatically the province and duty of the judicial department to say what the law is." This decision declared the basic principle that the federal judiciary is supreme in the exposition of the law of the Constitution, and that principle has ever since been respected by this Court and the Country as a permanent and indispensable feature of our constitutional system. It follows that the interpretation of the Fourteenth Amendment enunciated by this Court in the *Brown* case is the supreme law of the land, and Art. VI of the Constitution makes it of binding effect on the States "any Thing in the Constitution or Laws of any State to the Contrary notwithstanding. "Every state legislator and executive and judicial officer is solemnly committed by oath taken pursuant to Art. VI, § 3 "to support this Constitution." Chief Justice Taney, speaking for a unanimous Court in 1859, said that this requirement reflected the framers' "anxiety to preserve the Constitution in full force, in all its powers, and to guard against resistance to or evasion of its authority, on the part of a State."

No state legislator or executive or judicial officer can war against the Constitution without violating his undertaking to support it. Chief Justice Marshall spoke for a unanimous Court in 1809 saying that: "If the legislatures of the several states may, at will, annul the judgments of the courts of the United States, and destroy the rights acquired under those judgments, the constitution itself becomes a solemn mockery." A Governor who asserts a power to nullify a federal court order is similarly restrained. If he had such power, said Chief Justice Hughes, in 1932, also for a unanimous Court, "it is manifest that the fiat of a state Governor, and not the Constitution of the United States, would be the supreme law of the land; that the restrictions of the Federal Constitution upon the exercise of state power would be but impotent phrases."

It is, of course, quite true that the responsibility for public education is primarily the concern of the States, but it is equally true that such responsibilities, like all other state activity, must be exercised consistently with federal constitutional requirements as they apply to state action. The Constitution created a government dedicated to equal justice under law. The Fourteenth Amendment embodied and emphasized that ideal. State support of segregated schools through any arrangement, management, funds, or property cannot be squared with the Amendment's command that no State shall deny to any person within its jurisdiction the equal protection of the laws. The right of a student not to be segregated on racial grounds in schools so maintained is indeed so fundamental and pervasive that it is embraced in the concept of due process of law, as well. The basic decision in *Brown* was unanimously reached by this Court only after the case had been briefed and twice argued and the issues had been given the most serious consideration. Since the first *Brown* opinion three new Justices have come to the Court. They are at one with the Justices still on the Court who participated in that basic decision as to its correctness, and that decision is now unanimously reaffirmed. The principles announced in that decision and the obedience of the States to them, according to the command of the Constitution, are indispensable for the protection of the freedoms guaranteed by our fundamental charter for all of us. Our constitutional ideal of equal justice under law is thus made a living truth.

*The history and contemporary understanding
of the impeachment provisions support our reading of the constitutional language. The parties do
not offer evidence of a single word in the history of
the Constitutional Convention or in contemporary
commentary that even alludes to the possibility of
judicial review in the context of the impeachment
powers.*

— *William H. Rehnquist*

## Nixon v. United States
### 113 S.Ct. 732 (1993)

*Walter L. Nixon, Jr., a former Chief Judge of the
United States District Court for the Southern District of
Mississippi, was convicted by a jury of two counts of making false statements before a federal grand jury. The
grand jury investigation stemmed from reports that
Nixon had accepted a gratuity from a Mississippi businessman in exchange for asking a local district attorney
to halt the prosecution of the businessman's son. Because
Nixon refused to resign from his office as a United States
District Judge, he continued to collect his judicial salary
while serving out his prison sentence. The House of Representatives adopted articles of impeachment and the
Senate undertook its constitutional duty to "try" him. He
objected to the Senate's procedure and asked the courts to
review and reverse the decision to remove him from office.
The Chief Justice delivered an historical disquisition why
the courts could not define the word "try"—certainly a
term normally considered within the judicial ken—as
that word appears in Article I. This is only one of two
modern holdings declaring that a clause in the Constitution is beyond the power of judicial review. Notice the
worries about potential mischief for separation of powers,
including the prospects for Presidential impeachments,
that figure in the Court's reasoning.*

**Chief Justice Rehnquist:** Walter L. Nixon, Jr., asks this
court to decide whether Senate Rule XI, which allows a committee of Senators to hear evidence against an individual who has
been impeached and to report that evidence to the full Senate,
violates the Impeachment Trial Clause, Art. I, § 3, cl. 6. That

Clause provides that the "Senate shall have the sole Power to try all Impeachments." But before we reach the merits of such a claim, we must decide whether it is "justiciable," that is, whether it is a claim that may be resolved by the courts. We conclude that it is not.

On May 10, 1989, the House of Representatives adopted three articles of impeachment for high crimes and misdemeanors. The first two articles charged Nixon with giving false testimony before the grand jury and the third article charged him with bringing disrepute on the Federal Judiciary.

After the House presented the articles to the Senate, the Senate voted to invoke its own Impeachment Rule XI, under which the presiding officer appoints a committee of Senators to "receive evidence and take testimony." The Senate committee held four days of hearings, during which 10 witnesses, including Nixon, testified. Pursuant to Rule XI, the committee presented the full Senate with a complete transcript of the proceeding and a report stating the uncontested facts and summarizing the evidence on the contested facts. Nixon and the House impeachment managers submitted extensive final briefs to the full Senate and delivered arguments from the Senate floor during the three hours set aside for oral argument in front of that body. Nixon himself gave a personal appeal, and several Senators posed questions directly to both parties. The Senate voted by more than the constitutionally required two-thirds majority to convict Nixon on the first two articles. The presiding officer then entered judgment removing Nixon from his office as a United States District Judge.

Nixon thereafter commenced the present suit, arguing that Senate Rule XI violates the constitutional grant of authority to the Senate to "try" all impeachments because it prohibits the whole Senate from taking part in the evidentiary hearings. See Art. I, § 3, cl. 6. Nixon sought a declaratory judgment that his impeachment conviction was void and that his judicial salary and privileges should be reinstated.

A controversy is nonjusticiable—*i.e.*, involves a political question—where there is "a textually demonstrable constitutional commitment of the issue to a coordinate political department; or a lack of judicially discoverable and manageable standards for resolving it." But the courts must, in the first instance, interpret the text in question and determine whether and to what extent the issue is textually committed. As the discussion that follows makes clear, the concept of a textual

commitment to a coordinate political department is not completely separate from the concept of a lack of judicially discoverable and manageable standards for resolving it; the lack of
judicially manageable standards may strengthen the conclusion
that there is a textually demonstrable commitment to a coordinate branch.

In this case, we must examine Art. I, § 3, cl. 6, to determine
the scope of authority conferred upon the Senate by the Framers
regarding impeachment. It provides: "The Senate shall have the
sole Power to try all Impeachments. When sitting for that Purpose, they shall be on Oath or Affirmation. When the President
of the United States is tried, the Chief Justice shall preside:
And no Person shall be convicted without the Concurrence of
two thirds of the Members present." The language and structure
of this Clause are revealing. The first sentence is a grant of
authority to the Senate, and the word "sole" indicates that this
authority is reposed in the Senate and nowhere else. The next
two sentences specify requirements to which the Senate proceedings shall conform: the Senate shall be on oath or affirmation, a two-thirds vote is required to convict, and when the
President is tried the Chief Justice shall preside.

Nixon argues that the word "try" in the first sentence imposes by implication an additional requirement on the Senate in
that the proceedings must be in the nature of a judicial trial.
From there Nixon goes on to argue that this limitation precludes the Senate from delegating to a select committee the task
of hearing the testimony of witnesses, as was done pursuant to
Senate Rule XI. His brief argues, " 'try' means more than simply
'vote on' or 'review' or 'judge.' In 1787 and today, trying a case
means hearing the evidence, not scanning a cold record." Nixon
concludes from this that courts may review whether or not the
Senate "tried" him before convicting him.

There are several difficulties with this position which lead
us ultimately to reject it. The word "try," both in 1787 and later,
has considerably broader meanings than those to which Nixon
would limit it. Older dictionaries define try as "to examine" or
"to examine as a judge." 2 S. JOHNSON, A DICTIONARY OF THE
ENGLISH LANGUAGE (1785). In more modern usage the term has
various meanings. For example, try can mean "to examine or
investigate judicially," "to conduct the trial of," or "to put to the
test by experiment, investigation, or trial." WEBSTER'S THIRD
NEW INTERNATIONAL DICTIONARY 2457 (1971). Nixon submits
that "try," as contained in T. SHERIDAN, DICTIONARY OF THE

ENGLISH LANGUAGE (1796), means "to examine as a judge; to bring before a judicial tribunal." Based on the variety of definitions, however, we cannot say that the Framers used the word "try" as an implied limitation on the method by which the Senate might proceed in trying impeachments. This Court has observed, "As a rule the Constitution speaks in general terms, leaving Congress to deal with subsidiary matters of detail as the public interests and changing conditions may require."

The conclusion that the use of the word "try" in the first sentence of the Impeachment Trial Clause lacks sufficient precision to afford any judicially manageable standard of review of the Senate's actions is fortified by the existence of the three very specific requirements that the Constitution does impose on the Senate when trying impeachments: the members must be under oath, a two-thirds vote is required to convict, and the Chief Justice presides when the President is tried. These limitations are quite precise, and their nature suggests that the Framers did not intend to impose additional limitations on the form of the Senate proceedings by the use of the word "try" in the first sentence.

Nixon devotes only two pages in his brief to negating the significance of the word "sole" in the first sentence of Clause 6. As noted above, that sentence provides that "the Senate shall have the sole Power to try all Impeachments." We think that the word "sole" is of considerable significance. Indeed, the word "sole" appears only one other time in the Constitution—with respect to the House of Representatives' "sole Power of Impeachment." Art. I, § 2, cl. 5. The common sense meaning of the word "sole" is that the Senate alone shall have authority to determine whether an individual should be acquitted or convicted. The dictionary definition bears this out. "Sole" is defined as "having no companion," "solitary," "being the only one," and "functioning independently and without assistance or interference." WEBSTER'S THIRD NEW INTERNATIONAL DICTIONARY 2168 (1971). If the courts may review the actions of the Senate in order to determine whether that body "tried" an impeached official, it is difficult to see how the Senate would be "functioning independently and without assistance or interference."

Nixon asserts that the word "sole" has no substantive meaning. To support this contention, he argues that the word is nothing more than a mere "cosmetic edit" added by the Committee of Style after the delegates had approved the substance of the Impeachment Trial Clause. There are two difficulties with this argument. First, accepting as we must the proposition that the Committee of Style had no authority from the Constitutional Convention to alter the meaning of the Clause, we must presume that the Committee's reorganization or rephrasing accurately captured what the Framers meant in their unadorned language. That is, we must presume that the Committee did its job. This presumption is buttressed by the fact that the Constitutional Convention voted on, and accepted, the Committee of Style's linguistic version. We agree with the Government that "the word 'sole' is entitled to no less weight than any other word of the text, because the Committee revision perfected what 'had been agreed to.'" Second, carrying Nixon's argument to its logical conclusion would constrain us to say that the second to last draft would govern in every instance where the Committee of Style added an arguably substantive word. Such a result is at odds with the fact that the Convention passed the Committee's version, and with the well established rule that the plain language of the enacted text is the best indicator of intent.

Nixon also contends that the word "sole" should not bear on the question of justiciability because Art. II, § 2, cl. 1, of the Constitution grants the President pardon authority "except in Cases of Impeachment." He argues that such a limitation on the President's pardon power would not have been necessary if the Framers thought that the Senate alone had authority to deal with such questions. But the granting of a pardon is in no sense an overturning of a judgment of conviction by some other tribunal; it is "an executive action that mitigates or sets aside punishment for a crime." BLACK'S LAW DICTIONARY 1113 (6th ed. 1990). Authority in the Senate to determine procedures for trying an impeached official, unreviewable by the courts, is therefore not at all inconsistent with authority in the President to grant a pardon to the convicted official. The exception from the President's pardon authority of cases of impeachment was a separate determination by the Framers that executive clemency should not be available in such cases.

Nixon finally argues that even if significance be attributed to the word "sole" in the first sentence of the clause, the authority granted is to the Senate, and this means that "the Senate—not the courts, not a lay jury, not a Senate Committee—shall try impeachments." It would be possible to read the first sentence of the Clause this way, but it is not a natural reading. Nixon's interpretation would bring into judicial purview not merely the sort of claim made by Nixon, but other similar claims based on the conclusion that the word "Senate" has imposed by implication limitations on procedures which the Senate might adopt. Such limitations would be inconsistent with the construction of the Clause as a whole, which, as we have noted, sets out three express limitations in separate sentences.

The history and contemporary understanding of the impeachment provisions support our reading of the constitutional language. The parties do not offer evidence of a single word in the history of the Constitutional Convention or in contemporary commentary that even alludes to the possibility of judicial review in the context of the impeachment powers. This silence is quite meaningful in light of the several explicit references to the availability of judicial review as a check on the Legislature's power with respect to bills of attainder, *ex post facto* laws, and statutes. *The Federalist No. 78* ("Limitations can be preserved in practice no other way than through the medium of the courts of justice").

The Framers labored over the question of where the impeachment power should lie. Significantly, in at least two considered scenarios—in the Virginia Plan and in the New Jersey Plan—the power was placed with the Federal Judiciary. Indeed, Madison and the Committee of Detail proposed that the Supreme Court should have the power to determine impeachments. Despite these proposals, the Convention ultimately decided that the Senate would have "the sole Power to Try all Impeachments." Art. I, § 3, cl. 6. According to Alexander Hamilton in *The Federalist No. 65*, the Senate was the "most fit depositary of this important trust" because its members are representatives of the people. The Supreme Court was not the proper body because the Framers "doubted whether the members of that tribunal would, at all times, be endowed with so eminent a portion of fortitude as would be called for in the execution of so difficult a task" or whether the Court "would possess the degree of credit and authority" to carry out its judgment if it conflicted with the accusation brought by the Legislature—the people's representative. In addition, according to Hamilton, the Framers believed the Court was too small in number: "The awful discretion, which a court of impeachments must necessarily have, to doom to honor or to infamy the most confidential and the most distinguished characters of the community, forbids the commitment of the trust to a small number of persons."

There are two additional reasons why the Judiciary, and the Supreme Court in particular, were not chosen to have any role in impeachments. First, the Framers recognized that most likely there would be two sets of proceedings for individuals who commit impeachable offenses—the impeachment trial and a separate criminal trial. In fact, the Constitution explicitly provides for two separate proceedings. Art. I, § 3, cl. 7. The Framers deliberately separated the two forums to avoid raising the specter of bias and to ensure independent judgments: "Would it be proper that the persons, who had disposed of his fame and his most valuable rights as a citizen in one trial, should in another trial, for the same offence, be also the disposers of his life and his fortune? Would there not be the greatest reason to apprehend, that error in the first sentence would be the parent of error in the second sentence? That the strong bias of one decision would be apt to overrule the influence of any new lights, which might be brought to vary the complexion of another decision?" *The Federalist No. 65.* Certainly judicial review of the Senate's "trial" would introduce the same risk of bias as would participation in the trial itself.

Second, judicial review would be inconsistent with the Framers' insistence that our system be one of checks and balances. In our constitutional system, impeachment was designed to be the only check on the Judicial Branch by the Legislature. On the topic of judicial accountability, Hamilton wrote: "The precautions for their responsibility are comprised in the article respecting impeachments. They are liable to be impeached for mal-conduct by the house of representatives, and tried by the senate, and if convicted, may be dismissed from office and disqualified for holding any other. This is the only provision on the point, which is consistent with the necessary independence of the judicial character, and is the only one which we find in our own constitution in respect to our own judges." *The Federalist No. 79.* Judicial involvement in impeachment proceedings, even if only for purposes of judicial review, is counterintuitive because it would eviscerate the "important constitutional check," *The Federalist No. 81,* placed on the Judiciary by the Framers. Nixon's argument would place final reviewing authority with respect to impeachments in the hands of the same body that the impeachment process is meant to regulate.

Nevertheless, Nixon argues that judicial review is necessary in order to place a check on the Legislature. Nixon fears that if the Senate is given unreviewable authority to interpret the Impeachment Trial Clause, there is a grave risk that the Senate will usurp judicial power. The Framers anticipated this objection and created two constitutional safeguards to keep the Senate in check. The first safeguard is that the whole of the impeachment power is divided between the two legislative bodies, with the House given the right to accuse and the Senate given the right to judge. *The Federalist No. 66*. This split of authority "avoids the inconvenience of making the same persons both accusers and judges; and guards against the danger of persecution from the prevalency of a factious spirit in either of those branches." The second safeguard is the two-thirds supermajority vote requirement. Hamilton explained that "as the concurrence of two-thirds of the senate will be requisite to a condemnation, the security to innocence, from this additional circumstance, will be as complete as itself can desire."

In addition to the textual commitment argument, we are persuaded that the lack of finality and the difficulty of fashioning relief counsel against justiciability. We agree with the court below that opening the door of judicial review to the procedures used by the Senate in trying impeachments would "expose the political life of the country to months, or perhaps years, of chaos." This lack of finality would manifest itself most dramatically if the President were impeached. The legitimacy of any successor, and hence his effectiveness, would be impaired severely, not merely while the judicial process was running its course, but during any retrial that a differently constituted Senate might conduct if its first judgment of conviction were invalidated. Equally uncertain is the question of what relief a court may give other than simply setting aside the judgment of conviction. Could it order the reinstatement of a convicted federal judge, or order Congress to create an additional judgeship if the seat had been filled in the interim?

In the case before us, there is no separate provision of the Constitution which could be defeated by allowing the Senate final authority to determine the meaning of the word "try" in the Impeachment Trial Clause. We agree with Nixon that courts possess power to review either legislative or executive action that transgresses identifiable textual limits. As we have made clear once before, "whether the action of either the Legislative or Executive Branch exceeds whatever authority has been committed, is itself a delicate exercise in constitutional interpretation, and is a responsibility of this Court as ultimate interpreter of the Constitution." But we conclude, after exercising that delicate responsibility, that the word "try" in the Impeachment Clause does not provide an identifiable textual limit on the authority which is committed to the Senate.

*⁴There may be narrower scope for operation of the presumption of constitutionality . . . .*

— *Harlan F. Stone*

## United States v. Carolene Products Co.
### 58 S.Ct. 778, 304 U.S. 144 (1938)

*Footnote 4 to Justice Harlan F. Stone's opinion is probably the most important, the most famous, and the most controversial footnote in Supreme Court history. The otherwise forgettable decision upheld the 1923 federal ban on the interstate shipment of "filled-milk," skimmed milk compounded with non-milk fat or oils, like coconut oil, and blended to resemble whole milk. Just a few years before, the Supreme Court formally renounced its earlier decisions and abandoned the practice of reviewing the wisdom of legislation, under the guise of protecting the "liberty of contract." The Justices were not about to substitute their own social and economic beliefs for the legislative judgments about property rights, under the due process clauses in the 5th and 14th amendments. The text of Justice Stone's opinion explains that the courts generally presume the constitutional validity of duly-enacted statutes. The footnote, however tentatively though presciently, suggested what has become the modern paradigm for affording less deference to legislative judgments and applying greater judicial scrutiny to laws that affect fundamental rights or discriminate against certain groups. The first paragraph suggests that there is a greater role for the courts to protect rights enshrined in the Constitution. The second paragraph suggests greater judicial scrutiny of legislative measures that have the effect of restricting or limiting effective participation in self-government. The third paragraph suggests that groups who lack power or influence in politics might merit special protection from the courts. Taken as a whole, the footnote admits a constitutional distrust of democracy or majority rule. The Constitution protects antimajoritarian values and the Supreme Court is an antimajoritarian institution. Jurists and scholars have continued to debate these premises and their implications for the Court and the Constitution down to the present day.*

**Justice Stone:** The question for decision is whether the "Filled Milk Act" of Congress of March 4, 1923, which prohibits the shipment in interstate commerce of skimmed milk compounded with any fat or oil other than milk fat, so as to resemble milk or cream, transcends the power of Congress to regulate interstate commerce or infringes the Fifth Amendment.

We may assume for present purposes that no pronouncement of a Legislature can forestall attack upon the constitutionality of the prohibition which it enacts by applying opprobrious epithets to the prohibited act, and that a statute would deny due process which precluded the disproof in judicial proceedings of all facts which would show or tend to show that a statute depriving the suitor of life, liberty, or property had a rational basis.

But such we think is not the purpose or construction of the statutory characterization of filled milk as injurious to health and as a fraud upon the public. There is no need to consider it here as more than a declaration of the legislative findings deemed to support and justify the action taken as a constitutional exertion of the legislative power, aiding informed judicial review, as do the reports of legislative committees, by revealing the rationale of the legislation. Even in the absence of such aids, the existence of facts supporting the legislative judgment is to be presumed, for regulatory legislation affecting ordinary commercial transactions is not to be pronounced unconstitutional unless in the light of the facts made known or generally assumed it is of such a character as to preclude the assumption that it rests upon some rational basis within the knowledge and experience of the legislators.[4]

---

4. There may be narrower scope for operation of the presumption of constitutionality when legislation appears on its face to be within a specific prohibition of the Constitution, such as those of the first ten Amendments, which are deemed equally specific when held to be embraced within the Fourteenth.

It is unnecessary to consider now whether legislation which restricts those political processes which can ordinarily be expected to bring about repeal of undesirable legislation, is to be subjected to more exacting judicial scrutiny under the general prohibitions of the Fourteenth Amendment than are most other types of legislation.

Nor need we enquire whether similar considerations enter into the review of statutes directed at particular religious, or national, or racial minorities: whether prejudice against discrete and insular minorities may be a special condition, which tends seriously to curtail the operation of those political processes ordinarily to be relied upon to protect minorities, and which may call for a correspondingly more searching judicial inquiry.

Where the existence of a rational basis for legislation whose constitutionality is attacked depends upon facts beyond the sphere of judicial notice, such facts may properly be made the subject of judicial inquiry, and the constitutionality of a statute predicated upon the existence of a particular state of facts may be challenged by showing to the court that those facts have ceased to exist. Similarly, we recognize that the constitutionality of a statute, valid on its face, may be assailed by proof of facts tending to show that the statute as applied to a particular article is without support in reason because the article, although within the prohibited class, is so different from others of the class as to be without the reason for the prohibition, though the effect of such proof depends on the relevant circumstances of each case, as for example the administrative difficulty of excluding the article from the regulated class. But by their very nature such inquiries, where the legislative judgment is drawn in question, must be restricted to the issue whether any state of facts either known or which could reasonably be assumed affords support for it. Here the challenge is to the validity of the statute on its face and it is evident from all the considerations presented to Congress, and those of which we may take judicial notice, that the question is at least debatable whether commerce in filled milk should be left unregulated, or in some measure restricted, or wholly prohibited. As that decision was for Congress, neither the finding of a court arrived at by weighing the evidence, nor the verdict of a jury can be substituted for it. The prohibition of shipment in interstate commerce of the Defendant's product, as described in the indictment, is a constitutional exercise of the power to regulate interstate commerce.

> *While I am loath to overturn a century of prac-*
> *tice shared by almost all of the States, I believe the*
> *historical evidence from the framing outweighs re-*
> *cent tradition.*

> — *Clarence Thomas*

## McIntyre v. Ohio Elections Commission
### 115 S.Ct. 1511 (1995)

*Margaret McIntyre was fined $100 for distributing*
*anonymous leaflets at a public meeting that described her*
*opposition to a proposed tax increase. Justice Stevens*
*wrote a typical modern opinion applying doctrine and*
*precedent to hold that the Ohio statute prohibiting the*
*distribution of anonymous campaign literature was a*
*"law . . . abridging the freedom of speech within the*
*meaning of the first amendment." Justice Thomas con-*
*curred and Justice Scalia dissented. Both are proponents*
*of a jurisprudence of original meaning, which obliges the*
*interpreter to glean the historic meaning of the words of*
*the Constitution. They agreed that the majority's ap-*
*proach was mistaken, but they disagreed about the result*
*their shared approach should yield: Justice Thomas con-*
*cluded the Ohio law violated the 1st amendment and*
*Justice Scalia would have approved the statute. Their*
*opinions are juxtaposed here as a case study in the vaga-*
*ries of constitutional interpretation. Scholars of history*
*often shake their head at such attempts at "law office*
*history" by lawyers and judges. Somewhat curious, per-*
*haps revealing, is the fact that Justice Thomas wrote and*
*Justice Scalia joined an opinion in another 1st amend-*
*ment case announced the same day that followed a doc-*
*trine-and-precedent approach and failed altogether to*
*mention original intent.*

**Justice Thomas:** I agree with the majority's conclusion
that Ohio's election law is inconsistent with the First Amendment. I would apply, however, a different methodology to this
case. Instead of asking whether "an honorable tradition" of
anonymous speech has existed throughout American history, or
what the "value" of anonymous speech might be, we should de-

termine whether the phrase "freedom of speech, or of the press," as originally understood, protected anonymous political leafletting. I believe that it did.

The First Amendment states that the government "shall make no law abridging the freedom of speech, or of the press." When interpreting the Free Speech and Press Clauses, we must be guided by their original meaning, for "the Constitution is a written instrument. As such its meaning does not alter. That which it meant when adopted, it means now." We have long recognized that the meaning of the Constitution "must necessarily depend on the words of the constitution and the meaning and intention of the convention which framed and proposed it for adoption and ratification to the conventions in the several states." We should seek the original understanding when we interpret the Speech and Press Clauses, just as we do when we read the Religion Clauses of the First Amendment. When the Framers did not discuss the precise question at issue, we have turned to "what history reveals was the contemporaneous understanding of the Establishment Clause's guarantees." "The line we must draw between the permissible and the impermissible is one which accords with history and faithfully reflects the understanding of the Founding Fathers."

Unfortunately, we have no record of discussions of anonymous political expression either in the First Congress, which drafted the Bill of Rights, or in the state ratifying conventions. Thus, our analysis must focus on the practices and beliefs held by the Founders concerning anonymous political articles and pamphlets. As an initial matter, we can safely maintain that the leaflets at issue in this case implicate the freedom of the press. When the Framers thought of the press, they did not envision the large, corporate newspaper and television establishments of our modern world. Instead, they employed the term "the press" to refer to the many independent printers who circulated small newspapers or published a writer's pamphlets for a fee. This practice continued during the struggle for ratification. Regardless of whether one designates the right involved here as one of press or one of speech, however, it makes little difference in terms of our analysis, which seeks to determine only whether the First Amendment, as originally understood, protects anonymous writing.

There is little doubt that the Framers engaged in anonymous political writing. The essays in the *Federalist Papers*, published under the pseudonym of "Publius," are only the most famous example of the outpouring of anonymous political writing that occurred during the ratification of the Constitution. Of course, the simple fact that the Framers engaged in certain conduct does not necessarily prove that they forbade its prohibition by the government. In this case, however, the historical evidence indicates that Founding-era Americans opposed attempts to require that anonymous authors reveal their identities on the ground that forced disclosure violated the "freedom of the press."

For example, the earliest and most famous American experience with freedom of the press, the 1735 Zenger trial, centered around anonymous political pamphlets. The case involved a printer, John Peter Zenger, who refused to reveal the anonymous authors of published attacks on the Crown governor of New York. When the governor and his council could not discover the identity of the authors, they prosecuted Zenger himself for seditious libel. Although the case set the colonies afire for its example of a jury refusing to convict a defendant of seditious libel against Crown authorities, it also signified at an early moment the extent to which anonymity and the freedom of the press were intertwined in the early American mind.

During the Revolutionary and Ratification periods, the Framers' understanding of the relationship between anonymity and freedom of the press became more explicit. To be sure, there was some controversy among newspaper editors over publishing anonymous articles and pamphlets. But this controversy was resolved in a manner that indicates that the freedom of the press protected an author's anonymity.

The tempest began when a Federalist, writing anonymously himself, expressed fear that "emissaries" of "foreign enemies" would attempt to scuttle the Constitution by "filling the press with objections" against the proposal. He called upon printers to refrain from publishing when the author "chooses to remain concealed." Benjamin Russell, the editor of the prominent Federalist newspaper the *Massachusetts Centinel*, immediately adopted a policy of refusing to publish Anti-Federalist pieces unless the author provided his identity to be "handed to the publick, if required." A few days later, the *Massachusetts Gazette* announced that it would emulate the example set by the *Massachusetts Centinel*. In the same issue, the *Gazette* carried an article claiming that requiring an anonymous writer to leave his name with the printer, so that anyone who wished to know his identity could be informed, "appears perfectly reasonable, and is perfectly consistent with the liberty of the press." Federalists expressed similar thoughts in Philadelphia.

Ordinarily, the fact that some Founding-era editors as a matter of policy decided not to publish anonymous articles would seem to shed little light upon what the framers thought the government could do. The widespread criticism raised by the Anti-Federalists, however, who were the driving force behind the demand for a Bill of Rights, indicates that they believed the freedom of the press to include the right to author anonymous political articles and pamphlets. That most other Americans shared this understanding is reflected in the Federalists' hasty retreat before the withering criticism of their assault on the liberty of the press.

Opposition to Russell's declaration centered in Philadelphia. Three Philadelphia papers published the "Citizen" piece that had run in the *Massachusetts Gazette*. In response, one of the leading Anti-Federalist writers, the "Federal Farmer," attacked Russell's policy. Another Anti-Federalist, "Philadelphiensis," also launched a substantial attack on Russell and his defenders for undermining the freedom of the press. In Philadelphiensis' eyes, Federalist attempts to suppress the Anti-Federalist press by requiring the disclosure of authors' identities only foreshadowed the oppression permitted by the new Constitution: "Here we see pretty plainly through the Federalists' excellent regulation of the press, how things are to be carried on after the adoption of the new constitution." As a result of Federalist policies, according to Philadelphiensis, "In Boston the liberty of the press is now completely abolished; and hence all other privileges and rights of the people will in a short time be destroyed." Not limited to Philadelphia, the Anti-Federalist attack was repeated widely throughout the States.

The controversy over Federalist attempts to prohibit anonymous political speech is significant for several reasons. First, the Anti-Federalists clearly believed the right to author and publish anonymous political articles and pamphlets was protected by the liberty of the press. Second, although printers' editorial policies did not constitute state action, the Anti-Federalists believed that the Federalists were merely flexing the governmental powers they would fully exercise upon the Constitution's ratification. Third, and perhaps most significantly, it appears that the Federalists agreed with the Anti-Federalist critique. In Philadelphia, where opposition to the ban was strongest, there is no record that any newspaper adopted the non-anonymity policy, nor that of any city or State aside from Russell's *Massachusetts Centinel* and the Federalist *Massachusetts Gazette*. Moreover, these two papers' bark was worse than their bite. In the face of widespread criticism, it appears that Russell retreated from his policy and, as he put it, "readily" reprinted several anonymous Federalist and Anti-Federalist essays to show that claims that he had suppressed freedom of the press "had not any foundation in truth." Likewise, the *Massachusetts Gazette* refused to release the names of Anti-Federalist writers when requested. When Federalist attempts to ban anonymity are followed by a sharp, widespread Anti-Federalist defense in the name of the freedom of the press, and then by an open Federalist retreat on the issue, I must conclude that both Anti-Federalists and Federalists believed that the freedom of the press included the right to publish without revealing the author's name.

The historical record is not as complete or as full as I would desire. For example, there is no evidence that, after the adoption of the First Amendment, the Federal Government attempted to require writers to attach their names to political documents. Nor do we have any indication that the federal courts of the early Republic would have squashed such an effort as a violation of the First Amendment. The understanding described above, however, when viewed in light of the Framers' universal practice of publishing anonymous articles and pamphlets, indicates that the Framers shared the belief that such activity was firmly part of the freedom of the press. It is only an innovation of modern times that has permitted the regulation of anonymous speech.

The large quantity of newspapers and pamphlets the Framers produced during the various crises of their generation show the remarkable extent to which the Framers relied upon anonymity. During the break with Great Britain, the revolutionaries employed pseudonyms both to conceal their identity from Crown authorities and to impart a message. Often, writers would choose names to signal their point of view or to invoke specific classical and modern "crusaders in an age long struggle against tyranny." Thus, leaders of the struggle for independence would adopt descriptive names such as "Common Sense," a "Farmer," or "A True Patriot," or historical ones such as "Cato" (a name used by many to refer to the Roman Cato and to Cato's letters), or "Mucius Scaevola." The practice was even more prevalent during the great outpouring of political argument and commentary that accompanied the ratification of the Constitution. Besides "Publius," prominent Federalists signed their articles and pamphlets with names such as "An American Citizen," "Marcus," "A Landholder," "Americanus"; Anti-Federalists replied with the pseudonyms "Cato," "Centinel," "Brutus," the "Federal Farmer," and "The Impartial Examiner." The practice of publishing one's thoughts anonymously or under pseudonym was so widespread that only two major Federalist or Anti-Federalist pieces appear to have been signed by their true authors, and they may have had special reasons to do so.

If the practice of publishing anonymous articles and pamphlets fell into disuse after the Ratification, one might infer that the custom of anonymous political speech arose only in response to the unusual conditions of the 1776–1787 period. After all, the Revolution and the Ratification were not "elections," *per se*, either for candidates or for discrete issues. Records from the first federal elections indicate, however, that anonymous political pamphlets and newspaper articles remained the favorite medium for expressing views on candidates. In Pennsylvania, for example, writers for or against the Federalist and Anti-Federalist candidates wrote under the names "Numa," "Pompilius," "A Friend to Agriculture, Trade, and Good Laws," "A Federal Centinel," a "Freeman," "Centinel," "A Real Patriot to All True Federalists," "A Mechanic," "Justice," "A German Federalist," and so on. This appears to have been the practice in all of the major states of which we have substantial records today. It seems that actual names were used rarely, and usually only by candidates who wanted to explain their positions to the electorate.

The use of anonymous writing extended to issues as well as candidates. The ratification of the Constitution was not the only issue discussed *via* anonymous writings in the press. James Madison and Alexander Hamilton, for example, resorted to pseudonyms in the famous "Helvidius" and "Pacificus" debates over President Washington's declaration of neutrality in the war between the British and French. Anonymous writings continued in such Republican papers as the *Aurora* and Federalists organs such as the *Gazette of the United States* at least until the election of Thomas Jefferson.

This evidence leads me to agree with the majority's result, but not its reasoning. The majority fails to seek the original understanding of the First Amendment, and instead attempts to answer the question in this case by resorting to three approaches. First, the majority recalls the historical practice of anonymous writing from Shakespeare's works to the *Federalist Papers* to Mark Twain. Second, it finds that anonymous speech has an expressive value both to the speaker and to society that outweighs public interest in disclosure. Third, it finds that the Ohio statute cannot survive strict scrutiny because it is a "content-based" restriction on speech.

I cannot join the majority's analysis because it deviates from our settled approach to interpreting the Constitution and because it superimposes its modern theories concerning expression upon the constitutional text. Whether "great works of literature" by Voltaire or George Eliot have been published anonymously should be irrelevant to our analysis, because it sheds no light on what the phrases "free speech" or "free press" meant to the people who drafted and ratified the First Amendment. Similarly, whether certain types of expression have "value" today has little significance; what is important is whether the Framers in 1791 believed anonymous speech sufficiently valuable to deserve the protection of the Bill of Rights. And although the majority faithfully follows our doctrinal approach to "content-based" speech regulations, we need not undertake this analysis when the original understanding provides the answer.

While I am loath to overturn a century of practice shared by almost all of the States, I believe the historical evidence from the framing outweighs recent tradition. When interpreting other provisions of the Constitution, this Court has believed itself bound by the text of the Constitution and by the intent of those who drafted and ratified it. It should hold itself to no less a standard when interpreting the Speech and Press Clauses. After reviewing the weight of the historical evidence, it seems that the Framers understood the First Amendment to protect an author's right to express his thoughts on political candidates or issues in an anonymous fashion. Because the majority has adopted an analysis that is largely unconnected to the Constitution's text and history, I concur only in the judgment.

**Justice Scalia:** At a time when both political branches of Government and both political parties reflect a popular desire to leave more decisionmaking authority to the States, today's decision moves in the opposite direction, adding to the legacy of inflexible central mandates (irrevocable even by Congress) imposed by this Court's constitutional jurisprudence. In an opinion which reads as though it is addressing some peculiar law, the Court invalidates a species of protection for the election process that exists, in a variety of forms, in every State except California, and that has a pedigree dating back to the end of the 19th century. Preferring the views of the English utilitarian philosopher John Stuart Mill, to the considered judgment of the American people's elected representatives from coast to coast, the Court discovers a hitherto unknown right-to-be-unknown while engaging in electoral politics. I dissent from this imposition of free-speech imperatives that are demonstrably not those of the American people today, and that there is inadequate reason to believe were those of the society that begat the First Amendment or the Fourteenth.

The question posed by the present case is not the easiest sort to answer for those who adhere to the Court's (and the society's) traditional view that the Constitution bears its original meaning and is unchanging. Under that view, Thomas Jefferson explained, "on every question of construction, we should carry ourselves back to the time when the Constitution was adopted; recollect the spirit manifested in the debates; and instead of trying to find what meaning may be squeezed out of the text, or invented against it, conform to the probable one in which it was passed." That technique is simple of application when government conduct that is claimed to violate the Bill of Rights or the Fourteenth Amendment is shown, upon investigation, to have been engaged in without objection at the very time the Bill of Rights or the Fourteenth Amendment was adopted. There is no doubt, for example, that laws against libel and obscenity do not violate "the freedom of speech" to which the First Amendment refers; they existed and were universally approved in 1791. Application of the principle of an unchanging Constitution is also simple enough at the other extreme, where the government conduct at issue was not engaged in at the time of adoption, and there is ample evidence that the reason it was not engaged in is that it was thought to violate the right embodied in the constitutional guarantee. For example, racks and thumbscrews, well known instruments for inflicting pain, were not in use because they were regarded as cruel punishments.

The present case lies between those two extremes. Anonymous electioneering was not prohibited by law in 1791 or in 1868. In fact, it was widely practiced at the earlier date, an understandable legacy of the revolutionary era in which political dissent could produce governmental reprisal. I need not dwell upon the evidence of that, since it is described at length in Justice Thomas's concurrence. The practice of anonymous electioneering may have been less general in 1868, when the Fourteenth Amendment was adopted, but at least as late as 1837 it was respectable enough to be engaged in by Abraham Lincoln.

But to prove that anonymous electioneering was used frequently is not to establish that it is a constitutional right. Quite obviously, not every restriction upon expression that did not exist in 1791 or in 1868 is *ipso facto* unconstitutional, or else modern election laws would be prohibited, as would (to mention only a few other categories) modern antinoise regulation of the sort involved, and modern parade-permitting regulation.

Evidence that anonymous electioneering was regarded as a constitutional right is sparse, and as far as I am aware evidence that it was *generally* regarded as such is nonexistent. Justice Thomas points to "freedom of the press" objections that were made against the refusal of some Federalist newspapers to publish unsigned essays opposing the proposed constitution (on the ground that they might be the work of foreign agents). But of course if every partisan cry of "freedom of the press" were accepted as valid, our Constitution would be unrecognizable; and if one were to generalize from these particular cries, the First Amendment would be not only a protection *for* newspapers but a restriction *upon* them. Leaving aside, however, the fact that no governmental action was involved, the Anti-Federalists had a point, inasmuch as the editorial proscription applied only to *them*, and thus had the vice of viewpoint discrimination.

Justice Thomas recounts other pre- and post-Revolution examples of defense of anonymity in the name of "freedom of the press," but not a single one involves the context of restrictions imposed in connection with a free, democratic election, which is all that is at issue here. For many of them, moreover, such as the 1735 *Zenger* trial, the issue of anonymity was incidental to the (unquestionably free-speech) issue of whether criticism of the government could be *punished* by the state.

Thus, the sum total of the historical evidence marshalled by the concurrence for the principle of *constitutional entitlement* to anonymous electioneering is partisan claims in the debate on ratification (which was *almost* like an election) that a viewpoint-based restriction on anonymity by newspaper editors violates freedom of speech. This absence of historical testimony concerning the point before us is hardly remarkable. The issue of a governmental prohibition upon anonymous electioneering in particular (as opposed to a government prohibition upon anonymous publication in general) simply never arose. Indeed, there probably never arose even the abstract question of whether electoral openness and regularity was worth such a governmental restriction upon the normal right to anonymous speech. The idea of close government regulation of the electoral process is a more modern phenomenon, arriving in this country in the late 1800's.

What we have, then, is the most difficult case for determining the meaning of the Constitution. No accepted existence of governmental restrictions of the sort at issue here demonstrates their constitutionality, but neither can their nonexistence clearly be attributed to constitutional objections. In such a case, constitutional adjudication necessarily involves not just history but judgment: judgment as to whether the government action under challenge is consonant with the concept of the protected freedom (in this case, the freedom of speech and of the press) that existed when the constitutional protection was accorded. In the present case, *absent other indication* I would be inclined to agree with the concurrence that a society which used anonymous political debate so regularly would not regard as constitutional even moderate restrictions made to improve the election process. (I would, however, want further evidence of common practice in 1868, since I doubt that the Fourteenth Amendment time-warped the post-Civil War States back to the Revolution.)

But there *is* other indication, of the most weighty sort: the widespread and longstanding traditions of our people. Principles of liberty fundamental enough to have been embodied within constitutional guarantees are not readily erased from the Nation's consciousness. A governmental practice that has become general throughout the United States, and particularly one that has the validation of long, accepted usage, bears a strong presumption of constitutionality. And that is what we have before us here. This statute was enacted by the General Assembly of the State of Ohio almost 80 years ago. Even at the time of its adoption, there was nothing unique or extraordinary about it. The earliest statute of this sort was adopted by Massachusetts in 1890, little more than 20 years after the Fourteenth Amendment was ratified. No less than 24 States had similar laws by the end of World War I, and today every State of the Union except California has one, as does the District of Columbia, and as does the Federal Government. Of course, post-adoption tradition cannot alter the core meaning of a constitutional guarantee. But such a universal and long established American legislative practice must be given precedence, I think, over historical and academic speculation regarding a restriction that assuredly does not go to the heart of free speech.

The foregoing analysis suffices to decide this case for me. Where the meaning of a constitutional text (such as "the freedom of speech") is unclear, the widespread and long-accepted practices of the American people are the best indication of what fundamental beliefs it was intended to enshrine.

The Justices of the majority set their own views—on a practical matter that bears closely upon the real-life experience of elected politicians and not upon that of unelected judges—up against the views of 49 state legislatures and the federal Congress. We might also add to the list on the other side the legislatures of foreign democracies: Australia, Canada, and England, for example, all have prohibitions upon anonymous campaigning. How is it, one must wonder, that all of these elected legislators, from around the country and around the world, could not see what six Justices of this Court see so clearly that they are willing to require the entire Nation to act upon it: that requiring identification of the source of campaign literature does not improve the quality of the campaign?

I do not know where the Court derives its perception that "anonymous pamphleteering is not a pernicious, fraudulent practice, but an honorable tradition of advocacy and of dissent." I can imagine no reason why an anonymous leaflet is any more honorable, as a general matter, than an anonymous phone call or an anonymous letter. It facilitates wrong by eliminating accountability, which is ordinarily the very purpose of the anonymity. But to strike down the Ohio law in its general application—and similar laws of 48 other States and the Federal Government—on the ground that all anonymous communication is in our society traditionally sacrosanct, seems to me a distortion of the past that will lead to a coarsening of the future.

*If by the statement that what the Constitution meant at the time of its adoption it means to-day, it is intended to say that the great clauses of the Constitution must be confined to the interpretation which the framers, with the conditions and outlook of their time, would have placed upon them, the statement carries its own refutation.*

*— Charles Evans Hughes*

# Home Building & Loan Assoc. v. Blaisdell
## 54 S.Ct. 231, 290 U.S. 398 (1934)

*During the Great Depression, many States enacted debtors' relief statutes postponing the obligations of homeowners to meet their home mortgage payments; the Minnesota statute authorized state courts to exempt property from foreclosure for two years, so long as the debtor paid a reasonable rental value on the property. The historical understanding of the contract clause, Article I, § 10, and previous Supreme Court decisions, most assuredly would have invalidated the measure as an impairment of the obligation of contract. When he was Governor of New York, Charles Evans Hughes once remarked, "We are under a Constitution, but the Constitution is what the judges say it is. . . ." In this opinion, the Chief Justice said that the Constitution authorized the Minnesota statute as a valid exercise of a government power equal to the economic emergency. Four dissenters warned that the Constitution is the only true protection against abuse of the legislative prerogative and insisted that judges must be true to the meaning and intent of its Framers, even at a time of perceived emergency.*

**Chief Justice Hughes:** The Supreme Court of Minnesota upheld the statute as an emergency measure. Although conceding that the obligations of the mortgage contract were impaired, the court decided that what it thus described as an impairment was, notwithstanding the contract clause of the Federal Constitution, within the police power of the state as that power was called into exercise by the public economic emergency which the Legislature had found to exist.

In determining whether the provision for this temporary and conditional relief exceeds the power of the state by reason of the clause in the Federal Constitution prohibiting impairment of the obligations of contracts, we must consider the relation of emergency to constitutional power, the historical setting of the contract clause, the development of the jurisprudence of this Court in the construction of that clause, and the principles of construction which we may consider to be established.

Emergency does not create power. Emergency does not increase granted power or remove or diminish the restrictions imposed upon power granted or reserved. The Constitution was adopted in a period of grave emergency. Its grants of power to the federal government and its limitations of the power of the States were determined in the light of emergency, and they are not altered by emergency. What power was thus granted and what limitations were thus imposed are questions which have always been, and always will be, the subject of close examination under our constitutional system.

While emergency does not create power, emergency may furnish the occasion for the exercise of power. "Although an emergency may not call into life a power which has never lived, nevertheless emergency may afford a reason for the exertion of a living power already enjoyed." The constitutional question presented in the light of an emergency is whether the power possessed embraces the particular exercise of it in response to particular conditions. Thus, the war power of the federal government is not created by the emergency of war, but it is a power given to meet that emergency. It is a power to wage war successfully, and thus it permits the harnessing of the entire energies of the people in a supreme co-operative effort to preserve the nation. But even the war power does not remove constitutional limitations safeguarding essential liberties.

When the provisions of the Constitution, in grant or restriction, are specific, so particularized as not to admit of construction, no question is presented. Thus, emergency would not permit a state to have more than two Senators in the Congress, or permit the election of President by a general popular vote without regard to the number of electors to which the States are respectively entitled, or permit the States to "coin money" or to "make anything but gold and silver coin a tender in payment of debts."

But, where constitutional grants and limitations of power are set forth in general clauses, which afford a broad outline, the process of construction is essential to fill in the details. That is true of the contract clause. The necessity of construction is not obviated by the fact that the contract clause is associated in the same section with other and more specific prohibitions. Even the grouping of subjects in the same clause may not require the same application to each of the subjects, regardless of differences in their nature.

In the construction of the contract clause, the debates in the Constitutional Convention are of little aid. But the reasons which led to the adoption of that clause, and of the other prohibitions of section 10 of article 1, are not left in doubt, and have frequently been described with eloquent emphasis. The widespread distress following the revolutionary period and the plight of debtors had called forth in the States an ignoble array of legislative schemes for the defeat of creditors and the invasion of contractual obligations. Legislative interferences had been so numerous and extreme that the confidence essential to prosperous trade had been undermined and the utter destruction of credit was threatened. "The sober people of America" were convinced that some "thorough reform" was needed which would "inspire a general prudence and industry, and give a regular course to the business of society." *The Federalist, No. 44.* It was necessary to interpose the restraining power of a central authority in order to secure the foundations even of "private faith."

But full recognition of the occasion and general purpose of the clause does not suffice to fix its precise scope. Nor does an examination of the details of prior legislation in the States yield criteria which can be considered controlling. To ascertain the scope of the constitutional prohibition, we examine the course of judicial decisions in its application. These put it beyond question that the prohibition is not an absolute and is not to be read with literal exactness like a mathematical formula.

The inescapable problems of construction have been: What is a contract? What are the obligations of contracts? What constitutes impairment of these obligations? What residuum of power is there still in the States, in relation to the operation of contracts, to protect the vital interests of the community? Questions of this character, "of no small nicety and intricacy, have vexed the legislative halls, as well as the judicial tribunals, with an uncounted variety and frequency of litigation and speculation."

The obligation of a contract is the law which binds the parties to perform their agreement. This Court has said that "the laws which subsist at the time and place of the making of a contract, and where it is to be performed, enter into and form a part of it, as if they were expressly referred to or incorporated in its terms. This principle embraces alike those which affect its validity, construction, discharge, and enforcement. Nothing can be more material to the obligation than the means of enforcement. The ideas of validity and remedy are inseparable, and both are parts of the obligation, which is guaranteed by the Constitution against invasion." But this broad language cannot be taken without qualification. Chief Justice Marshall pointed out the distinction between obligation and remedy: "The distinction between the obligation of a contract, and the remedy given by the legislature to enforce that obligation, has been taken at the bar, and exists in the nature of things. Without impairing the obligation of the contract, the remedy may certainly be modified as the wisdom of the nation shall direct." And in a later case Chief Justice Waite added: "In all such cases the question becomes, therefore, one of reasonableness, and of that the legislature is primarily the judge."

The obligations of a contract are impaired by a law which renders them invalid, or releases or extinguishes them and impairment, as above noted, has been predicated of laws which without destroying contracts derogate from substantial contractual rights.

None of these cases we have cited is directly applicable to the question now before us in view of the conditions with which the Minnesota statute seeks to safeguard the interests of the mortgagee-purchaser during the extended period. And broad expressions contained in some of these opinions went beyond the requirements of the decision, and are not controlling.

Not only is the constitutional provision qualified by the measure of control which the state retains over remedial processes, but the state also continues to possess authority to safeguard the vital interests of its people. It does not matter that legislation appropriate to that end "has the result of modifying or abrogating contracts already in effect." Not only are existing laws read into contracts in order to fix obligations as between the parties, but the reservation of essential attributes of sovereign power is also read into contracts as a postulate of the legal order. The policy of protecting contracts against impairment presupposes the maintenance of a government by virtue of which contractual relations are worthwhile, a government which retains adequate authority to secure the peace and good order of society. This principle of harmonizing the constitutional prohibition with the necessary residuum of state power has had progressive recognition in the decisions of this Court.

While the charters of private corporations constitute contracts, a grant of exclusive privilege is not to be implied as against the state. And all contracts are subject to the right of eminent domain. The reservation of this necessary authority of the state is deemed to be a part of the contract.

The Legislature cannot "bargain away the public health or the public morals." Thus the constitutional provision against the impairment of contracts was held not to be violated by an amendment of the state Constitution which put an end to a lottery theretofore authorized by the Legislature. The states retain adequate power to protect the public health against the maintenance of nuisances despite insistence upon existing contracts. Legislation to protect the public safety comes within the same category of reserved power. This principle has had recent and noteworthy application to the regulation of the use of public highways by common carriers and "contract carriers," where the assertion of interference with existing contract rights has been without avail.

The economic interests of the state may justify the exercise of its continuing and dominant protective power notwithstanding interference with contracts. Said the Court, by Mr. Justice Holmes: "One whose rights, such as they are, are subject to state restriction, cannot remove them from the power of the state by making a contract about them. The contract will carry with it the infirmity of the subject-matter." The general authority of the Legislature to regulate, and thus to modify, the rates charged by public service corporations, affords another illustration. Similarly, where the protective power of the state is exercised in a manner otherwise appropriate in the regulation of a business, it is no objection that the performance of existing contracts may be frustrated by the prohibition of injurious practices.

The argument is pressed that in the cases we have cited the obligation of contracts was affected only incidentally. This argument proceeds upon a misconception. The question is not whether the legislative action affects contracts incidentally, or directly or indirectly, but whether the legislation is addressed to a legitimate end and the measures taken are reasonable and appropriate to that end. Another argument, which comes more closely to the point, is that the state power may be addressed directly to the prevention of the enforcement of contracts only when these are of a sort which the Legislature in its discretion may denounce as being in themselves hostile to public morals, or public health, safety, or welfare, or where the prohibition is merely of injurious practices; that interference with the enforcement of other and valid contracts according to appropriate legal procedure, although the interference is temporary and for a public purpose, is not permissible. This is but to contend that in the latter case the end is not legitimate in the view that it cannot be reconciled with a fair interpretation of the constitutional provision.

Undoubtedly, whatever is reserved of state power must be consistent with the fair intent of the constitutional limitation of that power. The reserved power cannot be construed so as to destroy the limitation, nor is the limitation to be construed to destroy the reserved power in its essential aspects. They must be construed in harmony with each other. This principle precludes a construction which would permit the state to adopt as its policy the repudiation of debts or the destruction of contracts or the denial of means to enforce them. But it does not follow that conditions may not arise in which a temporary restraint of enforcement may be consistent with the spirit and purpose of the constitutional provision and thus be found to be within the range of the reserved power of the state to protect the vital interests of the community. It cannot be maintained that the constitutional prohibition should be so construed as to prevent limited and temporary interpositions with respect to the enforcement of contracts if made necessary by a great public calamity such as fire, flood, or earthquake. The reservation of state power appropriate to such extraordinary conditions may be deemed to be as much a part of all contracts as is the reservation of state power to protect the public interest in the other situations to which we have referred. And, if state power exists to give temporary relief from the enforcement of contracts in the presence of disasters due to physical causes such as fire, flood, or earthquake, that power cannot be said to be nonexistent when the urgent public need demanding such relief is produced by other and economic causes.

Whatever doubt there may have been that the protective power of the state, its police power, may be exercised—without violating the true intent of the provision of the Federal Constitution—in directly preventing the immediate and literal enforcement of contractual obligations by a temporary and conditional restraint, where vital public interests would otherwise suffer, was removed by our decisions relating to the enforcement of provisions of leases during a period of scarcity of housing.

It is manifest from a review of our decisions that there has been a growing appreciation of public needs and of the necessity of finding ground for a rational compromise between individual rights and public welfare. The settlement and consequent contraction of the public domain, the pressure of a constantly increasing density of population, the interrelation of the activities of our people and the complexity of our economic interests, have inevitably led to an increased use of the organization of society in order to protect the very bases of individual opportunity. Where, in earlier days, it was thought that only the concerns of individuals or of classes were involved, and that those of the state itself were touched only remotely, it has later been found that the fundamental interests of the state are directly affected; and that the question is no longer merely that of one party to a contract as against another, but of the use of reasonable means to safeguard the economic structure upon which the good of all depends.

It is no answer to say that this public need was not apprehended a century ago, or to insist that what the provision of the Constitution meant to the vision of that day it must mean to the vision of our time. If by the statement that what the Constitution meant at the time of its adoption it means to-day, it is intended to say that the great clauses of the Constitution must be confined to the interpretation which the framers, with the conditions and outlook of their time, would have placed upon them, the statement carries its own refutation. It was to guard against such a narrow conception that Chief Justice Marshall uttered the memorable warning: "We must never forget, that it is a constitution we are expounding a constitution intended to endure for ages to come, and, consequently, to be adapted to the various crises of human affairs." When we are dealing with the words of the Constitution, said Justice Holmes for this Court in 1920, "we must realize that they have called into life a being the development of which could not have been foreseen completely by the most gifted of its begetters. The case before us must be considered in the light of our whole experience and not merely in that of what was said a hundred years ago."

Nor is it helpful to attempt to draw a fine distinction between the intended meaning of the words of the Constitution and their intended application. When we consider the contract clause and the decisions which have expounded it in harmony with the essential reserved power of the states to protect the security of their peoples, we find no warrant for the conclusion that the clause has been warped by these decisions from its proper significance or that the founders of our government would have interpreted the clause differently had they had occasion to assume that responsibility in the conditions of the later day. The vast body of law which has been developed was unknown to the fathers, but it is believed to have preserved the essential content and the spirit of the Constitution. With a growing recognition of public needs and the relation of individual right to public security, the court has sought to prevent the perversion of the clause through its use as an instrument to throttle the capacity of the states to protect their fundamental interests. This development is a growth from the seeds which the fathers planted. It is a development forecast by the prophetic words of various members of this Court. The principle of this development is, as we have seen, that the reservation of the reasonable exercise of the protective power of the state is read into all contracts.

Applying the criteria established by our decisions, we conclude:

1. An emergency existed in Minnesota which furnished a proper occasion for the exercise of the reserved power of the state to protect the vital interests of the community. The declarations of the existence of this emergency by the Legislature and by the Supreme Court of Minnesota cannot be regarded as a subterfuge or as lacking in adequate basis.

2. The legislation was addressed to a legitimate end; that is, the legislation was not for the mere advantage of particular individuals but for the protection of a basic interest of society.

3. In view of the nature of the contracts in question—mortgages of unquestionable validity—the relief afforded and justified by the emergency, in order not to contravene the constitutional provision, could only be of a character appropriate to that emergency, and could be granted only upon reasonable conditions.

4. The conditions upon which the period of redemption is extended do not appear to be unreasonable.

5. The legislation is temporary in operation. It is limited to the exigency which called it forth.

We are of the opinion that the Minnesota statute as here applied does not violate the contract clause of the Federal Constitution. Whether the legislation is wise or unwise as a matter of policy is a question with which we are not concerned.

*If, on the other hand, the Legislature of the Union, or the Legislature of any member of the Union, shall pass a law, within the general scope of their constitutional power, the Court cannot pronounce it to be void, merely because it is, in their judgment, contrary to the principles of natural justice.*

— *James Iredell*

## Calder v. Bull
### 3 U.S. (3 Dallas) 386 (1798)

The legislature of Connecticut passed a statute setting aside a decree of a probate court and granting a new hearing in the matter. The Supreme Court rejected the claim that the statute was an ex post facto law, prohibited under Article I, § 10 of the Constitution. As was the custom then, the Justices announced seriatim opinions, amounting to individual speeches delivered from the bench. One of the earliest decisions involving constitutional limits on government power, the holding remains an important precedent limiting the ex post facto clause to criminal matters. But the larger debate between Justice Chase and Justice Iredell—over the power of the Court to go beyond the text of the Constitution in search of higher principles for decision—has continued unabated over the intervening two centuries. Justice Chase believed that judges were duty bound to strike down acts of the legislature, federal or state, which the judge was persuaded contravened fundamental principles of republican government, as the judge understood those unwritten principles. That this is circular and subjective should be obvious. That it would aggrandize the power of the judicial branch at the expense of the legislative branches should be equally obvious. That Justice Chase had the losing side of this debate should not be so obvious. First, consider the countless case annotations, court opinions that seem to go on forever, applying such majestic generalities as "due process" and "equal protection." Second, consider how often the Justices escape to higher levels of abstraction to interpolate nontextual rights like the "right of privacy." Finally, consider how often the Justices rely on their own understandings of history and tradition.

*Thus, in many ways, the Supreme Court seems to have honored Justice Iredell's arguments for textualism and self-restraint primarily in the breach.*

**Justice Chase:** The decision of one question determines (in my opinion), the present dispute. I shall, therefore, state from the record no more of the case, than I think necessary for the consideration of that question only.

It appears to me a self-evident proposition, that the several State Legislatures retain all the powers of legislation, delegated to them by the State Constitutions; which are not expressly taken away by the Constitution of the United States. The establishing courts of justice, the appointment of Judges, and the making regulations for the administration of justice, within each State, according to its laws, on all subjects not entrusted to the Federal Government, appears to me to be the peculiar and exclusive province, and duty of the State Legislatures: All the powers delegated by the people of the United States to the Federal Government are defined, and no constructive powers can be exercised by it, and all the powers that remain in the State Governments are indefinite.

The sole enquiry is, whether this resolution or law of Connecticut, having such operation, is an *ex post facto* law, within the prohibition of the Federal Constitution?

I cannot subscribe to the omnipotence of a State Legislature, or that it is absolute and without control; although its authority should not be expressly restrained by the Constitution, or fundamental law, of the State. The people of the United States erected their Constitutions, or forms of government, to establish justice, to promote the general welfare, to secure the blessings of liberty; and to protect their persons and property from violence. The purposes for which men enter into society will determine the nature and terms of the social compact; and as they are the foundation of the legislative power, they will decide what are the proper objects of it: The nature, and ends of legislative power will limit the exercise of it. This fundamental principle flows from the very nature of our free Republican governments, that no man should be compelled to do what the laws do not require; nor to refrain from acts which the laws permit. There are acts which the Federal, or State, Legislature cannot do, without exceeding their authority. There are certain vital principles in our free Republican governments, which will determine and over-rule an apparent and flagrant abuse of legislative power; as to authorize manifest injustice by positive law; or to take away that security for personal liberty, or private property, for the protection whereof of the government was established. An act of the Legislature (for I cannot call it a law) contrary to the great first principles of the social compact, cannot be considered a rightful exercise of legislative authority. The obligation of a law in governments established on express compact, and on republican principles, must be determined by the nature of the power, on which it is founded.

A few instances will suffice to explain what I mean. A law that punished a citizen for an innocent action, or, in other words, for an act, which, when done, was in violation of no existing law; a law that destroys, or impairs, the lawful private contracts of citizens; a law that makes a man a Judge in his own cause; or a law that takes property from A and gives it to B: It is against all reason and justice, for a people to entrust a Legislature with such powers; and, therefore, it cannot be presumed that they have done it. The genius, the nature, and the spirit, of our State Governments, amount to a prohibition of such acts of legislation; and the general principles of law and reason forbid them. The Legislature may enjoin, permit, forbid, and punish; they may declare new crimes; and establish rules of conduct for all its citizens in future cases; they may command what is right, and prohibit what is wrong; but they cannot change innocence into guilt; or punish innocence as a crime; or violate the right of an antecedent lawful private contract; or the right of private property. To maintain that our Federal, or State, Legislature possesses such powers, if they had not been expressly restrained; would,in my opinion, be a political heresy, altogether inadmissible in our free republican governments.

The Constitution of the United States, article 1, section 9, prohibits the Legislature of the United States from passing any *ex post facto* law; and, in section 10, lays several restrictions on the authority of the Legislatures of the several states; and, among them, "that no state shall pass any *ex post facto* law."

I will state what laws I consider *ex post facto* laws, within the words and the intent of the prohibition. 1st. Every law that makes an action, done before the passing of the law, and which was innocent when done, criminal; and punishes such action. 2nd. Every law that aggravates a crime, or makes it greater than it was, when committed. 3rd. Every law that changes the punishment, and inflicts a greater punishment, than the law annexed to the crime, when committed. 4th. Every law that alters the legal rules of evidence, and receives less, or different, testimony, than the law required at the time of the commission of the offence, in order to convict the offender. All these, and similar laws, are manifestly unjust and oppressive. In my opinion, the true distinction is between *ex post facto* laws, and retrospective laws. Every *ex post facto* law must necessarily be retrospective; but every retrospective law is not an *ex post facto* law: The former, only, are prohibited. Every law that takes away, or impairs, rights vested, agreeably to existing laws, is retrospective, and is generally unjust; and may be oppressive; and it is a good general rule, that a law should have no retrospect: but there are cases in which laws may justly, and for the benefit of the community, and also of individuals, relate to a time antecedent to their commencement.

If the term *ex post facto* law is to be construed to include and to prohibit the enacting any law after a fact, it will greatly restrict the power of the federal and state legislatures; and the consequences of such a construction may not be foreseen.

It is not to be presumed, that the federal or state legislatures will pass laws to deprive citizens of rights vested in them by existing laws; unless for the benefit of the whole community; and on making full satisfaction. The restraint against making any *ex post facto* laws was not considered, by the framers of the constitution, as extending to prohibit the depriving a citizen even of a vested right to property; or the provision, "that private property should not be taken for public use, without just compensation," was unnecessary.

It seems to me, that the right of property, in its origin, could only arise from compact express, or implied, and I think it the better opinion, that the right, as well as the mode, or manner, of acquiring property, and of alienating or transferring, inheriting, or transmitting it, is conferred by society; is regulated by civil institution, and is always subject to the rules prescribed by positive law. When I say that a right is vested in a citizen, I mean, that he has the power to do certain actions; or to possess certain things, according to the law of the land.

I am under a necessity to give a construction, or explanation of the words, "*ex post facto* law," because they have not any certain meaning attached to them. But I will not go farther than I feel myself bound to do; and if I ever exercise the jurisdiction I will not decide any law to be void, but in a very clear case.

**Justice Iredell:** Though I concur in the general result of the opinions, which have been delivered, I cannot entirely adopt the reasons that are assigned upon the occasion.

From the best information to be collected, relative to the Constitution of Connecticut, it appears, that the Legislature of that State has been in the uniform, uninterrupted, habit of exercising a general superintending power over its courts of law, by granting new trials. It may, indeed, appear strange to some of us, that in any form, there should exist a power to grant, with respect to suits depending or adjudged, new rights of trial, new privileges of proceeding, not previously recognized and regulated by positive institutions; but such is the established usage of Connecticut, and it is obviously consistent with the general superintending authority of her Legislature. Nor is it altogether without some sanction for a Legislature to act as a court of justice. The power, however, is judicial in its nature; and whenever it is exercised, as in the present instance, it is an exercise of judicial, not of legislative, authority.

But, let us, for a moment, suppose, that the resolution, granting a new trial, was a legislative act, it will by no means follow, that it is an act affected by the constitutional prohibition, that "no State shall pass any *ex post facto* law." I will endeavor to state the general principles, which influence me, on this point, succinctly and clearly, though I have not had an opportunity to reduce my opinion to writing.

If, then, a government, composed of Legislative, Executive and Judicial departments, were established, by a Constitution, which imposed no limits on the legislative power, the consequence would inevitably be, that whatever the legislative power chose to enact, would be lawfully enacted, and the judicial power could never interpose to pronounce it void. It is true, that some speculative jurists have held, that a legislative act against natural justice must, in itself, be void; but I cannot think that, under such a government, any Court of Justice would possess a power to declare it so. Sir William Blackstone, having put the strong case of an act of Parliament, which should authorize a man to try his own cause, explicitly adds, that even in that case, "there is no court that has power to defeat the intent of the Legislature, when couched in such evident and express words, as leave no doubt whether it was the intent of the Legislature, or no."

In order, therefore, to guard against so great an evil, it has been the policy of all the American states, which have, individually, framed their state constitutions since the revolution, and of the people of the United States, when they framed the Federal Constitution, to define with precision the objects of the legislative power, and to restrain its exercise within marked and settled boundaries. If any act of Congress, or of the Legislature of a state, violates those constitutional provisions, it is unquestionably void; though, I admit, that as the authority to declare it void is of a delicate and awful nature, the Court will never resort to that authority, but in a clear and urgent case. If, on the other hand, the Legislature of the Union, or the Legislature of any member of the Union, shall pass a law, within the general scope of their constitutional power, the Court cannot pronounce it to be void, merely because it is, in their judgment, contrary to the principles of natural justice. The ideas of natural justice are regulated by no fixed standard: the ablest and the purest men have differed upon the subject; and all that the Court could properly say, in such an event, would be, that the Legislature (possessed of an equal right of opinion) had passed an act which, in the opinion of the judges, was inconsistent with the abstract principles of natural justice. There are then but two lights, in which the subject can be viewed: 1st. If the Legislature pursue the authority delegated to them, their acts are valid. 2nd. If they transgress the boundaries of that authority, their acts are invalid. In the former case, they exercise the discretion vested in them by the people, to whom alone they are responsible for the faithful discharge of their trust: but in the latter case, they violate a fundamental law, which must be our guide, whenever we are called upon as judges to determine the validity of a legislative act.

Still, however, in the present instance, the act or resolution of the Legislature of Connecticut, cannot be regarded as an *ex post facto* law; for, the true construction of the prohibition extends to criminal, not to civil, cases. It is only in criminal cases, indeed, in which the danger to be guarded against, is greatly to be apprehended. The history of every country in Europe will furnish flagrant instances of tyranny exercised under the pretext of penal dispensations. Rival factions, in their efforts to crush each other, have superseded all the forms, and suppressed all the sentiments, of justice; while attainders, on the principle of retaliation and proscription, have marked all the vicissitudes of party triumph. The temptation to such abuses of power is unfortunately too alluring for human virtue; and, therefore, the framers of the American Constitutions have wisely denied to the respective Legislatures, Federal as well as State, the possession of the power itself: They shall not pass any *ex post facto* law; or, in other words, they shall not inflict a punishment for any act, which was innocent at the time it was committed; nor increase the degree of punishment previously denounced for any specific offence.

The policy, the reason and humanity, of the prohibition, do not, I repeat, extend to civil cases, to cases that merely affect the private property of citizens. Some of the most necessary and important acts of Legislation are, on the contrary, founded upon the principle, that private rights must yield to public exigencies. Highways are run through private grounds. Fortifications, light-houses, and other public edifices, are necessarily sometimes built upon the soil owned by individuals. In such, and similar cases, if the owners should refuse voluntarily to accommodate the public, they must be constrained, as far as the public necessities require; and justice is done, by allowing them a reasonable equivalent. Without the possession of this power the operations of Government would often be obstructed, and society itself would be endangered. It is not sufficient to urge, that the power may be abused, for, such is the nature of all power, such is the tendency of every human institution: and, it might as fairly be said, that the power of taxation, which is only circumscribed by the discretion of the Body, in which it is vested, ought not to be granted, because the Legislature, disregarding its true objects, might, for visionary and useless projects, impose a tax to the amount of nineteen shillings in the pound. We must be content to limit power where we can, and where we cannot, consistently with its use, we must be content to repose a salutary confidence. It is our consolation that there never existed a Government, in ancient or modern times, more free from danger in this respect, than the Governments of America.

*We deal with a right of privacy older than the*
*Bill of Rights.*

— *William O. Douglas*

## Griswold v. Connecticut
### 85 S.Ct. 1678, 381 U.S. 479 (1965)

*The Supreme Court held that a Connecticut statute*
*forbidding the use of contraceptives for birth control un-*
*constitutionally intruded upon the right of marital pri-*
*vacy. Along the way, the Justices debated amongst*
*themselves when and how the Court ought to go beyond*
*the text of the Constitution in search for rules of deci-*
*sions. Justice Black was heard to shout in protest, "I like*
*my privacy as well as the next one, but I am nevertheless*
*compelled to admit that government has a right to invade*
*it unless prohibited by some specific constitutional provi-*
*sion." Academic critics lined up behind his Court col-*
*leagues to complain, perhaps unfairly, that Justice*
*Douglas—apparently at the quiet urging of Justice Bren-*
*nan—had skipped through the Bill of Rights like a cheer-*
*leader yelling, "Give me a P . . . give me an R . . . give me*
*an I . . . ." and found "P–R–I–V–A–C–Y" to be a protected*
*right. The importance and ongoing nature of this inter-*
*pretive debate is evidenced by two later related rulings:*
Roe v. Wade (1973), *extending the right of privacy to the*
*decision to have an abortion, and* Bowers v. Hardwick
(1986), *refusing to extend the right of privacy to adult*
*consensual homosexual conduct.*

**Justice Douglas:** Coming to the merits, we are met with a
wide range of questions that implicate the Due Process Clause
of the Fourteenth Amendment. We do not sit as a super-legisla-
ture to determine the wisdom, need, and propriety of laws that
touch economic problems, business affairs, or social conditions.
This law, however, operates directly on an intimate relation of
husband and wife and their physician's role in one aspect of that
relation.

The association of people is not mentioned in the Constitution nor in the Bill of Rights. The right to educate a child in a
school of the parents' choice—whether public or private or parochial—is also not mentioned. Nor is the right to study any par-

ticular subject or any foreign language. Yet the First Amendment has been construed to include certain of those rights.

The right to educate one's children as one chooses is made applicable to the States by the force of the First and Fourteenth Amendments. The State may not, consistently with the spirit of the First Amendment, contract the spectrum of available knowledge. The right of freedom of speech and press includes not only the right to utter or to print, but the right to distribute, the right to receive, the right to read and freedom of inquiry, freedom of thought, and freedom to teach—indeed the freedom of the entire university community. Without those peripheral rights the specific rights would be less secure.

We protected the "freedom to associate and privacy in one's associations," noting that freedom of association was a peripheral First Amendment right. In other words, the First Amendment has a penumbra where privacy is protected from governmental intrusion. In like context, we have protected forms of "association" that are not political in the customary sense but pertain to the social, legal, and economic benefit of the members.

Our prior cases suggest that specific guarantees in the Bill of Rights have penumbras, formed by emanations from those guarantees that help give them life and substance. Various guarantees create zones of privacy. The right of association contained in the penumbra of the First Amendment is one, as we have seen. The Third Amendment in its prohibition against the quartering of soldiers "in any house" in time of peace without the consent of the owner is another facet of that privacy. The Fourth Amendment explicitly affirms the "right of the people to be secure in their persons, houses, papers, and effects, against unreasonable searches and seizures." The Fifth Amendment in its Self-Incrimination Clause enables the citizen to create a zone of privacy which government may not force him to surrender to his detriment. The Ninth Amendment provides: "The enumeration in the Constitution, of certain rights, shall not be construed to deny or disparage others retained by the people."

We have had many controversies over these penumbral rights of "privacy and repose." These cases bear witness that the right of privacy which presses for recognition here is a legitimate one.

The present case, then, concerns a relationship lying within the zone of privacy created by several fundamental constitutional guarantees. And it concerns a law which, in forbidding the use of contraceptives rather than regulating their manufacture or sale, seeks to achieve its goals by means having a maximum destructive impact upon that relationship. Such a law cannot stand. Would we allow the police to search the sacred precincts of marital bedrooms for telltale signs of the use of contraceptives? The very idea is repulsive to the notions of privacy surrounding the marriage relationship.

We deal with a right of privacy older than the Bill of Rights—older than our political parties, older than our school system. Marriage is a coming together for better or for worse, hopefully enduring, and intimate to the degree of being sacred. It is an association that promotes a way of life, not causes; a harmony in living, not political faiths; a bilateral loyalty, not commercial or social projects. Yet it is an association for as noble a purpose as any involved in our prior decisions.

**Justice Goldberg:** The language and history of the Ninth Amendment reveal that the Framers of the Constitution believed that there are additional fundamental rights, protected from governmental infringement, which exist alongside those fundamental rights specifically mentioned in the first eight constitutional amendments.

The Amendment is almost entirely the work of James Madison. It was introduced in Congress by him and passed the House and Senate with little or no debate and virtually no change in language. It was proffered to quiet expressed fears that a bill of specifically enumerated rights could not be sufficiently broad to cover all essential rights and that the specific mention of certain rights would be interpreted as a denial that others were protected.

While this Court has had little occasion to interpret the Ninth Amendment, as Chief Justice Marshall noted "it cannot be presumed that any clause in the constitution is intended to be without effect." In interpreting the Constitution, this court more recently insisted, "real effect should be given to all the words it uses." The Ninth Amendment to the Constitution may be regarded by some as a recent discovery and may be forgotten by others, but since 1791 it has been a basic part of the Constitution which we are sworn to uphold. To hold that a right so basic and fundamental and so deep-rooted in our society as the right of privacy in marriage may be infringed because that right is not guaranteed in so many words by the first eight amendments to the Constitution is to ignore the Ninth Amendment and to give it no effect whatsoever. Moreover, a judicial construction that this fundamental right is not protected by the Constitution because it is not mentioned in explicit terms by one of the first eight amendments or elsewhere in the Constitution would violate the Ninth Amendment, which specifically states that "the enumeration in the Constitution, of certain rights shall not be construed to deny or disparage others retained by the people."

The Ninth Amendment shows a belief of the Constitution's authors that fundamental rights exist that are not expressly enumerated in the first eight amendments and an intent that the list of rights included there not be deemed exhaustive. As any student of this Court's opinions knows, this Court has held, often unanimously, that the Fifth and Fourteenth Amendments protect certain fundamental personal liberties from abridgment by the Federal Government or the States. The Ninth Amendment simply shows the intent of the Constitution's authors that other fundamental personal rights should not be denied such protection or disparaged in any other way simply because they are not specifically listed in the first eight constitutional amendments. I do not see how this broadens the authority of the Court; rather it serves to support what this Court has been doing in protecting fundamental rights.

The entire fabric of the Constitution and the purposes that clearly underlie its specific guarantees demonstrate that the rights to marital privacy and to marry and raise a family are of similar order and magnitude as the fundamental rights specifically protected.

Although the Constitution does not speak in so many words of the right of privacy in marriage, I cannot believe that it offers these fundamental rights no protection. The fact that no particular provision of the Constitution explicitly forbids the State from disrupting the traditional relation of the family—a relation as old and as fundamental as our entire civilization—surely does not show that the Government was meant to have the power to do so. Rather, as the Ninth Amendment expressly recognizes, there are fundamental personal rights such as this one, which are protected from abridgment by the Government though not specifically mentioned in the Constitution.

The logic of the dissents would sanction federal or state legislation that seems to me even more plainly unconstitutional than the statute before us. Surely the Government could not decree that all husbands and wives must be sterilized after two children have been born to them. Yet by their reasoning such an invasion of marital privacy would not be subject to constitutional challenge because, while it might be "silly," no provision of the Constitution specifically prevents the Government from curtailing the marital right to bear children and raise a family. While it may shock some of my Brethren that the Court today holds that the Constitution protects the right of marital privacy, in my view it is far more shocking to believe that the personal liberty guaranteed by the Constitution does not include protection against such totalitarian limitation. Yet, if a law outlawing voluntary birth control by married persons is valid, then, by the same reasoning, a law requiring compulsory birth control also would seem to be valid. In my view, however, both types of law would unjustifiably intrude upon rights of marital privacy which are constitutionally protected.

**Justice Harlan:** In my view, the proper constitutional inquiry in this case is whether this Connecticut statute infringes the Due Process Clause of the Fourteenth Amendment because the enactment violates basic values "implicit in the concept of ordered liberty." While the relevant inquiry may be aided by resort to one or more of the provisions of the Bill of Rights, it is not dependent on them or any of their radiations. The Due Process Clause of the Fourteenth Amendment stands on its own bottom.

While I could not more heartily agree that judicial "self restraint" is an indispensable ingredient of sound constitutional adjudication, I do submit that the formula suggested for achieving it is more hollow than real. "Specific" provisions of the Constitution, no less than "due process," lend themselves as readily to "personal" interpretations by judges whose constitutional outlook is simply to keep the Constitution in supposed "tune with the times."

Judicial self-restraint will be achieved in this area, as in other constitutional areas, only by continual insistence upon respect for the teachings of history, solid recognition of the basic values that underlie our society, and wise appreciation of the great roles that the doctrines of federalism and separation of powers have played in establishing and preserving American freedoms. Adherence to these principles will not, of course, obviate all constitutional differences of opinion among judges, nor should it. Their continued recognition will, however, go farther toward keeping most judges from roaming at large in the constitutional field than will the interpolation into the Constitution of an artificial and largely illusory restriction on the content of the Due Process Clause.

**Justice Black:** The Court talks about a constitutional "right of privacy" as though there is some constitutional provision or provisions forbidding any law ever to be passed which might abridge the "privacy" of individuals. But there is not. There are, of course, guarantees in certain specific constitutional provisions which are designed in part to protect privacy at certain times and places with respect to certain activities. Such, for example, is the Fourth Amendment's guarantee against "unreasonable searches and seizures." But I think it belittles that Amendment to talk about it as though it protects nothing but "privacy." To treat it that way is to give it a niggardly interpretation, not the kind of liberal reading I think any Bill of Rights provision should be given.

One of the most effective ways of diluting or expanding a constitutionally guaranteed right is to substitute for the crucial word or words of a constitutional guarantee another word or words, more or less flexible and more or less restricted in meaning. This fact is well illustrated by the use of the term "right of privacy" as a comprehensive substitute for the Fourth Amendment's guarantee against "unreasonable searches and seizures." "Privacy" is a broad, abstract and ambiguous concept which can easily be shrunken in meaning but which can also, on the other hand, easily be interpreted as a constitutional ban against many things other than searches and seizures.

I get nowhere in this case by talk about a constitutional "right or privacy" as an emanation from one or more constitutional provisions. I like my privacy as well as the next one, but I am nevertheless compelled to admit that government has a right to invade it unless prohibited by some specific constitutional provision.

The erroneous premise is that this Court is vested with power to invalidate all state laws that it considers to be arbitrary, capricious, unreasonable, or oppressive, or this Court's belief that a particular state law under scrutiny has no "rational or justifying" purpose, or is offensive to a "sense of fairness and justice." If these formulas based on "natural justice," or others which mean the same thing, are to prevail, they require judges to determine what is or is not constitutional on the basis of their own appraisal of what laws are unwise or unnecessary. The power to make such decisions is of course that of a legislative body. Surely it has to be admitted that no provision of the Constitution specifically gives such blanket power to courts to exercise such a supervisory veto over the wisdom and value of legislative policies and to hold unconstitutional those laws which they believe unwise or dangerous. I readily admit that no legislative body, state or national, should pass laws that can justly be given any of the invidious labels invoked as constitutional excuses to strike down state laws. But perhaps it is not too much to say that no legislative body ever does pass laws without believing that they will accomplish a sane, rational, wise and justifiable purpose. While I completely subscribe to the holding of *Marbury v. Madison (1803)*, and subsequent cases, that our Court has constitutional power to strike down statutes, state or federal, that violate commands of the Federal Constitution, I do not believe that we are granted power by the Due Process Clause or any other constitutional provision or provisions to measure constitutionality by our belief that legislation is arbitrary, capricious or unreasonable, or accomplishes no justifiable purpose, or is offensive to our own notions of "civilized standards of conduct." Such an appraisal of the wisdom of legislation is an attribute of the power to make laws, not of the power to interpret them. The use by federal courts of such a formula or doctrine or whatnot to veto federal or state laws simply takes away from Congress and States the power to make laws based on their own judgment of fairness and wisdom and transfers that power to this Court for ultimate determination— a power which was specifically denied to federal courts by the convention that framed the Constitution.

My Brother Goldberg has adopted the recent discovery that the Ninth Amendment as well as the Due Process Clause can be used by this Court as authority to strike down state legislation. He also states, without proof satisfactory to me, that in making decisions on this basis judges will not consider "their personal and private notions." One may ask how they can avoid considering them. Our Court certainly has no machinery with which to take a Gallup Poll. And the scientific miracles of this age have not yet produced a gadget which the Court can use to determine what traditions are rooted in the "collective conscience of our people." Moreover, one would certainly have to look far beyond the language of the Ninth Amendment to find that the Framers vested in this Court any such awesome veto powers over law-making, either by the States or by the Congress. Nor does anything in the history of the Amendment offer any support for such a shocking doctrine. That Amendment was passed, not to broaden the powers of this Court or any other department of "the General Government," but, as every student of history knows, to assure the people that the Constitution in all its provisions was intended to limit the Federal Government to the powers granted expressly or by necessary implication. If any broad, unlimited power to hold laws unconstitutional because they offend what this Court conceives to be the "collective conscience of our people" is vested in this Court by the Ninth Amendment, the Fourteenth Amendment, or any other provision of the Constitution, it was not given by the Framers, but rather has been bestowed on the Court by the Court. Use of any such broad, unbounded judicial authority would make of this Court's members a day-to-day constitutional convention.

This Court does have power, which it should exercise, to hold laws unconstitutional where they are forbidden by the Federal Constitution. My point is that there is no provision of the Constitution which either expressly or impliedly vests power in this Court to sit as a supervisory agency over acts of duly constituted legislative bodies and set aside their laws because of the Court's belief that the legislative policies adopted are unreasonable, unwise, arbitrary, capricious or irrational. The adoption of such a loose, flexible, uncontrolled standard for holding laws unconstitutional, if ever it is finally achieved, will amount to a great unconstitutional shift of power to the courts which I believe and am constrained to say will be bad for the courts and worse for the country. Subjecting federal and state laws to such an unrestrained and unrestrainable judicial control as to the wisdom of legislative enactments would, I fear, jeopardize the separation of governmental powers that the Framers set up and at the same time threaten to take away much of the power of States to govern themselves which the Constitution plainly intended them to have.

I realize that many good and able men have eloquently spoken and written, sometimes in rhapsodical strains, about the duty of this Court to keep the Constitution in tune with the times. The idea is that the Constitution must be changed from time to time and that this Court is charged with a duty to make those changes. For myself, I must with all deference reject that philosophy. The Constitution makers knew the need for change and provided for it. Amendments suggested by the people's elected representatives can be submitted to the people or their selected agents for ratification. That method of change was good for our Fathers, and being somewhat old fashioned I must add it is good enough for me. And so, I cannot rely on the Due Process Clause or the Ninth Amendment or any mysterious and uncertain natural law concept as a reason for striking down this state law. Any limitation upon judges using the natural law due process philosophy to strike down any state law, dealing with any activity whatever, will obviously be only self-imposed.

The late Judge Learned Hand, after emphasizing his view that judges should not use the due process formula to invalidate legislation offensive to their "personal preferences," made the statement, with which I fully agree, that: "For myself it would be most irksome to be ruled by a bevy of Platonic Guardians, even if I knew how to choose them, which I assuredly do not."

**Justice Stewart:** Since 1879, Connecticut has had on its books a law which forbids the use of contraceptives by anyone. I think this is an uncommonly silly law. As a practical matter, the law is obviously unenforceable, except in the oblique context of the present case. As a philosophical matter, I believe the use of contraceptives in the relationship of marriage should be left to personal and private choice, based upon each individual's moral, ethical, and religious beliefs. As a matter of social policy, I think professional counsel about methods of birth control should be available to all, so that each individual's choice can be meaningfully made. But we are not asked in this case to say whether we think this law is unwise, or even asinine. We are asked to hold that it violates the United States Constitution. And that I cannot do.

In the course of its opinion the Court refers to no less than six Amendments to the Constitution: the First, the Third, the Fourth, the Fifth, the Ninth, and the Fourteenth. But the Court does not say which of these Amendments, if any, it thinks is infringed by this Connecticut law.

I can find nothing in any of them to invalidate this Connecticut law. And surely, unless the solemn process of constitutional adjudication is to descend to the level of a play on words, there is not involved here any abridgment of "the freedom of speech, or of the press; or the right of the people peaceably to assemble, and to petition the Government for a redress of grievances." No soldier has been quartered in any house. There has been no search, and no seizure. Nobody has been compelled to be a witness against himself.

To say that the Ninth Amendment has anything to do with this case is to turn somersaults with history. The Ninth Amendment, like its companion the Tenth, which this Court held "states but a truism that all is retained which has not been surrendered," was framed by James Madison and adopted by the States simply to make clear that the adoption of the Bill of Rights did not alter the plan that the Federal Government was to be a government of express and limited powers, and that all rights and powers not delegated to it were retained by the people and the individual States. Until today no member of this Court has ever suggested that the Ninth Amendment meant anything else, and the idea that a federal court could ever use the Ninth Amendment to annul a law passed by the elected representatives of the people of the State of Connecticut would have caused James Madison no little wonder.

What provision of the Constitution, then, does make this state law invalid? The Court says it is the right of privacy "created by several fundamental constitutional guarantees." With all deference, I can find no such general right of privacy in the Bill of Rights, in any other part of the Constitution, or in any case ever before decided by this Court.

It is not the function of this Court to decide cases on the basis of community standards. We are here to decide cases "agreeably to the Constitution and laws of the United States." It is the essence of judicial duty to subordinate our own personal views, our own ideas of what legislation is wise and what is not. If, as I should surely hope, the law before us does not reflect the standards of the people of Connecticut, the people of Connecticut can freely exercise their true Ninth and Tenth Amendment rights to persuade their elected representatives to repeal it. That is the constitutional way to take this law off the books.

*The document that the plurality construes today is unfamiliar to me. It is not the living charter that I have taken to be our Constitution; it is instead a stagnant, archaic, hidebound document steeped in the prejudices and superstitions of a time long past. This Constitution does not recognize that times change, does not see that sometimes a practice or rule outlives its foundations. I cannot accept an interpretive method that does such violence to the charter that I am bound by oath to uphold.*

*— William J. Brennan*

## Michael H. and Victoria D. v. Gerald D.
### 109 S.Ct. 2333, 491 U.S. 110 (1989)

*Michael H. alleged that he was the natural or biological father of Victoria D., who was the legal daughter of another married couple, Gerald D. and Carole D. In fact, scientific blood testing established a 98.07% probability that Michael H. was Victoria D.'s biological father. But a California statute, which had been on the books for more than a hundred years and which was similar to the laws of most States, created a legal presumption that a child born to a married woman was the child of the woman's husband. This presumption could be rebutted only by the married couple themselves and only in limited situations; there was nothing the man claiming to be the biological father could do to overcome the legal presumption. Michael H. argued, unsuccessfully, that the statute denied him due process of law. A fractured Court issued five separate opinions. Only one other member of the Court formally accepted Justice Scalia's due process methodology; the other two Justices who joined the rest of his opinion distanced themselves from his footnote theory of interpretation and the remaining Justices expressly rejected it. Justice Scalia focused on the particular tradition disapproving of adultery and illegitimacy; Justice Brennan would have decided the case based on today's general understanding of parenthood and family. Both sound like Tevye in* Fiddler on the Roof *singing about the importance of "Tradition!," but each is singing about a different tradition. The philosophical debate between these two Justices takes us back to basic principles of constitutionalism. What is the nature of a written Constitution? Does it change over time? Should judges be trusted to rely on history and tradition to reinterpret the Constitution? Of what importance are contemporary understandings of society? This footnoted debate has since been rehearsed in numerous scholarly articles as well as in many subsequent opinions.*

**Justice Scalia:** The facts of this case are, we must hope, extraordinary. At the outset, it is necessary to clarify what Michael sought and what he was denied. California law, like nature itself, makes no provision for dual fatherhood. Michael was seeking to be declared the father of Victoria. The immediate benefit he evidently sought to obtain from that status was visitation rights. But if Michael were successful in being declared the father, other rights would follow—most importantly, the right to be considered as the parent who should have custody, a status which "embraces the sum of parental rights with respect to the rearing of a child, including the child's care; the right to the child's services and earnings; the right to direct the child's activities; the right to make decisions regarding the control, education, and health of the child; and the right, as well as the duty, to prepare the child for additional obligations, which includes the teaching of moral standards, religious beliefs, and elements of good citizenship." All parental rights, including visitation, were automatically denied by denying Michael status as the father.

Michael contends as a matter of substantive due process that, because he has established a parental relationship with Victoria, protection of Gerald's and Carole's marital union is an insufficient state interest to support termination of that relationship. This argument is, of course, predicated on the assertion that Michael has a constitutionally protected liberty interest in his relationship with Victoria.

It is an established part of our constitutional jurisprudence that the term "liberty" in the Due Process Clause extends beyond freedom from physical restraint. Without that core textual meaning as a limitation, defining the scope of the Due Process Clause "has at times been a treacherous field for this Court," giving "reason for concern lest the only limits to judicial intervention become the predilections of those who happen at the time to be Members of this Court." In an attempt to limit and guide interpretation of the Clause, we have insisted not merely that the interest denominated as a "liberty" be "fundamental" (a concept that, in isolation, is hard to objectify), but also that it be an interest traditionally protected by our society.[2] As we have put it, the Due Process Clause affords only those protections "so rooted in the traditions and conscience of our people as to be ranked as fundamental." Our cases reflect what Justice Harlan once called the "continual insistence upon respect for the teachings of history and solid recognition of the basic values that underlie our society."

This insistence that the asserted liberty interest be rooted in history and tradition is evident, as elsewhere, in our cases according constitutional protection to certain parental rights. Michael reads our prior cases as establishing that a liberty interest is created by biological fatherhood plus an established parental relationship—factors that exist in the present case as well. We think that distorts the rationale of those cases. As we view them, they rest not upon such isolated factors but upon the historic respect—indeed, sanctity would not be too strong a term—traditionally accorded to the relationships that develop within the unitary family.[3] As Justice Powell has stated: "Our decisions establish that the Constitution protects the sanctity of the family precisely because the institution of the family is deeply rooted in this Nation's history and tradition."

Thus, the legal issue in the present case reduces to whether the relationship between persons in the situation of Michael and

---

2. We do not understand what Justice Brennan has in mind by an interest "that society traditionally has thought important . . . without protecting it." The protection need not take the form of an explicit constitutional provision or statutory guarantee, but it must at least exclude (all that is necessary to decide the present case) a societal tradition of enacting laws denying the interest. Nor do we understand why our practice of limiting the Due Process Clause to traditionally protected interests turns the Clause "into a redundancy." Its purpose is to prevent future generations from lightly casting aside important traditional values—not to enable this Court to invent new ones.

3. Justice Brennan asserts that only a "pinched conception of 'the family'" would exclude Michael, Carole, and Victoria from protection. We disagree. The family unit accorded traditional respect in our society, which we have referred to as the "unitary family," is typified, of course, by the marital family, but also includes the household of unmarried parents and their children. Perhaps the concept can be expanded even beyond this, but it will bear no resemblance to traditionally respected relationships—and will thus cease to have any constitutional significance—if it is stretched so far as to include the relationship here established between a married woman, her lover, and their child.

Victoria has been treated as a protected family unit under the historic practices of our society, or whether on any other basis it has been accorded special protection. We think it impossible to find that it has. In fact, quite to the contrary, our traditions have protected the marital family (Gerald, Carole, and the child they acknowledge to be theirs) against the sort of claim Michael asserts.[4]

The presumption of legitimacy was a fundamental principle of the common law. Traditionally, that presumption could be rebutted only by proof that a husband was incapable of procreation or had had no access to his wife during the relevant period. As explained by Blackstone, nonaccess could only be proved "if the husband be out of the kingdom of England (or, as the law somewhat loosely phrases it, *extra quatuor maria*, "beyond the four seas") for above nine months." The primary policy rationale underlying the common law's severe restrictions on rebuttal of the presumption appears to have been an aversion to declaring children illegitimate, thereby depriving them of rights of inheritance and succession, and likely making them wards of the state. A secondary policy concern was the interest in promoting the "peace and tranquillity of States and families," a goal that is obviously impaired by facilitating suits against husband and wife asserting that their children are illegitimate. Even though, as bastardy laws became less harsh, "the law retained a strong bias against ruling the children of married women illegitimate."

We have found nothing in the older sources, nor in the older cases, addressing specifically the power of the natural father to assert parental rights over a child born into a woman's existing marriage with another man. Since it is Michael's burden to establish that such a power (at least where the natural father has established a relationship with the child) is so deeply embedded within our traditions as to be a fundamental right, the lack of

---

4. Justice Brennan insists that in determining whether a liberty interest exists we must look at Michael's relationship with Victoria in isolation, without reference to the circumstance that Victoria's mother was married to someone else when the child was conceived, and that that woman and her husband wish to raise the child as their own. We cannot imagine what compels this strange procedure of looking at the act which is assertedly the subject of a liberty interest in isolation from its effect upon other people— rather like inquiring whether there is a liberty interest in firing a gun where the case at hand happens to involve its discharge into another person's body. The logic of Justice Brennan's position leads to the conclusion that if Michael had begotten Victoria by rape, that fact would in no way affect his possession of a liberty interest in his relationship with her.

evidence alone might defeat his case. But the evidence shows that even in modern times—when, as we have noted, the rigid protection of the marital family has in other respects been relaxed—the ability of a person in Michael's position to claim paternity has not been generally acknowledged.

What Michael asserts here is a right to have himself declared the natural father and thereby to obtain parental prerogatives. What he must establish, therefore, is not that our society has traditionally allowed a natural father in his circumstances to establish paternity, but that it has traditionally accorded such a father parental rights, or at least has not traditionally denied them. What counts is whether the States in fact award substantive parental rights to the natural father of a child conceived within, and born into, an extant marital union that wishes to embrace the child. We are not aware of a single case, old or new, that has done so. This is not the stuff of which fundamental rights qualifying as liberty interests are made.[6]

It is a question of legislative policy and not constitutional law whether California will allow the presumed parenthood of a couple desiring to retain a child conceived within and born into

---

6. Justice Brennan criticizes our methodology in using historical traditions specifically relating to the rights of an adulterous natural father, rather than inquiring more generally "whether parenthood is an interest that historically has received our attention and protection." There seems to us no basis for the contention that this methodology is "novel." For example, in *Bowers v. Hardwick (1986)*, we noted that at the time the Fourteenth Amendment was ratified all but 5 of the 37 States had criminal sodomy laws, that all 50 of the States had such laws prior to 1961, and that 24 States and the District of Columbia continued to have them; and we concluded from that record, regarding that very specific aspect of sexual conduct, that "to claim that a right to engage in such conduct is 'deeply rooted in this Nation's history and tradition' or 'implicit in the concept of ordered liberty' is, at best, facetious." In *Roe v. Wade (1973)*, we spent about a fifth of our opinion negating the proposition that there was a longstanding tradition of laws proscribing abortion.

We do not understand why, having rejected our focus upon the societal tradition regarding the natural father's rights vis-a-vis a child whose mother is married to another man, Justice Brennan would choose to focus instead upon "parenthood." Why should the relevant category not be even more general—perhaps "family relationships"; or "personal relationships"; or even "emotional attachments in general"? Though the dissent has no basis for the level of generality it would select, we do: We refer to the most specific level at which a relevant tradition protecting, or denying protection to, the asserted right can be identified. If, for example, there were no societal tradition, either way, regarding the rights of the natural father of a child adulterously conceived, we would have to consult, and (if possible) reason from, the traditions regarding natural fathers in general. But there is such a more specific tradition, and it unqualifiedly denies protection to such a parent.

their marriage to be rebutted.[7] We do not accept Justice Brennan's criticism that this result "squashes" the liberty that consists of "the freedom not to conform." It seems to us that reflects the erroneous view that there is only one side to this controversy—that one disposition can expand a "liberty" of sorts without contracting an equivalent "liberty" on the other side. Such a happy choice is rarely available. Here, to provide protection to an adulterous natural father is to deny protection to a marital father, and *vice versa*. If Michael has a "freedom not to conform" (whatever that means), Gerald must equivalently have a "freedom to conform." One of them will pay a price for asserting that "freedom"—Michael by being unable to act as father of the child he has adulterously begotten, or Gerald by being unable to preserve the integrity of the traditional family unit he and Victoria have established. Our disposition does not choose between these two "freedoms," but leaves that to the people of California. Justice Brennan's approach chooses one of them as the constitutional imperative, on no apparent basis except that the unconventional is to be preferred.

---

*(Footnote 6 continued)*

One would think that Justice Brennan would appreciate the value of consulting the most specific tradition available, since he acknowledges that "even if we can agree that 'family' and 'parenthood' are part of the good life, it is absurd to assume that we can agree on the content of those terms and destructive to pretend that we do." Because such general traditions provide such imprecise guidance, they permit judges to dictate rather than discern the society's views. The need, if arbitrary decisionmaking is to be avoided, to adopt the most specific tradition as the point of reference—or at least to announce, as Justice Brennan declines to do, some other criterion for selecting among the innumerable relevant traditions that could be consulted—is well enough exemplified by the fact that in the present case the opinions which disapprove of this footnote both appeal to tradition, but on the basis of the tradition they select reach opposite results. Although assuredly having the virtue (if it be that) of leaving judges free to decide as they think best when the unanticipated occurs, a rule of law that binds neither by text nor by any particular, identifiable tradition is no rule of law at all.

Finally, we may note that this analysis is not inconsistent with the result in cases such as *Griswold v. Connecticut (1965)*. None of those cases acknowledged a longstanding and still extant societal tradition withholding the very right pronounced to be the subject of a liberty interest and then rejected it. Justice Brennan must do so here. In this case, the existence of such a tradition, continuing to the present day, refutes any possible contention that the alleged right is "so rooted in the traditions and conscience of our people as to be ranked as fundamental," or "implicit in the concept of ordered liberty."

7. Justice Brennan chides us for thus limiting our holding to situations in which, as here, the husband and wife wish to raise her child jointly. The dissent believes that without this limitation we would be unable to "rely on the State's

**Justice Brennan:** Once we recognized that the "liberty" protected by the Due Process Clause of the Fourteenth Amendment encompasses more than freedom from bodily restraint, today's plurality opinion emphasizes, the concept was cut loose from one natural limitation on its meaning. This innovation paved the way, so the plurality hints, for judges to substitute their own preferences for those of elected officials. Dissatisfied with this supposedly unbridled and uncertain state of affairs, the plurality casts about for another limitation on the concept of liberty.

fact that this concept can be as malleable and as elusive as "liberty" itself, the plurality pretends that tradition places a discernible border around the Constitution. The pretense is seductive; it would be comforting to believe that a search for "tradition" involves nothing more idiosyncratic or complicated than poring through dusty volumes on American history. Yet, as Justice White has observed, "What the deeply rooted traditions of the country are is arguable." Indeed, wherever I would begin to look for an interest "deeply rooted in the country's traditions," one thing is certain: I would not stop (as does the plurality) at Bracton, or Blackstone, or Kent, or even the American Law Reports in conducting my search. Because reasonable people can disagree about the content of particular traditions, and because they can disagree even about which traditions are relevant to the definition of "liberty," the plurality has not found the objective boundary that it seeks.

It finds this limitation in "tradition." Apparently oblivious to theEven if we could agree, moreover, on the content and significance of particular traditions, we still would be forced to identify the point at which a tradition becomes firm enough to be relevant to our definition of liberty and the moment at which it be-

---

*(Footnote 7 continued)*
asserted interest in protecting the 'unitary family' in denying that Michael and Victoria have been deprived of liberty." As we have sought to make clear, however, we rest our decision not upon our independent "balancing" of such interests, but upon the absence of any constitutionally protected right to legal parentage on the part of an adulterous natural father in Michael's situation, as evidenced by long tradition. That tradition reflects a "balancing" that has already been made by society itself. We limit our pronouncement to the relevant facts of this case because it is at least possible that our traditions lead to a different conclusion with regard to adulterous fathering of a child whom the marital parents do not wish to raise as their own. It seems unfair for those who disagree with our holding to include among their criticisms that we have not extended the holding more broadly.

comes too obsolete to be relevant any longer. The plurality supplies no objective means by which we might make these determinations. Indeed, as soon as the plurality sees signs that the tradition upon which it bases its decision is crumbling, it shifts ground and says that the case has nothing to do with that tradition, after all. The plurality's last-minute denial of this fact dramatically illustrates the subjectivity of its own analysis.

It is ironic that an approach so utterly dependent on tradition is so indifferent to our precedents. Citing barely a handful of this Court's numerous decisions defining the scope of the liberty protected by the Due Process Clause to support its reliance on tradition, the plurality acts as though English legal treatises and the American Law Reports always have provided the sole source for our constitutional principles. They have not. Just as common-law notions no longer define the "property" that the Constitution protects, neither do they circumscribe the "liberty" that it guarantees. On the contrary, " 'liberty' and 'property' are broad and majestic terms. They are among the 'great constitutional concepts purposely left to gather meaning from experience. They relate to the whole domain of social and economic fact, and the statesmen who founded this Nation knew too well that only a stagnant society remains unchanged.' "

It is not that tradition has been irrelevant to our prior decisions. Throughout our decisionmaking in this important area runs the theme that certain interests and practices—freedom from physical restraint, marriage, childbearing, childrearing, and others—form the core of our definition of "liberty." Our solicitude for these interests is partly the result of the fact that the Due Process Clause would seem an empty promise if it did not protect them, and partly the result of the historical and traditional importance of these interests in our society. In deciding cases arising under the Due Process Clause, therefore, we have considered whether the concrete limitation under consideration impermissibly impinges upon one of these more generalized interests.

Today's plurality, however, does not ask whether parenthood is an interest that historically has received our attention and protection; the answer to that question is too clear for dispute. Instead, the plurality asks whether the specific variety of parenthood under consideration—a natural father's relationship with a child whose mother is married to another man—has enjoyed such protection.

If we had looked to tradition with such specificity in past cases, many a decision would have reached a different result. Surely the use of contraceptives by unmarried couples, or even by married couples, the freedom from corporal punishment in schools, and even the right to raise one's natural but illegitimate children, were not "interests traditionally protected by our society," at the time of their consideration by this Court. That we did not ask this question in those cases highlights the novelty of the interpretive method that the plurality opinion employs today.

The plurality's interpretive method is more than novel; it is misguided. It ignores the good reasons for limiting the role of "tradition" in interpreting the Constitution's deliberately capacious language. In the plurality's constitutional universe, we may not take notice of the fact that the original reasons for the conclusive presumption of paternity are out of place in a world in which blood tests can prove virtually beyond a shadow of a doubt who sired a particular child and in which the fact of illegitimacy no longer plays the burdensome and stigmatizing role it once did. Nor, in the plurality's world, may we deny "tradition" its full scope by pointing out that the rationale for the conventional rule has changed over the years, as has the rationale for the California statutory presumption; instead, our task is simply to identify a rule denying the asserted interest and not to ask whether the basis for that rule—which is the true reflection of the values undergirding it—has changed too often or too recently to call the rule embodying that rationale a "tradition." Moreover, by describing the decisive question as whether Michael's and Victoria's interest is one that has been "traditionally protected by our society," rather than one that society traditionally has thought important (with or without protecting it), and by suggesting that our sole function is to "discern the society's views," the plurality acts as if the only purpose of the Due Process Clause is to confirm the importance of interests already protected by a majority of the States. Transforming the protection afforded by the Due Process Clause into a redundancy mocks those who, with care and purpose, wrote the Fourteenth Amendment.

In construing the Fourteenth Amendment to offer shelter only to those interests specifically protected by historical practice, moreover, the plurality ignores the kind of society in which our Constitution exists. We are not an assimilative, homogeneous society, but a facilitative, pluralistic one, in which we must be willing to abide someone else's unfamiliar or even repellent practice because the same tolerant impulse protects our own idiosyncracies. Even if we can agree, therefore, that "family" and "parenthood" are part of the good life, it is absurd to assume that we can agree on the content of those terms and destructive to pretend that we do. In a community such as ours, "liberty" must include the freedom not to conform. The plurality today squashes this freedom by requiring specific approval from history before protecting anything in the name of liberty.

The document that the plurality construes today is unfamiliar to me. It is not the living charter that I have taken to be our Constitution; it is instead a stagnant, archaic, hidebound document steeped in the prejudices and superstitions of a time long past. This Constitution does not recognize that times change, does not see that sometimes a practice or rule outlives its foundations. I cannot accept an interpretive method that does such violence to the charter that I am bound by oath to uphold.

The plurality's reworking of our interpretive approach is all the more troubling because it is unnecessary. This is not a case in which we face a "new" kind of interest, one that requires us to consider for the first time whether the Constitution protects it. On the contrary, we confront an interest—that of a parent and child in their relationship with each other—that was among the first that this Court acknowledged in its cases defining the "liberty" protected by the Constitution, and I think I am safe in saying that no one doubts the wisdom or validity of those decisions. Where the interest under consideration is a parent-child relationship, we need not ask, over and over again, whether that interest is one that society traditionally protects.

The plurality's exclusive rather than inclusive definition of the "unitary family" is out of step with other decisions as well. This pinched conception of "the family," crucial as it is in rejecting Michael's and Victoria's claims of a liberty interest, is jarring in light of our many cases preventing the States from denying important interests or statuses to those whose situations do not fit the government's narrow view of the family. We have declined to respect a State's notion, as manifested in its allocation of privileges and burdens, of what the family should be. Today's rhapsody on the "unitary family" is out of tune with such decisions.

The question before us, therefore, is whether California has an interest so powerful that it justifies granting Michael no hearing before terminating his parental rights. "Many controversies have raged about the cryptic and abstract words of the

Due Process Clause but there can be no doubt that at a minimum they require that deprivation of life, liberty or property by adjudication be preceded by notice and opportunity for hearing appropriate to the nature of the case." The purported state interests here, however, stem primarily from the State's antagonism to Michael's and Victoria's constitutionally protected interest in their relationship with each other and not from any desire to streamline procedures.

The atmosphere surrounding today's decision is one of make-believe. Beginning with the suggestion that the situation confronting us here does not repeat itself every day in every corner of the country, moving on to the claim that it is tradition alone that supplies the details of the liberty that the Constitution protects, and passing finally to the notion that the Court always has recognized a cramped vision of "the family," today's decision lets stand California's pronouncement that Michael—whom blood tests show to a 98 percent probability to be Victoria's father—is not Victoria's father. When and if the Court awakes to reality, it will find a world very different from the one it expects.

*But I had thought that the propriety of the exercise of a power admitted to exist in some cases was for the consideration of Congress alone and that this Court always had disavowed the right to intrude its judgment upon questions of policy or morals.*

— *Oliver W. Holmes, Jr.*

## Hammer v. Dagenhart
### 38 S.Ct. 529, 247 U.S. 251 (1918)

*"The powerful and now classic dissent of Mr. Justice Holmes," are the words Justice Stone later would use, writing in 1941 for a unanimous Court that vindicated this dissent. Back when this case was decided, however, in 1918, five members of the Court were unable or unwilling to sustain the Congressional regulation and voted to strike down the federal child-labor statute. Justice Holmes excoriated his colleagues for allowing their personal policy preferences to intrude into their judicial role. Congress responded by reenacting the measure under its taxing power and the Court for a second time held the legislation unconstitutional in 1922. Congress then proposed a constitutional amendment that would have authorized federal legislation to prohibit child labor, but the amendment languished in constitutional limbo when only 28 of the requisite 36 States ratified it between 1924 and 1938. The Fair Labor Standards Act of 1938, part of the New Deal reforms, contained an outright prohibition on child labor and* United States v. Darby (1941) *was the occasion for the high Court to praise Holmes and to overrule* Hammer. *Justice Holmes' dissent, upon a close reading, had more to do with judicial deference to majority rule and the political process than with a concern for the "have nots" or what he himself sometimes in private derisively called "moral uplift."*

**Justice Holmes:** The single question in this case is whether Congress has power to prohibit the shipment in interstate or foreign commerce of any product of a cotton mill situated in the United States, in which within thirty days before the removal of the product children under fourteen have been employed, or children between fourteen and sixteen have been employed more than eight hours in a day, or more than six days in any week, or between seven in the evening and six in the morning. The objection urged against the power is that the States have exclusive control over their methods of production and that Congress cannot meddle with them, and taking the proposition in the sense of direct intermeddling I agree to it and suppose that no one denies it. But if an act is within the powers specifically conferred upon Congress, it seems to me that it is not made any less constitutional because of the indirect effects that it may have, however obvious it may be that it will have those effects, and that we are not at liberty upon such grounds to hold it void.

The first step in my argument is to make plain what no one is likely to dispute—that the statute in question is within the power expressly given to Congress if considered only as to its immediate effects and that if invalid it is so only upon some collateral ground. The statute confines itself to prohibiting the carriage of certain goods in interstate or foreign commerce. Congress is given power to regulate such commerce in unqualified terms. It would not be argued today that the power to regulate does not include the power to prohibit. Regulation means the prohibition of something, and when interstate commerce is the matter to be regulated I cannot doubt that the regulation may prohibit any part of such commerce that Congress sees fit to forbid. At all events it is established by our cases that a law is not beyond the regulative power of Congress merely because it prohibits certain transportation out and out. So I repeat that this statute in its immediate operation is clearly within the Congress's constitutional power.

The question then is narrowed to whether the exercise of its otherwise constitutional power by Congress can be pronounced unconstitutional because of its possible reaction upon the conduct of the States in a matter upon which I have admitted that they are free from direct control. I should have thought that that matter had been disposed of so fully as to leave no room for doubt. I should have thought that the most conspicuous decisions of this Court had made it clear that the power to regulate commerce and other constitutional powers could not be cut down or qualified by the fact that it might interfere with the carrying out of the domestic policy of any State.

Once before the Court made short work of the argument made here as to the purpose of an Act: "The Judicial cannot prescribe to the Legislative Departments of the Government limitations upon the exercise of its acknowledged powers." The objection that the control of the States over production was interfered with was urged again and again in past cases but always in vain.

This Court's intimation that "no trade can be carried on between the States to which the power of Congress to regulate commerce does not extend," applies not merely to articles that the changing opinions of the time condemn as intrinsically harmful but to others innocent in themselves. It does not matter whether the supposed evil precedes or follows the transportation. It is enough that in the opinion of Congress the transportation encourages the evil. I may add that in this Court's cases it was established that the means adopted by Congress as convenient to the exercise of its power might have the character of police regulations. This Court has said, "a subject matter which has been confided exclusively to Congress by the Constitution is not within the jurisdiction of the police power of the State unless placed there by congressional action." I see no reason for that proposition not applying here.

The notion that prohibition is any less prohibition when applied to things now thought evil I do not understand. But if there is any matter upon which civilized countries have agreed—far more unanimously than they have with regard to intoxicants and some other matters over which this country is now emotionally aroused—it is the evil of premature and excessive child labor. I should have thought that if we were to introduce our own moral conceptions where in my opinion they do not belong, this was preeminently a case for upholding the exercise of all its powers by the United States.

But I had thought that the propriety of the exercise of a power admitted to exist in some cases was for the consideration of Congress alone and that this Court always had disavowed the right to intrude its judgment upon questions of policy or morals. It is not for this Court to pronounce when prohibition is necessary to regulation if it ever may be necessary—to say that it is permissible as against strong drink but not as against the product of ruined lives.

The Act does not meddle with anything belonging to the States. They may regulate their internal affairs and their domestic commerce as they like. But when they seek to send their products across the State line they are no longer within their rights. If there were no Constitution and no Congress their power to cross the line would depend upon their neighbors. Under the Constitution such commerce belongs not to the States but to Congress to regulate. It may carry out its views of public policy whatever indirect effect they may have upon the activities of the States. Instead of being encountered by a prohibitive tariff at her boundaries the State encounters the public policy of the United States which it is for Congress to express. The public policy of the United States is shaped with a view to the benefit of the nation as a whole. If, as has been the case within the memory of men still living, a State should take a different view of the propriety of sustaining a lottery from that which generally prevails, I cannot believe that the fact would require a different decision from that reached in our case upholding it. Yet in that case it would be said with quite as much force as in this, that Congress was attempting to intermeddle with the State's domestic affairs. The national welfare as understood by Congress may require a different attitude within its sphere from that of some self-seeking State. It seems to me entirely constitutional for Congress to enforce its understanding by all the means at its command.

*I would follow what I believe was the original purpose of the Fourteenth Amendment—to extend to all the people of the nation the complete protection of the Bill of Rights. To hold that this Court can determine what, if any, provisions of the Bill of Rights will be enforced, and if so to what degree, is to frustrate the great design of a written Constitution.*

— *Hugo L. Black*

## Adamson v. California
### 67 S.Ct. 1672, 332 U.S. 46 (1947)

*By a 5 to 4 vote, the Supreme Court upheld California laws that permitted the trial court and the prosecutor to ask the jury to consider a criminal defendant's failure to explain or deny the evidence against him. The 5th amendment right against self-incrimination—which would have prohibited the same procedure in a federal court—was held not to apply in a state criminal trial. This holding eventually would be overruled in* Griffin v. California (1965), *and so the majority opinion written by Justice Reed is omitted. The lasting importance of the Justices' side opinions, which are excerpted here, is their debate over how to interpret and define the word "liberty" in the 14th amendment. Does it incorporate and apply to the States all of the particular provisions found in the Bill of Rights? Only some of those federal rights? If only some of them, which ones? How should a judge go about answering these questions? This is called the incorporation doctrine. Concurring, Justice Frankfurter argued for a more gestalt approach to apply to the States those provisions in the Bill of Rights that the Justices deemed essential to "a scheme of ordered liberty." Dissenting, Justice Black argued for a complete and total incorporation. This debate would occupy the Court during most of the decade of the 1960s. In* Duncan v. Louisiana (1968), *which appears in the next Chapter, the majority developed a slightly different definition of "due process" to consider whether the particular procedure was "fundamental to the American scheme of justice." Eventually, nearly all of the guarantees in the Bill of Rights, one by one, were deemed to apply in state criminal proceedings. Thus, Jus-*

*tice Black lost the battle but won the war. Among the first
eight amendments, the eclectic provisions which have not
been incorporated are: 2d amendment right to bear arms;
3d amendment prohibition of forced quartering of troops;
5th amendment right to a grand jury indictment; and the
7th amendment right to a jury in civil suits for more than
$20. Neither the 9th nor the 10th amendment could be
incorporated, by their own terms.*

**Justice Frankfurter:** Between the incorporation of the
Fourteenth Amendment into the Constitution and the beginning
of the present membership of the Court—a period of 70 years—
the scope of that Amendment was passed upon by 43 judges. Of
all these judges, only one, who may respectfully be called an
eccentric exception, ever indicated the belief that the Fourteenth Amendment was a shorthand summary of the first eight
Amendments theretofore limiting only the Federal Government,
and that due process incorporated those eight Amendments as
restrictions upon the powers of the States. Among these judges
were not only those who would have to be included among the
greatest in the history of the Court, but—it is especially relevant to note—they included those whose services in the cause of
human rights and the spirit of freedom are the most conspicuous in our history. It is not invidious to single out Miller, Davis,
Bradley, Waite, Matthews, Gray, Fuller, Holmes, Brandeis,
Stone and Cardozo (to speak only of the dead) as judges who
were alert in safeguarding and promoting the interests of liberty
and human dignity through law. But they were also judges
mindful of the relation of our federal system to a progressively
democratic society and therefore duly regardful of the scope of
authority that was left to the States even after the Civil War.
And so they did not find that the Fourteenth Amendment, concerned as it was with matters fundamental to the pursuit of
justice, fastened upon the States procedural arrangements
which, in the language of Mr. Justice Cardozo, only those who
are "narrow or provincial" would deem essential to "a fair and
enlightened system of justice." To suggest that it is inconsistent
with a truly free society to begin prosecutions without an indictment, to try petty civil cases without the paraphernalia of a
common law jury, to take into consideration that one who has
full opportunity to make a defense remains silent is, in de Tocqueville's phrase, to confound the familiar with the necessary.

The short answer to the suggestion that the provision of the Fourteenth Amendment, which ordains "nor shall any State deprive any person of life, liberty, or property, without due process of law," was a way of saying that every State must thereafter initiate prosecutions through indictment by a grand jury, must have a trial by a jury of 12 in criminal cases, and must have trial by such a jury in common law suits where the amount in controversy exceeds $20, is that it is a strange way of saying it. It would be extraordinarily strange for a Constitution to convey such specific commands in such a roundabout and inexplicit way. After all, an amendment to the Constitution should be read in a "sense most obvious to the common understanding at the time of its adoption. For it was for public adoption that it was proposed."

Those reading the English language with the meaning which it ordinarily conveys, those conversant with the political and legal history of the concept of due process, those sensitive to the relations of the States to the central government as well as the relation of some of the provisions of the Bill of Rights to the process of justice, would hardly recognize the Fourteenth Amendment as a cover for the various explicit provisions of the first eight Amendments. Some of these are enduring reflections of experience with human nature, while some express the restricted views of Eighteenth-Century England regarding the best methods for the ascertainment of facts. The notion that the Fourteenth Amendment was a covert way of imposing upon the States all the rules which it seemed important to Eighteenth-Century statesmen to write into the Federal Amendments, was rejected by judges who were themselves witnesses of the process by which the Fourteenth Amendment became part of the Constitution.

Arguments that may now be adduced to prove that the first eight Amendments were concealed within the historic phrasing of the Fourteenth Amendment were not unknown at the time of its adoption. A surer estimate of their bearing was possible for judges at the time than distorting distance is likely to vouchsafe. Any evidence of design or purpose not contemporaneously known could hardly have influenced those who ratified the Amendment. Remarks of a particular proponent of the Amendment, no matter how influential, are not to be deemed part of the Amendment. What was submitted for ratification was his proposal, not his speech. Thus, at the time of the ratification of the Fourteenth Amendment the constitutions of nearly half of the ratifying States did not have the rigorous requirements of the Fifth Amendment for instituting criminal proceedings through a grand jury. It could hardly have occurred to these States that by ratifying the Amendment they uprooted their established methods for prosecuting crime and fastened upon themselves a new prosecutorial system.

Indeed, the suggestion that the Fourteenth Amendment incorporates the first eight Amendments as such is not unambiguously urged. Even the boldest innovator would shrink from that suggestion. There is suggested merely a selective incorporation of the first eight Amendments into the Fourteenth Amendment. Some are in and some are out, but we are left in the dark as to which are in and which are out. Nor are we given the calculus for determining which go in and which stay out. If the basis of selection is merely that those provisions of the first eight Amendments are incorporated which commend themselves to individual justices as indispensable to the dignity and happiness of a free man, we are thrown back to a merely subjective test. In the history of thought "natural law" has a much longer and much better founded meaning and justification than such subjective selection of the first eight Amendments for incorporation into the Fourteenth. If all that is meant is that due process contains within itself certain minimal standards which are "of the very essence of a scheme of ordered liberty," in the felicitous phrasing of Mr. Justice Cardozo, putting upon this Court the duty of applying these standards from time to time, then we have merely arrived at the insight which our predecessors long ago expressed. We are called upon to apply to the difficult issues of our own day the wisdom afforded by the great opinions in this field. This guidance bids us to be duly mindful of the heritage of the past, with its great lessons of how liberties are won and how they are lost. As judges charged with the delicate task of subjecting the government of a continent to the Rule of Law we must be particularly mindful that it is "a constitution we are expounding," so that it should not be imprisoned in what are merely legal forms even though they have the sanction of the Eighteenth Century.

It may not be amiss to restate the pervasive function of the Fourteenth Amendment in exacting from the States observance of basic liberties. The Amendment neither comprehends the specific provisions by which the founders deemed it appropriate to restrict the federal government nor is it confined to them. The Due Process Clause of the Fourteenth Amendment has an independent potency, precisely as does the Due Process Clause of the Fifth Amendment in relation to the Federal Government. It ought not to require argument to reject the notion that due process of law meant one thing in the Fifth Amendment and another in the Fourteenth. The Fifth Amendment precludes deprivation of "life, liberty, or property, without due process of law." Are Madison and his contemporaries in the framing of the Bill of Rights to be charged with writing into it a meaningless clause? To consider "due process of law" as merely a shorthand statement of other specific clauses in the same amendment is to attribute to the authors and proponents of this Amendment ignorance of, or indifference to, a historic conception which was one of the great instruments in the arsenal of constitutional freedom which the Bill of Rights was to protect and strengthen.

A construction which gives to due process no independent function but turns it into a summary of the specific provisions of the Bill of Rights would, as has been noted, tear up by the roots much of the fabric of law in the several States, and would deprive the States of opportunity for reforms in legal process designed for extending the area of freedom. It would assume that no other abuses would reveal themselves in the course of time than those which had become manifest in 1791. Such a view not only disregards the historic meaning of "due process." It leads inevitably to a warped construction of specific provisions of the Bill of Rights to bring within their scope conduct clearly condemned by due process but not easily fitting into the pigeon-holes of the specific provisions. It seems pretty late in the day to suggest that a phrase so laden with historic meaning should be given an improvised content consisting of some but not all of the provisions of the first eight Amendments, selected on an undefined basis, with improvisation of content for the provisions so selected.

And so, when, as in a case like the present, a conviction in a State court is here for review under a claim that a right protected by the Due Process Clause of the Fourteenth Amendment has been denied, the issue is not whether an infraction of one of the specific provisions of the first eight Amendments is disclosed by the record. The relevant question is whether the criminal proceedings which resulted in conviction deprived the accused of the due process of law to which the United States Constitution entitled him. Judicial review of that guaranty of the Fourteenth Amendment inescapably imposes upon this Court an exercise of judgment upon the whole course of the proceedings in order to ascertain whether they offend those canons of decency and fairness which express the notions of justice of English-speaking peoples even toward those charged with the most heinous offenses. These standards of justice are not authoritatively formulated anywhere as though they were prescriptions in a pharmacopoeia. But neither does the application of the Due Process Clause imply that judges are wholly at large. The judicial judgment in applying the Due Process Clause must move within the limits of accepted notions of justice and is not to be based upon the idiosyncrasies of a merely personal judgment. The fact that judges among themselves may differ whether in a particular case a trial offends accepted notions of justice is not disproof that general rather than idiosyncratic standards are applied. An important safeguard against such merely individual judgment is an alert deference to the judgment of the State court under review.

**Justice Black:** This decision reasserts a constitutional theory that this Court is endowed by the Constitution with boundless power under "natural law" periodically to expand and contract constitutional standards to conform to the Court's conception of what at a particular time constitutes "civilized decency" and "fundamental principles of liberty and justice." Invoking this rule, the Court concludes that although comment upon testimony in a federal court would violate the Fifth Amendment, identical comment in a state court does not violate today's fashion in civilized decency and fundamentals and is therefore not prohibited by the Federal Constitution as amended.

A case decided in 1908 was the first, as it is the only, decision of this Court which has squarely held that states were free, notwithstanding the Fifth and Fourteenth Amendments, to extort evidence from one accused of crime. I think that decision and the "natural law" theory of the Constitution upon which it relies, degrade the constitutional safeguards of the Bill of Rights and simultaneously appropriate for this Court a broad power which we are not authorized by the Constitution to exercise. My reasons can best be understood by reference to the constitutional, judicial, and general history that preceded and followed that case.

The first 10 amendments were proposed and adopted largely because of fear that Government might unduly interfere with prized individual liberties. The people wanted and demanded a Bill of Rights written into their Constitution. The amendments embodying the Bill of Rights were intended to curb all branches of the Federal Government in the fields touched by the amendments—Legislative, Executive, and Judicial. The Fifth, Sixth, and Eighth Amendments were pointedly aimed at confining exercise of power by courts and judges within precise boundaries, particularly in the procedure used for the trial of criminal cases. Past history provided strong reasons for the apprehensions which brought these procedural amendments into being and attest the wisdom of their adoption. For the fears of arbitrary court action sprang largely from the past use of courts in the imposition of criminal punishments to suppress speech, press, and religion. Hence the constitutional limitations of courts' powers were, in the view of the Founders, essential supplements to the First Amendment, which was itself designed to protect the widest scope for all people to believe and to express the most divergent political, religious, and other views.

But these limitations were not expressly imposed upon state court action. In 1833, Chief Justice John Marshall, speaking for a unanimous Court, specifically held inapplicable to the states that provision of the Fifth Amendment which declares: "nor shall private property be taken for public use, without just compensation." In deciding the particular point raised, the Court there said that it could not hold that the first eight amendments applied to the states. This was the controlling constitutional rule when the Fourteenth Amendment was proposed in 1866.

My study of the historical events that culminated in the Fourteenth Amendment, and the expressions of those who sponsored and favored, as well as those who opposed its submission and passage, persuades me that one of the chief objects that the provisions of the Amendment's first section, separately, and as a whole, were intended to accomplish was to make the Bill of Rights, applicable to the states. With full knowledge of the import of the 1833 decision, the framers and backers of the Fourteenth Amendment proclaimed its purpose to be to overturn the constitutional rule that case had announced. This historical purpose has never received full consideration or exposition in any opinion of this Court interpreting the Amendment.

In construing other constitutional provisions, this Court has almost uniformly followed the precept that "It is never to be forgotten that in the construction of the language of the Constitution, as indeed in all other instances where construction becomes necessary, we are to place ourselves as nearly as possible in the condition of the men who framed that instrument."

Investigation of the cases relied upon to support the conclusion that neither the Fifth Amendment's prohibition of compelled testimony, nor any of the Bill of Rights, applies to the

States, reveals an unexplained departure from this salutary practice. Neither the briefs nor opinions in any of these cases make reference to the legislative and contemporary history for the purpose of demonstrating that those who conceived, shaped, and brought about the adoption of the Fourteenth Amendment intended it to nullify this Court's decision in 1833, and thereby to make the Bill of Rights applicable to the States.

Thus the Court declined and again today declines, to appraise the relevant historical evidence of the intended scope of the first section of the Amendment. Instead it relied upon previous cases, none of which had analyzed the evidence showing that one purpose of those who framed, advocated, and adopted the Amendment had been to make the Bill of Rights applicable to the States. None of the cases relied upon by the Court today made such an analysis.

For this reason, I am attaching to this dissent, an appendix which contains a resume, by no means complete, of the Amendment's history. In my judgment, that history conclusively demonstrates that the language of the first section of the Fourteenth Amendment, taken as a whole, was thought by those responsible for its submission to the people, and by those who opposed its submission, sufficiently explicit to guarantee that thereafter no state could deprive its citizens of the privileges and protections of the Bill of Rights. Whether this Court ever will, or whether it now should, in the light of past decisions, give full effect to what the Amendment was intended to accomplish is not necessarily essential to a decision here. However that may be, our prior decisions, do not prevent our carrying out that purpose, at least to the extent of making applicable to the states, not a mere part, as the Court has, but the full protection of the Fifth Amendment's provision against compelling evidence from an accused to convict him of crime. And I further contend that the "natural law" formula which the Court uses to reach its conclusion in this case should be abandoned as an incongruous excrescence on our Constitution. I believe that formula to be itself a violation of our Constitution, in that it subtly conveys to courts, at the expense of legislatures, ultimate power over public policies in fields where no specific provision of the Constitution limits legislative power. And my belief seems to be in accord with the views expressed by this Court, at least for the first two decades after the Fourteenth Amendment was adopted.

The natural law arguments, so suggestive of the premises on which the present due process formula rest, were flatly rejected by a majority of the Court, in 1873, in the first opinion to construe the three Civil War amendments. The majority of the Court emphatically declined the invitation of counsel to hold that the Fourteenth Amendment subjected all state regulatory legislation to continuous censorship by this Court in order for it to determine whether it collided with this Court's opinion of "natural" right and justice. In effect, that decision rejected the very natural justice formula the Court today embraces. The Court did not meet the question of whether the safeguards of the Bill of Rights were protected against state invasion by the Fourteenth Amendment. And it specifically did not say as the Court now does, that particular provisions of the Bill of Rights could be breached by states in part, but not breached in other respects, according to this Court's notions of "civilized standards," "canons of decency," and "fundamental justice."

I cannot consider the Bill of Rights to be an outworn 18th Century "strait jacket." Its provisions may be thought outdated abstractions by some. And it is true that they were designed to meet ancient evils. But they are the same kind of human evils that have emerged from century to century wherever excessive power is sought by the few at the expense of the many. In my judgment the people of no nation can lose their liberty so long as a Bill of Rights like ours survives and its basic purposes are conscientiously interpreted, enforced and respected so as to afford continuous protection against old, as well as new, devices and practices which might thwart those purposes. I fear to see the consequences of the Court's practice of substituting its own concepts of decency and fundamental justice for the language of the Bill of Rights as its point of departure in interpreting and enforcing that Bill of Rights. If the choice must be between the selective process of the "natural law" approach apply some of the Bill of Rights to the States, or the rule applying none of them, I would choose the selective process. But rather than accept either of these choices, I would follow what I believe was the original purpose of the Fourteenth Amendment—to extend to all the people of the nation the complete protection of the Bill of Rights. To hold that this Court can determine what, if any, provisions of the Bill of Rights will be enforced, and if so to what degree, is to frustrate the great design of a written Constitution.

Conceding the possibility that this Court is now wise enough to improve on the Bill of Rights by substituting natural law concepts for the Bill of Rights, I think the possibility is entirely too speculative to agree to take that course. I would therefore hold in this case that the full protection of the Fifth Amendment's proscription against compelled testimony must be afforded by California. This I would do because of reliance upon the original purpose of the Fourteenth Amendment.

It is an illusory apprehension that literal application of some or all of the provisions of the Bill of Rights to the States would unwisely increase the sum total of the powers of this Court to invalidate state legislation. The Federal Government has not been harmfully burdened by the requirement that enforcement of federal laws affecting civil liberty conform literally to the Bill of Rights. Who would advocate its repeal? It must be conceded, of course, that the natural-law-due-process formula, which the Court today reaffirms, has been interpreted to limit substantially this Court's power to prevent state violations of the individual civil liberties guaranteed by the Bill of Rights. But this formula also has been used in the past and can be used in the future, to license this Court, in considering regulatory legislation, to roam at large in the broad expanses of policy and morals and to trespass, all too freely, on the legislative domain of the States as well as the Federal Government.

The practice has been firmly established, for better or worse, that courts can strike down legislative enactments which violate the Constitution. This process, of course, involves interpretation, and since words can have many meanings, interpretation obviously may result in contraction or extension of the original purpose of a constitutional provision thereby affecting policy. But to pass upon the constitutionality of statutes by looking to the particular standards enumerated in the Bill of Rights and other parts of the Constitution is one thing; to invalidate statutes because of application of "natural law" deemed to be above and undefined by the Constitution is another. "In the one instance, courts proceeding within clearly marked constitutional boundaries seek to execute policies written into the Constitution; in the other they roam at will in the limitless area of their own beliefs as to reasonableness and actually select policies, a responsibility which the Constitution entrusts to the legislative representatives of the people."

*This principle, if firmly established, would work a radical change in our governmental system. It would inaugurate a new era in the American judicial system and in the relations of the national and state governments. It would enable the subordinate Federal courts to supervise and control the official action of the states as if they were "dependencies" or provinces.*

— *John M. Harlan*

## Ex parte Young
## 28 S.Ct. 441, 209 U.S. 123 (1908)

*Although relatively obscure and somewhat obtuse, this case is one of the five most important the Supreme Court has ever decided. The issue was whether a citizen might resort to federal court to sue a state official in order to protect a federal right from being violated by a State. The Minnesota legislature passed a statute reducing railroad fares and imposing severe civil and criminal penalties if the railroads failed to comply. Shareholders of the railroads brought suit in federal court to keep the companies from complying and obtained a federal injunction directing the State Attorney General not to enforce the state law. Faced with a state statute commanding him to enforce the lower rates and a federal court order not to do so, Attorney General Young chose to go to state court to enforce the state law against the railroads. For this, the federal court found Young in contempt, and he was taken into custody by U.S. Marshals. Young took the case to the Supreme Court. The majority, with only the first Justice Harlan dissenting, concluded that the federal court could enter an injunction forbidding the State from acting, despite the 11th amendment, which provides that federal courts have no jurisdiction to hear suits by citizens (the shareholders) against a State (the Minnesota Attorney General). Justice Peckham relied on a legal fiction to reason that if the state Attorney General was acting pursuant to a state law that was unconstitutional under the 14th amendment he was not acting on behalf of the State for purposes of the 11th amendment. Just how the underlying dispute could be against "Mr." Young, for purposes of the 11th amendment, and against "Attorney General"*

*Young, for purposes of the 14th amendment, is downright metaphysical. Justice Harlan saw through the fiction and foresaw the implications for federalism. The fiction made it possible for federal courts, including the Supreme Court, to enforce the Supremacy Clause, Article VI, cl. 2, and to enjoin all levels of state government from violating federal rights. Without it, such famous federal cases as* Brown v. Bd. of Educ. (1954) *could not have been possible. Critics of the federal courts, however, have complained of the modern regime of "government by federal court injunction" by which a single judge sitting on a lower federal court can supervise and control such traditional state functions as schools and prisons.*

**Justice Peckham:** We recognize and appreciate to the fullest extent the very great importance of this case, not only to the parties now before the court, but also to the great mass of the citizens of this country, all of whom are interested in the practical working of the courts of justice throughout the land, both Federal and state, and in the proper exercise of the jurisdiction of the Federal courts, as limited and controlled by the Federal Constitution and the laws of Congress. The question of jurisdiction, whether of the lower federal circuit court or of this court, is frequently a delicate matter to deal with, and it is especially so in this case, where the material and most important objection to the jurisdiction of the circuit court is the assertion that the suit is, in effect, against one of the states of the Union. It is a question, however, which we are called upon, and which it is our duty to decide.

We conclude that the circuit court had jurisdiction in the case before it, because it involved the decision of Federal questions arising under the Constitution of the United States.

We have upon this record the case of an allegedly unconstitutional act of the state legislature and an intention by the attorney general of the state to endeavor to enforce its provisions, to the injury of the company, in compelling it, at great expense, to defend legal proceedings of a complicated and unusual character, and involving questions of vast importance to all employees and officers of the company, as well as to the company itself. The question that arises is whether there is a remedy that the parties interested may resort to, by going into a Federal court of equity, in a case involving a violation of the Federal Constitution, and obtaining a judicial investigation of the problem, and, pending its solution, obtain freedom from suits, civil or criminal, by a temporary injunction, and, if the question be finally decided favorably to the contention of the company, a permanent injunction restraining all such actions or proceedings.

This inquiry necessitates an examination of the most material and important objection made to the jurisdiction of the circuit court, the objection being that the suit is, in effect, one against the state of Minnesota, and that the injunction issued against the attorney general illegally prohibits state action, either criminal or civil, to enforce obedience to the statutes of the state. This objection is to be considered with reference to the 11th and 14th Amendments to the Federal Constitution. The 11th Amendment prohibits the commencement or prosecution of any suit against one of the United States by citizens of another state or citizens or subjects of any foreign state. The 14th Amendment provides that no state shall deprive any person of life, liberty, or property without due process of law, nor shall it deny to any person within its jurisdiction the equal protection of the laws.

The case before the circuit court proceeded upon the theory that the orders and acts heretofore mentioned would, if enforced, violate rights of the complainants protected by the latter amendment. We think that whatever the rights of complainants may be, they are largely founded upon that Amendment, but a decision of this case does not require an examination or decision of the question whether its adoption in any way altered or limited the effect of the earlier Amendment. We may assume that each exists in full force, and that we must give to the 11th Amendment all the effect it naturally would have, without cutting it down or rendering its meaning any more narrow than the language, fairly interpreted, would warrant. It applies to a suit brought against a state by one of its own citizens, as well as to a suit brought by a citizen of another state. It was adopted after the controversial decision of this court in 1792, where it was held that a state might be sued by a citizen of another state.

The prior cases we have reviewed do not include one exactly like this under discussion. They serve to illustrate the principles upon which many cases have been decided. The various authorities we have referred to furnish ample justification for the assertion that individuals who, as officers of the state, are clothed with some duty in regard to the enforcement of the laws of the state, and who threaten and are about to commence proceedings, either of a civil or criminal nature, to enforce against parties affected an unconstitutional act, violating the Federal Constitution, may be enjoined by a Federal court of equity from such action.

In making an officer of the state a party defendant in a suit to enjoin the enforcement of an act alleged to be unconstitutional, it is plain that such officer must have some connection with the enforcement of the act, or else it is merely making him a party as a representative of the state, and thereby attempting to make the state a party.

It is objected that as the Minnesota statute does not specifically make it the duty of the attorney general (assuming he has that general right) to enforce it, he has, under such circumstances, a full general discretion whether to attempt its enforcement or not, and the court cannot interfere to control him as attorney general in the exercise of his discretion.

In our view there is no interference with his discretion under the facts herein. There is no doubt that the court cannot control the actual exercise of the discretion of an officer. The general discretion regarding the enforcement of the laws when and as he deems appropriate is not interfered with by an injunction which restrains the state officer from taking any steps towards the enforcement of an unconstitutional enactment, to the injury of complainant. In such case no affirmative action of any nature is directed, and the officer is simply prohibited from doing an act which he had no legal right to do. An injunction to prevent him from doing that which he has no legal right to do is not an interference with the discretion of an officer.

It is also argued that the only proceeding which the attorney general could take to enforce the statute, so far as his office is concerned, was one by mandamus, which would be commenced by the state, in its sovereign and governmental character, and that the right to bring such action is a necessary attribute of a sovereign government. It is contended that the complainants do not complain and they care nothing about any action which Mr. Young might take or bring as an ordinary individual, but that he was complained of as an officer, to whose discretion is confided the use of the name of the state of Minnesota so far as litigation is concerned, and that when or how he shall use it is a matter resting in his discretion and cannot be controlled by any court.

The answer to all this is the same as made in every case where an official claims to be acting under the authority of the state. The act to be enforced is alleged to be unconstitutional; and if it be so, the use of the name of the state to enforce an unconstitutional act to the injury of complainants is a proceeding without the authority of, and one which does not affect, the state in its sovereign or governmental capacity. It is simply an illegal act upon the part of a state official in attempting, by the use of the name of the state, to enforce a legislative enactment which is void because unconstitutional. If the act which the state attorney general seeks to enforce be a violation of the Federal Constitution, the officer, in proceeding under such enactment, comes into conflict with the superior authority of that Constitution, and he is in that case stripped of his official or representative character and is subjected in his person to the consequences of his individual conduct. The state has no power to impart to him any immunity from responsibility to the supreme authority of the United States.

It is further objected (and the objection really forms part of the contention that the state cannot be sued) that a federal court of equity has no jurisdiction to enjoin criminal proceedings, by indictment or otherwise, under the state law. This, as a general rule, is true. But there are exceptions. When such indictment or proceeding is brought to enforce an alleged unconstitutional statute, which is the subject-matter of inquiry in a suit already pending in a Federal court, the latter court, having first obtained jurisdiction over the subject-matter, has the right, in both civil and criminal cases, to hold and maintain such jurisdiction, to the exclusion of all other courts, until its duty is fully performed.

It is still further objected that there is a plain and adequate remedy at law open to the complainants, and that a court of equity, therefore, has no jurisdiction in such case. It has been suggested that the proper way to test the constitutionality of the act is to disobey it, at least once, after which the company might obey the act pending subsequent proceedings to test its validity. But in the event of a single violation the prosecutor might not avail himself of the opportunity to make the test, as obedience to the law was thereafter continued, and he might think it unnecessary to start an inquiry. If, however, he should do so while the company was thereafter obeying the law, several years might elapse before there was a final determination of the question, and, if it should be determined that the law was invalid, the property of the company would have been taken during that time without due process of law, and there would be no possibility of its recovery.

Another obstacle to making the test on the part of the company might be to find an agent or employee who would disobey the law, with a possible fine and imprisonment staring him in the face if the act should be held valid. It is true the company might pay the fine, but the imprisonment the agent would have to suffer personally. It would not be wonderful if, under such circumstances, there would not be a crowd of agents offering to disobey the law. The wonder would be that a single agent should be found ready to take the risk. If, however, one should be found, and the State prosecutor should elect to proceed against him, the defense that the act was invalid, because the rates established by it were too low, would require a long and difficult examination of quite complicated facts upon which the validity of the act depended.

We do not say the company could not interpose this defense in an action to recover penalties or upon the trial of an indictment, but the facility of proving it in either case falls so far below that which would obtain in a court of equity that comparison is scarcely possible. To await proceedings against the company in a state court, grounded upon a disobedience of the act, and then, if necessary, obtain a review in this court by writ of error to the highest state court, would place the company in peril of large loss and its agents in great risk of fines and imprisonment if it should be finally determined that the act was valid. This risk the company ought not to be required to take. Over eleven thousand millions of dollars, it is estimated, are invested in railroad property, owned by many thousands of people, who are scattered over the whole country, from ocean to ocean, and they are entitled to equal protection from the laws and from the courts, with the owners of all other kinds of property, no more, no less. The courts having jurisdiction, Federal or state, should, at all times, be opened to them as well as to others, for the purpose of protecting their property and their legal rights.

All the objections to a remedy at law as being plainly inadequate are obviated by a suit in equity, making all who are directly interested parties to the suit, and enjoining the enforcement of the act until the decision of the court upon the legal question. It cannot be to the real interest of anyone to injure or cripple the resources of the railroad companies of the country, because the prosperity of both the railroads and the country is most intimately connected. The question of sufficiency of rates is important and controlling; and, being of a judicial nature, it ought to be settled at the earliest moment by some court, and when a Federal court first obtains jurisdiction it ought, on general principles of jurisprudence, to be permitted to finish the inquiry and make a conclusive judgment, to the exclusion of all other courts.

Finally, it is objected that the necessary result of upholding this suit in the circuit court will be to draw to the lower Federal courts a great flood of litigation of this character, where one Federal judge would have it in his power to enjoin proceedings by state officials to enforce the legislative acts of the state, either by criminal or civil actions. To this it may be answered, in the first place, that no injunction ought to be granted unless in a case reasonably free from doubt. We think such rule is, and will be, followed by all the judges of the Federal courts.

And, again, it must be remembered that jurisdiction of this general character has, in fact, been exercised by Federal courts from the earliest time up to the present; the only difference in regard to the case in hand being that in this case the injury complained of is the threatened commencement of suits, civil or criminal, to enforce the Minnesota act, instead of an actual and direct trespass upon or interference with tangible property. A bill filed to prevent the commencement of suits to enforce an unconstitutional act, under the circumstances already mentioned, is no new invention. The difference between an actual and direct interference with tangible property and the enjoining of state officers from enforcing an unconstitutional act, is not of a radical nature, and does not extend, in truth, the jurisdiction of the courts. Where the state official, instead of directly interfering with tangible property, is about to commence suits which have for their object the enforcement of an act which violates the Federal Constitution, to the great and irreparable injury of the complainants, he is seeking the same justification from the authority of the state as in other cases. The sovereignty of the state is, in reality, no more involved in one case than in the other. The state cannot, in either case, impart to the official immunity from responsibility to the supreme authority of the United States.

This supreme authority, which arises from the specific provisions of the Constitution itself, is nowhere more fully illustrated than in the series of decisions under the Federal habeas corpus statute, in some of which cases persons in the custody of state officers for alleged crimes against the state have been taken from that custody and discharged by a Federal court or judge, because the imprisonment was adjudged to be in violation of the Federal Constitution. The right to so discharge has not been doubted by this court, and it has never been supposed there was any suit against the state by reason of serving the writ upon one of the officers of the state in whose custody the person was found.

It is somewhat difficult to appreciate the distinction which, while admitting that the taking of such a person from the custody of the state by virtue of service of the writ on the state officer in whose custody he is found is not a suit against the state, and yet service of a writ on the attorney general, to prevent his enforcing an unconstitutional enactment of a state legislature, is a suit against the state. There is nothing in the case before us that ought properly to breed hostility to the customary operation of Federal courts of justice in cases of this character.

**Justice Harlan:** Let it be observed that the suit instituted in the circuit court of the United States was, as to the defendant Young, one against him as, and only because he was, attorney general of Minnesota. No relief was sought against him individually, but only in his capacity as attorney general. And the manifest, indeed the avowed and admitted, object of seeking such relief, was to tie the hands of the state so that it could not in any manner or by any mode of proceeding, in its own courts, test the validity of the statutes and orders in question. It would therefore seem clear that within the true meaning of the 11th Amendment the suit brought in the Federal court was one, in legal effect, against the state—as much so as if the state had been formally named on the record as a party—and therefore it was a suit to which, under the Amendment, so far as the state or its attorney general was concerned, the judicial power of the United States did not and could not extend. If this proposition be sound it will follow—indeed, it is conceded that if, so far as relief is sought against the attorney general of Minnesota, this be a suit against the state—then, the order of the Federal court enjoining that officer from taking any action, suit, step, or proceeding to compel the railway company to obey the Minnesota statute was beyond the jurisdiction of that court and wholly void; in which case, that officer was at liberty to proceed in the discharge of his official duties as defined by the laws of the state, and the order adjudging him to be in contempt for bringing the *mandamus* proceeding in the state court was a nullity.

The fact that the Federal circuit court had, prior to the institution of the mandamus suit in the state court, preliminarily (but not finally) held the statutes of Minnesota and the orders of its railroad and warehouse commission in question to be in violation of the Constitution of the United States, was no reason why that court should have laid violent hands upon the attorney general of Minnesota, and by its orders have deprived the state of the services of its constitutional law officer in its own courts. Yet that is what was done by the Federal circuit court; for the intangible thing called a state, however extensive its powers, can never appear or be represented or known in any court in a litigated case, except by and through its officers. When, therefore, the Federal court forbade the defendant Young, as attorney general of Minnesota, from taking any action, suit, step, or proceeding whatever looking to the enforcement of the statutes in question, it said in effect to the state of Minnesota: "It is true that the powers not delegated to the United States by the Constitution, nor prohibited by it to the states, are reserved to the states respectively or to its people, and it is true that, under the Constitution, the judicial power of the United States does not extend to any suit brought against a state by a citizen of another state or by a citizen or subject of a foreign state, yet the Federal court adjudges that you, the state, although a sovereign for many important governmental purposes, shall not appear in your own courts, by your law officer, with the view of enforcing, or even for determining the validity of, the state enactments which the Federal court has, upon a preliminary hearing, declared to be in violation of the Constitution of the United States."

This principle, if firmly established, would work a radical change in our governmental system. It would inaugurate a new era in the American judicial system and in the relations of the national and state governments. It would enable the subordinate Federal courts to supervise and control the official action of the states as if they were "dependencies" or provinces. It would place the states of the Union in a condition of inferiority never dreamed of when the Constitution was adopted or when the 11th Amendment was made a part of the supreme law of the land. I cannot suppose that the great men who framed the Constitution ever thought the time would come when a subordinate Federal court, having no power to compel a state, in its corporate capacity, to appear before it as a litigant, would yet assume to deprive a state of the right to be represented in its own courts by its regular law officer. That is what the court below did, as to Minnesota, when it adjudged that the appearance of the defendant Young in the state court, as the attorney general of Minnesota, representing his state as its chief law officer, was a contempt of the authority of the Federal court, punishable by fine and imprisonment. Too little consequence has been attached to the fact that the courts of the states are under an obligation equally strong with that resting upon the courts of the Union to respect and enforce the provisions of the Federal Constitution as the supreme law of the land, and to guard rights secured or guaranteed by that instrument. We must assume—a decent respect for the states requires us to assume—that the state courts will enforce every right secured by the Constitution. If they fail to do so, the party complaining has a clear remedy for the protection of his rights; for he can come by writ of error, in an orderly, judicial way, from the highest court of the state to this tribunal for redress in respect of every right granted or secured by that instrument and denied by the state court.

Upon the fullest consideration and after a careful examination of the authorities, my mind has been brought to the conclusion that no case heretofore determined by this court requires us to hold that the Federal circuit court had authority to forbid the attorney general of Minnesota from representing the state in the *mandamus* suit in the state court, or to adjudge that he was in contempt and liable to be fined and imprisoned simply because of his having, as attorney general, brought that suit for the state in one of its courts. On the contrary, my conviction is very strong that, if regard be had to former utterances of this court, the suit in the Federal court, in respect of the relief sought therein against Young, in his official capacity, as attorney general of Minnesota, is to be deemed a suit against the state, of which the circuit court of the United States could not take cognizance without violating the 11th Amendment of the Constitution. Neither the words nor the policy of the 11th Amendment will, under our former decisions, justify any order of a Federal court the necessary effect of which will be to exclude a state from its own courts. Such an order, attended by such results, cannot, I submit, be sustained consistently with the powers which the states, according to the uniform declarations of this court, possess under the Constitution. I am justified, by what this court has heretofore declared, in now saying that the men who framed the Constitution, and who caused the adoption of the 11th Amendment, would have been amazed by the suggestion that a state of the Union can be prevented, by an order of a subordinate Federal court, from being represented by its attorney general in a suit brought by it in one of its own courts; and that such an order would be inconsistent with the dignity of the states as involved in their constitutional immunity from the judicial process of the Federal courts (except in the limited cases in which they may constitutionally be made parties in this court), and would be attended by most pernicious results.

*One familiar with the profound debates that ushered our Federal Constitution into existence is bound to respect those who remain loyal to the ideals and dreams of "Our Federalism."*

— *Hugo L. Black*

## Younger v. Harris
### 91 S.Ct. 746, 401 U.S. 37 (1971)

*The leading scholar on the subject has noted there is no more controversial doctrine in the federal courts today than the doctrine of "Our Federalism." Justice Black's heartfelt phrase stands for the proposition that federal courts must refrain from hearing constitutional challenges to state laws when federal action would be an improper intrusion on the sovereignty of the State to enforce its laws in its own courts. Exceptions to this principle are exceedingly rare. The doctrine has been extended, some argue beyond its logic, in numerous later decisions obliging a federal court to defer to on-going state court proceedings and to withhold federal relief thus consigning litigants and their U.S. constitutional rights to state courts and state judges. But in fact, after the Supreme Court ordered this federal case dismissed, the California courts held the state syndicalism law was invalid. "Our Federalism" must be an important constitutional value to prevent a federal court from vindicating 1st amendment preferred freedoms.*

**Justice Black:** John Harris, Jr., was indicted in a California state court, charged with violation of the California Criminal Syndicalism Act. He then filed a civil complaint in the Federal District Court, asking that court to enjoin Younger, the District Attorney of Los Angeles County, from prosecuting him, and alleging that the prosecution and even the presence of the Act inhibited him in the exercise of his rights of free speech and press, rights guaranteed him by the First and Fourteenth Amendments. A three-judge Federal District Court held that it had jurisdiction and power to restrain the District Attorney from prosecuting, held that the State's Criminal Syndicalism Act was void for vagueness and overbreadth in violation of the First and Fourteenth Amendments, and accordingly restrained the District Attorney from "further prosecution of the currently pending action against plaintiff Harris for alleged violation of the Act."

Harris has been indicted, and was actually being prosecuted by California for a violation of its Criminal Syndicalism Act at the time this suit was filed. He thus has an acute, live controversy with the State and its prosecutor. A federal lawsuit to stop a prosecution in a state court is a serious matter. And persons having no fears of state prosecution except those that are imaginary or speculative, are not to be accepted as appropriate plaintiffs in such cases. Since Harris is actually being prosecuted under the challenged laws, however, we proceed with him as a proper party.

Since the beginning of this country's history Congress has, subject to few exceptions, manifested a desire to permit state courts to try state cases free from interference by federal courts. In 1793 an Act unconditionally provided: "Nor shall a writ of injunction be granted to stay proceedings in any court of a state." A comparison of the 1793 Act with its present-day successor, graphically illustrates how few and minor have been the exceptions granted from the flat, prohibitory language of the old Act. During all this lapse of years from 1793 to the present, the statutory exceptions to the 1793 congressional enactment have been only three. In addition, a judicial exception to the longstanding policy evidenced by the statute has been made where a person about to be prosecuted in a state court can show that he will, if the proceeding in the state court is not enjoined, suffer irreparable damages.

The precise reasons for this longstanding public policy against federal court interference with state court proceedings have never been specifically identified but the primary sources of the policy are plain. One is the basic doctrine of equity jurisprudence that courts of equity should not act, and particularly should not act to restrain a criminal prosecution, when the moving party has an adequate remedy at law and will not suffer irreparable injury if denied equitable relief. The doctrine may originally have grown out of circumstances peculiar to the English judicial system and not applicable in this country, but its fundamental purpose of restraining equity jurisdiction within narrow limits is equally important under our Constitution, in order to prevent erosion of the role of the jury and avoid a duplication of legal proceedings and legal sanctions where a single suit would be adequate to protect the rights asserted.

This underlying reason for restraining courts of equity from interfering with criminal prosecutions is reinforced by an even more vital consideration, the notion of "comity," that is, a proper respect for state functions, a recognition of the fact that the entire country is made up of a Union of separate state governments, and a continuance of the belief that the National Government will fare best if the States and their institutions are left free to perform their separate functions in their separate ways. This, perhaps for lack of a better and clearer way to describe it, is referred to by many as "Our Federalism," and one familiar with the profound debates that ushered our Federal Constitution into existence is bound to respect those who remain loyal to the ideals and dreams of "Our Federalism." The concept does not mean blind deference to "States' Rights" any more than it means centralization of control over every important issue in our National Government and its courts. The Framers rejected both these courses. What the concept does represent is a system in which there is sensitivity to the legitimate interests of both State and National Governments, and in which the National Government, anxious though it may be to vindicate and protect federal rights and federal interests, always endeavors to do so in ways that will not unduly interfere with the legitimate activities of the States. It should never be forgotten that this slogan, "Our Federalism," born in the early struggling days of our Union of States, occupies a highly important place in our Nation's history and its future.

This brief discussion should be enough to suggest some of the reasons why it has been perfectly natural for our cases to repeat time and time again that the normal thing to do when federal courts are asked to enjoin pending proceedings in state courts is not to issue such injunctions. These principles have been repeatedly followed and reaffirmed in other cases involving threatened prosecutions.

In all of these cases the Court stressed the importance of showing irreparable injury, the traditional prerequisite to obtaining an injunction. In addition, however, the Court also made clear that in view of the fundamental policy against federal interference with state criminal prosecutions, even irreparable injury is insufficient unless it is "both great and immediate." Certain types of injury, in particular, the cost, anxiety, and inconvenience of having to defend against a single criminal prosecution, could not by themselves be considered "irreparable" in the special legal sense of that term. Instead, the threat to the plaintiff's federally protected rights must be one that cannot be eliminated by his defense against a single criminal prosecution.

It is against the background of these principles that we must judge the propriety of an injunction under the circumstances of the present case. Here a proceeding was already pending in the state court, affording Harris an opportunity to raise his constitutional claims. There is no suggestion that this single prosecution against Harris is brought in bad faith or is only one of a series of repeated prosecutions to which he will be subjected. In other words, the injury that Harris faces is solely "that incidental to every criminal proceeding brought lawfully and in good faith," and therefore under the settled doctrine we have already described he is not entitled to equitable relief "even if such statutes are unconstitutional."

It is undoubtedly true, as the Court stated in 1965, that "a criminal prosecution under a statute regulating expression usually involves imponderables and contingencies that themselves may inhibit the full exercise of First Amendment freedoms." But this sort of "chilling effect," should not by itself justify federal intervention. In the first place, the chilling effect cannot be satisfactorily eliminated by federal injunctive relief. In that case itself the Court stated that the injunction to be issued there could be lifted if the State obtained an "acceptable limiting construction" from the state courts. The Court then made clear that once this was done, prosecutions could then be brought for conduct occurring before the narrowing construction was made, and proper convictions could stand so long as the defendants were not deprived of fair warning. The kind of relief granted in that case thus does not effectively eliminate uncertainty as to the coverage of the state statute and leaves most citizens with virtually the same doubts as before regarding the danger that their conduct might eventually be subjected to criminal sanctions. The chilling effect can, of course, be eliminated by an injunction that would prohibit any prosecution whatever for conduct occurring prior to a satisfactory rewriting of the statute. But the States would then be stripped of all power to prosecute even the socially dangerous and constitutionally unprotected conduct that had been covered by the statute, until a new statute could be passed by the state legislature and approved by the federal courts in potentially lengthy trial and appellate proceedings. Thus, in that case itself the Court carefully reaffirmed the principle that even in the direct prosecution in the State's own courts, a valid narrowing construction can be applied to conduct occurring prior to the date when the narrowing construction was made, in the absence of fair warning problems.

Moreover, the existence of a "chilling effect," even in the area of First Amendment rights, has never been considered a sufficient basis, in and of itself, for prohibiting state action. Where a statute does not directly abridge free speech, but—while regulating a subject within the State's power—tends to have the incidental effect of inhibiting First Amendment rights, it is well settled that the statute can be upheld if the effect on speech is minor in relation to the need for control of the conduct and the lack of alternative means for doing so. Just as the incidental "chilling effect" of such statutes does not automatically render them unconstitutional, so the chilling effect that admittedly can result from the very existence of certain laws on the statute books does not in itself justify prohibiting the State from carrying out the important and necessary task of enforcing these laws against socially harmful conduct that the State believes in good faith to be punishable under its laws and the Constitution.

Beyond all this is another, more basic consideration. Procedures for testing the constitutionality of a statute "on its face" in the manner apparently contemplated by our 1965 decision, and for then enjoining all action to enforce the statute until the State can obtain court approval for a modified version, are fundamentally at odds with the function of the federal courts in our constitutional plan. The power and duty of the judiciary to declare laws unconstitutional is in the final analysis derived from its responsibility for resolving concrete disputes brought before the courts for decision; a statute apparently governing a dispute cannot be applied by judges, consistently with their obligations under the Supremacy Clause, when such an application of the statute would conflict with the Constitution. But this vital responsibility, broad as it is, does not amount to an unlimited power to survey the statute books and pass judgment on laws before the courts are called upon to enforce them. Ever since the Constitutional Convention rejected a proposal for having members of the Supreme Court render advice concerning pending legislation it has been clear that, even when suits of this kind involve a "case or controversy" sufficient to satisfy the requirements of Article III of the Constitution, the task of analyzing a proposed statute, pinpointing its deficiencies, and requiring correction of these deficiencies before the statute is put into effect, is rarely if ever an appropriate task for the judiciary. The combination of the relative remoteness of the controversy, the impact on the legislative process of the relief sought, and above all the speculative and amorphous nature of the required line-by-line analysis of detailed statutes, ordinarily results in a kind of case that is wholly unsatisfactory for deciding constitutional questions, whichever way they might be decided. In light of this fundamental conception of the Framers as to the proper place of the federal courts in the governmental processes of passing and enforcing laws, it can seldom be appropriate for these courts to exercise any such power of prior approval or veto over the legislative process.

For these reasons, fundamental not only to our federal system but also to the basic functions of the Judicial Branch of the National Government under our Constitution, we hold that our 1965 decision should not be regarded as having upset the settled doctrines that have always confined very narrowly the availability of injunctive relief against state criminal prosecutions. We do not think that opinion stands for the proposition that a federal court can properly enjoin enforcement of a statute solely on the basis of a showing that the statute "on its face" abridges First Amendment rights. There may, of course, be extraordinary circumstances in which the necessary irreparable injury can be shown even in the absence of the usual prerequisites of bad faith and harassment. For example, in an earlier decision, we indicated: "It is of course conceivable that a statute might be flagrantly and patently violative of express constitutional prohibitions in every clause, sentence and paragraph, and in whatever manner and against whomever an effort might be made to apply it." Other unusual situations calling for federal intervention might also arise, but there is no point in our attempting now to specify what they might be. It is sufficient for purposes of the present case to hold, as we do, that the possible unconstitutionality of a statute "on its face" does not in itself justify an injunction against good-faith attempts to enforce it, and that appellee Harris has failed to make any showing of bad faith, harassment, or any other unusual circumstance that would call for equitable relief.

*From this day forward, I no longer shall tinker with the machinery of death. For more than 20 years I have endeavored—indeed, I have struggled—along with a majority of this Court, to develop procedural and substantive rules that would lend more than the mere appearance of fairness to the death penalty endeavor.*

— *Harry A. Blackmun*

## Callins v. Collins
### 114 S.Ct. 1127, 510 U.S. 1141 (1994)

*Justice Blackmun reveals his intellectual, moral, and emotional struggle to follow the Constitution in death penalty cases and declares, after 20 years, that he and the Court have failed. Because he cannot reconcile the two competing demands in the Constitution—the demand for consistency among all cases and the demand for mercy in individual cases—he goes on record to announce that he will no longer play a role in these macabre dramas. He retired from the Court a few months later. This opinion reveals something of what it must be like to be on the Supreme Court and illustrates a judge's conflict to know his mind and to follow his heart. One of the Court's most important death penalty decisions is included in Chapter Five.*

**Justice Blackmun:** On February 23, 1994, at approximately 1:00 a.m., Bruce Edwin Callins will be executed by the State of Texas. Intravenous tubes attached to his arms will carry the instrument of death, a toxic fluid designed specifically for the purpose of killing human beings. The witnesses, standing a few feet away, will behold Callins, no longer a defendant, an appellant, or a petitioner, but a man, strapped to a gurney, and seconds away from extinction.

Within days, or perhaps hours, the memory of Callins will begin to fade. The wheels of justice will churn again, and somewhere, another jury or another judge will have the unenviable task of determining whether some human being is to live or die. We hope, of course, that the defendant whose life is at risk will be represented by competent counsel—someone who is inspired by the awareness that a less-than-vigorous defense truly could have fatal consequences for the defendant. We hope that the attorney will investigate all aspects of the case, follow all evidentiary and procedural rules, and appear before a judge who is still committed to the protection of defendants' rights—even now, as the prospect of meaningful judicial oversight has diminished. In the same vein, we hope that the prosecution, in urging the penalty of death, will have exercised its discretion wisely, free from bias, prejudice, or political motive, and will be humbled, rather than emboldened, by the awesome authority conferred by the State.

But even if we can feel confident that these actors will fulfill their roles to the best of their human ability, our collective conscience will remain uneasy. Twenty years have passed since this Court declared that the death penalty must be imposed fairly and with reasonable consistency, or not at all and, despite the effort of the States and courts to devise legal formulas and procedural rules to meet this daunting challenge, the death penalty remains fraught with arbitrariness, discrimination, caprice, and mistake. This is not to say that the problems with the death penalty today are identical to those that were present 20 years ago. Rather, the problems that were pursued down one hole with procedural rules and verbal formulas have come to the surface somewhere else, just as virulent and pernicious as they were in their original form. Experience has taught us that the constitutional goal of eliminating arbitrariness and discrimination from the administration of death can never be achieved without compromising an equally essential component of fundamental fairness—individualized sentencing.

It is tempting, when faced with conflicting constitutional commands, to sacrifice one for the other or to assume that an acceptable balance between them already has been struck. In the context of the death penalty, however, such jurisprudential maneuvers are wholly inappropriate. The death penalty must be imposed, this Court has written, "fairly, and with reasonable consistency, or not at all."

To be fair, a capital sentencing scheme must treat each person convicted of a capital offense with that "degree of respect due the uniqueness of the individual." That means affording the sentencer the power and discretion to grant mercy in a particular case, and providing avenues for the consideration of any and all relevant mitigating evidence that would justify a sentence less than death. Reasonable consistency, on the other hand, requires that the death penalty be inflicted evenhandedly, in accordance with reason and objective standards, rather than by whim, caprice, or prejudice. Finally, because human error is inevitable, and because our criminal justice system is less than perfect, searching appellate review of death sentences and their underlying convictions is a prerequisite to a constitutional death penalty scheme.

On their face, these goals of individual fairness, reasonable consistency, and absence of error appear to be attainable: Courts are in the very business of erecting procedural devices from which fair, equitable, and reliable outcomes are presumed to flow. Yet, in the death penalty area, this Court, in my view, has engaged in a futile effort to balance these constitutional demands, and now is retreating not only from the promise of consistency and rationality, but from the requirement of individualized sentencing as well. Having virtually conceded that both fairness and rationality cannot be achieved in the administration of the death penalty, the Court has chosen to deregulate the entire enterprise, replacing, it would seem, substantive constitutional requirements with mere aesthetics, and abdicating its statutorily and constitutionally imposed duty to provide meaningful judicial oversight to the administration of death by the States.

From this day forward, I no longer shall tinker with the machinery of death. For more than 20 years I have endeavored—indeed, I have struggled—along with a majority of this Court, to develop procedural and substantive rules that would lend more than the mere appearance of fairness to the death penalty endeavor. Earlier in my judicial career, as a member of the United States Court of Appeals, I voted to enforce the death penalty, even as I stated publicly that I doubted its moral, social, and constitutional legitimacy.

Rather than continue to coddle the Court's delusion that the desired level of fairness has been achieved and the need for regulation eviscerated, I feel morally and intellectually obligated simply to concede that the death penalty experiment has failed. It is virtually self-evident to me now that no combination of procedural rules or substantive regulations ever can save the death penalty from its inherent constitutional deficiencies. The basic question—does the system accurately and consistently determine which defendants "deserve" to die?—cannot be answered in the affirmative. It is not simply that this Court has allowed vague aggravating circumstances to be employed, and vital judicial review to be blocked. The problem is that the inevitability of factual, legal, and moral error gives us a system that we know must wrongly kill some defendants, a system that fails to deliver the fair, consistent, and reliable sentences of death required by the Constitution. Because I conclude that no sentence of death may be constitutionally imposed under our death penalty scheme, I do not address Callins' individual claims of error.

Although most of the public seems to desire, and the Constitution appears to permit, the penalty of death, it surely is beyond dispute that if the death penalty cannot be administered consistently and rationally, it may not be administered at all. Delivering on this promise, however, has proved to be another matter. Over the years, serious efforts were made to comply with its mandate. State legislatures and appellate courts struggled to provide judges and juries with sensible and objective guidelines for determining who should live and who should die. Some States attempted to define in statutes who is "deserving" of the death penalty through the use of carefully chosen adjectives, reserving the death penalty for those who commit crimes that are "especially heinous, atrocious, or cruel," or "wantonly vile, horrible or inhuman." Other States enacted mandatory death penalty statutes, attempting to eliminate sentencer discretion altogether. Still other States specified aggravating and mitigating factors that were to be considered by the sentencer and weighed against one another in a calculated and rational manner.

It soon became apparent that discretion could not be eliminated from capital sentencing without threatening the fundamental fairness due a defendant when life is at stake. Just as contemporary society was no longer tolerant of the random or discriminatory infliction of the penalty of death, evolving standards of decency required due consideration of the uniqueness of each individual defendant when imposing society's ultimate penalty.

This development in the American conscience would have presented no constitutional dilemma if fairness to the individual could be achieved without sacrificing the consistency and rationality promised. But over the past two decades, efforts to balance these competing constitutional commands have been to no avail. Experience has shown that the consistency and rationality promised are inversely related to the fairness owed the individual when considering a sentence of death. A step toward consistency is a step away from fairness.

There is a heightened need for fairness in the administration of death. This unique level of fairness is born of the appreciation that death truly is different from all other punishments a society inflicts upon its citizens. Because of the qualitative difference of the death penalty, Justice Stewart noted, "there is a corresponding difference in the need for reliability in the determination that death is the appropriate punishment in a specific case." While the risk of mistake in the determination of the appropriate penalty may be tolerated in other areas of the criminal law, "in capital cases the fundamental respect for humanity underlying the Eighth Amendment requires consideration of the character and record of the individual offender and the circumstances of the particular offense as a constitutionally indispensable part of the process of inflicting the penalty of death." Thus, although individualized sentencing in capital cases was not considered essential at the time the Constitution was adopted, this Court recognized that American standards of decency could no longer tolerate a capital sentencing process that failed to afford a defendant individualized consideration in the determination whether he or she should live or die.

I believe this line of analysis to be fundamentally sound and rooted in American standards of decency that have evolved over time. The notion of prohibiting a sentencer from exercising its discretion "to dispense mercy on the basis of factors too intangible to write into a statute," is offensive to our sense of fundamental fairness and respect for the uniqueness of the individual. I once wrote in dissent: "The sentencer's ability to respond with mercy towards a defendant has always struck me as a particularly valuable aspect of the capital sentencing procedure. We adhere so strongly to our belief that a sentencer should have the opportunity to spare a capital defendant's life on account of compassion for the individual because, recognizing that the capital sentencing decision must be made in the context of 'contemporary values,' we see in the sentencer's expression of mercy a distinctive feature of our society that we deeply value."

Yet, as several Members of the Court have recognized, there is real "tension" between the need for fairness to the individual and the consistency promised. On the one hand, discretion in capital sentencing must be "controlled by clear and objective standards so as to produce non-discriminatory and reasoned application." On the other hand, the Constitution also requires that the sentencer be able to consider "any relevant mitigating evidence regarding the defendant's character or background, and the circumstances of the particular offense." The power to consider mitigating evidence that would warrant a sentence less than death is meaningless unless the sentencer has the discretion and authority to dispense mercy based on that evidence. Thus, the Constitution, by requiring a heightened degree of fairness to the individual, and also a greater degree of equality and rationality in the administration of death, demands sentencer discretion that is at once generously expanded and severely restricted.

Over time, I have come to conclude that even this approach is unacceptable: It simply reduces, rather than eliminates, the number of people subject to arbitrary sentencing. It is the decision to sentence a defendant to death—not merely the decision to make a defendant eligible for death—that may not be arbitrary. While one might hope that providing the sentencer with as much relevant mitigating evidence as possible will lead to more rational and consistent sentences, experience has taught otherwise. It seems that the decision whether a human being should live or die is so inherently subjective—rife with all of life's understandings, experiences, prejudices, and passions—that it inevitably defies the rationality and consistency required by the Constitution.

The arbitrariness inherent in the sentencer's discretion to afford mercy is exacerbated by the problem of race. Even under the most sophisticated death penalty statutes, race continues to play a major role in determining who shall live and who shall die. Perhaps it should not be surprising that the biases and prejudices that infect society generally would influence the determination of who is sentenced to death, even within the narrower pool of death-eligible defendants selected according to objective standards. No matter how narrowly the pool of death-eligible defendants is drawn according to objective standards, the promise of consistency still will go unfulfilled so long as the sentencer is free to exercise unbridled discretion within the smaller group and thereby to discriminate. "The power to be lenient also is the power to discriminate."

I have come to wonder whether there was truth in the suggestion that discrimination and arbitrariness could not be purged from the administration of capital punishment without sacrificing the equally essential component of fairness—individualized sentencing. Viewed in this way, the promised consistency and the fairness to the individual are not only inversely related, but irreconcilable in the context of capital punishment. Any statute or procedure that could effectively eliminate arbitrariness from the administration of death would also restrict the sentencer's discretion to such an extent that the sentencer would be unable to give full consideration to the unique characteristics of each defendant and the circumstances of the offense. By the same token, any statute or procedure that would provide the sentencer with sufficient discretion to consider fully and act upon the unique circumstances of each defendant would "throw open the back door to arbitrary and irrational sentencing." All efforts to strike an appropriate balance between these conflicting constitutional commands are futile because there is a heightened need for both in the administration of death.

The Court is unmoved by this dilemma, however; it prefers "finality" in death sentences to reliable determinations of a capital defendant's guilt. Because I no longer can state with any confidence that this Court is able to reconcile the Eighth Amendment's competing constitutional commands, or that the federal judiciary will provide meaningful oversight to the state courts as they exercise their authority to inflict the penalty of death, I believe that the death penalty, as currently administered, is unconstitutional.

Perhaps one day this Court will develop procedural rules or verbal formulas that actually will provide consistency, fairness, and reliability in a capital-sentencing scheme. I am not optimistic that such a day will come. I am more optimistic, though, that this Court eventually will conclude that the effort to eliminate arbitrariness while preserving fairness "in the infliction of death is so plainly doomed to failure that it—and the death penalty— must be abandoned altogether." I may not live to see that day, but I have faith that eventually it will arrive. The path the Court has chosen lessens us all. I dissent.

*The hard fact is that sometimes we must make decisions we do not like. We make them because they are right, right in the sense that the law and the Constitution, as we see them, compel the result.*

— *Anthony M. Kennedy*

## Texas v. Johnson
### 109 S.Ct. 2533, 491 U.S. 397 (1989)

*At an anti-government demonstration during the 1984 Republican National Convention, Gregory Lee Johnson burned an American flag and led his fellow protesters in the chant, "America, the red, white, and blue, we spit on you." There were no acts or threats of violence, although several witnesses testified that they were seriously offended. When the crowd dispersed, an on-looker collected the flag's remains and buried them in his back yard. Johnson was charged under a Texas misdemeanor statute prohibiting the "desecration of venerated objects." The Justices divided 5 to 4, with a majority ruling that what Johnson did was protected free speech, and so he could not be punished for it. The dissenters complained that Justice Brennan's majority opinion at best discounted the "uniquely deep awe and respect for our flag felt by virtually all of us" and at worst amounted to a "regrettably patronizing civics lesson." Reactions in the Congress, from the White House, and in public opinion, were immediate and angry. Bills were introduced in Congress to change the language of the 1st amendment. Many defenders of the Court and the Constitution worried that overwhelming public support would allow those proposals to succeed with the consequence that settled understandings of the freedom of speech might be undone. A federal statute protecting the flag was passed to placate public opinion. Flag burners lined up to be the first to violate the new law the day it went into effect. The next year, the Court held the new federal statute to be unconstitutional for the same reasons and by the same vote as it had invalidated the Texas law.* United States v. Eichman (1990). *In this opinion Justice Kennedy, reluctantly concurs with the decision in favor of Defendant Johnson. But he takes pains to emphasize that Justices have a duty to the law of the Constitution that goes beyond their personal likes and dislikes.*

**Justice Kennedy:** I write not to qualify the words Justice Brennan chooses so well, for he says with power all that is necessary to explain our ruling. I join his opinion without reservation, but with a keen sense that this case, like others before us from time to time, exacts its personal toll. This prompts me to add to our pages these few remarks.

The case before us illustrates better than most that the judicial power is often difficult in its exercise. We cannot here ask another Branch to share responsibility, as when the argument is made that a statute is flawed or incomplete. For we are presented with a clear and simple statute to be judged against a pure command of the Constitution. The outcome can be laid at no door but ours.

The hard fact is that sometimes we must make decisions we do not like. We make them because they are right, right in the sense that the law and the Constitution, as we see them, compel the result. And so great is our commitment to the process that, except in the rare case, we do not pause to express distaste for the result, perhaps for fear of undermining a valued principle that dictates the decision. This is one of those rare cases.

Our colleagues in dissent advance powerful arguments why the Defendant may be convicted for his expression, reminding us that among those who will be dismayed by our holding will be some who have had the singular honor of carrying the flag in battle. And I agree that the flag holds a lonely place of honor in an age when absolutes are distrusted and simple truths are burdened by unneeded apologetics.

With all respect to those views, I do not believe the Constitution gives us the right to rule as the dissenting Members of the Court urge, however painful this judgment is to announce. Though symbols often are what we ourselves make of them, the flag is constant in expressing beliefs Americans share, beliefs in law and peace and that freedom which sustains the human spirit. The case here today forces recognition of the costs to which those beliefs commit us. It is poignant but fundamental that the flag protects those who hold it in contempt.

For all the record shows, this Defendant was not a philosopher and perhaps did not even possess the ability to comprehend how repellent his statements must be to the Republic itself. But whether or not he could appreciate the enormity of the offense he gave, the fact remains that his acts were speech, in both the technical and the fundamental meaning of the Constitution. So I agree with the Court that he must go free.

# CHAPTER FIVE

# CIVIL RIGHTS AND CIVIL LIBERTIES

*No State shall make or enforce any law
which shall abridge the privileges and
immunities of citizens of the United States; nor
shall any State deprive any person of life,
liberty, or property, without due process of law;
nor deny to any person within its jurisdiction
the equal protection of the laws.*

---

"The Constitution is one of the great achievements of political philosophy; and it may be the only political achievement of philosophy in our society," writes legal philosopher Donald H. Regan. The overarching philosophy of the Constitution is the philosophy of individual rights. This is exemplified in the critical sentence quoted above from the 14th amendment. Though it was ratified in 1868, our constitutional preoccupation with individual rights, which is the subject of this last Chapter, began long before.

The subject of individual rights takes us back to the Madisonian dilemma, which was introduced in Chapter One. There is, at bottom, a fundamental contradiction in liberal political theory. "Liberal," of course, refers to the political traditions of western democracies and includes Federalists and Antifederalists, Democrats and Republicans, liberals and conservatives. The fundamental contradiction is that the justification of the state, ultimately, is to provide the legal force necessary to protect all individual rights, including basic rights in property as well as political and civil rights. Thus, liberal political theory calls the state into existence, and the citizen needs the state to protect individual rights. The state, at the same time, represents the greatest threat to our realization of our rights. How is it possible to make government more powerful without making those subject to its authority less free? That is the constitutional paradox. This explains, in large part, how and why constitutional law issues are so open-ended, forever being reconsidered and reargued, never being fully and finally settled. The relationship between individual liberty and government power, by theoretical and practical necessity, is subtle and complex and is constantly evolving.

Liberalism, with its emphasis on the individual, is the ideology of rights, of capitalism, and of the limited state. It is at the opposite end of the ideological spectrum from communitarianism, the ideology of relatedness, of social solidarity, of an activist state with an emphasis on the collective. The United States always has been a country of rights. Lockean or liberal constitutionalism posits a sphere of individual liberty, guaranteed by property rights writ large, with a fixed government constituted by majority consent. A liberal constitutional government is representative, responsible, and limited, and its great powers are separated among coordinate branches. It is maintained by a perpetual threat of popular revolution, at least in theory. In practice, the consent of the governed is expressed in regular elections participated in by an enfranchised citizenry. "Here the people rule," remarked Gerald Ford, upon taking the oath of office as President.

Indeed, the idea of rights was part of the United States even before there was a Constitution. In the beginning, there was the dramatic invocation of unalienable rights in the *Declaration of Independence*, based on the belief that the governed could withdraw or withhold their consent from government: "We hold these Truths to be self-evident, that all Men are created equal, that they are endowed by their Creator with certain unalienable Rights, that among these are Life, Liberty, and the Pursuit of Happiness." Though this familiar declaration is now more than two centuries old, it was a quite radical departure in its day. The English constitution, by comparison, had been limited only by the rule of law and by established procedures as were to be found in the *Magna Carta*. English constitutional history, the legal history of the colonists, could not imagine any limits in principle on the purposes of government. Americans would be different. We would have a written Constitution and then a written Bill of Rights—no one in the 18th century could even imagine a British version of the 1st amendment, "Parliament shall make no law . . ."—and with those formative documents our liberal constitutionalism became forever rights-centered. We need only compare the nearly contemporaneous revolution in France to understand the uniqueness of this development at the time. The French people followed Rousseau toward more equality and fraternity than liberty; these values were expressed in the general will of the community; but importantly there were no individual "rights" against the general will. The people in the French republic, as in England, enjoyed rights only by laws, by legislative grace, because only the parliament spoke for the general will. Our *Declaration* insisted otherwise. Our political creed was based on the fundamental tenet that certain rights were inherent in human nature, that individual human dignity did not depend on government authority and was superior to it. While the *Magna Carta* granted rights, our Constitution grants no rights, not because we do not value individual rights, but because our understanding is that liberty is not a matter of governmental grace.

The Framers' first line of defense of individual rights was to be found in the structure of their government. Government power always and everywhere was to be mistrusted; it had to be divided to be limited. Federalism principles divided power vertically between the States and the national government. Separation of powers divided power horizontally within the national government. The most powerful branch, the legislative branch, was further subdivided by bicameralism. Their system of checks and balances was designed with all the complexity of the inner workings of a clock. Their purpose was to prevent government power from becoming concentrated in one institution that would then lord over individual liberty.

The new government would have necessary and proper powers, no less nor no more. The Framers sought to empower the government sufficiently for its essential tasks and, at the same time to prevent it from overreaching the individual. Thus, the Constitution, as originally intended and understood, was arranged in its entirety to protect the individual. This is why the delegates did not take long to consider and reject a proposal to add a bill of rights—suggested almost as an afterthought near the end of the Constitutional Convention—by a 10–0 State vote. It was not that the delegates were opposed to a bill of rights. Rather they deemed one unnecessary. For Federalists like Alexander Hamilton, "the Constitution is itself, in every rational sense, and to every useful purpose, a bill of rights." *The Federalist Paper No. 84*. He concluded, "why declare that things shall not be done which there is no power to do?" There was no need to elaborate further and declare what the national government could *not* do, in the first place because it could only do what it was expressly empowered to do, and in the second place because of the peril that any list of rights might be incomplete and overlook some freedom or fail to anticipate some essential liberty.

Federalists' protestations notwithstanding, it soon became apparent that the lack of a bill of rights, like the ones to be found in the contemporary state constitutions, was a serious flaw in the proposed Constitution. Virginia's George Mason refused to sign the Constitution for this reason. Thomas Jefferson chastised his friend James Madison for leaving out a bill of rights. In the ratifying conventions in State after State, Antifederalists raised the alarm for individual liberties. For a time, it looked like the Federalists had made a serious political miscalculation since these opponents of the proposed Constitution were prominent and influential and their attacks on the Constitution gained momentum. It was only after Federalist leaders, Madison included, had pledged to add a bill of rights immediately upon ratification that the proposed Constitution garnered the necessary support and then only by slim margins in several state conventions.

One of James Madison's claims to fame as a statesman of integrity is that he kept his campaign promise to sponsor a federal bill of rights. After defeating the Antifederalists' candidate James Monroe, one of the first things Madison did as a member of the House of Representatives was to sponsor a set of constitutional amendments. In a speech on June 8, 1789, he pledged: "I shall proceed to bring the amendments before you and advocate them until they shall be finally adopted or rejected." He continued, "this House is bound by every motive of prudence, not to let the first session pass over without proposing to the State legislatures some things to be incorporated into the constitution, that will render it acceptable to the whole people of the United States." He explained his belief that most of those who had opposed the Constitution "disliked it because it did not contain effectual provisions against encroachments on particular rights." The newly-elected President, George Washington, who had presided at the Convention and then lent his critical support to the proposed Constitution, had himself made note of the fact of the widespread demand for a bill of rights in his first official message to Congress. Now, Madison insisted, it was up to the Congress under Article V "to provide those securities for liberty and expressly declare the great rights of mankind secured under this constitution." In his cogent history, THE GREAT RIGHTS OF MANKIND (1977), Bernard Schwartz gives Madison credit for being the "prime mover" behind the proposed bill of rights. He framed it and he shepherded it through the Congress. Madison's own Virginia was the necessary eleventh State to ratify on December 15, 1791, making the Bill of Rights part of the Constitution.

The Bill of Rights has amounted to more than a parchment barrier to the majority will. Each guarantee represents a hard fought victory for human dignity and individual integrity in the centuries-old struggle between the individual and government. More than any other part of the Constitution, the Bill of Rights is deeply ingrained in our peoples' collective consciousness, as a cherished part of our political heritage. But there was no small constitutional difficulty that had to be overcome to realize its full potential. This was a consequence of federalism. The Constitution of the United States, after all, is a national document which, for the most part, establishes the terms of the social compact between citizens and the national government. Consequently, there was no room for disagreement or dispute when Chief Justice Marshall and a unanimous Supreme Court ruled, in *Barron v. Baltimore (1833)*, that the provisions in the Bill of Rights were effective only against the national government and not the States. This was the original understanding, demonstrated by the text itself, as for example the 1st amendment entreaty that "Congress shall make no law . . ." The national government was bound by the Bill of Rights, but the States could have their way with individual liberties.

Additional amendments and the Supreme Court's power of interpretation changed all this. The 14th amendment was ratified in 1868, in the aftermath of the constitutional paroxysm of the Civil War. Along with the 13th amendment, which abolished slavery and forever banished that witch of the 1787 christening, and the 15th amendment, which guaranteed the freedmen the franchise, the 14th amendment was addressed directly to the States. For the longest time, however, its constitutional potential went unrealized because of niggardly Supreme Court interpretations. Tentatively at first, later more insistently during the Warren Court years (1953–69) and then primarily at the instigation of Justice Hugo L. Black, the Supreme Court "interpreted" the 14th amendment "due process" to include almost all of the particulars of the Bill of Rights. This intellectual legerdemain is known in constitutional circles as the "incorporation doctrine," because it conceptualizes that the 1868 due process clause incorporated the particular 1791 Bill of Right protection and made it applicable to the States. The national and state governments today are both obliged to respect the same Bill of Rights guarantees, with few exceptions. That this process of incorporation is virtually complete and now taken for granted is demonstrated when Supreme Court Justices lapse into the *lingua franca* of referring to a State violating the 1st amendment freedom of speech, for example, even though, correctly speaking, the amendment being violated is the 14th. All the varieties of rights derived from the Constitution of the United States are displayed in this Chapter.

Nothing is rooted more deeply in our constitutional culture and political tradition than the American creed of individual civil liberties and civil rights. The vocabulary of rights is the dominant dialectic of modern constitutional law. This has been true from the beginning. From the *Declaration of Independence*, through the Bill of Rights and the Reconstruction Amendments, the debate has never been whether individuals hold rights against their government. That truth has been self-evident. The debate has been over the scope and content of rights, how the balance ought to be struck in particular situations. This debate often fuses legal and moral issues. The Supreme Court must balance the Madisonian dilemma. Our Constitution demonstrates a profound bias against claims of absoluteness from either side, individual or the government. Rights and powers are balanced in tension. "America's genius, at least in her own legend, is in not taking any abstract doctrine to its logical extreme," explains legal philosopher Ronald Dworkin, but he goes on to insist, "If the Government does not take rights seriously, then it does not take law seriously either." The opinions sampled in this Chapter represent some of the Justices' most inspired writings about the great rights of mankind. The Supreme Court takes rights very seriously.

* * * *

Perhaps because this country was the first ever to be argued into existence, many constitutionalists, on and off the Supreme Court, deem the 1st amendment to be preferred over other freedoms, though not everyone agrees on the significance of this preference, beyond repeating the paean to those freedoms of conscience. Three opinions included here deal with the freedom of speech. Justice Holmes defends the freedom of speech of those who disavow the Constitution and advocate extra-constitutional violence, in his famous dissent in *Abrams v. United States*

*(1919)*. In *Roth v. United States (1957)*, Justice Brennan explains that the freedom of speech is not absolute, despite the phrasing "Congress shall make no law. . ." Taking a categorical approach, he reasons that obscene speech is not part of the protected freedom. And in *Whitney v. California (1927)*, Justice Brandeis delivers a manifesto of his own on the importance of the freedom of speech in a democracy and the right to be a dissenter. In this classical peroration, he teaches us that the founders valued liberty over order and he seeks to inspire us that we should be brave enough to do the same.

The 1st amendment contains two provisions relating to religion in one grammatical clause; one provision prohibits any establishment of religion but the other provision guarantees free exercise of religion. These provisions often are understood as being in tension with each other. It would indeed be a gross understatement to describe the Supreme Court's religion pronouncements over the years as highly controversial. The divisiveness the Framers feared from religious differences often has manifested itself in the constitutional debate. Justice Black is responsible for borrowing Thomas Jefferson's "wall-of-separation" metaphor as a rule for decision in cases involving the establishment clause. He authored two of the High Court's most controversial decisions which are included here: *Everson v. Bd. of Educ. (1947)*, holding that a State could afford transportation to parochial school children, and *Engel v. Vitale (1962)*, holding that a non-denominational prayer could not be made an official part of the opening-school proceedings at a public school. The free exercise clause has met with decidedly mixed results. Chief Justice Morrison R. Waite sides with Utah officials against a Mormon believer who practiced polygamy in *Reynolds v. United States (1878)*. Justice Robert H. Jackson's opinion in *West Virginia Bd. of Educ. v. Barnette (1943)* is a soaring affirmation of individual conscience. It is all the more remarkable because it overrules a contrary 8 to 1 decision from only three years before, and because, in the middle of World War II, he calls on all Americans loyal to the Constitution to respect Jehovah's Witnesses' refusal to show respect for the flag.

Of the twenty-three separate rights mentioned in the first eight amendments, twelve relate to criminal procedure. The Framers themselves were cognizant of the historical and potential abuses of the criminal prosecution and therefore erected elaborate procedural safeguards between the government-as-prosecutor and the individual. That these protections still perform a critical service in the cause of freedom is vividly demonstrated by even a casual inquiry into modern totalitarian regimes where the government relies on criminal prosecutions *in terrorem* to imprison individuals and destroy the spirit of their people. Those who cannot imagine this, in the past or in the present, need only read the art-imitating-life novels of Aleksandr Solzhenitsyn and Fyodor Dostoyevsky. To paraphrase Justice Holmes, such terrible things are not possible in the United States, so long as the Supreme Court sits to enforce the law of the Constitution.

Once the Supreme Court became attuned to this due process priority for procedure, the process of incorporation resulted in the large scale federalization of state criminal procedures. After the Supreme Court ruled that a specific provision of the Bill of Rights applied to the States through the 14th amendment, any state defendant charged with any state crime who alleges a violation of that right gets to invoke the Constitution of the United States. The debate over the incorporation doctrine came into play in Chapter Four on the proper role of the Third Branch. In this Chapter on individual liberty, the emphasis is on the constitutional importance of specific rights.

Our criminal justice system values procedural fairness both as a means to an end and as end in itself. Our Constitution, in effect, says that it is better that a guilty person go free than that an innocent person be wrongly convicted. And sometimes, as counter-intuitive as it may seem, "The criminal is to go free because the constable blundered," to quote Justice Cardozo's aphorism. Justice Bradley's opinion in *Boyd v. United States (1886)* is one of the earliest criminal procedure decisions from the Supreme Court. He writes about the history of affording rights to those who are accused of crime and points out that this is a hallmark of a free society. In *Papachristou v. City of Jacksonville (1972)*, Justice Douglas reminds us that equality and justice sometimes are supposed to get in the way of the police. Even crooks have rights, including a right to privacy, according to the 4th amendment as understood by Justice Stewart in *Katz v. United States (1967)*. The same Justice balks in *Schneckloth v. Bustamonte (1973)*, however, at the seemingly logical and commonsensical argument that a person must be aware of a constitutional right in order to give it up. If the police ask your permission and you agree to a search, it does not matter that under the circumstances you could have and would have refused if only you had known better. Other rights are different in the way they are protected and in the way they are waived. *Miranda v. Arizona (1966)* establishes the famous *Miranda* warning, included in every Hollywood screenplay but required by the Constitution on the streets. Chief Justice Warren's opinion became a symbol used by critics of the Supreme Court to protest that the judges were reaching into the stationhouse to police the police. Justice White's opinion in *Duncan v. Louisiana (1968)*, highlights what a jury of his peers can mean to a person accused of a crime. Finally, Justice Black takes center stage to deliver a dramatic soliloquy about the singular significance for an accused to have a lawyer, in the landmark decision *Gideon v. Wainwright (1963)*.

Moving to the 14th amendment proper, three opinions mark the boundaries of due process and substantive rights and liberties. First, Justice Holmes penned one of the most celebrated opinions in Supreme Court annals to explain why he could not join the majority in *Lochner v. New York (1905)*. His main thesis was that judges should not second guess legislative majorities unless expressly authorized to do so by the Constitution in terms more specific than "due process." His sentiments eventually prevailed, at least so far as legislative regulations of social and economic matters are concerned. But "liberty" has always been a rallying cry of judges who are convinced that they know better than the rest. Individual liberties are not limited to the list found in the text of the Bill of Rights. Justices roam beyond the text, into history and tradition and even into philosophy, to demarcate non-textual fundamental rights. That this is a long-standing practice is illustrated by Justice James C. McReynolds' opinion in *Meyer v. Nebraska (1923)*, holding that the parents' fundamental right to raise their children would not allow Nebraska to prohibit the teaching and learning of a foreign language. One can train a magnifying glass on the parchment until it begins to darken and smolder and still not find a clause stating that proposition, at least not in so many words. But many argue that this is why we have judges, to view the text through a glass darkly. Others insist that these strained readings are illegitimate, that they more resemble the escapades of platonic guardians in an oligarchy rather than judges interpreting a written Constitution with fealty in a republic. This debate is rehearsed down to the present day regarding the right of privacy, manifested most controversially in judicial protection of a woman's decisionmaking whether to have an abortion. This was first announced in 1973 in *Roe v. Wade*, the decision which registered the highest disturbance on the constitutional Richter scale over the last forty years. Included in this Chapter is the plurality opinion in *Planned Parenthood of Southeastern Pennsylvania v. Casey (1992)*, which reaffirmed the 1973 decision, and caused some aftershocks of its own. This opinion seems to signal that the present configuration of Justices deems the constitutional issue to be settled for the time being.

Besides due process, the other great engine for civil rights in the 14th amendment is the equal protection clause. In their leading treatise on CONSTITUTIONAL LAW (5th ed. 1995), Professors Nowak and Rotunda state, matter of factly, "In recent years the equal protection guarantee has become the single most important concept in the Constitution for the protection of individual rights." The government runs afoul of this guarantee when it draws lines, when two groups of citizens are distinguished and then treated differently for no good reason or for a constitutionally bad reason. In other words, a constitutional violation is not made out by the simple fact of different treatment, because the 14th amendment does not require that the government treat everyone the same. For example, a State is expected to treat someone convicted of crime far differently than a law-abiding citizen. Rather, the equality principle is more subtle to require that similarly situated persons must be treated similarly. The landmark decision in *Brown v. Bd. of Educ. (1954)* was anything but subtle. Chief Justice Warren boldly declared that separate but equal public schools were unconstitutional *"per se,"* as lawyers say when they mean inherently, *i.e.*, by their very nature of separating children based on race. Thus, the High Court withdrew its own constitutional *imprimatur* and signalled an end to American apartheid, euphemistically named "Jim Crow," after the title of a 19th century minstrel song.

That issues of race continue to plague the body politic is underscored by the juxtaposition here of two separate opinions on the issue of affirmative action or reverse discrimination. The two opinions were authored by the only two African-Americans ever to don Supreme Court robes, in two different Supreme Court decisions, separated by a generation and more. Justice Thurgood Marshall makes the "pro" arguments in *Regents of the University of California v. Bakke (1978)*. Justice Clarence Thomas makes the "con" arguments in *Adarand Constructors, Inc. v. Pena (1995)*.

Derrick Bell, prominent professor of constitutional law, took Jeremiah's Old Testament lament "we are not saved" as the title of his recent book on race relations to express the conventional frustration with the *status quo* and the lack of meaningful progress. Certainly, our Nation's history demonstrates that our national capacity for discrimination against people on the basis of race, gender, and creed is far more profound than we generally admit or fully understand. Our constitutional history more importantly demonstrates that America is committed, in its ideals, to the equal treatment of all people. Our American regime is not unique in the world for our repeated failures to live up to our ideals. Our uniqueness rather is to be found in the constancy of our people's striving to live up to the promise of the *Declaration of Independence* and in the unforgiving perseverance of the ideal of equality in our constitutional beliefs.

Equality has proven to be as elusive a social norm as it is a rule for deciding cases. Three decisions illustrate the difficulty the Supreme Court has experienced in moving from the level of philosophical abstraction down to resolving constitutional disputes. Justice Brennan's plurality opinion in *Frontiero v. Richardson (1973)* took a direct and simple approach to equate discrimination based on gender with discrimination based on race, a short-lived approach from which subsequent Supreme Court decisions have backed away. In *Plyler v. Doe (1982)*, writing for another plurality, Justice Brennan managed to cobble together a holding that Texas could not discriminate against the children of illegal aliens by excluding them from its public schools. And in *Romer* v. *Evans (1996)* a majority of the Justices weigh in and choose sides, at least tentatively, in what the dissent calls the "culture war" over gay rights.

Closing this Chapter on individual rights, two decisions demonstrate that the phrase "life, liberty or property," quite explicitly, reveals all the fearsome power of government. The Constitution, quite literally, can be a matter of life or death. On the civil side, in *Cruzan v. Director, Missouri Department of Health (1990)*, the Justices argue about what, if anything, the Constitution has to say about a person's decision to forego life-sustaining treatment when the medical prognosis promises no hope for anything but flat lines. The poignancy of this issue, for Nancy Cruzan and her family, is beyond our ken. On the criminal side, under the rubric of the 8th amendment prohibition on "cruel and unusual punishments," we encounter the perennial debate over the death penalty. In the last and longest set of opinions in this volume, *Furman v. Georgia (1972)*, the Justices describe their innermost constitutional thoughts about that ultimate punishment and whether it can be reconciled with the value of human dignity that animates the Bill of Rights. The mystery of life and death revealed in these two decisions seems to be much larger than the Constitution and the Supreme Court.

The Supreme Court plays a central role in defining constitutional rights and liberties. But Judge Learned Hand, who was the Nestor of the federal courts in his day, understood that ultimately freedom must be yoked with individual responsibility. In the critical World War II year of 1944, he delivered an inspired speech on what it means to be an American entitled *The Spirit of Liberty*. "I often wonder whether we do not rest our hopes too much upon constitutions, upon laws and upon courts," Judge Hand mused, "These are false hopes; believe me, these are false hopes. Liberty lies in the hearts of men and women; when it dies there, no constitution, no law, no court can save it; no constitution, no law, no court can even do much to help it. While it lies there it needs no constitution, no law, no court to save it."

What French Prime Minister Georges Clemenceau said about war and generals applies in kind to "the most wonderful work ever struck off at a given time by the brain and purpose of man." Our Constitution is too important to be left to the Justices.

*But when men have realized that time has up-
set many fighting faiths, they may come to believe
even more than they believe the very foundations
of their own conduct that the ultimate good desired is better reached by free trade in ideas—that
the best test of truth is the power of the thought to
get itself accepted in the competition of the market, and that truth is the only ground upon which
their wishes safely can be carried out.*

— *Oliver W. Holmes, Jr.*

## Abrams v. United States
### 40 S.Ct. 17, 250 U.S. 616 (1919)

*Earlier, in* Schenck v. United States (1919), *Justice
Holmes wrote an opinion for the Court affirming the convictions under the Espionage Act of 1917 of defendants
who had mailed leaflets opposing the World War I draft
to potential draftees. There he got off the famous line,
"The most stringent protection of free speech would not
protect a man in falsely shouting fire in a theatre and
causing a panic." The idea behind his example is that the
government can punish or prevent speech if, and only if,
there is a "clear and present danger" that something very
bad will happen immediately; otherwise, the only appropriate response to controversial speech is to answer it
with more speech and then to allow people to make up
their mind. Here in* Abrams, *Justice Holmes dissents to
complain that the majority is not applying his analysis
correctly and he argues that the 1st amendment should
protect the defendants' campaign to support the Russian
revolution of 1917. Later relying on his marketplace-of-
ideas metaphor in* Gitlow v. New York (1925), *he would
use even "more impressive words" to defend free speech
even for those who do not believe in the very Constitution
they invoke in their defense: "Every idea is an incitement.
It offers itself for belief and if believed it is acted on
unless some other belief outweighs it or some failure of
energy stifles the movement at its birth. The only difference between the expression of an opinion and an incitement in the narrower sense is the speaker's enthusiasm
for the result. Eloquence may set fire to reason. If in the
long run the beliefs expressed in proletarian dictatorship*

*are destined to be accepted by the dominant forces of the community, the only meaning of free speech is that they should be given their chance and have their way." Today the Supreme Court continues to struggle with issues—like racist-hate speech and flag burning—which invoke what Justice Holmes once called "freedom for the thought we hate."*

**Justice Holmes:** This indictment is founded wholly upon the publication of two leaflets. The first of these leaflets says that the President's cowardly silence about the intervention in Russia reveals the hypocrisy of the plutocratic gang in Washington. It intimates that "German militarism combined with allied capitalism to crush the Russian revolution"—goes on that the tyrants of the world fight each other until they see a common enemy—working class enlightenment, when they combine to crush it; and that now militarism and capitalism combined, though not openly, to crush the Russian revolution. It says that there is only one enemy of the workers of the world and that is capitalism; that it is a crime for workers of America, etc., to fight the workers' republic of Russia, and ends "Awake! Awake, you workers of the world! Revolutionists." A note adds "It is absurd to call us pro-German. We hate and despise German militarism more than do you hypocritical tyrants. We have more reason for denouncing German militarism than has the coward of the White House."

The other leaflet, headed "Workers—Wake Up," with abusive language says that America together with the Allies will march for Russia to help the Czecko-Slovaks in their struggle against the Bolsheviki, and that this time the hypocrites shall not fool the Russian emigrants and friends of Russia in America. It tells the Russian emigrants that they now must spit in the face of the false military propaganda by which their sympathy and help to the prosecution of the war have been called forth and says that with the money they have lent or are going to lend "they will make bullets not only for the Germans but also for the Workers Soviets of Russia," and further, "Workers in the ammunition factories, you are producing bullets, bayonets, cannon to murder not only the Germans, but also your dearest, best, who are in Russia fighting for freedom." It then appeals to the same Russian emigrants at some length not to consent to the "inquisitionary expedition in Russia," and says that the destruction of the Russian revolution is "the politics of the march on Russia." The leaflet winds up by saying: "Workers, our reply to this barbaric intervention has to be a general strike!" and after a few words on the spirit of revolution, exhortations not to be afraid, and some usual tall talk ends, "Woe unto those who will be in the way of progress. Let solidarity live! The Rebels."

No argument seems to be necessary to show that these pronunciamentos in no way attack the form of government of the United States, or that they do not support either of the first two counts in the indictment. What little I have to say about the third count may be postponed until I have considered the fourth. With regard to that it seems too plain to be denied that the suggestion to workers in the ammunition factories that they are producing bullets to murder their dearest, and the further advocacy of a general strike, both in the second leaflet, do urge curtailment of production of things necessary to the prosecution of the war within the meaning of the 1917 Espionage Act as amended by the 1918 Sedition Act. But to make the conduct criminal that statute requires that it should be "with intent by such curtailment to cripple or hinder the United States in the prosecution of the war." It seems to me that no such intent is proved.

It seems to me that this statute must be taken to use its words in a strict and accurate sense. They would be absurd in any other. A patriot might think that we were wasting money on aeroplanes, or making more cannon of a certain kind than we needed, and might advocate curtailment with success, yet even if it turned out that the curtailment hindered and was thought by other minds to have been obviously likely to hinder the United States in the prosecution of the war, no one would hold such conduct a crime. I admit that my illustration does not answer all that might be said, but it is enough to show what I think and to let me pass to a more important aspect of the case. I refer to the First Amendment to the Constitution that Congress shall make no law abridging the freedom of speech.

I never have seen any reason to doubt that the questions of law that alone were before this Court in our previous First Amendment cases were rightly decided. I do not doubt for a moment that by the same reasoning that would justify punishing persuasion to murder, the United States constitutionally may punish speech that produces or is intended to produce a clear and imminent danger that it will bring about forthwith certain substantive evils that the United States constitutionally may seek to prevent. The power undoubtedly is greater in time of war than in time of peace because war opens dangers that do not exist at other times.

But as against dangers peculiar to war, as against others, the principle of the right to free speech is always the same. It is only the present danger of immediate evil or an intent to bring it about that warrants Congress in setting a limit to the expression of opinion where private rights are not concerned. Congress certainly cannot forbid all effort to change the mind of the country. Now nobody can suppose that the surreptitious publishing of a silly leaflet by an unknown man, without more, would present any immediate danger that its opinions would hinder the success of the government arms or have any appreciable tendency to do so. Publishing those opinions for the very purpose of obstructing, however, might indicate a greater danger and at any rate would have the quality of an attempt. So I assume that the second leaflet if published for the purposes alleged in the fourth count, might be punishable. But it seems pretty clear to me that nothing less than that would bring these papers within the scope of this law. An actual intent, in the sense that I have explained, is necessary to constitute an attempt, where a further act of the same individual is required to complete the substantive crime. It is necessary where the success of the attempt depends upon others because if that intent is not present, the actor's aim may be accomplished without bringing about the evils sought to be checked. An intent to prevent interference with the revolution in Russia might have been satisfied without any hindrance to carrying on the war in which we were engaged.

I do not see how anyone can find the intent required by the statute in any of the defendant's words. The second leaflet is the only one that affords even a foundation for the charge, and there, without invoking the hatred of German militarism expressed in the former one, it is evident from the beginning to the end that the only object of the paper is to help Russia and stop American intervention there against the popular government—not to impede the United States in the war that it was carrying on. To say that two phrases taken literally might import a suggestion of conduct that would have interference with the war as an indirect and probably undesired effect seems to me by no means enough to show an attempt to produce that effect.

I return for a moment to the third count of the indictment. That charges an intent to provoke resistance to the United States in its war with Germany. Taking the clause in the statute that deals with that in connection with the other elaborate provisions of the Act, I think that resistance to the United States means some forcible act of opposition to some proceeding of the United States in pursuance of the war. I think the intent must be the specific intent that I have described and for the reasons that I have given I think that no such intent was proved or existed in fact. I also think that there is no hint at resistance to the United States as I construe the phrase.

In this case, sentences of twenty years imprisonment have been imposed for the publishing of two leaflets that I believe the defendants had as much right to publish as the Government has to publish the Constitution of the United States now vainly invoked by them. Even if I am technically wrong and enough can be squeezed from these poor and puny anonymities to turn the color of legal litmus paper; I will add, even if what I think the necessary intent were shown; the most nominal punishment seems to me all that possibly could be inflicted, unless the defendants are to be made to suffer not for what the indictment alleges but for the creed that they avow—a creed that I believe to be the creed of ignorance and immaturity when honestly held, as I see no reason to doubt that it was held here but which, although made the subject of examination at the trial, no one has a right even to consider in dealing with the charges before the Court.

Persecution for the expression of opinions seems to me perfectly logical. If you have no doubt of your premises or your power and want a certain result with all your heart you naturally express your wishes in law and sweep away all opposition. To allow opposition by speech seems to indicate that you think the speech impotent, as when a man says that he has squared the circle, or that you do not care whole-heartedly for the result, or that you doubt either your power or your premises. But when men have realized that time has upset many fighting faiths, they may come to believe even more than they believe the very foundations of their own conduct that the ultimate good desired is better reached by free trade in ideas—that the best test of truth is the power of the thought to get itself accepted in the competition of the market, and that truth is the only ground upon which their wishes safely can be carried out. That at any rate is the theory of our Constitution. It is an experiment, as all life is an experiment. Every year if not every day we have to wager our salvation upon some prophecy based upon imperfect knowledge. While that experiment is part of our system I think that we should be eternally vigilant against attempts to check the expression of opinions that we loathe and believe to be fraught with death, unless they so imminently threaten immediate interference with the lawful and pressing purposes of the law that an immediate check is required to save the country. I wholly disagree with the argument of the Government that the First Amendment left the common law as to seditious libel in force. History seems to me against the notion. I had conceived that the United States through many years had shown its repentance for the Sedition Act of 1798, by repaying fines that it imposed. Only the emergency that makes it immediately dangerous to leave the correction of evil counsels to time warrants making any exception to the sweeping command, "Congress shall make no law abridging the freedom of speech." Of course I am speaking only of expressions of opinion and exhortations, which were all that were uttered here, but I regret that I cannot put into more impressive words my belief that in their conviction upon this indictment the defendants were deprived of their rights under the Constitution of the United States.

*In light of this history, it is apparent that the unconditional phrasing of the First Amendment was not intended to protect every utterance.*

*— William J. Brennan*

## Roth v. United States
### 77 S.Ct. 1304, 354 U.S. 476 (1957)

*The 1st amendment protects "the freedom of speech," not all speech, but that begs the question what speech is protected and what is not. The difficulty of answering this question is illustrated by what Justice Harlan once described as "the intractable obscenity problem:" if a work is obscene it is not constitutionally protected, but how should the line be drawn and how should a court determine whether a particular book, movie, or magazine is over the line. In this, the Court's first obscenity decision, Justice Brennan takes a definitional approach. Dissenting Justices argued for an absolute theory that all speech, including obscene speech, was protected. In the aftermath of this opinion, the Supreme Court was overwhelmed with these cases as it felt obliged to review lower court decisions, performing as a censorship board for the Nation. In an attempt to extirpate itself, the Court further refined the definition of obscenity in* Miller v. California *(1973) as follows: (a) whether the average person, applying contemporary community standards would find the work, taken as a whole, appeals to the prurient interest; (b) whether the work depicts or describes, in a patently offensive way, sexual conduct specifically defined by the applicable statute; and (c) whether the work, taken as a whole, lacks serious literary, artistic, political or scientific value. By that point, Justice Brennan announced that he was giving up because he had become convinced that it is impossible to define and apply such a test. Since obscenity cases are decided by juries, what materials are protected or tolerated may vary from Las Vegas, Nevada, to Lubbock, Texas. The Court has looked favorably on municipal zoning regulations applied to so-called "adult businesses," either clustering them in one area or dispersing them, in order to regulate their secondary effects. An-*

*other important case decided in 1982 relaxed the consti-*
*tutional standard and gave the States more leeway to*
*control child pornography.*

**Justice Brennan:** The constitutionality of a criminal obscenity statute is the question in each of these two cases, one
based on a federal statute and the other based on a state law
from California. The dispositive question is whether obscenity is
utterance within the area of protected speech and press.

Although this is the first time the question has been
squarely presented to this Court, either under the First Amendment or under the Fourteenth Amendment, expressions found
in numerous opinions indicate that this Court has always assumed that obscenity is not protected by the freedoms of speech
and press. No issue of fact is presented in either case concerning
the obscenity of the materials involved, which are presumed to
be obscene.

The guaranties of freedom of expression in effect in 10 of the
14 States which by 1792 had ratified the Constitution, gave no
absolute protection for every utterance. Thirteen of the 14
States provided for the prosecution of libel, and all of those
States made either blasphemy or profanity, or both, statutory
crimes. As early as 1712, Massachusetts made it criminal to
publish "any filthy, obscene, or profane song, pamphlet, libel or
mock sermon" in imitation or mimicking of religious services.
Thus, profanity and obscenity were related offenses.

In light of this history, it is apparent that the unconditional
phrasing of the First Amendment was not intended to protect
every utterance. This phrasing did not prevent this Court from
concluding that libelous utterances are not within the area of
constitutionally protected speech. At the time of the adoption of
the First Amendment, obscenity law was not as fully developed
as libel law, but there is sufficiently contemporaneous evidence
to show that obscenity, too, was outside the protection intended
for speech and press.

The protection given speech and press was fashioned to assure unfettered interchange of ideas for the bringing about of
political and social changes desired by the people. This objective
was made explicit as early as 1774 in a letter of the Continental
Congress to the inhabitants of Quebec: "The last right we shall
mention, regards the freedom of the press. The importance of
this consists, besides the advancement of truth, science, morality, and arts in general, in its diffusion of liberal sentiments on

the administration of Government, its ready communication of thoughts between subjects, and its consequential promotion of union among them, whereby oppressive officers are shamed or intimidated, into more honourable and just modes of conducting affairs." All ideas having even the slightest redeeming social importance—unorthodox ideas, controversial ideas, even ideas hateful to the prevailing climate of opinion—have the full protection of the guaranties, unless excludable because they encroach upon the limited area of more important interests. But implicit in the history of the First Amendment is the rejection of obscenity as utterly without redeeming social importance. This rejection for that reason is mirrored in the universal judgment that obscenity should be restrained, reflected in the international agreement of over 50 nations, in the obscenity laws of all of the 48 States, and in the 20 obscenity laws enacted by the Congress from 1842 to 1956. This is the same judgment expressed by this Court in a 1942 decision: "There are certain well-defined and narrowly limited classes of speech, the prevention and punishment of which have never been thought to raise any Constitutional problem. These include the lewd and obscene. It has been well observed that such utterances are no essential part of any exposition of ideas, and are of such slight social value as a step to truth that any benefit that may be derived from them is clearly outweighed by the social interest in order and morality." We hold that obscenity is not within the area of constitutionally protected speech or press.

However, sex and obscenity are not synonymous. Obscene material is material which deals with sex in a manner appealing to prurient interest, *i.e.*, material having a tendency to excite lustful thoughts. WEBSTER'S NEW INTERNATIONAL DICTIONARY (1949) defines prurient, in pertinent part, as follows: "itching; longing; uneasy with desire or longing; of persons, having itching, morbid, or lascivious longings; of desire, curiosity, or propensity, lewd." The portrayal of sex, *e.g.*, in art, literature and scientific works, is not itself sufficient reason to deny material the constitutional protection of freedom of speech and press. Sex, a great and mysterious motive force in human life, has indisputably been a subject of absorbing interest to mankind through the ages; it is one of the vital problems of human interest and public concern.

The fundamental freedom of speech and press have contributed greatly to the development and well-being of our free society and are indispensable to its continued growth. Ceaseless vigilance is the watchword to prevent their erosion by Congress or by the States. The door barring federal and state intrusion into this area cannot be left ajar; it must be kept tightly closed and opened only the slightest crack necessary to prevent encroachment upon more important interests. It is therefore vital that the standards for judging obscenity safeguard the protection of freedom of speech and press for material which does not treat sex in a manner appealing to prurient interest.

The early English common law standard of obscenity, allowed material to be judged merely by the effect of an isolated excerpt upon particularly susceptible persons. Some American courts adopted this standard but later decisions have rejected it and substituted this test: whether to the average person, applying contemporary community standards, the dominant theme of the material taken as a whole appeals to prurient interest. The English test, judging obscenity by the effect of isolated passages upon the most susceptible persons, might well encompass material legitimately treating with sex, and so it must be rejected as unconstitutionally restrictive of the freedoms of speech and press. On the other hand, the substituted standard provides safeguards adequate to withstand the charge of constitutional infirmity.

It is argued that the statutes before the Court do not provide reasonably ascertainable standards of guilt and therefore violate the constitutional requirements of due process. The federal obscenity statute makes punishable the mailing of material that is "obscene, lewd, lascivious, or filthy or other publication of an indecent character." The California statute makes punishable, inter alia, the keeping for sale or advertising material that is "obscene or indecent." The thrust of the argument is that these words are not sufficiently precise because they do not mean the same thing to all people, all the time, everywhere.

Many decisions have recognized that these terms of obscenity statutes are not precise. This Court, however, has consistently held that lack of precision is not itself offensive to the requirements of due process: "The Constitution does not require impossible standards;" all that is required is that the language "conveys sufficiently definite warning as to the proscribed conduct when measured by common understanding and practices." These words, applied according to the proper standard for judging obscenity, already discussed, give adequate warning of the conduct proscribed and mark "boundaries sufficiently distinct for judges and juries fairly to administer the law. That there may be marginal cases in which it is difficult to determine the side of the line on which a particular fact situation falls is no sufficient reason to hold the language too ambiguous to define a criminal offense."

In summary, then, we hold that these statutes, applied according to the proper standard for judging obscenity, do not offend constitutional safeguards against convictions based upon protected material, or fail to give men in acting adequate notice of what is prohibited.

*Those who won our independence by revolution were not cowards. They did not fear political change. They did not exalt order at the cost of liberty.*

— *Louis D. Brandeis*

## Whitney v. California
### 47 S.Ct. 641, 274 U.S. 357 (1927)

*Charlotte Anita Whitney was convicted of a felony for organizing and being a member of the Communist Party of California in 1919. The Supreme Court approved the state criminal statute and affirmed her conviction, even though she had tried to persuade the Party to work for political reform through the democratic process. Justice Brandeis reluctantly agreed with the result, but wrote a concurring opinion that emphasized the value to a democracy of freedom of speech, even for dissidents. This is a masterful example of the freedom of thought and expression that is so eloquently defended by the Justice F.D.R. respectfully called "Old Isaiah." The Governor pardoned Whitney based on this concurring opinion. And eventually the Supreme Court fully embraced Justice Brandeis's constitutional reasoning in a 1969 decision.*

**Justice Brandeis:** It is settled that the due process clause of the Fourteenth Amendment applies to matters of substantive law as well as to matters of procedure. Thus all fundamental rights comprised within the term liberty are protected by the federal Constitution from invasion by the states. The right of free speech, the right to teach and the right of assembly are, of course, fundamental rights. These may not be denied or abridged. But, although the rights of free speech and assembly are fundamental, they are not in their nature absolute. Their exercise is subject to restriction, if the particular restriction proposed is required in order to protect the state from destruction or from serious injury, political, economic or moral. That the necessity which is essential to a valid restriction does not exist unless speech would produce, or is intended to produce, a clear and imminent danger of some substantive evil which the state constitutionally may seek to prevent has been settled.

It is said to be the function of the Legislature to determine whether at a particular time and under the particular circumstances the formation of, or assembly with, a society organized to advocate criminal syndicalism constitutes a clear and present danger of substantive evil; and that by enacting the law here in question the Legislature of California determined that question in the affirmative. The Legislature must obviously decide, in the first instance, whether a danger exists which calls for a particular protective measure. But where a statute is valid only in case certain conditions exist, the enactment of the statute cannot alone establish the facts which are essential to its validity.

This court has not yet fixed the standard by which to determine when a danger shall be deemed clear; how remote the danger may be and yet be deemed present; and what degree of evil shall be deemed sufficiently substantial to justify resort to abridgment of free speech and assembly as the means of protection. To reach sound conclusions on these matters, we must bear in mind why a state is, ordinarily, denied the power to prohibit dissemination of social, economic and political doctrine which a vast majority of its citizens believes to be false and fraught with evil consequence.

Those who won our independence believed that the final end of the state was to make men free to develop their faculties, and that in its government the deliberative forces should prevail over the arbitrary. They valued liberty both as an end and as a means. They believed liberty to the secret of happiness and courage to be the secret of liberty. They believed that freedom to think as you will and to speak as you think are means indispensable to the discovery and spread of political truth; that without free speech and assembly discussion would be futile; that with them, discussion affords ordinarily adequate protection against the dissemination of noxious doctrine; that the greatest menace to freedom is an inert people; that public discussion is a political duty; and that this should be a fundamental principle of the American government.[3] They recognized the risks to which all

---

3. Compare Thomas Jefferson: "We have nothing to fear from the demoralizing reasonings of some, if others are left free to demonstrate their errors and especially when the law stands ready to punish the first criminal act produced by the false reasonings; these are safer corrections than the conscience of the judge." Also in his first Inaugural Address: "If there be any among us who would wish to dissolve this union or change its republican form, let them stand undisturbed as monuments of the safety with which error of opinion may be tolerated where reason is left free to combat it."

human institutions are subject. But they knew that order cannot be secured merely through fear of punishment for its infraction; that it is hazardous to discourage thought, hope and imagination; that fear breeds repression; that repression breeds hate; that hate menaces stable government; that the path of safety lies in the opportunity to discuss freely supposed grievances and proposed remedies; and that the fitting remedy for evil counsels is good ones. Believing in the power of reason as applied through public discussion, they eschewed silence coerced by law—the argument of force in its worst form. Recognizing the occasional tyrannies of governing majorities, they amended the Constitution so that free speech and assembly should be guaranteed.

Fear of serious injury cannot alone justify suppression of free speech and assembly. Men feared witches and burnt women. It is the function of speech to free men from the bondage of irrational fears. To justify suppression of free speech there must be reasonable ground to fear that serious evil will result if free speech is practiced. There must be reasonable ground to believe that the danger apprehended is imminent. There must be reasonable ground to believe that the evil to be prevented is a serious one. Every denunciation of existing law tends in some measure to increase the probability that there will be violation of it. Condonation of a breach enhances the probability. Expressions of approval add to the probability. Propagation of the criminal state of mind by teaching syndicalism increases it. Advocacy of lawbreaking heightens it still further. But even advocacy of violation, however reprehensible morally, is not a justification for denying free speech where the advocacy falls short of incitement and there is nothing to indicate that the advocacy would be immediately acted on. The wide difference between advocacy and incitement, between preparation and attempt, between assembling and conspiracy, must be borne in mind. In order to support a finding of clear and present danger, it must be shown either that immediate serious violence was to be expected or was advocated, or that the past conduct furnished reason to believe that such advocacy was then contemplated.

Those who won our independence by revolution were not cowards. They did not fear political change. They did not exalt order at the cost of liberty. To courageous, self-reliant men, with confidence in the power of free and fearless reasoning applied through the processes of popular government, no danger flowing from speech can be deemed clear and present, unless the incidence of the evil apprehended is so imminent that it may befall before there is opportunity for full discussion. If there be time to expose through discussion the falsehood and fallacies, to avert the evil by the processes of education, the remedy to be applied is more speech, not enforced silence. Only an emergency can justify repression. Such must be the rule if authority is to be reconciled with freedom. Such, in my opinion, is the command of the Constitution. It is therefore always open to Americans to challenge a law abridging free speech and assembly by showing that there was no emergency justifying it.

Moreover, even imminent danger cannot justify resort to prohibition of these functions essential to effective democracy, unless the evil apprehended is relatively serious. Prohibition of free speech and assembly is a measure so stringent that it would be inappropriate as the means for averting a relatively trivial harm to society. A police measure may be unconstitutional merely because the remedy, although effective as means of protection, is unduly harsh or oppressive. Thus, a state might, in the exercise of its police power, make any trespass upon the land of another a crime, regardless of the results or of the intent or purpose of the trespasser. It might, also, punish an attempt, a conspiracy, or an incitement to commit the trespass. But it is hardly conceivable that this court would hold constitutional a statute which punished as a felony the mere voluntary assembly with a society formed to teach that pedestrians had the moral right to cross uninclosed, unposted, waste lands and to advocate their doing so, even if there was imminent danger that advocacy would lead to a trespass. The fact that speech is likely to result in some violence or in destruction of property is not enough to justify its suppression. There must be the probability of serious injury to the State. Among free men, the deterrents ordinarily to be applied to prevent crime are education and punishment for violations of the law, not abridgment of the rights of free speech and assembly.

> *In the words of Jefferson, the clause against establishment of religion by law was intended to erect "a wall of separation between Church and State."*
>
> — *Hugo L. Black*

## Everson v. Bd. of Educ.
### 67 S.Ct. 504, 330 U.S. 1 (1947)

*This was the first in what has been a zig-zag of back-and-forth holdings whether this or that particular government program in education does or does not contravene the establishment clause in the 1st amendment. It is sometimes referred to as the "non-establishment clause" for its Ten Commandment phrasing: "Congress shall make no law respecting an establishment of religion." This continues to be one of the least predictable and most uncertain areas of constitutional law today. A New Jersey statute authorized local school boards to reimburse parents for the cost of public transportation of their children to both public and private (mostly Catholic) schools. By a 5 to 4 vote, the Court upheld the statute. Justice Jackson dissented to accuse the majority of reaching a conclusion "utterly discordant" with its own reasoning. Justice Rutledge wrote a separate dissent that invoked the writings of Madison and Jefferson against the majority's history and insisted that the transportation program did not realistically further the goal of public safety. Justice Black's non sequitur majority opinion— written in strict separation-of-church-and-state rhetoric but nonetheless upholding the State's accommodation of religion—likewise failed to satisfy both sides of the public debate over government aid to religious schools, back in 1947 and ever since.*

**Justice Black:** The New Jersey statute is challenged as a "law respecting an establishment of religion." The First Amendment, as made applicable to the states by the Fourteenth, commands that a state "shall make no law respecting an establishment of religion, or prohibiting the free exercise thereof." These words of the First Amendment reflected in the minds of early Americans a vivid mental picture of conditions and practices which they fervently wished to stamp out in order to preserve liberty for themselves and for their posterity. Doubtless their goal has not been entirely reached; but so far has the Nation moved toward it that the expression "law respecting an establishment of religion," probably does not so vividly remind present-day Americans of the evils, fears, and political problems that caused that expression to be written into our Bill of Rights. Whether this New Jersey law is one respecting the "establishment of religion" requires an understanding of the meaning of that language, particularly with respect to the imposition of taxes. Therefore, it is not inappropriate briefly to review the background and environment of the period in which that constitutional language was fashioned and adopted.

A large proportion of the early settlers of this country came here from Europe to escape the bondage of laws which compelled them to support and attend government favored churches. The centuries immediately before and contemporaneous with the colonization of America had been filled with turmoil, civil strife, and persecutions, generated in large part by established sects determined to maintain their absolute political and religious supremacy. With the power of government supporting them, at various times and places, Catholics had persecuted Protestants, Protestants had persecuted Catholics, Protestant sects had persecuted other Protestant sects, Catholics of one shade of belief had persecuted Catholics of another shade of belief, and all of these had from time to time persecuted Jews. In efforts to force loyalty to whatever religious group happened to be on top and in league with the government of a particular time and place, men and women had been fined, cast in jail, cruelly tortured, and killed. Among the offenses for which these punishments had been inflicted were such things as speaking disrespectfully of the views of ministers of government-established churches, nonattendance at those churches, expressions of non-belief in their doctrines, and failure to pay taxes and tithes to support them.

These practices of the old world were transplanted to and began to thrive in the soil of the new America. The very charters granted by the English Crown to the individuals and companies designated to make the laws which would control the destinies of the colonials authorized these individuals and companies to erect religious establishments which all, whether believers or non-believers, would be required to support and attend. An exercise of this authority was accompanied by a repetition of many of the old world practices and persecutions. Catholics found themselves hounded and proscribed because of their faith;

Quakers who followed their conscience went to jail; Baptists were peculiarly obnoxious to certain dominant Protestant sects; men and women of varied faiths who happened to be in a minority in a particular locality were persecuted because they steadfastly persisted in worshipping God only as their own consciences dictated. And all of these dissenters were compelled to pay tithes and taxes to support government-sponsored churches whose ministers preached inflammatory sermons designed to strengthen and consolidate the established faith by generating a burning hatred against dissenters.

These practices became so commonplace as to shock the freedom-loving colonials into a feeling of abhorrence. The imposition of taxes to pay ministers' salaries and to build and maintain churches and church property aroused their indignation. It was these feelings which found expression in the First Amendment. No one locality and no one group throughout the Colonies can rightly be given entire credit for having aroused the sentiment that culminated in adoption of the Bill of Rights' provisions embracing religious liberty. But Virginia, where the established church had achieved a dominant influence in political affairs and where many excesses attracted wide public attention, provided a great stimulus and able leadership for the movement. The people there, as elsewhere, reached the conviction that individual religious liberty could be achieved best under a government which was stripped of all power to tax, to support, or otherwise to assist any or all religions, or to interfere with the beliefs of any religious individual or group.

The movement toward this end reached its dramatic climax in Virginia in 1785–86 when the Virginia legislative body was about to renew Virginia's tax levy for the support of the established church. Thomas Jefferson and James Madison led the fight against this tax. Madison wrote his great *Memorial and Remonstrance* against the law. In it, he eloquently argued that a true religion did not need the support of law; that no person, either believer or non-believer, should be taxed to support a religious institution of any kind; that the best interest of a society required that the minds of men always be wholly free; and that cruel persecutions were the inevitable result of government-established religions. Madison's *Remonstrance* received strong support throughout Virginia, and the Assembly postponed consideration of the proposed tax measure until its next session. When the proposal came up for consideration at that session, it not only died in committee, but the Assembly enacted the famous "Virginia Bill for Religious Liberty" originally written by Thomas Jefferson. The preamble to that Bill stated among other things that "Almighty God hath created the mind free; that all attempts to influence it by temporal punishments, or burthens, or by civil incapacitations, tend only to beget habits of hypocrisy and meanness, and are a departure from the plan of the Holy author of our religion who being Lord both of body and mind, yet chose not to propagate it by coercions on either that to compel a man to furnish contributions of money for the propagation of opinions which he disbelieves, is sinful and tyrannical; that even the forcing him to support this or that teacher of his own religious persuasion, is depriving him of the comfortable liberty of giving his contributions to the particular pastor, whose morals he would make his pattern."

And the statute itself enacted "That no man shall be compelled to frequent or support any religious worship, place, or ministry whatsoever, nor shall be enforced, restrained, molested, or burthened, in his body or goods, nor shall otherwise suffer on account of his religious opinions or belief."

This Court has previously recognized that the provisions of the First Amendment, in the drafting and adoption of which Madison and Jefferson played such leading roles, had the same objective and were intended to provide the same protection against governmental intrusion on religious liberty as the Virginia statute.

The meaning and scope of the First Amendment, preventing establishment of religion or prohibiting the free exercise thereof, in the light of its history and the evils it was designed forever to suppress, have been several times elaborated by the decisions of this Court. The broad meaning given the Amendment by these earlier cases has been accepted by this Court in its decisions concerning an individual's religious freedom rendered since the Fourteenth Amendment was interpreted to make the prohibitions of the First applicable to state action abridging religious freedom. There is every reason to give the same application and broad interpretation to the "establishment of religion" clause.

The "establishment of religion" clause of the First Amendment means at least this: Neither a state nor the Federal Government can set up a church. Neither can pass laws which aid one religion, aid all religions, or prefer one religion over another. Neither can force nor influence a person to go to or to remain away from church against his will or force him to profess a belief or disbelief in any religion. No person can be punished for entertaining or professing religious beliefs or disbeliefs, for church attendance or non-attendance. No tax in any amount, large or small, can be levied to support any religious activities or institutions, whatever they may be called, or whatever form they may adopt to teach or practice religion. Neither a state nor the Federal Government can, openly or secretly, participate in the affairs of any religious organizations or groups and vice versa. In the words of Jefferson, the clause against establishment of religion by law was intended to erect "a wall of separation between Church and State."

We must consider the New Jersey statute in accordance with the foregoing limitations imposed by the First Amendment. But we must not strike that state statute down if it is within the state's constitutional power even though it approaches the verge of that power. New Jersey cannot consistently with the "establishment of religion" clause of the First Amendment contribute tax-raised funds to the support of an institution which teaches the tenets and faith of any church. On the other hand, other language of the amendment commands that New Jersey cannot hamper its citizens in the free exercise of their own religion. Consequently, it cannot exclude individual Catholics, Lutherans, Mohammedans, Baptists, Jews, Methodists, Non-believers, Presbyterians, or the members of any other faith, because of their faith, or lack of it, from receiving the benefits of public welfare legislation. While we do not mean to intimate that a state could not provide transportation only to children attending public schools, we must be careful, in protecting the citizens of New Jersey against state-established churches, to be sure that we do not inadvertently prohibit New Jersey from extending its general State law benefits to all its citizens without regard to their religious belief.

Measured by these standards, we cannot say that the First Amendment prohibits New Jersey from spending tax-raised funds to pay the bus fares of parochial school pupils as a part of a general program under which it pays the fares of pupils attending public and other schools. It is undoubtedly true that children are helped to get to church schools. There is even a possibility that some of the children might not be sent to the church schools if the parents were compelled to pay their children's bus fares out of their own pockets when transportation to a public school would have been paid for by the State. The same possibility exists where the state requires a local transit company to provide reduced fares to school children including those attending parochial schools, or where a municipally owned transportation system undertakes to carry all school children free of charge. Moreover, state-paid policemen, detailed to protect children going to and from church schools from the very real hazards of traffic, would serve much the same purpose and accomplish much the same result as state provisions intended to guarantee free transportation of a kind which the state deems to be best for the school children's welfare. And parents might refuse to risk their children to the serious danger of traffic accidents going to and from parochial schools, the approaches to which were not protected by policemen. Similarly, parents might be reluctant to permit their children to attend schools which the state had cut off from such general government services as ordinary police and fire protection, connections for sewage disposal, public highways and sidewalks. Of course, cutting off church schools from these services, so separate and so indisputably marked off from the religious function, would make it far more difficult for the schools to operate. But such is obviously not the purpose of the First Amendment. That Amendment requires the state to be a neutral in its relations with groups of religious believers and non-believers; it does not require the state to be their adversary. State power is no more to be used so as to handicap religions, than it is to favor them.

This Court has said that parents may, in the discharge of their duty under state compulsory education laws, send their children to a religious rather than a public school if the school meets the secular educational requirements which the state has power to impose. It appears that these parochial schools meet New Jersey's requirements. The State contributes no money to the schools. It does not support them. Its legislation, as applied, does no more than provide a general program to help parents get their children, regardless of their religion, safely and expeditiously to and from accredited schools.

The First Amendment has erected a wall between church and state. That wall must be kept high and impregnable. We could not approve the slightest breach. New Jersey has not breached it here.

*We think that the constitutional prohibition against laws respecting an establishment of religion must at least mean that in this country it is no part of the business of government to compose official prayers for any group of the American people to recite as a part of a religious program carried on by government.*

— *Hugo L. Black*

## Engel v. Vitale
### 82 S.Ct. 1261, 370 U.S. 421 (1962)

*This is among the most controversial decisions of modern times. "I think this decision is wrong," Justice Stewart insisted in his solo dissent, "I cannot see how an 'official religion' is established by letting those who want to say a prayer say it." Attempts to overrule this holding by amending the Constitution to allow prayer in public schools were begun immediately and continue to the present day. In* Lemon v. Kurtzman *(1971), the Court announced a formalistic three-part test for determining whether a government action is a "law respecting the establishment of religion:" (1) the law must have a secular purpose; (2) the primary effect of the law must be one that neither advances nor inhibits religion; and (3) the law must not foster an excessive entanglement with religion. The on-going problem is that the Justices have been unable to agree how to apply this test. Consequently, later holdings have been entirely inconsistent and an analytical chaos has characterized establishment clause jurisprudence. The lines of Court-critics form on the political right and on the political left, depending on the particular outcome, and the queues often are long and angry.*

**Justice Black:** The Board of Education of Union Free School District No. 9, New Hyde Park, New York, acting in its official capacity under state law, directed the School District's principal to cause the following prayer to be said aloud by each class in the presence of a teacher at the beginning of each school day: "Almighty God, we acknowledge our dependence upon Thee, and we beg Thy blessings upon us, our parents, our teachers and our Country." This daily procedure was adopted on the recommendation of the State Board of Regents, a governmental agency created by the State Constitution to which the New York Legislature has granted broad supervisory, executive, and legislative powers over the State's public school system. These state officials composed the prayer which they recommended and published as a part of their *Statement on Moral and Spiritual Training in the Schools,* saying: "We believe that this *Statement* will be subscribed to by all men and women of good will, and we call upon all of them to aid in giving life to our program."

Shortly after the practice of reciting the Regents' prayer was adopted by the School District, the parents of ten pupils brought this action in a New York State Court insisting that use of this official prayer in the public schools was contrary to the beliefs, religions, or religious practices of both themselves and their children. We granted *certiorari* to review this important decision involving rights protected by the First and Fourteenth Amendments.

We think that by using its public school system to encourage recitation of the Regents' prayer, the State of New York has adopted a practice wholly inconsistent with the Establishment Clause. There can, of course, be no doubt that New York's program of daily classroom invocation of God's blessings as prescribed in the Regents' prayer is a religious activity. It is a solemn avowal of divine faith and supplication for the blessings of the Almighty. The nature of such a prayer has always been religious, none of the government defendants has denied this and the trial court expressly so found.

The plaintiffs contend among other things that the state laws requiring or permitting use of the Regents' prayer must be struck down as a violation of the Establishment Clause because that prayer was composed by governmental officials as a part of a governmental program to further religious beliefs. For this reason, plaintiffs argue, the State's use of the Regents' prayer in its public school system breaches the constitutional wall of separation between Church and State. We agree with that contention since we think that the constitutional prohibition against laws respecting an establishment of religion must at least mean that in this country it is no part of the business of government to compose official prayers for any group of the American people to recite as a part of a religious program carried on by government.

It is a matter of history that this very practice of establishing governmentally composed prayers for religious services was one of the reasons which caused many of our early colonists to leave England and seek religious freedom in America. The *Book of Common Prayer*, which was created under governmental direction and which was approved by Acts of Parliament in 1548 and 1549, set out in minute detail the accepted form and content of prayer and other religious ceremonies to be used in the established, tax-supported Church of England. The controversies over the *Book* and what should be its content repeatedly threatened to disrupt the peace of that country as the accepted forms of prayer in the established church changed with the views of the particular ruler that happened to be in control at the time. Powerful groups representing some of the varying religious views of the people struggled among themselves to impress their particular views upon the Government and obtain amendments of the *Book* more suitable to their respective notions of how religious services should be conducted in order that the official religious establishment would advance their particular religious beliefs. Other groups, lacking the necessary political power to influence the Government on the matter, decided to leave England and its established church and seek freedom in America from England's governmentally ordained and supported religion.

It is an unfortunate fact of history that when some of the very groups which had most strenuously opposed the established Church of England found themselves sufficiently in control of colonial governments in this country to write their own prayers into law, they passed laws making their own religion the official religion of their respective colonies. Indeed, as late as the time of the Revolutionary War, there were established churches in at least eight of the thirteen former colonies and established religions in at least four of the other five. But the successful Revolution against English political domination was shortly followed by intense opposition to the practice of establishing religion by law. This opposition crystallized rapidly into an effective political force in Virginia where the minority religious groups such as Presbyterians, Lutherans, Quakers and Baptists had gained such strength that the adherents to the established Episcopal Church were actually a minority themselves. In 1785–1786, those opposed to the established Church, led by James Madison and Thomas Jefferson, who, though themselves not members of any of these dissenting religious groups, opposed all religious establishments by law on grounds of principle, obtained the enactment of the famous "Virginia Bill for Religious Liberty" by which all religious groups were placed on an equal footing so far as the State was concerned. Similar though less far-reaching legislation was being considered and passed in other States.

By the time of the adoption of the Constitution, our history shows that there was a widespread awareness among many Americans of the dangers of a union of Church and State. These people knew, some of them from bitter personal experience, that one of the greatest dangers to the freedom of the individual to worship in his own way lay in the Government's placing its official stamp of approval upon one particular kind of prayer or one particular form of religious services. They knew the anguish, hardship and bitter strife that could come when zealous religious groups struggled with one another to obtain the Government's stamp of approval from each King, Queen, or Protector that came to temporary power. The Constitution was intended to avert a part of this danger by leaving the government of this country in the hands of the people rather than in the hands of any monarch. But this safeguard was not enough. Our Founders were no more willing to let the content of their prayers and their privilege of praying whenever they pleased be influenced by the ballot box than they were to let these vital matters of personal conscience depend upon the succession of monarchs. The First Amendment was added to the Constitution to stand as a guarantee that neither the power nor the prestige of the Federal Government would be used to control, support or influence the kinds of prayer the American people can say—that the people's religions must not be subjected to the pressures of government for change each time a new political administration is elected to office. Under that Amendment's prohibition against governmental establishment of religion, as reinforced by the provisions of the Fourteenth Amendment, government in this country, be it state or federal, is without power to prescribe by law any particular form of prayer which is to be used as an official prayer in carrying on any program of governmentally sponsored religious activity.

There can be no doubt that New York's state prayer program officially establishes the religious beliefs embodied in the Regents' prayer. The defendants' argument to the contrary, which is largely based upon the contention that the Regents' prayer is "nondenominational" and the fact that the program, as modified and approved by state courts, does not require all pupils to recite the prayer but permits those who wish to do so to remain silent or be excused from the room, ignores the essential nature of the program's constitutional defects. Neither the fact that the prayer may be denominationally neutral nor the fact that its observance on the part of the students is voluntary can serve to free it from the limitations of the Establishment Clause, as it might from the Free Exercise Clause, of the First Amendment, both of which are operative against the States by virtue of the Fourteenth Amendment. Although these two clauses may in certain instances overlap, they forbid two quite different kinds of governmental encroachment upon religious freedom. The Establishment Clause, unlike the Free Exercise Clause, does not depend upon any showing of direct governmental compulsion and is violated by the enactment of laws which establish an official religion whether those laws operate directly to coerce nonobserving individuals or not. This is not to say, of course, that laws officially prescribing a particular form of religious worship do not involve coercion of such individuals. When the power, prestige and financial support of government is placed behind a particular religious belief, the indirect coercive pressure upon religious minorities to conform to the prevailing officially approved religion is plain. But the purposes underlying the Establishment Clause go much further than that. Its first and most immediate purpose rested on the belief that a union of government and religion tends to destroy government and to degrade religion. The history of governmentally established religion, both in England and in this country, showed that whenever government had allied itself with one particular form of religion, the inevitable result had been that it had incurred the hatred, disrespect and even contempt of those who held contrary beliefs. That same history showed that many people had lost their respect for any religion that had relied upon the support for government to spread its faith. The Establishment Clause thus stands as an expression of principle on the part of the Founders of our Constitution that religion is too personal, too sacred, too holy, to permit its "unhallowed perversion" by a civil magistrate.

Another purpose of the Establishment Clause rested upon an awareness of the historical fact that governmentally established religions and religious persecutions go hand in hand. The Founders knew that only a few years after the *Book of Common Prayer* became the only accepted form of religious services in the established Church of England, an Act of Uniformity was passed to compel all Englishmen to attend those services and to make it a criminal offense to conduct or attend religious gatherings of any other kind—a law which was consistently flouted by dissenting religious groups in England and which contributed to widespread persecutions of people like John Bunyan who persisted in holding "unlawful religious meetings to the great disturbance and distraction of the good subjects of this kingdom." And they knew that similar persecutions had received the sanction of law in several of the colonies in this country soon after the establishment of official religions in those colonies. It was in large part to get completely away from this sort of systematic religious persecution that the Founders brought into being our Nation, our Constitution, and our Bill of Rights with its prohibition against any governmental establishment of religion. The New York laws officially prescribing the Regents' prayer are inconsistent both with the purposes of the Establishment Clause and with the Establishment Clause itself.

It has been argued that to apply the Constitution in such a way as to prohibit state laws respecting an establishment of religious services in public schools is to indicate a hostility toward religion or toward prayer. Nothing, of course, could be more wrong. The history of man is inseparable from the history of religion. And perhaps it is not too much to say that since the beginning of that history many people have devoutly believed that "More things are wrought by prayer than this world dreams of." It was doubtless largely due to men who believed this that there grew up a sentiment that caused men to leave the cross-currents of officially established state religions and religious persecution in Europe and come to this country filled with the hope that they could find a place in which they could pray when they pleased to the God of their faith in the language they chose. And there were men of this same faith in the power of prayer who led the fight for adoption of our Constitution and also for our Bill of Rights with the very guarantees of religious freedom that forbid the sort of governmental activity which New York has attempted here. These men knew that the First Amendment, which tried to put an end to governmental control of religion and of prayer, was not written to destroy either. They knew rather that it was written to quiet well-justified fears which nearly all of them felt arising out of an awareness that governments of the past had shackled men's tongues to make them speak only the religious thoughts that government wanted them to speak and to pray only to the God that government wanted them to pray to. It is neither sacrilegious nor antireligious to say that each separate government in this country should stay out of the business of writing or sanctioning official prayers and leave that purely religious function to the people themselves and to those the people choose to look to for religious guidance.

It is true that New York's establishment of its Regents' prayer as an officially approved religious doctrine of that State does not amount to a total establishment of one particular religious sect to the exclusion of all others—that, indeed, the governmental endorsement of that prayer seems relatively insignificant when compared to the governmental encroachments upon religion which were commonplace 200 years ago. To those who may subscribe to the view that because the Regents' official prayer is so brief and general there can be no danger to religious freedom in its governmental establishment, however, it may be appropriate to say in the words of James Madison, the author of the First Amendment: "It is proper to take alarm at the first experiment on our liberties. Who does not see that the same authority which can establish Christianity, in exclusion of all other Religions, may establish with the same ease any particular sect of Christians, in exclusion of all other Sects? That the same authority which can force a citizen to contribute three pence only of his property for the support of any one establishment, may force him to conform to any other establishment in all cases whatsoever?"

*Laws are made for the government of actions, and while they cannot interfere with mere religious belief and opinions, they may with practices.*
— *Morrison R. Waite*

## Reynolds v. United States
### 98 U.S. 145 (1878)

*Because under our Constitution, "Man's relation to his God was made no concern of the state," Justice Douglas proclaimed in a 1944 opinion, "Men may believe what they cannot prove. They may not be put to the proof of their religious doctrines or beliefs." Ever since 1878, however, the Justices have conceded the government a power to regulate a citizen's actions or conduct, even though motivated by a religious belief. George Reynolds, secretary to Brigham Young, lost his challenge to the federal law in the Utah territory and went to prison for acting on his sincere religious belief in polygamy. In a controversial recent decision applying this 1878 principle, the Supreme Court approved a state decision to refuse unemployment compensation to two drug abuse rehabilitation counsellors who were fired for using the hallucinogen peyote in a Native-American religious ceremony; the plurality reasoned that the State was not obliged under the free exercise clause to grant a religious exemption from such an otherwise valid, neutral law.* Employment Division, Dept. of Human Services v. Smith (1990). *By a statute enacted in 1993, the Religious Freedom Restoration Act, Congress has made it more difficult for the States and the national government to regulate actual religious practices themselves, thus restoring some of the lost protection for religious exercises.*

**Chief Justice Waite:** On the trial, the accused proved that at the time of his alleged second marriage he was, and for many years before had been, a member of the Church of Jesus Christ of Latter-Day Saints, commonly called the Mormon Church, and a believer in its doctrines; that it was an accepted doctrine of that church "that it was the duty of male members of said church, circumstances permitting, to practise polygamy; that this duty was enjoined by different books which the members of said church believed to be of divine origin, and among others the

Holy Bible, and also that the members of the church believed that the practice of polygamy was directly enjoined upon the male members thereof by the Almighty God, in a revelation to Joseph Smith, the founder and prophet of said church; that the failing or refusing to practise polygamy by such male members of said church, when circumstances would admit, would be punished, and that the penalty for such failure and refusal would be damnation in the life to come." He also proved "that he had received permission from the recognized authorities in said church to enter into polygamous marriage; that Daniel H. Wells, one having authority in said church to perform the marriage ceremony, married the said defendant on or about the time the crime is alleged to have been committed, to some woman by the name of Schofield, and that such marriage ceremony was performed under and pursuant to the doctrines of said church."

The question is raised whether religious belief can be accepted as a justification of an overt act made criminal by the law of the land. The inquiry is not as to the power of Congress to prescribe criminal laws for the Territories, but as to the guilt of one who knowingly violates a law which has been properly enacted, if he entertains a religious belief that the law is wrong.

Congress cannot pass a law for the government of the Territories which shall prohibit the free exercise of religion. The first amendment to the Constitution expressly forbids such legislation. Religious freedom is guaranteed everywhere throughout the United States, so far as congressional interference is concerned. The question to be determined is, whether the law now under consideration comes within this prohibition.

The word "religion" is not defined in the Constitution. We must go elsewhere, therefore, to ascertain its meaning, and nowhere more appropriately, we think, than to the history of the times in the midst of which the provision was adopted. The precise point of the inquiry is, what is the religious freedom which has been guaranteed.

Before the adoption of the Constitution, attempts were made in some of the colonies and States to legislate not only in respect to the establishment of religion, but in respect to its doctrines and precepts as well. The people were taxed, against their will, for the support of religion, and sometimes for the support of particular sects to whose tenets they could not and did not subscribe. Punishments were prescribed for a failure to attend upon public worship, and sometimes for entertaining heretical opinions. The controversy upon this general subject was animated in many of the States, but seemed at last to culminate in Virginia. In 1784, the House of Delegates of that State having under consideration "a bill establishing provision for teachers of the Christian religion," postponed it until the next session, and directed that the bill should be published and distributed, and that the people be requested "to signify their opinion respecting the adoption of such a bill at the next session of assembly."

This brought out a determined opposition. Amongst others, Mr. Madison prepared a *Memorial and Remonstrance*, which was widely circulated and signed, and in which he demonstrated "that religion, or the duty we owe the Creator," was not within the cognizance of civil government. At the next session the proposed bill was not only defeated, but another, "for establishing religious freedom," drafted by Mr. Jefferson, was passed. In the preamble of this act, religious freedom is defined; and after a recital "that to suffer the civil magistrate to intrude his powers into the field of opinion, and to restrain the profession or propagation of principles on supposition of their ill tendency, is a dangerous fallacy which at once destroys all religious liberty," it is declared "that it is time enough for the rightful purposes of civil government for its officers to interfere when principles break out into overt acts against peace and good order." In these two sentences is found the true distinction between what properly belongs to the church and what to the State.

In a little more than a year after the passage of this statute, the convention met which prepared the Constitution of the United States. Of this convention Mr. Jefferson was not a member, he being then absent as minister to France. As soon as he saw the draft of the Constitution proposed for adoption, he, in a letter to a friend, expressed his disappointment at the absence of an express declaration insuring the freedom of religion, but was willing to accept it as it was, trusting that the good sense and honest intentions of the people would bring about the necessary alterations. Five of the States, while adopting the Constitution, proposed amendments. Three—New Hampshire, New York, and Virginia—included in one form or another a declaration of religious freedom in the changes they desired to have made, as did also North Carolina, where the convention at first declined to ratify the Constitution until the proposed amendments were acted upon. Accordingly, at the first session of the first Congress the amendment now under consideration was proposed with others by Mr. Madison. It met the views of the advocates of religious freedom, and was adopted. Mr. Jefferson afterwards, in reply to an address to him by a committee of the

Danbury Baptist Association, took occasion to say: "Believing with you that religion is a matter which lies solely between man and his God; that he owes account to none other for his faith or his worship; that the legislative powers of the government reach actions only, and not opinions—I contemplate with sovereign reverence that act of the whole American people which declared that their legislature should 'make no law respecting an establishment of religion or prohibiting the free exercise thereof,' thus building a wall of separation between church and State. Adhering to this expression of the supreme will of the nation in behalf of the rights of conscience, I shall see with sincere satisfaction the progress of those sentiments which tend to restore man to all his natural rights, convinced he has no natural right in opposition to his social duties." Coming as this does from an acknowledged leader of the advocates of the measure, it may be accepted almost as an authoritative declaration of the scope and effect of the amendment thus secured. Congress was deprived of all legislative power over mere opinion, but was left free to reach actions which were in violation of social duties or subversive of good order.

Polygamy has always been odious among the northern and western nations of Europe, and, until the establishment of the Mormon Church, was almost exclusively a feature of the life of Asiatic and of African people. At common law, the second marriage was always void, and from the earliest history of England polygamy has been treated as an offence against society. By a statute passed in the reign of James I, the offence, if committed in England or Wales, was made punishable in the civil courts, and the penalty was death. As this statute was limited in its operation to England and Wales, it was at a very early period re-enacted, generally with some modifications, in all the colonies. In connection with the case we are now considering, it is a significant fact that on the 8th of December, 1788, after the passage of the act establishing religious freedom, and after the convention of Virginia had recommended as an amendment to the Constitution of the United States the declaration in a bill of rights that "all men have an equal, natural, and unalienable right to the free exercise of religion, according to the dictates of conscience," the legislature of that State substantially enacted the statute of James I, death penalty included, because, as recited in the preamble, "it hath been doubted whether bigamy or polygamy be punishable by the laws of this Commonwealth." From that day to this we think it may safely be said there never has been a time in any State of the Union when polygamy has not been an offence against society, cognizable by the civil courts and punishable with more or less severity. In the face of all this evidence, it is impossible to believe that the constitutional guaranty of religious freedom was intended to prohibit legislation in respect to this most important feature of social life. Marriage, while from its very nature a sacred obligation, is nevertheless, in most civilized nations, a civil contract, and usually regulated by law. Upon it society may be said to be built, and out of its fruits spring social relations and social obligations and duties, with which government is necessarily required to deal. In fact, according as monogamous or polygamous marriages are allowed, do we find the principles on which the government of the people, to a greater or less extent, rests. Polygamy leads to the patriarchal principle, and which, when applied to large communities, fetters the people in stationary despotism, while that principle cannot long exist in connection with monogamy. An exceptional colony of polygamists under an exceptional leadership may sometimes exist for a time without appearing to disturb the social condition of the people who surround it; but there cannot be a doubt that, unless restricted by some form of constitution, it is within the legitimate scope of the power of every civil government to determine whether polygamy or monogamy shall be the law of social life under its dominion.

In our opinion, the statute immediately under consideration is within the legislative power of Congress. It is constitutional and valid as prescribing a rule of action for all those residing in the Territories, and in places over which the United States have exclusive control. This being so, the only question which remains is, whether those who make polygamy a part of their religion are excepted from the operation of the statute. If they are, then those who do not make polygamy a part of their religious belief may be found guilty and punished, while those who do, must be acquitted and go free. This would be introducing a new element into criminal law. Laws are made for the government of actions, and while they cannot interfere with mere religious belief and opinions, they may with practices. Suppose one believed that human sacrifices were a necessary part of religious worship, would it be seriously contended that the civil government under which he lived could not interfere to prevent a sacrifice? Or if a wife religiously believed it was her duty to burn herself upon the funeral pile of her dead husband, would it be beyond the power of the civil government to prevent her carrying her belief into practice?

So here, as a law of the organization of society under the exclusive dominion of the United States, it is provided that plural marriages shall not be allowed. Can a man excuse his practices to the contrary because of his religious belief? To permit this would be to make the professed doctrines of religious belief superior to the law of the land, and in effect to permit every citizen to become a law unto himself. Government could exist only in name under such circumstances.

A criminal intent is generally an element of crime, but every man is presumed to intend the necessary and legitimate consequences of what he knowingly does. Here the accused knew he had been once married, and that his first wife was living. He also knew that his second marriage was forbidden by law. When, therefore, he married the second time, he is presumed to have intended to break the law. And the breaking of the law is the crime. Every act necessary to constitute the crime was knowingly done, and the crime was therefore knowingly committed. Ignorance of a fact may sometimes be taken as evidence of a want of criminal intent, but not ignorance of the law. The only defence of the accused in this case is his belief that the law ought not to have been enacted. It matters not that his belief was a part of his professed religion: it was still belief, and belief only. When the offence consists of a positive act which is knowingly done, it would be dangerous to hold that the offender might escape punishment because he religiously believed the law which he had broken ought never to have been made. No case, we believe, can be found that has gone so far.

*If there is any fixed star in our constitutional
constellation, it is that no official, high or petty,
can prescribe what shall be orthodox in politics,
nationalism, religion, or other matters of opinion
or force citizens to confess by word or act their
faith therein.*

— *Robert H. Jackson*

## West Virginia Bd. of Educ. v. Barnette
### 63 S.Ct. 1178, 319 U.S. 624 (1943)

*In Minersville School District v. Gobitis (1940), the
Supreme Court upheld a state law mandating flag salute
and recitation of the Pledge of Allegiance in public
schools and ruled against Jehovah's Witness children
and their parents, by a vote of 8 to 1. Similar provisions
were enacted around the country. Public outrages against
the group, including physical attacks, became widespread
with the World War II emphasis on loyalty and patriotism. Only three years later, however, the Justices reversed
themselves by a vote of 6 to 3 with this opinion, so power-
fully written by Justice Jackson, which has become a
hallmark of the freedom of conscience.*

**Justice Jackson:** The freedom asserted by these children
does not bring them into collision with rights asserted by any
other individual. It is such conflicts which most frequently require intervention of the State to determine where the rights of
one end and those of another begin. But the refusal of these
persons to participate in the ceremony does not interfere with or
deny rights of others to do so. Nor is there any question in this
case that their behavior is peaceable and orderly. The sole conflict is between authority and rights of the individual. The State
asserts power to condition access to public education on making
a prescribed sign and profession and at the same time to coerce
attendance by punishing both parent and child. The latter stand
on a right of self-determination in matters that touch individual
opinion and personal attitude.

As the present Chief Justice said in his solitary dissent in
the *Gobitis* case, the State may "require teaching by instruction
and study of all in our history and in the structure and organization of our government, including the guaranties of civil liberty which tend to inspire patriotism and love of country." Here,

however, we are dealing with a compulsion of students to declare a belief. They are not merely made acquainted with the
flag salute so that they may be informed as to what it is or even
what it means. The issue here is whether this slow and easily
neglected route to aroused loyalties constitutionally may be
short-cut by substituting a compulsory salute and slogan.

There is no doubt that, in connection with the pledges, the
flag salute is a form of utterance. Symbolism is a primitive but
effective way of communicating ideas. The use of an emblem or
flag to symbolize some system, idea, institution, or personality,
is a short cut from mind to mind. Causes and nations, political
parties, lodges and ecclesiastical groups seek to knit the loyalty
of their followings to a flag or banner, a color or design. The
State announces rank, function, and authority through crowns
and maces, uniforms and black robes; the church speaks
through the Cross, the Crucifix, the altar and shrine, and cleri-
cal raiment. Symbols of State often convey political ideas just as
religious symbols come to convey theological ones. Associated
with many of these symbols are appropriate gestures of acceptance or respect: a salute, a bowed or bared head, a bended
knee. A person gets from a symbol the meaning he puts into it,
and what is one man's comfort and inspiration is another's jest
and scorn.

Over a decade ago Chief Justice Hughes led this Court in
holding that the display of a red flag as a symbol of opposition
by peaceful and legal means to organized government was protected by the free speech guaranties of the Constitution. Here it
is the State that employs a flag as a symbol of adherence to
government as presently organized. It requires the individual to
communicate by word and sign his acceptance of the political
ideas it thus bespeaks. Objection to this form of communication
when coerced is an old one, well known to the framers of the Bill
of Rights.[13]

It is also to be noted that the compulsory flag salute and
pledge requires affirmation of a belief and an attitude of mind.
It is not clear whether the regulation contemplates that pupils
forego any contrary convictions of their own and become unwill-

---

13. Early Christians were frequently persecuted for their refusal to
participate in ceremonies before the statue of the emperor or other symbol
of imperial authority. The story of William Tell's sentence to shoot an
apple off his son's head for refusal to salute a bailiff's hat is an ancient one.
The Quakers, William Penn included, suffered punishment rather than
uncover their heads in deference to any civil authority.

ing converts to the prescribed ceremony or whether it will be acceptable if they simulate assent by words without belief and by a gesture barren of meaning. It is now a commonplace that censorship or suppression of expression of opinion is tolerated by our Constitution only when the expression presents a clear and present danger of action of a kind the State is empowered to prevent and punish. It would seem that involuntary affirmation could be commanded only on even more immediate and urgent grounds than silence. But here the power of compulsion is invoked without any allegation that remaining passive during a flag salute ritual creates a clear and present danger that would justify an effort even to muffle expression. To sustain the compulsory flag salute we are required to say that a Bill of Rights which guards the individual's right to speak his own mind, left it open to public authorities to compel him to utter what is not in his mind.

Whether the First Amendment to the Constitution will permit officials to order observance of ritual of this nature does not depend upon whether as a voluntary exercise we would think it to be good, bad or merely innocuous. Any credo of nationalism is likely to include what some disapprove or to omit what others think essential, and to give off different overtones as it takes on different accents or interpretations.[14] If official power exists to coerce acceptance of any patriotic creed, what it shall contain cannot be decided by courts, but must be largely discretionary with the ordaining authority, whose power to prescribe would no doubt include power to amend. Hence validity of the asserted power to force an American citizen publicly to profess any statement of belief or to engage in any ceremony of assent to one presents questions of power that must be considered independently of any idea we may have as to the utility of the ceremony in question.

Nor does the issue as we see it turn on one's possession of particular religious views or the sincerity with which they are held. While religion supplies these persons' motive for enduring the discomforts of making the issue in this case, many citizens

---

14. For example: Use of "Republic," if rendered to distinguish our government from a "democracy," or the words "one Nation," if intended to distinguish it from a "federation," open up old and bitter controversies in our political history; "liberty and justice for all," if it must be accepted as descriptive of the present order rather than an ideal, might to some seem an overstatement.

who do not share these religious views hold such a compulsory rite to infringe constitutional liberty of the individual. It is not necessary to inquire whether non-conformist beliefs will exempt from the duty to salute unless we first find power to make the salute a legal duty.

The *Gobitis* decision, however, assumed, as did the argument in that case and in this, that power exists in the State to impose the flag salute discipline upon school children in general. The Court only examined and rejected a claim based on religious beliefs of immunity from an unquestioned general rule. The question which underlies the flag salute controversy is whether such a ceremony so touching matters of opinion and political attitude may be imposed upon the individual by official authority under powers committed to any political organization under our Constitution. We examine rather than assume existence of this power and, against this broader definition of issues in this case, re-examine specific grounds assigned for the *Gobitis* decision.

It was said that the flag-salute controversy confronted the Court with "the problem which Lincoln cast in memorable dilemma: 'Must a government of necessity be too strong for the liberties of its people, or too weak to maintain its own existence?'" and that the answer must be in favor of strength.

It may be doubted whether Mr. Lincoln would have thought that the strength of government to maintain itself would be impressively vindicated by our confirming power of the state to expel a handful of children from school. Such oversimplification, so handy in political debate, often lacks the precision necessary to postulates of judicial reasoning. If validly applied to this problem, the utterance cited would resolve every issue of power in favor of those in authority and would require us to override every liberty thought to weaken or delay execution of their policies.

Government of limited power need not be anemic government. Assurance that rights are secure tends to diminish fear and jealousy of strong government, and by making us feel safe to live under it makes for its better support. Without promise of a limiting Bill of Rights it is doubtful if our Constitution could have mustered enough strength to enable its ratification. To enforce those rights today is not to choose weak government over strong government. It is only to adhere as a means of strength to individual freedom of mind in preference to officially disciplined uniformity for which history indicates a disappointing and disastrous end.

The subject now before us exemplifies this principle. Free public education, if faithful to the ideal of secular instruction and political neutrality, will not be partisan or enemy of any class, creed, party, or faction. If it is to impose any ideological discipline, however, each party or denomination must seek to control, or failing that, to weaken the influence of the educational system. Observance of the limitations of the Constitution will not weaken government in the field appropriate for its exercise.

The very purpose of a Bill of Rights was to withdraw certain subjects from the vicissitudes of political controversy, to place them beyond the reach of majorities and officials and to establish them as legal principles to be applied by the courts. One's right to life, liberty, and property, to free speech, a free press, freedom of worship and assembly, and other fundamental rights may not be submitted to vote; they depend on the outcome of no elections.

Nor does our duty to apply the Bill of Rights to assertions of official authority depend upon our possession of marked competence in the field where the invasion of rights occurs. True, the task of translating the majestic generalities of the Bill of Rights, conceived as part of the pattern of liberal government in the eighteenth century, into concrete restraints on officials dealing with the problems of the twentieth century, is one to disturb self-confidence. These principles grew in soil which also produced a philosophy that the individual was the center of society, that his liberty was attainable through mere absence of governmental restraints, and that government should be entrusted with few controls and only the mildest supervision over men's affairs. We must transplant these rights to a soil in which the laissez-faire concept or principle of non-interference has withered at least as to economic affairs, and social advancements are increasingly sought through closer integration of society and through expanded and strengthened governmental controls. These changed conditions often deprive precedents of reliability and cast us more than we would choose upon our own judgment. But we act in these matters not by authority of our competence but by force of our commissions. We cannot, because of modest estimates of our competence in such specialties as public education, withhold the judgment that history authenticates as the function of this Court when liberty is infringed.

National unity as an end which officials may foster by persuasion and example is not in question. The problem is whether under our Constitution compulsion as here employed is a permissible means for its achievement.

Struggles to coerce uniformity of sentiment in support of some end thought essential to their time and country have been waged by many good as well as by evil men. Nationalism is a relatively recent phenomenon but at other times and places the ends have been racial or territorial security, support of a dynasty or regime, and particular plans for saving souls. As first and moderate methods to attain unity have failed, those bent on its accomplishment must resort to an ever-increasing severity. As governmental pressure toward unity becomes greater, so strife becomes more bitter as to whose unity it shall be. Probably no deeper division of our people could proceed from any provocation than from finding it necessary to choose what doctrine and whose program public educational officials shall compel youth to unite in embracing. Ultimate futility of such attempts to compel coherence is the lesson of every such effort from the Roman drive to stamp out Christianity as a disturber of its pagan unity, the Inquisition, as a means to religious and dynastic unity, the Siberian exiles as a means to Russian unity, down to the fast failing efforts of our present totalitarian enemies. Those who begin coercive elimination of dissent soon find themselves exterminating dissenters. Compulsory unification of opinion achieves only the unanimity of the graveyard.

It seems trite but necessary to say that the First Amendment to our Constitution was designed to avoid these ends by avoiding these beginnings. There is no mysticism in the American concept of the State or of the nature or origin of its authority. We set up government by consent of the governed, and the Bill of Rights denies those in power any legal opportunity to coerce that consent. Authority here is to be controlled by public opinion, not public opinion by authority.

The case is made difficult not because the principles of its decision are obscure but because the flag involved is our own. Nevertheless, we apply the limitations of the Constitution with no fear that freedom to be intellectually and spiritually diverse or even contrary will disintegrate the social organization. To believe that patriotism will not flourish if patriotic ceremonies are voluntary and spontaneous instead of a compulsory routine is to make an unflattering estimate of the appeal of our institutions to free minds. We can have intellectual individualism and the rich cultural diversities that we owe to exceptional minds only at the price of occasional eccentricity and abnormal attitudes. When they are so harmless to others or to the State as those we deal with here, the price is not too great. But freedom to differ is not limited to things that do not matter much. That would be a mere shadow of freedom. The test of its substance is the right to differ as to things that touch the heart of the existing order.

If there is any fixed star in our constitutional constellation, it is that no official, high or petty, can prescribe what shall be orthodox in politics, nationalism, religion, or other matters of opinion or force citizens to confess by word or act their faith therein. If there are any circumstances which permit an exception, they do not now occur to us.

We think the action of the local authorities in compelling the flag salute and pledge transcends constitutional limitations on their power and invades the sphere of intellect and spirit which it is the purpose of the First Amendment to our Constitution to reserve from all official control.

*And any compulsory discovery by extorting the party's oath, or compelling the production of his private books and papers, to convict him of crime, or to forfeit his property, is contrary to the principles of a free government.*

*— Joseph P. Bradley*

## Boyd v. United States
### 6 S.Ct. 524, 116 U.S. 616 (1886)

*This was the first important decision dealing with the 4th amendment right against unreasonable search and seizure and the 5th amendment right against self-incrimination. Although later decisions have narrowed its precedential authority, Justice Bradley's opinion for the Court remains a landmark of individual rights. The noble sentiments he expressed continue to be invoked down to the present day. This was a civil action by the Government to forfeit goods imported without paying the required duty, in violation of customs laws. An 1874 statute, first enacted in 1863, obliged the importer to produce in court all relevant records pertaining to the goods in question (35 cases of plate glass) or else the offense of not paying the duty would be deemed "confessed" and a civil forfeiture of the goods would follow automatically. The automatic penalty, in the Court's view, effectively made the production of the records compulsory. In his own famous opinion in* Olmstead v. United States *(1928), Justice Brandeis proclaimed this was "a case that will be remembered as long as civil liberty lives in the United States."*

**Justice Bradley:** The clauses of the constitution, to which it is contended that these customs laws are repugnant, are the fourth and fifth amendments. But, in regard to the fourth amendment, it is contended that, whatever might have been alleged against the constitutionality of prior statutes, the current statute, under which the order in the present case was made, is free from constitutional objection, because it does not authorize the search and seizure of books and papers, but only requires the defendant or claimant to produce them. That is so; but it declares that if he does not produce them, the allegations which it is affirmed they will prove shall be taken as confessed.

This is tantamount to compelling their production, for the prosecuting attorney will always be sure to state the evidence expected to be derived from them as strongly as the case will admit of. It is true that certain aggravating incidents of actual search and seizure, such as forcible entry into a man's house and searching among his papers, are wanting, and to this extent the proceeding under the current statute is a mitigation of that which was authorized by the former acts; but it accomplishes the substantial object of those acts in forcing from a party evidence against himself. It is our opinion, therefore, that a compulsory production of a man's private papers to establish a criminal charge against him, or to forfeit his property, is within the scope of the fourth amendment to the constitution, in all cases in which a search and seizure would be, because it is a material ingredient, and effects the sole object and purpose of search and seizure.

The principal question, however, remains to be considered. Is a search and seizure, or, what is equivalent thereto, a compulsory production of a man's private papers, to be used in evidence against him in a proceeding to forfeit his property for alleged fraud against the revenue laws—is such a proceeding for such a purpose an "unreasonable search and seizure" within the meaning of the fourth amendment of the constitution? or is it a legitimate proceeding? It is contended by the counsel for the government, that it is a legitimate proceeding, sanctioned by long usage, and the authority of judicial decision. No doubt long usage, acquiesced in by the courts, goes a long way to prove that there is some plausible ground or reason for it in the law, or in the historical facts which have imposed a particular construction of the law favorable to such usage. But we do not find any long usage or any contemporary construction of the constitution, which would justify any of the acts of congress now under consideration.

In order to ascertain the nature of the proceedings intended by the fourth amendment to the constitution under the terms "unreasonable searches and seizures," it is only necessary to recall the contemporary or then recent history of the controversies on the subject, both in this country and in England. The practice had obtained in the colonies of issuing writs of assistance to the revenue officers, empowering them, in their discretion, to search suspected places for smuggled goods, which James Otis pronounced "the worst instrument of arbitrary power, the most destructive of English liberty and the fundamental principles of law, that ever was found in an English law book;" since they placed "the liberty of every man in the hands of every petty officer." This was in February, 1761, in Boston, and the famous debate in which it occurred was perhaps the most prominent event which inaugurated the resistance of the colonies to the oppressions of the mother country.

"Then and there," said John Adams, "then and there was the first scene of the first act of opposition to the arbitrary claims of Great Britain. Then and there the child Independence was born." These things, and the events which took place in England immediately following the argument about writs of assistance in Boston, were fresh in the memories of those who achieved our independence and established our form of government. In the period from 1762, when the *North Briton* newspaper was started by John Wilkes, to April, 1766, when the house of commons passed resolutions condemnatory of general warrants, whether for the seizure of persons or papers, occurred the bitter controversy between the English government and Wilkes, in which the latter appeared as the champion of popular rights, and was, indeed, the pioneer in the contest which resulted in the abolition of some grievous abuses which had gradually crept into the administration of public affairs. Prominent and principal among these was the practice of issuing general warrants by the secretary of state, for searching private houses for the discovery and seizure of books and papers that might be used to convict their owner of the charge of libel. The *North Briton* had been very bold in denunciation of the government, and were esteemed heinously libelous. By authority of the secretary's warrant Wilkes' house was searched, and his papers were indiscriminately seized. For this outrage he sued the perpetrators and obtained a verdict of 1,000 pounds sterling against Wood, one of the party who made the search, and 4,000 pounds sterling against Lord Halifax, the secretary of state, who issued the warrant.

The case, however, which will always be celebrated as being the occasion of Lord Camden's memorable discussion of the subject, was that of *Entick v. Carrington and Three Other King's Messengers.* The action was trespass for entering the plaintiff's dwelling-house in November, 1762, and breaking open his desks, boxes, etc., and searching and examining his papers. The jury rendered a special verdict, and the case was twice solemnly argued at the bar. Lord Camden pronounced the judgment of the court in Michaelmas term, 1765, and the law, as expounded by him, has been regarded as settled from that time to this, and his great judgment on that occasion is considered as on of the landmarks of English liberty. It was welcomed and applauded by the lovers of liberty in the colonies as well as in the mother country. It is regarded as one of the permanent monuments of the British constitution, and is quoted as such by the English authorities on that subject down to the present time.

As every American statesman, during our revolutionary and formative period as a nation, was undoubtedly familiar with this monument of English freedom, and considered it as the true and ultimate expression of constitutional law, it may be confidently asserted that its propositions were in the minds of those who framed the fourth amendment to the constitution, and were considered as sufficiently explanatory of what was meant by unreasonable searches and seizures. We think, therefore, it is pertinent to the present subject of discussion to quote somewhat largely from this celebrated judgment. After describing the power claimed by the secretary of state for issuing general search-warrants, and the manner in which they were executed, Lord Camden says:

The great end for which men entered into society was to secure their property. That right is preserved sacred and incommunicable in all instances where it has not been taken away or abridged by some public law for the good of the whole. By the laws of England, every invasion of private property, be it ever so minute, is a trespass. No man can set his foot upon my ground without my license, but he is liable to an action, though the damage be nothing, which is proved by every declaration in trespass where the defendant is called upon to answer for bruising the grass and even treading upon the soil. If he admits the fact, he is bound to show, by way of justification, that some positive law has justified or excused him. The justification is submitted to the judges, who are to look into the books, and see if such a justification can be maintained by the text of the statute law, or by the principles of the common law. If that cannot be done, it is a trespass.

Papers are the owner's goods and chattels; they are his dearest property, and are so far from enduring a seizure, that they will hardly bear an inspection; and though the eye cannot by the laws of England be guilty of a trespass, yet where private papers are removed and carried away the secret nature of those goods will be an aggravation of the trespass, and demand more considerable damages in that respect. Where is the written law that gives any magistrate such a power? I can safely answer, there is none; and therefore it is too much for us, without such authority, to pronounce a practice legal which would be subversive of all the comforts of society.

Lastly it is urged as an argument of utility that such a search is a means of detecting offenders by discovering evidence. It is very certain that the law obligeth no man to accuse himself, because the necessary means of compelling self-accusation, falling upon the innocent as well as the guilty, would be both cruel and unjust; and it would seem that search for evidence is disallowed upon the same principle. Then, too, the innocent would be confounded with the guilty.

After a few further observations, his lordship concluded thus: "I have now taken notice of everything that has been urged upon the present point; and upon the whole we are all of opinion that the warrant to seize and carry away the party's papers in the case of a seditious libel is illegal and void."

The principles laid down in this opinion affect the very essence of constitutional liberty and security. They reach further than the concrete form of the case then before the court, with its adventitious circumstances; they apply to all invasions on the part of the government and its employees of the sanctity of a man's home and the privacies of life. It is not the breaking of his doors, and the rummaging of his drawers, that constitutes the essence of the offense; but it is the invasion of his indefeasible right of personal security, personal liberty, and private property, where that right has never been forfeited by his conviction of some public offense—it is the invasion of this sacred right which underlies and constitutes the essence of Lord Camden's judgment. Breaking into a house and opening boxes and drawers are circumstances of aggravation; but any forcible and compulsory extortion of a man's own testimony, or of his private papers to be used as evidence to convict him of crime, or to forfeit his goods, is within the condemnation of that judgment. In this regard the fourth and fifth amendments run almost into each other. Can we doubt that when the fourth and fifth amendments to the constitution of the United States were penned and adopted, the language of Lord Camden was relied on as expressing the true doctrine on the subject of searches and seizures, and as furnishing the true criteria of the reasonable and 'unreasonable" character of such seizures? Could the men who proposed those amendments, in the light of Lord Camden's opinion, have put their hands to a law like the predecessor statute of

1863? If they could not, would they have approved the act of 1874, which was adopted as a substitute for the previous statute? It seems to us that the question cannot admit of a doubt. They never would have approved of them. The struggles against arbitrary power in which they had been engaged for more than 20 years would have been too deeply engraved in their memories to have allowed them to approve of such insidious disguises of the old grievance which they had so deeply abhorred.

The views of the first congress on the question of compelling a man to produce evidence against himself may be inferred from a remarkable section of the judiciary act of 1789. The fifteenth section of that act introduced a great improvement in the law of procedure for the production of documents. The restriction of this section to "cases and under circumstances where they the parties might be compelled to produce the same books or writings by the ordinary rules of proceeding in chancery," shows the wisdom of the congress of 1789. The court of chancery had for generations been weighing and balancing the rules to be observed in granting discovery on bills filed for that purpose, in the endeavor to fix upon such as would best secure the ends of justice. To go beyond the point to which that court had gone may well have been thought hazardous. Now it is elementary knowledge that one cardinal rule of the court of chancery is never to decree a discovery which might tend to convict the party of a crime, or to forfeit his property. And any compulsory discovery by extorting the party's oath, or compelling the production of his private books and papers, to convict him of crime, or to forfeit his property, is contrary to the principles of a free government. It is abhorrent to the instincts of an Englishman; it is abhorrent to the instincts of an American. It may suit the purposes of despotic power, but it cannot abide the pure atmosphere of political liberty and personal freedom.

We have already noticed the intimate relation between the two amendments. They throw great light on each other. For the "unreasonable searches and seizures" condemned in the fourth amendment are almost always made for the purpose of compelling a man to give evidence against himself, which in criminal cases is condemned in the fifth amendment; and compelling a man "in a criminal case to be a witness against himself," which is condemned in the fifth amendment, throws light on the question as to what is an "unreasonable search and seizure" within the meaning of the fourth amendment. And we have been unable to perceive that the seizure of a man's private books and papers to be used in evidence against him is substantially different from compelling him to be a witness against himself. We think it is within the clear intent and meaning of those terms. We are also clearly of opinion that proceedings instituted for the purpose of declaring the forfeiture of a man's property by reason of offenses committed by him, though they may be civil in form, are in their nature criminal. In this very case the ground of forfeiture consists of certain acts of fraud committed against the public revenue in relation to imported merchandise which are made criminal by statute; and it is declared, that the offender shall be fined or be imprisoned, or both; and in addition such merchandise shall be forfeited. These are the penalties affixed to the criminal acts, the forfeiture sought by this suit being one of them. As, therefore, suits for penalties and forfeitures, incurred by the commission of offenses against the law, are of this quasi criminal nature, we think that they are within the reason of criminal proceedings for all the purposes of the fourth amendment of the constitution, and of that portion of the fifth amendment which declares that no person shall be compelled in any criminal case to be a witness against himself; and we are further of opinion that a compulsory production of the private books and papers of the owner of goods sought to be forfeited in such a suit is compelling him to be a witness against himself, within the meaning of the fifth amendment to the constitution, and is the equivalent of a search and seizure—and an unreasonable search and seizure—within the meaning of the fourth amendment. Though the proceeding in question is divested of many of the aggravating incidents of actual search and seizure, yet, as before said, it contains their substance and essence, and effects their substantial purpose. It may be that it is the obnoxious thing in its mildest and least repulsive form; but illegitimate and unconstitutional practices get their first footing in that way, namely, by silent approaches and slight deviations from legal modes of procedure. This can only be obviated by adhering to the rule that constitutional provisions for the security of person and property should be liberally construed. A close and literal construction deprives them of half their efficacy, and leads to gradual depreciation of the right, as if it consisted more in sound than in substance.

It is the duty of courts to be watchful for the constitutional rights of the citizen, and against any stealthy encroachments thereon. Their motto should be *obsta principiis*. We have no doubt that the legislative body is actuated by the same motives; but the vast accumulation of public business brought before it sometimes prevents it, on a first presentation, from noticing objections which become developed by time and the practical application of the objectionable law. We think that the notice to produce the invoice in this case, the order by virtue of which it was issued, and the law which authorized the order, were unconstitutional and void, and that the inspection by the district attorney of said invoice, when produced in obedience to said notice, and its admission in evidence by the court, were erroneous and unconstitutional proceedings.

*Of course, vagrancy statutes are useful to the police. Of course, they are nets making easy the roundup of so-called undesirables. But the rule of law implies equality and justice in its application.*
— *William O. Douglas*

## Papachristou v. City of Jacksonville
### 92 S.Ct. 839, 405 U.S. 156 (1972)

*This unanimous decision consolidated several appeals from convictions under the same city ordinance. Some of the defendants had prior arrest records and were in fact engaged in suspicious activity, according to the police. Some had never been arrested before and were able to provide lawful and credible explanations for what they were doing when police arrested them. Before and after this case, the Supreme Court has given vagrancy prosecutions short shrift. In the famous "Shuffling Sam" case,* Thompson v. City of Louisville (1960), *the Court took the extraordinary step of granting review in a case from a local Police Court and summarily reversed a conviction for loitering and disorderly conduct because the record was totally devoid of evidence of any wrongdoing. In* Kolender v. Lawson (1983), *the Court invalidated for vagueness a California statute that required persons loitering or wandering to provide police with "credible and reliable" identification. "The majestic egalitarianism of the law," French writer Anatole France remarked near the turn of the century, "forbids rich and poor alike to sleep under bridges, to beg in the streets, and to steal bread." Justice Douglas, perhaps the most eccentric individualist ever to sit on the Supreme Court, would insist that in a free country, free people—rich and poor alike—have a constitutional right to loaf.*

**Justice Douglas:** This case involves eight defendants who were convicted in a Florida municipal court of violating a Jacksonville, Florida, vagrancy ordinance, which provided at the time of these arrests and convictions as follows:

Rogues and vagabonds, or dissolute persons who go about begging, common gamblers, persons who use juggling or unlawful games or plays, common drunkards, common night walkers, thieves, pilferers or pickpockets, traders in stolen property, lewd, wanton and lascivious persons, keepers of gambling places, common railers and brawlers, persons wandering or strolling around from place to place without any lawful purpose or object, habitual loafers, disorderly persons, persons neglecting all lawful business and habitually spending their time by frequenting houses of ill fame, gaming houses, or places where alcoholic beverages are sold or served, persons able to work but habitually living upon the earnings of their wives or minor children shall be deemed vagrants and, upon conviction in the Municipal Court shall be punished as provided for Class D offenses.

Class D offenses were punishable by 90 days' imprisonment, $500 fine, or both. The State of Florida also has a vagrancy statute which reads quite closely on the Jacksonville ordinance.

Jacksonville's ordinance and Florida's statute were "derived from early English law," and employ "archaic language" in their definitions of vagrants. The history is an often-told tale. The break-up of feudal estates in England led to labor shortages which in turn resulted in the Statutes of Laborers, designed to stabilize the labor force by prohibiting increases in wages and prohibiting the movement of workers from their home areas in search of improved conditions. Later vagrancy laws became criminal aspects of the poor laws. The series of laws passed in England on the subject became increasingly severe. But today "the theory of the Elizabethan poor laws no longer fits the facts." The conditions which spawned these laws may be gone, but the archaic classifications remain.

This ordinance is void for vagueness, both in the sense that it "fails to give a person of ordinary intelligence fair notice that his contemplated conduct is forbidden by the statute," and because it encourages arbitrary and erratic arrests and convictions.

Living under a rule of law entails various suppositions, one of which is that "all persons are entitled to be informed as to what the State commands or forbids." There is a well-recognized group of cases insisting that the law give fair notice of the offending conduct. In the field of regulatory statutes governing business activities, where the acts limited are in a narrow category, greater leeway is allowed.

The poor among us, the minorities, the average householder are not in business and not alerted to the regulatory schemes of vagrancy laws; and we assume they would have no understanding of their meaning and impact if they read them. Nor are they protected from being caught in the vagrancy net by the necessity of having a specific intent to commit an unlawful act.

The Jacksonville ordinance makes criminal activities which by modern standards are normally innocent. "Nightwalking" is one. Florida construes the ordinance not to make criminal one night's wandering, only the "habitual" wanderer or, as the ordinance describes it, "common night walkers." We know, however, from experience that sleepless people often walk at night, perhaps hopeful that sleep-inducing relaxation will result.

Luis Munoz-Marin, former Governor of Puerto Rico, commented once that "loafing" was a national virtue in his Commonwealth and that it should be encouraged. It is, however, a crime in Jacksonville, Florida.

"Persons able to work but habitually living upon the earnings of their wives or minor children"—like habitually living "without visible means of support"—might implicate unemployed pillars of the community who have married rich wives.

"Persons able to work but habitually living upon the earnings of their wives or minor children" may also embrace unemployed people out of the labor market, by reason of a recession or disemployed by reason of technological or so-called structural displacements.

Persons "wandering or strolling" from place to place have been extolled by Walt Whitman and Vachel Lindsay. The qualification "without any lawful purpose or object" may be a trap for innocent acts. Persons "neglecting all lawful business and habitually spending their time by frequenting places where alcoholic beverages are sold or served" would literally embrace many members of golf clubs and city clubs.

Walkers and strollers and wanderers may be going to or coming from a burglary. Loafers or loiterers may be "casing" a place for a holdup. Letting one's wife support him is an intrafamily matter, and normally of no concern to the police. Yet it may, of course, be the setting for numerous crimes.

The difficulty is that these activities are historically part of the amenities of life as we have known them. They are not mentioned in the Constitution or in the Bill of Rights. These unwritten amenities have been in part responsible for giving our people the feeling of independence and self-confidence, the feeling of creativity. These amenities have dignified the right of dissent and have honored the right to be nonconformists and the right to defy submissiveness. They have encouraged lives of high spirits rather than hushed, suffocating silence.

They are embedded in Walt Whitman's writings, especially in his "Song of the Open Road." They are reflected too, in the spirit of Vachel Lindsay's "I Want to Go Wandering," and by Henry D. Thoreau ("I have met with but one or two persons in the course of my life who understood the art of Walking, that is, of taking walks,—who had a genius so to speak, for sauntering. He who sits still in a house all the time may be the greatest vagrant of all; but the saunterer, in the good sense, is no more vagrant than the meandering river, which is all the while sedulously seeking the shortest course to the sea.").

This aspect of the vagrancy ordinance before us is suggested by what this Court said in 1876 about a broad criminal statute enacted by Congress: "It would certainly be dangerous if the legislature could set a net large enough to catch all possible offenders, and leave it to the courts to step inside and say who could be rightfully detained, and who should be set at large." While that was a federal case, the due process implications are equally applicable to the States and to this vagrancy ordinance. Here the net cast is large, not to give the courts the power to pick and choose but to increase the arsenal of the police. Where the list of crimes is so all-inclusive and generalized as the one in this ordinance, those convicted may be punished for no more than vindicating affronts to police authority.

Another aspect of the ordinance's vagueness appears when we focus, not on the lack of notice given a potential offender, but on the effect of the unfettered discretion it places in the hands of the Jacksonville police. Professor Caleb Foote, an early student of this subject, has called the vagrancy-type law as offering "punishment by analogy." Such crimes, though long common in Russia, are not compatible with our constitutional system. We allow our police to make arrests only on "probable cause," a Fourth and Fourteenth Amendment standard applicable to the States as well as to the Federal Government. Arresting a person on suspicion, like arresting a person for investigation, is foreign to our system, even when the arrest is for past criminality. Future criminality, however, is the common justification for the presence of vagrancy statutes. Florida has, indeed, construed her vagrancy statute "as necessary regulations," *inter alia*, "to deter vagabondage and prevent crimes."

A direction by a legislature to the police to arrest all "suspicious" persons would not pass constitutional muster. A vagrancy prosecution may be merely the cloak for a conviction which could not be obtained on the real but undisclosed grounds for the arrest.

Those generally implicated by the imprecise terms of the ordinance—poor people, nonconformists, dissenters, idlers— may be required to comport themselves according to the life style deemed appropriate by the Jacksonville police and the state courts. Where, as here, there are no standards governing the exercise of the discretion granted by the ordinance, the scheme permits and encourages an arbitrary and discriminatory enforcement of the law. It furnishes a convenient tool for "harsh and discriminatory enforcement by local prosecuting officials, against particular groups deemed to merit their displeasure." It results in a regime in which the poor and the unpopular are permitted to "stand on a public sidewalk only at the whim of any police officer." Under these kinds of ordinances, as Professor Anthony Amsterdam has explained, "If some carefree type of fellow is satisfied to work just so much, and no more, as will pay for one square meal, some wine, and a flophouse daily, but a court thinks this kind of living subhuman, the fellow can be forced to raise his sights or go to jail as a vagrant."

A presumption that people who might walk or loaf or loiter or stroll or frequent houses where liquor is sold, or who are supported by their wives or who look suspicious to the police are to become future criminals is too precarious for a rule of law. The implicit presumption in these generalized vagrancy standards—that crime is being nipped in the bud—is too extravagant to deserve extended treatment. Of course, vagrancy statutes are useful to the police. Of course, they are nets making easy the roundup of so-called undesirables. But the rule of law implies equality and justice in its application. Vagrancy laws of the Jacksonville type teach that the scales of justice are so tipped that even-handed administration of the law is not possible. The rule of law, evenly applied to minorities as well as majorities, to the poor as well as the rich, is the great mucilage that holds society together.

The Jacksonville ordinance cannot be squared with our constitutional standards and is plainly unconstitutional.

*For the Fourth Amendment protects people, not places.*

*— Potter Stewart*

## Katz v. United States
### 88 S.Ct. 507, 389 U.S. 347 (1967)

*This landmark holding marks the modern under-standing of the 4th amendment's protection. Charles Katz was suspected of bookmaking. Federal agents "bugged" a public telephone booth he frequented, without first ob-taining a warrant or court order, by installing an elec-tronic eavesdropping device outside the booth. Earlier decisions had rested on fine distinctions whether the gov-ernment agents had physically trespassed on the property of a defendant based on elaborate common law rules. The majority finally gave up on that approach and started all over. From this case forward, the law of the 4th amend-ment would be based on the assumption that the right of privacy from government intrusion is individual and per-sonal. It includes private conversations. Justice Harlan wrote an important concurring opinion to explain the twofold requirement of the new* Katz *formula: a person must exhibit an actual or subjective expectation of pri-vacy plus the expectation must be one that society is pre-pared to accept as reasonable.*

**Justice Stewart:** The defendant has phrased the questions as follows: "(1) Whether a public telephone booth is a constitu-tionally protected area so that evidence obtained by attaching an electronic listening recording device to the top of such a booth is obtained in violation of the right to privacy of the user of the booth. (2) Whether physical penetration of a constitution-ally protected area is necessary before a search and seizure can be said to be violative of the Fourth Amendment to the United States Constitution."

We decline to adopt this formulation of the issues. In the first place, the correct solution of Fourth Amendment problems is not necessarily promoted by incantation of the phrase "consti-tutionally protected area." Secondly, the Fourth Amendment cannot be translated into a general constitutional "right to pri-vacy." That Amendment protects individual privacy against cer-tain kinds of governmental intrusion, but its protections go further, and often have nothing to do with privacy at all. Other provisions of the Constitution protect personal privacy from other forms of governmental invasion. But the protection of a person's general right to privacy—his right to be let alone by other people—is, like the protection of his property and of his very life, left largely to the law of the individual States.

Because of the misleading way the issues have been formulated, the parties have attached great significance to the characterization of the telephone booth from which the defendant placed his calls. The defendant has strenuously argued that the booth was a "constitutionally protected area." The Government has maintained with equal vigor that it was not. But this effort to decide whether or not a given "area," viewed in the abstract, is "constitutionally protected" deflects attention from the problem presented by this case. It is true that this Court has occasionally described its conclusions in terms of "constitutionally protected areas," but we have never suggested that this concept can serve as a talismanic solution to every Fourth Amendment problem. For the Fourth Amendment protects people, not places. What a person knowingly exposes to the public, even in his own home or office, is not a subject of Fourth Amendment protection. But what he seeks to preserve as private, even in an area accessible to the public, may be constitutionally protected.

The Government stresses the fact that the telephone booth from which the defendant made his calls was constructed partly of glass, so that he was as visible after he entered it as he would have been if he had remained outside. But what he sought to exclude when he entered the booth was not the intruding eye—it was the uninvited ear. He did not shed his right to do so simply because he made his calls from a place where he might be seen. No less than an individual in a business office, in a friend's apartment, or in a taxicab, a person in a telephone booth may rely upon the protection of the Fourth Amendment. One who occupies it, shuts the door behind him, and pays the toll that permits him to place a call is surely entitled to assume that the words he utters into the mouthpiece will not be broadcast to the world. To read the Constitution more narrowly is to ignore the vital role that the public telephone has come to play in private communication.

The Government contends, however, that the activities of its agents in this case should not be tested by Fourth Amendment requirements, for the surveillance technique they employed involved no physical penetration of the telephone booth from which the defendant placed his calls. It is true that the absence of such penetration was at one time thought to foreclose further Fourth Amendment inquiry, for that Amendment was thought to limit only searches and seizures of tangible property. But "the premise that property interests control the right of the Government to search and seize has been discredited." Thus, although a closely divided Court supposed back in 1928 that surveillance without any trespass and without the seizure of any material object fell outside the ambit of the Constitution, we have since departed from the narrow view on which that decision rested. Indeed, we have expressly held that the Fourth Amendment governs not only the seizure of tangible items, but extends as well to the recording of oral statements overheard without any "technical trespass under local property law." Once this much is acknowledged, and once it is recognized that the Fourth Amendment protects people—and not simply "areas"—against unreasonable searches and seizures it becomes clear that the reach of that Amendment cannot turn upon the presence or absence of a physical intrusion into any given enclosure.

We conclude that the underpinnings of our older precedents have been so eroded by our subsequent decisions that the "trespass" doctrine there enunciated can no longer be regarded as controlling. The Government's activities in electronically listening to and recording the defendant's words violated the privacy upon which he justifiably relied while using the telephone booth and thus constituted a "search and seizure" within the meaning of the Fourth Amendment. The fact that the electronic device employed to achieve that end did not happen to penetrate the wall of the booth can have no constitutional significance.

*Neither this Court's prior cases, nor the tradi-
tional definition of "voluntariness" requires proof
of knowledge of a right to refuse as the* sine qua
non *of an effective consent to a search.*

— *Potter Stewart*

## Schneckloth v. Bustamonte
### 93 S.Ct. 2041, 412 U.S. 218 (1973)

*Can you waive a constitutional right without knowing
about it? Around 3 a.m., the police stopped a car with one
headlight and a burned-out license plate light carrying
Robert Bustamonte and five others. The driver could not
produce a license. One of the others explained that the car
belonged to his brother. When the police asked him for
permission to search the vehicle without telling him he
could refuse, he said, "Sure, go ahead." Under the rear
seat, they found three wadded up checks that had been
stolen in a burglary of a car wash. The checks, along with
other evidence, were used to convict Bustamonte and the
others. The issue presented is whether a person must
know about a right before it can be waived. The Court's
answer was "no" in the context of a search and seizure,
even though in other cases here distinguished the Court
had previously ruled that a waiver of some constitutional
rights, like the right to counsel at trial, had to be knowing
and voluntary in order to be valid. In* Miranda v. Arizona
(1966), *which appears next in this Chapter, the Court
had imposed a duty on police to give a suspect a warning
about the right to remain silent and the right to have an
attorney before they can ask any questions. Here the
Court explains that the validity of a waiver of a constitutional right varies with the nature of the right being
waived. When the police have no warrant and there is no
excuse for them to search without a warrant, they must
ask for your permission before they can conduct a search.
But they do not have to tell you that you have a right to
refuse. Justice Brennan dissented to exclaim, "It wholly
escapes me how our citizens can meaningfully be said to
have waived something as precious as a constitutional
guarantee without ever being aware of its existence."*

**Justice Stewart:** It is important to make it clear at the outset what is not involved in this case. The defendant concedes that a search conducted pursuant to a valid consent is constitutionally permissible. And similarly the State concedes that when a prosecutor seeks to rely upon consent to justify the lawfulness of a search, he has the burden of proving that the consent was, in fact, freely and voluntarily given. The precise question in this case, then, is what must the prosecution prove to demonstrate that a consent was "voluntarily" given.

Our previous cases yield no talismanic definition of "voluntariness," mechanically applicable to the host of situations where the question has arisen. "The notion of "voluntariness," Justice Frankfurter once wrote, "is itself an amphibian." Rather, "voluntariness" has reflected an accommodation of a complex of values. At one end of the spectrum is the acknowledged need for effective enforcement of criminal laws. At the other end of the spectrum is the set of values reflecting society's deeply felt belief that the criminal law cannot be used as an instrument of unfairness, and that the possibility of unfair and even brutal police tactics poses a real and serious threat to civilized notions of justice. This Court's decisions reflect a frank recognition that the Constitution requires the sacrifice of neither security nor liberty.

The question whether a consent to a search was in fact "voluntary" or was the product of duress or coercion, express or implied, is a question of fact to be determined from the totality of all the circumstances. While knowledge of the right to refuse consent is one factor to be taken into account, the government need not establish such knowledge as the *sine qua non* of an effective consent. Two competing concerns must be accommodated in determining the meaning of a "voluntary" consent—the legitimate need for such searches and the equally important requirement of assuring the absence of coercion.

In situations where the police have some evidence of illicit activity, but lack probable cause to arrest or search, a search authorized by a valid consent may be the only means of obtaining important and reliable evidence. In the present case for example, while the police had reason to stop the car for traffic violations, the State does not contend that there was probable cause to search the vehicle or that the search was incident to a valid arrest of any of the occupants. Yet, the search yielded tangible evidence that served as a basis for a prosecution, and provided some assurance that others, wholly innocent of the crime, were not mistakenly brought to trial. And in those cases where there is probable cause to arrest or search, but where the police lack a warrant, a consent search may still be valuable. If the search is conducted and proves fruitless, that in itself may convince the police that an arrest with its possible stigma and embarrassment is unnecessary, or that a far more extensive search pursuant to a warrant is not justified. In short, a search pursuant to consent may result in considerably less inconvenience for the subject of the search, and, properly conducted, is a constitutionally permissible and wholly legitimate aspect of effective police activity.

But the Fourth and Fourteenth Amendments require that a consent not be coerced, by explicit or implicit means, by implied threat or covert force. For, no matter how subtly the coercion was applied, the resulting "consent" would be no more than a pretext for the unjustified police intrusion against which the Fourth Amendment is directed.

The problem of reconciling the recognized legitimacy of consent searches with the requirement that they be free from any aspect of official coercion cannot be resolved by any infallible touchstone. To approve such searches without the most careful scrutiny would sanction the possibility of official coercion; to place artificial restrictions upon such searches would jeopardize their basic validity. The requirement of a "voluntary" consent reflects a fair accommodation of the constitutional requirements involved. In examining all the surrounding circumstances to determine if in fact the consent to search was coerced, account must be taken of subtly coercive police questions, as well as the possibly vulnerable subjective state of the person who consents. Those searches that are the product of police coercion can thus be filtered out without undermining the continuing validity of consent searches. In sum, there is no reason for us to depart in the area of consent searches, from the traditional definition of "voluntariness."

To rule that the State must affirmatively prove that the subject of the search knew that he had a right to refuse consent, would, in practice, create serious doubt whether consent searches could continue to be conducted. There might be rare cases where it could be proved from the record that a person in fact affirmatively knew of his right to refuse. But more commonly where there was no evidence of any coercion, explicit or implicit, the prosecution would nevertheless be unable to demonstrate that the subject of the search in fact had known of his right to refuse consent.

The very object of the inquiry—the nature of a person's subjective understanding—underlines the difficulty of the prosecution's burden under the rule we reject in this case. Any defendant who was the subject of a search authorized solely by his consent could effectively frustrate the introduction into evidence of the fruits of that search by simply failing to testify that he in fact knew he could refuse to consent. And the near impossibility of meeting this prosecutorial burden suggests why this Court has never previously accepted any such litmus-paper test of voluntariness.

One alternative that would go far toward proving that the subject of a search did know he had a right to refuse consent would be to advise him of that right before eliciting his consent. That, however, is a suggestion that has been almost universally repudiated by both federal and state courts, and, we think, rightly so. For it would be thoroughly impractical to impose on the normal consent search the detailed requirements of an effective warning. Consent searches are part of the standard investigatory techniques of law enforcement agencies. They normally occur on the highway, or in a person's home or office, and under informal and unstructured conditions. The circumstances that prompt the initial request to search may develop quickly or be a logical extension of investigative police questioning. The police may seek to investigate further suspicious circumstances or to follow up leads developed in questioning persons at the scene of a crime. These situations are a far cry from the structured atmosphere of a trial where, assisted by counsel if he chooses, a defendant is informed of his trial rights. And, while surely a closer question, these situations are still immeasurably, far removed from "custodial interrogation" where, in 1966, we found that the Constitution required certain now familiar warnings as a prerequisite to police interrogation.

It is only by analyzing all the circumstances of an individual consent that it can be ascertained whether in fact it was voluntary or coerced. It is this careful sifting of the unique facts and circumstances of each case that is evidenced in our prior decisions involving consent searches. Conversely, if under all the circumstances it has appeared that the consent was not given voluntarily—that it was coerced by threats or force, or granted only in submission to a claim of lawful authority—then we have found the consent invalid and the search unreasonable.

Implicit in all of these cases is the recognition that knowledge of a right to refuse is not a prerequisite of a voluntary consent. Neither this Court's prior cases, nor the traditional definition of "voluntariness" requires proof of knowledge of a right to refuse as the *sine qua non* of an effective consent to a search.

It is said, however, that a "consent" is a "waiver" of a person's rights under the Fourth and Fourteenth Amendments. The argument is that by allowing the police to conduct a search, a person "waives" whatever right he had to prevent the police from searching. It is argued that to establish such a "waiver" the State must demonstrate "an intentional relinquishment or abandonment of a known right or privilege." But this standard was enunciated in the context of the safeguards of a fair criminal trial. Our cases do not reflect an uncritical demand for a knowing and intelligent waiver in every situation where a person has failed to invoke a constitutional protection. As Justice Black once observed for the Court: "Waiver" is a vague term used for a great variety of purposes, good and bad, in the law."

The general requirement of a "knowing" and "intelligent" waiver was articulated in a case involving the validity of a defendant's decision to forego a right constitutionally guaranteed to protect a fair trial and the reliability of the truth-determining process. The particular case dealt with the denial of counsel in a federal criminal trial. Almost without exception, the requirement of a knowing and intelligent waiver has been applied only to those rights which the Constitution guarantees to a criminal defendant in order to preserve a fair trial.

There is a vast difference between those rights that protect a fair criminal trial and the rights guaranteed under the Fourth Amendment. Nothing, either in the purposes behind requiring a "knowing" and "intelligent" waiver of trial rights, or in the practical application of such a requirement suggests that it ought to be extended to the constitutional guarantee against unreasonable searches and seizures.

A strict standard of waiver has been applied to those rights guaranteed to a criminal defendant to insure that he will be accorded the greatest possible opportunity to utilize every facet of the constitutional model of a fair criminal trial. Any trial conducted in derogation of that model leaves open the possibility that the trial reached an unfair result precisely because all the protections specified in the Constitution were not provided. A prime example is the right to counsel. For without that right, a wholly innocent accused faces the real and substantial danger that simply because of his lack of legal expertise he may be convicted.

The protections of the Fourth Amendment are of a wholly different order, and have nothing whatever to do with promoting the fair ascertainment of truth at a criminal trial. Rather, as Justice Frankfurter put it, the Fourth Amendment protects the "security of one's privacy against arbitrary intrusion by the police." This Court has emphasized that "there is no likelihood of unreliability or coercion present in a search-and-seizure case." The Fourth Amendment "is not an adjunct to the ascertainment of truth." The guarantees of the Fourth Amendment stand "as a protection of quite different constitutional values—values reflecting the concern of our society for the right of each individual to be let alone. To recognize this is no more than to accord those values undiluted respect."

Nor can it even be said that a search, as opposed to an eventual trial, is somehow "unfair" if a person consents to a search. While the Fourth and Fourteenth Amendments limit the circumstances under which the police can conduct a search, there is nothing constitutionally suspect in a person's voluntarily allowing a search. The actual conduct of the search may be precisely the same as if the police had obtained a warrant. And, unlike those constitutional guarantees that protect a defendant at trial, it cannot be said every reasonable presumption ought to be indulged against voluntary relinquishment. We have only recently stated: "It is no part of the policy underlying the Fourth and Fourteenth Amendments to discourage citizens from aiding to the utmost of their ability in the apprehension of criminals." Rather, the community has a real interest in encouraging consent, for the resulting search may yield necessary evidence for the solution and prosecution of crime, evidence that may insure that a wholly innocent person is not wrongly charged with a criminal offense.

It would be next to impossible to apply to a consent search the standard of "an intentional relinquishment or abandonment of a known right or privilege." It would be unrealistic to expect that in the informal, unstructured context of a consent search, a policeman, upon pain of tainting the evidence obtained, could make the detailed type of examination demanded by the defendant. And, if for this reason a diluted form of "waiver" were found acceptable, that would itself be ample recognition of the fact that there is no universal standard that must be applied in every situation where a person forgoes a constitutional right. In short, there is nothing in the purposes or application of the waiver requirement that justifies, much less compels, the easy equation of a knowing waiver with a consent search.

We hold only that when the subject of a search is not in custody and the State attempts to justify a search on the basis of his consent, the Fourth and Fourteenth Amendments require that it demonstrate that the consent was in fact voluntarily given, and not the result of duress or coercion, express or implied. Voluntariness is a question of fact to be determined from all the circumstances, and while the subject's knowledge of a right to refuse is a factor to be taken into account, the prosecution is not required to demonstrate such knowledge as a prerequisite to establishing a voluntary consent.

*The accused must be adequately and effectively
apprised of his rights and the exercise of those
rights must be fully honored.*

*— Earl Warren*

## Miranda v. Arizona
### 86 S.Ct. 1602, 384 U.S. 436 (1966)

*This is the best known and most criticized criminal
justice decision of the Warren Court. The majority here
abandons the traditional due process totality-of-the-cir-
cumstances analysis for determining whether a confession was voluntary and admissible. Chief Justice Warren
composed the obligatory warning that has become such a
standard police practice that anyone who watches enough
television can recite it. He went on to declare the statements of the four different defendants to be inadmissible.
The four dissenting Justices accused the majority of
straight-jacketing the police, a charge echoed with vehe-
mence by many in the law enforcement community at the
time. Numerous cases over the last thirty years, however,
have qualified the warning requirements, as more conservative Justices have swung the pendulum back in the
direction of law enforcement. Today, law enforcement officials have so internalized the warning in their training
and procedures that they have come to rely on it as a
formula that guarantees the in-court admissibility of a
confession.*

**Chief Justice Warren:** The cases before us raise questions
which go to the roots of our concepts of American criminal jurisprudence: the restraints society must observe consistent with
the Federal Constitution in prosecuting individuals for crime.
More specifically, we deal with the admissibility of statements
obtained from an individual who is subjected to custodial police
interrogation and the necessity for procedures which assure that
the individual is accorded his privilege under the Fifth Amendment to the Constitution not to be compelled to incriminate
himself.

In each of these four cases, the defendant was questioned by
police officers, detectives, or a prosecuting attorney in a room in
which he was cut off from the outside world. In none of these
cases was the defendant given a full and effective warning of his

rights at the outset of the interrogation process. In all the cases, the questioning elicited oral admissions, and in three of them, signed statements as well which were admitted at their trials. They all thus share salient features—incommunicado interrogation of individuals in a police-dominated atmosphere, resulting in self-incriminating statements without full warnings of constitutional rights.

An understanding of the nature and setting of this in-custody interrogation is essential to our decisions today. The difficulty in depicting what transpires at such interrogations stems from the fact that in this country they have largely taken place incommunicado. From extensive factual studies undertaken in the early 1930's, including the famous Wickersham Report to Congress by a Presidential Commission, it is clear that police violence and the "third degree" flourished at that time. In a series of cases decided by this Court long after these studies, the police resorted to physical brutality—beatings, hanging, whipping—and to sustained and protracted questioning incommunicado in order to extort confessions. The Commission on Civil Rights in 1961 found much evidence to indicate that "some policemen still resort to physical force to obtain confessions." The use of physical brutality and violence is not, unfortunately, relegated to the past or to any part of the country. These are undoubtedly the exception now, but they are sufficiently widespread to be the object of concern. Unless a proper limitation upon custodial interrogation is achieved—such as these decisions will advance—there can be no assurance that practices of this nature will be eradicated in the foreseeable future.

Again we stress that the modern practice of in-custody interrogation is psychologically rather than physically oriented. Interrogation still takes place in privacy. Privacy results in secrecy and this in turn results in a gap in our knowledge as to what in fact goes on in the interrogation rooms. A valuable source of information about present police practices, however, may be found in various police manuals and texts which document procedures employed with success in the past, and which recommend various other effective tactics. These texts are used by law enforcement agencies themselves as guides. It should be noted that these texts professedly present the most enlightened and effective means presently used to obtain statements through custodial interrogation. By considering these texts and other data, it is possible to describe procedures observed and noted around the country.

The officers are told by the manuals that the "principal psychological factor contributing to a successful interrogation is privacy—being alone with the person under interrogation." To highlight the isolation and unfamiliar surroundings, the manuals instruct the police to display an air of confidence in the suspect's guilt and from outward appearance to maintain only an interest in confirming certain details. The guilt of the subject is to be posited as a fact. The interrogator should direct his comments toward the reasons why the subject committed the act, rather than court failure by asking the subject whether he did it. Like other men, perhaps the subject has had a bad family life, had an unhappy childhood, had too much to drink, had an unrequited desire for women. The officers are instructed to minimize the moral seriousness of the offense, to cast blame on the victim or on society. These tactics are designed to put the subject in a psychological state where his story is but an elaboration of what the police purport to know already—that he is guilty. Explanations to the contrary are dismissed and discouraged. The texts thus stress that the major qualities an interrogator should possess are patience and perseverance.

When the techniques described above prove unavailing, the texts recommend they be alternated with a show of some hostility. One ploy often used has been termed the "friendly-unfriendly" or the "Mutt and Jeff" act. The interrogators sometimes are instructed to induce a confession out of trickery. The technique here is quite effective in crimes which require identification or which run in series. In the identification situation, the interrogator may take a break in his questioning to place the subject among a group of men in a line-up. "The witness or complainant (previously coached, if necessary) studies the line-up and confidently points out the subject as the guilty party." Then the questioning resumes "as though there were now no doubt about the guilt of the subject."

The manuals also contain instructions for police on how to handle the individual who refuses to discuss the matter entirely, or who asks for an attorney or relatives. The examiner is to concede him the right to remain silent. "This usually has a very undermining effect. First of all, he is disappointed in his expectation of an unfavorable reaction on the part of the interrogator. Secondly, a concession of this right to remain silent impresses the subject with the apparent fairness of his interrogator." After this psychological conditioning, however, the officer is told to point out the incriminating significance of the suspect's refusal to talk. Few will persist in their initial refusal to talk, it is said, if this technique is employed correctly.

In the event that the subject wishes to speak to a relative or an attorney, the following advice is tendered: "The interrogator should respond by suggesting that the subject first tell the truth to the interrogator himself rather than get anyone else involved in the matter. If the request is for an attorney, the interrogator may suggest that the subject save himself or his family the expense of any such professional service, particularly if he is innocent of the offense under investigation."

From these representative samples of interrogation techniques, the setting prescribed by the manuals and observed in practice becomes clear. In essence, it is this: To be alone with the subject is essential to prevent distraction and to deprive him of any outside support. The aura of confidence in his guilt undermines his will to resist. He merely confirms the preconceived story the police seek to have him describe. Patience and persistence, at times relentless questioning, are employed. To obtain a confession, the interrogator must "patiently maneuver himself or his quarry into a position from which the desired objective may be attained." When normal procedures fail to produce the needed result, the police may resort to deceptive stratagems such as giving false legal advice. It is important to keep the subject off balance, for example, by trading on his insecurity about himself or his surroundings. The police then persuade, trick, or cajole him out of exercising his constitutional rights.

Even without employing brutality, the "third degree" or the specific stratagems described above, the very fact of custodial interrogation exacts a heavy toll on individual liberty and trades on the weakness of individuals. In the cases before us today, given this background, we concern ourselves primarily with this interrogation atmosphere and the evils it can bring.

In these cases, we might not find the defendants' statements to have been involuntary in traditional terms. Our concern for adequate safeguards to protect precious Fifth Amendment rights is, of course, not lessened in the slightest. In each of the cases, the defendant was thrust into an unfamiliar atmosphere and run through menacing police interrogation procedures. The potentiality for compulsion is forcefully apparent. To be sure, the records do not evince overt physical coercion or patent psychological ploys. The fact remains that in none of these cases did the officers undertake to afford appropriate safeguards at the outset of the interrogation to insure that the statements were truly the product of free choice.

It is obvious that such an interrogation environment is created for no purpose other than to subjugate the individual to the will of his examiner. This atmosphere carries its own badge of intimidation. To be sure, this is not physical intimidation, but it is equally destructive of human dignity. The current practice of incommunicado interrogation is at odds with one of our Nation's most cherished principles—that the individual may not be compelled to incriminate himself. Unless adequate protective devices are employed to dispel the compulsion inherent in custodial surroundings, no statement obtained from the defendant can truly be the product of his free choice.

We sometimes forget how long it has taken to establish the privilege against self-incrimination, the sources from which it came and the fervor with which it was defended. Its roots go back into ancient times. Those who framed our Constitution and the Bill of Rights were ever aware of subtle encroachments on individual liberty. They knew that "illegitimate and unconstitutional practices get their first footing by silent approaches and slight deviations from legal modes of procedure." The privilege was elevated to constitutional status and has always been "as broad as the mischief against which it seeks to guard." We cannot depart from this noble heritage. Thus we may view the historical development of the privilege as one which groped for the proper scope of governmental power over the citizen. We have recently noted that the privilege against self-incrimination—the essential mainstay of our adversary system—is founded on a complex of values. All these policies point to one overriding thought: the constitutional foundation underlying the privilege is the respect a government—state or federal—must accord to the dignity and integrity of its citizens. To maintain a "fair state-individual balance," to require the government "to shoulder the entire load," to respect the inviolability of the human personality, our accusatory system of criminal justice demands that the government seeking to punish an individual produce the evidence against him by its own independent labors, rather than by the cruel, simple expedient of compelling it from his own mouth. In sum, the privilege is fulfilled only when the person is guaranteed the right "to remain silent unless he chooses to speak in the unfettered exercise of his own will."

The question in these cases is whether the privilege is fully applicable during a period of custodial interrogation. In this Court, the privilege has consistently been accorded a liberal construction. We are satisfied that all the principles embodied in the privilege apply to informal compulsion exerted by law-enforcement officers during in-custody questioning. An individual swept from familiar surroundings into police custody, surrounded by antagonistic forces, and subjected to the techniques of persuasion described above cannot be otherwise than under compulsion to speak. As a practical matter, the compulsion to speak in the isolated setting of the police station may well be greater than in courts or other official investigations, where there are often impartial observers to guard against intimidation or trickery.

Today, then, there can be no doubt that the Fifth Amendment privilege is available outside of criminal court proceedings and serves to protect persons in all settings in which their freedom of action is curtailed in any significant way from being compelled to incriminate themselves. We have concluded that without proper safeguards the process of in-custody interrogation of persons suspected or accused of crime contains inherently compelling pressures which work to undermine the individual's will to resist and to compel him to speak where he would not otherwise do so freely. In order to combat these pressures and to permit a full opportunity to exercise the privilege against self-incrimination, the accused must be adequately and effectively apprised of his rights and the exercise of those rights must be fully honored.

It is impossible for us to foresee the potential alternatives for protecting the privilege which might be devised by Congress or the States in the exercise of their creative rule-making capacities. Therefore we cannot say that the Constitution necessarily requires adherence to any particular solution for the inherent compulsions of the interrogation process as it is presently conducted. Our decision in no way creates a constitutional straitjacket which will handicap sound efforts at reform, nor is it intended to have this effect. We encourage Congress and the States to continue their laudable search for increasingly effective ways of protecting the rights of the individual while promoting efficient enforcement of our criminal laws. However, unless we are shown other procedures which are at least as effective in apprising accused persons of their right of silence and in assuring a continuous opportunity to exercise it, the following safeguards must be observed.

We hold that when an individual is taken into custody or otherwise deprived of his freedom by the authorities in any significant way and is subjected to questioning, the privilege against self-incrimination is jeopardized. Procedural safeguards must be employed to protect the privilege and unless other fully effective means are adopted to notify the person of his right of silence and to assure that the exercise of the right will be scrupulously honored, the following measures are required. He must be warned prior to any questioning that he has the right to remain silent, that anything he says can be used against him in a court of law, that he has the right to the presence of an attorney, and that if he cannot afford an attorney one will be appointed for him prior to any questioning if he so desires. Opportunity to exercise these rights must be afforded to him throughout the interrogation. After such warnings have been given, and such opportunity afforded him, the individual may knowingly and intelligently waive these rights and agree to answer questions or make a statement. But unless and until such warnings and waiver are demonstrated by the prosecution at trial, no evidence obtained as a result of interrogation can be used against him.

A recurrent argument made in these cases is that society's need for interrogation outweighs the privilege. This argument is not unfamiliar to this Court. The whole thrust of our foregoing discussion demonstrates that the Constitution has prescribed the rights of the individual when confronted with the power of government when it provided in the Fifth Amendment that an individual cannot be compelled to be a witness against himself. That right cannot be abridged. It has been pointed out: "The quality of a nation's civilization can be largely measured by the methods it uses in the enforcement of its criminal law." If the individual desires to exercise his privilege, he has the right to do so. This is not for the authorities to decide. An attorney may advise his client not to talk to police until he has had an opportunity to investigate the case, or he may wish to be present with his client during any police questioning. In doing so an attorney is merely exercising the good professional judgment he has been taught. This is not cause for considering the attorney a menace to law enforcement. He is merely carrying out what he is sworn to do under his oath—to protect to the extent of his ability the rights of his client. In fulfilling this responsibility the attorney plays a vital role in the administration of criminal justice under our Constitution.

In announcing these principles, we are not unmindful of the burdens which law enforcement officials must bear, often under trying circumstances. We also fully recognize the obligation of all citizens to aid in enforcing the criminal laws. This Court, while protecting individual rights, has always given ample latitude to law enforcement agencies in the legitimate exercise of their duties. The limits we have placed on the interrogation process should not constitute an undue interference with a proper system of law enforcement. As we have noted, our decision does not in any way preclude police from carrying out their traditional investigatory functions. Although confessions may play an important role in some convictions, the cases before us present graphic examples of the overstatement of the "need" for confessions. In each case, authorities conducted interrogations ranging up to five days in duration despite the presence, through standard investigating practices, of considerable evidence against each defendant. Further examples are chronicled in our prior cases.

It is also urged that an unfettered right to detention for interrogation should be allowed because it will often redound to the benefit of the person questioned. When police inquiry determines that there is no reason to believe that the person has committed any crime, it is said, he will be released without need for further formal procedures. The person who has committed no offense, however, will be better able to clear himself after warnings with counsel present than without. It can be assumed that in such circumstances a lawyer would advise his client to talk freely to police in order to clear himself.

Custodial interrogation, by contrast, does not necessarily afford the innocent an opportunity to clear themselves. A serious consequence of the present practice of the interrogation alleged to be beneficial for the innocent is that many arrests "for investigation" subject large numbers of innocent persons to detention and interrogation. In one of the cases before us, police held four persons, who were in the defendant's house at the time of the arrest, in jail for five days until defendant confessed. At that time they were finally released. Police stated that there was "no evidence to connect them with any crime." Available statistics on the extent of this practice where it is condoned indicate that these four are far from alone in being subjected to arrest, prolonged detention, and interrogation without the requisite probable cause.

Over the years, the Federal Bureau of Investigation has compiled an exemplary record of effective law enforcement while advising any suspect or arrested person, at the outset of an interview, that he is not required to make a statement, that any statement may be used against him in court, that the individual may obtain the services of an attorney of his own choice and, more recently, that he has a right to free counsel if he is unable to pay. The practice of the FBI can readily be emulated by state and local enforcement agencies. The experience in some other countries also suggests that the danger to law enforcement in curbs on interrogation is overplayed. Similarly, in our country the Uniform Code of Military Justice has long provided comparable safeguards for custodial interrogation. There appears to have been no marked detrimental effect on criminal law enforcement in these jurisdictions as a result of these rules. We deal here with rights grounded in a specific requirement of the Fifth Amendment of the Constitution, whereas other jurisdictions arrived at their conclusions on the basis of principles of justice not so specifically defined.

We have already pointed out that the Constitution does not require any specific code of procedures for protecting the privilege against self-incrimination during custodial interrogation. Congress and the States are free to develop their own safeguards for the privilege, so long as they are fully as effective as those described above in informing accused persons of their right of silence and in affording a continuous opportunity to exercise it. In any event, however, the issues presented are of constitutional dimensions and must be determined by the courts. The admissibility of a statement in the face of a claim that it was obtained in violation of the defendant's constitutional rights is an issue the resolution of which has long since been undertaken by this Court. Judicial solutions to problems of constitutional dimension have evolved decade by decade. As courts have been presented with the need to enforce constitutional rights, they have found means of doing so. That is our responsibility today. Where rights secured by the Constitution are involved, there can be no rule making or legislation which would abrogate them.

Because of the nature of the problem and because of its recurrent significance in numerous cases, we have to this point discussed the relationship of the Fifth Amendment privilege to police interrogation without specific concentration on the facts of the cases before us. We turn now to these facts to consider the application to these cases of the constitutional principles discussed above. In each instance, we have concluded that statements were obtained from the defendant under circumstances that did not meet constitutional standards for protection of the privilege.

*Beyond this, the jury trial provisions in the Federal and State Constitutions reflect a fundamental decision about the exercise of official power—a reluctance to entrust plenary powers over the life and liberty of the citizen to one judge or to a group of judges.*

*— Byron R. White*

## Duncan v. Louisiana
### 88 S.Ct. 1444, 391 U.S. 145 (1968)

*Gary Duncan, a 19 year-old African-American, got involved in an argument between his younger cousins and four White boys over the integration of the local high school. After allegedly slapping one of the White boys on the arm, he was charged and convicted before a judge for the misdemeanor of battery and sentenced to 60 days and $150 fine. He insisted that his right to due process was violated because state procedures did not authorize a jury trial. Justice White agreed with Duncan and set out a new, improved definition of due process that asked if a procedure was "fundamental to the American scheme of justice." Under this standard, most all of the specific provisions of the Bill of Rights have been applied to state criminal prosecutions. The Justices have disagreed from time to time over the content of the fundamental right, however, and have countenanced state procedures that are at variance with the parallel federal procedures. For example, the Court has sustained criminal procedures in some States that provide for fewer than twelve jurors or less-than-unanimous verdicts. In opinions not reproduced here, Justices Black and Harlan continued the larger debate over the "incorporation doctrine" that Black and Justice Frankfurter began in* Adamson v. California *(1947), which is excerpted Chapter 4. Here the focus is on the value of the right to a jury.*

**Justice White:** The Fourteenth Amendment denies the States the power to "deprive any person of life, liberty, or property, without due process of law." In resolving conflicting claims concerning the meaning of this spacious language, the Court has looked increasingly to the Bill of Rights for guidance; many of the rights guaranteed by the first eight Amendments to the

Constitution have been held to be protected against state action by the Due Process Clause of the Fourteenth Amendment. That clause now protects the right to compensation for property taken by the State; the rights of speech, press, and religion covered by the First Amendment; the Fourth Amendment rights to be free from unreasonable searches and seizures and to have excluded from criminal trials any evidence illegally seized; the right guaranteed by the Fifth Amendment to be free of compelled self-incrimination; and the Sixth Amendment rights to counsel, to a speedy and public trial, to confrontation of opposing witnesses, and to compulsory process for obtaining witnesses.

The test for determining whether a right extended by the Fifth and Sixth Amendments with respect to federal criminal proceedings is also protected against state action by the Fourteenth Amendment has been phrased in a variety of ways in the opinions of this Court. The question has been asked whether a right is among those "fundamental principles of liberty and justice which lie at the base of all our civil and political institutions," whether it is "basic in our system of jurisprudence," and whether it is "a fundamental right, essential to a fair trial."

In one sense recent cases applying provisions of the first eight Amendments to the States represent a new approach to the "incorporation" debate. Earlier the Court can be seen as having asked, when inquiring into whether some particular procedural safeguard was required of a State, if a civilized system could be imagined that would not accord the particular protection. The recent cases, on the other hand, have proceeded upon the valid assumption that state criminal processes are not imaginary and theoretical schemes but actual systems bearing virtually every characteristic of the common-law system that has been developing contemporaneously in England and in this country. The question thus is whether given this kind of system a particular procedure is fundamental—whether, that is, a procedure is necessary to an Anglo-American regime of ordered liberty. Of immediate relevance for this case are the Court's holdings that the States must comply with certain provisions of the Sixth Amendment, specifically that the States may not refuse a speedy trial, confrontation of witnesses, and the assistance, at state expense if necessary, of counsel. Of each of these determinations that a constitutional provision originally written to bind the Federal Government should bind the States as well it might be said that the limitation in question is not necessarily fundamental to fairness in every criminal system that might be imagined but is fundamental in the context of the criminal processes maintained by the American States. When the inquiry is approached in this way the question whether the States can impose criminal punishment without granting a jury trial appears quite different from the way it appeared in the older cases opining that States might abolish jury trial. A criminal process which was fair and equitable but used no juries is easy to imagine. It would make use of alternative guarantees and protections which would serve the purposes that the jury serves in the English and American systems. Yet no American State has undertaken to construct such a system. Instead, every American State, including Louisiana, uses the jury extensively, and imposes very serious punishments only after a trial at which the defendant has a right to a jury's verdict. In every State, including Louisiana, the structure and style of the criminal process—the supporting framework and the subsidiary procedures—are of the sort that naturally complement jury trial, and have developed in connection with and in reliance upon jury trial.

Duncan's claim is that the right to trial by jury guaranteed by the Sixth Amendment meets these tests. The position of Louisiana, on the other hand, is that the Constitution imposes upon the States no duty to give a jury trial in any criminal case, regardless of the seriousness of the crime or the size of the punishment which may be imposed. Because we believe that trial by jury in criminal cases is fundamental to the American scheme of justice, we hold that the Fourteenth Amendment guarantees a right of jury trial in all criminal cases which—were they to be tried in a federal court—would come within the Sixth Amendment's guarantee. Since we consider the appeal before us to be such a case, we hold that the Constitution was violated when Duncan's demand for jury trial was refused.

The history of trial by jury in criminal cases has been frequently told. It is sufficient for present purposes to say that by the time our Constitution was written, jury trial in criminal cases had been in existence in England for several centuries and carried impressive credentials traced by many to *Magna Carta*. Its preservation and proper operation as a protection against arbitrary rule were among the major objectives of the revolutionary settlement which was expressed in the English Declaration and Bill of Rights of 1689.

Jury trial came to America with English colonists, and received strong support from them. Royal interference with the jury trial was deeply resented. Among the resolutions adopted by the First Congress of the American Colonies (the Stamp Act Congress) on October 19, 1765—resolutions deemed by their authors to state "the most essential rights and liberties of the colonists"—was the declaration: "That trial by jury is the inherent and invaluable right of every British subject in these colonies." The First Continental Congress, in the resolve of October 14, 1774, objected to trials before judges dependent upon the Crown alone for their salaries and to trials in England for alleged crimes committed in the colonies; the Congress therefore declared: "That the respective colonies are entitled to the common law of England, and more especially to the great and inestimable privilege of being tried by their peers of the vicinage, according to the course of that law."

The *Declaration of Independence* stated solemn objections to the King's making "judges dependent on his will alone, for the tenure of their offices, and the amount and payment of their salaries," to his "depriving us in many cases, of the benefits of Trial by Jury," and to his "transporting us beyond Seas to be tried for pretended offenses." The Constitution itself, in Art. III, § 2, commanded: "The Trial of all Crimes, except in Cases of Impeachment, shall be by Jury; and such Trial shall be held in the State where the said Crimes shall have been committed." Objections to the Constitution because of the absence of a bill of rights were met by the immediate submission and adoption of the Bill of Rights. Included was the Sixth Amendment which, among other things, provided: "In all criminal prosecutions, the accused shall enjoy the right to a speedy and public trial, by an impartial jury of the State and district wherein the crime shall have been committed."

The constitutions adopted by the original States guaranteed jury trial. Also, the constitution of every State entering the Union thereafter in one form or another protected the right to jury trial in criminal cases.

Even such skeletal history is impressive support for considering the right to jury trial in criminal cases to be fundamental to our system of justice, an importance frequently recognized in the opinions of this Court.

Jury trial continues to receive strong support. The laws of every State guarantee a right to jury trial in serious criminal cases; no State has dispensed with it; nor are there significant movements underway to do so. Indeed, the three most recent state constitutional revisions, in Maryland, Michigan, and New York, carefully preserved the right of the accused to have the judgment of a jury when tried for a serious crime.

We are aware of prior cases in this Court in which the prevailing opinion contains statements contrary to our holding today that the right to jury trial in serious criminal cases is a fundamental right and hence must be recognized by the States as part of their obligation to extend due process of law to all persons within their jurisdiction. Louisiana relies especially on these decisions. None of these cases, however, dealt with a State which had purported to dispense entirely with a jury trial in serious criminal cases. Respectfully, we reject the prior *dicta* regarding jury trial in criminal cases.

The guarantees of jury trial in the Federal and State Constitutions reflect a profound judgment about the way in which law should be enforced and justice administered. A right to jury trial is granted to criminal defendants in order to prevent oppression by the Government. Those who wrote our constitutions knew from history and experience that it was necessary to protect against unfounded criminal charges brought to eliminate enemies and against judges too responsive to the voice of higher authority. The framers of the constitutions strove to create an independent judiciary but insisted upon further protection against arbitrary action. Providing an accused with the right to be tried by a jury of his peers gave him an inestimable safeguard against the corrupt or overzealous prosecutor and against the compliant, biased, or eccentric judge. If the defendant preferred the common-sense judgment of a jury to the more tutored but perhaps less sympathetic reaction of the single judge, he was to have it. Beyond this, the jury trial provisions in the Federal and State Constitutions reflect a fundamental decision about the exercise of official power—a reluctance to entrust plenary powers over the life and liberty of the citizen to one judge or to a group of judges. Fear of unchecked power, so typical of our State and Federal Governments in other respects, found expression in the criminal law in this insistence upon community participation in the determination of guilt or innocence. The deep commitment of the Nation to the right of jury trial in serious criminal cases as a defense against arbitrary law enforcement qualifies for protection under the Due Process Clause of the Fourteenth Amendment, and must therefore be respected by the States.

*In our adversary system of criminal justice, any person haled into court, who is too poor to hire a lawyer, cannot be assured a fair trial unless counsel is provided for him.*

— *Hugo L. Black*

## Gideon v. Wainwright
### 83 S.Ct. 792, 372 U.S. 335 (1963)

*Anthony Lewis's classic book* GIDEON'S TRUMPET *tells the story of this remarkable case. Clarence Earl Gideon, a ne'er-do-well charged with breaking and entering the Bay Harbor Poolroom in Panama City, Florida, made constitutional law representing himself "about as well as could be expected." Gideon insisted that he was entitled to appointed counsel, but he would have to convince the Supreme Court to change its mind.* Betts v. Brady (1942) *had held there was no such right in non-capital cases, over the dissent of Justice Hugo L. Black. Gideon filed his own petition for review from prison, hand-printed in pencil on lined prison-issue paper, and the Supreme Court of the United States agreed to hear his case. The Court appointed Abe Fortas, one of the most prominent lawyers of the day who later would serve on the High Court bench, to brief and argue the appeal. In an historic vindication, Justice Black authored the opinion in an unanimous decision overruling* Betts. *The right to counsel since has been extended to require appointment whenever the defendant is subject to imprisonment and to guarantee a minimum level of effective representation.*

**Justice Black:** Petitioner Gideon was charged in a Florida state court with having broken and entered a poolroom with intent to commit a misdemeanor. This offense is a felony under Florida law. Appearing in court without funds and without a lawyer, Gideon asked the court to appoint counsel for him, whereupon the following colloquy took place:

The COURT: Mr. Gideon, I am sorry, but I cannot appoint Counsel to represent you in this case. Under the laws of the State of Florida, the only time the Court can appoint Counsel to represent a Defendant is when that person is charged with a capital offense. I am sorry, but I will have to deny your request to appoint Counsel to defend you in this case.

The DEFENDANT: The United States Supreme Court says I am entitled to be represented by Counsel.

Put to trial before a jury, Gideon conducted his defense about as well as could be expected from a layman. He made an opening statement to the jury, cross-examined the State's witnesses, presented witnesses in his own defense, declined to testify himself, and made a short argument "emphasizing his innocence to the charge contained in the Information filed in this case." The jury returned a verdict of guilty, and Gideon was sentenced to serve five years in the state prison. Later, Gideon filed in the Florida Supreme Court this habeas corpus petition attacking his conviction and sentence on the ground that the trial court's refusal to appoint counsel for him denied him rights "guaranteed by the Constitution and the Bill of Rights by the United States Government." Treating the petition for habeas corpus as properly before it, the State Supreme Court, "upon consideration thereof" but without an opinion, denied all relief.

Since 1942, when *Betts v. Brady*, was decided by a divided Court, the problem of a defendant's federal constitutional right to counsel in a state court has been a continuing source of controversy and litigation in both state and federal courts. To give this problem another review here, we granted certiorari. Since Gideon was proceeding in forma pauperis, we appointed counsel to represent him and requested both sides to discuss in their briefs and oral arguments the following: "Should this Court's holding in *Betts v. Brady* be reconsidered?"

The facts upon which Betts claimed that he had been unconstitutionally denied the right to have counsel appointed to assist him are strikingly like the facts upon which Gideon here bases his federal constitutional claim. It was held that a refusal to appoint counsel for an indigent defendant charged with a felony did not necessarily violate the Due Process Clause of the Fourteenth Amendment, which for reasons given the Court deemed to be the only applicable federal constitutional provision. The Court said: "Asserted denial (of due process) is to be tested by an appraisal of the totality of facts in a given case. That which may, in one setting, constitute a denial of fundamental fairness, shocking to the universal sense of justice, may, in other circumstances, and in the light of other considerations, fall short of such denial." The Court held that refusal to appoint counsel under the particular facts and circumstances in the *Betts* case was not so "offensive to the common and fundamental ideas of fairness" as to amount to a denial of due process. Since the facts and circumstances of the two cases are so nearly indistinguishable, we think the *Betts v. Brady* holding if left standing would require us to reject Gideon's claim that the Constitution guarantees him the assistance of counsel. Upon full reconsideration, we conclude that *Betts v. Brady* should be overruled.

The Sixth Amendment provides, "In all criminal prosecutions, the accused shall enjoy the right to have the Assistance of Counsel for his defence." We have construed this to mean that in federal courts counsel must be provided for defendants unable to employ counsel unless the right is competently and intelligently waived. Betts argued that this right is extended to indigent defendants in state courts by the Fourteenth Amendment. In response the Court stated that, while the Sixth Amendment laid down "no rule for the conduct of the states, the question recurs whether the constraint laid by the amendment upon the national courts expresses a rule so fundamental and essential to a fair trial, and so, to due process of law, that it is made obligatory upon the states by the Fourteenth Amendment." In order to decide whether the Sixth Amendment's guarantee of counsel is of this fundamental nature, the Court in *Betts* set out and considered "relevant data on the subject afforded by constitutional and statutory provisions subsisting in the colonies and the states prior to the inclusion of the Bill of Rights in the national Constitution, and in the constitutional, legislative, and judicial history of the states to the present date." On the basis of this historical data the Court concluded that "appointment of counsel is not a fundamental right, essential to a fair trial." It was for this reason the *Betts* Court refused to accept the contention that the Sixth Amendment's guarantee of counsel for indigent federal defendants was extended to or, in the words of that Court, "made obligatory upon the states by the Fourteenth Amendment". Plainly, had the Court concluded that appointment of counsel for an indigent criminal defendant was "a fundamental right, essential to a fair trial," it would have held that the Fourteenth Amendment requires appointment of counsel in a state court, just as the Sixth Amendment requires in a federal court.

We think the Court in *Betts* had ample precedent for acknowledging that those guarantees of the Bill of Rights which are fundamental safeguards of liberty immune from federal abridgment are equally protected against state invasion by the Due Process Clause of the Fourteenth Amendment. This same principle was recognized, explained, and applied in a 1932 case upholding the right of counsel in a state capital prosecution, where the Court held that the Fourteenth Amendment "embraced" those "fundamental principles of liberty and justice which lie at the base of all our civil and political institutions," even though they had been "specifically dealt with in another part of the Federal Constitution."

In many other cases, this Court has looked to the fundamental nature of original Bill of Rights guarantees to decide whether the Fourteenth Amendment makes them obligatory on the States. On the other hand, in a 1937 case refused to hold that the Fourteenth Amendment made the double jeopardy provision of the Fifth Amendment obligatory on the States. In so refusing, however, the Court, speaking through Mr. Justice Cardozo, was careful to emphasize that "immunities that are valid as against the federal government by force of the specific pledges of particular amendments have been found to be implicit in the concept of ordered liberty, and thus, through the Fourteenth Amendment, become valid as against the states' and that guarantees "in their origin effective against the federal government alone" had by prior cases "been taken over from the earlier articles of the Federal Bill of Rights and brought within the Fourteenth Amendment by a process of absorption."

We accept *Betts v. Brady*'s assumption, based as it was on our prior cases, that a provision of the Bill of Rights which is "fundamental and essential to a fair trial" is made obligatory upon the States by the Fourteenth Amendment. We think the Court in *Betts* was wrong, however, in concluding that the Sixth Amendment's guarantee of counsel is not one of these fundamental rights.

In light of many other prior decisions of this Court, it is not surprising that the *Betts* Court, when faced with the contention that "one charged with crime, who is unable to obtain counsel, must be furnished counsel by the state," conceded that "expressions in the opinions of this court lend color to the argument." The fact is that in deciding as it did—that "appointment of counsel is not a fundamental right, essential to a fair trial"—the Court in *Betts v. Brady* made an abrupt break with its own well-considered precedents. In returning to these old precedents, sounder we believe than the new, we but restore constitutional principles established to achieve a fair system of justice. Not only these precedents but also reason and reflection require us to recognize that in our adversary system of criminal justice, any person haled into court, who is too poor to hire a lawyer, cannot be assured a fair trial unless counsel is provided for him.

This seems to us to be an obvious truth. Governments, both state and federal, quite properly spend vast sums of money to establish machinery to try defendants accused of crime. Lawyers to prosecute are everywhere deemed essential to protect the public's interest in an orderly society. Similarly, there are few defendants charged with crime, few indeed, who fail to hire the best lawyers they can get to prepare and present their defenses. That government hires lawyers to prosecute and defendants who have the money hire lawyers to defend are the strongest indications of the wide-spread belief that lawyers in criminal courts are necessities, not luxuries. The right of one charged with crime to counsel may not be deemed fundamental and essential to fair trials in some countries, but it is in ours. From the very beginning, our state and national constitutions and laws have laid great emphasis on procedural and substantive safeguards designed to assure fair trials before impartial tribunals in which every defendant stands equal before the law. This noble ideal cannot be realized if the poor man charged with crime has to face his accusers without a lawyer to assist him. A defendant's need for a lawyer is nowhere better stated than in the moving words of Mr. Justice Sutherland:

> The right to be heard would be, in many cases, of little avail if it did not comprehend the right to be heard by counsel. Even the intelligent and educated layman has small and sometimes no skill in the science of law. If charged with crime, he is incapable, generally, of determining for himself whether the indictment is good or bad. He is unfamiliar with the rules of evidence. Left without the aid of counsel he may be put on trial without a proper charge, and convicted upon incompetent evidence, or evidence irrelevant to the issue or otherwise inadmissible. He lacks both the skill and knowledge adequately to prepare his defense, even though he have a perfect one. He requires the guiding hand of counsel at every step in the proceedings against him. Without it, though he be not guilty, he faces the danger of conviction because he does not know how to establish his innocence.

Florida, supported by two other States, has asked that *Betts v. Brady* be left intact. Twenty-two States, as friends of the Court, argue that *Betts* was "an anachronism when handed down" and that it should now be overruled. We agree.

*I think that the word "liberty," in the 14th Amendment, is perverted when it is held to prevent the natural outcome of a dominant opinion, unless it can be said that a rational and fair man necessarily would admit that the statute proposed would infringe fundamental principles as they have been understood by the traditions of our people and our law.*

*— Oliver W. Holmes, Jr.*

## Lochner v. New York
### 25 S.Ct. 539, 198 U.S. 45 (1905)

*This dissenting opinion has been called "the most famous opinion of our most famous judge." It ushered in a new era of legal realism and it marked the beginning of modern constitutional law. The majority invalidated a New York law that set a maximum of 60 hours per week that bakery employees could work, under an interpretation of the 14th amendment due process clause. During this old era, Supreme Court majorities routinely would set aside state legislation basically because they disapproved of the measures, using a "liberty of contract" theory. This substantive due process approach eventually was rejected, and Justice Holmes was vindicated, in the 1930s, when the Court finally admitted that the wisdom of public policy was for the legislative branch alone to decide. So long as a measure is rational—and most statutes are reasonably related to a legitimate purpose—it is valid, unless it interferes with some fundamental right. Judges cannot use the Constitution to substitute their own social and economic beliefs for the judgment of elected legislators.*

**Justice Holmes:** I regret sincerely that I am unable to agree with the judgment in this case, and that I think it my duty to express my dissent.

This case is decided upon an economic theory which a large part of the country does not entertain. If it were a question whether I agreed with that theory, I should desire to study it further and long before making up my mind. But I do not conceive that to be my duty, because I strongly believe that my agreement or disagreement has nothing to do with the right of a majority to embody their opinions in law. It is settled by various decisions of this court that state constitutions and state laws may regulate life in many ways which we as legislators might think as injudicious, or if you like as tyrannical, as this, and which, equally with this, interfere with the liberty to contract. Sunday laws and usury laws are ancient examples. A more modern one is the prohibition of lotteries. The liberty of the citizen to do as he likes so long as he does not interfere with the liberty of others to do the same, which has been a shibboleth for some well-known writers, is interfered with by school laws, by the Postoffice, by every state or municipal institution which takes his money for purposes thought desirable, whether he likes it or not. The 14th Amendment does not enact Mr. Herbert Spencer's Social Statics. The other day we sustained the Massachusetts vaccination law. United States and state statutes and decisions cutting down the liberty to contract by way of combination are familiar to this court. Some of these laws embody convictions or prejudices which judges are likely to share. Some may not. But a Constitution is not intended to embody a particular economic theory, whether of paternalism and the organic relation of the citizen to the state or of *laissez faire*. It is made for people of fundamentally differing views, and the accident of our finding certain opinions natural and familiar, or novel, and even shocking, ought not to conclude our judgment upon the question whether statutes embodying them conflict with the Constitution of the United States.

General propositions do not decide concrete cases. The decision will depend on a judgment or intuition more subtle than any articulate major premise. But I think that the proposition just stated, if it is accepted, will carry us far toward the end. Every opinion tends to become a law. I think that the word "liberty," in the 14th Amendment, is perverted when it is held to prevent the natural outcome of a dominant opinion, unless it can be said that a rational and fair man necessarily would admit that the statute proposed would infringe fundamental principles as they have been understood by the traditions of our people and our law. It does not need research to show that no such sweeping condemnation can be passed upon the statute before us. A reasonable man might think it a proper measure on the score of health. Men whom I certainly could not pronounce unreasonable would uphold it as a first installment of a general regulation of the hours of work. Whether in the latter aspect it would be open to the charge of inequality I think it unnecessary to discuss.

*That the state may do much, go very far, indeed,
in order to improve the quality of its citizens,
physically, mentally and morally, is clear; but the
individual has certain fundamental rights which
must be respected.*

— *James C. McReynolds*

## Meyer v. Nebraska
### 43 S.Ct. 625, 262 U.S. 390 (1923)

*This is an early precedent for the "right of privacy"
cases decided in the 1960s. The constitutional principle
being enforced is one of personal autonomy or individual
decisionmaking free from governmental interference. The
14th amendment guarantee of liberty protects the individual from government control over important matters.
Under the Constitution of the United States, unlike in
Plato's republic, the legislature's expression of the common good does not always prevail. In our regime of individual rights, rights not spelled out in the text—the right
to teach, the right to learn, the right to rear children—
come under the aegis of the Constitution and the Court.
Nebraska could not give in to the general xenophobia and
the anti-German attitudes after World War I to make it a
crime for a school teacher to teach German to a 10 year-
old boy.*

**Justice McReynolds:** The problem for our determination is
whether the statute as construed and applied unreasonably infringes the liberty guaranteed to the plaintiff in error by the
Fourteenth Amendment: "No state . . . shall deprive any person
of life, liberty or property without due process of law."

While this court has not attempted to define with exactness
the liberty thus guaranteed, the term has received much consideration and some of the included things have been definitely
stated. Without doubt, it denotes not merely freedom from bodily restraint, but also the right of the individual to contract, to
engage in any of the common occupations of life, to acquire
useful knowledge, to marry, establish a home and bring up children, to worship God according to the dictates of his own conscience, and generally to enjoy those privileges long recognized
at common law as essential to the orderly pursuit of happiness
by free men. The established doctrine is that this liberty may

not be interfered with, under the guise of protecting the public interest, by legislative action which is arbitrary or without reasonable relation to some purpose within the competency of the state to effect. Determination by the Legislature of what constitutes proper exercise of police power is not final or conclusive but is subject to supervision by the courts.

The American people have always regarded education and acquisition of knowledge as matters of supreme importance which should be diligently promoted. The Northwest Ordinance of 1787 declares: "Religion, morality and knowledge being necessary to good government and the happiness of mankind, schools and the means of education shall forever be encouraged."

Corresponding to the right of control, it is the natural duty of the parent to give his children education suitable to their station in life; and nearly all the states, including Nebraska, enforce this obligation by compulsory laws.

Practically, education of the young is only possible in schools conducted by especially qualified persons who devote themselves thereto. The calling always has been regarded as useful and honorable, essential, indeed, to the public welfare. Mere knowledge of the German language cannot reasonably be regarded as harmful. Heretofore it has been commonly looked upon as helpful and desirable. Defendant taught this language in school as part of his occupation. His right thus to teach and the right of parents to engage him so to instruct their children, we think, are within the liberty of the amendment.

The challenged statute forbids the teaching in school of any subject except in English; also the teaching of any other language until the pupil has attained and successfully passed the eighth grade, which is not usually accomplished before the age of twelve. The Supreme Court of the state has held that "the so-called ancient or dead languages" are not "within the spirit or the purpose of the act." Latin, Greek, Hebrew are not proscribed; but German, French, Spanish, Italian, and every other alien speech are within the ban. Evidently the Legislature has attempted materially to interfere with the calling of modern language teachers, with the opportunities of pupils to acquire knowledge, and with the power of parents to control the education of their own.

It is said the purpose of the legislation was to promote civic development by inhibiting training and education of the immature in foreign tongues and ideals before they could learn English and acquire American ideals, and "that the English language should be and become the mother tongue of all children reared in this state." It is also affirmed that the foreign born population is very large, that certain communities commonly use foreign words, follow foreign leaders, move in a foreign atmosphere, and that the children are thereby hindered from becoming citizens of the most useful type and the public safety is imperiled.

That the state may do much, go very far, indeed, in order to improve the quality of its citizens, physically, mentally and morally, is clear; but the individual has certain fundamental rights which must be respected. The protection of the Constitution extends to all, to those who speak other languages as well as to those born with English on the tongue. Perhaps it would be highly advantageous if all had ready understanding of our ordinary speech, but this cannot be coerced by methods which conflict with the Constitution—a desirable end cannot be promoted by prohibited means.

For the welfare of his Ideal Commonwealth, Plato suggested a law which should provide: "That the wives of our guardians are to be common, and their children are to be common, and no parent is to know his own child, nor any child his parent. The proper officers will take the offspring of the good parents to the pen or fold, and there they will deposit them with certain nurses who dwell in a separate quarter; but the offspring of the inferior, or of the better when they chance to be deformed, will be put away in some mysterious, unknown place, as they should be."

In order to submerge the individual and develop ideal citizens, Sparta assembled the males at seven into barracks and intrusted their subsequent education and training to official guardians. Although such measures have been deliberately approved by men of great genius, their ideas touching the relation between individual and state were wholly different from those upon which our institutions rest; and it hardly will be affirmed that any Legislature could impose such restrictions upon the people of a state without doing violence to both letter and spirit of the Constitution.

The desire of the Legislature to foster a homogeneous people with American ideals prepared readily to understand current discussions of civic matters is easy to appreciate. Unfortunate experiences during the late war and aversion toward every character of truculent adversaries were certainly enough to quicken that aspiration. But the means adopted, we think, exceed the limitations upon the power of the state and conflict with rights assured to Defendant. The interference is plain enough and no adequate reason therefor in time of peace and domestic tranquility has been shown.

The power of the state to compel attendance at some school and to make reasonable regulations for all schools, including a requirement that they shall give instructions in English, is not questioned. Nor has challenge been made of the state's power to prescribe a curriculum for institutions which it supports. Those matters are not within the present controversy. No emergency has arisen which renders knowledge by a child of some language other than English so clearly harmful as to justify its inhibition with the consequent infringement of rights long freely enjoyed. We are constrained to conclude that the statute as applied is arbitrary and without reasonable relation to any end within the competency of the state.

*After considering the fundamental constitu-*
*tional questions resolved by Roe, principles of*
*institutional integrity, and the rule of stare deci-*
*sis, we are led to conclude this: the essential*
*holding of Roe v. Wade should be retained and*
*once again reaffirmed.*

— *Sandra Day O'Connor,*
*Anthony M. Kennedy &*
*David H. Souter*

## Planned Parenthood of Southeastern Pennsylvania v. Casey
### 112 S.Ct. 2791, 505 U.S. 833 (1992)

*In* Roe v. Wade (1973), *the Supreme Court held state laws prohibiting abortions to be unconstitutional. This proved to be one of the most controversial decisions of all time. The ensuing debate within the Court over the right to privacy was fierce, but not nearly as fierce as in the rest of the country. "Pro-choice" and "pro-life" advocates clashed in every conceivable political venue: Congress, state legislatures, political party conventions, political campaigns at all levels, and even in the streets. The issue figured prominently in Presidential politics, as well as in separation of powers battles over the Court itself, exemplified by President Reagan's nomination and the Senate's rejection of Robert H. Bork in 1987. This plurality opinion, written jointly by Justices O'Connor, Kennedy, and Souter, surprised many Court watchers who at the time confidently were predicting an outright overruling of* Roe, *as had been promised by dissenting Justices in cases decided just before this one. But the votes to reverse simply were not there. The essential holding in* Roe *was reaffirmed. This decision effectively ended the debate within the Supreme Court, at least for the foreseeable future. The four dissenters were beside themselves, especially because Justice O'Connor and Justice Kennedy, who had themselves criticized* Roe *in earlier cases, had been counted on to join in an overruling. Justice Scalia took after the plurality in a vehement dissent written in a mocking tone. Appointments to the Court since 1992 have made the* Roe *precedent even more stable and far less vulnerable to overruling. The acrimonious debate beyond the marble palace, however, shows no sign whatsoever of subsiding.*

**Justices O'Connor, Kennedy & Souter:** Liberty finds no refuge in a jurisprudence of doubt. Yet 19 years after our holding that the Constitution protects a woman's right to terminate her pregnancy in its early stages, *Roe v. Wade* (1973), that definition of liberty is still questioned. After considering the fundamental constitutional questions resolved by *Roe*, principles of institutional integrity, and the rule of *stare decisis*, we are led to conclude this: the essential holding of *Roe v. Wade* should be retained and once again reaffirmed.

It must be stated at the outset and with clarity that *Roe's* essential holding, the holding we reaffirm, has three parts. First is a recognition of the right of the woman to choose to have an abortion before viability and to obtain it without undue interference from the State. Before viability, the State's interests are not strong enough to support a prohibition of abortion or the imposition of a substantial obstacle to the woman's effective right to elect the procedure. Second is a confirmation of the State's power to restrict abortions after fetal viability, if the law contains exceptions for pregnancies which endanger a woman's life or health. And third is the principle that the State has legitimate interests from the outset of the pregnancy in protecting the health of the woman and the life of the fetus that may become a child. These principles do not contradict one another; and we adhere to each.

Constitutional protection of the woman's decision to terminate her pregnancy derives from the Due Process Clause of the Fourteenth Amendment. It declares that no State shall "deprive any person of life, liberty, or property, without due process of law." The controlling word in the case before us is "liberty." Neither the Bill of Rights nor the specific practices of States at the time of the adoption of the Fourteenth Amendment marks the outer limits of the substantive sphere of liberty which the Fourteenth Amendment protects. It is settled now, as it was when the Court heard arguments in *Roe v. Wade*, that the Constitution places limits on a State's right to interfere with a person's most basic decisions about family and parenthood, as well as bodily integrity.

The inescapable fact is that adjudication of substantive due process claims may call upon the Court in interpreting the Constitution to exercise that same capacity which by tradition courts always have exercised: reasoned judgment. Its boundaries are not susceptible of expression as a simple rule. That does not mean we are free to invalidate state policy choices with which we disagree; yet neither does it permit us to shrink from the duties of our office.

Men and women of good conscience can disagree, and we suppose some always shall disagree, about the profound moral and spiritual implications of terminating a pregnancy, even in its earliest stage. Some of us as individuals find abortion offensive to our most basic principles of morality, but that cannot control our decision. Our obligation is to define the liberty of all, not to mandate our own moral code. The underlying constitutional issue is whether the State can resolve these philosophic questions in such a definitive way that a woman lacks all choice in the matter, except perhaps in those rare circumstances in which the pregnancy is itself a danger to her own life or health, or is the result of rape or incest.

It is conventional constitutional doctrine that where reasonable people disagree the government can adopt one position or the other. That theorem, however, assumes a state of affairs in which the choice does not intrude upon a protected liberty. Thus, while some people might disagree about whether or not the flag should be saluted, or disagree about the proposition that it may not be defiled, we have ruled that a State may not compel or enforce one view or the other.

Our law affords constitutional protection to personal decisions relating to marriage, procreation, contraception, family relationships, child rearing, and education. Our cases recognize "the right of the individual, married or single, to be free from unwarranted governmental intrusion into matters so fundamentally affecting a person as the decision whether to bear or beget a child." Our precedents "have respected the private realm of family life which the state cannot enter." These matters, involving the most intimate and personal choices a person may make in a lifetime, choices central to personal dignity and autonomy, are central to the liberty protected by the Fourteenth Amendment. At the heart of liberty is the right to define one's own concept of existence, of meaning, of the universe, and of the mystery of human life. Beliefs about these matters could not define the attributes of personhood were they formed under compulsion of the State.

These considerations begin our analysis of the woman's interest in terminating her pregnancy but cannot end it, for this reason: though the abortion decision may originate within the zone of conscience and belief, it is more than a philosophic exercise. Abortion is a unique act. It is an act fraught with consequences for others: for the woman who must live with the implications of her decision; for the persons who perform and assist in the procedure; for the spouse, family, and society which must confront the knowledge that these procedures exist, procedures some deem nothing short of an act of violence against innocent human life; and, depending on one's beliefs, for the life or potential life that is aborted. Though abortion is conduct, it does not follow that the State is entitled to proscribe it in all instances. That is because the liberty of the woman is at stake in a sense unique to the human condition and so unique to the law. The mother who carries a child to full term is subject to anxieties, to physical constraints, to pain that only she must bear. That these sacrifices have from the beginning of the human race been endured by woman with a pride that ennobles her in the eyes of others and gives to the infant a bond of love cannot alone be grounds for the State to insist she make the sacrifice. Her suffering is too intimate and personal for the State to insist, without more, upon its own vision of the woman's role, however dominant that vision has been in the course of our history and our culture. The destiny of the woman must be shaped to a large extent on her own conception of her spiritual imperatives and her place in society.

It should be recognized, moreover, that in some critical respects the abortion decision is of the same character as the decision to use contraception, to which our precedents afford constitutional protection. We have no doubt as to the correctness of those decisions. They support the reasoning in *Roe* relating to the woman's liberty because they involve personal decisions concerning not only the meaning of procreation but also human responsibility and respect for it. As with abortion, reasonable people will have differences of opinion about these matters. One view is based on such reverence for the wonder of creation that any pregnancy ought to be welcomed and carried to full term no matter how difficult it will be to provide for the child and ensure its well-being. Another is that the inability to provide for the nurture and care of the infant is a cruelty to the child and an anguish to the parent. These are intimate views with infinite variations, and their deep, personal character underlay our previous decisions. The same concerns are present when the woman confronts the reality that, perhaps despite her attempts to avoid it, she has become pregnant.

It was this dimension of personal liberty that *Roe* sought to protect, and its holding invoked the reasoning and the tradition of the precedents we have discussed, granting protection to substantive liberties of the person. *Roe* was, of course, an extension of those cases and, as the decision itself indicated, the separate States could act in some degree to further their own legitimate interests in protecting pre-natal life. The extent to which the legislatures of the States might act to outweigh the interests of the woman in choosing to terminate her pregnancy was a subject of debate both in *Roe* itself and in decisions following it.

While we appreciate the weight of the arguments made on behalf of the State in the case before us, arguments which in their ultimate formulation conclude that *Roe* should be overruled, the reservations any of us may have in reaffirming the central holding of *Roe* are outweighed by the explication of individual liberty we have given combined with the force of *stare decisis*. We turn now to that doctrine.

The obligation to follow precedent begins with necessity, and a contrary necessity marks its outer limit. With Justice Cardozo, we recognize that no judicial system could do society's work if it eyed each issue afresh in every case that raised it. Indeed, the very concept of the rule of law underlying our own Constitution requires such continuity over time that a respect for precedent is, by definition, indispensable. At the other extreme, a different necessity would make itself felt if a prior judicial ruling should come to be seen so clearly as error that its enforcement was for that very reason doomed.

Even when the decision to overrule a prior case is not, as in the rare, latter instance, virtually foreordained, it is common wisdom that the rule of *stare decisis* is not an "inexorable command," and certainly it is not such in every constitutional case. Rather, when this Court reexamines a prior holding, its judgment is customarily informed by a series of prudential and pragmatic considerations designed to test the consistency of overruling a prior decision with the ideal of the rule of law, and to gauge the respective costs of reaffirming and overruling a prior case. So in this case we may inquire whether *Roe*'s central rule has been found unworkable; whether the rule's limitation on state power could be removed without serious inequity to those who have relied upon it or significant damage to the stability of the society governed by the rule in question; whether the law's growth in the intervening years has left *Roe*'s central rule a doctrinal anachronism discounted by society; and whether *Roe*'s premises of fact have so far changed in the ensuing two decades as to render its central holding somehow irrelevant or unjustifiable in dealing with the issue it addressed.

Although *Roe* has engendered opposition, it has in no sense proven "unworkable," representing as it does a simple limitation beyond which a state law is unenforceable. While *Roe* has, of course, required judicial assessment of state laws affecting the exercise of the choice guaranteed against government infringement, and although the need for such review will remain as a consequence of today's decision, the required determinations fall within judicial competence.

The inquiry into reliance counts the cost of a rule's repudiation as it would fall on those who have relied reasonably on the rule's continued application. For two decades of economic and social developments, people have organized intimate relationships and made choices that define their views of themselves and their places in society, in reliance on the availability of abortion in the event that contraception should fail. The ability of women to participate equally in the economic and social life of the Nation has been facilitated by their ability to control their reproductive lives. The Constitution serves human values, and while the effect of reliance on *Roe* cannot be exactly measured, neither can the certain cost of overruling *Roe* for people who have ordered their thinking and living around that case be dismissed.

No evolution of legal principle has left *Roe*'s doctrinal footings weaker than they were in 1973. No development of constitutional law since the case was decided has implicitly or explicitly left *Roe* behind as a mere survivor of obsolete constitutional thinking. The *Roe* Court itself placed its holding in the succession of cases most prominently exemplified by *Griswold v. Connecticut (1965)*. Subsequent constitutional developments have neither disturbed, nor do they threaten to diminish, the scope of recognized protection accorded to the liberty relating to intimate relationships, the family, and decisions about whether or not to beget or bear a child. *Roe* may be seen not only as an exemplar of *Griswold* liberty but as a rule (whether or not mistaken) of personal autonomy and bodily integrity, with doctrinal affinity to cases recognizing limits on governmental power to mandate medical treatment or to bar its rejection. If so, our cases since *Roe* accord with *Roe*'s view that a State's interest in the protection of life falls short of justifying any plenary override of individual liberty claims. Finally, one could classify *Roe* as *sui generis*. If the case is so viewed, then there clearly has been no erosion of its central determination. The original holding resting on the concurrence of seven Members of the Court in 1973 was expressly affirmed by a majority of six in 1983, and by a majority of five in 1986, expressing adherence to the constitutional ruling despite legislative efforts in some States to test its limits. More recently, in 1989, a majority of the Court either decided to reaffirm or declined to address the constitutional validity of the central holding of *Roe*.

Nor will courts building upon *Roe* be likely to hand down erroneous decisions as a consequence. Even on the assumption that the central holding of *Roe* was in error, that error would go only to the strength of the state interest in fetal protection, not to the recognition afforded by the Constitution to the woman's liberty. The latter aspect of the decision fits comfortably within the framework of the Court's numerous prior decisions, the holdings of which are "not a series of isolated points," but mark a "rational continuum."

The soundness of this prong of the *Roe* analysis is apparent from a consideration of the alternative. If indeed the woman's interest in deciding whether to bear and beget a child had not been recognized as in *Roe*, the State might as readily restrict a woman's right to choose to carry a pregnancy to term as to terminate it, to further asserted state interests in population control, or eugenics, for example. Yet *Roe* has been sensibly relied upon to counter any such suggestions. In any event, because *Roe*'s scope is confined by the fact of its concern with postconception potential life, a concern otherwise likely to be implicated only by some forms of contraception protected independently under *Griswold* and later cases, any error in *Roe* is unlikely to have serious ramifications in future cases.

We have seen how time has overtaken some of *Roe*'s factual assumptions: advances in maternal health care allow for abortions safe to the mother later in pregnancy than was true in 1973, and advances in neonatal care have advanced viability to a point somewhat earlier. But these facts go only to the scheme of time limits on the realization of competing interests, and the divergences from the factual premises of 1973 have no bearing on the validity of *Roe*'s central holding, that viability marks the earliest point at which the State's interest in fetal life is constitutionally adequate to justify a legislative ban on nontherapeutic abortions. The soundness or unsoundness of that constitutional judgment in no sense turns on whether viability occurs at approximately 28 weeks, as was usual at the time of *Roe*, at 23 to 24 weeks, as it sometimes does today, or at some moment even slightly earlier in pregnancy, as it may if fetal respiratory capacity can somehow be medically enhanced in the future. Whenever it may occur, the attainment of viability may continue to serve as the critical fact, just as it has done since *Roe* was decided; which is to say that no change in *Roe*'s factual underpinning has left its central holding obsolete, and none supports an argument for overruling it.

The sum of the precedential inquiry to this point shows *Roe*'s underpinnings unweakened in any way affecting its central holding. While it has engendered disapproval, it has not been unworkable. An entire generation has come of age free to assume *Roe*'s concept of liberty in defining the capacity of women to act in society, and to make reproductive decisions; no erosion of principle going to liberty or personal autonomy has left *Roe*'s central holding a doctrinal remnant; *Roe* portends no developments at odds with other precedent for the analysis of personal liberty; and no changes of fact have rendered viability more or less appropriate as the point at which the balance of interests tips. Within the bounds of normal *stare decisis* analysis, then, and subject to the considerations on which it customarily turns, the stronger argument is for affirming *Roe*'s central holding, with whatever degree of personal reluctance any of us may have, not for overruling it.

In a less significant case, *stare decisis* analysis could, and would, stop at the point we have reached. But the sustained and widespread debate *Roe* has provoked calls for some comparison between that case and others of comparable dimension that have responded to national controversies and taken on the impress of the controversies addressed. Only two such decisional lines from the past century present themselves for examination, and in each instance the result reached by the Court accorded with the principles we apply today.

The first example is that line of cases identified with *Lochner v. New York (1905)*, which imposed substantive limitations on legislation limiting economic autonomy in favor of health and welfare regulation, adopting, in Justice Holmes' dissenting view, the theory of laissez-faire. In the meantime, the Depression had come and, with it, the lesson that seemed unmistakable to most people by 1937, that the interpretation of contractual freedom protected in earlier decisions had rested on fundamentally false factual assumptions about the capacity of a relatively unregulated market to satisfy minimal levels of human welfare. As Justice Jackson wrote of the constitutional crisis of 1937, shortly before he came on the bench, "The older world of *laissez-faire* was recognized everywhere outside the Court to be dead." The facts upon which the earlier case had premised a constitutional resolution of social controversy had proved to be untrue, and history's demonstration of their untruth not only justified but required the new choice of constitutional principle overruling that line of decisions. Of course, it was true that the Court lost something by its misperception, or its lack of prescience, and the Court-packing crisis only magnified the loss; but the clear demonstration that the facts of economic life were different from those previously assumed warranted the repudiation of the old law.

The second comparison that 20th century history invites is with the cases employing the separate-but-equal rule for applying the Fourteenth Amendment's equal protection guarantee. They began with *Plessy v. Ferguson (1896)*. The *Plessy* Court considered "the underlying fallacy of the plaintiff's argument to consist in the assumption that the enforced separation of the two races stamps the colored race with a badge of inferiority. If this be so, it is not by reason of anything found in the act, but solely because the colored race chooses to put that construction upon it." But this understanding of the facts and the rule it was stated to justify were repudiated in *Brown v. Board of Education (1954)*. The Court in *Brown* observed that whatever may have been the understanding in *Plessy*'s time of the power of segregation to stigmatize those who were segregated with a "badge of inferiority," it was clear by 1954 that legally sanctioned segregation had just such an effect, to the point that racially separate public educational facilities were deemed inherently unequal. Society's understanding of the facts upon which a constitutional ruling was sought in 1954 was thus fundamentally different from the basis claimed for the decision in 1896. While we think *Plessy* was wrong the day it was decided, we must also recognize that the *Plessy* Court's explanation for its decision was so clearly at odds with the facts apparent to the Court in 1954 that the decision to reexamine *Plessy* was on this ground alone not only justified but required.

These two lines of decisions each rested on facts, or an understanding of facts, changed from those which furnished the claimed justifications for the earlier constitutional resolutions. Each case was comprehensible as the Court's response to facts that the country could understand, or had come to understand already, but which the Court of an earlier day, as its own declarations disclosed, had not been able to perceive. As the decisions were thus comprehensible, they were also defensible, not merely as the victories of one doctrinal school over another by dint of numbers (victories though they were), but as applications of constitutional principle to facts as they had not been seen by the Court before. In constitutional adjudication, as elsewhere in life, changed circumstances may impose new obligations, and the thoughtful part of the Nation could accept each decision to overrule a prior case as a response to the Court's constitutional duty.

Because the case before us presents no such occasion it could be seen as no such response. Because neither the factual underpinnings of *Roe*'s central holding nor our understanding of it has changed (and because no other indication of weakened precedent has been shown) the Court could not pretend to be reexamining the prior law with any justification beyond a present doctrinal disposition to come out differently from the Court of 1973. To overrule prior law for no other reason than that would run counter to the view repeated in our cases, that a decision to overrule should rest on some special reason over and above the belief that a prior case was wrongly decided. As Justice Stewart insisted in 1974, "A basic change in the law upon a ground no firmer than a change in our membership invites the popular misconception that this institution is little different from the two political branches of the Government. No misconception could do more lasting injury to this Court and to the system of law which it is our abiding mission to serve."

The examination of the conditions justifying the these two repudiations of earlier precedents is enough to suggest the terrible price that would have been paid if the Court had not overruled as it did. In the present case, however, as our analysis to this point makes clear, the terrible price would be paid for overruling. Our analysis would not be complete, however, without explaining why overruling *Roe*'s central holding would not only reach an unjustifiable result under principles of *stare decisis*, but would seriously weaken the Court's capacity to exercise the judicial power and to function as the Supreme Court of a Nation dedicated to the rule of law. To understand why this would be so it is necessary to understand the source of this Court's authority, the conditions necessary for its preservation, and its relationship to the country's understanding of itself as a constitutional Republic.

The root of American governmental power is revealed most clearly in the instance of the power conferred by the Constitution upon the Judiciary of the United States and specifically upon this Court. As Americans of each succeeding generation are rightly told, the Court cannot buy support for its decisions by spending money and, except to a minor degree, it cannot independently coerce obedience to its decrees. The Court's power lies, rather, in its legitimacy, a product of substance and perception that shows itself in the people's acceptance of the Judiciary as fit to determine what the Nation's law means and to declare what it demands.

The underlying substance of this legitimacy is of course the warrant for the Court's decisions in the Constitution and the lesser sources of legal principle on which the Court draws. That substance is expressed in the Court's opinions, and our contemporary understanding is such that a decision without principled justification would be no judicial act at all. But even when justification is furnished by apposite legal principle, something more is required. Because not every conscientious claim of principled justification will be accepted as such, the justification claimed must be beyond dispute. The Court must take care to speak and act in ways that allow people to accept its decisions on the terms the Court claims for them, as grounded truly in principle, not as compromises with social and political pressures having, as such, no bearing on the principled choices that the Court is obliged to make. Thus, the Court's legitimacy depends on making legally principled decisions under circumstances in which their principled character is sufficiently plausible to be accepted by the Nation.

The need for principled action to be perceived as such is implicated to some degree whenever this, or any other appellate court, overrules a prior case. This is not to say, of course, that this Court cannot give a perfectly satisfactory explanation in most cases. People understand that some of the Constitution's language is hard to fathom and that the Court's Justices are sometimes able to perceive significant facts or to understand principles of law that eluded their predecessors and that justify departures from existing decisions. However upsetting it may be to those most directly affected when one judicially derived rule replaces another, the country can accept some correction of error without necessarily questioning the legitimacy of the Court.

In two circumstances, however, the Court would almost certainly fail to receive the benefit of the doubt in overruling prior cases. There is, first, a point beyond which frequent overruling would overtax the country's belief in the Court's good faith. Despite the variety of reasons that may inform and justify a decision to overrule, we cannot forget that such a decision is usually perceived (and perceived correctly) as, at the least, a statement that a prior decision was wrong. There is a limit to the amount of error that can plausibly be imputed to prior courts. If that limit should be exceeded, disturbance of prior rulings would be taken as evidence that justifiable reexamination of principle had given way to drives for particular results in the short term. The legitimacy of the Court would fade with the frequency of its vacillation.

That first circumstance can be described as hypothetical; the second is to the point here and now. Where, in the performance of its judicial duties, the Court decides a case in such a way as to resolve the sort of intensely divisive controversy reflected in *Roe* and those rare, comparable cases, its decision has a dimension that the resolution of the normal case does not carry. It is the dimension present whenever the Court's interpretation of the Constitution calls the contending sides of a national controversy to end their national division by accepting a common mandate rooted in the Constitution.

The Court is not asked to do this very often, having thus addressed the Nation only twice in our lifetime, in the decisions of *Brown* and *Roe*. But when the Court does act in this way, its decision requires an equally rare precedential force to counter the inevitable efforts to overturn it and to thwart its implementation. Some of those efforts may be mere unprincipled emotional reactions; others may proceed from principles worthy of profound respect. But whatever the premises of opposition may be, only the most convincing justification under accepted standards of precedent could suffice to demonstrate that a later decision overruling the first was anything but a surrender to political pressure, and an unjustified repudiation of the principle on which the Court staked its authority in the first instance. So to overrule under fire in the absence of the most compelling reason to reexamine a watershed decision would subvert the Court's legitimacy beyond any serious question.

The country's loss of confidence in the judiciary would be underscored by an equally certain and equally reasonable condemnation for another failing in overruling unnecessarily and under pressure. Some cost will be paid by anyone who approves or implements a constitutional decision where it is unpopular, or who refuses to work to undermine the decision or to force its reversal. The price may be criticism or ostracism, or it may be violence. An extra price will be paid by those who themselves disapprove of the decision's results when viewed outside of constitutional terms, but who nevertheless struggle to accept it, because they respect the rule of law. To all those who will be so tested by following, the Court implicitly undertakes to remain steadfast, lest in the end a price be paid for nothing. The promise of constancy, once given, binds its maker for as long as the power to stand by the decision survives and the understanding of the issue has not changed so fundamentally as to render the commitment obsolete. From the obligation of this promise this Court cannot and should not assume any exemption when duty requires it to decide a case in conformance with the Constitution. A willing breach of it would be nothing less than a breach of faith, and no Court that broke its faith with the people could sensibly expect credit for principle in the decision by which it did that.

It is true that diminished legitimacy may be restored, but only slowly. Unlike the political branches, a Court thus weakened could not seek to regain its position with a new mandate from the voters, and even if the Court could somehow go to the polls, the loss of its principled character could not be retrieved by the casting of so many votes. Like the character of an individual, the legitimacy of the Court must be earned over time. So, indeed, must be the character of a Nation of people who aspire to live according to the rule of law. Their belief in themselves as such a people is not readily separable from their understanding of the Court invested with the authority to decide their constitutional cases and speak before all others for their constitutional ideals. If the Court's legitimacy should be undermined, then, so would the country be in its very ability to see itself through its constitutional ideals. The Court's concern with legitimacy is not for the sake of the Court but for the sake of the Nation to which it is responsible.

The Court's duty in the present case is clear. In 1973, it confronted the already-divisive issue of governmental power to limit personal choice to undergo abortion, for which it provided a new resolution based on the due process guaranteed by the

Fourteenth Amendment. Whether or not a new social consensus is developing on that issue, its divisiveness is no less today than in 1973, and pressure to overrule the decision, like pressure to retain it, has grown only more intense. A decision to overrule *Roe*'s essential holding under the existing circumstances would address error, if error there was, at the cost of both profound and unnecessary damage to the Court's legitimacy, and to the Nation's commitment to the rule of law. It is therefore imperative to adhere to the essence of *Roe*'s original decision, and we do so today.

From what we have said so far it follows that it is a constitutional liberty of the woman to have some freedom to terminate her pregnancy. We conclude that the basic decision in *Roe* was based on a constitutional analysis which we cannot now repudiate. The woman's liberty is not so unlimited, however, that from the outset the State cannot show its concern for the life of the unborn, and at a later point in fetal development the State's interest in life has sufficient force so that the right of the woman to terminate the pregnancy can be restricted.

That brings us, of course, to the point where much criticism has been directed at *Roe*, a criticism that always inheres when the Court draws a specific rule from what in the Constitution is but a general standard. We conclude, however, that the urgent claims of the woman to retain the ultimate control over her destiny and her body, claims implicit in the meaning of liberty, require us to perform that function. Liberty must not be extinguished for want of a line that is clear. And it falls to us to give some real substance to the woman's liberty to determine whether to carry her pregnancy to full term.

We conclude the line should be drawn at viability, so that before that time the woman has a right to choose to terminate her pregnancy. We adhere to this principle for two reasons. First, as we have said, is the doctrine of *stare decisis*. Any judicial act of line-drawing may seem somewhat arbitrary, but *Roe* was a reasoned statement, elaborated with great care. We have twice reaffirmed it in the face of great opposition. The central premise of those cases represents an unbroken commitment by this Court to the essential holding of *Roe*. It is that premise which we reaffirm today.

The second reason is that the concept of viability, as we noted in *Roe*, is the time at which there is a realistic possibility of maintaining and nourishing a life outside the womb, so that the independent existence of the second life can in reason and all fairness be the object of state protection that now overrides the rights of the woman. Consistent with other constitutional norms, legislatures may draw lines which appear arbitrary without the necessity of offering a justification. But courts may not. We must justify the lines we draw. And there is no line other than viability which is more workable. To be sure, as we have said, there may be some medical developments that affect the precise point of viability, but this is an imprecision within tolerable limits given that the medical community and all those who must apply its discoveries will continue to explore the matter. The viability line also has, as a practical matter, an element of fairness. In some broad sense it might be said that a woman who fails to act before viability has consented to the State's intervention on behalf of the developing child.

The woman's right to terminate her pregnancy before viability is the most central principle of *Roe v. Wade*. It is a rule of law and a component of liberty we cannot renounce.

On the other side of the equation is the interest of the State in the protection of potential life. The *Roe* Court recognized the State's "important and legitimate interest in protecting the potentiality of human life." The weight to be given this state interest, not the strength of the woman's interest, was the difficult question faced in *Roe*. We do not need to say whether each of us, had we been Members of the Court when the valuation of the State interest came before it as an original matter, would have concluded, as the *Roe* Court did, that its weight is insufficient to justify a ban on abortions prior to viability even when it is subject to certain exceptions. The matter is not before us in the first instance, and coming as it does after nearly 20 years of litigation in *Roe*'s wake we are satisfied that the immediate question is not the soundness of *Roe*'s resolution of the issue, but the precedential force that must be accorded to its holding. And we have concluded that the essential holding of *Roe* should be reaffirmed.

Yet it must be remembered that *Roe v. Wade* speaks with clarity in establishing not only the woman's liberty but also the State's "important and legitimate interest in potential life." That portion of the decision in *Roe* has been given too little acknowledgement and implementation by the Court in its subsequent cases. Not all of the cases decided under that formulation can be reconciled with the holding in *Roe* itself that the

State has legitimate interests in the health of the woman and in protecting the potential life within her. In resolving this tension, we choose to rely upon *Roe*, as against the later cases.

*Roe* established a trimester framework to govern abortion regulations. Under this elaborate but rigid construct, almost no regulation at all is permitted during the first trimester of pregnancy; regulations designed to protect the woman's health, but not to further the State's interest in potential life, are permitted during the second trimester; and during the third trimester, when the fetus is viable, prohibitions are permitted provided the life or health of the mother is not at stake. Most of our cases since *Roe* have involved the application of rules derived from the trimester framework.

The trimester framework no doubt was erected to ensure that the woman's right to choose not become so subordinate to the State's interest in promoting fetal life that her choice exists in theory but not in fact. We do not agree, however, that the trimester approach is necessary to accomplish this objective. A framework of this rigidity was unnecessary and in its later interpretation sometimes contradicted the State's permissible exercise of its powers.

Though the woman has a right to choose to terminate or continue her pregnancy before viability, it does not at all follow that the State is prohibited from taking steps to ensure that this choice is thoughtful and informed. Even in the earliest stages of pregnancy, the State may enact rules and regulations designed to encourage her to know that there are philosophic and social arguments of great weight that can be brought to bear in favor of continuing the pregnancy to full term and that there are procedures and institutions to allow adoption of unwanted children as well as a certain degree of state assistance if the mother chooses to raise the child herself. "The Constitution does not forbid a State or city, pursuant to democratic processes, from expressing a preference for normal childbirth." It follows that States are free to enact laws to provide a reasonable framework for a woman to make a decision that has such profound and lasting meaning. This, too, we find consistent with *Roe*'s central premises, and indeed the inevitable consequence of our holding that the State has an interest in protecting the life of the unborn.

We reject the trimester framework, which we do not consider to be part of the essential holding of *Roe*. Measures aimed at ensuring that a woman's choice contemplates the consequences for the fetus do not necessarily interfere with the right recognized in *Roe*, although those measures have been found to be inconsistent with the rigid trimester framework announced in that case. A logical reading of the central holding in *Roe* itself, and a necessary reconciliation of the liberty of the woman and the interest of the State in promoting prenatal life, require, in our view, that we abandon the trimester framework as a rigid prohibition on all previability regulation aimed at the protection of fetal life. The trimester framework suffers from these basic flaws: in its formulation it misconceives the nature of the pregnant woman's interest; and in practice it undervalues the State's interest in potential life, as recognized in *Roe*.

As our jurisprudence relating to all liberties save perhaps abortion has recognized, not every law which makes a right more difficult to exercise is, *ipso facto*, an infringement of that right. An example clarifies the point. We have held that not every ballot access limitation amounts to an infringement of the right to vote. Rather, the States are granted substantial flexibility in establishing the framework within which voters choose the candidates for whom they wish to vote.

The abortion right is similar. Numerous forms of state regulation might have the incidental effect of increasing the cost or decreasing the availability of medical care, whether for abortion or any other medical procedure. The fact that a law which serves a valid purpose, one not designed to strike at the right itself, has the incidental effect of making it more difficult or more expensive to procure an abortion cannot be enough to invalidate it. Only where state regulation imposes an undue burden on a woman's ability to make this decision does the power of the State reach into the heart of the liberty protected by the Due Process Clause.

For the most part, the Court's early abortion cases adhered to this view. These considerations of the nature of the abortion right illustrate that it is an overstatement to describe it as a right to decide whether to have an abortion "without interference from the State." All abortion regulations interfere to some degree with a woman's ability to decide whether to terminate her pregnancy. It is, as a consequence, not surprising that despite the protestations contained in the original *Roe* opinion to the effect that the Court was not recognizing an absolute right, the Court's experience applying the trimester framework has led to the striking down of some abortion regulations which in no real sense deprived women of the ultimate decision. Those

judicial decisions went too far because the right recognized by
*Roe* is a right "to be free from unwarranted governmental intrusion into matters so fundamentally affecting a person as the
decision whether to bear or beget a child." Not all governmental
intrusion is of necessity unwarranted; and that brings us to the
other basic flaw in the trimester framework: even in *Roe*'s
terms, in practice it undervalues the State's interest in the potential life within the woman. *Roe v. Wade* was express in its
recognition of the State's "important and legitimate interests in
preserving and protecting the health of the pregnant woman
and in protecting the potentiality of human life." The trimester
framework, however, does not fulfill *Roe*'s own promise that the
State has an interest in protecting fetal life or potential life. *Roe*
began the contradiction by using the trimester framework to
forbid any regulation of abortion designed to advance that interest before viability. Before viability, *Roe* and subsequent cases
treat all governmental attempts to influence a woman's decision
on behalf of the potential life within her as unwarranted. This
treatment is, in our judgment, incompatible with the recognition
that there is a substantial state interest in potential life
throughout pregnancy.

The very notion that the State has a substantial interest in
potential life leads to the conclusion that not all regulations
must be deemed unwarranted. Not all burdens on the right to
decide whether to terminate a pregnancy will be undue. In our
view, the undue burden standard is the appropriate means of
reconciling the State's interest with the woman's constitutionally protected liberty.

A finding of an undue burden is a shorthand for the conclusion that a state regulation has the purpose or effect of placing a
substantial obstacle in the path of a woman seeking an abortion
of a nonviable fetus. A statute with this purpose is invalid because the means chosen by the State to further the interest in
potential life must be calculated to inform the woman's free
choice, not hinder it. And a statute which, while furthering the
interest in potential life or some other valid state interest, has
the effect of placing a substantial obstacle in the path of a
woman's choice cannot be considered a permissible means of
serving its legitimate ends. Understood another way, we answer
the question, left open in previous opinions discussing the undue burden formulation, whether a law designed to further the
State's interest in fetal life which imposes an undue burden on
the woman's decision before fetal viability could be constitutional. The answer is no.

Some guiding principles should emerge. What is at stake is the woman's right to make the ultimate decision, not a right to be insulated from all others in doing so. Regulations which do no more than create a structural mechanism by which the State, or the parent or guardian of a minor, may express profound respect for the life of the unborn are permitted, if they are not a substantial obstacle to the woman's exercise of the right to choose. Unless it has that effect on her right of choice, a state measure designed to persuade her to choose childbirth over abortion will be upheld if reasonably related to that goal. Regulations designed to foster the health of a woman seeking an abortion are valid if they do not constitute an undue burden.

Our Constitution is a covenant running from the first generation of Americans to us and then to future generations. It is a coherent succession. Each generation must learn anew that the Constitution's written terms embody ideas and aspirations that must survive more ages than one. We accept our responsibility not to retreat from interpreting the full meaning of the covenant in light of all of our precedents. We invoke it once again to define the freedom guaranteed by the Constitution's own promise, the promise of liberty.

*We conclude that in the field of public educa-*
*tion the doctrine of "separate but equal" has no*
*place. Separate educational facilities are inher-*
*ently unequal.*

*— Earl Warren*

## Brown v. Bd. of Educ.
### 74 S.Ct. 686, 347 U.S. 483 (1954)

*The Supreme Court overruled its own mistaken "sepa-*
*rate but equal" doctrine, established in* Plessy v. Ferguson *(1896), which had made the Jim Crow era*
*possible. In a brief but unanimous opinion, written in the*
*grand style of John Marshall, Chief Justice Warren*
*asked the question: what does equality mean in our time?*
*And he gave the only answer morally possible. On reargu-*
*ment, the States were ordered to desegregate public*
*schools "with all deliberate speed," a formula that re-*
*sulted in more deliberateness than speed. Notwithstand-*
*ing Chief Justice Warren's focus and emphasis on the*
*importance of public education, the equal protection prin-*
*ciple announced here was extended in later cases to every*
*sort of government facility.*

**Chief Justice Warren:** These cases come to us from the
States of Kansas, South Carolina, Virginia, and Delaware. They
are premised on different facts and different local conditions,
but a common legal question justifies their consideration together in this consolidated opinion.

In each of the cases, minors of the Negro race, through their
legal representatives, seek the aid of the courts in obtaining
admission to the public schools of their community on a non-
segregated basis. In each instance, they have been denied admission to schools attended by white children under laws
requiring or permitting segregation according to race. This segregation was alleged to deprive the plaintiffs of the equal protection of the laws under the Fourteenth Amendment. In each of
the cases other than the Delaware case, a three-judge federal
district court denied relief to the plaintiffs on the so-called
"separate but equal" doctrine announced by this Court in *Plessy*
*v. Ferguson (1896).* Under that doctrine, equality of treatment is
accorded when the races are provided substantially equal facilities, even though these facilities be separate. In the Delaware

case, the Supreme Court of Delaware adhered to that doctrine, but ordered that the plaintiffs be admitted to the white schools because of their superiority to the Negro schools.

The plaintiffs contend that segregated public schools are not "equal" and cannot be made "equal," and that hence they are deprived of the equal protection of the laws. Because of the obvious importance of the question presented, the Court took jurisdiction. Argument was heard in the 1952 Term, and reargument was heard this Term on certain questions propounded by the Court.

Reargument was largely devoted to the circumstances surrounding the adoption of the Fourteenth Amendment in 1868. It covered exhaustively consideration of the Amendment in Congress, ratification by the states, then existing practices in racial segregation, and the views of proponents and opponents of the Amendment. This discussion and our own investigation convince us that, although these sources cast some light, it is not enough to resolve the problem with which we are faced. At best, they are inconclusive. The most avid proponents of the post-War Amendments undoubtedly intended them to remove all legal distinctions among "all persons born or naturalized in the United States." Their opponents, just as certainly, were antagonistic to both the letter and the spirit of the Amendments and wished them to have the most limited effect. What others in Congress and the state legislatures had in mind cannot be determined with any degree of certainty.

An additional reason for the inconclusive nature of the Amendment's history, with respect to segregated schools, is the status of public education at that time. In the South, the movement toward free common schools, supported by general taxation, had not yet taken hold. Education of white children was largely in the hands of private groups. Education of Negroes was almost nonexistent, and practically all of the race were illiterate. In fact, any education of Negroes was forbidden by law in some states. Today, in contrast, many Negroes have achieved outstanding success in the arts and sciences as well as in the business and professional world. It is true that public school education at the time of the Amendment had advanced further in the North, but the effect of the Amendment on Northern States was generally ignored in the congressional debates. Even in the North, the conditions of public education did not approximate those existing today. The curriculum was usually rudimentary; ungraded schools were common in rural areas; the

—— 597 ——

school term was but three months a year in many states; and compulsory school attendance was virtually unknown. As a consequence, it is not surprising that there should be so little in the history of the Fourteenth Amendment relating to its intended effect on public education.

In the first cases in this Court construing the Fourteenth Amendment, decided shortly after its adoption, the Court interpreted it as proscribing all state-imposed discriminations against the Negro race. The doctrine of "separate but equal" did not make its appearance in this court until 1896 in the case *Plessy v. Ferguson*, involving not education but transportation. American courts have since labored with the doctrine for over half a century. In this Court, there have been six cases involving the "separate but equal" doctrine in the field of public education. In more recent cases, all on the graduate school level, inequality was found in that specific benefits enjoyed by white students were denied to Negro students of the same educational qualifications. In none of these cases was it necessary to re-examine the doctrine to grant relief to the Negro plaintiff. And in 1950 the Court expressly reserved decision on the question whether *Plessy v. Ferguson* should be held inapplicable to public education.

In the instant cases, that question is directly presented. Here, unlike the 1950 case, there are findings below that the Negro and white schools involved have been equalized, or are being equalized, with respect to buildings, curricula, qualifications and salaries of teachers, and other "tangible" factors. Our decision, therefore, cannot turn on merely a comparison of these tangible factors in the Negro and white schools involved in each of the cases. We must look instead to the effect of segregation itself on public education.

In approaching this problem, we cannot turn the clock back to 1868 when the Amendment was adopted, or even to 1896 when *Plessy v. Ferguson* was written. We must consider public education in the light of its full development and its present place in American life throughout the Nation. Only in this way can it be determined if segregation in public schools deprives these plaintiffs of the equal protection of the laws.

Today, education is perhaps the most important function of state and local governments. Compulsory school attendance laws and the great expenditures for education both demonstrate our recognition of the importance of education to our democratic society. It is required in the performance of our most basic public responsibilities, even service in the armed forces. It is the very foundation of good citizenship. Today it is a principal instrument in awakening the child to cultural values, in preparing him for later professional training, and in helping him to adjust normally to his environment. In these days, it is doubtful that any child may reasonably be expected to succeed in life if he is denied the opportunity of an education. Such an opportunity, where the state has undertaken to provide it, is a right which must be made available to all on equal terms.

We come then to the question presented: Does segregation of children in public schools solely on the basis of race, even though the physical facilities and other "tangible" factors may be equal, deprive the children of the minority group of equal educational opportunities? We believe that it does.

In a 1950 decision, in finding that a segregated law school for Negroes could not provide them equal educational opportunities, this Court relied in large part on "those qualities which are incapable of objective measurement but which make for greatness in a law school." In the companion case, the Court, in requiring that a Negro admitted to a white graduate school be treated like all other students, again resorted to intangible considerations: "his ability to study, to engage in discussions and exchange views with other students, and, in general, to learn his profession." Such considerations apply with added force to children in grade and high schools. To separate them from others of similar age and qualifications solely because of their race generates a feeling of inferiority as to their status in the community that may affect their hearts and minds in a way unlikely ever to be undone. The effect of this separation on their educational opportunities was well stated by a finding in the Kansas case by a court which nevertheless felt compelled to rule against the Negro plaintiffs: "Segregation of white and colored children in public schools has a detrimental effect upon the colored children. The impact is greater when it has the sanction of the law; for the policy of separating the races is usually interpreted as denoting the inferiority of the negro group. A sense of inferiority affects the motivation of a child to learn. Segregation with the sanction of law, therefore, has a tendency to retard the educational and mental development of Negro children and to deprive them of some of the benefits they would receive in a racially integrated school system."

Whatever may have been the extent of psychological knowledge at the time of *Plessy v. Ferguson*, this finding is amply supported by modern authority in psychology and the other social sciences. Any language in *Plessy v. Ferguson* contrary to this finding is rejected.

We conclude that in the field of public education the doctrine of "separate but equal" has no place. Separate educational facilities are inherently unequal. Therefore, we hold that the plaintiffs and others similarly situated for whom the actions have been brought are, by reason of the segregation complained of, deprived of the equal protection of the laws guaranteed by the Fourteenth Amendment.

*In light of the sorry history of discrimination
and its devastating impact on the lives of Negroes,
bringing the Negro into the mainstream of American life should be a state interest of the highest
order. To fail to do so is to ensure that America
will forever remain a divided society.*

— *Thurgood Marshall*

*In my mind, government-sponsored racial
discrimination based on benign prejudice is just
as noxious as discrimination inspired by
malicious prejudice. In each instance, it is
racial discrimination, plain and simple.*

— *Clarence Thomas*

## Regents of the University of California v. Bakke
### 98 S.Ct. 2733, 438 U.S. 265 (1978)

## Adarand Constructors, Inc. v. Pena
### 115 S.Ct. 2097, (1995)

*These two excerpts are different from all the others in
this book. Here are two opinions from two different cases
written by two Justices who never served with each other:
Justice Marshall's opinion in* Bakke—*the first major affirmative action/reverse discrimination decision—and
Justice Thomas' opinion in* Adarand—*the most recent but
surely not the last decision on this issue. They are juxtaposed to demonstrate how extremely polarizing this subject is today.*

*In 1978,* Bakke *allowed for the possibility of awarding
a "plus" to an individual applicant to a state university
for having a racial or ethnic background that would contribute to the diversity of the student body, but held that
the Medical School at the University of California at
Davis could not set aside a specific number of seats to be
filled only by persons of color. Justice Thurgood Marshall, the great-grandson of a slave, achieved historical
greatness as the NAACP lawyer-strategist of the move-*

*ment to declare "Jim Crow" de jure segregation unconsti-*
*tutional. The first African-American to be appointed to*
*the Supreme Court, he served from 1967–1991.*

*In 1995, Adarand ruled that a federal program which*
*provided general contractors a financial incentive to hire*
*subcontractors controlled by "socially and economically*
*disadvantaged individuals," particularly racial minori-*
*ties, could be challenged by a majority-owned company*
*and would be upheld only if it was narrowly tailored to*
*serve a compelling governmental interest. The decision*
*sent the Clinton Administration scrambling to decide*
*what programs would be defended before the Congress*
*and in the Courts. Justice Clarence Thomas replaced*
*Justice Marshall and is the second African-American*
*Justice. His Senate confirmation was one of the most vi-*
*tuperative in history, including a charge of sexual har-*
*assment brought by law professor and former staffer*
*Anita Hill as well as general attacks that amounted to*
*calling him an "Uncle Tom."*

*The constitutional debate illustrated here will remain*
*on America's constitutional agenda for a long time to*
*come.*

**Justice Marshall:** I agree with the judgment of the Court
only insofar as it permits a university to consider the race of an
applicant in making admissions decisions. I do not agree that
the University's admissions program violates the Constitution.
For it must be remembered that, during most of the past 200
years, the Constitution as interpreted by this Court did not
prohibit the most ingenious and pervasive forms of discrimination against the Negro. Now, when a State acts to remedy the
effects of that legacy of discrimination, I cannot believe that this
same Constitution stands as a barrier.

Three hundred and fifty years ago, the Negro was dragged to
this country in chains to be sold into slavery. Uprooted from his
homeland and thrust into bondage for forced labor, the slave
was deprived of all legal rights. It was unlawful to teach him to
read; he could be sold away from his family and friends at the
whim of his master; and killing or maiming him was not a
crime. The system of slavery brutalized and dehumanized both
master and slave.

The denial of human rights was etched into the American Colonies' first attempts at establishing self-government. When the colonists determined to seek their independence from England, they drafted a unique document cataloguing their grievances against the King and proclaiming as "self-evident" that "all men are created equal" and are endowed "with certain unalienable Rights," including those to "Life, Liberty and the pursuit of Happiness." The self-evident truths and the unalienable rights were intended, however, to apply only to white men. An earlier draft of the *Declaration of Independence*, submitted by Thomas Jefferson to the Continental Congress, had included among the charges against the King that "he has waged cruel war against human nature itself, violating its most sacred rights of life and liberty in the persons of a distant people who never offended him, captivating and carrying them into slavery in another hemisphere, or to incur miserable death in their transportation thither." The Southern delegation insisted that the charge be deleted; the colonists themselves were implicated in the slave trade, and inclusion of this claim might have made it more difficult to justify the continuation of slavery once the ties to England were severed. Thus, even as the colonists embarked on a course to secure their own freedom and equality, they ensured perpetuation of the system that deprived a whole race of those rights.

The implicit protection of slavery embodied in the *Declaration of Independence* was made explicit in the Constitution, which treated a slave as being equivalent to three-fifths of a person for purposes of apportioning representatives and taxes among the States. Art. I, § 2. The Constitution also contained a clause ensuring that the "Migration or Importation" of slaves into the existing States would be legal until at least 1808, Art. I, § 9, and a fugitive slave clause requiring that when a slave escaped to another State, he must be returned on the claim of the master, Art. IV, § 2. In their declaration of the principles that were to provide the cornerstone of the new Nation, therefore, the Framers made it plain that "we the people," for whose protection the Constitution was designed, did not include those whose skins were the wrong color.

The individual States likewise established the machinery to protect the system of slavery through the promulgation of the Slave Codes, which were designed primarily to defend the property interest of the owner in his slave. The position of the Negro slave as mere property was confirmed by this Court in *Dred Scott v. Sandford (1857)*, holding that the Missouri Compromise—which prohibited slavery in the portion of the Louisiana Purchase Territory north of Missouri—was unconstitutional because it deprived slave owners of their property without due process. The Court declared that under the Constitution a slave was property, and "the right to traffic in it, like an ordinary article of merchandise and property, was guaranteed to the citizens of the United States." The Court further concluded that Negroes were not intended to be included as citizens under the Constitution but were "regarded as beings of an inferior order altogether unfit to associate with the white race, either in social or political relations; and so far inferior, that they had no rights which the white man was bound to respect."

The status of the Negro as property was officially erased by his emancipation at the end of the Civil War. But the long-awaited emancipation, while freeing the Negro from slavery, did not bring him citizenship or equality in any meaningful way. Slavery was replaced by a system of "laws which imposed upon the colored race onerous disabilities and burdens, and curtailed their rights in the pursuit of life, liberty, and property to such an extent that their freedom was of little value," in the words of an 1873 decision of this Court. Despite the passage of the Thirteenth, Fourteenth, and Fifteenth Amendments, the Negro was systematically denied the rights those Amendments were supposed to secure. The combined actions and inactions of the State and Federal Governments maintained Negroes in a position of legal inferiority for another century after the Civil War.

The Southern States took the first steps to re-enslave the Negroes. Immediately following the end of the Civil War, many of the provisional legislatures passed Black Codes, similar to the Slave Codes, which, among other things, limited the rights of Negroes to own or rent property and permitted imprisonment for breach of employment contracts. Over the next several decades, the South managed to disenfranchise the Negroes in spite of the Fifteenth Amendment by various techniques, including poll taxes, deliberately complicated balloting processes, property and literacy qualifications, and finally the white primary.

Congress responded to the legal disabilities being imposed in the Southern States by passing the Reconstruction Acts and the Civil Rights Acts. Congress also responded to the needs of the Negroes at the end of the Civil War by establishing the Bureau of Refugees, Freedmen, and Abandoned Lands, better known as the Freedmen's Bureau, to supply food, hospitals, land, and education to the newly freed slaves. Thus, for a time it seemed as if the Negro might be protected from the continued denial of his civil rights and might be relieved of the disabilities that prevented him from taking his place as a free and equal citizen.

That time, however, was short-lived. Reconstruction came to a close, and, with the assistance of this Court, the Negro was rapidly stripped of his new civil rights. In the words of the premier scholar of the period, C. Vann Woodward: "By narrow and ingenious interpretation the Supreme Court's decisions over a period of years had whittled away a great part of the authority presumably given the government for protection of civil rights."

The Court began by interpreting the Civil War Amendments in a manner that sharply curtailed their substantive protections in the *Slaughter-House Cases (1873)*. Then in the notorious *Civil Rights Cases (1883)*, the Court strangled Congress' efforts to use its power to promote racial equality. In those cases the Court invalidated sections of the Civil Rights Act of 1875 that made it a crime to deny equal access to "inns, public conveyances, theatres and other places of public amusement." According to the Court, the Fourteenth Amendment gave Congress the power to proscribe only discriminatory action by the State. The Court ruled that the Negroes who were excluded from public places suffered only an invasion of their social rights at the hands of private individuals, and Congress had no power to remedy that. "When a man has emerged from slavery, and by the aid of beneficent legislation has shaken off the inseparable concomitants of that state," the Court concluded, "there must be some stage in the progress of his elevation when he takes the rank of a mere citizen, and ceases to be the special favorite of the laws." As Mr. Justice Harlan noted in dissent, however, the Civil War Amendments and Civil Rights Acts did not make the Negroes the "special favorite" of the laws but instead "sought to accomplish in reference to that race what had already been done in every State of the Union for the white race—to secure and protect rights belonging to them as freemen and citizens; nothing more."

The Court's ultimate blow to the Civil War Amendments and to the equality of Negroes came in *Plessy v. Ferguson (1896)*. In upholding a Louisiana law that required railway companies to provide "equal but separate" accommodations for whites and Negroes, the Court held that the Fourteenth Amendment was not intended "to abolish distinctions based upon color, or to enforce social, as distinguished from political equality, or a commingling of the two races upon terms unsatisfactory to either." Ignoring totally the realities of the positions of the two races, the Court remarked: "We consider the underlying fallacy of the plaintiff's argument to consist in the assumption that the enforced separation of the two races stamps the colored race with a badge of inferiority. If this be so, it is not by reason of anything found in the act, but solely because the colored race chooses to put that construction upon it."

Mr. Justice Harlan's dissenting opinion recognized the bankruptcy of the Court's reasoning. He noted that the "real meaning" of the legislation was "that colored citizens are so inferior and degraded that they cannot be allowed to sit in public coaches occupied by white citizens." He expressed his fear that if like laws were enacted in other States, "the effect would be in the highest degree mischievous." Although slavery would have disappeared, the States would retain the power "to interfere with the full enjoyment of the blessings of freedom; to regulate civil rights, common to all citizens, upon the basis of race; and to place in a condition of legal inferiority a large body of American citizens."

The fears of Mr. Justice Harlan were soon to be realized. In the wake of *Plessy*, many States expanded their Jim Crow laws, which had up until that time been limited primarily to passenger trains and schools. The segregation of the races was extended to residential areas, parks, hospitals, theaters, waiting rooms, and bathrooms. There were even statutes and ordinances which authorized separate phone booths for Negroes and whites, which required that textbooks used by children of one race be kept separate from those used by the other, and which required that Negro and white prostitutes be kept in separate districts. In 1898, after *Plessy*, the *Charlestown News and Courier* printed a parody of Jim Crow laws: "If there must be Jim Crow cars on the railroads, there should be Jim Crow cars on the street railways. Also on all passenger boats. If there are to be Jim Crow cars, moreover, there should be Jim Crow waiting saloons at all stations, and Jim Crow eating houses. There should be Jim Crow sections of the jury box, and a separate Jim Crow dock and witness stand in every court—and a Jim Crow Bible for colored witnesses to kiss." The irony is that before many years had passed, with the exception of the Jim Crow witness stand, "all the improbable applications of the principle suggested by the editor in derision had been put into practice—down to and including the Jim Crow Bible."

Nor were the laws restricting the rights of Negroes limited solely to the Southern States. In many of the Northern States, the Negro was denied the right to vote, prevented from serving on juries, and excluded from theaters, restaurants, hotels, and inns. Under President Wilson, the Federal Government began to require segregation in Government buildings; desks of Negro employees were curtained off; separate bathrooms and separate tables in the cafeterias were provided; and even the galleries of the Congress were segregated. When his segregationist policies were attacked, President Wilson responded that segregation was "not humiliating but a benefit" and that he was "rendering the Negroes more safe in their possession of office and less likely to be discriminated against."

The enforced segregation of the races continued into the middle of the 20th century. In both World Wars, Negroes were for the most part confined to separate military units; it was not until 1948 that an end to segregation in the military was ordered by President Truman. And the history of the exclusion of Negro children from white public schools is too well known and recent to require repeating here. That Negroes were deliberately excluded from public graduate and professional schools—and thereby denied the opportunity to become doctors, lawyers, engineers, and the like—is also well established. It is of course true that some of the Jim Crow laws (which the decisions of this Court had helped to foster) were struck down by this Court in a series of decisions leading up to *Brown v. Board of Education (1954)*. Those decisions, however, did not automatically end segregation, nor did they move Negroes from a position of legal inferiority to one of equality. The legacy of years of slavery and of years of second-class citizenship in the wake of emancipation could not be so easily eliminated.

The position of the Negro today in America is the tragic but inevitable consequence of centuries of unequal treatment. Measured by any benchmark of comfort or achievement, meaningful equality remains a distant dream for the Negro.

A Negro child today has a life expectancy which is shorter by more than five years than that of a white child. The Negro child's mother is over three times more likely to die of complications in childbirth, and the infant mortality rate for Negroes is nearly twice that for whites. The median income of the Negro family is only 60% that of the median of a white family, and the percentage of Negroes who live in families with incomes below the poverty line is nearly four times greater than that of whites.

When the Negro child reaches working age, he finds that America offers him significantly less than it offers his white counterpart. For Negro adults, the unemployment rate is twice that of whites, and the unemployment rate for Negro teenagers is nearly three times that of white teenagers. A Negro male who completes four years of college can expect a median annual income of merely $110 more than a white male who has only a high school diploma. Although Negroes represent 11.5% of the population, they are only 1.2% of the lawyers, and judges, 2% of the physicians, 2.3% of the dentists, 1.1% of the engineers and 2.6% of the college and university professors.

The relationship between those figures and the history of unequal treatment afforded to the Negro cannot be denied. At every point from birth to death the impact of the past is reflected in the still disfavored position of the Negro.

In light of the sorry history of discrimination and its devastating impact on the lives of Negroes, bringing the Negro into the mainstream of American life should be a state interest of the highest order. To fail to do so is to ensure that America will forever remain a divided society.

I do not believe that the Fourteenth Amendment requires us to accept that fate. Neither its history nor our past cases lend any support to the conclusion that a university may not remedy the cumulative effects of society's discrimination by giving consideration to race in an effort to increase the number and percentage of Negro doctors.

It is plain that the Fourteenth Amendment was not intended to prohibit measures designed to remedy the effects of the Nation's past treatment of Negroes. The Congress that passed the Fourteenth Amendment is the same Congress that passed the 1866 Freedmen's Bureau Act, an Act that provided many of its benefits only to Negroes. Despite the objection to the special treatment the bill would provide for Negroes, it was passed by Congress. President Johnson vetoed this bill; one of his principal objections to the bill was that it gave special benefits to Negroes. Rejecting the concerns of the President and the bill's opponents, Congress overrode the President's veto. Since the Congress that considered and rejected the objections to the 1866 Freedmen's Bureau Act concerning special relief to Negroes also proposed the Fourteenth Amendment, it is inconceivable that the Fourteenth Amendment was intended to prohibit all race-conscious relief measures.

This Court's past cases establish the constitutionality of race-conscious remedial measures. Beginning with the school desegregation cases, we recognized that even absent a judicial or legislative finding of constitutional violation, a school board constitutionally could consider the race of students in making school-assignment decisions. As we have observed, "any other approach would freeze the status quo that is the very target of all desegregation processes." We have been willing to sanction the remedial use of a racial classification even though it disadvantaged otherwise "innocent" individuals. We have recognized the permissibility of remedying past societal discrimination through the use of otherwise disfavored classifications.

Nothing in our prior cases suggests that a university cannot similarly act to remedy past discrimination. There is thus ample support for the conclusion that a university can employ race-conscious measures to remedy past societal discrimination, without the need for a finding that those benefited were actually victims of that discrimination.

While I applaud the judgment of the Court that a university may consider race in its admissions process, it is more than a little ironic that, after several hundred years of class-based discrimination against Negroes, the Court is unwilling to hold that a class-based remedy for that discrimination is permissible. In declining to so hold, today's judgment ignores the fact that for several hundred years Negroes have been discriminated against, not as individuals, but rather solely because of the color of their skins. It is unnecessary in 20th-century America to have individual Negroes demonstrate that they have been victims of racial discrimination; the racism of our society has been so pervasive that none, regardless of wealth or position, has managed to escape its impact. The experience of Negroes in America has been different in kind, not just in degree, from that of other ethnic groups. It is not merely the history of slavery alone but also that a whole people were marked as inferior by the law. And that mark has endured. The dream of America as the great melting pot has not been realized for the Negro; because of his skin color he never even made it into the pot.

These differences in the experience of the Negro make it difficult for me to accept that Negroes cannot be afforded greater protection under the Fourteenth Amendment where it is necessary to remedy the effects of past discrimination. In the *Civil Rights Cases*, the Court wrote that the Negro emerging from slavery must cease "to be the special favorite of the laws."

We cannot in light of the history of the last century yield to that view. Had the Court in that decision and others been willing to "do for human liberty and the fundamental rights of American citizenship, what it did for the protection of slavery and the rights of the masters of fugitive slaves," Justice Harlan insisted, we would not need now to permit the recognition of any "special wards."

Most importantly, had the Court been willing in 1896, in *Plessy v. Ferguson* to hold that the Equal Protection Clause forbids differences in treatment based on race, we would not be faced with this dilemma in 1978. We must remember, however, that the principle that the "Constitution is color-blind" appeared only in the opinion of the lone dissenter. The majority of the Court rejected the principle of color-blindness, and for the next 58 years, from *Plessy* to *Brown v. Board of Education*, ours was a Nation where, by law, an individual could be given "special" treatment based on the color of his skin.

It is because of a legacy of unequal treatment that we now must permit the institutions of this society to give consideration to race in making decisions about who will hold the positions of influence, affluence, and prestige in America. For far too long, the doors to those positions have been shut to Negroes. If we are ever to become a fully integrated society, one in which the color of a person's skin will not determine the opportunities available to him or her, we must be willing to take steps to open those doors. I do not believe that anyone can truly look into America's past and still find that a remedy for the effects of that past is impermissible.

I fear that we have come full circle. After the Civil War, our Government started several "affirmative action" programs. This Court in the *Civil Rights Cases* and *Plessy v. Ferguson* destroyed the movement toward complete equality. For almost a century no action was taken, and this nonaction was with the tacit approval of the courts. Then we had *Brown v. Board of Education* and the Civil Rights Acts of Congress, followed by numerous affirmative-action programs. Now, we have this Court again stepping in, this time to stop affirmative-action programs of the type used by the University of California.

**Justice Thomas:** I write separately to express my disagreement with the premise underlying the dissents: that there is a racial paternalism exception to the principle of equal protection. I believe that there is a "moral and constitutional equivalence," between laws designed to subjugate a race and those that distribute benefits on the basis of race in order to foster some current notion of equality. Government cannot make us equal; it can only recognize, respect, and protect us as equal before the law.

That these programs may have been motivated, in part, by good intentions cannot provide refuge from the principle that under our Constitution, the government may not make distinctions on the basis of race. As far as the Constitution is concerned, it is irrelevant whether a government's racial classifications are drawn by those who wish to oppress a race or by those who have a sincere desire to help those thought to be disadvantaged. There can be no doubt that the paternalism that appears to lie at the heart of this program is at war with the principle of inherent equality that underlies and infuses our Constitution. See *The Declaration of Independence* ("We hold these truths to be self-evident, that all men are created equal, that they are endowed by their Creator with certain unalienable Rights, that among these are Life, Liberty, and the pursuit of Happiness").

These programs not only raise grave constitutional questions, they also undermine the moral basis of the equal protection principle. Purchased at the price of immeasurable human suffering, the equal protection principle reflects our Nation's understanding that such classifications ultimately have a destructive impact on the individual and our society. Unquestionably, "invidious racial discrimination is an engine of oppression." It is also true that "remedial" racial preferences may reflect "a desire to foster equality in society." But there can be no doubt that racial paternalism and its unintended consequences can be as poisonous and pernicious as any other form of discrimination. So-called "benign" discrimination teaches many that because of chronic and apparently immutable handicaps, minorities cannot compete with them without their patronizing indulgence. Inevitably, such programs engender attitudes of superiority or, alternatively, provoke resentment among those who believe that they have been wronged by the government's use of race. These programs stamp minorities with a badge of inferiority and may cause them to develop dependencies or to adopt an attitude that they are "entitled" to preferences.

It should be obvious that every racial classification helps, in a narrow sense, some races and hurts others. As to the races benefitted, the classification could surely be called "benign." Accordingly, whether a law relying upon racial taxonomy is "benign" or "malign," either turns on "whose ox is gored," or on distinctions found only in the eye of the beholder.

In my mind, government-sponsored racial discrimination based on benign prejudice is just as noxious as discrimination inspired by malicious prejudice. In each instance, it is racial discrimination, plain and simple.

*With these considerations in mind, we can only conclude that classifications based upon sex, like classifications based upon race, alienage, or national origin, are inherently suspect, and must therefore be subjected to strict judicial scrutiny.*

— *William J. Brennan*

## Frontiero v. Richardson
### 93 S.Ct. 1764, 411 U.S. 677 (1973)

*Sharron A. Frontiero, a Lieutenant in the U.S. Air Force, challenged the denial of her application for dependant benefits for her husband Joseph. The previous term, in* Reed v. Reed *(1971), a unanimous Court had in fact struck down a state law giving men a preference to serve as administrators of decedents' estates. In this case, only a plurality of four Justices, one short of a majority, agreed with all of Justice Brennan's analysis to extend the principle farther. Justice Stewart concurred only in the judgment and Justice Rehnquist dissented altogether. Justice Powell, joined by Chief Justice Burger and Justice Blackmun, concurred in a separate opinion to explain why he did not agree with the plurality's analysis equating gender discrimination with race discrimination. Further, he insisted that the plurality should have deferred to the democratic political process and should not have imposed by judicial fiat what the then-pending Equal Rights Amendment would have guaranteed. The ERA eventually failed to garner the ratifications of the necessary two-thirds of the States. A few years later, in* Craig v. Boren *(1976), the Court revisited the issue of gender discrimination and the Justices seemed to compromise to treat gender classifications somewhere in between racial classifications, which are presumed to be unconstitutional, and socio-economic classifications, which are presumed to be constitutional. In a 1996 decision declaring that the Virginia Military Institute's exclusion of women denied them the equal protection of the laws, Justice Ruth Bader Ginsburg—only the second woman to serve as a High Court Justice—insisted that the Supreme Court would continue to demand an "exceedingly persuasive justification" for any state policy that "closes a door or denies opportunity to women (or to men)." Interestingly enough, back when this case was being decided she was one of the lawyers who filed a friend-of-the-court brief encouraging Justice Brennan's even stricter approach here.*

**Justice Brennan:** The question before us concerns the right of a female member of the uniformed services to claim her spouse as a "dependent" for the purposes of obtaining increased quarters allowances and medical and dental benefits on an equal footing with male members. Under these statutes, a serviceman may claim his wife as a "dependent" without regard to whether she is in fact dependent upon him for any part of her support. A servicewoman, on the other hand, may not claim her husband as a "dependent" under these programs unless he is in fact dependent upon her for over one-half of his support. Thus, the question for decision is whether this difference in treatment constitutes an unconstitutional discrimination against servicewomen in violation of the Due Process Clause of the Fifth Amendment.

In essence, the Frontieros asserted that the discriminatory impact of the statutes is twofold: first, as a procedural matter, a female member is required to demonstrate her spouse's dependency, while no such burden is imposed upon male members; and, second, as a substantive matter, a male member who does not provide more than one-half of his wife's support receives benefits, while a similarly situated female member is denied such benefits.

Although the legislative history of these statutes sheds virtually no light on the purposes underlying the differential treatment accorded male and female members, the District Court surmised that Congress might reasonably have concluded that, since the husband in our society is generally the "breadwinner" in the family—and the wife typically the "dependent" partner— "it would be more economical to require married female members claiming husbands to prove actual dependency than to extend the presumption of dependency to such members." Indeed, given the fact that approximately 99% of all members of the uniformed services are male, the District Court speculated that such differential treatment might conceivably lead to a "considerable saving of administrative expense and manpower."

At the outset, the Frontieros contend that classifications based upon sex, like classifications based upon race, alienage, and national origin, are inherently suspect and must therefore be subjected to close judicial scrutiny. We agree and, indeed, find at least implicit support for such an approach in our unanimous decision only last Term.

In that case, the Court considered the constitutionality of an Idaho statute providing that, when two individuals are otherwise equally entitled to appointment as administrator of an estate, the male applicant must be preferred to the female. The Court noted that the Idaho statute "provides that different treatment be accorded to the applicants on the basis of their sex; it thus establishes a classification subject to scrutiny under the Equal Protection Clause." Under "traditional" equal protection analysis, a legislative classification must be sustained unless it is "patently arbitrary" and bears no rational relationship to a legitimate governmental interest.

In an effort to meet this standard, it was contended that the statutory scheme was a reasonable measure designed to reduce the workload on probate courts by eliminating one class of contests. Moreover, it was argued that the mandatory preference for male applicants was in itself reasonable since "men are as a rule more conversant with business affairs than women." Indeed, it was maintained that "it is a matter of common knowledge, that women still are not engaged in politics, the professions, business or industry to the extent that men are." And the Idaho Supreme Court, in upholding the constitutionality of this statute, suggested that the Idaho Legislature might reasonably have "concluded that in general men are better qualified to act as an administrator than are women."

Despite these contentions, however, the Court held the statutory preference for male applicants unconstitutional. In reaching this result, the Court implicitly rejected these apparently rational explanations of the statutory scheme, and concluded that, by ignoring the individual qualifications of particular applicants, the challenged statute provide "dissimilar treatment for men and women who are similarly situated." The Court therefore held that, even though the State's interest in achieving administrative efficiency "is not without some legitimacy," "to give a mandatory preference to members of either sex over members of the other, merely to accomplish the elimination of hearings on the merits, is to make the very kind of arbitrary legislative choice forbidden by the Constitution." This departure from "traditional" rational-basis analysis with respect to sex-based classifications is clearly justified.

There can be no doubt that our Nation has had a long and unfortunate history of sex discrimination. Indeed, the position of women in this country at its inception is reflected in the view expressed by Thomas Jefferson that women should be neither seen nor heard in society's decisionmaking councils. Traditionally, such discrimination was rationalized by an attitude of "romantic paternalism" which, in practical effect, put women, not on a pedestal, but in a cage. Indeed, this paternalistic attitude became so firmly rooted in our national consciousness that, 100 years ago, a distinguished Member of this Court was able to proclaim: "Man is, or should be, women's protector and defender. The natural and proper timidity and delicacy which belongs to the female sex evidently unfits it for many of the occupations of civil life. The constitution of the family organization, which is founded in the divine ordinance, as well as in the nature of things, indicates the domestic sphere as that which properly belongs to the domain and functions of womanhood. The harmony, not to say identity, of interests and views which belong, or should belong, to the family institution is repugnant to the idea of a woman adopting a distinct and independent career from that of her husband. The paramount destiny and mission of woman are to fulfil the noble and benign offices of wife and mother. This is the law of the Creator."

As a result of notions such as these, our statute books gradually became laden with gross, stereotyped distinctions between the sexes and, indeed, throughout much of the 19th century the position of women in our society was, in many respects, comparable to that of blacks under the pre-Civil War slave codes. Neither slaves nor women could hold office, serve on juries, or bring suit in their own names, and married women traditionally were denied the legal capacity to hold or convey property or to serve as legal guardians of their own children. And although blacks were guaranteed the right to vote in 1870, women were denied even that right—which is itself "preservative of other basic civil and political rights"—until adoption of the Nineteenth Amendment half a century later.

It is true, of course, that the position of women in America has improved markedly in recent decades. Nevertheless, it can hardly be doubted that, in part because of the high visibility of the sex characteristic, women still face pervasive, although at times more subtle, discrimination in our educational institutions, in the job market and, perhaps most conspicuously, in the political arena. It is true, of course, that when viewed in the abstract, women do not constitute a small and powerless minority. Nevertheless, in part because of past discrimination, women are vastly underrepresented in this Nation's decisionmaking councils. There has never been a female President, nor a female member of this Court. Not a single woman presently sits in the United States Senate, and only 14 women hold seats in the House of Representatives. And, as the Frontieros point out, this underrepresentation is present throughout all levels of our State and Federal Government.

Moreover, since sex, like race and national origin, is an immutable characteristic determined solely by the accident of birth, the imposition of special disabilities upon the members of a particular sex because of their sex would seem to violate "the basic concept of our system that legal burdens should bear some relationship to individual responsibility. And what differentiates sex from such non-suspect statuses as intelligence or physical disability, and aligns it with the recognized suspect criteria, is that the sex characteristic frequently bears no relation to ability to perform or contribute to society. As a result, statutory distinctions between the sexes often have the effect of invidiously relegating the entire class of females to inferior legal status without regard to the actual capabilities of its individual members.

We might also note that, over the past decade, Congress has itself manifested an increasing sensitivity to sex-based classifications. In the Civil Rights Act of 1964, for example, Congress expressly declared that no employer, labor union, or other organization subject to the provisions of the Act shall discriminate against any individual on the basis of "race, color, religion, sex, or national origin." Similarly, the Equal Pay Act of 1963 provides that no employer covered by the Act "shall discriminate between employees on the basis of sex." And Section 1 of the Equal Rights Amendment, passed by Congress on March 22, 1972, and submitted to the legislatures of the States for ratification, declares that "equality of rights under the law shall not be denied or abridged by the United States or by any State on account of sex." In conformity with these principles, Congress in recent years has amended various statutory schemes similar to those presently under consideration so as to eliminate the differential treatment of men and women. Thus, Congress itself has concluded that classifications based upon sex are inherently invidious, and this conclusion of a coequal branch of Government is not without significance to the question presently under consideration.

With these considerations in mind, we can only conclude that classifications based upon sex, like classifications based upon race, alienage, or national origin, are inherently suspect, and must therefore be subjected to strict judicial scrutiny. Applying the analysis mandated by that stricter standard of review, it is clear that the statutory scheme now before us is constitutionally invalid.

The sole basis of the classification established in the challenged statutes is the sex of the individuals involved. A female member of the uniformed services seeking to obtain housing and medical benefits for her spouse must prove his dependency in fact, whereas no such burden is imposed upon male members. In addition, the statutes operate so as to deny benefits to a female member, such as Lieutenant Frontiero, who provides less than one-half of her spouse's support, while at the same time granting such benefits to a male member who likewise provides less than one-half of his spouse's support. Thus, to this extent at least, it may fairly be said that these statutes command "dissimilar treatment for men and women who are similarly situated."

Moreover, the Government concedes that the differential treatment accorded men and women under these statutes serves no purpose other than mere "administrative convenience." In essence, the Government maintains that, as an empirical matter, wives in our society frequently are dependent upon their husbands, while husbands rarely are dependent upon their wives. Thus, the Government argues that Congress might reasonably have concluded that it would be both cheaper and easier simply conclusively to presume that wives of male members are financially dependent upon their husbands, while burdening female members with the task of establishing dependency in fact.

It should be noted that these statutes are not in any sense designed to rectify the effects of past discrimination against women. On the contrary, these statutes seize upon a group—women—who have historically suffered discrimination in employment, and rely on the effects of this past discrimination as a justification for heaping on additional economic disadvantages.

The Government offers no concrete evidence, however, tending to support its view that such differential treatment in fact saves the Government any money. In order to satisfy the demands of strict judicial scrutiny, the Government must demonstrate, for example, that it is actually cheaper to grant increased benefits with respect to all male members, than it is to determine which male members are in fact entitled to such benefits and to grant increased benefits only to those members whose wives actually meet the dependency requirement. Here, however, there is substantial evidence that, if put to the test, many of the wives of male members would fail to qualify for benefits. And in light of the fact that the dependency determination with respect to the husbands of female members is presently made solely on the basis of affidavits rather than through the more costly hearing process, the Government's explanation of the statutory scheme is, to say the least, questionable.

In any case, our prior decisions make clear that, although efficacious administration of governmental programs is not without some importance, "the Constitution recognizes higher values than speed and efficiency." And when we enter the realm of "strict judicial scrutiny," there can be no doubt that "administrative convenience" is not a shibboleth, the mere recitation of which dictates constitutionality. On the contrary, any statutory scheme which draws a sharp line between the sexes, *solely* for the purpose of achieving administrative convenience, necessarily commands "dissimilar treatment for men and women who are similarly situated," and therefore involves the "very kind of arbitrary legislative choice forbidden by the Constitution." We therefore conclude that, by according differential treatment to male and female members of the uniformed services for the sole purpose of achieving administrative convenience, the challenged statutes violate the Due Process Clause of the Fifth Amendment insofar as they require a female member to prove the dependency of her husband.

*If the State is to deny a discrete group of inno-*
*cent children the free public education that it*
*offers to other children residing within its bor-*
*ders, that denial must be justified by a showing*
*that it furthers some substantial state interest. No*
*such showing was made here.*

*— William J. Brennan*

## Plyler v. Doe
### 102 S.Ct. 2382, 457 U.S. 202 (1982)

*"Were it our business to set the Nation's social policy, I*
*would agree without hesitation that it is senseless for an*
*enlightened society to deprive any children—including il-*
*legal aliens—of an elementary education . . . it would be*
*folly—and wrong," Chief Justice Burger's strident dissent*
*in this case begins, "However, the Constitution does not*
*constitute us as 'Platonic Guardians' nor does it vest in*
*this Court the authority to strike down laws because they*
*do not meet our standards of desirable social policy, 'wis-*
*dom,' or 'common sense.'" Demonstrating his prowess at*
*reaching the "right result," Justice Brennan poured new*
*meaning into the 14th amendment phrase "equal protec-*
*tion of the laws." He massed the Court behind an opinion*
*that is a rhetorical masterpiece, though not a stellar ex-*
*ample of constitutional logic. The Texas state policy to*
*refuse free public education to the children of illegal ali-*
*ens was irrational and hence invalid. It was a crazy idea,*
*constitutionally speaking, according to a narrow majority*
*of five Justices. On its face, his opinion is limited to these*
*somewhat peculiar facts, but his reasoning surely will*
*help shape the public debate over immigration, legal and*
*illegal, for the years to come.*

**Justice Brennan:** The question presented by these cases is
whether, consistent with the Equal Protection Clause of the
Fourteenth Amendment, Texas may deny to undocumented
school-age children the free public education that it provides to
children who are citizens of the United States or legally admitted aliens.

Highland Park Public Library
Information & Imagination
--- CHECKOUT RECEIPT ---
--       847-432-0216

User ID: 1000101821576

Date charged: 12/27/2011,17:
Title: "The most wonderful
work..." : our constitution i
Item ID: 00010471592
Date due: 1/24/2012,23:59

Library Hours:
Monday - Thursday 9a.m.-9p.m.
Friday 9a.m.-6p.m.
Saturday 9a.m.-5p.m.
Sunday 1-5p.m.

--- www.hplibrary.org ---
-

Since the late 19th century, the United States has restricted immigration into this country. Unsanctioned entry into the United States is a crime, and those who have entered unlawfully are subject to deportation. But despite the existence of these legal restrictions, a substantial number of persons have succeeded in unlawfully entering the United States, and now live within various States, including the State of Texas.

In May 1975, the Texas Legislature revised its education laws to withhold from local school districts any state funds for the education of children who were not "legally admitted" into the United States. The 1975 revision also authorized local school districts to deny enrollment in their public schools to children not "legally admitted" to the country.

The Equal Protection Clause must be understood to require that "all persons similarly circumstanced shall be treated alike." But so too, "the Constitution does not require things which are different in fact or opinion to be treated in law as though they were the same." The initial discretion to determine what is "different" and what is "the same" resides in the legislatures of the States. A legislature must have substantial latitude to establish classifications that roughly approximate the nature of the problem perceived, that accommodate competing concerns both public and private, and that account for limitations on the practical ability of the State to remedy every ill. In applying the Equal Protection Clause to most forms of state action, we thus seek only the assurance that the classification at issue bears some fair relationship to a legitimate public purpose. But we judges would not be faithful to our obligations under the Fourteenth Amendment if we applied so deferential a standard to every classification. The Equal Protection Clause was intended as a restriction on state legislative action inconsistent with elemental constitutional premises. We have sought the assurance that the classification reflects a reasoned judgment consistent with the ideal of equal protection by inquiring whether it may fairly be viewed as furthering a substantial interest of the State.

Sheer incapability or lax enforcement of the laws barring entry into this country, coupled with the failure to establish an effective bar to the employment of undocumented aliens, has resulted in the creation of a substantial "shadow population" of illegal migrants—numbering in the millions—within our borders. This situation raises the specter of a permanent caste of undocumented resident aliens, encouraged by some to remain here as a source of cheap labor, but nevertheless denied the benefits that our society makes available to citizens and lawful residents. The existence of such an underclass presents most difficult problems for a Nation that prides itself on adherence to principles of equality under law.

The children who are plaintiffs in these cases are special members of this underclass. Persuasive arguments support the view that a State may withhold its beneficence from those whose very presence within the United States is the product of their own unlawful conduct. These arguments do not apply with the same force to classifications imposing disabilities on the minor children of such illegal entrants. At the least, those who elect to enter our territory by stealth and in violation of our law should be prepared to bear the consequences, including, but not limited to, deportation. But the children of those illegal entrants are not comparably situated. Their "parents have the ability to conform their conduct to societal norms," and presumably the ability to remove themselves from the State's jurisdiction; but the children who are plaintiffs in these cases "can affect neither their parents' conduct nor their own status." Even if the State found it expedient to control the conduct of adults by acting against their children, legislation directing the onus of a parent's misconduct against his children does not comport with fundamental conceptions of justice.

Of course, undocumented status is not irrelevant to any proper legislative goal. Nor is undocumented status an absolutely immutable characteristic since it is the product of conscious, indeed unlawful, action. But the Texas statute is directed against children, and imposes its discriminatory burden on the basis of a legal characteristic over which children can have little control. It is thus difficult to conceive of a rational justification for penalizing these children for their presence within the United States. Yet that appears to be precisely the effect of the statute.

Furthermore, it is well-settled that public education is not a "right" granted to individuals by the U.S. Constitution. But neither is it merely some governmental "benefit" indistinguishable from other forms of social welfare legislation. Both the importance of education in maintaining our basic institutions, and the lasting impact of its deprivation on the life of the child, mark the distinction. The "American people have always regarded education and the acquisition of knowledge as matters of supreme importance." We have recognized "the public schools as a most vital civic institution for the preservation of a democratic system of government," and as the primary vehicle for transmitting "the values on which our society rests." "As pointed out early in our history, some degree of education is necessary to prepare citizens to participate effectively and intelligently in our open political system if we are to preserve freedom and independence." And these historic "perceptions of the public schools as inculcating fundamental values necessary to the maintenance of a democratic political system have been confirmed by the observations of social scientists." In addition, education provides the basic tools by which individuals might lead economically productive lives to the benefit of us all. In sum, education has a fundamental role in maintaining the fabric of our society. We cannot ignore the significant social costs borne by our Nation when select groups are denied the means to absorb the values and skills upon which our social order rests.

In addition to the pivotal role of education in sustaining our political and cultural heritage, denial of education to some isolated group of children poses an affront to one of the goals of the Equal Protection Clause: the abolition of governmental barriers presenting unreasonable obstacles to advancement on the basis of individual merit. Paradoxically, by depriving the children of any disfavored group of an education, we foreclose the means by which that group might raise the level of esteem in which it is held by the majority. But more directly, "education prepares individuals to be self-reliant and self-sufficient participants in society." Illiteracy is an enduring disability. The inability to read and write will handicap the individual deprived of a basic education each and every day of his life. The inestimable toll of that deprivation on the social economic, intellectual, and psychological well-being of the individual, and the obstacle it poses to individual achievement, make it most difficult to reconcile the cost or the principle of a status-based denial of basic education with the framework of equality embodied in the Equal Protection Clause.

Well-settled principles of Constitutional law allow us to determine the proper level of deference to be afforded the Texas statute. Undocumented aliens cannot be treated as a suspect class because their presence in this country in violation of federal law is not a "constitutional irrelevancy." Nor is education a fundamental right; a State need not justify by compelling necessity every variation in the manner in which education is provided to its population. But more is involved in these cases than the abstract question whether the state law discriminates against a suspect class, or whether education is a fundamental right. The Texas statute imposes a lifetime hardship on a discrete class of children not accountable for their disabling status. The stigma of illiteracy will mark them for the rest of their lives. By denying these children a basic education, we deny them the ability to live within the structure of our civic institutions, and foreclose any realistic possibility that they will contribute in even the smallest way to the progress of our Nation. In determining the rationality of this law, we may appropriately take into account its costs to the Nation and to the innocent children who are its victims. In light of these countervailing costs, the discrimination contained in this statute can hardly be considered rational unless it furthers some substantial goal of the State.

It is the State's principal argument, and apparently the view of the dissenting Justices, that the undocumented status of these children *vel non* establishes a sufficient rational basis for denying them benefits that a State might choose to afford other residents. The State notes that while other aliens are admitted "on an equality of legal privileges with all citizens under nondiscriminatory laws," the asserted right of these children to an education can claim no implicit congressional *imprimatur*. Indeed, in the State's view, Congress' apparent disapproval of the presence of these children within the United States, and the evasion of the federal regulatory program that is the mark of undocumented status, provides authority for its decision to impose upon them special disabilities. Faced with an equal protection challenge respecting the treatment of aliens, we agree that the courts must be attentive to congressional policy; the exercise of congressional power might well affect the State's prerogatives to afford differential treatment to a particular class of aliens. But we are unable to find in the congressional immigration scheme any statement of policy that might weigh significantly in arriving at an equal protection balance concerning the State's authority to deprive these children of an education.

The Constitution grants Congress the power to "establish an uniform Rule of Naturalization." Art. I, § 8, cl. 4. Drawing upon this power, upon its plenary authority with respect to foreign relations and international commerce, and upon the inherent power of a sovereign to close its borders, Congress has developed a complex scheme governing admission to our Nation and status within our borders. The obvious need for delicate policy judgments has counseled the Judicial Branch to avoid intrusion into this field. But this traditional caution does not persuade us that unusual deference must be shown the classification embodied in the Texas statute. The States enjoy no power with respect to the classification of aliens. This power is "committed to the political branches of the Federal Government." Although it is "a routine and normally legitimate part" of the business of the Federal Government to classify on the basis of alien status, and to "take into account the character of the relationship between the alien and this country," only rarely are such matters relevant to legislation by a State.

To be sure, like all persons who have entered the United States unlawfully, these children are subject to deportation. But there is no assurance that a child subject to deportation will ever be deported. An illegal entrant might be granted federal permission to continue to reside in this country, or even to become a citizen. In light of the discretionary federal power to grant relief from deportation, a State cannot realistically determine that any particular undocumented child will in fact be deported until after deportation proceedings have been completed. It would of course be most difficult for the State to justify a denial of education to a child enjoying an inchoate federal permission to remain.

We are reluctant to impute to Congress the intention to withhold from these children, for so long as they are present in this country through no fault of their own, access to a basic education. In other contexts, undocumented status, coupled with some articulable federal policy, might enhance state authority with respect to the treatment of undocumented aliens. But in the area of special constitutional sensitivity presented by these cases, and in the absence of any contrary indication fairly discernible in the present legislative record, we perceive no national policy that supports the State in denying these children an elementary education. The State may borrow the federal classification. But to justify its use as a criterion for its own discriminatory policy, the State must demonstrate that the classification is reasonably adapted to "the purposes for which the state desires to use it." We therefore turn to the state objectives that are said to support the Texas law.

The Texas school officials argue that the classification at issue furthers an interest in the "preservation of the state's limited resources for the education of its lawful residents." Of course, a concern for the preservation of resources standing alone can hardly justify the classification used in allocating those resources. The State must do more than justify its classification with a concise expression of an intention to discriminate.

Apart from the asserted state prerogative to act against undocumented children solely on the basis of their undocumented status—an asserted prerogative that carries only minimal force in the circumstances of these cases—we discern three colorable state interests that might support the Texas statute.

First, the school officials appear to suggest that the State may seek to protect itself from an influx of illegal immigrants. While a State might have an interest in mitigating the potentially harsh economic effects of sudden shifts in population, this statute hardly offers an effective method of dealing with an urgent demographic or economic problem. There is no evidence in the record suggesting that illegal entrants impose any significant burden on the State's economy. To the contrary, the available evidence suggests that illegal aliens underutilize public services, while contributing their labor to the local economy and tax money to the state fisc. The dominant incentive for illegal entry into the State of Texas is the availability of employment; few if any illegal immigrants come to this country, or presumably to the State of Texas, in order to avail themselves of a free education. Thus, even making the doubtful assumption that the net impact of illegal aliens on the economy of the State is negative, we think the District Court was clearly correct, "charging tuition to undocumented children constitutes a ludicrously ineffectual attempt to stem the tide of illegal immigration," at least when compared with the alternative of prohibiting the employment of illegal aliens.

Second, while it is apparent that a State may "not reduce expenditures for education by barring some arbitrarily chosen class of children from its schools," the school officials suggest that undocumented children are appropriately singled out for exclusion because of the special burdens they impose on the State's ability to provide high-quality public education. But the record in no way supports the claim that exclusion of undocumented children is likely to improve the overall quality of education in the State. As the District Court noted, the State failed to offer any "credible supporting evidence that a proportionately small diminution of the funds spent on each child which might result from devoting some state funds to the education of the excluded group will have a grave impact on the quality of education." And, after reviewing the State's school financing mechanism, the District Court concluded that barring undocumented children from local schools would not necessarily improve the quality of education provided in those schools. Of course, even if improvement in the quality of education were a likely result of barring some number of children from the schools of the State, the State must support its selection of this group as the appropriate target for exclusion. In terms of educational cost and need, however, undocumented children are "basically indistinguishable" from legally resident alien children.

Finally, the school officials suggest that undocumented children are appropriately singled out because their unlawful presence within the United States renders them less likely than other children to remain within the boundaries of the State, and to put their education to productive social or political use within the State. Even assuming that such an interest is legitimate, it is an interest that is most difficult to quantify. The State has no assurance that any child, citizen or not, will employ the education provided by the State within the confines of the State's borders. In any event, the record is clear that many of the undocumented children disabled by this classification will remain in this country indefinitely, and that some will become lawful residents or citizens of the United States. It is difficult to understand precisely what the State hopes to achieve by promoting the creation and perpetuation of a subclass of illiterates within our boundaries, surely adding to the problems and costs of unemployment, welfare, and crime. It is thus clear that whatever savings might be achieved by denying these children an education, they are wholly insubstantial in light of the costs involved to these children, the State, and the Nation.

If the State is to deny a discrete group of innocent children the free public education that it offers to other children residing within its borders, that denial must be justified by a showing that it furthers some substantial state interest. No such showing was made here.

*We must conclude that Amendment 2 classifies homosexuals not to further a proper legislative end but to make them unequal to everyone else. This Colorado cannot do. A State cannot so deem a class of persons a stranger to its laws.*

— *Anthony M. Kennedy*

## Romer v. Evans,
### 116 S.Ct. 1620 (1996)

*In a controversial decision,* Bowers v. Hardwick *(1986), the Justices voted five to four to uphold a Georgia statute that made sodomy a crime punishable by imprisonment for up to twenty years. Justice White concluded for a majority that the claim that the 14th amendment protected homosexual conduct, even for consenting adults in private, was "at best, facetious." Justice Blackmun dissented and insisted that what was at stake was the most comprehensive and important of rights, "the right to be left alone" by the government. Justice Powell filed an enigmatic concurring opinion, but would later recant his deciding vote, only after he retired from the Court. Ten years later, Justices White, Blackmun, Powell, and three others who sat in the 1986 case, were gone from the bench and had been replaced. In this 1996 case, the Court returned to the debate over the meaning of equality as it relates to sexual orientation, voting six to three to invalidate an amendment to the Colorado state constitution that at once abolished and prohibited any and all state and local laws that protected gays, lesbians, and bisexuals from discrimination. Justice Scalia dissents and accuses the Court of imposing its political will against the democratic will of the voters. This area of constitutional law is in a state of flux and what the Justices say in these opinions will not be the last word, any more than what was said ten years before.*

**Justice Kennedy:** One century ago, the first Justice Harlan admonished this Court that the Constitution "neither knows nor tolerates classes among citizens." Unheeded then, those words now are understood to state a commitment to the law's neutrality where the rights of persons are at stake. The Equal Protection Clause enforces this principle and today requires us to hold invalid a provision of Colorado's Constitution.

The enactment challenged in this case is an amendment to the Constitution of the State of Colorado, adopted in a 1992 statewide referendum. The parties and the state courts refer to it as "Amendment 2," its designation when submitted to the voters. The impetus for the amendment and the contentious campaign that preceded its adoption came in large part from ordinances that had been passed in various Colorado municipalities. For example, the cities of Aspen and Boulder and the City and County of Denver each had enacted ordinances which banned discrimination in many transactions and activities, including housing, employment, education, public accommodations, and health and welfare services. What gave rise to the statewide controversy was the protection the ordinances afforded to persons discriminated against by reason of their sexual orientation. Amendment 2 repeals these ordinances to the extent they prohibit discrimination on the basis of "homosexual, lesbian or bisexual orientation, conduct, practices or relationships."

Yet Amendment 2, in explicit terms, does more than repeal or rescind these provisions. It prohibits all legislative, executive or judicial action at any level of state or local government designed to protect the named class, a class we shall refer to as homosexual persons or gays and lesbians. The amendment reads: "No Protected Status Based on Homosexual, Lesbian, or Bisexual Orientation. Neither the State of Colorado, through any of its branches or departments, nor any of its agencies, political subdivisions, municipalities or school districts, shall enact, adopt or enforce any statute, regulation, ordinance or policy whereby homosexual, lesbian or bisexual orientation, conduct, practices or relationships shall constitute or otherwise be the basis of or entitle any person or class of persons to have or claim any minority status, quota preferences, protected status or claim of discrimination."

The State's principal argument in defense of Amendment 2 is that it puts gays and lesbians in the same position as all other persons. So, the State says, the measure does no more than deny homosexuals special rights. This reading of the amendment's language is implausible. Sweeping and comprehensive is the change in legal status effected by this law. Homosexuals, by state decree, are put in a solitary class with respect to transactions and relations in both the private and governmental spheres.

The amendment withdraws from homosexuals, but no others, specific legal protection from the injuries caused by discrimination, and it forbids reinstatement of these laws and policies. The change that Amendment 2 works in the legal status of gays and lesbians in the private sphere is far-reaching, both on its own terms and when considered in light of the structure and operation of modern anti-discrimination laws, including contemporary statutes and ordinances prohibiting discrimination by providers of public accommodations. Amendment 2 bars homosexuals from securing protection against the injuries that these public-accommodations laws address. That in itself is a severe consequence, but there is more. Amendment 2, in addition, nullifies specific legal protections for this targeted class in all transactions in housing, sale of real estate, insurance, health and welfare services, private education, and employment.

Not confined to the private sphere, Amendment 2 also operates to repeal and forbid all laws or policies providing specific protection for gays or lesbians from discrimination by every level of Colorado government. The repeal of these measures and the prohibition against their future reenactment demonstrates that Amendment 2 has the same force and effect in Colorado's governmental sector as it does elsewhere and that it applies to policies as well as ordinary legislation.

We cannot accept the view that Amendment 2's prohibition on specific legal protections does no more than deprive homosexuals of special rights. To the contrary, the amendment imposes a special disability upon those persons alone. Homosexuals are forbidden the safeguards that others enjoy or may seek without constraint. They can obtain specific protection against discrimination only by enlisting the citizenry of Colorado to amend the state constitution or perhaps, on the State's view, by trying to pass helpful laws of general applicability. This is so no matter how local or discrete the harm, no matter how public and widespread the injury. We find nothing special in the protections Amendment 2 withholds. These are protections taken for granted by most people either because they already have them or do not need them; these are protections against exclusion from an almost limitless number of transactions and endeavors that constitute ordinary civic life in a free society.

The Fourteenth Amendment's promise that no person shall be denied the equal protection of the laws must co-exist with the practical necessity that most legislation classifies for one purpose or another, with resulting disadvantage to various groups or persons. We have attempted to reconcile the principle with the reality by stating that, if a law neither burdens a fundamental right nor targets a suspect class, we will uphold the legislative classification so long as it bears a rational relation to some legitimate end.

Amendment 2 fails, indeed defies, even this conventional inquiry. First, the amendment has the peculiar property of imposing a broad and undifferentiated disability on a single named group, an exceptional and, as we shall explain, invalid form of legislation. Second, its sheer breadth is so discontinuous with the reasons offered for it that the amendment seems inexplicable by anything but animus toward the class that it affects; it lacks a rational relationship to legitimate state interests.

Amendment 2 confounds this normal process of judicial review. It is at once too narrow and too broad. It identifies persons by a single trait and then denies them protection across the board. The resulting disqualification of a class of persons from the right to seek specific protection from the law is unprecedented in our jurisprudence. The absence of precedent for Amendment 2 is itself instructive; "discriminations of an unusual character especially suggest careful consideration to determine whether they are obnoxious to the constitutional provision."

It is not within our constitutional tradition to enact laws of this sort. Central both to the idea of the rule of law and to our own Constitution's guarantee of equal protection is the principle that government and each of its parts remain open on impartial terms to all who seek its assistance. "Equal protection of the laws is not achieved through indiscriminate imposition of inequalities." Respect for this principle explains why laws singling out a certain class of citizens for disfavored legal status or general hardships are rare. A law declaring that in general it shall be more difficult for one group of citizens than for all others to seek aid from the government is itself a denial of equal protection of the laws in the most literal sense. "The guaranty of equal protection of the laws is a pledge of the protection of equal laws."

Laws of the kind now before us raise the inevitable inference that the disadvantage imposed is born of animosity toward the class of persons affected. "If the constitutional conception of 'equal protection of the laws' means anything, it must at the very least mean that a bare desire to harm a politically unpopular group cannot constitute a legitimate governmental interest." Even laws enacted for broad and ambitious purposes often can be explained by reference to legitimate public policies which justify the incidental disadvantages they impose on certain persons. Amendment 2, however, in making a general announcement that gays and lesbians shall not have any particular protections from the law, inflicts on them immediate, continuing, and real injuries that outrun and belie any legitimate justifications that may be claimed for it.

The primary rationale the State offers for Amendment 2 is respect for other citizens' freedom of association, and in particular the liberties of landlords or employers who have personal or religious objections to homosexuality. Colorado also cites its interest in conserving resources to fight discrimination against other groups. The breadth of the Amendment is so far removed from these particular justifications that we find it impossible to credit them. We cannot say that Amendment 2 is directed to any identifiable legitimate purpose or discrete objective. It is a status-based enactment divorced from any factual context from which we could discern a relationship to legitimate state interests; it is a classification of persons undertaken for its own sake, something the Equal Protection Clause does not permit. "Class legislation is obnoxious to the prohibitions of the Fourteenth Amendment."

We must conclude that Amendment 2 classifies homosexuals not to further a proper legislative end but to make them unequal to everyone else. This Colorado cannot do. A State cannot so deem a class of persons a stranger to its laws. Amendment 2 violates the Equal Protection Clause.

**Justice Scalia:** The Court has mistaken a Kulturkampf for a fit of spite. The constitutional amendment before us here is not the manifestation of a "bare desire to harm" homosexuals, but is rather a modest attempt by seemingly tolerant Coloradans to preserve traditional sexual mores against the efforts of a politically powerful minority to revise those mores through use of the laws. That objective, and the means chosen to achieve it, are not only unimpeachable under any constitutional doctrine hitherto pronounced (hence the opinion's heavy reliance upon principles of righteousness rather than judicial holdings); they have been specifically approved by the Congress of the United States and by this Court.

In holding that homosexuality cannot be singled out for disfavorable treatment, the Court contradicts a decision, unchallenged here, pronounced only 10 years ago, *Bowers v. Hardwick (1986)*, and places the prestige of this institution behind the proposition that opposition to homosexuality is as reprehensible as racial or religious bias. Whether it is or not is precisely the cultural debate that gave rise to the Colorado constitutional amendment (and to the preferential laws against which the amendment was directed). Since the Constitution of the United States says nothing about this subject, it is left to be resolved by normal democratic means, including the democratic adoption of provisions in state constitutions. This Court has no business imposing upon all Americans the resolution favored by the elite class from which the Members of this institution are selected, pronouncing that "animosity" toward homosexuality is evil. I vigorously dissent.

Despite all of its hand-wringing, the only denial of equal treatment the majority contends homosexuals have suffered is this: They may not obtain preferential treatment without amending the state constitution. That is to say, the principle underlying the majority opinion is that one who is accorded equal treatment under the laws, but cannot as readily as others obtain preferential treatment under the laws, has been denied equal protection of the laws. If merely stating this alleged "equal protection" violation does not suffice to refute it, our constitutional jurisprudence has achieved terminal silliness.

The central thesis of the majority's reasoning is that any group is denied equal protection when, to obtain advantage (or, presumably, to avoid disadvantage), it must have recourse to a more general and hence more difficult level of political decisionmaking than others. The world has never heard of such a principle, which is why the majority's opinion is so long on emotive utterance and so short on relevant legal citation. And it seems to me most unlikely that any multilevel democracy can function under such a principle. For whenever a disadvantage is imposed, or conferral of a benefit is prohibited, at one of the higher levels of democratic decisionmaking (i.e., by the state legislature rather than local government, or by the people at large in the state constitution rather than the legislature), the affected group has (under this theory) been denied equal protection. It is ridiculous to consider this a denial of equal protection, which is why the majority's theory is unheard-of. The majority's entire novel theory rests upon the proposition that there is something special—something that cannot be justified by normal "rational basis" analysis—in making a disadvantaged group (or a non-preferred group) resort to a higher decisionmaking level. That proposition finds no support in law or logic.

I turn next to whether there was a legitimate rational basis for the substance of the constitutional amendment—for the prohibition of special protection for homosexuals. It is unsurprising that the Court avoids discussion of this question, since the answer is so obviously yes. The case most relevant to the issue before us today is not even mentioned in the majority's opinion: In *Bowers v. Hardwick (1986)*, we held that the Constitution does not prohibit what virtually all States had done from the founding of the Republic until very recent years—making homosexual conduct a crime. That holding is unassailable, except by those who think that the Constitution changes to suit current fashions. But in any event it is a given in the present case: Plaintiffs' briefs challenging Amendment 2 did not urge overruling *Bowers*, and at oral argument Plaintiffs' counsel expressly disavowed any intent to seek such overruling. If it is constitutionally permissible for a State to make homosexual conduct criminal, surely it is constitutionally permissible for a State to enact other laws merely disfavoring homosexual conduct. And *a fortiori* it is constitutionally permissible for a State to adopt a provision not even disfavoring homosexual conduct, but merely prohibiting all levels of state government from bestowing special protections upon homosexual conduct. If it is rational to criminalize the conduct, surely it is rational to deny special favor and protection to those with a self-avowed tendency or desire to engage in the conduct. Indeed, where criminal sanctions are not involved, homosexual "orientation" is an acceptable stand-in for homosexual conduct. A State "does not violate the Equal Protection Clause merely because the classifications made by its laws are imperfect." Amendment 2 is not constitutionally invalid simply because it could have been drawn more precisely so as to withdraw special antidiscrimination protections only from those of homosexual "orientation" who actually engage in homosexual conduct.

The foregoing suffices to establish what the majority's failure to cite any case remotely in point would lead one to suspect: No principle set forth in the Constitution, nor even any imagined by this Court in the past 200 years, prohibits what Colorado has done here. But the case for Colorado is much stronger than that. What it has done is not only unprohibited, but eminently reasonable, with close, congressionally approved precedent in earlier constitutional practice.

First, as to its eminent reasonableness. The majority's opinion contains grim, disapproving hints that Coloradans have been guilty of "animus" or "animosity" toward homosexuality, as though that has been established as Unamerican. Of course it is our moral heritage that one should not hate any human being or class of human beings. But I had thought that one could consider certain conduct reprehensible—murder, for example, or polygamy, or cruelty to animals—and could exhibit even "animus" toward such conduct. Surely that is the only sort of "animus" at issue here: moral disapproval of homosexual conduct, the same sort of moral disapproval that produced the centuries-old criminal laws that we held constitutional in *Bowers*. The Colorado amendment does not, to speak entirely precisely, prohibit giving favored status to people who are homosexuals; they can be favored for many reasons, for example, because they are senior citizens or members of racial minorities. But it prohibits giving them favored status because of their homosexual conduct—that is, it prohibits favored status for homosexuality.

But though Coloradans are, as I say, entitled to be hostile toward homosexual conduct, the fact is that the degree of hostility reflected by Amendment 2 is the smallest conceivable. The Court's portrayal of Coloradans as a society fallen victim to pointless, hate-filled "gay-bashing" is so false as to be comical. Colorado not only is one of the 25 States that have repealed their antisodomy laws, but was among the first to do so. But the society that eliminates criminal punishment for homosexual acts does not necessarily abandon the view that homosexuality is morally wrong and socially harmful; often, abolition simply reflects the view that enforcement of such criminal laws involves unseemly intrusion into the intimate lives of citizens.

There is a problem, however, which arises when criminal sanction of homosexuality is eliminated but moral and social disapprobation of homosexuality is meant to be retained. The majority cannot be unaware of that problem; it is evident in many cities of the country, and occasionally bubbles to the surface of the news, in heated political disputes over such matters as the introduction into local schools of books teaching that homosexuality is an optional and fully acceptable "alternate life style." The problem (a problem, that is, for those who wish to retain social disapprobation of homosexuality) is that, because those who engage in homosexual conduct tend to reside in disproportionate numbers in certain communities, have high disposable income, and of course care about homosexual-rights issues much more ardently than the public at large, they possess political power much greater than their numbers, both locally and statewide. Quite understandably, they devote this political power to achieving not merely a grudging social toleration, but full social acceptance, of homosexuality.

By the time Coloradans were asked to vote on Amendment 2, their exposure to homosexuals' quest for social endorsement was not limited to newspaper accounts of happenings in places such as New York, Los Angeles, San Francisco, and Key West. Three Colorado cities—Aspen, Boulder, and Denver—had enacted ordinances that listed "sexual orientation" as an impermissible ground for discrimination, equating the moral disapproval of homosexual conduct with racial and religious bigotry. The phenomenon had even appeared statewide: the Governor of Colorado had signed an executive order pronouncing that "in the State of Colorado we recognize the diversity in our pluralistic society and strive to bring an end to discrimination in any form," and directing state agency-heads to "ensure non-discrimination" in hiring and promotion based on, among other things, "sexual orientation." I do not mean to be critical of these legislative successes; homosexuals are as entitled to use the legal system for reinforcement of their moral sentiments as are the rest of society. But they are subject to being countered by lawful, democratic countermeasures as well.

That is where Amendment 2 came in. It sought to counter both the geographic concentration and the disproportionate political power of homosexuals by (1) resolving the controversy at the statewide level, and (2) making the election a single-issue contest for both sides. It put directly, to all the citizens of the State, the question: Should homosexuality be given special protection? They answered no. The majority today asserts that this most democratic of procedures is unconstitutional. Lacking any cases to establish that facially absurd proposition, it simply asserts that it must be unconstitutional, because it has never happened before.

This is proved false every time a state law prohibiting or disfavoring certain conduct is passed, because such a law prevents the adversely affected group—whether drug addicts, or smokers, or gun owners, or motorcyclists—from changing the policy thus established in "each of the parts" of the State. What the majority says is even demonstrably false at the constitutional level. The Eighteenth Amendment to the Federal Constitution, for example, deprived those who drank alcohol not only of the power to alter the policy of prohibition locally or through state legislation, but even of the power to alter it through state constitutional amendment or federal legislation. The Establishment Clause of the First Amendment prevents theocrats from having their way by converting their fellow citizens at the local, state, or federal statutory level; as does the Republican Form of Government Clause prevent monarchists.

But there is a much closer analogy, one that involves precisely the effort by the majority of citizens to preserve its view of sexual morality statewide, against the efforts of a geographically concentrated and politically powerful minority to undermine it. The constitutions of the States of Arizona, Idaho, New Mexico, Oklahoma, and Utah to this day contain provisions stating that polygamy is "forever prohibited." Polygamists, and those who have a polygamous "orientation," have been "singled out" by these provisions for much more severe treatment than merely denial of favored status; and that treatment can only be changed by achieving amendment of the state constitutions. The majority's disposition today suggests that these provisions are unconstitutional, and that polygamy must be permitted in these States on a state-legislated, or perhaps even local-option, basis—unless, of course, polygamists for some reason have fewer constitutional rights than homosexuals.

The United States Congress, by the way, required the inclusion of these antipolygamy provisions in the constitutions of Arizona, New Mexico, Oklahoma, and Utah, as a condition of their admission to statehood and Idaho adopted the constitutional provision on its own. Thus, this "singling out" of the sexual practices of a single group for statewide, democratic vote—so utterly alien to our constitutional system, the majority would have us believe—has not only happened before, but has received the explicit approval of the United States Congress.

Has the majority concluded that the perceived social harm of polygamy is a "legitimate concern of government," and the perceived social harm of homosexuality is not? I strongly suspect that the answer to the last question is yes, which leads me to the last point I wish to make: The majority today employs a constitutional theory heretofore unknown to frustrate Colorado's reasonable effort to preserve traditional American moral values. The majority's stern disapproval of "animosity" towards homosexuality might be compared with what an earlier Court said in 1885, rejecting a constitutional challenge to a United States statute that denied the franchise in federal territories to those who engaged in polygamous cohabitation: "Certainly no legislation can be supposed more wholesome and necessary in the founding of a free, self-governing commonwealth, fit to take rank as one of the co-ordinate States of the Union, than that which seeks to establish it on the basis of the idea of the family, as consisting in and springing from the union for life of one man and one woman in the holy estate of matrimony; the sure foundation of all that is stable and noble in our civilization; the best guaranty of that reverent morality which is the source of all beneficent progress in social and political improvement." I would not myself indulge in such official praise for heterosexual monogamy, because I think it no business of the courts (as opposed to the political branches) to take sides in this culture war.

But the majority today has done so, not only by inventing a novel and extravagant constitutional doctrine to take the victory away from traditional forces, but even by verbally disparaging as bigotry adherence to traditional attitudes. To suggest, for example, that this constitutional amendment springs from nothing more than "a bare desire to harm a politically unpopular group," is nothing short of insulting. (It is also nothing short of preposterous to call "politically unpopular" a group which enjoys enormous influence in American media and politics, and which, as the trial court here noted, though composing no more than 4% of the population had the support of 46% of the Colorado voters, the percentage who voted against Amendment 2.)

Today's opinion has no foundation in American constitutional law, and barely pretends to. The people of Colorado have adopted an entirely reasonable provision which does not even disfavor homosexuals in any substantive sense, but merely denies them preferential treatment. Amendment 2 is designed to prevent piecemeal deterioration of the sexual morality favored by a majority of Coloradans, and is not only an appropriate means to that legitimate end, but a means that Americans have employed before. Striking it down is an act, not of judicial judgment, but of political will.

*Choices about death touch the core of liberty. The more precise constitutional significance of death is difficult to describe; not much may be said with confidence about death unless it is said from faith, and that alone is reason enough to protect the freedom to conform choices about death to individual conscience.*

— *John Paul Stevens*

# Cruzan v. Director, Missouri Department of Health
### 110 S.Ct. 2841, 497 U.S. 261 (1990)

*The opinion Chief Justice Rehnquist drafted for the majority, omitted here, "assumed" for purposes of this case that the Constitution would grant a competent person a constitutionally protected right to refuse lifesaving food and water. But the sad fact was that Nancy Beth Cruzan was not legally competent. She had been injured back in 1983 in an automobile accident and suffered severe brain damage rendering her in a persistent vegetative state, a condition in which a person exhibits motor reflexes but evinces no indications of significant cognitive function. After it became apparent that Nancy had virtually no chance of regaining her mental faculties, her parents obtained a state court order requiring doctors to remove her feeding and hydration tube, but the highest court in Missouri set aside the order because her parents had not clearly proven their decision was consistent with Nancy's own intentions, as manifested to others before the accident. By a 5 to 4 vote, the Supreme Court affirmed that decision. Mr. and Mrs. Cruzan went back to the state courts, and on the basis of new and additional evidence obtained the removal order; Nancy died twelve days later, in December 1990. Her case continues to be one of the most famous "right to die" precedents. Here Justices Scalia and Stevens square-off robe-to-robe over the constitutional issue, reasoning from different premises to opposite conclusions.*

**Justice Scalia:** The various opinions in this case portray quite clearly the difficult, indeed agonizing, questions that are presented by the constantly increasing power of science to keep the human body alive for longer than any reasonable person would want to inhabit it. The States have begun to grapple with these problems through legislation. While I agree with the Court's analysis today, and therefore join in its opinion, I would have preferred that we announce, clearly and promptly, that the federal courts have no business in this field; that American law has always accorded the State the power to prevent, by force if necessary, suicide—including suicide by refusing to take appropriate measures necessary to preserve one's life; that the point at which life becomes "worthless," and the point at which the means necessary to preserve it become "extraordinary" or "inappropriate," are neither set forth in the Constitution nor known to the nine Justices of this Court any better than they are known to nine people picked at random from the Kansas City telephone directory; and hence, that even when it is demonstrated by clear and convincing evidence that a patient no longer wishes certain measures to be taken to preserve his or her life, it is up to the citizens of Missouri to decide, through their elected representatives, whether that wish will be honored. It is quite impossible (because the Constitution says nothing about the matter) that those citizens will decide upon a line less lawful than the one we would choose; and it is unlikely (because we know no more about "life and death" than they do) that they will decide upon a line less reasonable.

The text of the Due Process Clause does not protect individuals against deprivations of liberty *simpliciter*. It protects them against deprivations of liberty "without due process of law." It is at least true that no "substantive due process" claim can be maintained unless the claimant demonstrates that the State has deprived him of a right historically and traditionally protected against state interference. That cannot possibly be established here.

At common law in England, a suicide—defined by Blackstone as one who "deliberately puts an end to his own existence, or commits any unlawful malicious act, the consequence of which is his own death"—was criminally liable. Although the States abolished the penalties imposed by the common law (*i.e.*, forfeiture and ignominious burial), they did so to spare the innocent family and not to legitimize the act. Case law at the time of the adoption of the Fourteenth Amendment generally held that assisting suicide was a criminal offense. And most States that did not explicitly prohibit assisted suicide in 1868 recognized, when the issue arose in the 50 years following the Fourteenth Amendment's ratification, that assisted and (in some cases) attempted suicide were unlawful. Thus, "there is no significant support for the claim that a right to suicide is so rooted in our tradition that it may be deemed 'fundamental' or 'implicit in the concept of ordered liberty.'"

Her parents rely on three distinctions to separate Nancy Cruzan's case from ordinary suicide: (1) that she is permanently incapacitated and in pain; (2) that she would bring on her death not by any affirmative act but by merely declining treatment that provides nourishment; and (3) that preventing her from effectuating her presumed wish to die requires violation of her bodily integrity. None of these suffices. First, suicide was not excused even when committed, in Blackstone's words, "to avoid those ills which persons had not the fortitude to endure." Nor would the imminence of the patient's death have affected liability at the common law.

The second asserted distinction—suggested by the recent cases concerning the right to refuse medical treatment—relies on the dichotomy between action and inaction. Suicide, it is said, consists of an affirmative act to end one's life; refusing treatment is not an affirmative act "causing" death, but merely a passive acceptance of the natural process of dying. I readily acknowledge that the distinction between action and inaction has some bearing upon the legislative judgment of what ought to be prevented as suicide—though even there it would seem to me unreasonable to draw the line precisely between action and inaction, rather than between various forms of inaction. It would not make much sense to say that one may not kill oneself by walking into the sea, but may sit on the beach until submerged by the incoming tide; or that one may not intentionally lock oneself into a cold storage locker, but may refrain from coming indoors when the temperature drops below freezing. Even as a legislative matter, in other words, the intelligent line does not fall between action and inaction but between those forms of inaction that consist of abstaining from "ordinary" care and those that consist of abstaining from "excessive" or "heroic" measures. Unlike action versus inaction, that is not a line to be discerned by logic or legal analysis, and we should not pretend that it is.

But to return to the principal point for present purposes: the irrelevance of the action-inaction distinction. Starving oneself to death is no different from putting a gun to one's temple as far as the common-law definition of suicide is concerned; the cause of death in both cases is the suicide's conscious decision to "put an end to his own existence." Furthermore, the common law rejected the action-inaction distinction in other contexts involving the taking of human life as well, as for examples, in the prosecution of a parent for the starvation death of her infant or regarding a physician's criminal liability for failure to provide care that could have extended a patient's life though the death was immediately caused by the underlying disease that the physician failed to treat.

The third asserted basis of distinction—that frustrating Nancy Cruzan's wish to die in the present case requires interference with her bodily integrity—is likewise inadequate, because such interference is impermissible only if one begs the question whether her refusal to undergo the treatment on her own is suicide. It has always been lawful not only for the State, but even for private citizens, to interfere with bodily integrity to prevent a felony. That general rule has of course been applied to suicide. It is not even reasonable, much less required by the Constitution, to maintain that although the State has the right to prevent a person from slashing his wrists, it does not have the power to apply physical force to prevent him from doing so, nor the power, should he succeed, to apply, coercively if necessary, medical measures to stop the flow of blood.

The dissent of Justice Stevens makes a plausible case for our intervention here only by embracing a political principle that the States are free to adopt, but that is demonstrably not imposed by the Constitution. One who accepts this principle must also accept, I think, that the State has no such legitimate interest that could outweigh the person's choice to put an end to her life. For insofar as balancing the relative interests of the State and the individual is concerned, there is nothing distinctive about accepting death through the refusal of "medical treatment," as opposed to accepting it through the refusal of food, or through the failure to shut off the engine and get out of the car after parking in one's garage after work. Suppose that Nancy Cruzan were in precisely the condition she is in today, except that she could be fed and digest food and water without artificial assistance. How is the State's "interest" in keeping her alive thereby increased, or her interest in deciding whether she wants to continue living reduced? It seems to me, in other words, that the dissenters' position ultimately rests upon the proposition that it is none of the State's business if a person wants to commit suicide. Justice Stevens is explicit on the point: "Choices about death touch the core of liberty." This is a view that some societies have held, and that our States are free to adopt if they wish. But it is not a view imposed by our constitutional traditions, in which the power of the State to prohibit suicide is unquestionable.

What I have said above is not meant to suggest that I would think it desirable, if we were sure that Nancy Cruzan wanted to die, to keep her alive by the means at issue here. I assert only that the Constitution has nothing to say about the subject. To raise up a constitutional right here we would have to create out of nothing (for it exists neither in text nor tradition) some constitutional principle whereby, although the State may insist that an individual come in out of the cold and eat food, it may not insist that he take medicine; and although it may pump his stomach empty of poison he has ingested, it may not fill his stomach with food he has failed to ingest. Are there, then, no reasonable and humane limits that ought not to be exceeded in requiring an individual to preserve his own life? There obviously are, but they are not set forth in the Due Process Clause. What assures us that those limits will not be exceeded is the same constitutional guarantee that is the source of most of our protection—what protects us, for example, from being assessed a tax of 100% of our income above the subsistence level, from being forbidden to drive cars, or from being required to send our children to school for 10 hours a day, none of which horribles are categorically prohibited by the Constitution. Our salvation is the Equal Protection Clause, which requires the democratic majority to accept for themselves and their loved ones what they impose on you and me. This Court need not, and has no authority to, inject itself into every field of human activity where irrationality and oppression may theoretically occur, and if it tries to do so it will destroy itself.

**Justice Stevens:** Our Constitution is born of the proposition that all legitimate governments must secure the equal right of every person to "Life, Liberty, and the pursuit of Happiness." In the ordinary case we quite naturally assume that these three ends are compatible, mutually enhancing, and perhaps even coincident.

This case is the first in which we consider whether, and how, the Constitution protects the liberty of seriously ill patients to be free from life-sustaining medical treatment. So put, the question is both general and profound. We need not, however, resolve the question in the abstract. Our responsibility as judges both enables and compels us to treat the problem as it is illuminated by the facts of the controversy before us.

The most important of those facts are these: "Clear and convincing evidence" established that Nancy Cruzan is "oblivious to her environment except for reflexive responses to sound and perhaps to painful stimuli"; that "she has no cognitive or reflexive ability to swallow food or water"; that "she will never recover" these abilities; and that her "cerebral cortical atrophy is irreversible, permanent, progressive and ongoing." Recovery and consciousness are impossible; the highest cognitive brain function that can be hoped for is a grimace in "recognition of ordinarily painful stimuli" or an "apparent response to sound."

The independent guardian *ad litem* endorsed the critical finding that "it was in Nancy Cruzan's best interests to have the tube feeding discontinued." That important conclusion thus was not disputed by the litigants. One might reasonably suppose that it would be dispositive: If Nancy Cruzan has no interest in continued treatment, and if she has a liberty interest in being free from unwanted treatment, and if the cessation of treatment would have no adverse impact on third parties, and if no reason exists to doubt the good faith of Nancy's parents, then what possible basis could the State have for insisting upon continued medical treatment?

It is perhaps predictable that courts might undervalue the liberty at stake here. Because death is so profoundly personal, public reflection upon it is unusual. As this sad case shows, however, such reflection must become more common if we are to deal responsibly with the modern circumstances of death. Medical advances have altered the physiological conditions of death in ways that may be alarming: Highly invasive treatment may perpetuate human existence through a merger of body and machine that some might reasonably regard as an insult to life rather than as its continuation. But those same advances, and the reorganization of medical care accompanying the new science and technology, have also transformed the political and social conditions of death: People are less likely to die at home, and more likely to die in relatively public places, such as hospitals or nursing homes.

Ultimate questions that might once have been dealt with in intimacy by a family and its physician have now become the concern of institutions. When the institution is a state hospital, as it is in this case, the government itself becomes involved. Nevertheless, this Court has long recognized that the liberty to make the decisions and choices constitutive of private life is so fundamental to our "concept of ordered liberty," that those choices must occasionally be afforded more direct protection.

Respect for these choices has guided our recognition of rights pertaining to bodily integrity. The constitutional decisions identifying those rights, like the common-law tradition upon which they built, are mindful that the "makers of our Constitution recognized the significance of man's spiritual nature." It may truly be said that "our notions of liberty are inextricably entwined with our idea of physical freedom and self-determination." Thus we have construed the Due Process Clause to preclude physically invasive recoveries of evidence not only because such procedures are "brutal" but also because they are "offensive to human dignity." We have interpreted the Constitution to interpose barriers to a State's efforts to sterilize some criminals not only because the proposed punishment would do "irreparable injury" to bodily integrity, but because "marriage and procreation" concern "the basic civil rights of man." The sanctity, and individual privacy, of the human body is obviously fundamental to liberty. "Every violation of a person's bodily integrity is an invasion of his or her liberty."

It is against this background of decisional law, and the constitutional tradition which it illuminates, that the right to be free from unwanted life-sustaining medical treatment must be understood. That right presupposes no abandonment of the desire for life. Nor is it reducible to a protection against batteries undertaken in the name of treatment, or to a guarantee against the infliction of bodily discomfort. Choices about death touch the core of liberty. Our duty, and the concomitant freedom, to come to terms with the conditions of our own mortality are undoubtedly "so rooted in the traditions and conscience of our people as to be ranked as fundamental," and indeed are essential incidents of the unalienable rights to life and liberty endowed us by our Creator.

The more precise constitutional significance of death is difficult to describe; not much may be said with confidence about death unless it is said from faith, and that alone is reason enough to protect the freedom to conform choices about death to individual conscience. We may also, however, justly assume that death is not life's simple opposite, or its necessary terminus, but rather its completion. Our ethical tradition has long regarded an appreciation of mortality as essential to understanding life's significance. It may, in fact, be impossible to live for anything without being prepared to die for something. Many philosophies and religions have, for example, long venerated the idea that there is a "life after death," and that the human soul endures even after the human body has perished.

These considerations cast into stark relief the injustice, and unconstitutionality, of Missouri's treatment of Nancy Beth Cruzan. Nancy Cruzan's death, when it comes, cannot be an historic act of heroism; it will inevitably be the consequence of her tragic accident. But Nancy Cruzan's interest in life, no less than that of any other person, includes an interest in how she will be thought of after her death by those whose opinions mattered to her. There can be no doubt that her life made her dear to her family and to others. How she dies will affect how that life is remembered.

To be constitutionally permissible, Missouri's intrusion upon these fundamental liberties must, at a minimum, bear a reasonable relationship to a legitimate state end. Missouri asserts that its policy is related to a state interest in the protection of life. In my view, however, it is an effort to define life, rather than to protect it, that is the heart of Missouri's policy. Missouri insists, without regard to Nancy Cruzan's own interests, upon equating her life with the biological persistence of her bodily functions. Nancy Cruzan, it must be remembered, is not now simply incompetent. She is in a persistent vegetative state and has been so for seven years. The trial court found, and no party contested, that Nancy has no possibility of recovery and no consciousness.

It seems to me that the Court errs insofar as it characterizes this case as involving "judgments about the 'quality' of life that a particular individual may enjoy." Nancy Cruzan is obviously "alive " in a physiological sense. But for patients like Nancy Cruzan, who have no consciousness and no chance of recovery, there is a serious question as to whether the mere persistence of their bodies is "life " as that word is commonly understood, or as it is used in both the Constitution and the Declaration of Independence. The State's unflagging determination to perpetuate Nancy Cruzan's physical existence is comprehensible only as an effort to define life's meaning, not as an attempt to preserve its sanctity.

Life, particularly human life, is not commonly thought of as a merely physiological condition or function. Its sanctity is often thought to derive from the impossibility of any such reduction. When people speak of life, they often mean to describe the experiences that comprise a person's history, as when it is said that somebody "led a good life." They may also mean to refer to the practical manifestation of the human spirit, a meaning captured by the familiar observation that somebody "added life" to an assembly. If there is a shared thread among the various opinions on this subject, it may be that life is an activity which is at once the matrix for, and an integration of, a person's interests. In any event, absent some theological abstraction, the idea of life is not conceived separately from the idea of a living person. Yet, it is by precisely such a separation that Missouri asserts an interest in Nancy Cruzan's life in opposition to Nancy Cruzan's own interests. The resulting definition is uncommon indeed.

The laws punishing homicide, upon which the Court relies, do not support a contrary inference. Obviously, such laws protect both the life and interests of those who would otherwise be victims. Even laws against suicide pre-suppose that those inclined to take their own lives have some interest in living, and, indeed, that the depressed people whose lives are preserved may later be thankful for the State's intervention. Likewise, decisions that address the "quality of life" of incompetent, but conscious, patients rest upon the recognition that these patients have some interest in continuing their lives, even if that interest pales in some eyes when measured against interests in dignity or comfort. Not so here. Contrary to the Court's suggestion, Missouri's protection of life in a form abstracted from the living is not commonplace; it is aberrant.

In short, there is no reasonable ground for believing that Nancy Beth Cruzan has any personal interest in the perpetuation of what the State has decided is her life. As I have already suggested, it would be possible to hypothesize such an interest on the basis of theological or philosophical conjecture. But even to posit such a basis for the State's action is to condemn it. It is not within the province of secular government to circumscribe the liberties of the people by regulations designed wholly for the purpose of establishing a sectarian definition of life.

Only because Missouri has arrogated to itself the power to define life, and only because the Court permits this usurpation, are Nancy Cruzan's life and liberty put into disquieting conflict. If Nancy Cruzan's life were defined by reference to her own interests, so that her life expired when her biological existence ceased serving any of her own interests, then her constitutionally protected interest in freedom from unwanted treatment would not come into conflict with her constitutionally protected interest in life. Conversely, if there were any evidence that

Nancy Cruzan herself defined life to encompass every form of biological persistence by a human being, so that the continuation of treatment would serve Nancy's own liberty, then once again there would be no conflict between life and liberty. The opposition of life and liberty in this case are thus not the result of Nancy Cruzan's tragic accident, but are instead the artificial consequence of Missouri's effort, and this Court's willingness, to abstract Nancy Cruzan's life from Nancy Cruzan's person.

This Court's majority expresses great deference to the policy choice made by the state legislature. That deference is, in my view, based upon a severe error in the Court's constitutional logic. The Court's deference seems ultimately to derive from the premise that chronically incompetent persons have no constitutionally cognizable interests at all, and so are not persons within the meaning of the Constitution. Deference of this sort is patently unconstitutional. It is also dangerous in ways that may not be immediately apparent. Today the State of Missouri has announced its intent to spend several hundred thousand dollars in preserving the life of Nancy Beth Cruzan in order to vindicate its general policy favoring the preservation of human life. Tomorrow, another State equally eager to champion an interest in the "quality of life" might favor a policy designed to ensure quick and comfortable deaths by denying treatment to categories of marginally hopeless cases. If the State in fact has an interest in defining life, and if the State's policy with respect to the termination of life-sustaining treatment commands deference from the judiciary, it is unclear how any resulting conflict between the best interests of the individual and the general policy of the State would be resolved. I believe the Constitution requires that the individual's vital interest in liberty should prevail over the general policy in that case, just as in this.

That a contrary result is readily imaginable under the majority's theory makes manifest that this Court cannot defer to any state policy that drives a theoretical wedge between a person's life, on the one hand, and that person's liberty or happiness, on the other. The consequence of such a theory is to deny the personhood of those whose lives are defined by the State's interests rather than their own. This consequence may be acceptable in theology or in speculative philosophy, but it is radically inconsistent with the foundation of all legitimate government. Our Constitution presupposes a respect for the personhood of every individual, and nowhere is strict adherence to that principle more essential than in the judicial branch.

*These death sentences are cruel and unusual in the same way that being struck by lightning is cruel and unusual.*

— *Potter Stewart*

## Furman v. Georgia
### 92 S.Ct. 2726, 408 U.S. 238 (1972)

*The constitutionality of the death penalty has been hanging over the Supreme Court for more than two decades. This landmark 1972 decision voided statutes in 40 States and commuted the executions of more than 600 prisoners then on death row. All nine Justices wrote separate personal opinions. But the Justices could only agree that the statutes on the books at that time were unfair. A majority did not declare that the death penalty was unconstitutional once and for all. After* Furman, *a few state legislatures decided not to reinstitute the death penalty. But 35 state legislatures passed new statutes. Responding to the Justices' concerns for arbitrariness, several state legislatures enacted mandatory statutes that automatically imposed the death penalty for certain crimes. The more typical new statute separated the determination of guilt from the determination of punishment and prescribed elaborate guidelines identifying aggravating and mitigating factors for juries to apply in each case in order to determine which murderers should live and which should be put to death. In 1976, the Court would return to the constitutional issue, reviewing a batch of the then-new state statutes.* Woodson v. North Carolina (1976) *disapproved of the mandatory approach. But the Justices approved of the guidelines approach in* Gregg v. Georgia (1976). *Thus, the constitutional moratorium ended, and state executions resumed, although the controversy surrounding the death penalty continues in terms of its manner, methods, and morality. The* Furman *opinions— which fill 120 pages of the official reports with argumentation, statistics, history, and social science studies—give a full account of this pitched debate. Whatever your personal views, these opinions inform a deeper understanding of what is at stake as a matter of constitutional law. Every member of the Court is allowed a few pages here to sample each Justice's individual thinking and to*

*demonstrate the Court's collegial decisionmaking appara-
tus. This is an excellent example of how constitutional
law is so much more than merely nine lawyers counting
to five.*

**Justice Douglas:** The words "cruel and unusual" certainly
include penalties that are barbaric. But the words, at least
when read in light of the English proscription against selective
and irregular use of penalties, suggest that it is "cruel and unusual" to apply the death penalty—or any other penalty—selectively to minorities whose numbers are few, who are outcasts of
society, and who are unpopular, but whom society is willing to
see suffer though it would not countenance general application
of the same penalty across the board. Juries (or judges, as the
case may be) have practically untrammeled discretion to let an
accused live or insist that he die.

A scientific study of capital cases reached the conclusion:
"Application of the death penalty is unequal: most of those executed were poor, young, and ignorant." Former Attorney General Ramsey Clark has said, "It is the poor, the sick, the
ignorant, the powerless and the hated who are executed." One
searches our chronicles in vain for the execution of any member
of the affluent strata of this society. The Leopolds and Loebs are
given prison terms, not sentenced to death.

We cannot say from facts disclosed in these records before us
that these individual Defendants were sentenced to death because they were black. Yet our task is not restricted to an effort
to divine what motives impelled these death penalties. Rather,
we deal with a system of law and of justice that leaves to the
uncontrolled discretion of judges or juries the determination
whether defendants committing these crimes should die or be
imprisoned. Under these laws no standards govern the selection
of the penalty. People live or die, dependent on the whim of one
man or of 12.

Those who wrote the Eighth Amendment knew what price
their forebears had paid for a system based, not on equal justice,
but on discrimination. In those days the target was not the
blacks or the poor, but the dissenters, those who opposed absolutism in government, who struggled for a parliamentary regime, and who opposed governments' recurring efforts to foist a
particular religion on the people. But the tool of capital punishment was used with vengeance against the opposition and those
unpopular with the regime. One cannot read this history with-

out realizing that the desire for equality was reflected in the ban against "cruel and unusual punishments" contained in the Eighth Amendment.

In a Nation committed to equal protection of the laws, there is no permissible "caste" aspect of law enforcement. Yet we know that the discretion of judges and juries in imposing the death penalty enables the penalty to be selectively applied, feeding prejudices against the accused if he is poor and despised, and lacking political clout, or if he is a member of a suspect or unpopular minority, and saving those who by social position may be in a more protected position. In ancient Hindu law a Brahman was exempt from capital punishment, and under that law, "generally, in the law books, punishment increased in severity as social status diminished." We have, I fear, taken in practice the same position, partially as a result of making the death penalty discretionary and partially as a result of the ability of the rich to purchase the services of the most respected and most resourceful legal talent in the Nation.

A law that stated that anyone making more than $50,000 would be exempt from the death penalty would plainly fall, as would a law that in terms said that blacks, those who never went beyond the fifth grade in school, those who made less than $3,000 a year, or those who were unpopular or unstable should be the only people executed. A law which in the overall view reaches that result in practice has no more sanctity than a law which in terms provides the same.

**Justice Brennan:** We have very little evidence of the Framers' intent in including the Cruel and Unusual Punishments Clause among those restraints upon the new Government enumerated in the Bill of Rights. Several conclusions emerge from the history of the adoption of the Clause. We know that the Framers' concern was directed specifically at the exercise of legislative power. They included in the Bill of Rights a prohibition upon "cruel and unusual punishments" precisely because the legislature would otherwise have had the unfettered power to prescribe punishments for crimes. Yet we cannot now know exactly what the Framers thought "cruel and unusual punishments" were. Certainly they intended to ban torturous punishments, but the available evidence does not support the further conclusion that only torturous punishments were to be outlawed. The Framers were well aware that the reach of the Clause was not limited to the proscription of unspeakable atrocities. Nor did they intend simply to forbid punishments considered "cruel and unusual" at the time. The "import" of the Clause is, indeed, "indefinite," and for good reason.

We know "that the words of the Clause are not precise, and that their scope is not static." We know, therefore that the Clause, in Chief Justice Warren's words, "must take its meaning from the evolving standards of decency that mark the progress of a maturing society." It has been explained that: "The basic concept underlying the Clause is nothing less than the dignity of man. While the State has the power to punish, the Clause stands to assure that this power be exercised within the limits of civilized standards." At bottom, then, the Cruel and Unusual Punishments Clause prohibits the infliction of uncivilized and inhuman punishments. The State, even as it punishes, must treat its members with respect for their intrinsic worth as human beings. A punishment is "cruel and unusual," therefore, if it does not comport with human dignity. If a punishment is unusually severe, if there is a strong probability that it is inflicted arbitrarily, if it is substantially rejected by contemporary society, and if there is no reason to believe that it serves any penal purpose more effectively than some less severe punishment, then the continued infliction of that punishment violates the command of the Clause that the State may not inflict inhuman and uncivilized punishments upon those convicted of crimes.

There is, first, a textual consideration raised by the Bill of Rights itself. The Fifth Amendment declares that if a particular crime is punishable by death, a person charged with that crime is entitled to certain procedural protections. We can thus infer that the Framers recognized the existence of what was then a common punishment. We cannot, however, make the further inference that they intended to exempt this particular punishment from the express prohibition of the Cruel and Unusual Punishments Clause. Nor is there any indication in the debates on the Clause that a special exception was to be made for death. If anything, the indication is to the contrary, for the congressional debates specifically mentioned death as a candidate for future proscription under the Clause. It does not advance analysis simply to insist that the Framers did not believe that adoption of the Bill of Rights would immediately prevent the infliction of the punishment of death. The question, then, is whether the deliberate infliction of death is today consistent with the command of the Clause that the State may not inflict punishments that do not comport with the principle of human dignity.

Death is a unique punishment in the United States. In a society that so strongly affirms the sanctity of life, not surprisingly the common view is that death is the ultimate sanction. This natural human feeling appears all about us. There has been no national debate about punishment, in general or by imprisonment, comparable to the debate about the punishment of death. No other punishment has been so continuously restricted, nor has any State yet abolished prisons, as some have abolished this punishment. And those States that still inflict death reserve it for the most heinous crimes. Juries, of course, have always treated death cases differently, as have governors exercising their commutation powers. This Court, too, almost always treats death cases as a class apart. And the unfortunate effect of this punishment upon the functioning of the judicial process is well known; no other punishment has a similar effect.

The only explanation for the uniqueness of death is its extreme severity. Death is today an unusually severe punishment, unusual in its pain, in its finality, and in its enormity. No other existing punishment is comparable to death in terms of physical and mental suffering.

The unusual severity of death is manifested most clearly in its finality and enormity. Death, in these respects, is in a class by itself. Death is truly an awesome punishment. The calculated killing of a human being by the State involves, by its very nature, a denial of the executed person's humanity. The contrast with the plight of a person punished by imprisonment is evident. An individual in prison does not lose "the right to have rights." A prisoner remains a member of the human family. Moreover, he retains the right of access to the courts. His punishment is not irrevocable. Apart from the common charge, grounded upon the recognition of human fallibility, that the punishment of death must inevitably be inflicted upon innocent men, we know that death has been the lot of men whose convictions were unconstitutionally secured in view of later holdings of this Court. The punishment itself may have been unconstitutionally inflicted, yet the finality of death precludes relief. An executed person has indeed "lost the right to have rights."

In comparison to all other punishments today, then, the deliberate extinguishment of human life by the State is uniquely degrading to human dignity. I would not hesitate to hold, on this first principle alone, that death is today a "cruel and un-usual" punishment, were it not that death is a punishment of longstanding usage and acceptance in this country.

Turning to the second principle—that the State may not arbitrarily inflict an unusually severe punishment—the out-standing characteristic of our present practice of punishing criminals by death is the infrequency with which we resort to it. The evidence is conclusive that death is not the ordinary pun-ishment for any crime.

There has been a steady decline in the infliction of this pun-ishment in every decade since the 1930's, the earliest period for which accurate statistics are available. Yet our population and the number of capital crimes committed have increased greatly over the past four decades. The contemporary rarity of the inflic-tion of this punishment is thus the end result of a long-contin-ued decline. Although there are no exact figures available, we know that thousands of murders and rapes are committed annu-ally in States where death is an authorized punishment for those crimes. How much rarer, after all, could the infliction of death be? When the punishment of death is inflicted in a trivial number of the cases in which it is legally available, the conclu-sion is virtually inescapable that it is being inflicted arbitrarily. Indeed, it smacks of little more than a lottery system.

Informed selectivity, of course, is a value not to be deni-grated. When the rate of infliction is at this low level, it is highly implausible that only the worst criminals or the crimi-nals who commit the worst crimes are selected for this punish-ment. No one has yet suggested a rational basis that could differentiate in those terms the few who die from the many who go to prison. Crimes and criminals simply do not admit of a distinction that can be drawn so finely as to explain, on that ground, the execution of such a tiny sample of those eligible. Certainly the laws that provide for this punishment do not at-tempt to draw that distinction; all cases to which the laws apply are necessarily "extreme." In other words, our procedures are not constructed to guard against the totally capricious selection of criminals for the punishment of death.

Turning to the third principle, an examination of the history and present operation of the American practice of punishing criminals by death reveals that this punishment has been al-most totally rejected by contemporary society.

From the beginning of our Nation, the punishment of death has stirred acute public controversy. Although pragmatic arguments for and against the punishment have been frequently advanced, this longstanding and heated controversy cannot be explained solely as the result of differences over the practical wisdom of a particular government policy. At bottom, the battle has been waged on moral grounds. The country has debated whether a society for which the dignity of the individual is the supreme value can, without a fundamental inconsistency, follow the practice of deliberately putting some of its members to death.

Our practice of punishing criminals by death has changed greatly over the years. Hanging and shooting have virtually ceased. No longer does our society countenance the spectacle of public executions, once thought desirable as a deterrent to criminal behavior by others. Today we reject public executions as debasing and brutalizing to us all.

Also significant is the drastic decrease in the crimes for which the punishment of death is actually inflicted. In addition, the crime of capital murder has itself been limited. Virtually all death sentences today are discretionarily imposed. Finally, it is significant that nine States no longer inflict the punishment of death under any circumstances, and five others have restricted it to extremely rare crimes.

Thus, although "the death penalty has been employed throughout our history," in fact the history of this punishment is one of successive restriction. What was once a common punishment has become, in the context of a continuing moral debate, increasingly rare. The result of this movement is our current system of administering the punishment, under which death sentences are rarely imposed and death is even more rarely inflicted. It is, of course, "We, the People" who are responsible for the rarity both of the imposition and the carrying out of this punishment. Juries, "expressing the conscience of the community on the ultimate question of life or death," have been able to bring themselves to vote for death in a mere 100 or so cases among the thousands tried each year where the punishment is available. Governors, elected by and acting for us, have regularly commuted a substantial number of those sentences. And it is our society that insists upon due process of law to the end that no person will be unjustly put to death, thus ensuring that many more of those sentences will not be carried out. In sum, we have made death a rare punishment today.

The progressive decline in, and the current rarity of, the infliction of death demonstrate that our society seriously questions the appropriateness of this punishment today. The objective indicator of society's view of an unusually severe punishment is what society does with it, and today society will inflict death upon only a small sample of the eligible criminals. Rejection could hardly be more complete without becoming absolute. At the very least, I must conclude that contemporary society views this punishment with substantial doubt.

The final principle to be considered is that an unusually severe and degrading punishment may not be excessive in view of the purposes for which it is inflicted. The States' primary claim is that death is a necessary punishment because it prevents the commission of capital crimes more effectively than any less severe punishment. The sufficient answer to this is that if a criminal convicted of a capital crime poses a danger to society, effective administration of the State's pardon and parole laws can delay or deny his release from prison, and techniques of isolation can eliminate or minimize the danger while he remains confined.

The more significant argument is that the threat of death prevents the commission of capital crimes because it deters potential criminals who would not be deterred by the threat of imprisonment. The argument is not based upon evidence that the threat of death is a superior deterrent. Because people fear death the most, the argument runs, the threat of death must be the greatest deterrent.

It is not, denied that many, and probably most, capital crimes cannot be deterred by the threat of punishment. The concern, then, is with a particular type of potential criminal, the rational person who will commit a capital crime knowing that the punishment is long-term imprisonment, which may well be for the rest of his life, but will not commit the crime knowing that the punishment is death. On the face of it, the assumption that such persons exist is implausible.

Proponents of this argument necessarily admit that its validity depends upon the existence of a system in which the punishment of death is invariably and swiftly imposed. Our system, of course, satisfies neither condition. A rational person contemplating a murder or rape is confronted, not with the certainty of a speedy death, but with the slightest possibility that he will be executed in the distant future. The risk of death is remote and improbable; in contrast, the risk of long-term imprisonment is near and great. In short, whatever the speculative validity of the assumption that the threat of death is a superior deterrent, there is no reason to believe that as currently administered the punishment of death is necessary to deter the commission of capital crimes.

There is, however, another aspect to the argument that the punishment of death is necessary for the protection of society. The infliction of death, the States urge, serves to manifest the community's outrage at the commission of the crime. It is, they say, a concrete public expression of moral indignation that inculcates respect for the law and helps assure a more peaceful community. Moreover, we are told, not only does the punishment of death exert this widespread moralizing influence upon community values, it also satisfies the popular demand for grievous condemnation of abhorrent crimes and thus prevents disorder, lynching, and attempts by private citizens to take the law into their own hands.

The question, however, is not whether death serves these supposed purposes of punishment, but whether death serves them more effectively than imprisonment. If capital crimes require the punishment of death in order to provide moral reinforcement for the basic values of the community, those values can only be undermined when death is so rarely inflicted upon the criminals who commit the crimes. Furthermore, it is certainly doubtful that the infliction of death by the State does in fact strengthen the community's moral code; if the deliberate extinguishment of human life has any effect at all, it more likely tends to lower our respect for life and brutalize our values. That, after all, is why we no longer carry out public executions. There is, then, no substantial reason to believe that the punishment of death, as currently administered, is necessary for the protection of society.

The only other purpose suggested, one that is independent of protection for society, is retribution. Shortly stated, retribution in this context means that criminals are put to death because they deserve it.

Although it is difficult to believe that any State today wishes to proclaim adherence to "naked vengeance," the States claim, in reliance upon its statutory authorization, that death is the only fit punishment for capital crimes and that this retributive purpose justifies its infliction. Obviously, concepts of justice change; no immutable moral order requires death for murderers and rapists. The claim that death is a just punishment necessarily refers to the existence of certain public beliefs. The claim must be that for capital crimes death alone comports with society's notion of proper punishment. When the overwhelming number of criminals who commit capital crimes go to prison, it cannot be concluded that death serves the purpose of retribution more effectively than imprisonment. The asserted public belief that murderers and rapists deserve to die is flatly inconsistent with the execution of a random few. As the history of the punishment of death in this country shows, our society wishes to prevent crime; we have no desire to kill criminals simply to get even with them.

**Justice Stewart:** The penalty of death differs from all other forms of criminal punishment, not in degree but in kind. It is unique in its total irrevocability. It is unique in its rejection of rehabilitation of the convict as a basic purpose of criminal justice. And it is unique, finally, in its absolute renunciation of all that is embodied in our concept of humanity.

The death sentences now before us are the product of a legal system that brings them, I believe, within the very core of the Eighth Amendment's guarantee against cruel and unusual punishments. These sentences are "cruel" in the sense that they excessively go beyond, not in degree but in kind, the punishments that the state legislatures have determined to be necessary. These sentences are "unusual" in the sense that the penalty of death is infrequently imposed for murder, and that its imposition for rape is extraordinarily rare.

These death sentences are cruel and unusual in the same way that being struck by lightning is cruel and unusual. For, of all the people convicted of rapes and murders, many just as reprehensible as these, these Defendants are among a capriciously selected random handful upon whom the sentence of death has in fact been imposed. I simply conclude that the Eighth and Fourteenth Amendments cannot tolerate the infliction of a sentence of death under legal systems that permit this unique penalty to be so wantonly and so freakishly imposed.

**Justice White:** The imposition and execution of the death penalty are obviously cruel in the dictionary sense. But the penalty has not been considered cruel and unusual punishment in the constitutional sense because it was thought justified by the social ends it was deemed to serve. At the moment that it ceases realistically to further these purposes, however, the emerging question is whether its imposition in such circumstances would violate the Eighth Amendment. It is my view that it would, for its imposition would then be the pointless and needless extinction of life with only marginal contributions to any discernible social or public purposes. A penalty with such negligible returns to the State would be patently excessive and cruel and unusual punishment violative of the Eighth Amendment.

I must arrive at judgment; and I can do no more than state a conclusion based on 10 years of almost daily exposure to the facts and circumstances of hundreds and hundreds of federal and state criminal cases involving crimes for which death is the authorized penalty. That conclusion is that the death penalty is exacted with great infrequency even for the most atrocious crimes and that there is no meaningful basis for distinguishing the few cases in which it is imposed from the many cases in which it is not. The short of it is that the policy of vesting sentencing authority primarily in juries—a decision largely motivated by the desire to mitigate the harshness of the law and to bring community judgment to bear on the sentence as well as guilt or innocence—has so effectively achieved its aims that capital punishment within the confines of the statutes now before us has for all practical purposes run its course.

Past and present legislative judgment with respect to the death penalty loses much of its force when viewed in light of the recurring practice of delegating sentencing authority to the jury and the fact that a jury, in its own discretion and without violating its trust or any statutory policy, may refuse to impose the death penalty no matter what the circumstances of the crime. Legislative "policy" is thus necessarily defined not by what is legislatively authorized but by what juries and judges do in exercising the discretion so regularly conferred upon them. In my judgment what was done in these cases violated the Eighth Amendment.

**Justice Marshall:** The criminal acts with which we are confronted are ugly, vicious, reprehensible acts. Their sheer brutality cannot and should not be minimized. But, we are not called upon to condone the penalized conduct; we are asked only to examine the penalty imposed on each of these Defendants and to determine whether or not it violates the Eighth Amendment. The question then is not whether we condone rape or murder, for surely we do not; it is whether capital punishment is "a punishment no longer consistent with our own self-respect" and, therefore, violative of the Eighth Amendment. The elasticity of the constitutional provision under consideration presents dangers of too little or too much self-restraint. Hence, we must proceed with caution to answer the question presented.

Since capital punishment is not a recent phenomenon, if it violates the Constitution, it does so because it is excessive or unnecessary, or because it is abhorrent to currently existing moral values.

In order to assess whether or not death is an excessive or unnecessary penalty, it is necessary to consider the reasons why a legislature might select it as punishment for one or more offenses, and examine whether less severe penalties would satisfy the legitimate legislative wants as well as capital punishment. There are six purposes conceivably served by capital punishment: retribution, deterrence, prevention of repetitive criminal acts, encouragement of guilty pleas and confessions, eugenics, and economy.

If retribution alone could serve as a justification for any particular penalty, then all penalties selected by the legislature would by definition be acceptable means for designating society's moral approbation of a particular act. But the Eighth Amendment is our insulation from our baser selves. The "cruel and unusual" language limits the avenues through which vengeance can be channeled. The history of the Eighth Amendment supports only the conclusion that retribution for its own sake is improper.

The most hotly contested issue regarding capital punishment is whether it is better than life imprisonment as a deterrent to crime. Despite the fact that abolitionists have not proved non-deterrence beyond a reasonable doubt, they have succeeded in showing by clear and convincing evidence that capital punishment is not necessary as a deterrent to crime in our society. This is all that they must do. We would shirk our judicial responsibilities if we failed to accept the presently existing statistics and demanded more proof. In light of the massive amount of evidence before us, I see no alternative but to conclude that capital punishment cannot be justified on the basis of its deterrent effect.

Much of what must be said about the death penalty as a device to prevent recidivism is obvious—if a murderer is executed, he cannot possibly commit another offense. The fact is, however, that murderers are extremely unlikely to commit other crimes either in prison or upon their release. For the most part, they are first offenders, and when released from prison they are known to become model citizens. Furthermore, most persons who commit capital crimes are not executed. With respect to those who are sentenced to die, it is critical to note that the jury is never asked to determine whether they are likely to be recidivists. If capital punishment were justified purely on the basis of preventing recidivism, it would have to be considered to be excessive; no general need to obliterate all capital offenders could have been demonstrated, nor any specific need in individual cases.

If the death penalty is used to encourage guilty pleas and thus to deter suspects from exercising their rights under the Sixth Amendment to jury trials, it is unconstitutional.

Any suggestions concerning the eugenic benefits of capital punishment are obviously meritless. This Nation has never formally professed eugenic goals, and the history of the world does not look kindly on them.

As for the argument that it is cheaper to execute a capital offender than to imprison him for life, even assuming that such an argument, if true, would support a capital sanction, it is simply incorrect. When all is said and done, there can be no doubt that it costs more to execute a man than to keep him in prison for life.

It is not improper at this point to take judicial notice of the fact that for more than 200 years men have labored to demonstrate that capital punishment serves no purpose that life imprisonment could not serve equally well. And they have done so with great success. Little, if any, evidence has been adduced to prove the contrary. The point has now been reached at which deference to the legislatures is tantamount to abdication of our judicial roles as factfinders, judges, and ultimate arbiters of the Constitution. We know that at some point the presumption of constitutionality accorded legislative acts gives way to a realistic assessment of those acts. This point comes when there is sufficient evidence available so that judges can determine, not whether the legislature acted wisely, but whether it had any rational basis whatsoever for acting. We have this evidence before us now. There is no rational basis for concluding that capital punishment is not excessive.

Even if capital punishment is not excessive, it nonetheless violates the Eighth Amendment because it is morally unacceptable to the people of the United States at this time in their history.

In judging whether or not a given penalty is morally acceptable, most courts have said that the punishment is valid unless "it shocks the conscience and sense of justice of the people." The question with which we must deal is not whether a substantial proportion of American citizens would today, if polled, opine that capital punishment is barbarously cruel, but whether they would find it to be so in the light of all information presently available. With respect to this judgment, a violation of the Eighth Amendment is totally dependent on the predictable subjective, emotional reactions of informed citizens.

It has often been noted that American citizens know almost nothing about capital punishment. This information would almost surely convince the average citizen that the death penalty was unwise, but a problem arises as to whether it would convince him that the penalty was morally reprehensible. I cannot believe that at this stage in our history, the American people would ever knowingly support purposeless vengeance. Thus, I believe that the great mass of citizens would conclude on the basis of the material already considered that the death penalty is immoral and therefore unconstitutional.

I believe that the following facts would serve to convince even the most hesitant of citizens to condemn death as a sanction: capital punishment is imposed discriminatorily against certain identifiable classes of people; there is evidence that innocent people have been executed before their innocence can be proved; and the death penalty wreaks havoc with our entire criminal justice system.

Regarding discrimination, it has been said that "it is usually the poor, the illiterate, the underprivileged, the member of the minority group—the man who, because he is without means, and is defended by a court-appointed attorney—who becomes society's sacrificial lamb." Just as Americans know little about who is executed and why, they are unaware of the potential dangers of executing an innocent man. While it is difficult to ascertain with certainty the degree to which the death penalty is discriminatorily imposed or the number of innocent persons sentenced to die, there is one conclusion about the penalty that is universally accepted—i.e., it "tends to distort the course of the criminal law." Assuming knowledge of all the facts presently available regarding capital punishment, the average citizen would, in my opinion, find it shocking to his conscience and sense of justice.

At a time in our history when the streets of the Nation's cities inspire fear and despair, rather than pride and hope, it is difficult to maintain objectivity and concern for our fellow citizens. But, the measure of a country's greatness is its ability to retain compassion in time of crisis. No nation in the recorded history of man has a greater tradition of revering justice and fair treatment for all its citizens in times of turmoil, confusion, and tension than ours. This is a country which stands tallest in troubled times, a country that clings to fundamental principles, cherishes its constitutional heritage, and rejects simple solutions that compromise the values that lie at the roots of our democratic system.

In striking down capital punishment, this Court does not malign our system of government. On the contrary, it pays homage to it. Only in a free society could right triumph in difficult times, and could civilization record its magnificent advancement. In recognizing the humanity of our fellow beings, we pay ourselves the highest tribute. We achieve "a major milestone in the long road up from barbarism" and join the approximately 70 other jurisdictions in the world which celebrate their regard for civilization and humanity by shunning capital punishment.

**Chief Justice Burger:** Although the Eighth Amendment literally reads as prohibiting only those punishments that are both "cruel" and "unusual," history compels the conclusion that the Constitution prohibits all punishments of extreme and barbarous cruelty, regardless of how frequently or infrequently imposed. From every indication, the Framers of the Eighth Amendment intended to give the phrase a meaning far different from that of its English precursor. The records of the debates in several of the state conventions called to ratify the 1789 draft Constitution submitted prior to the addition of the Bill of Rights show that the Framers' exclusive concern was the absence of any ban on tortures. The later inclusion of the "cruel and unusual punishment" clause was in response to these objections.

The cases decided under the Eighth Amendment are consistent with the tone of the ratifying debates. I view these cases as turning on the single question whether capital punishment is "cruel" in the constitutional sense. The term "unusual" cannot be read as limiting the ban on "cruel" punishments or as somehow expanding the meaning of the term "cruel." For this reason

I am unpersuaded by the facile argument that since capital punishment has always been cruel in the everyday sense of the word, and has become unusual due to decreased use, it is, therefore, now "cruel and unusual."

Capital punishment was not impermissibly cruel at the time of the adoption of the Eighth Amendment. Not only do the records of the debates indicate that the Founding Fathers were limited in their concern to the prevention of torture, but it is also clear from the language of the Constitution itself that there was no thought whatever of the elimination of capital punishment. The opening sentence of the Fifth Amendment is a guarantee that the death penalty not be imposed "unless on a presentment or indictment of a Grand Jury." The Double Jeopardy Clause of the Fifth Amendment is a prohibition against being "twice put in jeopardy of life" for the same offense. Similarly, the Due Process Clause commands "due process of law" before an accused can be "deprived of life, liberty, or property." Thus, the explicit language of the Constitution affirmatively acknowledges the legal power to impose capital punishment. Since the Eighth Amendment was adopted on the same day in 1791 as the Fifth Amendment, it hardly needs more to establish that the death penalty was not "cruel" in the constitutional sense at that time. In the 181 years since the enactment of the Eighth Amendment, not a single decision of this Court has cast the slightest shadow of a doubt on the constitutionality of capital punishment.

It is apparent that there has been no change of constitutional significance in the nature of the punishment itself. Twentieth century modes of execution surely involve no greater physical suffering than the means employed at the time of the Eighth Amendment's adoption. And although a man awaiting execution must inevitably experience extraordinary mental anguish, no one suggests that this anguish is materially different from that experienced by condemned men in 1791, even though protracted appellate review processes have greatly increased the waiting time on "death row."

However, the inquiry cannot end here. The Eighth Amendment prohibition cannot fairly be limited to those punishments thought excessively cruel and barbarous at the time of the adoption of the Eighth Amendment. A punishment is inordinately cruel, in the sense we must deal with it in these cases, chiefly as perceived by the society so characterizing it. The standard of extreme cruelty is not merely descriptive, but necessarily embodies a moral judgment. The standard itself remains the same, but its applicability must change as the basic mores of society change.

Nevertheless, the Court up to now has never actually held that a punishment has become impermissibly cruel due to a shift in the weight of accepted social values; nor has the Court suggested judicially manageable criteria for measuring such a shift in moral consensus. The Court's quiescence in this area can be attributed to the fact that in a democratic society legislatures, not courts, are constituted to respond to the will and consequently the moral values of the people. The paucity of judicial decisions invalidating legislatively prescribed punishments is powerful evidence that in this country legislatures have in fact been responsive—albeit belatedly at times—to changes in social attitudes and moral values.

There are no obvious indications that capital punishment offends the conscience of society to such a degree that our traditional deference to the legislative judgment must be abandoned. Capital punishment is authorized by statute in 40 States, the District of Columbia, and in the federal courts for the commission of certain crimes. On four occasions in the last 11 years Congress has added to the list of federal crimes punishable by death.

One conceivable source of evidence that legislatures have abdicated their essentially barometric role with respect to community values would be public opinion polls, of which there have been many in the past decade addressed to the question of capital punishment. Without assessing the reliability of such polls, or intimating that any judicial reliance could ever be placed on them, it need only be noted that the reported results have shown nothing approximating the universal condemnation of capital punishment that might lead us to suspect that the legislatures in general have lost touch with current social values.

It cannot be gainsaid that by the choice of juries—and sometimes judges—the death penalty is imposed in far fewer than half the cases in which it is available. To go further and characterize the rate of imposition as "freakishly rare" is unwarranted hyperbole.

The selectivity of juries in imposing the punishment of death is properly viewed as a refinement on, rather than a repudiation of, the statutory authorization for that penalty. Legislatures prescribe the categories of crimes for which the death penalty should be available, and, acting as "the conscience of the community," juries are entrusted to determine in individual cases that the ultimate punishment is warranted. Juries are undoubtedly influenced in this judgment by myriad factors. The motive or lack of motive of the perpetrator, the degree of injury or suffering of the victim or victims, and the degree of brutality in the commission of the crime would seem to be prominent among these factors. Given the general awareness that death is no longer a routine punishment for the crimes for which it is made available, it is hardly surprising that juries have been increasingly meticulous in their imposition of the penalty. But to assume from the mere fact of relative infrequency that only a random assortment of pariahs are sentenced to death, is to cast grave doubt on the basic integrity of our jury system.

It would, of course, be unrealistic to assume that juries have been perfectly consistent in choosing the cases where the death penalty is to be imposed, for no human institution performs with perfect consistency. There are doubtless prisoners on death row who would not be there had they been tried before a different jury or in a different State. In this sense their fate has been controlled by a fortuitous circumstance. However, this element of fortuity does not stand as an indictment either of the general functioning of juries in capital cases or of the integrity of jury decisions in individual cases. There is no empirical basis for concluding that juries have generally failed to discharge in good faith the responsibility of choosing between life and death in individual cases according to the dictates of community values. For, if selective imposition evidences a rejection of capital punishment in those cases where it is not imposed, it surely evidences a correlative affirmation of the penalty in those cases where it is imposed.

The Eighth Amendment was included in the Bill of Rights to guard against the use of torturous and inhuman punishments, not those of limited efficacy. There is no authority suggesting that the Eighth Amendment was intended to purge the law of its retributive elements, and the Court has consistently assumed that retribution is a legitimate dimension of the punishment of crimes. It would be reading a great deal into the Eighth Amendment to hold that the punishments authorized by legislatures cannot constitutionally reflect a retributive purpose.

The less esoteric but no less controversial question is whether the death penalty acts as a superior deterrent. Those favoring abolition find no evidence that it does. Those favoring retention start from the intuitive notion that capital punishment should act as the most effective deterrent and note that there is no convincing evidence that it does not. Escape from this empirical stalemate is sought by placing the burden of proof on the States and concluding that they have failed to demonstrate that capital punishment is a more effective deterrent than life imprisonment. Numerous justifications have been advanced for shifting the burden, and they are not without their rhetorical appeal. However, these arguments are not descended from established constitutional principles, but are born of the urge to bypass an unresolved factual question. Comparative deterrence is not a matter that lends itself to precise measurement; to shift the burden to the States is to provide an illusory solution to an enormously complex problem. If it were proper to put the States to the test of demonstrating the deterrent value of capital punishment, we could just as well ask them to prove the need for life imprisonment or any other punishment. In fact, there are some who go so far as to challenge the notion that any punishments deter crime. If the States are unable to adduce convincing proof rebutting such assertions, does it then follow that all punishments are suspect as being "cruel and unusual" within the meaning of the Constitution? On the contrary, I submit that the questions raised by the necessity approach are beyond the pale of judicial inquiry under the Eighth Amendment.

Since there is no majority of the Court on the ultimate issue presented in these cases, the future of capital punishment in this country has been left in an uncertain limbo. Rather than providing a final and unambiguous answer on the basic constitutional question, the collective impact of the majority's ruling is to demand an undetermined measure of change from the various state legislatures and the Congress. While I cannot endorse the process of decisionmaking that has yielded today's result and the restraints that that result imposes on legislative action, I am not altogether displeased that legislative bodies have been given the opportunity, and indeed unavoidable responsibility, to make a thorough re-evaluation of the entire subject of capital punishment. If today's opinions demonstrate nothing else, they starkly show that this is an area where legislatures can act far more effectively than courts.

The world-wide trend toward limiting the use of capital punishment, a phenomenon to which we have been urged to give great weight, hardly points the way to a judicial solution in this country under a written Constitution. Rather, the change has generally come about through legislative action, often on a trial basis and with the retention of the penalty for certain limited classes of crimes. Virtually nowhere has change been wrought by so crude a tool as the Eighth Amendment. The complete and unconditional abolition of capital punishment in this country by judicial fiat would have undermined the careful progress of the legislative trend and foreclosed further inquiry on many as yet unanswered questions in this area.

Quite apart from the limitations of the Eighth Amendment itself, the preference for legislative action is justified by the inability of the courts to participate in the debate at the level where the controversy is focused. The case against capital punishment is not the product of legal dialectic, but rests primarily on factual claims, the truth of which cannot be tested by conventional judicial processes. Legislatures will have the opportunity to make a more penetrating study of these claims with the familiar and effective tools available to them as they are not to us.

**Justice Blackmun:** Cases such as these provide for me an excruciating agony of the spirit. I yield to no one in the depth of my distaste, antipathy, and, indeed, abhorrence, for the death penalty, with all its aspects of physical distress and fear and of moral judgment exercised by finite minds. That distaste is buttressed by a belief that capital punishment serves no useful purpose that can be demonstrated. For me, it violates childhood's training and life's experiences, and is not compatible with the philosophical convictions I have been able to develop. It is antagonistic to any sense of "reverence for life." Were I a legislator, I would vote against the death penalty for the policy reasons argued by counsel and expressed and adopted in the several opinions filed by the Justices who vote to reverse these judgments.

My problem, however, is the suddenness of the Court's perception of progress in the human attitude since decisions of only a short while ago. To reverse the judgments in these cases is, of course, the easy choice. It is easier to strike the balance in favor of life and against death. It is comforting to relax in the thoughts—perhaps the rationalizations—that this is the compassionate decision for a maturing society; that this is the moral and the "right" thing to do; that thereby we convince ourselves that we are moving down the road toward human decency; that we value life even though that life has taken another or others or has grievously scarred another or others and their families; and that we are less barbaric than we were.

This, for me, is good argument, and it makes some sense. But it is good argument and it makes sense only in a legislative and executive way and not as a judicial expedient. As I have said above, were I a legislator, I would do all I could to sponsor and to vote for legislation abolishing the death penalty. And were I the chief executive of a sovereign State, I would be sorely tempted to exercise executive clemency. There—on the Legislative Branch of the State or Federal Government, and secondarily, on the Executive Branch—is where the authority and responsibility for this kind of action lies. The authority should not be taken over by the judiciary in the modern guise of an Eighth Amendment issue.

I do not sit on these cases, however, as a legislator, responsive, at least in part, to the will of constituents. Our task here, as must so frequently be emphasized and re-emphasized, is to pass upon the constitutionality of legislation that has been enacted and that is challenged. This is the sole task for judges. We should not allow our personal preferences as to the wisdom of legislative and congressional action, or our distaste for such action, to guide our judicial decision in cases such as these. The temptations to cross that policy line are very great. In fact, as today's decision reveals, they are almost irresistible.

It is impossible for me to believe that the many lawyer-members of the House and Senate—including, I might add, outstanding leaders and prominent candidates for higher office—were callously unaware and insensitive of constitutional overtones in legislation of this type. The answer, of course, is that these elected representatives of the people—far more conscious of the temper of the times, of the maturing of society, and of the contemporary demands for man's dignity, than are we who sit cloistered on this Court—took it as settled that the death penalty then, as it always had been, was not in itself unconstitutional.

It is not without interest, also, to note the misery the Defendants' crimes occasioned to the victims, to the families of the victims, and to the communities where the offenses took place. There is risk, of course, in a comment such as this, for it opens one to the charge of emphasizing the retributive. Nevertheless, these cases are here because offenses to innocent victims were perpetrated. This fact, and the terror that occasioned it, and the fear that stalks the streets of many of our cities today perhaps deserve not to be entirely overlooked. Let us hope that, with the

Court's decision, the terror imposed will be forgotten by those upon whom it was visited, and that our society will reap the hoped-for benefits of magnanimity.

Although personally I may rejoice at the Court's result, I find it difficult to accept or to justify as a matter of history, of law, or of constitutional pronouncement. I fear the Court has overstepped. It has sought and has achieved an end.

**Justice Powell:** Whatever uncertainties may hereafter surface, several of the consequences of today's decision are unmistakably clear. The Court's judgment removes the death sentences previously imposed on some 600 persons awaiting punishment in state and federal prisons throughout the country. At least for the present, it also bars the States and the Federal Government from seeking sentences of death for defendants awaiting trial on charges for which capital punishment was heretofore a potential alternative. Less measurable, but certainly of no less significance, is the shattering effect this collection of views has on the root principles of *stare decisis*, federalism, judicial restraint and—most importantly—separation of powers.

Perhaps enough has been said to demonstrate the unswerving position that this Court has taken in opinions spanning the last hundred years. On virtually every occasion that any opinion has touched on the question of the constitutionality of the death penalty, it has been asserted affirmatively, or tacitly assumed, that the Constitution does not prohibit the penalty. No Justice of the Court, until today, has dissented from this consistent reading of the Constitution. *Stare decisis*, if it is a doctrine founded on principle, surely applies where there exists a long line of cases endorsing or necessarily assuming the validity of a particular matter of constitutional interpretation. While these oft-repeated expressions of unchallenged belief in the constitutionality of capital punishment may not justify a summary disposition of the constitutional question before us, they are views expressed and joined in over the years by no less than 29 Justices of this Court and therefore merit the greatest respect. Those who now resolve to set those views aside indeed have a heavy burden.

The prior opinions of this Court point with great clarity to reasons why those of us who sit on this Court at a particular time should act with restraint before assuming, contrary to a century of precedent, that we now know the answer for all time to come. First, where as here, the language of the applicable provision provides great leeway and where the underlying social policies are felt to be of vital importance, the temptation to read personal preference into the Constitution is understandably great. It is too easy to propound our subjective standards of wise policy under the rubric of more or less universally held standards of decency.

The second consideration dictating judicial self-restraint arises from a proper recognition of the respective roles of the legislative and judicial branches. The designation of punishments for crimes is a matter peculiarly within the sphere of the state and federal legislative bodies. When asked to encroach on the legislative prerogative we are well counseled to proceed with the utmost reticence.

Although determining the range of available punishments for a particular crime is a legislative function, the very presence of the Cruel and Unusual Punishments Clause within the Bill of Rights requires, in the context of a specific case, that courts decide whether particular acts of the Congress offend that Amendment. The Due Process Clause of the Fourteenth Amendment imposes on the judiciary a similar obligation to scrutinize state legislation. But the proper exercise of that constitutional obligation in the cases before us today must be founded on a full recognition of the several considerations set forth above—the affirmative references to capital punishment in the Constitution, the prevailing precedents of this Court, the limitations on the exercise of our power imposed by tested principles of judicial self-restraint, and the duty to avoid encroachment on the powers conferred upon state and federal legislatures. In the face of these considerations, only the most conclusive of objective demonstrations could warrant this Court in holding capital punishment per se unconstitutional. The burden of seeking so sweeping a decision against such formidable obstacles is almost insuperable. Viewed from this perspective, as I believe it must be, the case against the death penalty falls far short.

Members of this Court know, from the petitions and appeals that come before us regularly, that brutish and revolting murders continue to occur with disquieting frequency. Indeed, murders are so commonplace in our society that only the most sensational receive significant and sustained publicity. It could hardly be suggested that in any of these highly publicized murder cases—the several senseless assassinations or the too numerous shocking multiple murders that have stained this country's recent history—the public has exhibited any signs of "revulsion" at the thought of executing the convicted murderers. The public outcry, as we all know, has been quite to the contrary. Furthermore, there is little reason to suspect that the public's reaction would differ significantly in response to other less publicized murders. It is certainly arguable that many such murders, because of their senselessness or barbarousness, would evoke a public demand for the death penalty rather than a public rejection of that alternative. Nor is there any rational basis for arguing that the public reaction to any of these crimes would be muted if the murderer were "rich and powerful." The demand for the ultimate sanction might well be greater, as a wealthy killer is hardly a sympathetic figure. While there might be specific cases in which capital punishment would be regarded as excessive and shocking to the conscience of the community, it can hardly be argued that the public's dissatisfaction with the penalty in particular cases would translate into a demand for absolute abolition.

Much is made of the undeniable fact that the death penalty has a greater impact on the lower economic strata of society, which include a relatively higher percentage of persons of minority racial and ethnic group backgrounds. The argument drawn from this fact is two-pronged. The two contentions seem to require contradictory assumptions regarding the public's moral attitude toward capital punishment. The apathy argument is predicated on the assumption that the penalty is used against the less influential elements of society, that the public is fully aware of this, and that it tolerates use of capital punishment only because of a callous indifference to the offenders who are sentenced. The ignorance argument, on the other hand, rests on the contrary assumption that the public does not know against whom the penalty is enforced and that if the public were educated to this fact it would find the punishment intolerable. Neither assumption can claim to be an entirely accurate portrayal of public attitude; for some acceptance of capital punishment might be a consequence of hardened apathy based on the knowledge of infrequent and uneven application, while for others acceptance may grow only out of ignorance.

Certainly the claim is justified that this criminal sanction falls more heavily on the relatively impoverished and underprivileged elements of society. The "have-nots" in every society always have been subject to greater pressure to commit crimes and to fewer constraints than their more affluent fellow citizens. This is, indeed, a tragic byproduct of social and economic deprivation, but it is not an argument of constitutional proportions under the Eighth or Fourteenth Amendment. The same discriminatory impact argument could be made with equal force and logic with respect to those sentenced to prison terms. The Due Process Clause admits of no distinction between the deprivation of "life" and the deprivation of "liberty." If discriminatory impact renders capital punishment cruel and unusual, it likewise renders invalid most of the prescribed penalties for crimes of violence. The root causes of the higher incidence of criminal penalties on "minorities and the poor" will not be cured by abolishing the system of penalties. Nor, indeed, could any society have a viable system of criminal justice if sanctions were abolished or ameliorated because most of those who commit crimes happen to be underprivileged. The basic problem results not from the penalties imposed for criminal conduct but from social and economic factors that have plagued humanity since the beginning of recorded history, frustrating all efforts to create in any country at any time the perfect society in which there are no "poor," no "minorities" and no "underprivileged." The causes underlying this problem are unrelated to the constitutional issue before the Court.

I now return to the overriding question in these cases: whether this Court, acting in conformity with the Constitution, can justify its judgment to abolish capital punishment as heretofore known in this country. It is important to keep in focus the enormity of the step undertaken by the Court today. Not only does it invalidate hundreds of state and federal laws, it deprives those jurisdictions of the power to legislate with respect to capital punishment in the future, except in a manner consistent with the cloudily outlined views of those Justices who do not purport to undertake total abolition. Nothing short of an amendment to the United States Constitution can reverse the Court's judgments. Meanwhile, all flexibility is foreclosed. The normal democratic process, as well as the opportunities for the several States to respond to the will of their people expressed through ballot referenda is now shut off. The sobering disadvantage of constitutional adjudication of this magnitude is the universality and permanence of the judgment. The enduring merit of legislative action is its responsiveness to the democratic process, and to revision and change: mistaken judgments may be corrected and refinements perfected.

With deference and respect for the views of the Justices who differ, it seems to me that all the studies—both in this country and elsewhere—suggest that, as a matter of policy and precedent, this is a classic case for the exercise of our oft-announced allegiance to judicial restraint. I know of no case in which greater gravity and delicacy have attached to the duty that this Court is called on to perform whenever legislation—state or federal—is challenged on constitutional grounds. It seems to me that the sweeping judicial action undertaken today reflects a basic lack of faith and confidence in the democratic process. Many may regret, as I do, the failure of some legislative bodies to address the capital punishment issue with greater frankness or effectiveness. Many might decry their failure either to abolish the penalty entirely or selectively, or to establish standards for its enforcement. But impatience with the slowness, and even the unresponsiveness, of legislatures is no justification for judicial intrusion upon their historic powers.

**Justice Rehnquist:** The Court's judgments today strike down a penalty that our Nation's legislators have thought necessary since our country was founded. Whatever its precise rationale, today's holding necessarily brings into sharp relief the fundamental question of the role of judicial review in a democratic society. How can government by the elected representatives of the people co-exist with the power of the federal judiciary, whose members are constitutionally insulated from responsiveness to the popular will, to declare invalid laws duly enacted by the popular branches of government?

The answer, of course, is found in Hamilton's *Federalist Paper No. 78* and in Chief Justice Marshall's classic opinion in *Marbury v. Madison (1803)*. An oft-told story since then, it bears summarization once more. Sovereignty resides ultimately in the people as a whole and, by adopting through their States a written Constitution for the Nation and subsequently adding amendments to that instrument, they have both granted certain powers to the National Government, and denied other powers to the National and the State Governments. Courts are exercising no more than the judicial function conferred upon them by Article III of the Constitution when they assess, in a case before them, whether or not a particular legislative enactment is within the authority granted by the Constitution to the enacting body, and whether it runs afoul of some limitation placed by the Constitution on the authority of that body. For the theory is that the people themselves have spoken in the Constitution, and therefore its commands are superior to the commands of the legislature, which is merely an agent of the people.

The courts in cases properly before them have been entrusted under the Constitution with the last word, short of constitutional amendment, as to whether a law passed by the legislature conforms to the Constitution. Rigorous attention to the limits of this Court's authority is likewise enjoined because of the natural desire that beguiles judges along with other human beings into imposing their own views of goodness, truth, and justice upon others. Judges differ only in that they have the power, if not the authority, to enforce their desires. This is doubtless why nearly two centuries of judicial precedent from this Court counsel the sparing use of that power. The most expansive reading of the leading constitutional cases does not remotely suggest that this Court has been granted a roving commission, either by the Founding Fathers or by the framers of the Fourteenth Amendment, to strike down laws that are based upon notions of policy or morality suddenly found unacceptable by a majority of this Court.

A separate reason for deference to the legislative judgment is the consequence of human error on the part of the judiciary with respect to the constitutional issue before it. Human error there is bound to be, judges being men and women, and men and women being what they are. But an error in mistakenly sustaining the constitutionality of a particular enactment, while wrongfully depriving the individual of a right secured to him by the Constitution, nonetheless does so by simply letting stand a duly enacted law of a democratically chosen legislative body. The error resulting from a mistaken upholding of an individual's constitutional claim against the validity of a legislative enactment is a good deal more serious. For the result in such a case is not to leave standing a law duly enacted by a representative assembly, but to impose upon the Nation the judicial fiat of a majority of a court of judges whose connection with the popular will is remote at best.

The task of judging constitutional cases imposed by Article III cannot for this reason be avoided, but it must surely be approached with the deepest humility and genuine deference to legislative judgment. Today's decision to invalidate capital punishment is, I respectfully submit, significantly lacking in those attributes. I conclude that this decision holding unconstitutional capital punishment is not an act of judgment, but rather an act of will.

If there can be said to be one dominant theme in the Constitution, perhaps more fully articulated in the *Federalist Papers* than in the instrument itself, it is the notion of checks and balances. This philosophy of the Framers is best described by one of the ablest and greatest of their number, James Madison, in *Federalist No. 51*: "In framing a government which is to be administered by men over men, the great difficulty lies in this: You must first enable the government to controul the governed; and in the next place, oblige it to controul itself."

Madison's observation applies to the Judicial Branch with at least as much force as to the Legislative and Executive Branches. While overreaching by the Legislative and Executive Branches may result in the sacrifice of individual protections that the Constitution was designed to secure against action of the State, judicial overreaching may result in sacrifice of the equally important right of the people to govern themselves.

# *Bibliography*

*[The literature on the Constitution and the Supreme Court would fill an entire library. What follows is a list of books that likely would be of interest to a reader who wants to learn more about the constitutional principles found in this volume. The books are arranged in eight broad categories: Civil Rights and Civil Liberties; Constitutional History; Constitutional Law; Constitutional Philosophy; Constitutional Politics; Supreme Court Biography; Supreme Court Cases; and Supreme Court History. Each book is listed only once, in the interest of space, so the careful reader ought to peruse the entire list. Works marked with an asterisk "\*" are likely to be more accessible to more readers.]*

## Civil Rights and Civil Liberties

George Anastaplo, The Amendments to the Constitution: A Commentary (Johns Hopkins Univ. Press 1995)

Herman Belz, Emancipation and Equal Rights: Politics and Constitutionalism in the Civil War Era (W. W. Norton & Co. 1978)

Michael L. Benedict, A Compromise of Principle: Congressional Republicans and Reconstruction 1863–1869 (W. W. Norton & Co. 1974)

Raoul Berger, Government by Judiciary: The Transformation of the Fourteenth Amendment (Harvard Univ. Press 1977)

Walter Berns, For Capital Punishment: Crime and the Morality of the Death Penalty (Basic Books 1979)

Charles L. Black, Jr., Capital Punishment: The Inevitability of Caprice and Mistake (2d ed. W. W. Norton & Co. 1981)

*Stephen L. Carter, Reflections of an Affirmative Action Baby (Basic Books 1991)

Patrick T. Conely & John P. Kaminski, eds., The Bill of Rights and the States: The Colonial and Revolutionary Origins of American Liberties (Madison House 1992)

Derek Davis, Original Intent: Chief Justice Rehnquist and the Course of American Church/State Relations (Prometheus Books 1991)

Ward E. Y. Elliott, The Rise of Guardian Democracy: The Supreme Court's Role in Voting Rights Disputes, 1845–1969 (Harvard Univ. Press 1974)

Stanley Fish, There's No Such Thing as Free Speech . . . And It's a Good Thing Too (Oxford Univ. Press 1994)

John Hope Franklin, From Slavery to Freedom: A History of Negro Americans (5th ed. Alfred A. Knopf 1980)

John Hope Franklin & Genna Rae McNeil, eds., African Americans and the Living Constitution (Smithsonian Institution Press 1995)

*Mary Ann Glendon, Rights Talk: The Impoverishment of Political Discourse (The Free Press 1991)

Kent Greenawalt, Fighting Words: Individuals, Communities, and Liberties of Speech (Princeton Univ. Press 1995)

*Learned Hand, The Bill of Rights (Harvard Univ. Press 1958)

*Eugene W. Hickock, Jr., ed., The Bill of Rights: Original Meaning and Current Understanding (Univ. Press of Virginia 1993)

Harold M. Hyman & William M. Wiecek, Equal Justice Under Law: Constitutional Development, 1835–1875 (Harper & Rowe 1982)

David Kairys, With Liberty and Justice for Some: A Critique of the Conservative Supreme Court (The New Press 1993)

*Richard Kluger, Simple Justice: The History of Brown v. Board of Education and Black America's Struggle for Equality (Alfred A. Knopf 1975)

Andrew Kull, The Color-Blind Constitution (Harvard Univ. Press 1992)

Michael J. Lacey & Knud Haakonssen, eds., A Culture of Rights: The Bill of Rights in Philosophy, Politics, and Law, 1791 and 1991 (Cambridge Univ. Press 1992)

Leonard W. Levy, Origins of the Fifth Amendment: The Right Against Self-Incrimination (MacMillan 1986)

Roald Y. Mykkeltvedt, The Nationalization of the Bill of Rights: Fourteenth Amendment Due Process and Procedural Rights (Associated Faculty Press 1983)

William E. Nelson, The Fourteenth Amendment: From Political Principle to Judicial Doctrine (Harvard Univ. Press 1988)

Robert Allen Rutland, The Birth of the Bill of Rights, 1776–1791 (Bicentennial ed. Northeastern Univ. Press 1991)

*Bernard Schwartz, The Great Rights of Mankind: A History of the American Bill of Rights (Oxford Univ. Press 1977)

Steven D. Smith, Foreordained Failure: The Quest for a Constitutional Principle of Religious Freedom (Oxford Univ. Press 1995)

Girardeau A. Spann, Race Against the Court: Supreme Court and Minorities in Contemporary America (New York Univ. Press 1993)

J. Harvie Wilkinson, III, From Brown to Bakke: The Supreme Court and School Integration: 1954–1978 (Oxford Univ. Press 1979)

*Susan Ford Wiltshire, Greece, Rome, and the Bill of Rights (Univ. of Oklahoma Press 1992)

*C. Vann Woodward, The Strange Career of Jim Crow (3d rev. ed. Oxford Univ. Press 1974)

Elizabeth H. Wolgast, Equality and the Rights of Women (Cornell Univ. Press 1980)

## Constitutional History

Bruce A. Ackerman, We the People: Foundations (Belknap Press 1991)

John Agresto, The Supreme Court and Constitutional Democracy (Cornell Univ. Press 1984)

*George Anastaplo, The Constitution of 1787: A Commentary (Johns Hopkins Univ. Press 1989)

Bernard Bailyn, The Ideological Origins of the American Revolution (Enlarged ed. Belknap Press 1992)

Joseph M. Bessette, ed., Toward a More Perfect Union—Writings of Herbert J. Storing (The AEI Press 1995)

*Catherine Drinker Bowen, Miracle at Philadelphia—The Story of the Constitutional Convention: May to September 1787 (Little, Brown & Co. 1986)

Irving Brant, The Bill of Rights: Its Origin and Meaning (Bobbs-Merrill 1965)

David P. Currie, The Constitution in the Supreme Court: The First Hundred Years, 1789–1888 (Univ. of Chicago Press 1985)

David P. Currie, The Constitution in the Supreme Court: The Second Century, 1888–1986 (Univ. of Chicago Press 1990)

S. Rufus Davis, The Federal Principle: A Journey Through Time in Quest of a Meaning (Univ. of California Press 1978)

George M. Dennison, The Dorr War: Republicanism on Trial, 1831–1861 (Univ. Press of Kentucky 1976)

*Kermit L. Hall, James W. Ely, Jr., Joel B. Grossman & William M. Wiecek, eds., The Oxford Companion to the Supreme Court of the United States (Oxford Univ. Press 1992)

*Robert H. Jackson, The Supreme Court in the American System of Government (Harvard Univ. Press 1955)

Journal of Supreme Court History, Annual Yearbook of the Supreme Court Historical Society

*Michael Kammen, A Machine That Would Go of Itself (Alfred A. Knopf 1986)

Alfred H. Kelly, Winfred A. Harbison & Herman Belz, The American Constitution: Its Origins and Development (W. W. Norton & Co. 1991)

*Ralph Ketcham, The Anti-Federalist Papers and the Constitutional Convention Debates (Mentor Books 1986)

*Leonard W. Levy, Kenneth L. Karst & Dennis J. Mahoney, eds., Encyclopedia of the American Constitution (MacMillan 1986)

Jackson Turner Main, The Anti-Federalists: Critics of the Constitution, 1781–1788 (Univ. of North Carolina Press 1961)

Drew R. McCoy, The Last of the Fathers: James Madison and the Republican Legacy (Cambridge Univ. Press 1991)

*Forrest McDonald, Novus Ordo Seclorum—The Intellectual Origins of the Constitution (Univ. Press of Kansas 1985)

Marvin Meyers, ed., The Mind of the Founder: Sources of the Political Thought of James Madison (rev. ed. Brandeis Univ. Press 1981)

Charles A. Miller, The Supreme Court and the Uses of History (Belknap Press 1969)

Edmund S. Morgan, The Birth of the Republic, 1763–1789 (3d ed. Univ. of Chicago Press 1992)

*Richard B. Morris, The Forging of the Union, 1781–89 (Harper & Row 1987)

*Richard B. Morris, Witnesses at the Creation: Hamilton, Madison, Jay, and the Constitution (Holt, Rinehart & Winston 1985)

Paul L. Murphy, The Constitution in Crisis Times, 1918–1969 (Harper & Rowe 1972)

Drew Pearson & Robert S. Allen, The Nine Old Men (Da Capo Press 1974)

*Clinton Rossiter, 1787: The Grand Convention (MacMillan 1966)

*Bernard Schwartz, A Basic History of the U.S. Supreme Court (Van Nostrand Co. 1968)

*Robert Shnayerson, The Illustrated History of the Supreme Court of the United States (Harry N. Abrams 1986)

Leonard R. Sorenson, Madison on the "General Welfare" of America (Rowman & Littlefield Publishers 1995)

Herbert J. Storing, What the Antifederalists Were For (Univ. of Chicago Press 1981)

*Alan F. Westin, ed., An Autobiography of the Supreme Court: Off-the-Bench Commentary by the Justices (Greenwood Press 1978)

*G. Edward White, The American Judicial Tradition (2d ed. Oxford Univ. Press 1988)

William M. Wiecek, The Guarantee Clause of the U.S. Constitution (Cornell Univ. Press 1972)

*William M. Wiecek, Liberty Under Law: The Supreme Court in American Life (Johns Hopkins Univ. Press 1988)

Christopher Wolfe, The Rise of Modern Judicial Review: From Constitutional Interpretation to Judge-Made Law (Basic Books 1986)

*Gordon S. Wood, The Creation of the American Republic, 1776–1787 (Univ. of North Carolina Press 1969)

## Constitutional Law

Sotirios A. Barber, On What the Constitution Means (Johns Hopkins Univ. Press 1984)

Alexander M. Bickel, The Unpublished Opinions of Mr. Justice Brandeis: The Supreme Court at Work (Univ. of Chicago Press 1967)

Charles L. Black, Jr., The People and the Court (Prentice-Hall 1960)

*Hugo L. Black, A Constitutional Faith (Alfred A. Knopf 1969)

Lee C. Bollinger, The Tolerant Society: Freedom of Speech and Extremist Speech in America (Oxford Univ. Press 1986)

*Edward S. Corwin, The Constitution and What It Means Today (Princeton Univ. Press 1947)

*Edward S. Corwin & Jack W. Peltason, Understanding the Constitution (4th ed. Holt, Rinehart & Winston 1969)

*David P. Currie, The Constitution of the United States: A Primer for the People (Univ. of Chicago Press 1988)

Thomas I. Emerson, The System of Freedom of Expression (Random House 1970)

Richard A. Epstein, Takings: Private Property and the Power of Eminent Domain (Harvard Univ. Press 1985)

Mark DeWolfe Howe, The Garden and the Wilderness: Religion and Government in American Constitutional History (Univ. of Chicago Press 1965)

Harry Kalven, Jr., A Worthy Tradition: Freedom of Speech in America (Harper & Rowe 1988)

Leonard W. Levy, Emergence of a Free Press (Oxford Univ. Press 1985)

Leonard W. Levy, The Establishment Clause: Religion and the First Amendment (2d rev. ed. Univ. of North Carolina Press 1994)

John E. Nowak & Ronald D. Rotunda, Constitutional Law (5th ed. West Publishing Co. 1995)

Martin H. Redish, Freedom of Expression: A Critical Analysis (The Michie Co. 1984)

Winnifred Fallers Sullivan, Paying the Words Extra: Religious Discourse in the Supreme Court of the United States (Harvard Univ. Press 1994)

The Supreme Court Term, Harvard Law Review (November annual issue)

Laurence H. Tribe, American Constitutional Law (2d ed. Foundation Press 1988)

## Constitutional Philosophy

*Mortimer J. Adler, We Hold These Truths—Understanding the Ideas and Ideals of the Constitution (MacMillan 1987)

Hadley Arkes, Beyond the Constitution (Princeton Univ. Press 1990)

Richard Beeman, Stephen Botein & Edward C. Carter, II, eds., Beyond Confederation: Origins of the Constitution and American National Identity (Univ. of North Carolina Press 1987)

Samuel H. Beer, To Make a Nation: The Rediscovery of American Federalism (Harvard Univ. Press 1993)

*Alexander M. Bickel, The Supreme Court and the Idea of Progress (Yale Univ. Press 1978)

Philip Bobbitt, Constitutional Interpretation (Basil Blackwell 1991)

*Edward S. Corwin, The Twilight of the Supreme Court: A History of Our Constitutional Theory (Archon Books 1970)

Ronald Dworkin, Taking Rights Seriously (Harvard Univ. Press 1977)

*John Hart Ely, Democracy and Distrust: A Theory of Judicial Review (Harvard Univ. Press 1980)

John H. Garvey & T. Alexander Aleinikoff, Modern Constitutional Theory: A Reader (3d ed. West Publishing Co. 1994)

Michael J. Gerhardt & Thomas D. Rowe, Jr., Constitutional Theory: Arguments and Perspectives (The Michie Co. 1993)

Joseph Goldstein, The Intelligible Constitution (Oxford Univ. Press 1992)

William F. Harris, II, The Interpretable Constitution (Johns Hopkins Univ. Press 1993)

Samuel J. Konefsky, The Legacy of Holmes and Brandeis: A Study in the Influence of Ideas (MacMillan 1956)

Ralph Lerner, The Thinking Revolutionary: Principle and Practice in the New Republic (Cornell Univ. Press 1987)

Sanford Levinson, Constitutional Faith (Princeton Univ. Press 1988)

Leonard W. Levy, Original Intent and the Framer's Constitution (MacMillan 1988)

Jules Lobel, ed., A Less Than Perfect Union: Alternative Perspectives on the U.S. Constitution (Monthly Review Press 1988)

Louis Lusky, By What Right?: A Commentary on the Supreme Court's Power to Revise the Constitution (The Michie Co. 1975)

*Burke Marshall, ed., A Workable Government?: The Constitution After 200 Years (W. W. Norton & Co. 1987)

Alpheus T. Mason & William M. Beaney, The Supreme Court in a Free Society (Prentice-Hall 1959)

Arthur S. Miller, Politics, Democracy, and the Supreme Court: Essays on the Frontier of Constitutional Theory (Greenwood Press 1985)

Michael J. Perry, The Constitution in the Courts: Law or Politics? (Oxford Univ. Press 1994)

Thomas Reed Powell, Vagaries and Varieties in Constitutional Interpretation (AMS Press 1967)

*Clinton Rossiter, ed., The Federalist Papers: Alexander Hamilton, James Madison, John Jay (Mentor Books 1961)

*Eugene V. Rostow, The Sovereign Prerogative: The Supreme Court and the Quest for Law (Yale Univ. Press 1962)

Frederick Schauer, Free Speech: A Philosophical Inquiry (Cambridge Univ. Press 1982)

Steven H. Shiffrin, The First Amendment, Democracy, and Romance (Harvard Univ. Press 1990)

Cass R. Sunstein, The Partial Constitution (Harvard Univ. Press 1993)

*Laurence H. Tribe, Constitutional Choices (Harvard Univ. Press 1985)

Laurence H. Tribe & Michael C. Dorf, On Reading the Constitution (Harvard Univ. Press 1991)

Mark Tushnet, Red, White and Blue: A Critical Analysis of Constitutional Law (Harvard Univ. Press 1988)

Morton White, Philosophy, The Federalist, and the Constitution (Oxford Univ. Press 1987)

*Woodrow Wilson, Constitutional Government in the United States (Columbia Univ. Press (1908)

## Constitutional Politics

*Henry J. Abraham, Justices and Presidents: A Political History of Appointments to the Supreme Court (3d ed. Oxford Univ. Press 1992)

Henry J. Abraham, The Judiciary: The Supreme Court in the Governmental Process (9th ed. Brown & Benchmark 1994)

Raoul Berger, Congress v. The Supreme Court (Harvard Univ. Press 1969)

## BIBLIOGRAPHY

*Richard B. Bernstein & Jerome Agel, Amending America: If We Love America So Much, Why Do We Keep Trying to Change It? (Random House 1993)

Joseph M. Bessette & Jeffrey Tulis, eds., The Presidency in the Constitutional Order (Louisiana State Univ. Press 1981)

*Alexander M. Bickel, The Least Dangerous Branch: The Supreme Court at the Bare of Politics (2d ed. Yale Univ. Press 1986)

Susan Low Bloch & Thomas G. Krattenmaker, eds., Supreme Court Politics: The Institution and Its Procedures (West Publishing Co. 1994)

Allan Bloom, ed., Confronting the Constitution (American Enterprise Institute 1990)

*Robert H. Bork, The Tempting of America: The Political Seduction of the Law (The Free Press 1990)

Ethan Bronner, Battle for Justice: How the Bork Nomination Shook America (W. W. Norton & Co. 1989)

*Robert A. Burt, The Constitution in Conflict (Harvard Univ. Press 1992)

*Mark M. Cannon & David M. O'Brien, eds., Views From the Bench: The Judiciary and Constitutional Politics (Chatham House 1985)

*Lincoln Caplan, The Tenth Justice: The Solicitor General and the Rule of Law (Alfred A. Knopf 1987)

Jesse H. Choper, Judicial Review and the National Political Process: A Functional Reconsideration of the Role of the Supreme Court (Univ. of Chicago Press 1980)

Archibald Cox, The Role of the Supreme Court in American Government (Oxford Univ. Press 1976)

David J. Danelski, A Supreme Court Justice is Appointed (Random House 1964)

William Eaton, Who Killed the Constitution?—The Judges v. The Law (Regnery Gateway 1988)

Sam J. Ervin, Jr. & Ramsey Clark, The Role of the Supreme Court: Policymaker or Adjudicator? (American Enterprise Institute 1970)

Louis Fisher, Constitutional Conflicts Between Congress and the President (3d ed. Univ. Press of Kansas 1991)

*Louis Fisher, Constitutional Dialogues: Interpretation and Political Process (Princeton Univ. Press 1988)

*Fred W. Friendly & Martha J. H. Elliott, The Constitution: That Delicate Balance (Random House 1984)

William Gangi, Saving the Constitution from the Courts (Univ. of Oklahoma Press 1995)

Louis Henkin, Constitutionalism, Democracy, and Foreign Affairs (Columbia Univ. Press 1990)

Robert H. Jackson, The Struggle for Judicial Supremacy: A Study of a Crisis in American Power Politics (Caravelle ed. Vintage Books 1962)

Harold H. Koh, The National Security Constitution: Sharing Power After the Iran-Contra Affair (Yale Univ. Press 1990)

# BIBLIOGRAPHY

Samuel Krislov, The Supreme Court in the Political Process (MacMillan 1965)

Philip B. Kurland, Politics, the Constitution and the Warren Court (Univ. of Chicago Press 1970)

Philip B. Kurland, Watergate and the Constitution (Univ. of Chicago Press 1978)

Stanley I. Kutler, Judicial Power and Reconstruction Politics (Univ. of Chicago Press 1968)

Sanford Levinson, ed., Responding to Imperfection: The Theory and Practice of Constitutional Amendment (Princeton Univ. Press 1995)

Robert A. Licht, ed., Is the Supreme Court the Gaurdian of the Constituion? (The AEI Press 1993)

John F. Manley & Kenneth M. Dolbeare, eds., The Case Against the Constitution: From the Antifederalists to the Present (M.E. Sharpe 1987)

*Robert G. McCloskey, The American Supreme Court (Sanford Levinson rev. 2d ed. Univ. of Chicago Press 1994)

*Forrest McDonald, The American Presidency: An Intellectual History (Univ. Press of Kansas 1994)

Catherine A. MacKinnon, Toward a Feminist Theory of the State (Harvard Univ. Press 1989)

Walter F. Murphy, Congress and the Court: A Case Study in the American Political Process (Univ. of Chicago Press 1962)

Richard E. Neustadt, Presidential Power: The Politics of Leadership (John Wiley & Sons 1960)

Bertell Ollman & Johanthan Birnbaum, eds., The United States Constitution: 200 Years of Anti-Federalist, Abolitionist, Feminist, Muckraking, Progressive, and Especially Socialist Criticism (New York Univ. Press 1990)

*Richard D. Parker, "Here, the People Rule"—A Constitutional Populist Manifesto (Harvard Univ. Press 1994)

*C. Herman Pritchett, The American Constitution (3d ed. McGraw-Hill 1977)

C. Herman Pritchett, Congress versus the Supreme Court 1957–1960 (Univ. of Minnesota 1961)

C. Herman Pritchett, Constitutional Law of the Federal System (Prentice-Hall 1984)

Merlo John Pusey, The Supreme Court Crisis (Da Capo Press 1973)

David G. Savage, Turning Right: The Making of the Rehnquist Supreme Court (John Wiley & Sons 1993)

John R. Schmidhauser & Larry L. Berg, The Supreme Court and the Congress: Conflict and Interaction, 1945–1968 (The Free Press 1972)

Robert J. Steamer, The Supreme Court in Crisis: A History of Conflict (Univ. of Massachusetts Press 1971)

Harry P. Stumpf, The Politics of State Courts (Longman 1992)

Clinton L. Rossiter, Constitutional Dictatorship: Crisis Government in Modern Democracies (Princeton Univ. Press 1948)

M. J. C. Vile, Constitutionalism and the Separation of Powers (Clarendon Press 1967)

Charles Warren, Congress, the Constitution, and the Supreme Court (Johnson Reprint Corp. 1968)

Elder Witt, A Different Justice: Reagan and the Supreme Court (Cong. Quarterly 1986)

## Supreme Court Biography

Leonard Baker, Brandeis and Frankfurter: A Dual Biography (Harper & Rowe 1984)

*Leonard Baker, John Marshall: A Life in Law (Collier MacMillan 1974)

*Liva Baker, The Justice from Beacon Hill: The Life and Times of Oliver Wendell Holmes (Harper Collins 1991)

Howard Ball & Phillip J. Cooper, Of Power and Right: Hugo Black, William O. Douglas, and America's Constitutional Revolution (Oxford Univ. Press 1992)

Albert J. Beveridge, The Life of John Marshall (4 vols. Houghton-Mifflin Co. 1916–19)

Robert A. Burt, Two Jewish Justices: Outcasts in the Promised Land (Univ. of California Press 1988)

*Jesse H. Choper, ed., The Supreme Court and Its Justices (ABA 1987)

*Clare Cushman, ed., The Supreme Court Justices: Illustrated Biographies, 1789–1993 (Cong. Quarterly 1993)

Sue Davis, Justice Rehnquist and the Constitution (Princeton Univ. Press 1989)

*William O. Douglas, The Court Years, 1939–75 (Random House 1980)

*Gerald T. Dunne, Hugo Black and the Judicial Revolution (Simon & Schuster 1977)

Kim I. Eisler, A Justice for All: William J. Brennan, Jr., and the Decisions that Transformed America (Simon & Schuster 1993)

*Felix Frankfurter, Mr. Justice Holmes and the Supreme Court (Belknap Press 1961)

Leon Friedman, ed., The Justices of the United States Supreme Court, Their Lives and Major Opinions: Volume V, The Burger Court 1969–1978 (Chelsea House 1978)

Roger Goldman, Justice William J. Brennan, Jr.: Freedom First (Carroll & Graf 1994)

*John C. Jeffries, Jr., Justice Lewis F. Powell, Jr. and the Era of Judicial Balance (Charles Scribner's Sons 1994)

Charles M. Lamb & Stephen C. Halpern, eds., The Burger Court: Political and Judicial Profiles (Univ. of Illinois Press 1991)

Joseph P. Lash, From the Diaries of Felix Frankfurter (W. W. Norton & Co. 1975)

Alpheus T. Mason, Harlan Fiske Stone: Pillar of the Law (Archon Books 1968)

Alpheus T. Mason, William Howard Taft: Chief Justice (Simon & Schuster 1964)

Bruce Allen Murphy, The Brandeis/Frankfurter Connection (Anchor Books 1982)

*Bruce Allen Murphy, Fortas: The Rise and Ruin of a Supreme Court Justice (William Morrow & Co. 1988)

R. Kent Newmyer, Supreme Court Justice Joseph Story: Statesman of the Old Republic (Univ. of North Carolina Press 1985)

*Sheldon M. Novick, Honorable Justice: The Life of Oliver Wendell Holmes (Little, Brown & Co. 1989)

Lewis J. Paper, Brandeis (Prentice-Hall 1983)

William D. Pederson & Norman W. Provizer, eds., Great Justices of the U.S. Supreme Court (Peter Lang 1994)

Richard A. Posner, Cardozo: A Study in Reputation (Univ. of Chicago Press 1990)

Richard A. Posner, ed., The Essential Holmes—Selections from Letters, Speeches, Judicial Opinions, and Other Writings of Oliver Wendell Holmes, Jr. (Univ. of Chicago Press 1992)

*Carl T. Rowan, Dream Makers, Dream Breakers: The World of Justice Thurgood Marshall (Little, Brown & Co. 1993)

*Bernard Schwartz, Super Chief: Earl Warren and His Supreme Court—A Judicial Biography (New York Univ. Press 1983)

Philippa Strum, Louis D. Brandeis: Justice for the People (Harvard Univ. Press 1984)

Kenneth Bernard Umbreit, Our Eleven Chief Justices: A History of the Supreme Court in Terms of Their Personalities (Kennikat Press 1969)

Melvin I. Urofsky, The Supreme Court Justices: A Biographical Dictionary (Garland Publishing 1994)

*G. Edward White, Earl Warren: A Public Life (Oxford Univ. Press 1982)

*G. Edward White, Justice Oliver Wendell Holmes: Law and the Inner Self (Oxford Univ. Press 1993)

*Tinsley E. Yarbrough, John Marshall Harlan: Great Dissenter of the Warren Court (Oxford Univ. Press 1992)

*Tinsley E. Yarbrough, Judicial Enigma: The First Justice Harlan (Oxford Univ. Press 1995)

## Supreme Court Cases

Theodore L. Becker, ed., The Impact of Supreme Court Decisions: Empirical Studies (Oxford Univ. Press 1969)

Barbara Hinkson Craig, Chadha: The Story of an Epic Constitutional Struggle (Oxford Univ. Press 1988)

Don E. Fehrenbacher, The Dred Scott Case: Its Significance in American Law and Politics (Oxford Univ. Press 1978)

*John A. Garraty, ed., Quarrels That Have Shaped the Constitution (rev. ed. Harper & Row 1987)

David J. Garrow, Liberty and Sexuality: The Right to Privacy and the Making of Roe v. Wade (MacMillan 1994)

*Peter H. Irons, The Courage of Their Convictions (The Free Press 1988)

*Peter H. Irons, Justice at War (Oxford Univ. Press 1983)

*Peter H. Irons & Stephanie Guitton, eds., May It Please the Court: The Most Significant Oral Arguments Made Before the Supreme Court Since 1955 (The New Press 1993)

*Max Lerner, Nine Scorpions in a Bottle: Great Judges and Cases of the Supreme Court (Arcade 1994)

*Anthony Lewis, Gideon's Trumpet (Random House 1964)

*Anthony Lewis, Make No Law: The Sullivan Case and the First Amendment (Random House 1991)

David R. Manwaring, Render Unto Caesar: The Flag-Salute Controversy (Univ. of Chicago Press 1962)

Maeva Marcus, Truman and the Steel Seizure Case: The Limits of Presidential Power (Columbia Univ. Press 1977)

Michael Meltsner, Cruel and Unusual: The Supreme Court and Capital Punishment (Random House 1973)

Walter F. Murphy, Wiretapping on Trial: A Case Study in the Judicial Process (Random House 1965)

Preview of United States Supreme Court Cases, A Publication of the American Bar Association's Division for Public Education (Annual Periodical)

Doris Marie Provine, Case Selection in the United States Supreme Court (Univ. of Chicago Press 1980)

Gerald N. Rosenberg, The Hollow Hope: Can Courts Bring About Social Change (Univ. of Chicago Press 1991)

*Rodney A. Smolla, Jerry Falwell v. Larry Flynt: The First Amendment on Trial (St. Martin's Press 1988)

*Rodney A. Smolla, A Year in the Life of the Supreme Court (Duke Univ. Press 1995)

Harold J. Spaeth, Supreme Court Policy Making: Explanation and Prediction (W. H. Freeman & Co. 1979)

Laurence H. Tribe, Abortion: The Clash of Absolutes (W. W. Norton & Co. 1990)

Stephen L. Wasby, The Impact of the United States Supreme Court: Some Perspectives (Dorsey Press 1970)

Sarah Weddington, A Question of Choice (Putnam's Sons 1992)

Alan F. Westin, The Anatomy of a Constitutional Law Case: Youngstown Sheet and Tube Co. v. Sawyer: The Steel Seizure Decision (Columbia Univ. Press 1990)

## Supreme Court History

Leonard Baker, Back to Back: The Duel Between F.D.R. and the Supreme Court (MacMillan 1967)

Lawrence Baum, The Supreme Court (5th ed. Cong. Qtrly. 1995)

Charles A. Beard, An Economic Interpretation of the Constitution of the United States (MacMillan 1913)

Alexander M. Bickel & Benno C. Schmidt, Jr., The Judiciary and the Responsible Government 1910–1921 (MacMillan 1984)

Vincent Blasi, ed., The Burger Court: The Counter-Revolution That Wasn't (Yale Univ. Press 1983)

John Brigham, The Cult of the Court (Temple Univ. Press 1987)

*Warren E. Burger, It Is So Ordered: A Constitution Unfolds (William Morrow & Co. 1995)

William R. Casto, The Supreme Court in the Early Republic: The Chief Justiceships of John Jay and Oliver Ellsworth (Univ. of South Carolina Press 1995)

James W. Ely, Jr., The Chief Justiceship of Melville W. Fuller, 1888–1910 (Univ. of South Carolina Press 1995)

Lee Epstein, Jeffrey A. Segal, Harold J. Spaeth & Thomas G. Walker, The Supreme Court Compendium: Data, Decisions, and Developments (Cong. Quarterly 1994)

Charles Fairman, Five Justices and the Electoral Commission of 1877 (MacMillan 1988)

Charles Fairman, Part I: Reconstruction and Reunion 1864–88 (MacMillan 1971)

Charles Fairman, Part II: Reconstruction and Reunion 1864–88 (MacMillan 1987)

Owen M. Fiss, Troubled Beginnings of the Modern State, 1888–1910 (MacMillan 1993)

*John P. Frank, Marble Palace: The Supreme Court in American Life (Alfred A. Knopf 1958)

Felix Frankfurter & James M. Landis, The Business of the Supreme Court: A Study in the Federal Judicial System (Johnson Reprint Corp. 1972)

Richard D. Friedman, The Crucible of the Modern Constitution, 1930–1941 (MacMillan 1995)

Julius Goebel, Jr., Antecedents and Beginnings to 1801 (MacMillan 1971)

Arthur J. Goldberg, Equal Justice: The Warren Era of the Supreme Court (Northwestern Univ. Press 1971)

George L. Haskins & Herbert A. Johnson, Foundations of Power: John Marshall, 1801–1815 (MacMillan 1981)

Charles Evans Hughes, The Supreme Court of the United States: Its Foundation, Methods and Achievements: An Interpretation (Columbia Univ. Press 1928)

Peter H. Irons, Brennan vs. Rehnquist: The Battle for the Constitution (Alfred A. Knopf 1994)

William E. Leuchtenburg, The Supreme Court Reborn: The Constitutional Revolution in the Age of Roosevelt (Oxford Univ. Press 1995)

Alpheus T. Mason, The Supreme Court from Taft to Warren (Louisiana State Univ. Press 1958)

## BIBLIOGRAPHY

*Arthur Selwyn Miller, The Supreme Court: Myth and Reality (Greenwood Press 1978)

*David M. O'Brien, Storm Center: The Supreme Court in American Politics (3d ed. W. W. Norton & Co. 1993)

*Leo Pfeffer, This Honorable Court: A History of the United States Supreme Court (Beacon Press 1965)

Robert C. Post, Constitutional Rights and the Regulatory State, 1921–1930 (MacMillan 1995)

C. Herman Pritchett, The Roosevelt Court: A Study in Judicial Politics and Values 1937–1947 (MacMillan 1948)

*William H. Rehnquist, The Supreme Court: How It Was, How It Is (William Morrow & Co. 1987)

*Fred Rodell, Nine Men: A Political History of the Supreme Court of the United States from 1790 to 1955 (Random House 1955)

John D. Sprague, Voting Patterns of the United States Supreme Court: Cases in Federalism, 1889–1959 (Bobbs-Merrill Co. 1968)

Carl B. Swisher, The Taney Period 1836–64 (MacMillan 1974)

*Laurence H. Tribe, God Save This Honorable Court: How the Choice of Supreme Court Justices Shapes Our History (Random House 1985)

Mark Tushnet, ed., The Warren Court In Historical and Political Perspective (Univ. Press of Virginia 1993)

Melvin I. Urofsky, A March of Liberty: A Constitutional History of the United States (Alfred A. Knopf 1988)

Clement E. Vose, Constitutional Change: Amendment Politics and Supreme Court Litigation Since 1900 (Lexington Books 1972)

Charles Warren, The Supreme Court in United States History (rev. ed. Little, Brown & Co. 1926)

Alan F. Westin, ed., The Supreme Court: Views from Inside (W. W. Norton & Co. 1961)

G. Edward White, The Marshall Court and Cultural Change, 1815–1835 (MacMillan 1988)

Elder Witt, Congressional Quarterly's Guide to the U. S. Supreme Court (2d ed. Cong. Quarterly 1990)

*Bob Woodward & Scott Armstrong, The Brethren: Inside the Supreme Court (Simon & Schuster 1979)

# Justices of the Supreme Court

*Originally prepared by John J. Cound*
*Professor of Law, University of Minnesota*

In the data, the first dates in parentheses are those of birth and death; these are followed by the name of the appointing President, and the dates of service on the Court. The state in which the justice was residing when appointed and his political affiliation at that time are then given. In detailing prior careers, I have followed chronological order, with two exceptions: I have listed first that a justice was a signer of the Declaration of Independence or the Federal Constitution, and I have indicated state legislative experience only once for each justice. I have not distinguished between different bodies in the state legislature, and I have omitted service in the Continental Congresses. Private practice, except where deemed especially signficant, and law teaching have been omitted, except where the justice was primarily engaged therein upon his appointment. (Blackmun, Breyer, Burger, Douglas, Fortas, Ginsburg, Holmes, Hughes, Kennedy, L.Q.C. Lamar, Lurton, McReynolds, Murphy, Roberts, W. Rutledge, Scalia, Stevens, Stone and Van Devanter in addition to Taft and Frankfurter, had all taught before going on the Court; Story, Strong and Wilson taught while on the court or after leaving it). The activity in which a justice was engaged upon appointment has been italicized. Figures in parentheses indicate years of service in the position. In only a few cases, a justice's extra-Court or post-Court activity has been indicated, or some other note made. An asterisk designates the Chief Justices.

For detailed information on the men and women who have served as members of the Supreme Court, see L. Friedman & F. Israel, eds., *The Justices of the United States Supreme Court 1789–1997: Their Lives and Major Opinions* (Chelsea House, 1997), and the bibliographical references collected therein.

The accompanying Table of Justices has been planned so that the composition of the Court at any time can be readily ascertained.

BALDWIN, HENRY (1780–1844; Jackson 1830–1844). Pa.Dem.—U.S., House of Representatives (5). *Private practice.*

BARBOUR, PHILIP P. (1783–1841; Jackson, 1836–1841). Va.Dem.—Va., Legislature (2). U.S., House of Representatives (14). Va., Judge, General Court (2); President, State Constitutional Convention, 1829–30, *U.S., Judge, District Court (5).*

BLACK, HUGO L. (1886–1971; F.D. Roosevelt, 1937–1971). Ala.Dem.—Captain, Field Artillery, World War I. Ala., Judge, Police Court (1); County Solicitor (2). *U.S., Senate (10).*

BLACKMUN, HARRY A. (1908–___; Nixon, 1970–1994). Minn.Rep.—Resident Counsel, Mayo Clinic, (10). *U.S., Judge, Court of Appeals (11).*

BLAIR, JOHN (1732–1800; Washington, 1789–1796). Va.Fed.—Signer, U.S. Constitution, 1787. Va., Legislature (9); Judge and Chief Justice, General Court (2), *Court of Appeals (9).* His opinion in *Commonwealth v. Caton,* 4 Call 5, 20 (Va.1782), is one of the earliest expressions of the doctrine of judicial review.

BLATCHFORD, SAMUEL (1820–1893; Arthur, 1882–1893). N.Y.Rep.—U.S., Judge, District Court (5); *Circuit Court (10).*

BRADLEY, JOSEPH P. (1803–1892; Grant, 1870–1892). N.J.Rep.—Actuary. *Private practice.*

BRANDEIS, LOUIS D. (1856–1941; Wilson, 1916–1939). Mass.Dem.—*Private practice.* Counsel, variously for the government, for industry, and "for the people", in numerous administrative and judicial proceedings, both state and federal.

BRENNAN, WILLIAM J. (1906–___; Eisenhower, 1956–1990). N.J.Dem.—U.S. Army, World War II. N.J., Judge, Superior Court (1); Appellate Division (2); *Supreme Court (4).*

BREWER, DAVID J. (1837–1910; B. Harrison, 1889–1910). Kans.Rep.—Kans., Judge, County Criminal and Probate Court (1), District Court (4); County Attorney (1); Judge, Supreme Court (14), *U.S., Judge, Circuit Court (5).*

BREYER, STEPHEN GERALD (1937–___; Clinton, 1994–___); Mass.Dem.: U.S., *Judge, Court of Appeals (13 1/2).*

BROWN, HENRY, B. (1836–1913; B. Harrison, 1890–1906). Mich.Rep.—U.S., Assistant U.S. Attorney (5). Mich., Judge, Circuit Court (1). *U.S., Judge, District Court (15).*

*BURGER, WARREN E. (1907–1995; Nixon, 1969–1986). Va.Rep.—U.S., Assistant Attorney General, Civil Division (3), *Judge, Court of Appeals (13)*.

BURTON, HAROLD H. (1888–1964; Truman, 1945–1958). Ohio Rep.—Capt., U.S.A., World War I. Ohio, Legislature (2). Mayor, Cleveland, O. (5). *U.S., Senate (4)*.

BUTLER, PIERCE (1866–1939; Harding, 1922–1939). Minn.Dem.—Minn., County Attorney (4). *Private practice.*

BYRNES, JAMES F. (1879–1972; F.D. Roosevelt, 1941–1942). S.C.Dem.—S.C., Solicitor, Circuit Court (2). U.S., House of Representatives (14); *Senate (12)*. Resigned from the Court to become U.S. Director of Economic Stabilization.

CAMPBELL, JOHN A. (1811–1889; Pierce, 1853–1861). Ala.Dem.—*Private practice*. After his resignation, he became Assistant Secretary of War, C.S.A.

CARDOZO, BENJAMIN N. (1870–1938; Hoover, 1932–1938). N.Y.Dem.—N.Y., Judge, Supreme Court (6 weeks); Associate Judge and *Chief Judge, Court of Appeals (18)*.

CATRON, JOHN (1778–1865; Van Buren, 1837–1865). Tenn.Dem.—Tenn., Judge and Chief Justice, Supreme Court of Errors and Appeals (10). *Private practice.*

*CHASE, SALMON P. (1808–1873; Lincoln 1864–1873). Ohio Rep.—U.S., Senate (6). Ohio, Governor (4). *U.S., Secretary of the Treasury (3)*.

CHASE, SAMUEL (1741–1811; Washington, 1796–1811). Md.Fed.—Signer, U.S., Declaration of Independence, 1776. Md., Legislature (20); Chief Judge, Court of Oyer and Terminer (2), *General Court (5)*. Impeached and acquitted, 1804–05.

CLARK, TOM C. (1899–1977; Truman, 1949–1967). Tex.Dem.—U.S. Army, World War I. Tex., Civil District Attorney (5). U.S., Assistant Attorney General (2), *Attorney General (4)*.

CLARKE, JOHN H. (1857–1945; Wilson, 1916–1922). Ohio Dem.—*U.S. Judge, District Court (2)*.

CLIFFORD, NATHAN (1803–1881; Buchanan, 1858–1881). Me.Dem.—Me., Legislature (4); Attorney General (4). U.S., House of Representatives (4); Attorney General (2); Minister Plenipotentiary to Mexico, 1848. *Private practice.*

CURTIS, BENJAMIN R. (1809–1874; Fillmore, 1851–1857). Mass.Whig.—Mass., Legislature (1). *Private practice.*

CUSHING, WILLIAM (1732–1810; Washington, 1789–1810). Mass.Fed.—Mass., Judge, Superior Court (3); Justice and *Chief Justice, Supreme Judicial Court (14).*

DANIEL, PETER V. (1784–1860; Van Buren, 1841–1860). Va.Dem.—Va., Legislature (3); Member, Privy Council (23). *U.S., Judge, District Court (5).*

DAVIS, DAVID (1815–1886; Lincoln, 1862–1877). Ill.Rep.—Ill., Legislature (2); *Judge, Circuit Court (14).* His resignation to become U.S. Senator upset the agreed-upon composition of the Hayes-Tilden Electoral Commission.

DAY, WILLIAM R. (1849–1923; T. Roosevelt, 1903–1922). Ohio Rep.—Ohio, Judge, Court of Common Pleas (4). U.S., Assistant Secretary of State (1), Secretary of State (1/2); Chairman, U.S. Peace Commissioners, 1898; Judge, Circuit Court of Appeals (4).

DOUGLAS, WILLIAM O. (1898–1980; F.D. Roosevelt, 1939–1975). Conn.Dem.—Pvt., U.S. Army, World War I. *U.S., Chairman, Securities and Exchange Commission (3).* His was the longest tenure in the history of the Court.

DUVAL(L), GABRIEL (1752–1844; Madison, 1811–1935). Md.Rep.—Declined to serve as delegate, U.S. Constitutional Convention, 1787. Md., State Council (3). U.S., House of Representatives (2). Md., Judge, General Court (6). *U.S., Comptroller of the Treasury (9).*

*ELLSWORTH, OLIVER (1745–1807; Washington, 1796–1800). Conn.Fed.—Delegate, U.S. Constitutional Convention, 1787. Conn., Legislature (2); Member, Governor's Council (4); Judge, Superior Court (5). *U.S., Senate (7).*

FIELD, STEPHEN J. (1816–1899; Lincoln, 1863–1897). Calif.Dem.—*Calif.,* Justice, and *Chief Justice, Supreme Court (6).*

FORTAS, ABE (1910–1982; L.B. Johnson, 1965–1969). Tenn.Dem.—U.S. Government attorney and consultant (A.A.A., S.E.C., P.W.A., Dep't of Interior (9); Undersecretary of Interior (4). *Private practice in Washington, D.C.* Nominated as Chief Justice; nomination withdrawn, 1968. Resigned.

FRANKFURTER, FELIX (1882–1965; F.D. Roosevelt, 1939–1962). Mass. Independent.—U.S., Assistant U.S. Attorney (4); Law Officer, War Department, Bureau of Insular Affairs (3); Assistant to Secretary of War (1). *Professor of Law (25).*

*FULLER, MELVILLE W. (1833–1910; Cleveland, 1888–1910). Ill.Dem.—Ill., Legislature (2). *Private practice.*

GINSBURG, RUTH BADER (1933–___; Clinton 1993–___); N.Y.Dem.; U.S., *Judge, Court of Appeals* (13).

GOLDBERG, ARTHUR J. (1908–1990; Kennedy, 1962–1965). Ill.Dem.—Major, U.S.A., World War II. General Counsel, USW–AFL–CIO (13). *U.S., Secretary of Labor (1).* Resigned to become Ambassador to U.N.

GRAY, HORACE (1828–1902; Arthur, 1881–1902). Mass.Rep.—*Mass., Associate Justice and *Chief Justice, Supreme Judicial Court (18).*

GRIER, ROBERT O. (1794–1870; Polk, 1846–1870). Pa.Dem.—*Pa., Presiding Judge, District Court (13).*

HARLAN, JOHN M. (1833–1911; Hayes, 1877–1911). Ky.Rep.—Ky., Judge, County Court (1). Col., Union Army, 1861–63. Ky., Attorney General (4). U.S., Member, President's Louisiana Commission, 1877. *Private practice.* Grandfather of:

HARLAN, JOHN M. (1899–1971; Eisenhower, 1955–1971). N.Y.Rep.—Col., U.S.A.A.F., World War II. N.Y. Chief Counsel, State Crime Commission (2). *U.S., Judge, Court of Appeals (1).*

HOLMES, OLIVER W., JR. (1841–1935; T. Roosevelt, 1902–1932). Mass.Rep.—Lt. Col., Mass. Volunteers, Civil War. *Mass., Associate Justice, and *Chief Justice, Supreme Judicial Court (20).*

*HUGHES, CHARLES E. (1862–1948; Taft, 1910–1916, and Hoover, 1930–1941). N.Y.Rep.—N.Y., Counsel, legislative committees investigating gas and insurance industries, 1905–06. U.S., Special Assistant to Attorney General for Coal Investigation, 1906. *N.Y., Governor (3).* [Between appointments to the Supreme Court: Presidential Nominee, Republican Party, 1916. U.S., Secretary of State (4). *Member, Permanent Court of Arbitration, The Hague (4). Judge, Permanent Court of International Justice (2).*] Chief Justice on second appointment.

HUNT, WARD (1810–1886; Grant, 1872–1882). N.Y.Rep.—N.Y., Legislature (2). Mayor of Utica, N.Y. (1). N.Y. Associate Judge, and Chief Judge, Court of Appeals (4); *Commissioner of Appeals (4).* He did not sit from 1879 to his retirement in 1882.

IREDELL, JAMES (1750–1799; Washington, 1790–1799). N.C.Fed.—Comptroller of Customs (6), Collector of Port (2), Edenton, N.C., N.C., Judge, Superior Court (1/2); Attorney General (2); Member, Council of State, 1787; Reviser of Statutes (3).

JACKSON, HOWELL E. (1832–1895; B. Harrison, 1893–1895). Tenn.Dem.—Tenn., Judge, Court of Arbitration (4); Legislature (1). U.S. Senate (5); *Judge, Circuit Court of Appeals (7).*

JACKSON, ROBERT H. (1892–1954; F.D. Roosevelt, 1941–1954). N.Y.Dem.—U.S., General Counsel, Bureau of Internal Revenue (2); Assistant Attorney General (2); Solicitor General (2); *Attorney General (1).*

*JAY, JOHN (1745–1829; Washington, 1789–1795). N.Y.Fed.—N.Y., Chief Justice, Supreme Court (2). U.S., Envoy to Spain (2); Commissioner, Treaty of Paris, 1782–83; Secretary for Foreign Affairs (6). Co-author, The Federalist.

JOHNSON, THOMAS (1732–1819; Washington, 1791–1793). Md.Fed.—Md., Brigadier-General, Militia (1); Legislature (5); Governor (2); *Chief Judge, General Court (1).*

JOHNSON, WILLIAM (1771–1834; Jefferson, 1804–1834). S.C.Rep.—S.C., Legislature (4); *Judge, Court of Common Pleas (6).*

KENNEDY, ANTHONY M. (1936–____); Reagan (1988–____); Calif.Rep.; U.S., *Judge, Court of Appeals* (11).

LAMAR, JOSEPH R. (1857–1916; Taft, 1910–1916). Ga.Dem.—Ga., Legislature (3); Commissioner to Codify Laws (3); Associate Justice, Supreme Court (4). *Private practice.*

LAMAR, LUCIUS Q.C. (1825–1893; Cleveland, 1888–1893). Miss.Dem.—Ga., Legislature (2). U.S., House of Representatives (4). Draftsman, Mississippi Ordinance of Secession, 1861. C.S.A., Lt. Col. (1); Commissioner to Russia (1); Judge-Advocate, III Corps. Army of No. Va. (1). U.S., House of Representatives (4); Senate (8); *Secretary of the Interior (3).*

LIVINGSTON, (HENRY) BROCKHOLST (1757–1823; Jefferson, 1806–1823). N.Y.Rep.—Lt. Col., Continental Army. *N.Y., Judge, Supreme Court (4).*

LURTON, HORACE H. (1844–1914; Taft, 1909–1914). Tenn.Dem.—Sgt. Major, C.S.A. Tenn., Chancellor (3); Associate Justice and Chief Justice, Supreme Court (7). *U.S., Judge, Circuit Court of Appeals (16).*

McKENNA, JOSEPH (1843–1926; McKinley, 1898–1925). Calif.Rep.—Calif., District Attorney (2); Legislature (2). U.S., House of Representatives (7); *Judge, Circuit Court of Appeals (5); Attorney General (1).*

McKINLEY, JOHN (1780–1852; Van Buren, 1837–1852). Ala.Dem.—Legislature (4). U.S., Senate (5); House of Representatives (2); *re-elected to Senate,* but appointed to Court before taking seat.

McLEAN, JOHN (1785–1861; Jackson, 1829–1861). Ohio Dem.—U.S., House of Representatives (4). Ohio, Judge, Supreme Court (6). U.S., Commissioner, General Land Office (1); *Postmaster-General (6).*

McREYNOLDS, JAMES C. (1862–1946; Wilson, 1914–1941). Tenn.Dem.—U.S., Assistant Attorney General (4); *Attorney General (1).*

*MARSHALL, JOHN (1755–1835; J. Adams, 1801–1835). Va.Fed.—Va., Legislature (7); U.S., Envoy to France (1); House of Representatives (1); *Secretary of State (1).*

MARSHALL, THURGOOD (1908–1993; L.B. Johnson, 1967–1991). N.Y.Dem.—Counsel, Legal Defense and Educational Fund, NAACP (21). U.S., Judge, Court of Appeals (4); *Solicitor General (2).*

MATTHEWS, STANLEY (1824–1889; Garfield, 1881–1889). Ohio Rep.—Ohio, Judge, Court of Common Pleas (2); Legislature (3). U.S., District Attorney (3). Col., Ohio Volunteers. Ohio, Judge, Superior Court (2). Counsel before Hayes-Tilden Electoral Commission, 1877. U.S., Senate (2). *Private practice.* His first appointment to the Court by Hayes in 1881 was not acted upon by the Senate.

MILLER, SAMUEL F. (1816–1890; Lincoln, 1862–1890). Iowa Rep.—Physician. *Private practice.*

MINTON, SHERMAN (1890–1965; Truman, 1949–1956). Ind.Dem.—Capt., Inf., World War I. U.S., Senate (6); *Judge, Court of Appeals (8).*

MOODY, WILLIAM H. (1853–1917; T. Roosevelt, 1906–1910). Mass.Rep.—U.S., District Attorney (5), House of Representatives (7); Secretary of the Navy (2); *Attorney General (2).*

MOORE, ALFRED (1755–1810; J. Adams, 1799–1804). N.C.Fed.—N.C., Col. of Militia; Legislature (2); Attorney General (9). U.S. Commissioner, Treaty with Cherokee Nation (1); *N.C., Judge, Superior Court (1).*

MURPHY, FRANK (1893–1949; F.D. Roosevelt, 1940–1949). Mich.Dem.—Capt., Inf., World War I. U.S., Assistant U.S. Attorney (1). Mich., Judge, Recorder's Court (7). Mayor, Detroit, Mich. (3). U.S., Governor-General, and High Commissioner, P.I. (3). Mich., Governor (2). *U.S., Attorney General (1).*

NELSON, SAMUEL (1792–1873; Tyler, 1845–1872). N.Y.Dem.—N.Y., Judge, Circuit Court (8); Associate Justice, and *Chief Justice, Supreme Court (14).*

O'CONNOR, SANDRA DAY (1930–____; Reagan, 1981–____. Ariz.Rep.—Ariz., Assistant Attorney General (4); Legislature (6). Ariz., Judge, Superior Court (4); *Court of Appeals (2).*

PATERSON, WILLIAM (1745–1806; Washington, 1793–1806). N.J.Fed.—Signer, U.S. Constitution, 1787. N.J., Legislature (2); Attorney General (7). U.S., Senate (1). *N.J., Governor (3).* Reviser of English Pre-Revolutionary Statutes in Force in N.J.

PECKHAM, RUFUS W. (1838–1909; Cleveland, 1895–1909). N.Y.Dem.—N.Y., District Attorney (1); Justice, Supreme Court (3); *Associate Judge, Court of Appeals (9).*

PITNEY, MAHLON (1858–1924; Taft, 1912–1922). N.J.Rep.—U.S., House of Representatives (4). N.J., Legislature (2); Associate Justice, Supreme Court (7); Chancellor (4).

POWELL, LEWIS F. (1907–____; Nixon, 1972–1987). Va. Dem.—Col., U.S.A.A.F., World War II. *Private practice.*

REED, STANLEY F. (1884–1980; F.D. Roosevelt, 1938–1957). Ky.Dem.—Ky., Legislature (4). 1st Lt., U.S.A., World War I. U.S., General Counsel, Federal Farm Board (3); General Counsel, Reconstruction Finance Corporation (3); *Solicitor General (3).*

*REHNQUIST, WILLIAM H. (1924–____; Nixon, 1972–____). Ariz.Rep.—U.S.A.F., World War II. Law Clerk, Justice Jackson, 1952–53. *U.S., Assistant Attorney General (3).*

ROBERTS, OWEN J. (1875–1955; Hoover, 1930–1945). Pa.Rep.—Pa., Assistant District Attorney (3). U.S., Special Deputy Attorney General in Espionage Act Cases, World War I; Special Prosecutor, Oil Cases, 1924. *Private practice.*

*RUTLEDGE, JOHN (1739–1800; Washington, 1789–1791, and Washington, 1795). S.C.Fed.—Signer, U.S. Constitution, 1787. S.C., Legislature (18); Attorney General (1); President and Governor (6); *Chancellor (7).* [Between appointments to the Supreme Court: *S.C., Chief Justice, Court of Common Pleas and Sessions (4).*] He did not sit under his first appointment; he sat with a recess appointment as Chief Justice, but his regular appointment was rejected by the Senate.

RUTLEDGE, WILEY B. (1894–1949; F.D. Roosevelt, 1943–1949). Iowa Dem.—Mo., then Iowa, Member, National Conference of Commissioners on Uniform State Laws (10). *U.S., Judge, Court of Appeals (4).*

SANFORD, EDWARD T. (1865–1930; Harding, 1923–1930). Tenn.Rep.—U.S., Assistant Attorney General (1); *Judge, District Court (15).*

SCALIA, ANTONIN (1936–____); Reagan (1986–____); Va.Rep.—U.S., Assistant Attorney General (3); *Judge, Court of Appeals* (4).

SHIRAS, GEORGE (1832–1924; B. Harrison, 1892–1903). Pa.Rep. *Private practice.*

SOUTER, DAVID H. (1939–____); Bush (1990–____); N.H.Rep.; N.H., Deputy Attorney General (5); Attorney General (2); Associate Justice, Superior Court (5), Associate Justice, Supreme Court (7); U.S., *Judge, Court of Appeals* (5 mo.).

STEVENS, JOHN PAUL (1920–____; Ford, 1975–____). Ill.Independent.—U.S.N.R., World War II. Law Clerk, Justice Wiley Rutledge, 1947–48. *Judge, Court of Appeals (5).*

STEWART, POTTER (1915–1985; Eisenhower, 1958–1981). Ohio Rep.—Lt., U.S.N.R., World War II. *U.S., Judge, Court of Appeals (4).*

*STONE, HARLAN F. (1872–1946; Coolidge, later F.D. Roosevelt, 1925–1946). N.Y.Rep.—*U.S., Attorney General (1).* Chief Justice, 1941–1946.

STORY, JOSEPH (1779–1845; Madison, 1811–1845). Mass.Rep.—Mass., Legislature (5). U.S., House of Representatives (2). *Private practice.*

STRONG, WILLIAM (1808–1895; Grant, 1870–1880). Pa.Rep.—U.S., House of Representatives (4). Pa., Justice, Supreme Court (11). *Private practice.*

SUTHERLAND, GEORGE (1862–1942; Harding, 1922–1938). Utah Rep.—Utah, Legislature (4). U.S., House of Representatives (2); Senate (12). *Private practice.*

SWAYNE, NOAH H. (1804–1884; Lincoln, 1862–1881). Ohio Rep.—Ohio, County Attorney (4); Legislature (2). U.S., District Attorney (9). *Private practice.*

*TAFT, WILLIAM H. (1857–1930; Harding, 1921–1930). Conn.Rep.—U.S., Collector of Internal Revenue (1). Ohio, Judge, Superior Court (3). U.S., Solicitor General (2); Judge, Circuit Court of Appeals (8); Governor-General, P.I. (3); Secretary of War (4); President (4). *Professor of Law.*

*TANEY, ROGER B. (1777–1864; Jackson, 1836–1864). Md.Dem.—Md., Legislature (7); Attorney General (2). U.S., Attorney General (2), Secretary of the Treasury (3/4; rejected by the Senate). Private practice.

THOMAS, CLARENCE (1948–____; Bush 1991–____); Ga.Rep.; Mo., Assistant Attorney General (3); U.S., Chair, E.E.O.C. (8), *Judge, Court of Appeals (1 1/2).*

THOMPSON, SMITH (1768–1843; Monroe, 1823–1843). N.Y.Rep.—N.Y., Legislature (2); Associate Justice, and Chief Justice, Supreme Court (16). *U.S., Secretary of the Navy (4).*

TODD, THOMAS (1765–1826; Jefferson, 1807–1826). Ky.Rep.—*Ky., Judge, and Chief Justice, Court of Appeals (6).*

TRIMBLE, ROBERT (1777–1828; J.Q. Adams, 1826–1828). Ky.Rep.—Ky., Legislature (2). Judge, Court of Appeals (2). U.S., District Attorney (4); *Judge, District Court (9).*

VAN DEVANTER, WILLIS (1859–1941; Taft, 1910–1937). Wyo.Rep.—Wyo., Legislature (2); Chief Justice, Supreme Court (1). U.S., Assistant Attorney General (Interior Department) (6); *Judge, Circuit Court of Appeals (7).*

*VINSON, FRED M. (1890–1953; Truman, 1946–1953). Ky.Dem.—Ky., Commonwealth Attorney (3). U.S., House of Representatives (14); Judge, Court of Appeals (5); Director, Office of Economic Stabilization (2); Federal Loan Administrator (1 mo.); Director, Office of War Mobilization and Reconversion (3 mo.); *Secretary of the Treasury (1).*

*WAITE, MORRISON R. (1816–1888; Grant, 1874–1888). Ohio Rep.—Ohio, Legislature (2). Counsel for United States, U.S.—Gr. Brit. Arbitration ("Alabama" Claims), 1871–72. *Private practice.*

*WARREN, EARL (1891–1974; Eisenhower, 1953–1969). Calif.Rep.—1st Lt., Inf., World War I. Deputy City Attorney (1); Deputy District Attorney (5); District Attorney (14); Attorney General (4); *Governor (10).*

WASHINGTON, BUSHROD (1762–1829; J. Adams, 1798–1829). Pa.Fed.—Va., Legislature (1). *Private practice.*

WAYNE, JAMES M. (1790–1867; Jackson, 1835–1867). Ga.Dem.—Ga., Officer, Hussars, War of 1812; Legislature (2). Mayor of Savannah, Ga. (2). Ga., Judge, Superior Court (5). *U.S., House of Representatives (6).*

WHITE, BYRON R. (1917–___; Kennedy, 1962–1993). Colo.Dem.—U.S.N.R., World War II. Law Clerk, Chief Justice Vinson, 1946–47. *U.S., Deputy Attorney General (1).*

*WHITE, EDWARD D. (1845–1921; Cleveland, later Taft, 1894–1921). La.Dem.—La., Legislature (4); Justice, Supreme Court (2). *U.S., Senate (3).* Chief Justice, 1910–1921.

WHITTAKER, CHARLES E. (1901–1973; Eisenhower, 1957–1962). Mo.Rep.—U.S., Judge, District Court (2); *Court of Appeals (1).*

WILSON, JAMES (1724–1798; Washington, 1789–1798). Pa.Fed.—Signer, U.S. Declaration of Independence, 1776, and U.S. Constitution, 1787. Although he was strongly interested in western-land development companies for several years prior to his appointment, his primary activity in the period immediately preceding his appointment was in obtaining ratification of the Federal and Pennsylvania Constitutions.

WOODBURY, LEVI (1789–1851; Polk, 1845–1851). N.H. Dem.—N.H., Associate Justice, Superior Court (6); Governor (2); Legislature (1). U.S., Senate (6); Secretary of the Navy (3); Secretary of the Treasury (7); *Senate (4).*

WOODS, WILLIAM B. (1824–1887; Hayes, 1880–1887). Ga.Rep.—Mayor, Newark, O. (1). Ohio, Legislature (4). Brevet Major General, U.S. Vol., Civil War. Ala., Chancellor (1). *U.S., Judge, Circuit Court (11).*

Years (column headers): 1789, 1790, 1791, 1793, 1795, 1796, 1798, 1799, 1801, 1804, 1806, 1807, 1811, 1823, 1826, 1829, 1830, 1835, 1836, 1837, 1841, 1845, 1846, 1851, 1853, 1858, 1862, 1863, 1864, 1865, 1867, 1870, 1872, 1874, 1877, 1880, 1881, 1882, 1888, 1889, 1890, 1892, 1893, 1894, 1895, 1898, 1902, 1903, 1906

Succession of justices by seat (in chronological order within each seat):

**Seat 1 (Chief Justice):** Jay — Rutledge, J. — Ellsworth — Marshall, J. — Taney — Chase, Salmon — Waite — Fuller

**Seat 2:** Rutledge, J. — Johnson, T. — Paterson — Livingston — Thompson — Nelson — Hunt — Blatchford — White, E.

**Seat 3:** Cushing — Story — Woodbury — Curtis — Clifford — Gray — Holmes

**Seat 4:** Wilson — Washington — Baldwin — Grier — Strong — Woods — Lamar, L. — Jackson, H. — Peckham

**Seat 5:** Blair — Chase, Samuel — Duval — Barbour — Daniel — Miller — Brown — Shiras — Day — Moody

**Seat 6:** Iredell — Moore — Johnson, W. — Wayne — Bradley

**Seat 7:** Todd — Trimble — McLean — Swayne — Matthews — Brewer

**Seat 8:** Catron — Harlan

**Seat 9:** McKinley — Campbell — Davis — Field — McKenna

* Catron died in 1865, Wayne in 1867; their positions were abolished by Congress to prevent their being filled by President Johnson; a new position was created in 1869, which traditionally has been regarded as a re-creation of Wayne's seat.

| Year | Chief Justices | Seat 2 | Seat 3 | Seat 4 | Seat 5 | Seat 6 | Seat 7 | Seat 8 |
|------|----------------|--------|--------|--------|--------|--------|--------|--------|
| 1909 | White, E. | ** Van Devanter | Lurton | Lamar, J. | | Hughes | Pitney | Stone |
| 1910 | | | | | | | | |
| 1912 | Taft | | McReynolds | Brandeis | | Clarke | | |
| 1914 | | | | | | | | |
| 1916 | | | | | Butler | Sutherland | Sanford | |
| 1921 | | | | | | | Roberts | |
| 1922 | | | | | | | | |
| 1923 | | | | | | | | |
| 1925 | Hughes | Cardozo | | | | | | |
| 1930 | | Black | | | Reed | | | ** |
| 1932 | | | | | | | | Jackson, R. |
| 1937 | Stone | Frankfurter | Byrnes | Douglas | | | | |
| 1938 | | | Rutledge | | Murphy | | | |
| 1939 | | | | | | | | |
| 1940 | | | | | | | | |
| 1941 | Vinson | | | | | | Burton | |
| 1943 | | | Minton | | Clark | | | |
| 1945 | Warren | | | | | | | Harlan |
| 1946 | | | | | | | | |
| 1949 | | | Brennan | | | | | |
| 1953 | | | | | | | | |
| 1955 | | | | | | Whittaker | Stewart | |
| 1956 | | Goldberg | | | | White, B. | | |
| 1957 | | Fortas | | | | | | |
| 1958 | | Blackmun | | | Marshall, T. | | | Rehnquist |
| 1962 | Burger | | | Stevens | | | | |
| 1965 | | | | | | | | |
| 1967 | | Powell | | | | | O'Connor | ** |
| 1969 | Rehnquist | Kennedy | | | | | | Scalia |
| 1970 | | | Souter | | Thomas | Ginsburg | | |
| 1972 | | Breyer | | | | | | |
| ... | | | | | | | | |

**Fuller died in 1910 and White was named Chief Justice. Hughes resigned in 1941, and Stone was named Chief Justice. Burger resigned in 1986, and Rehnquist was named Chief Justice.

# Index of Cases

†